GUARDIANS
OF THE GALAXY

BY JIM VALENTINO

FRONT COVER ARTISTS: Jim Valentino, Bob Wiacek & Matt Milla
BACK COVER ARTISTS: Jim Valentino, Al Williamson & Thomas Mason

RESEARCH & LAYOUT: Jeph York
PRODUCTION: ColorTek and Joe Frontirre
BOOK DESIGNER: Nelson Ribeiro

COLLECTION EDITOR: Mark D. Beazley
DIGITAL TRAFFIC COORDINATOR: Joe Hochstein
ASSOCIATE MANAGING EDITOR: Alex Starbuck
EDITOR, SPECIAL PROJECTS: Jennifer Grünwald
SENIOR EDITOR, SPECIAL PROJECTS: Jeff Youngquist
SVP PRINT, SALES & MARKETING: David Gabriel

EDITOR IN CHIEF: Axel Alonso
CHIEF CREATIVE OFFICER: Joe Quesada
PUBLISHER: Dan Buckley
EXECUTIVE PRODUCER: Alan Fine

3 1969 02304 3523

GUARDIANS OF THE GALAXY BY JIM VALENTINO VOL. 2. Contains material originally published in magazine form as GUARDIANS OF THE GALAXY #8-20. First printing 2014. ISBN# 978-0-7851-8563-5. Published by MARVEL WORLDWIDE, INC., a subsidiary of MARVEL ENTERTAINMENT, LLC. OFFICE OF PUBLICATION: 135 West 50th Street, New York, NY 10020. Copyright © 1991, 1992 and 2014 Marvel Characters, Inc. All rights reserved. All characters featured in this issue and the distinctive names and likenesses thereof, and all related indicia are trademarks of Marvel Characters, Inc. No similarity between any of the names, characters, persons, and/or institutions in this magazine with those of any living or dead person or institution is intended, and any such similarity which may exist is purely coincidental. **Printed in the U.S.A.** ALAN FINE, EVP - Office of the President, Marvel Worldwide, Inc. and EVP & CMO Marvel Characters B.V.; DAN BUCKLEY, Publisher & President - Print, Animation & Digital Divisions; JOE QUESADA, Chief Creative Officer; TOM BREVOORT, SVP of Publishing; DAVID BOGART, SVP of Operations & Procurement, Publishing; C.B. CEBULSKI, SVP of Creator & Content Development; DAVID GABRIEL, SVP Print, Sales & Marketing; JIM O'KEEFE, VP of Operations & Logistics; DAN CARR, Executive Director of Publishing Technology; SUSAN CRESPI, Editorial Operations Manager; ALEX MORALES, Publishing Operations Manager; STAN LEE, Chairman Emeritus. For information regarding advertising in Marvel Comics or on Marvel.com, please contact Niza Disla, Director of Marvel Partnerships, at ndisla@marvel.com. For Marvel subscription inquiries, please call 800-217-9158. **Manufactured between 5/16/2014 and 6/23/2014 by R.R. DONNELLEY, INC., SALEM, VA, USA.**

10 9 8 7 6 5 4 3 2 1

GUARDIANS OF THE GALAXY

BY JIM VALENTINO

WRITER & PENCILER
JIM VALENTINO

INKER
STEVE MONTANO

COLORISTS
EVELYN STEIN, DANIEL VOZZO, MIKE THOMAS & MARIE JAVINS

LETTERERS
KEN LOPEZ, BRAD K. JOYCE & PHIL FELIX

ASSISTANT EDITORS
RENEÉ WITTERSTAETTER & JOHN LEWANDOWSKI

EDITORS
CRAIG ANDERSON

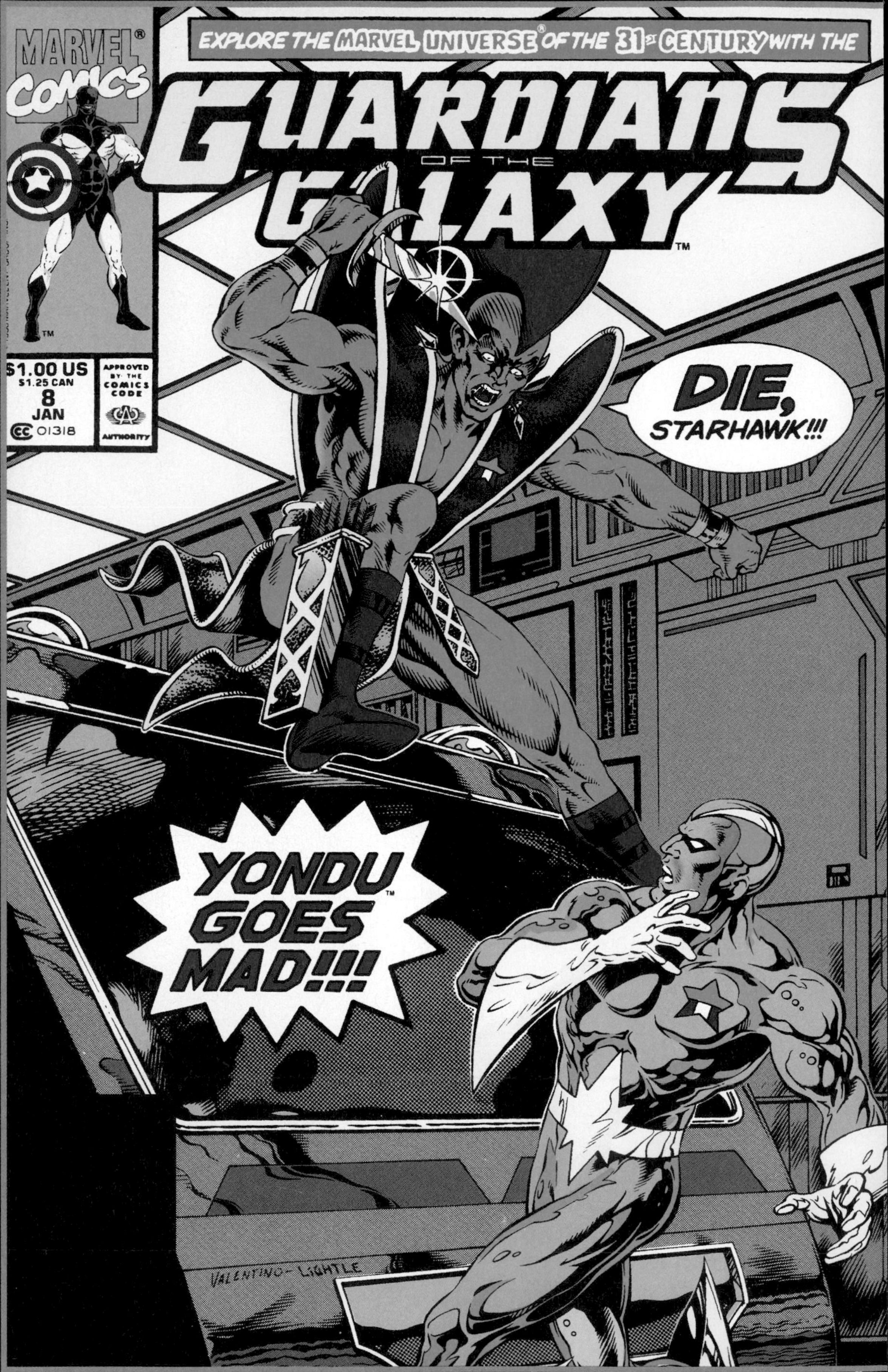
MARVEL® COMICS
EXPLORE THE MARVEL UNIVERSE® OF THE 31st CENTURY WITH THE
GUARDIANS OF THE GALAXY™
$1.00 US
$1.25 CAN
8
JAN
APPROVED BY THE COMICS CODE AUTHORITY
DIE, STARHAWK!!!
YONDU™ GOES MAD!!!
VALENTINO-LIGHTLE

CHARLIE 27! MARTINEX! NIKKI! VANCE ASTRO! YONDU! ALETA! STARHAWK! SEVEN EXTRAORDINARY SUPER-BEINGS, ALL SURVIVORS OF INTERSTELLAR WAR. NOW THEY ROAM THE COSMOS OF THE 31ST CENTURY ABOARD THE STARSHIP CAPTAIN AMERICA, THEIR MISSION—TO SAFEGUARD THE MILKY WAY! STAN LEE PRESENTS . . . THE GUARDIANS OF THE GALAXY!

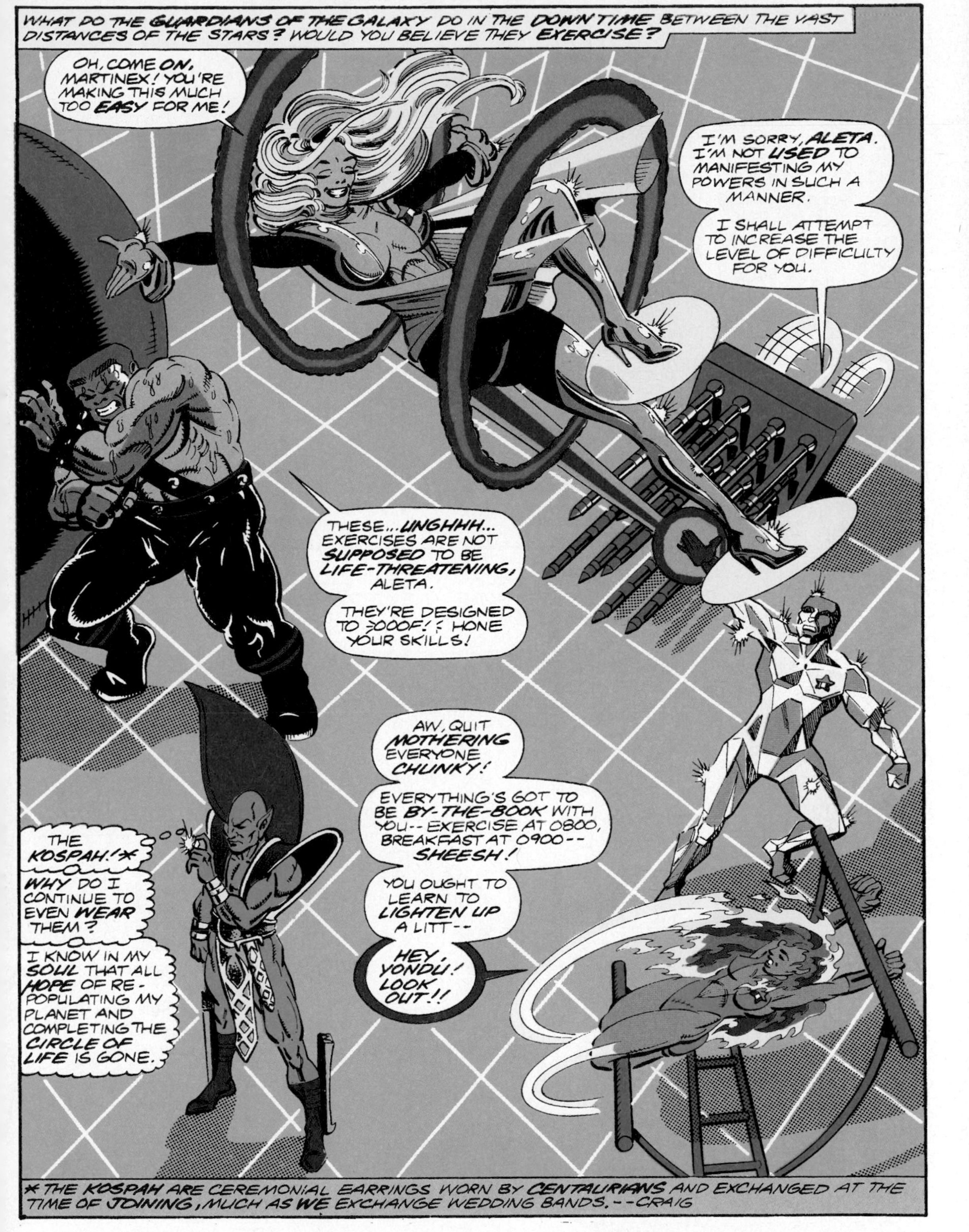
WHAT DO THE GUARDIANS OF THE GALAXY DO IN THE DOWN TIME BETWEEN THE VAST DISTANCES OF THE STARS? WOULD YOU BELIEVE THEY EXERCISE?
OH, COME ON, MARTINEX! YOU'RE MAKING THIS MUCH TOO EASY FOR ME!
I'M SORRY, ALETA. I'M NOT USED TO MANIFESTING MY POWERS IN SUCH A MANNER.
I SHALL ATTEMPT TO INCREASE THE LEVEL OF DIFFICULTY FOR YOU.
THESE... UNGHHH... EXERCISES ARE NOT SUPPOSED TO BE LIFE-THREATENING, ALETA.
THEY'RE DESIGNED TO >OOOF!< HONE YOUR SKILLS!
AW, QUIT MOTHERING EVERYONE, CHUNKY!
EVERYTHING'S GOT TO BE BY-THE-BOOK WITH YOU-- EXERCISE AT 0800, BREAKFAST AT 0900-- SHEESH!
YOU OUGHT TO LEARN TO LIGHTEN UP A LITT--
THE KOSPAH!*
WHY DO I CONTINUE TO EVEN WEAR THEM?
I KNOW IN MY SOUL THAT ALL HOPE OF RE-POPULATING MY PLANET AND COMPLETING THE CIRCLE OF LIFE IS GONE.
HEY, YONDU! LOOK OUT!!
* THE KOSPAH ARE CEREMONIAL EARRINGS WORN BY CENTAURIANS AND EXCHANGED AT THE TIME OF JOINING, MUCH AS WE EXCHANGE WEDDING BANDS. --CRAIG

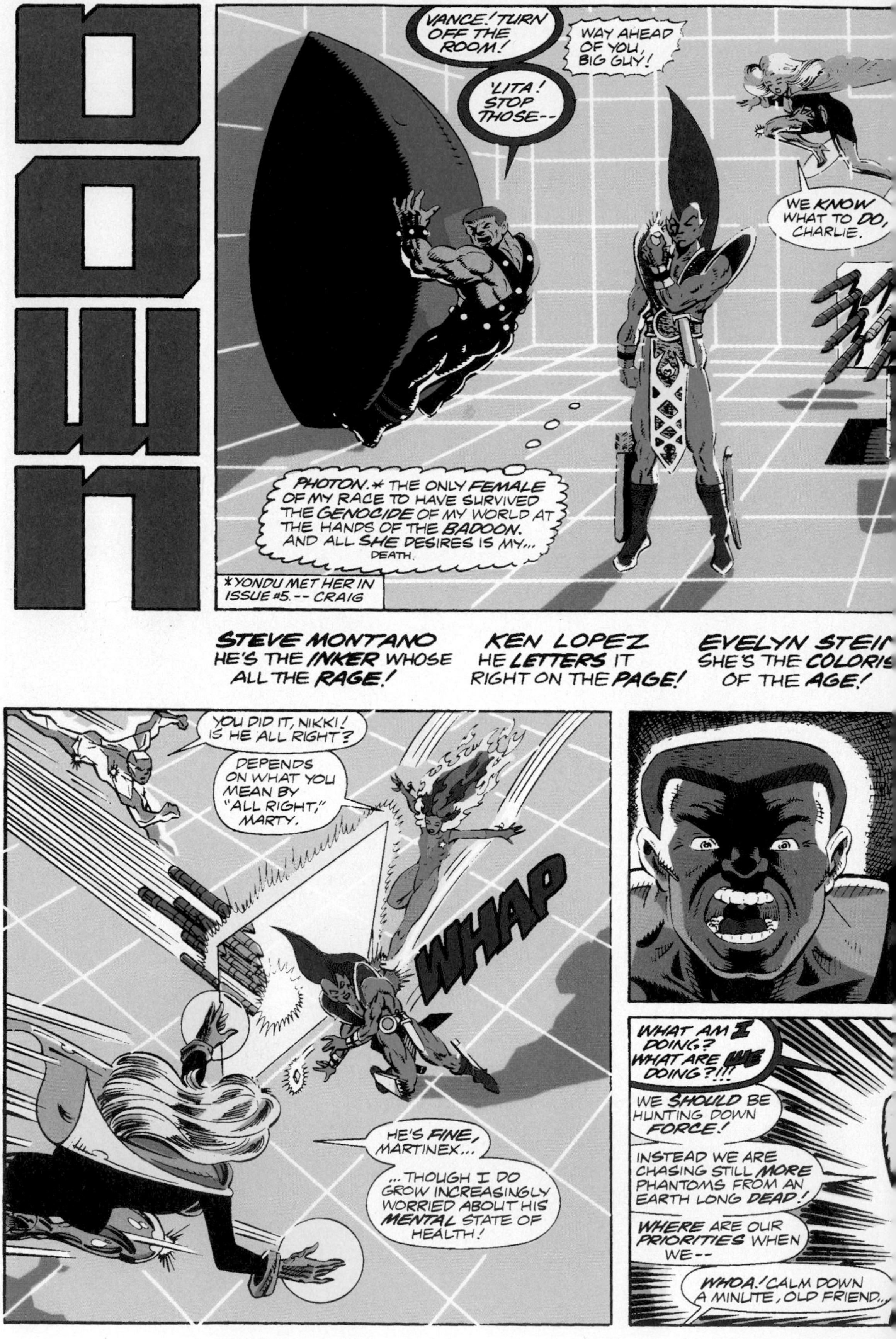
DOWN
VANCE! TURN OFF THE ROOM!
WAY AHEAD OF YOU, BIG GUY!
'LITA! STOP THOSE--
WE KNOW WHAT TO DO, CHARLIE.
PHOTON.* THE ONLY FEMALE OF MY RACE TO HAVE SURVIVED THE GENOCIDE OF MY WORLD AT THE HANDS OF THE BADOON. AND ALL SHE DESIRES IS MY... DEATH.
*YONDU MET HER IN ISSUE #5.-- CRAIG
STEVE MONTANO HE'S THE INKER WHOSE ALL THE RAGE!
KEN LOPEZ HE LETTERS IT RIGHT ON THE PAGE!
EVELYN STEI
SHE'S THE COLORIS
OF THE AGE!
YOU DID IT, NIKKI! IS HE ALL RIGHT?
DEPENDS ON WHAT YOU MEAN BY "ALL RIGHT," MARTY.
WHAP
HE'S FINE, MARTINEX...
...THOUGH I DO GROW INCREASINGLY WORRIED ABOUT HIS MENTAL STATE OF HEALTH!
WHAT AM I DOING? WHAT ARE WE DOING?!!!
WE SHOULD BE HUNTING DOWN FORCE!
INSTEAD WE ARE CHASING STILL MORE PHANTOMS FROM AN EARTH LONG DEAD!
WHERE ARE OUR PRIORITIES WHEN WE--
WHOA! CALM DOWN A MINUTE, OLD FRIEND...

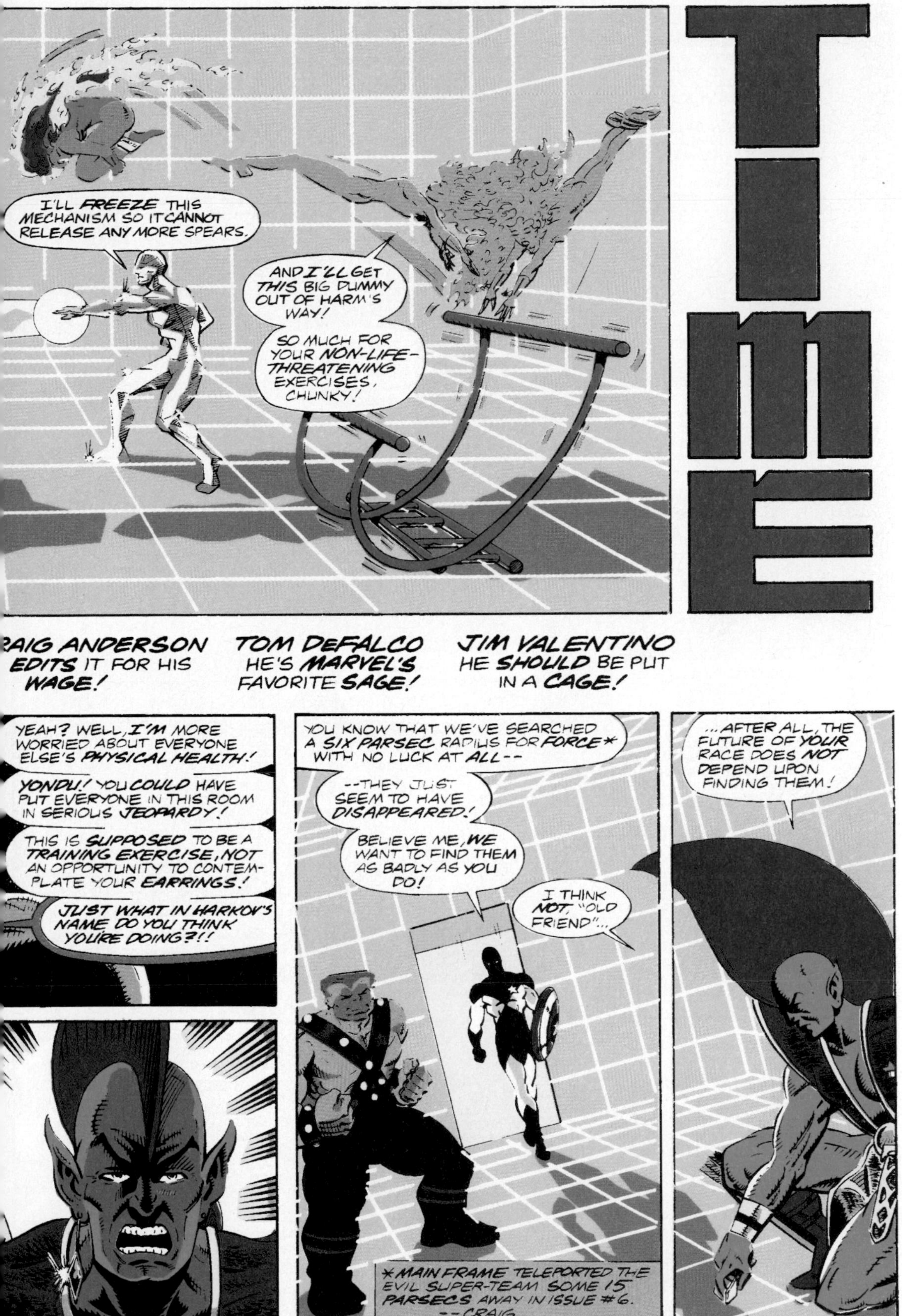
TIME
I'LL FREEZE THIS MECHANISM SO IT CANNOT RELEASE ANY MORE SPEARS.
AND I'LL GET THIS BIG DUMMY OUT OF HARM'S WAY!
SO MUCH FOR YOUR NON-LIFE-THREATENING EXERCISES, CHUNKY!
RAIG ANDERSON EDITS IT FOR HIS WAGE!
TOM DeFALCO HE'S MARVEL'S FAVORITE SAGE!
JIM VALENTINO HE SHOULD BE PUT IN A CAGE!
YEAH? WELL, I'M MORE WORRIED ABOUT EVERYONE ELSE'S PHYSICAL HEALTH!
YONDU! YOU COULD HAVE PUT EVERYONE IN THIS ROOM IN SERIOUS JEOPARDY!
THIS IS SUPPOSED TO BE A TRAINING EXERCISE, NOT AN OPPORTUNITY TO CONTEMPLATE YOUR EARRINGS!
JUST WHAT IN HARKOV'S NAME DO YOU THINK YOU'RE DOING?!!
YOU KNOW THAT WE'VE SEARCHED A SIX PARSEC RADIUS FOR FORCE* WITH NO LUCK AT ALL--
--THEY JUST SEEM TO HAVE DISAPPEARED!
BELIEVE ME, WE WANT TO FIND THEM AS BADLY AS YOU DO!
I THINK NOT, "OLD FRIEND"...
*MAIN FRAME TELEPORTED THE EVIL SUPER-TEAM SOME 15 PARSECS AWAY IN ISSUE #6. --CRAIG
...AFTER ALL, THE FUTURE OF YOUR RACE DOES NOT DEPEND UPON FINDING THEM!

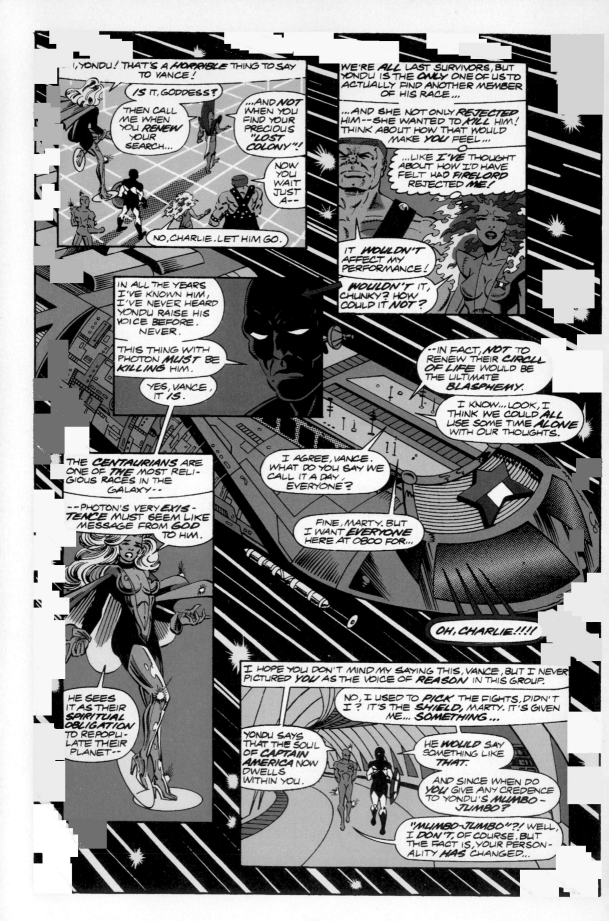

I, YONDU! THAT'S A *HORRIBLE* THING TO SAY TO VANCE!

IS IT, GODDESS?

THEN CALL ME WHEN YOU *RENEW* YOUR SEARCH...

...AND *NOT* WHEN YOU FIND YOUR PRECIOUS *"LOST COLONY"!*

NOW YOU WAIT JUST A--

NO, CHARLIE. LET HIM GO.

WE'RE *ALL* LAST SURVIVORS, BUT YONDU IS THE *ONLY* ONE OF US TO ACTUALLY FIND ANOTHER MEMBER OF HIS RACE...

...AND SHE NOT ONLY *REJECTED* HIM-- SHE WANTED TO *KILL* HIM! THINK ABOUT HOW THAT WOULD MAKE *YOU* FEEL...

...LIKE *I'VE* THOUGHT ABOUT HOW I'D HAVE FELT HAD *FIRELORD* REJECTED *ME!*

IT *WOULDN'T* AFFECT MY PERFORMANCE!

WOULDN'T IT, CHUNKY? HOW COULD IT *NOT?*

IN ALL THE YEARS I'VE KNOWN HIM, I'VE NEVER HEARD YONDU RAISE HIS VOICE BEFORE. NEVER.

THIS THING WITH PHOTON *MUST* BE KILLING HIM.

YES, VANCE, IT *IS.*

--IN FACT, *NOT* TO RENEW THEIR *CIRCLE OF LIFE* WOULD BE THE ULTIMATE *BLASPHEMY.*

I KNOW...LOOK, I THINK WE COULD *ALL* USE SOME TIME *ALONE* WITH OUR THOUGHTS.

THE *CENTAURIANS* ARE ONE OF *THE* MOST RELIGIOUS RACES IN THE GALAXY--

--PHOTON'S VERY *EXISTENCE* MUST SEEM LIKE MESSAGE FROM *GOD* TO HIM.

I AGREE, VANCE. WHAT DO YOU SAY WE CALL IT A DAY, EVERYONE?

FINE, MARTY. BUT I WANT *EVERYONE* HERE AT 0800 FOR...

OH, CHARLIE!!!!

HE SEES IT AS THEIR *SPIRITUAL OBLIGATION* TO REPOPULATE THEIR PLANET--

I HOPE YOU DON'T MIND MY SAYING THIS, VANCE, BUT I NEVER PICTURED *YOU* AS THE VOICE OF *REASON* IN THIS GROUP.

NO, I USED TO *PICK* THE FIGHTS, DIDN'T I? IT'S THE *SHIELD,* MARTY. IT'S GIVEN ME.... *SOMETHING...*

YONDU SAYS THAT THE SOUL OF *CAPTAIN AMERICA* NOW DWELLS WITHIN YOU.

HE *WOULD* SAY SOMETHING LIKE *THAT.*

AND SINCE WHEN DO *YOU* GIVE ANY CREDENCE TO YONDU'S *MUMBO-JUMBO?*

"MUMBO-JUMBO"?! WELL, I *DON'T,* OF COURSE. BUT THE FACT IS, YOUR PERSONALITY *HAS* CHANGED...

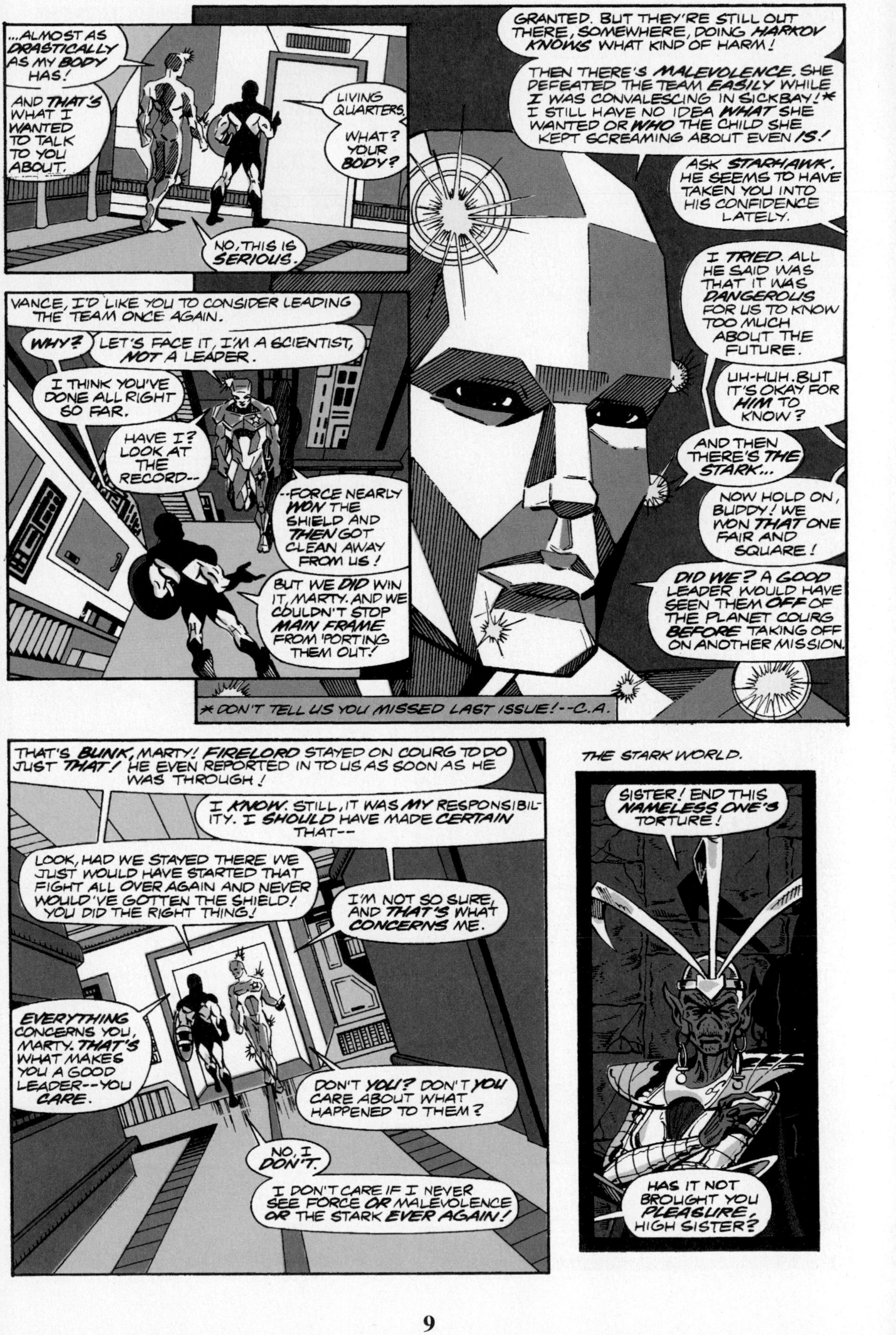

...ALMOST AS DRASTICALLY AS MY BODY HAS!
AND THAT'S WHAT I WANTED TO TALK TO YOU ABOUT.
LIVING QUARTERS.
WHAT? YOUR BODY?
NO, THIS IS SERIOUS.
GRANTED. BUT THEY'RE STILL OUT THERE, SOMEWHERE, DOING HARKOV KNOWS WHAT KIND OF HARM!
THEN THERE'S MALEVOLENCE. SHE DEFEATED THE TEAM EASILY WHILE I WAS CONVALESCING IN SICKBAY!* I STILL HAVE NO IDEA WHAT SHE WANTED OR WHO THE CHILD SHE KEPT SCREAMING ABOUT EVEN IS!
ASK STARHAWK. HE SEEMS TO HAVE TAKEN YOU INTO HIS CONFIDENCE LATELY.
I TRIED. ALL HE SAID WAS THAT IT WAS DANGEROUS FOR US TO KNOW TOO MUCH ABOUT THE FUTURE.
UH-HUH. BUT IT'S OKAY FOR HIM TO KNOW?
AND THEN THERE'S THE STARK...
NOW HOLD ON, BUDDY! WE WON THAT ONE FAIR AND SQUARE!
DID WE? A GOOD LEADER WOULD HAVE SEEN THEM OFF OF THE PLANET COURG BEFORE TAKING OFF ON ANOTHER MISSION.
VANCE, I'D LIKE YOU TO CONSIDER LEADING THE TEAM ONCE AGAIN.
WHY?
LET'S FACE IT, I'M A SCIENTIST, NOT A LEADER.
I THINK YOU'VE DONE ALL RIGHT SO FAR.
HAVE I? LOOK AT THE RECORD--
--FORCE NEARLY WON THE SHIELD AND THEN GOT CLEAN AWAY FROM US!
BUT WE DID WIN IT, MARTY. AND WE COULDN'T STOP MAIN FRAME FROM 'PORTING THEM OUT!
* DON'T TELL US YOU MISSED LAST ISSUE! --C.A.
THAT'S BUNK, MARTY! FIRELORD STAYED ON COURG TO DO JUST THAT! HE EVEN REPORTED IN TO US AS SOON AS HE WAS THROUGH!
I KNOW. STILL, IT WAS MY RESPONSIBILITY. I SHOULD HAVE MADE CERTAIN THAT--
LOOK, HAD WE STAYED THERE WE JUST WOULD HAVE STARTED THAT FIGHT ALL OVER AGAIN AND NEVER WOULD'VE GOTTEN THE SHIELD! YOU DID THE RIGHT THING!
I'M NOT SO SURE, AND THAT'S WHAT CONCERNS ME.
EVERYTHING CONCERNS YOU, MARTY. THAT'S WHAT MAKES YOU A GOOD LEADER--YOU CARE.
DON'T YOU? DON'T YOU CARE ABOUT WHAT HAPPENED TO THEM?
NO, I DON'T.
I DON'T CARE IF I NEVER SEE FORCE OR MALEVOLENCE OR THE STARK EVER AGAIN!
THE STARK WORLD.
SISTER! END THIS NAMELESS ONE'S TORTURE!
HAS IT NOT BROUGHT YOU PLEASURE, HIGH SISTER?

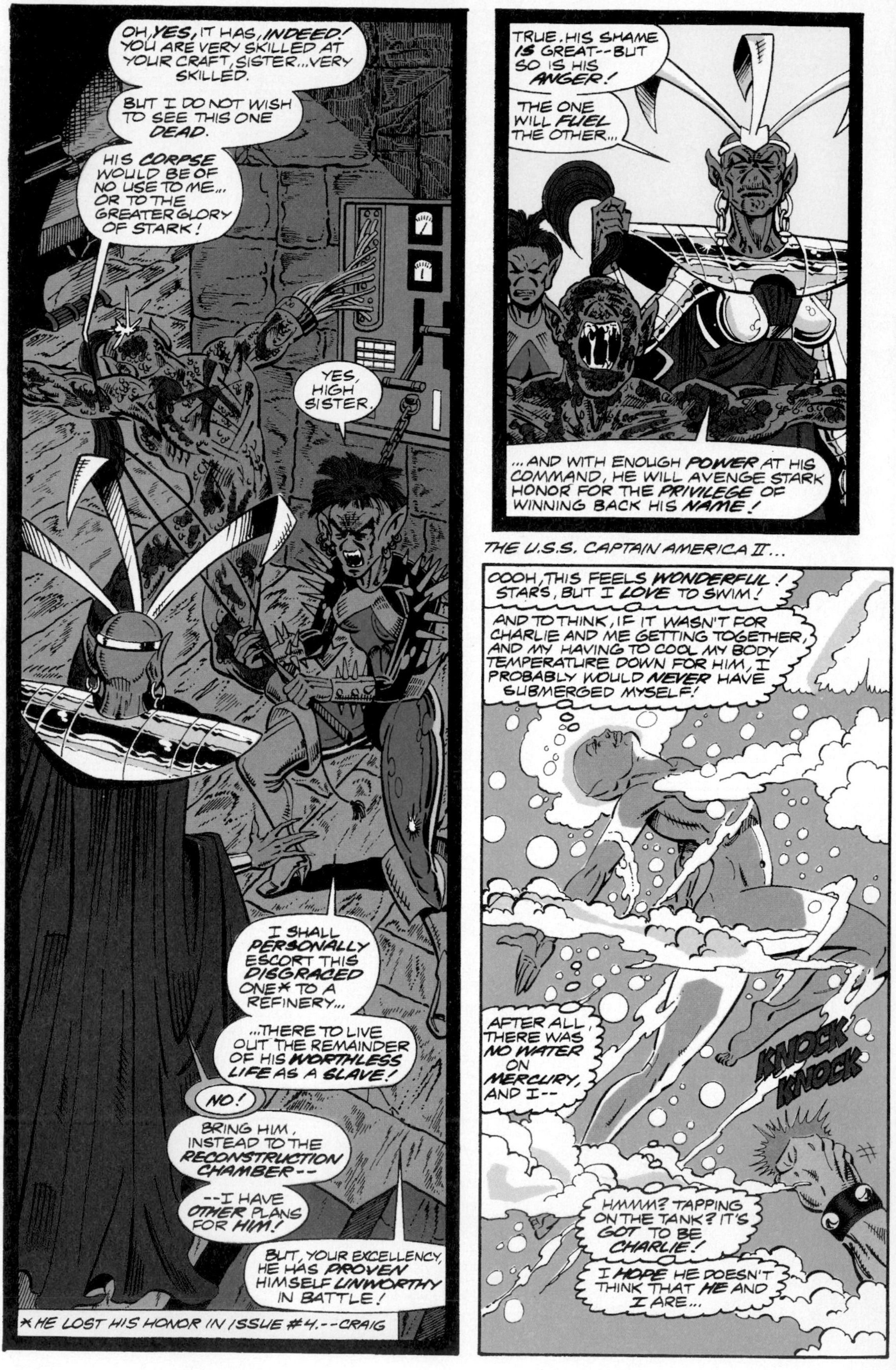
OH, YES, IT HAS, INDEED! YOU ARE VERY SKILLED AT YOUR CRAFT, SISTER... VERY SKILLED.
BUT I DO NOT WISH TO SEE THIS ONE DEAD.
HIS CORPSE WOULD BE OF NO USE TO ME... OR TO THE GREATER GLORY OF STARK!
YES, HIGH SISTER.
I SHALL PERSONALLY ESCORT THIS DISGRACED ONE* TO A REFINERY...
...THERE TO LIVE OUT THE REMAINDER OF HIS WORTHLESS LIFE AS A SLAVE!
NO!
BRING HIM, INSTEAD TO THE RECONSTRUCTION CHAMBER--
--I HAVE OTHER PLANS FOR HIM!
BUT, YOUR EXCELLENCY, HE HAS PROVEN HIMSELF UNWORTHY IN BATTLE!
*HE LOST HIS HONOR IN ISSUE #4.--CRAIG
TRUE. HIS SHAME IS GREAT--BUT SO IS HIS ANGER!
THE ONE WILL FUEL THE OTHER...
...AND WITH ENOUGH POWER AT HIS COMMAND, HE WILL AVENGE STARK HONOR FOR THE PRIVILEGE OF WINNING BACK HIS NAME!
THE U.S.S. CAPTAIN AMERICA II...
OOOH, THIS FEELS WONDERFUL! STARS, BUT I LOVE TO SWIM!
AND TO THINK, IF IT WASN'T FOR CHARLIE AND ME GETTING TOGETHER, AND MY HAVING TO COOL MY BODY TEMPERATURE DOWN FOR HIM, I PROBABLY WOULD NEVER HAVE SUBMERGED MYSELF!
AFTER ALL, THERE WAS NO WATER ON MERCURY, AND I--
KNOCK KNOCK
HMMM? TAPPING ON THE TANK? IT'S GOT TO BE CHARLIE!
I HOPE HE DOESN'T THINK THAT HE AND I ARE...

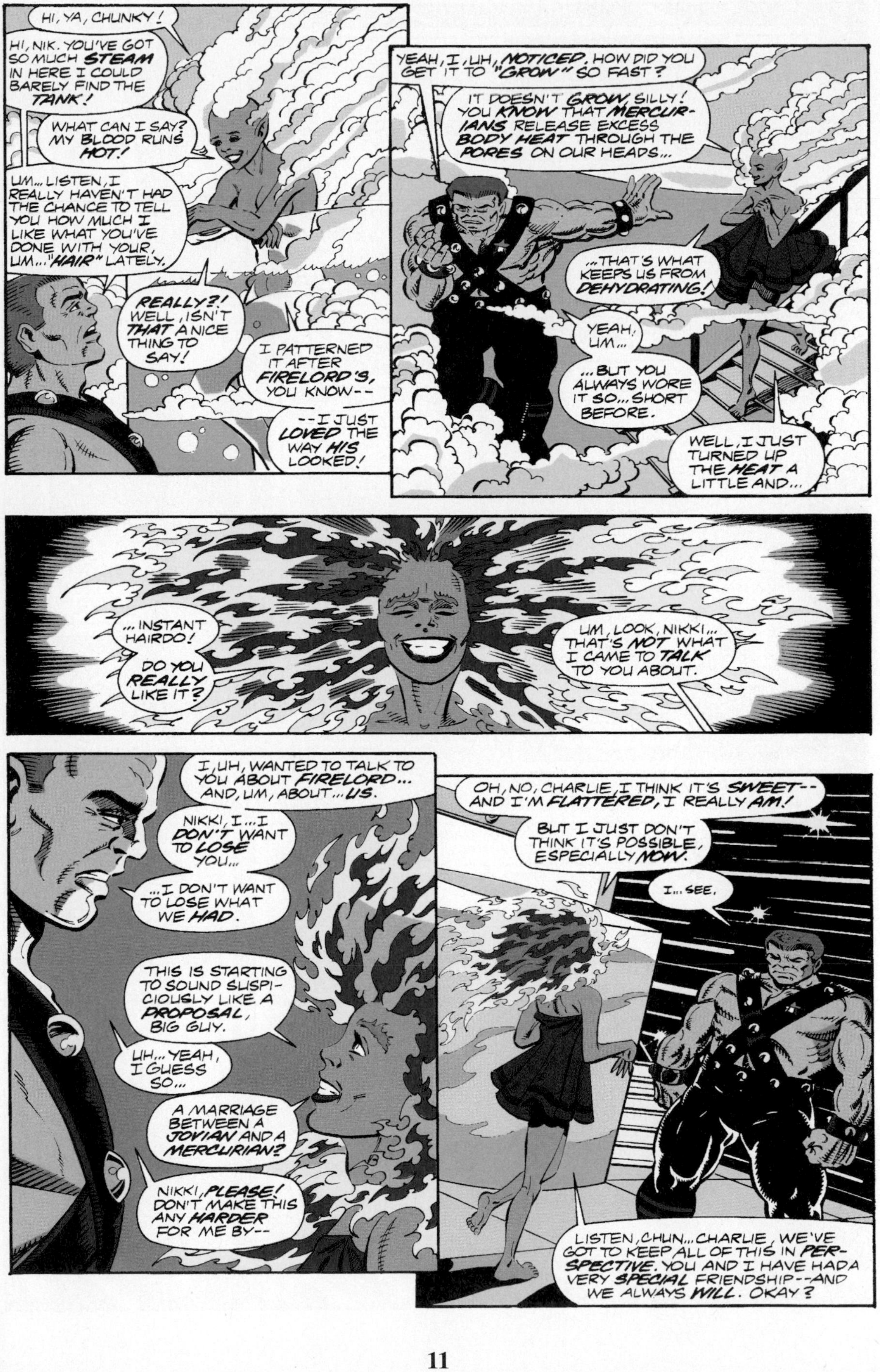

HI, YA, CHUNKY!
HI, NIK. YOU'VE GOT SO MUCH STEAM IN HERE I COULD BARELY FIND THE TANK!
WHAT CAN I SAY? MY BLOOD RUNS HOT!
UM... LISTEN, I REALLY HAVEN'T HAD THE CHANCE TO TELL YOU HOW MUCH I LIKE WHAT YOU'VE DONE WITH YOUR, UM..."HAIR" LATELY.
REALLY?! WELL, ISN'T THAT A NICE THING TO SAY!
I PATTERNED IT AFTER FIRELORD'S, YOU KNOW--
--I JUST LOVED THE WAY HIS LOOKED!
YEAH, I, UH, NOTICED. HOW DID YOU GET IT TO "GROW" SO FAST?
IT DOESN'T GROW, SILLY! YOU KNOW THAT MERCURIANS RELEASE EXCESS BODY HEAT THROUGH THE PORES ON OUR HEADS...
...THAT'S WHAT KEEPS US FROM DEHYDRATING!
YEAH, UM...
...BUT YOU ALWAYS WORE IT SO... SHORT BEFORE.
WELL, I JUST TURNED UP THE HEAT A LITTLE AND...
...INSTANT HAIRDO!
DO YOU REALLY LIKE IT?
UM, LOOK, NIKKI... THAT'S NOT WHAT I CAME TO TALK TO YOU ABOUT.
I, UH, WANTED TO TALK TO YOU ABOUT FIRELORD... AND, UM, ABOUT... US.
NIKKI, I...I DON'T WANT TO LOSE YOU...
...I DON'T WANT TO LOSE WHAT WE HAD.
THIS IS STARTING TO SOUND SUSPICIOUSLY LIKE A PROPOSAL, BIG GUY.
UH... YEAH, I GUESS SO...
A MARRIAGE BETWEEN A JOVIAN AND A MERCURIAN?
NIKKI, PLEASE! DON'T MAKE THIS ANY HARDER FOR ME BY--
OH, NO, CHARLIE, I THINK IT'S SWEET-- AND I'M FLATTERED, I REALLY AM!
BUT I JUST DON'T THINK IT'S POSSIBLE, ESPECIALLY NOW.
I... SEE.
LISTEN, CHUN... CHARLIE, WE'VE GOT TO KEEP ALL OF THIS IN PERSPECTIVE. YOU AND I HAVE HAD A VERY SPECIAL FRIENDSHIP--AND WE ALWAYS WILL. OKAY?

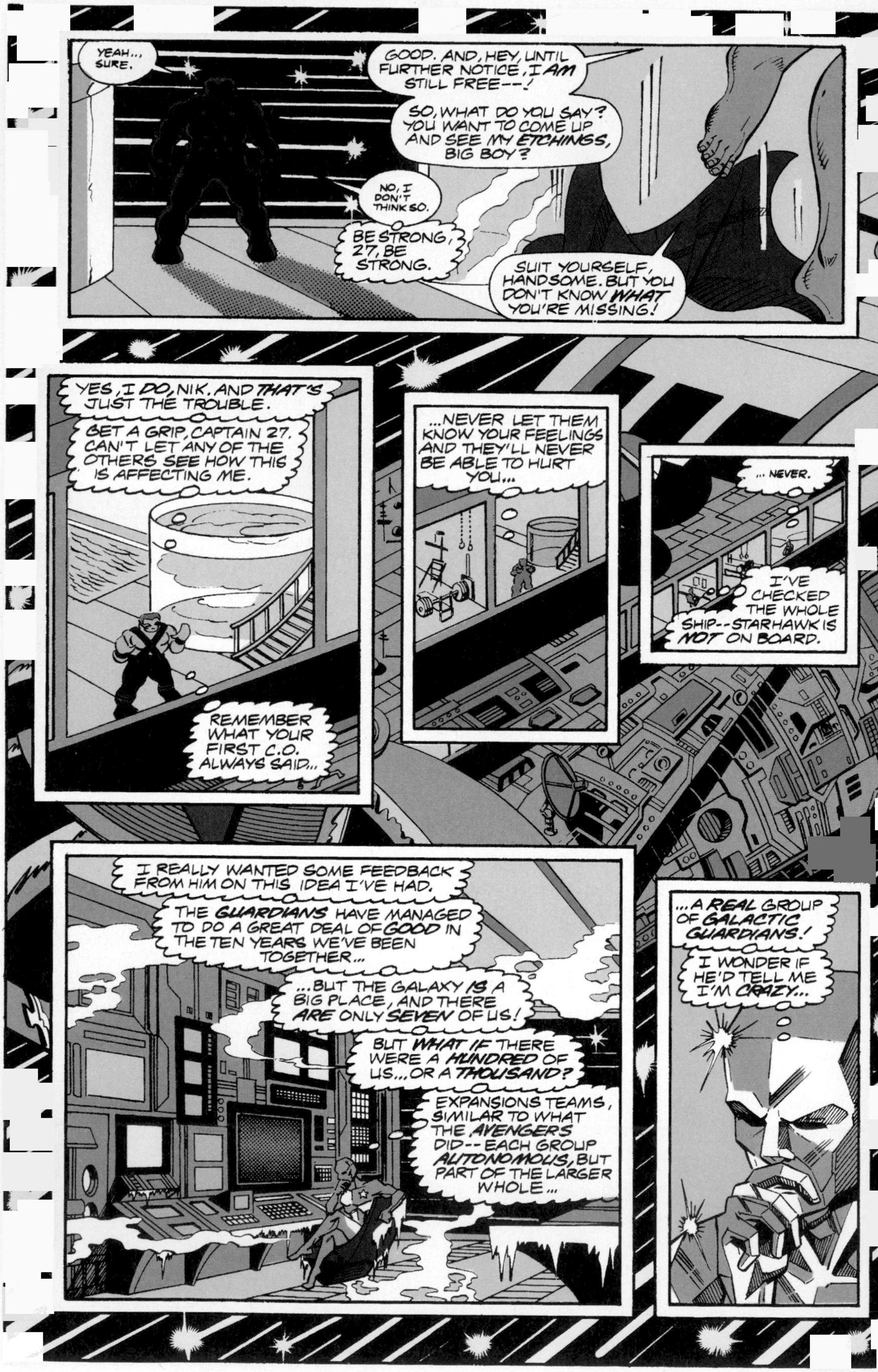

YEAH... SURE.
GOOD. AND, HEY, UNTIL FURTHER NOTICE, I AM STILL FREE--!
SO, WHAT DO YOU SAY? YOU WANT TO COME UP AND SEE MY ETCHINGS, BIG BOY?
NO, I DON'T THINK SO.
BE STRONG, 27, BE STRONG.
SUIT YOURSELF, HANDSOME. BUT YOU DON'T KNOW WHAT YOU'RE MISSING!
YES, I DO, NIK. AND THAT'S JUST THE TROUBLE.
GET A GRIP, CAPTAIN 27. CAN'T LET ANY OF THE OTHERS SEE HOW THIS IS AFFECTING ME.
REMEMBER WHAT YOUR FIRST C.O. ALWAYS SAID...
...NEVER LET THEM KNOW YOUR FEELINGS AND THEY'LL NEVER BE ABLE TO HURT YOU...
... NEVER.
I'VE CHECKED THE WHOLE SHIP--STARHAWK IS NOT ON BOARD.
I REALLY WANTED SOME FEEDBACK FROM HIM ON THIS IDEA I'VE HAD.
THE GUARDIANS HAVE MANAGED TO DO A GREAT DEAL OF GOOD IN THE TEN YEARS WE'VE BEEN TOGETHER...
...BUT THE GALAXY IS A BIG PLACE, AND THERE ARE ONLY SEVEN OF US!
BUT WHAT IF THERE WERE A HUNDRED OF US...OR A THOUSAND?
EXPANSIONS TEAMS, SIMILAR TO WHAT THE AVENGERS DID-- EACH GROUP AUTONOMOUS, BUT PART OF THE LARGER WHOLE...
...A REAL GROUP OF GALACTIC GUARDIANS!
I WONDER IF HE'D TELL ME I'M CRAZY...

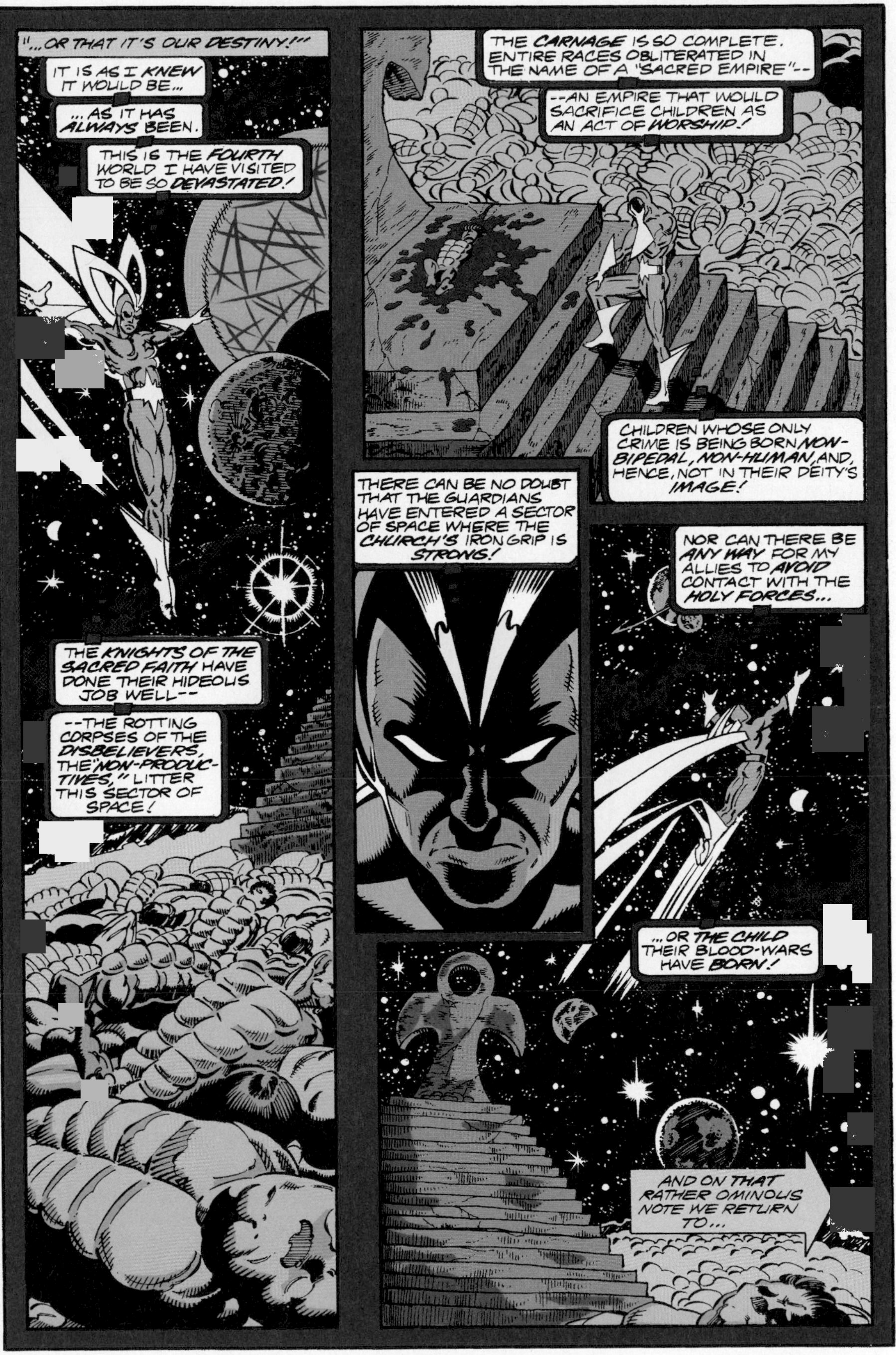
"...OR THAT IT'S OUR DESTINY!"
IT IS AS I KNEW IT WOULD BE...
...AS IT HAS ALWAYS BEEN.
THIS IS THE FOURTH WORLD I HAVE VISITED TO BE SO DEVASTATED!
THE KNIGHTS OF THE SACRED FAITH HAVE DONE THEIR HIDEOUS JOB WELL--
--THE ROTTING CORPSES OF THE DISBELIEVERS, THE "NON-PRODUCTIVES," LITTER THIS SECTOR OF SPACE!
THE CARNAGE IS SO COMPLETE. ENTIRE RACES OBLITERATED IN THE NAME OF A "SACRED EMPIRE"--
--AN EMPIRE THAT WOULD SACRIFICE CHILDREN AS AN ACT OF WORSHIP!
CHILDREN WHOSE ONLY CRIME IS BEING BORN NON-BIPEDAL, NON-HUMAN, AND, HENCE, NOT IN THEIR DEITY'S IMAGE!
THERE CAN BE NO DOUBT THAT THE GUARDIANS HAVE ENTERED A SECTOR OF SPACE WHERE THE CHURCH'S IRON GRIP IS STRONG!
NOR CAN THERE BE ANY WAY FOR MY ALLIES TO AVOID CONTACT WITH THE HOLY FORCES...
...OR THE CHILD THEIR BLOOD-WARS HAVE BORN!
AND ON THAT RATHER OMINOUS NOTE WE RETURN TO...

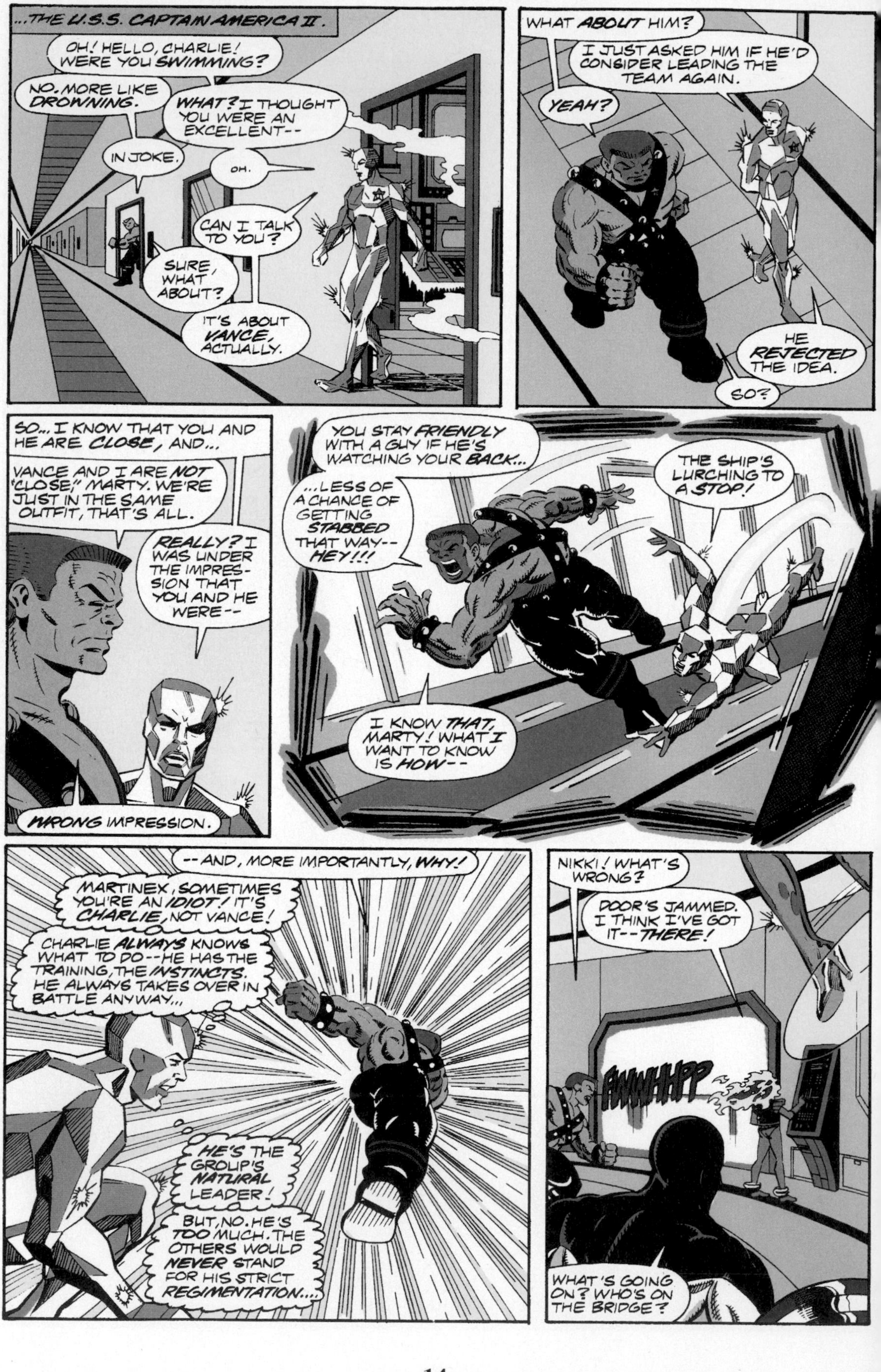

...THE U.S.S. CAPTAIN AMERICA II.
OH! HELLO, CHARLIE! WERE YOU SWIMMING?
NO. MORE LIKE DROWNING.
WHAT? I THOUGHT YOU WERE AN EXCELLENT--
IN JOKE.
OH.
CAN I TALK TO YOU?
SURE, WHAT ABOUT?
IT'S ABOUT VANCE, ACTUALLY.
WHAT ABOUT HIM?
I JUST ASKED HIM IF HE'D CONSIDER LEADING THE TEAM AGAIN.
YEAH?
HE REJECTED THE IDEA.
SO?
SO... I KNOW THAT YOU AND HE ARE CLOSE, AND...
VANCE AND I ARE NOT "CLOSE," MARTY. WE'RE JUST IN THE SAME OUTFIT, THAT'S ALL.
REALLY? I WAS UNDER THE IMPRESSION THAT YOU AND HE WERE--
WRONG IMPRESSION.
YOU STAY FRIENDLY WITH A GUY IF HE'S WATCHING YOUR BACK...
...LESS OF A CHANCE OF GETTING STABBED THAT WAY-- HEY!!!
THE SHIP'S LURCHING TO A STOP!
I KNOW THAT, MARTY! WHAT I WANT TO KNOW IS HOW--
--AND, MORE IMPORTANTLY, WHY!
MARTINEX, SOMETIMES YOU'RE AN IDIOT! IT'S CHARLIE, NOT VANCE!
CHARLIE ALWAYS KNOWS WHAT TO DO--HE HAS THE TRAINING, THE INSTINCTS. HE ALWAYS TAKES OVER IN BATTLE ANYWAY...
HE'S THE GROUP'S NATURAL LEADER!
BUT, NO. HE'S TOO MUCH. THE OTHERS WOULD NEVER STAND FOR HIS STRICT REGIMENTATION...
NIKKI! WHAT'S WRONG?
DOOR'S JAMMED. I THINK I'VE GOT IT--THERE!
FWWHHPP
WHAT'S GOING ON? WHO'S ON THE BRIDGE?

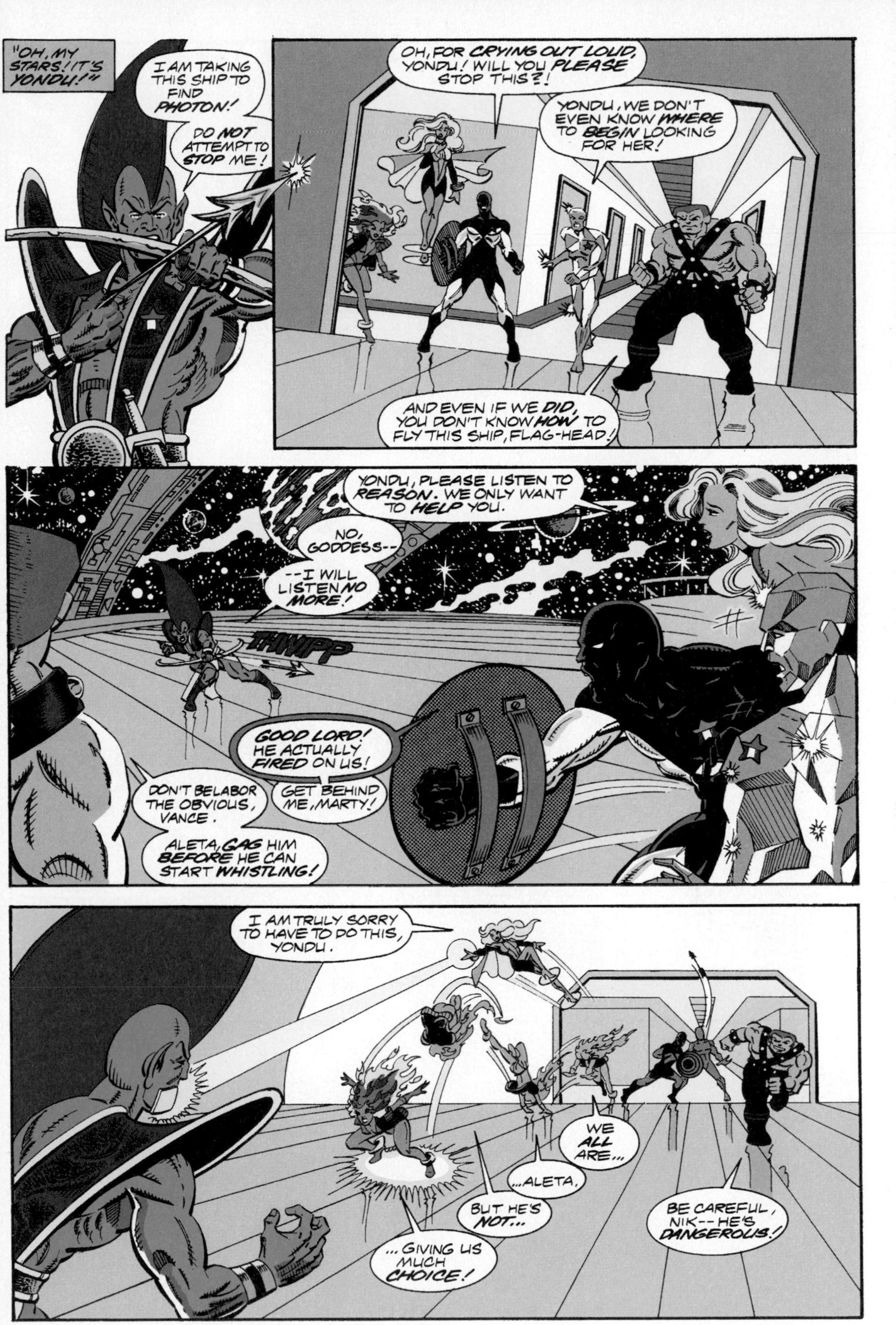
"OH, MY STARS! IT'S YONDU!"
I AM TAKING THIS SHIP TO FIND PHOTON!
DO NOT ATTEMPT TO STOP ME!
OH, FOR CRYING OUT LOUD, YONDU! WILL YOU PLEASE STOP THIS?!
YONDU, WE DON'T EVEN KNOW WHERE TO BEGIN LOOKING FOR HER!
AND EVEN IF WE DID, YOU DON'T KNOW HOW TO FLY THIS SHIP, FLAG-HEAD!
YONDU, PLEASE LISTEN TO REASON. WE ONLY WANT TO HELP YOU.
NO, GODDESS--
--I WILL LISTEN NO MORE!
THWIPP
GOOD LORD! HE ACTUALLY FIRED ON US!
GET BEHIND ME, MARTY!
DON'T BELABOR THE OBVIOUS, VANCE.
ALETA, GAG HIM BEFORE HE CAN START WHISTLING!
I AM TRULY SORRY TO HAVE TO DO THIS, YONDU.
WE ALL ARE...
...ALETA,
BUT HE'S NOT...
...GIVING US MUCH CHOICE!
BE CAREFUL, NIK--HE'S DANGEROUS!

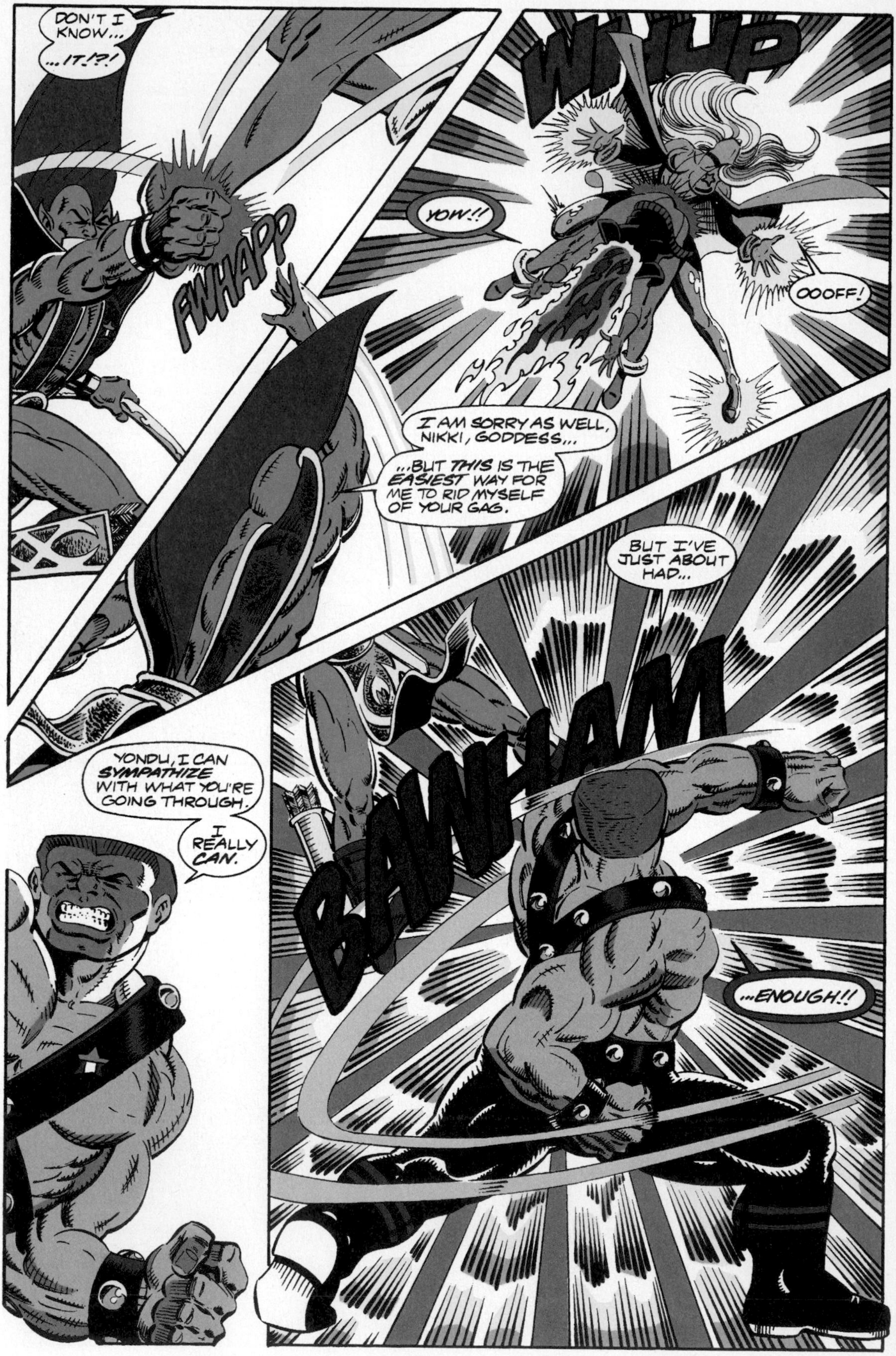
DON'T I KNOW... ...IT!?!
FWHAPP
WHUP
YOW!!
OOOFF!
I AM SORRY AS WELL, NIKKI, GODDESS...
...BUT THIS IS THE EASIEST WAY FOR ME TO RID MYSELF OF YOUR GAG.
YONDU, I CAN SYMPATHIZE WITH WHAT YOU'RE GOING THROUGH.
I REALLY CAN.
BUT I'VE JUST ABOUT HAD...
BAWHAM
...ENOUGH!!

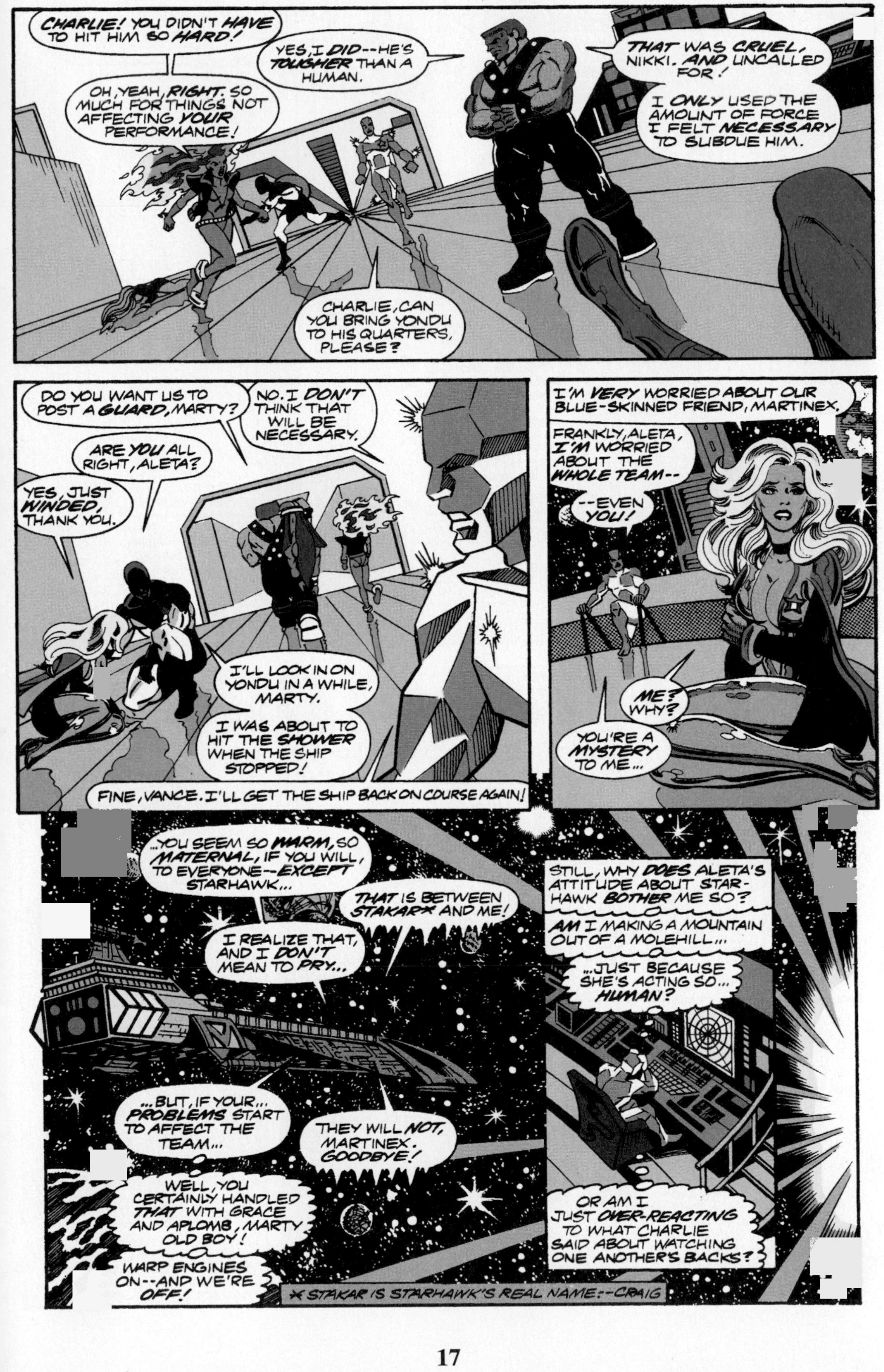
CHARLIE! YOU DIDN'T HAVE TO HIT HIM SO HARD!
OH, YEAH, RIGHT. SO MUCH FOR THINGS NOT AFFECTING YOUR PERFORMANCE!
YES, I DID--HE'S TOUGHER THAN A HUMAN.
THAT WAS CRUEL, NIKKI. AND UNCALLED FOR!
I ONLY USED THE AMOUNT OF FORCE I FELT NECESSARY TO SUBDUE HIM.
CHARLIE, CAN YOU BRING YONDU TO HIS QUARTERS, PLEASE?
DO YOU WANT US TO POST A GUARD, MARTY?
NO. I DON'T THINK THAT WILL BE NECESSARY.
ARE YOU ALL RIGHT, ALETA?
YES, JUST WINDED, THANK YOU.
I'LL LOOK IN ON YONDU IN A WHILE, MARTY.
I WAS ABOUT TO HIT THE SHOWER WHEN THE SHIP STOPPED!
FINE, VANCE. I'LL GET THE SHIP BACK ON COURSE AGAIN!
I'M VERY WORRIED ABOUT OUR BLUE-SKINNED FRIEND, MARTINEX.
FRANKLY, ALETA, I'M WORRIED ABOUT THE WHOLE TEAM--
--EVEN YOU!
ME? WHY?
YOU'RE A MYSTERY TO ME...
...YOU SEEM SO WARM, SO MATERNAL, IF YOU WILL, TO EVERYONE--EXCEPT STARHAWK...
THAT IS BETWEEN STAKAR* AND ME!
I REALIZE THAT, AND I DON'T MEAN TO PRY...
...BUT, IF YOUR... PROBLEMS START TO AFFECT THE TEAM...
THEY WILL NOT, MARTINEX. GOODBYE!
STILL, WHY DOES ALETA'S ATTITUDE ABOUT STAR-HAWK BOTHER ME SO?
AM I MAKING A MOUNTAIN OUT OF A MOLEHILL...
...JUST BECAUSE SHE'S ACTING SO... HUMAN?
WELL, YOU CERTAINLY HANDLED THAT WITH GRACE AND APLOMB, MARTY OLD BOY!
WARP ENGINES ON--AND WE'RE OFF!
OR AM I JUST OVER-REACTING TO WHAT CHARLIE SAID ABOUT WATCHING ONE ANOTHER'S BACKS?
* STAKAR IS STARHAWK'S REAL NAME: --CRAIG

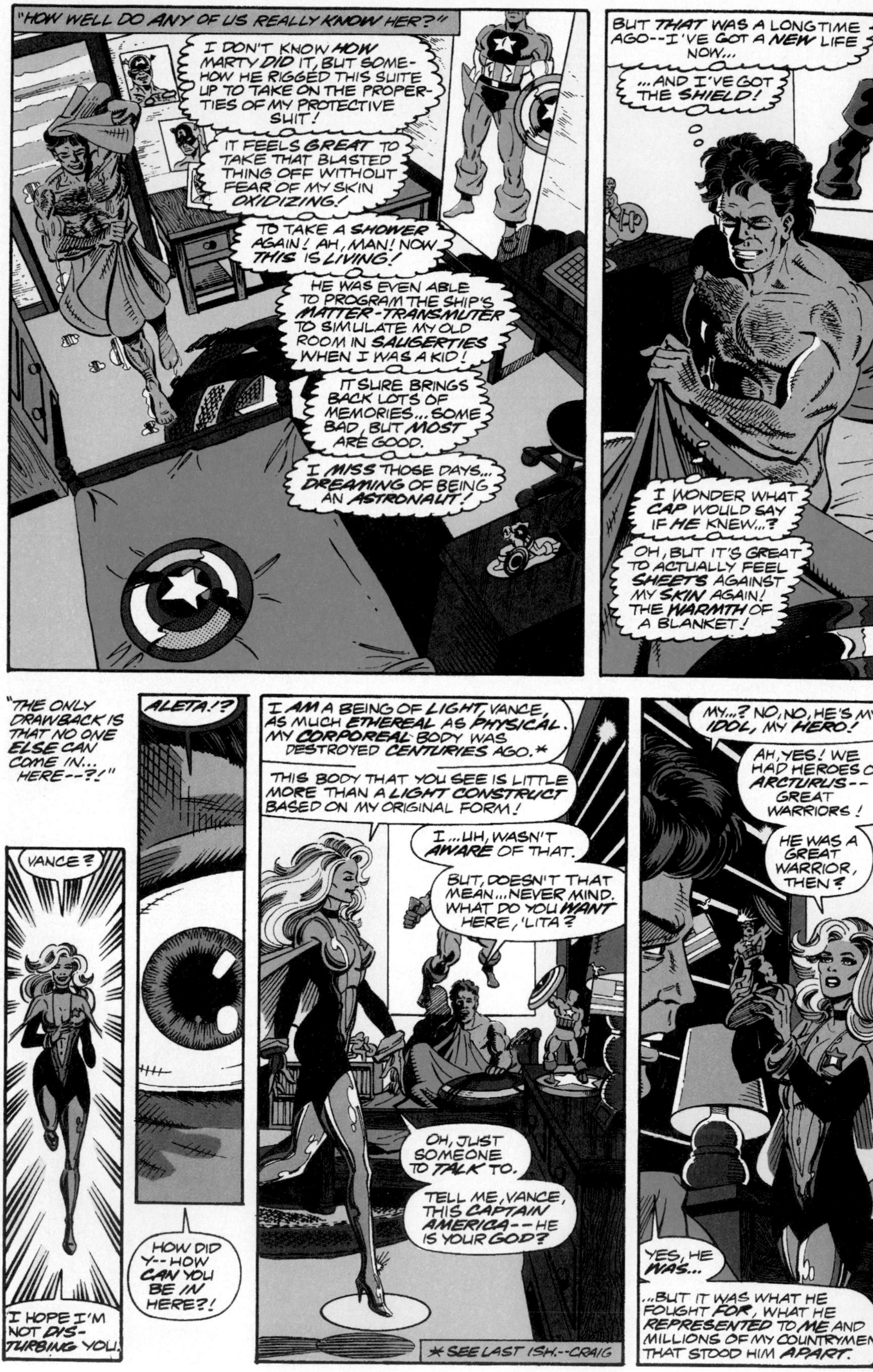
"HOW WELL DO ANY OF US REALLY KNOW HER?"
I DON'T KNOW HOW MARTY DID IT, BUT SOMEHOW HE RIGGED THIS SUITE UP TO TAKE ON THE PROPERTIES OF MY PROTECTIVE SUIT!
IT FEELS GREAT TO TAKE THAT BLASTED THING OFF WITHOUT FEAR OF MY SKIN OXIDIZING!
TO TAKE A SHOWER AGAIN! AH, MAN! NOW THIS IS LIVING!
HE WAS EVEN ABLE TO PROGRAM THE SHIP'S MATTER-TRANSMUTER TO SIMULATE MY OLD ROOM IN SAUGERTIES WHEN I WAS A KID!
IT SURE BRINGS BACK LOTS OF MEMORIES... SOME BAD, BUT MOST ARE GOOD.
I MISS THOSE DAYS... DREAMING OF BEING AN ASTRONAUT!
BUT THAT WAS A LONG TIME AGO--I'VE GOT A NEW LIFE NOW...
...AND I'VE GOT THE SHIELD!
I WONDER WHAT CAP WOULD SAY IF HE KNEW...?
OH, BUT IT'S GREAT TO ACTUALLY FEEL SHEETS AGAINST MY SKIN AGAIN! THE WARMTH OF A BLANKET!
"THE ONLY DRAWBACK IS THAT NO ONE ELSE CAN COME IN... HERE--?!"
VANCE?
I HOPE I'M NOT DISTURBING YOU.
ALETA!?
HOW DID Y--HOW CAN YOU BE IN HERE?!
I AM A BEING OF LIGHT, VANCE, AS MUCH ETHEREAL AS PHYSICAL. MY CORPOREAL BODY WAS DESTROYED CENTURIES AGO.*
THIS BODY THAT YOU SEE IS LITTLE MORE THAN A LIGHT CONSTRUCT BASED ON MY ORIGINAL FORM!
I... UH, WASN'T AWARE OF THAT.
BUT, DOESN'T THAT MEAN... NEVER MIND. WHAT DO YOU WANT HERE, 'LITA?
OH, JUST SOMEONE TO TALK TO.
TELL ME, VANCE, THIS CAPTAIN AMERICA--HE IS YOUR GOD?
*SEE LAST ISH.--CRAIG
MY...? NO, NO, HE'S MY IDOL, MY HERO!
AH, YES! WE HAD HEROES ON ARCTURUS--GREAT WARRIORS!
HE WAS A GREAT WARRIOR, THEN?
YES, HE WAS...
...BUT IT WAS WHAT HE FOUGHT FOR, WHAT HE REPRESENTED TO ME AND MILLIONS OF MY COUNTRYMEN, THAT STOOD HIM APART.

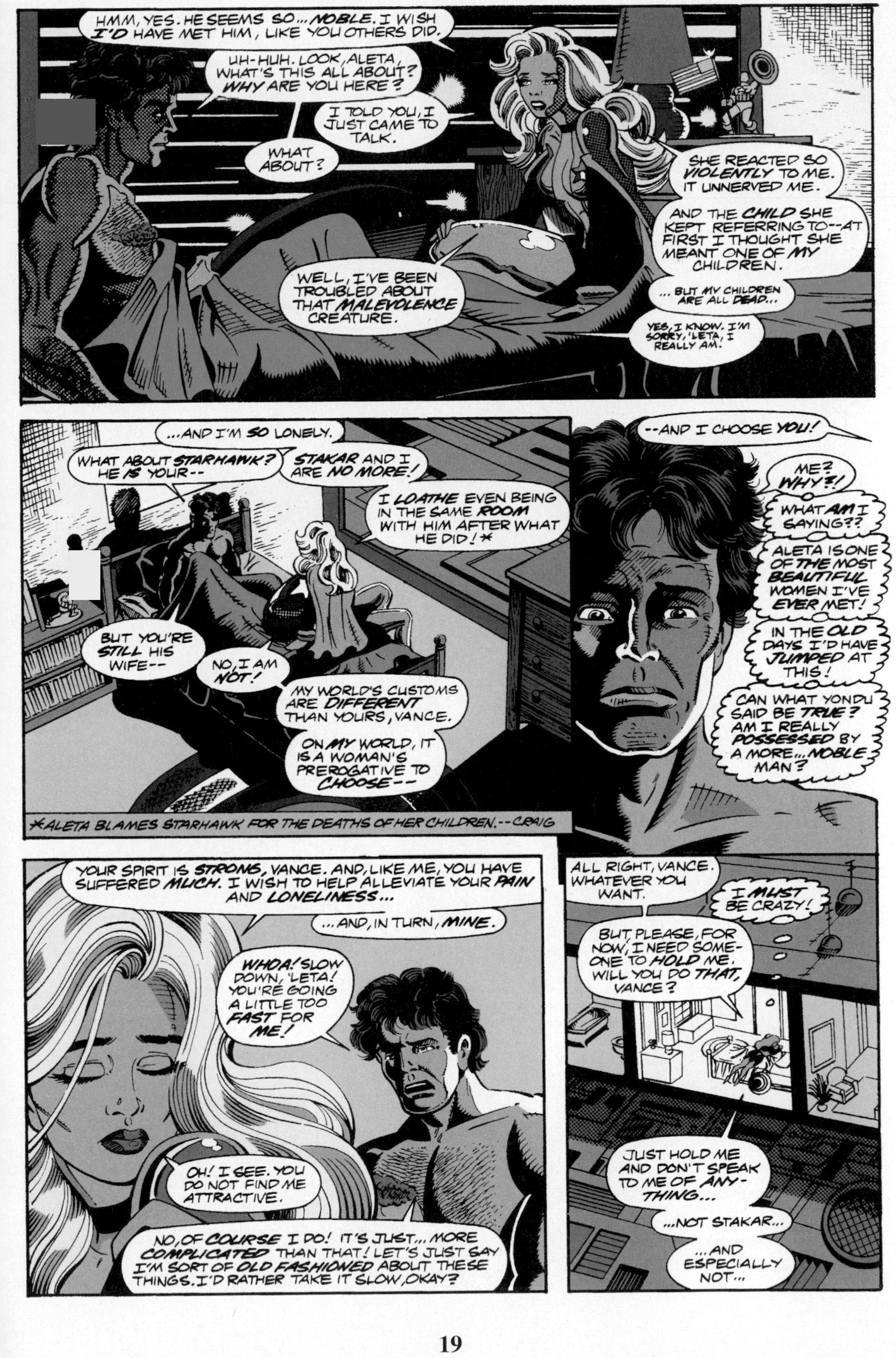
HMM, YES. HE SEEMS SO... NOBLE. I WISH I'D HAVE MET HIM, LIKE YOU OTHERS DID.
UH-HUH. LOOK, ALETA, WHAT'S THIS ALL ABOUT? WHY ARE YOU HERE?
I TOLD YOU, I JUST CAME TO TALK.
WHAT ABOUT?
WELL, I'VE BEEN TROUBLED ABOUT THAT MALEVOLENCE CREATURE.
SHE REACTED SO VIOLENTLY TO ME. IT UNNERVED ME.
AND THE CHILD SHE KEPT REFERRING TO--AT FIRST I THOUGHT SHE MEANT ONE OF MY CHILDREN.
...BUT MY CHILDREN ARE ALL DEAD...
YES, I KNOW. I'M SORRY, 'LETA, I REALLY AM.
...AND I'M SO LONELY.
WHAT ABOUT STARHAWK? HE IS YOUR--
STAKAR AND I ARE NO MORE!
I LOATHE EVEN BEING IN THE SAME ROOM WITH HIM AFTER WHAT HE DID!*
BUT YOU'RE STILL HIS WIFE--
NO, I AM NOT!
MY WORLD'S CUSTOMS ARE DIFFERENT THAN YOURS, VANCE.
ON MY WORLD, IT IS A WOMAN'S PREROGATIVE TO CHOOSE--
*ALETA BLAMES STARHAWK FOR THE DEATHS OF HER CHILDREN. --CRAIG
--AND I CHOOSE YOU!
ME? WHY?!
WHAT AM I SAYING??
ALETA IS ONE OF THE MOST BEAUTIFUL WOMEN I'VE EVER MET!
IN THE OLD DAYS I'D HAVE JUMPED AT THIS!
CAN WHAT YONDU SAID BE TRUE? AM I REALLY POSSESSED BY A MORE... NOBLE MAN?
YOUR SPIRIT IS STRONG, VANCE. AND, LIKE ME, YOU HAVE SUFFERED MUCH. I WISH TO HELP ALLEVIATE YOUR PAIN AND LONELINESS...
...AND, IN TURN, MINE.
WHOA! SLOW DOWN, 'LETA! YOU'RE GOING A LITTLE TOO FAST FOR ME!
OH! I SEE. YOU DO NOT FIND ME ATTRACTIVE.
NO, OF COURSE I DO! IT'S JUST... MORE COMPLICATED THAN THAT! LET'S JUST SAY I'M SORT OF OLD FASHIONED ABOUT THESE THINGS. I'D RATHER TAKE IT SLOW, OKAY?
ALL RIGHT, VANCE. WHATEVER YOU WANT.
I MUST BE CRAZY!
BUT, PLEASE, FOR NOW, I NEED SOMEONE TO HOLD ME. WILL YOU DO THAT, VANCE?
JUST HOLD ME AND DON'T SPEAK TO ME OF ANYTHING...
...NOT STAKAR...
...AND ESPECIALLY NOT...

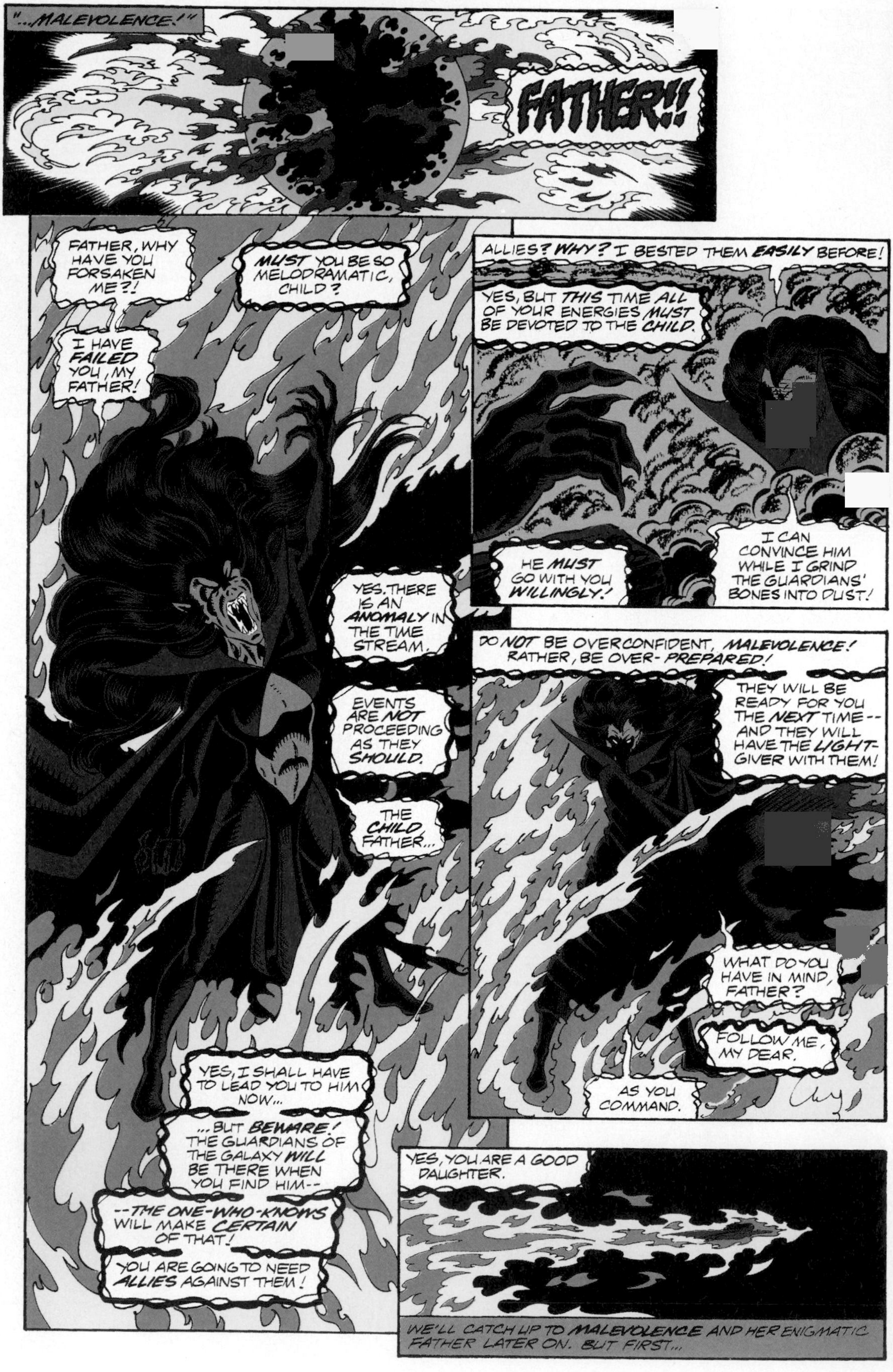
"...MALEVOLENCE!"
FATHER!!
FATHER, WHY HAVE YOU FORSAKEN ME?!
MUST YOU BE SO MELODRAMATIC, CHILD?
I HAVE FAILED YOU, MY FATHER!
YES. THERE IS AN ANOMALY IN THE TIME STREAM.
EVENTS ARE NOT PROCEEDING AS THEY SHOULD.
THE CHILD, FATHER...
YES, I SHALL HAVE TO LEAD YOU TO HIM NOW...
...BUT BEWARE! THE GUARDIANS OF THE GALAXY WILL BE THERE WHEN YOU FIND HIM--
--THE ONE-WHO-KNOWS WILL MAKE CERTAIN OF THAT!
YOU ARE GOING TO NEED ALLIES AGAINST THEM!
ALLIES? WHY? I BESTED THEM EASILY BEFORE!
YES, BUT THIS TIME ALL OF YOUR ENERGIES MUST BE DEVOTED TO THE CHILD.
HE MUST GO WITH YOU WILLINGLY!
I CAN CONVINCE HIM WHILE I GRIND THE GUARDIANS' BONES INTO DUST!
DO NOT BE OVERCONFIDENT, MALEVOLENCE! RATHER, BE OVER-PREPARED!
THEY WILL BE READY FOR YOU THE NEXT TIME-- AND THEY WILL HAVE THE LIGHT-GIVER WITH THEM!
WHAT DO YOU HAVE IN MIND, FATHER?
FOLLOW ME, MY DEAR.
AS YOU COMMAND.
YES, YOU ARE A GOOD DAUGHTER.
WE'LL CATCH UP TO MALEVOLENCE AND HER ENIGMATIC FATHER LATER ON. BUT FIRST...

...LET US RETURN TO THE *U.S.S. CAPTAIN AMERICA II,* AND, MORE SPECIFICALLY, THE GREENHOUSE IN THE AFT OF THE SHIP.

IT IS NO USE.

I CANNOT EVEN *MEDITATE.*

I HAVE LOST MY *CENTER,* THE CORE OF MY FAITH.

EVEN HERE AMONG THE GREEN, I AM *TORMENTED* BY HER.

SHE IS THE KEY TO OUR RACE'S FUTURE. IT IS ONLY THROUGH HER THAT THE SACRED CIRCLE OF LIFE CAN BE MENDED -- YET SHE WILL HAVE NO PART OF *THE WAY.*

I CANNOT *ACCEPT* THIS! I *MUST* GO TO HER...

...I *MUST* CONVINCE HER OF THE RIGHTNESS OF THE CIRCLE!

BREE BREE BREE

HAS YONDU GONE *INSANE?*

YELLOW ALERT--ALL HANDS...

...YONDU HAS JUST TRANSPORTED TO THE SHUTTLE BAY...

...THOUGH HARKOV KNOWS WHAT HE INTENDS TO *DO* THERE!

THIS VEHICLE WILL TAKE ME TO HER.

THOUGH I KNOW NOT HOW TO MAKE IT WORK...

...I *HAVE* WATCHED CHARLIE OPERATE IT.

HE SEEMS TO MERELY *SPEAK* TO IT!

SHIP, GO!

NOTHING HAPPENED. PERHAPS I DID NOT SPEAK *LOUDLY* ENOUGH TO IT.

SHIP, I SAID-- GO!

STILL NOTHING!

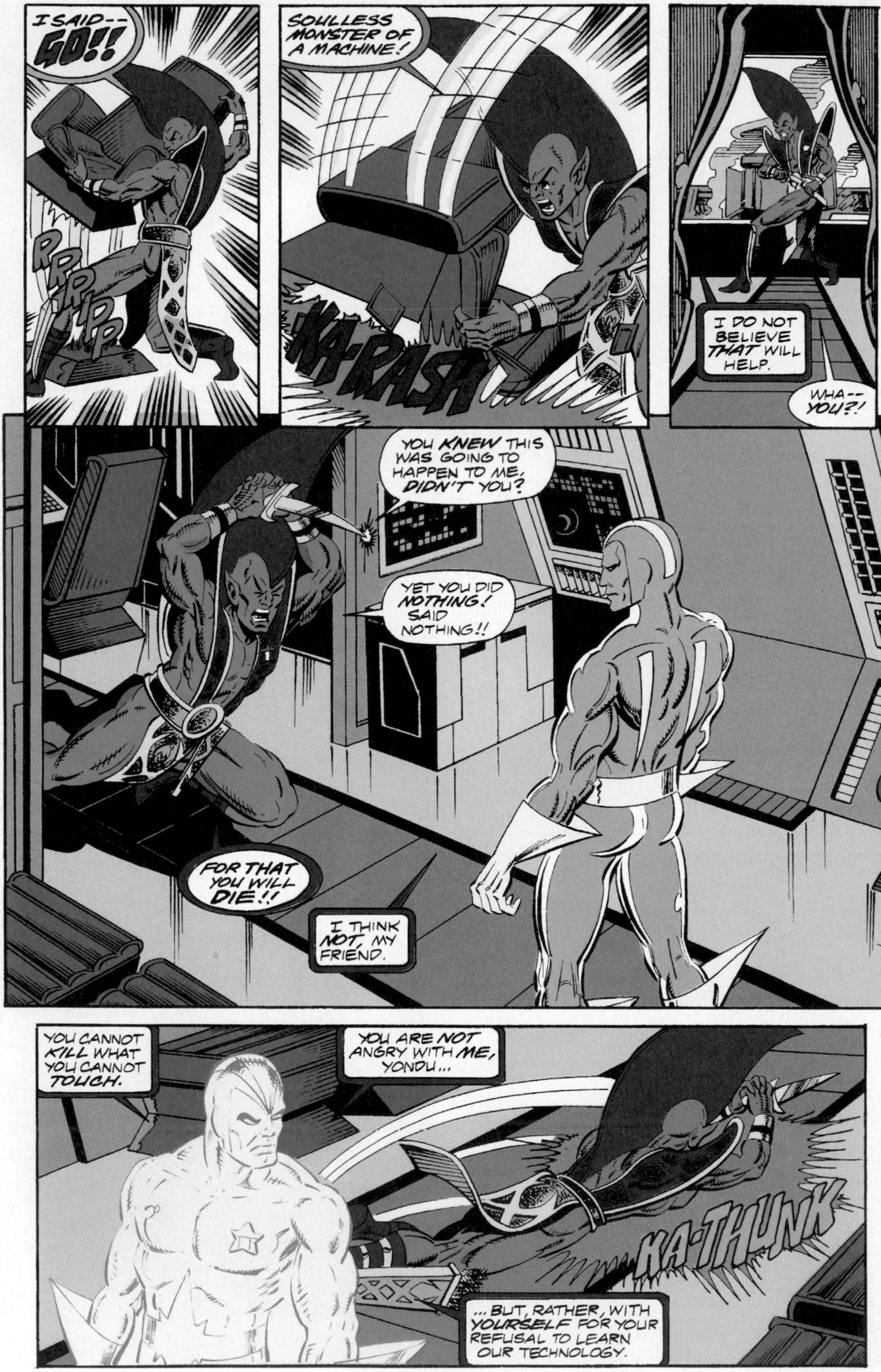
I SAID-- GO!!
RRRIPP
SOULLESS MONSTER OF A MACHINE!
KA-RASH
I DO NOT BELIEVE THAT WILL HELP.
WHA-- YOU?!
YOU KNEW THIS WAS GOING TO HAPPEN TO ME, DIDN'T YOU?
YET YOU DID NOTHING! SAID NOTHING!!
FOR THAT YOU WILL DIE!!
I THINK NOT, MY FRIEND.
YOU CANNOT KILL WHAT YOU CANNOT TOUCH.
YOU ARE NOT ANGRY WITH ME, YONDU...
KA-THUNK
...BUT, RATHER, WITH YOURSELF FOR YOUR REFUSAL TO LEARN OUR TECHNOLOGY.

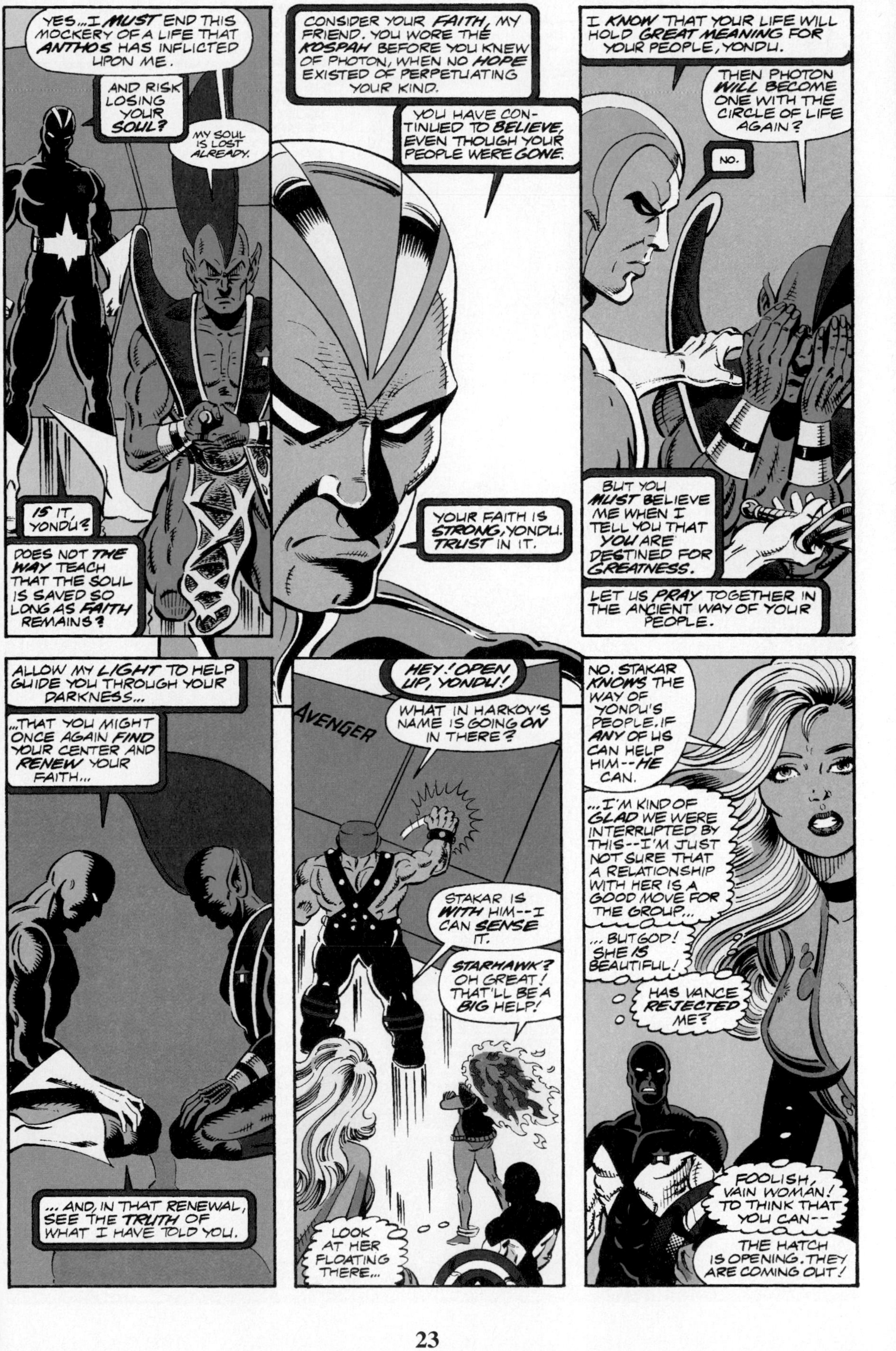

YES...I MUST END THIS MOCKERY OF A LIFE THAT ANTHOS HAS INFLICTED UPON ME.
AND RISK LOSING YOUR SOUL?
MY SOUL IS LOST ALREADY.
IS IT, YONDU?
DOES NOT THE WAY TEACH THAT THE SOUL IS SAVED SO LONG AS FAITH REMAINS?
CONSIDER YOUR FAITH, MY FRIEND. YOU WORE THE KOSPAH BEFORE YOU KNEW OF PHOTON, WHEN NO HOPE EXISTED OF PERPETUATING YOUR KIND.
YOU HAVE CONTINUED TO BELIEVE, EVEN THOUGH YOUR PEOPLE WERE GONE.
YOUR FAITH IS STRONG, YONDU. TRUST IN IT.
I KNOW THAT YOUR LIFE WILL HOLD GREAT MEANING FOR YOUR PEOPLE, YONDU.
THEN PHOTON WILL BECOME ONE WITH THE CIRCLE OF LIFE AGAIN?
NO.
BUT YOU MUST BELIEVE ME WHEN I TELL YOU THAT YOU ARE DESTINED FOR GREATNESS.
LET US PRAY TOGETHER IN THE ANCIENT WAY OF YOUR PEOPLE.
ALLOW MY LIGHT TO HELP GUIDE YOU THROUGH YOUR DARKNESS...
...THAT YOU MIGHT ONCE AGAIN FIND YOUR CENTER AND RENEW YOUR FAITH...
...AND, IN THAT RENEWAL, SEE THE TRUTH OF WHAT I HAVE TOLD YOU.
HEY! OPEN UP, YONDU!
WHAT IN HARKOV'S NAME IS GOING ON IN THERE?
AVENGER
STAKAR IS WITH HIM--I CAN SENSE IT.
STARHAWK? OH GREAT! THAT'LL BE A BIG HELP!
LOOK AT HER FLOATING THERE...
NO. STAKAR KNOWS THE WAY OF YONDU'S PEOPLE. IF ANY OF US CAN HELP HIM--HE CAN.
...I'M KIND OF GLAD WE WERE INTERRUPTED BY THIS--I'M JUST NOT SURE THAT A RELATIONSHIP WITH HER IS A GOOD MOVE FOR THE GROUP...
...BUT GOD! SHE IS BEAUTIFUL!
HAS VANCE REJECTED ME?
FOOLISH, VAIN WOMAN! TO THINK THAT YOU CAN--
THE HATCH IS OPENING. THEY ARE COMING OUT!

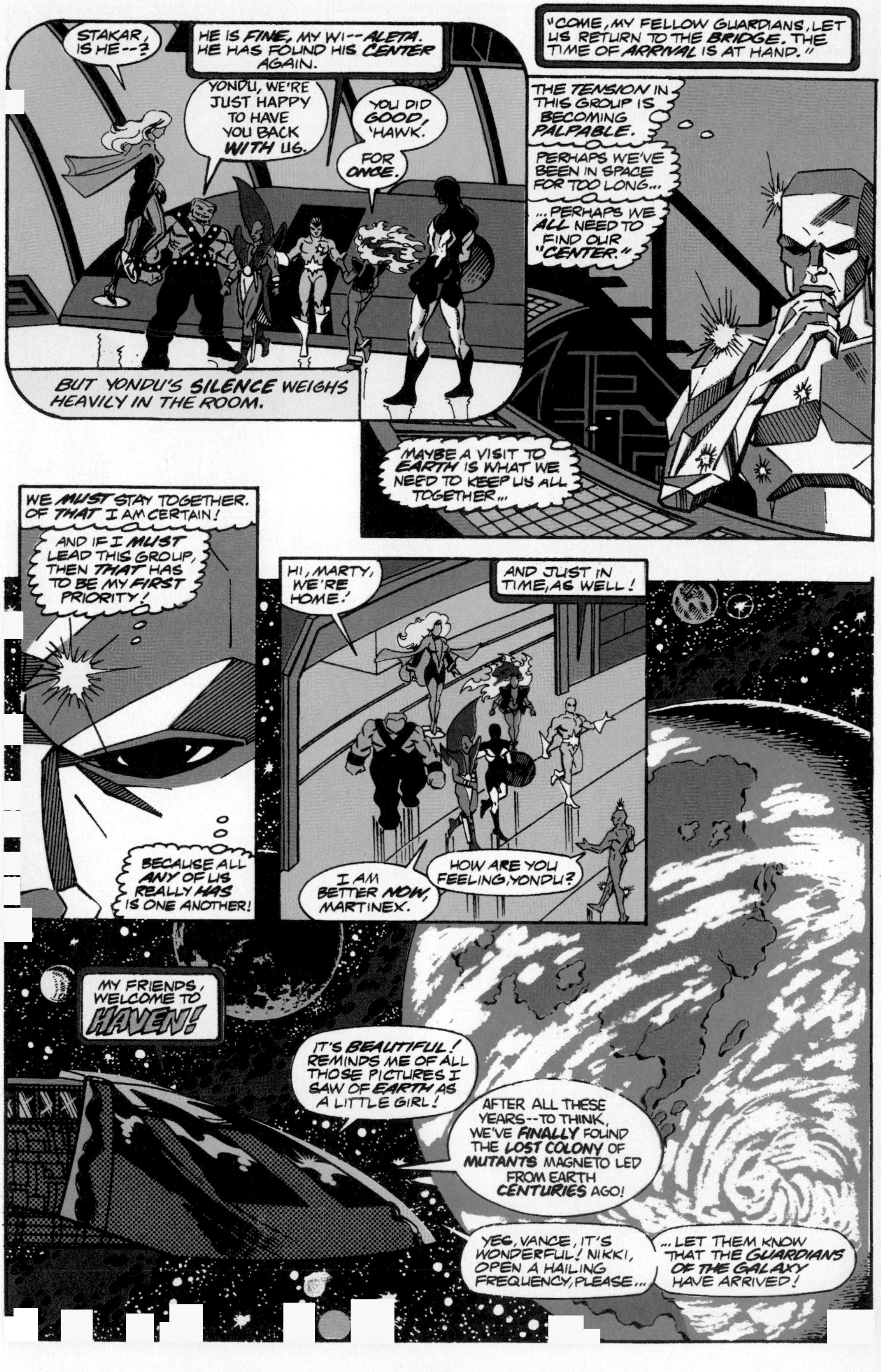
STAKAR, IS HE--?
HE IS FINE, MY WI-- ALETA. HE HAS FOUND HIS CENTER AGAIN.
YONDU, WE'RE JUST HAPPY TO HAVE YOU BACK WITH US.
YOU DID GOOD, 'HAWK.
FOR ONCE.
BUT YONDU'S SILENCE WEIGHS HEAVILY IN THE ROOM.
"COME, MY FELLOW GUARDIANS, LET US RETURN TO THE BRIDGE. THE TIME OF ARRIVAL IS AT HAND."
THE TENSION IN THIS GROUP IS BECOMING PALPABLE.
PERHAPS WE'VE BEEN IN SPACE FOR TOO LONG...
...PERHAPS WE ALL NEED TO FIND OUR "CENTER."
MAYBE A VISIT TO EARTH IS WHAT WE NEED TO KEEP US ALL TOGETHER...
WE MUST STAY TOGETHER. OF THAT I AM CERTAIN!
AND IF I MUST LEAD THIS GROUP, THEN THAT HAS TO BE MY FIRST PRIORITY!
BECAUSE ALL ANY OF US REALLY HAS IS ONE ANOTHER!
HI, MARTY, WE'RE HOME!
AND JUST IN TIME, AS WELL!
HOW ARE YOU FEELING, YONDU?
I AM BETTER NOW, MARTINEX.
MY FRIENDS, WELCOME TO HAVEN!
IT'S BEAUTIFUL! REMINDS ME OF ALL THOSE PICTURES I SAW OF EARTH AS A LITTLE GIRL!
AFTER ALL THESE YEARS--TO THINK, WE'VE FINALLY FOUND THE LOST COLONY OF MUTANTS MAGNETO LED FROM EARTH CENTURIES AGO!
YES, VANCE, IT'S WONDERFUL! NIKKI, OPEN A HAILING FREQUENCY, PLEASE...
...LET THEM KNOW THAT THE GUARDIANS OF THE GALAXY HAVE ARRIVED!

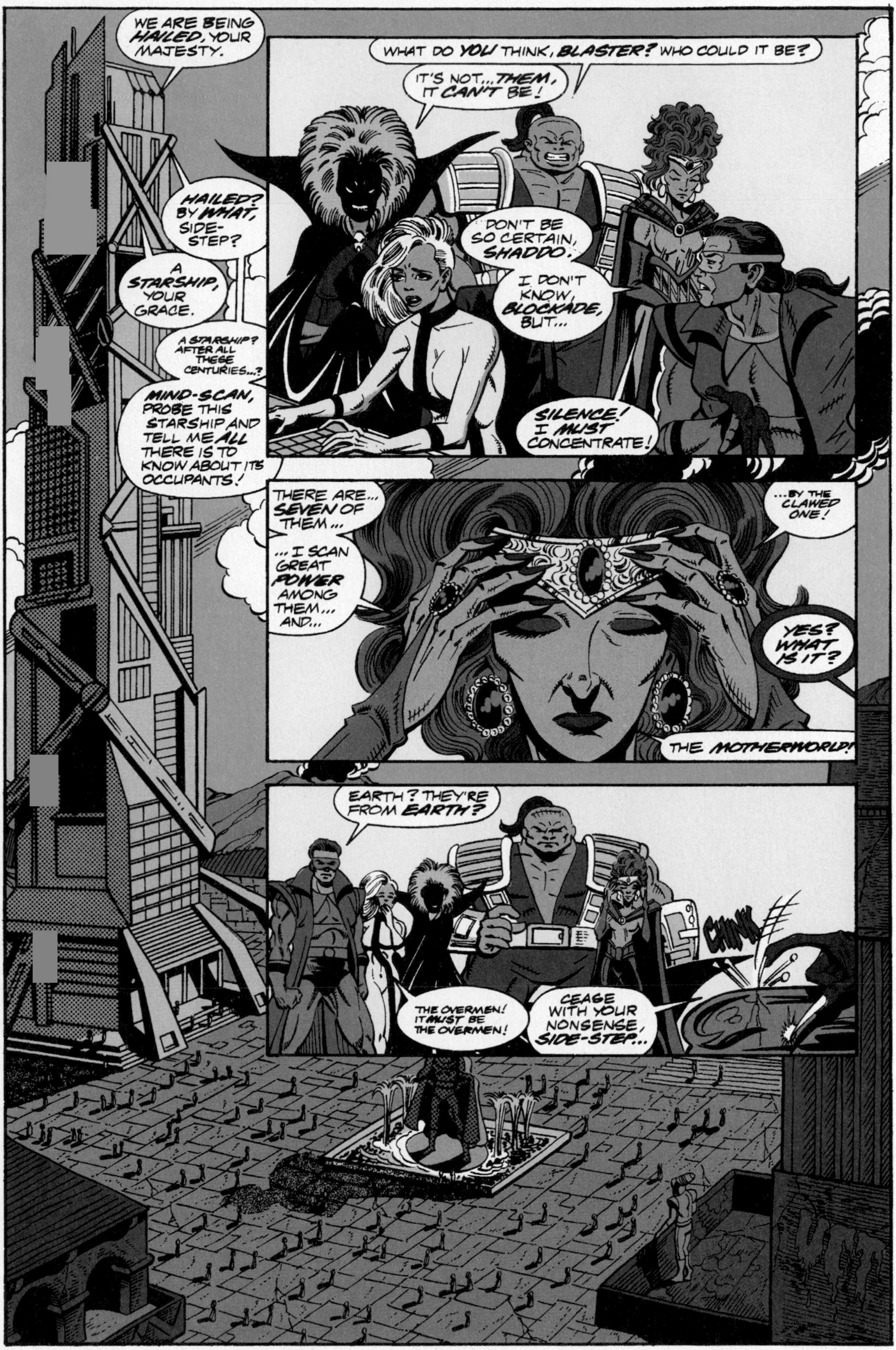
WE ARE BEING HAILED, YOUR MAJESTY.
WHAT DO YOU THINK, BLASTER? WHO COULD IT BE?
IT'S NOT...THEM, IT CAN'T BE!
HAILED? BY WHAT, SIDE-STEP?
A STARSHIP, YOUR GRACE.
DON'T BE SO CERTAIN, SHADDO.
I DON'T KNOW, BLOCKADE, BUT...
A STARSHIP? AFTER ALL THESE CENTURIES...?
MIND-SCAN, PROBE THIS STARSHIP AND TELL ME ALL THERE IS TO KNOW ABOUT ITS OCCUPANTS!
SILENCE! I MUST CONCENTRATE!
THERE ARE... SEVEN OF THEM...
...I SCAN GREAT POWER AMONG THEM... AND...
...BY THE CLAWED ONE!
YES? WHAT IS IT?
THE MOTHERWORLD!
EARTH? THEY'RE FROM EARTH?
THE OVERMEN! IT MUST BE THE OVERMEN!
CEASE WITH YOUR NONSENSE, SIDE-STEP...
CHINK

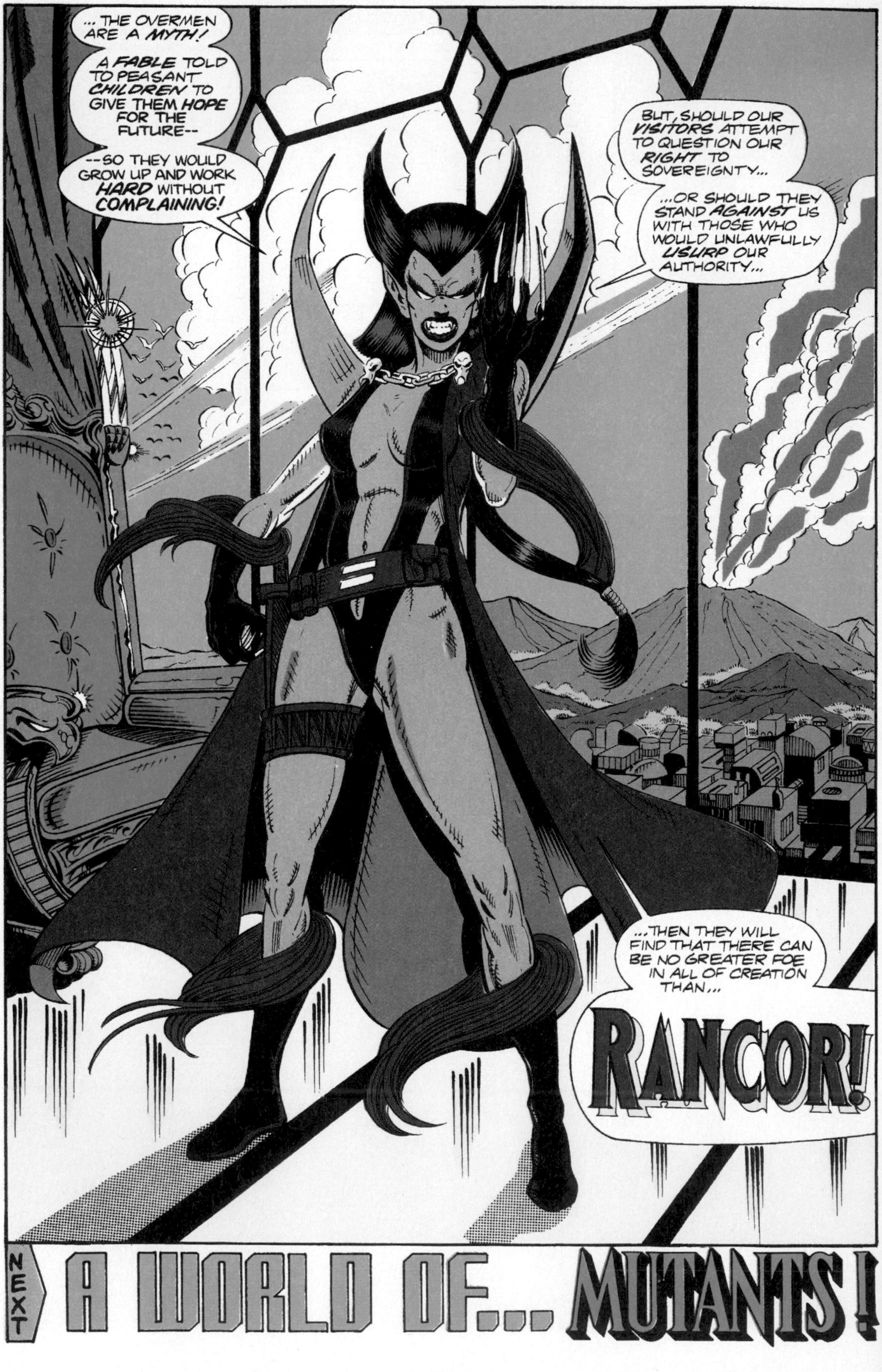
...THE OVERMEN ARE A MYTH!
A FABLE TOLD TO PEASANT CHILDREN TO GIVE THEM HOPE FOR THE FUTURE--
--SO THEY WOULD GROW UP AND WORK HARD WITHOUT COMPLAINING!
BUT, SHOULD OUR VISITORS ATTEMPT TO QUESTION OUR RIGHT TO SOVEREIGNTY...
...OR SHOULD THEY STAND AGAINST US WITH THOSE WHO WOULD UNLAWFULLY USURP OUR AUTHORITY...
...THEN THEY WILL FIND THAT THERE CAN BE NO GREATER FOE IN ALL OF CREATION THAN...
RANCOR!
NEXT A WORLD OF... MUTANTS!

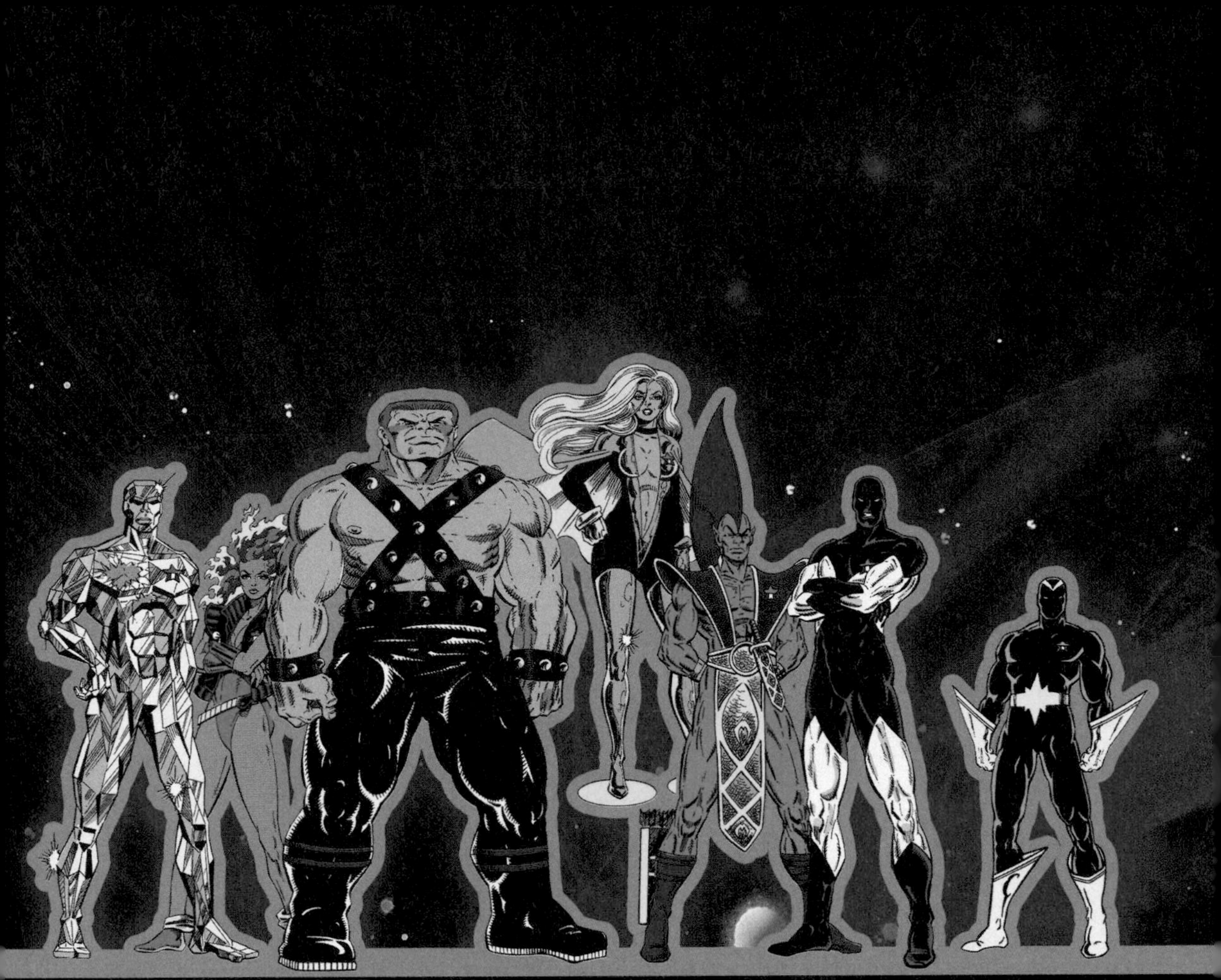

GUARDIANS OF THE GALAXY

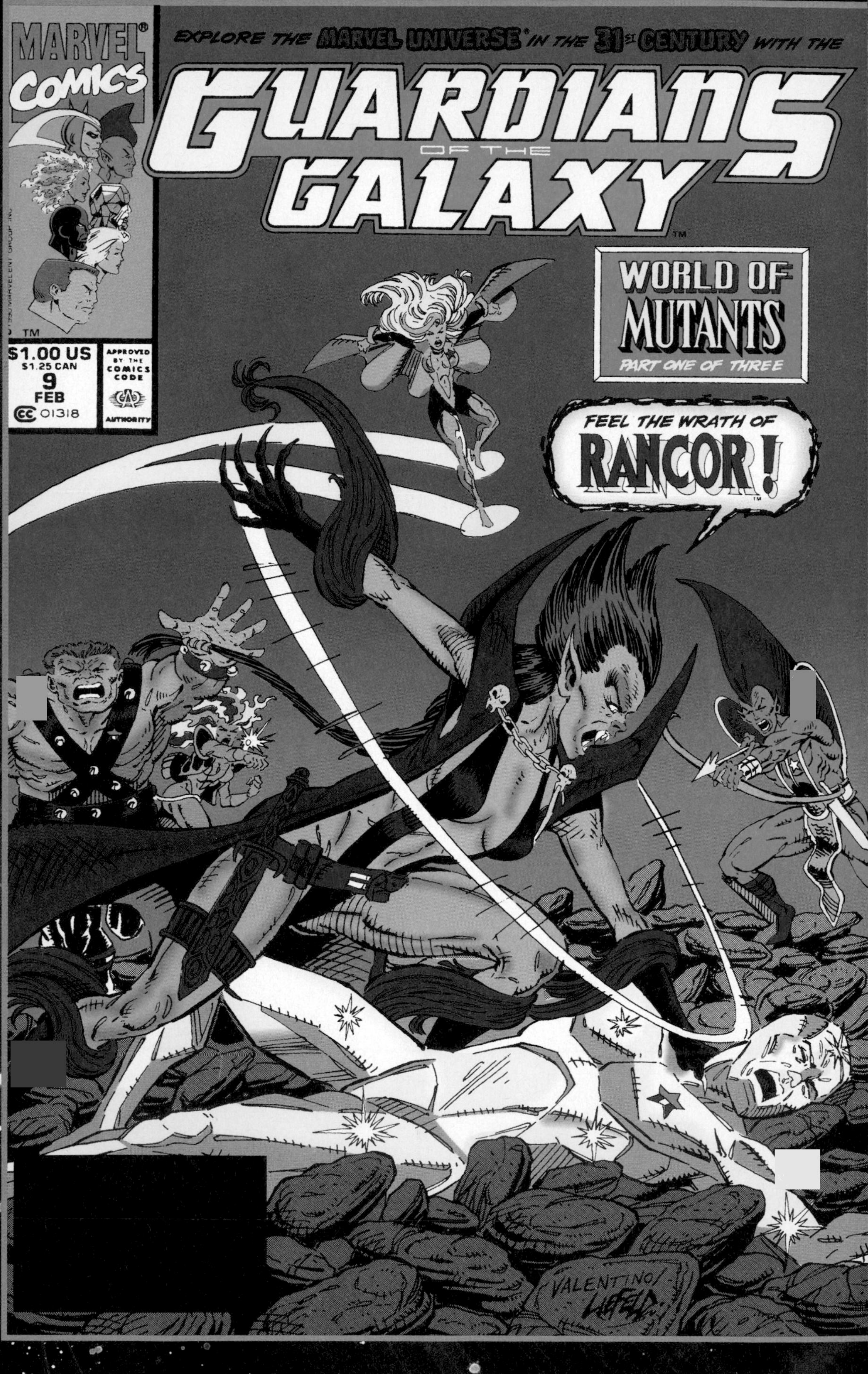

MARVEL COMICS
EXPLORE THE MARVEL UNIVERSE IN THE 31ST CENTURY WITH THE
GUARDIANS OF THE GALAXY
$1.00 US
$1.25 CAN
9
FEB
APPROVED BY THE COMICS CODE AUTHORITY
WORLD OF MUTANTS
PART ONE OF THREE
FEEL THE WRATH OF
RANCOR!
VALENTINO/ LIEFELD

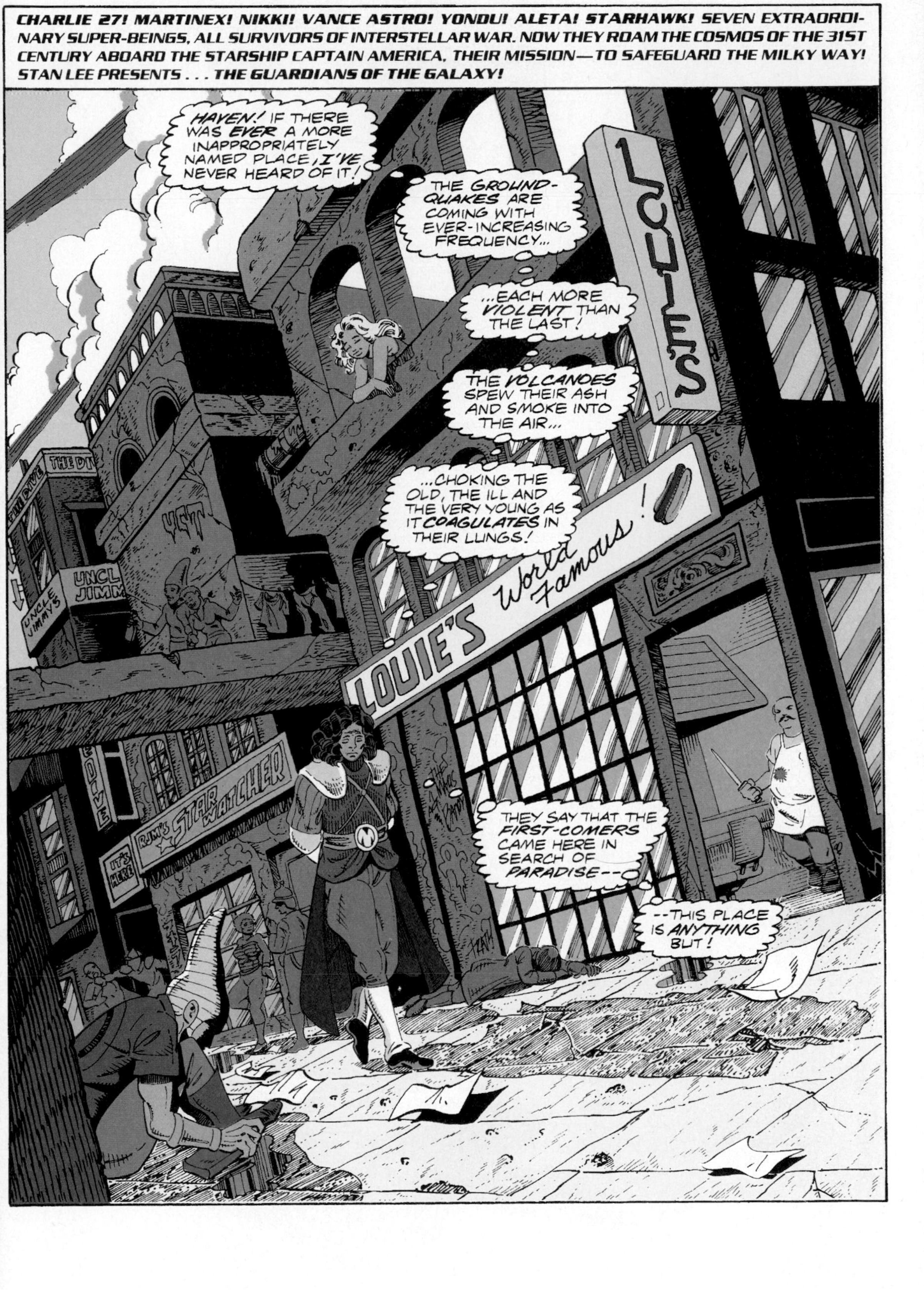
CHARLIE 27! MARTINEX! NIKKI! VANCE ASTRO! YONDU! ALETA! STARHAWK! SEVEN EXTRAORDINARY SUPER-BEINGS, ALL SURVIVORS OF INTERSTELLAR WAR. NOW THEY ROAM THE COSMOS OF THE 31ST CENTURY ABOARD THE STARSHIP CAPTAIN AMERICA, THEIR MISSION—TO SAFEGUARD THE MILKY WAY! STAN LEE PRESENTS . . . THE GUARDIANS OF THE GALAXY!
HAVEN! IF THERE WAS EVER A MORE INAPPROPRIATELY NAMED PLACE, I'VE NEVER HEARD OF IT!
THE GROUND-QUAKES ARE COMING WITH EVER-INCREASING FREQUENCY...
...EACH MORE VIOLENT THAN THE LAST!
THE VOLCANOES SPEW THEIR ASH AND SMOKE INTO THE AIR...
...CHOKING THE OLD, THE ILL AND THE VERY YOUNG AS IT COAGULATES IN THEIR LUNGS!
THEY SAY THAT THE FIRST-COMERS CAME HERE IN SEARCH OF PARADISE--
--THIS PLACE IS ANYTHING BUT!
LOUIE'S
LOUIE'S World Famous!
UNCLE JIMMY'S
RJM'S STAR WATCHER
IT'S HERE

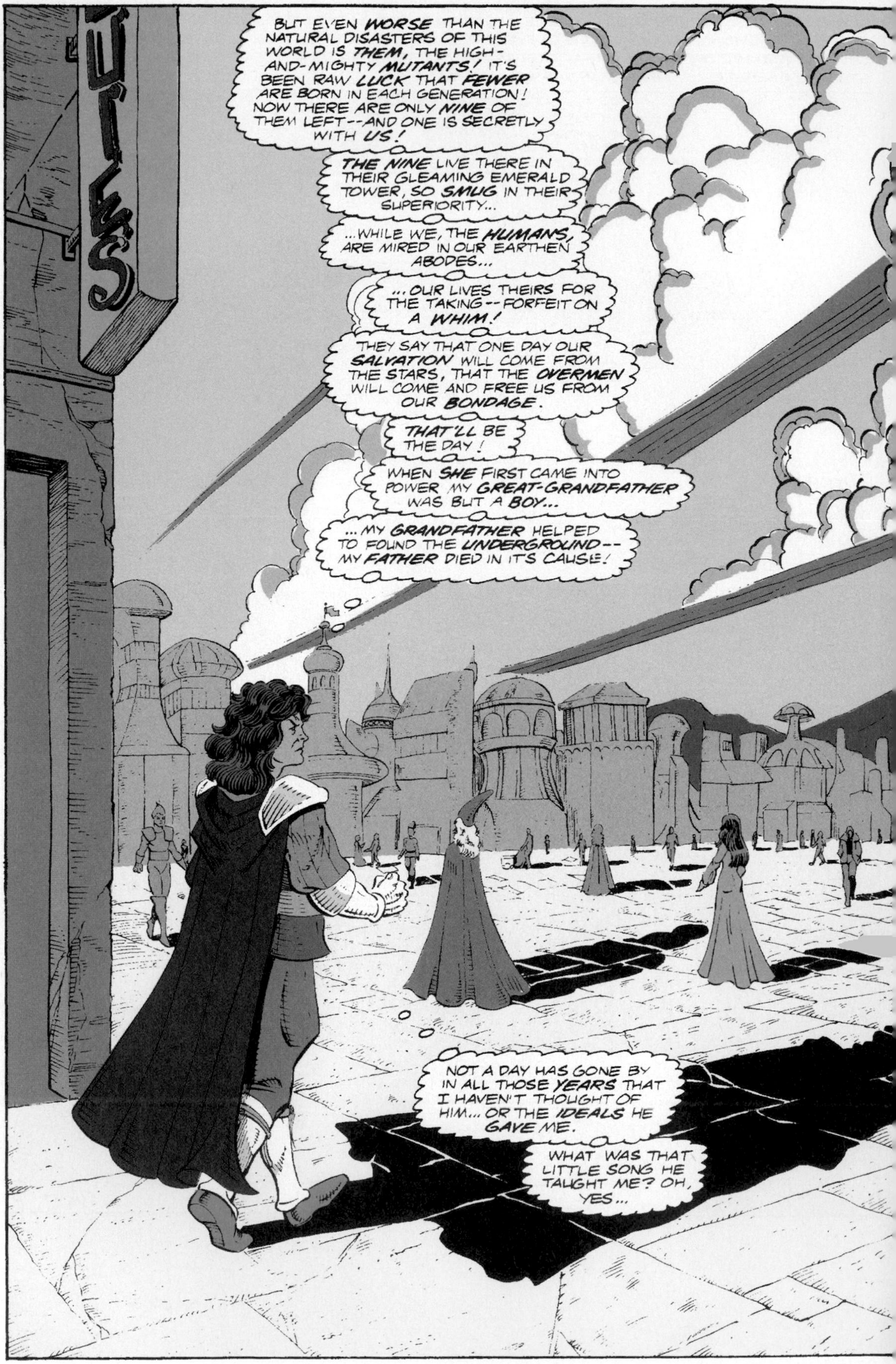
BUT EVEN WORSE THAN THE NATURAL DISASTERS OF THIS WORLD IS THEM, THE HIGH-AND-MIGHTY MUTANTS! IT'S BEEN RAW LUCK THAT FEWER ARE BORN IN EACH GENERATION! NOW THERE ARE ONLY NINE OF THEM LEFT--AND ONE IS SECRETLY WITH US!
THE NINE LIVE THERE IN THEIR GLEAMING EMERALD TOWER, SO SMUG IN THEIR SUPERIORITY...
...WHILE WE, THE HUMANS, ARE MIRED IN OUR EARTHEN ABODES...
...OUR LIVES THEIRS FOR THE TAKING--FORFEIT ON A WHIM!
THEY SAY THAT ONE DAY OUR SALVATION WILL COME FROM THE STARS, THAT THE OVERMEN WILL COME AND FREE US FROM OUR BONDAGE.
THAT'LL BE THE DAY!
WHEN SHE FIRST CAME INTO POWER MY GREAT-GRANDFATHER WAS BUT A BOY...
...MY GRANDFATHER HELPED TO FOUND THE UNDERGROUND--MY FATHER DIED IN IT'S CAUSE!
NOT A DAY HAS GONE BY IN ALL THOSE YEARS THAT I HAVEN'T THOUGHT OF HIM... OR THE IDEALS HE GAVE ME.
WHAT WAS THAT LITTLE SONG HE TAUGHT ME? OH, YES...

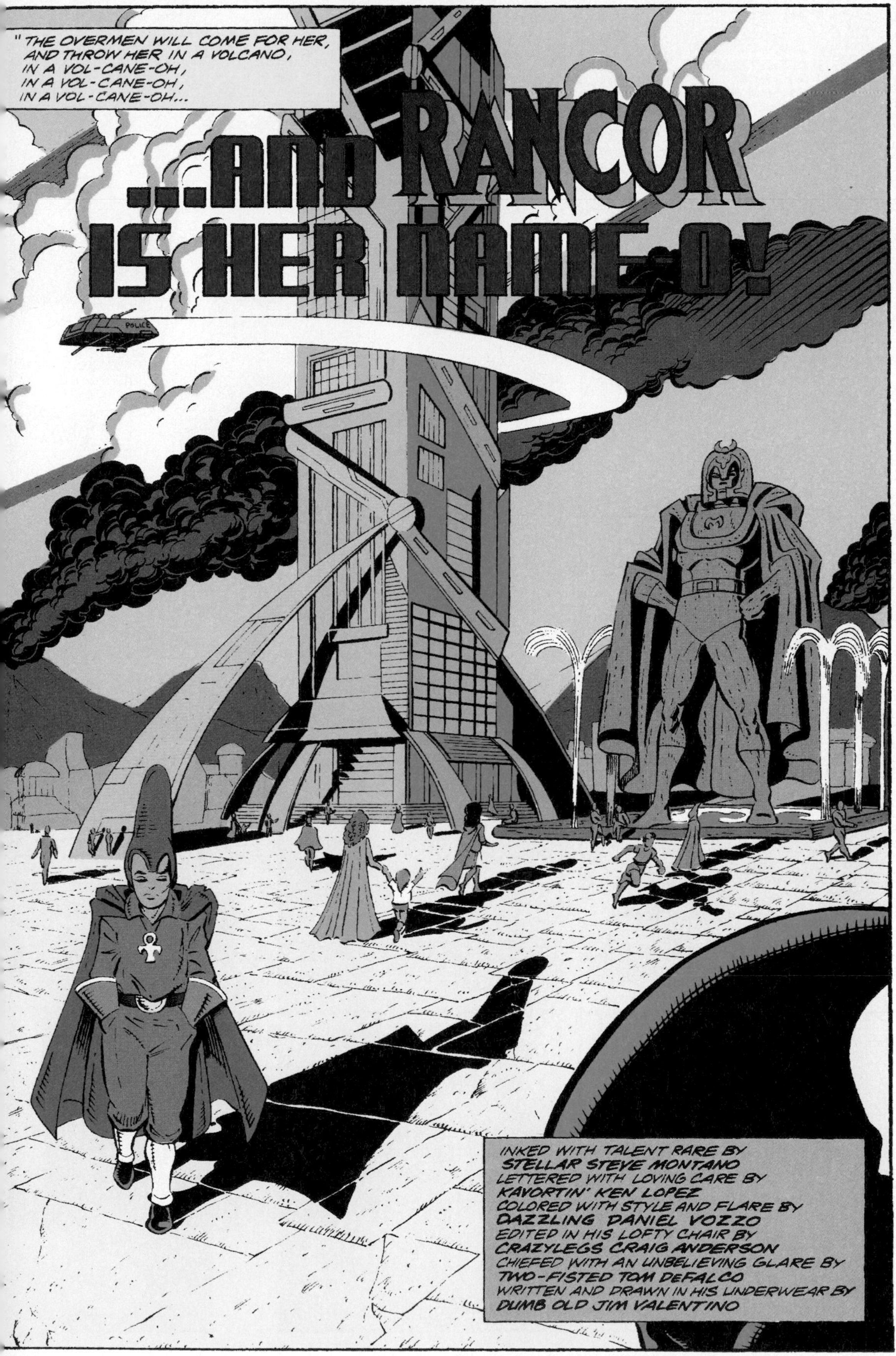
"THE OVERMEN WILL COME FOR HER, AND THROW HER IN A VOLCANO, IN A VOL-CANE-OH, IN A VOL-CANE-OH, IN A VOL-CANE-OH...
...AND RANCOR IS HER NAME-O!
POLICE
INKED WITH TALENT RARE BY STELLAR STEVE MONTANO
LETTERED WITH LOVING CARE BY KAVORTIN' KEN LOPEZ
COLORED WITH STYLE AND FLARE BY DAZZLING DANIEL VOZZO
EDITED IN HIS LOFTY CHAIR BY CRAZYLEGS CRAIG ANDERSON
CHIEFED WITH AN UNBELIEVING GLARE BY TWO-FISTED TOM DEFALCO
WRITTEN AND DRAWN IN HIS UNDERWEAR BY DUMB OLD JIM VALENTINO

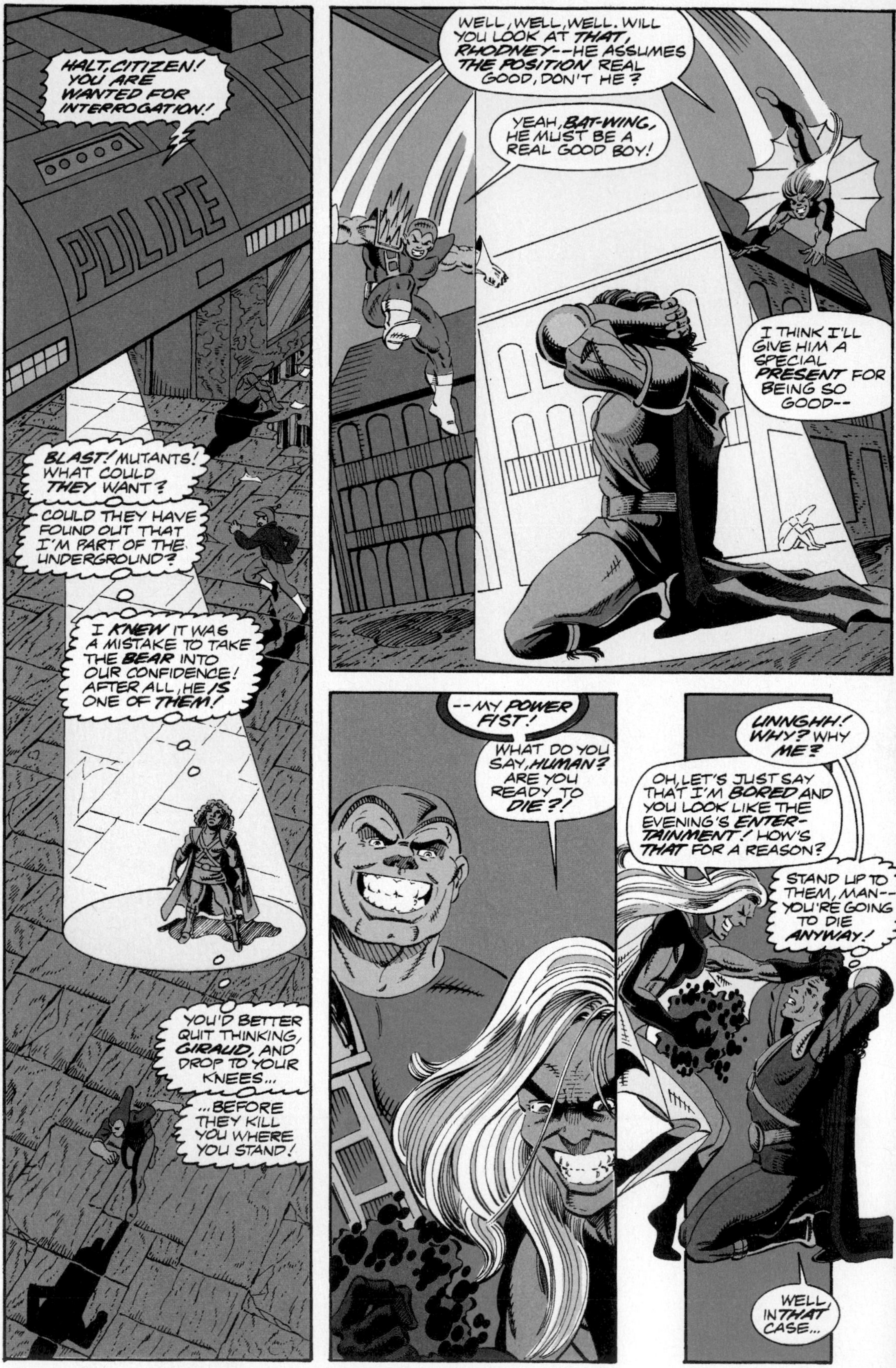
HALT, CITIZEN! YOU ARE WANTED FOR INTERROGATION!
BLAST! MUTANTS! WHAT COULD THEY WANT?
COULD THEY HAVE FOUND OUT THAT I'M PART OF THE UNDERGROUND?
I KNEW IT WAS A MISTAKE TO TAKE THE BEAR INTO OUR CONFIDENCE! AFTER ALL, HE IS ONE OF THEM!
YOU'D BETTER QUIT THINKING, GIRAUD, AND DROP TO YOUR KNEES...
...BEFORE THEY KILL YOU WHERE YOU STAND!
WELL, WELL, WELL. WILL YOU LOOK AT THAT, RHODNEY--HE ASSUMES THE POSITION REAL GOOD, DON'T HE?
YEAH, BAT-WING, HE MUST BE A REAL GOOD BOY!
I THINK I'LL GIVE HIM A SPECIAL PRESENT FOR BEING SO GOOD--
--MY POWER FIST!
WHAT DO YOU SAY, HUMAN? ARE YOU READY TO DIE?!
UNNGHH! WHY? WHY ME?
OH, LET'S JUST SAY THAT I'M BORED AND YOU LOOK LIKE THE EVENING'S ENTERTAINMENT! HOW'S THAT FOR A REASON?
STAND UP TO THEM, MAN--YOU'RE GOING TO DIE ANYWAY!
WELL, IN THAT CASE...

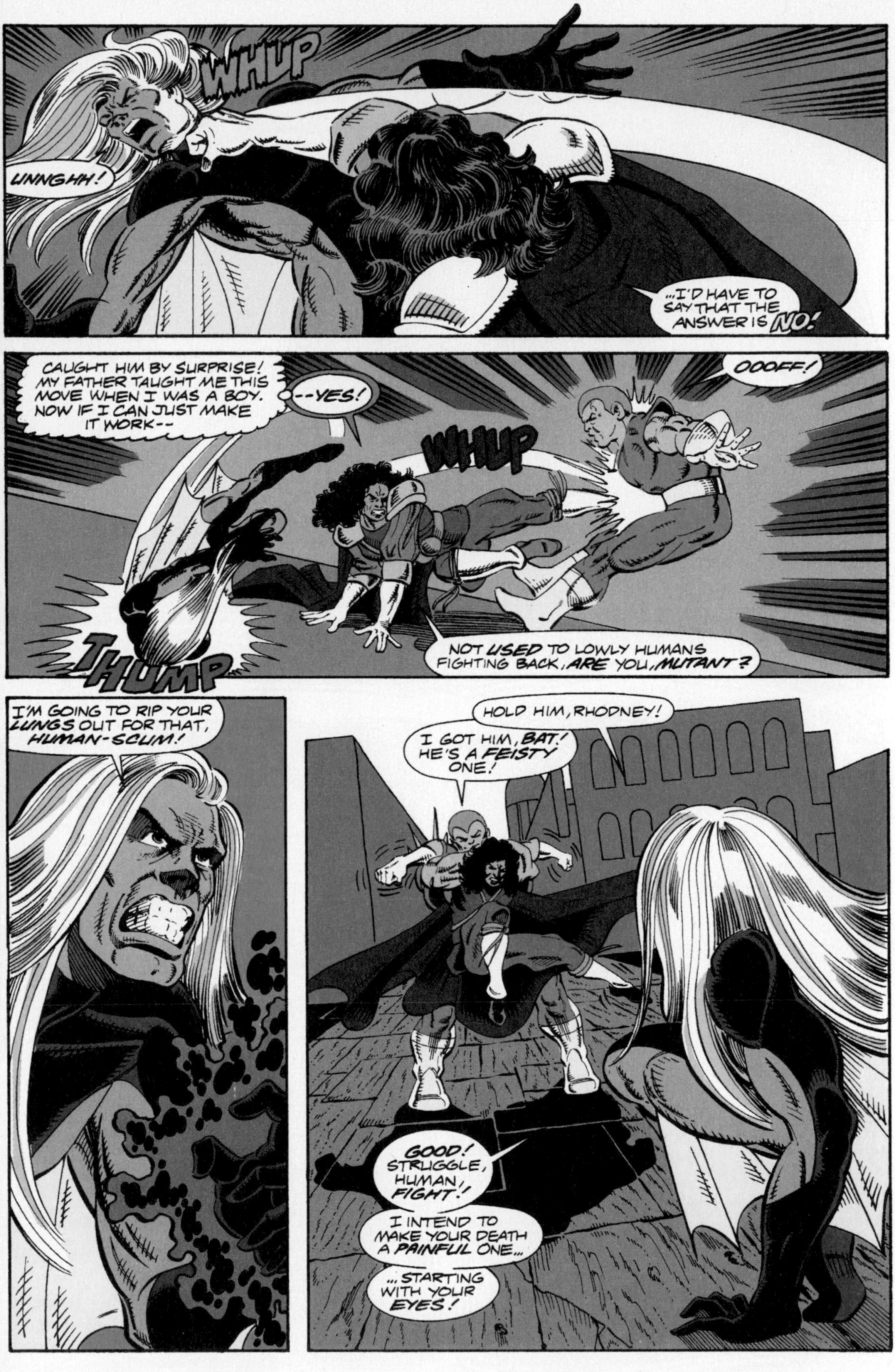
WHUP
UNNGHH!
...I'D HAVE TO SAY THAT THE ANSWER IS NO!
CAUGHT HIM BY SURPRISE! MY FATHER TAUGHT ME THIS MOVE WHEN I WAS A BOY. NOW IF I CAN JUST MAKE IT WORK--
--YES!
OOOFF!
WHUP
THUMP
NOT USED TO LOWLY HUMANS FIGHTING BACK, ARE YOU, MUTANT?
I'M GOING TO RIP YOUR LUNGS OUT FOR THAT, HUMAN-SCUM!
HOLD HIM, RHODNEY!
I GOT HIM, BAT! HE'S A FEISTY ONE!
GOOD! STRUGGLE, HUMAN, FIGHT!
I INTEND TO MAKE YOUR DEATH A PAINFUL ONE...
...STARTING WITH YOUR EYES!

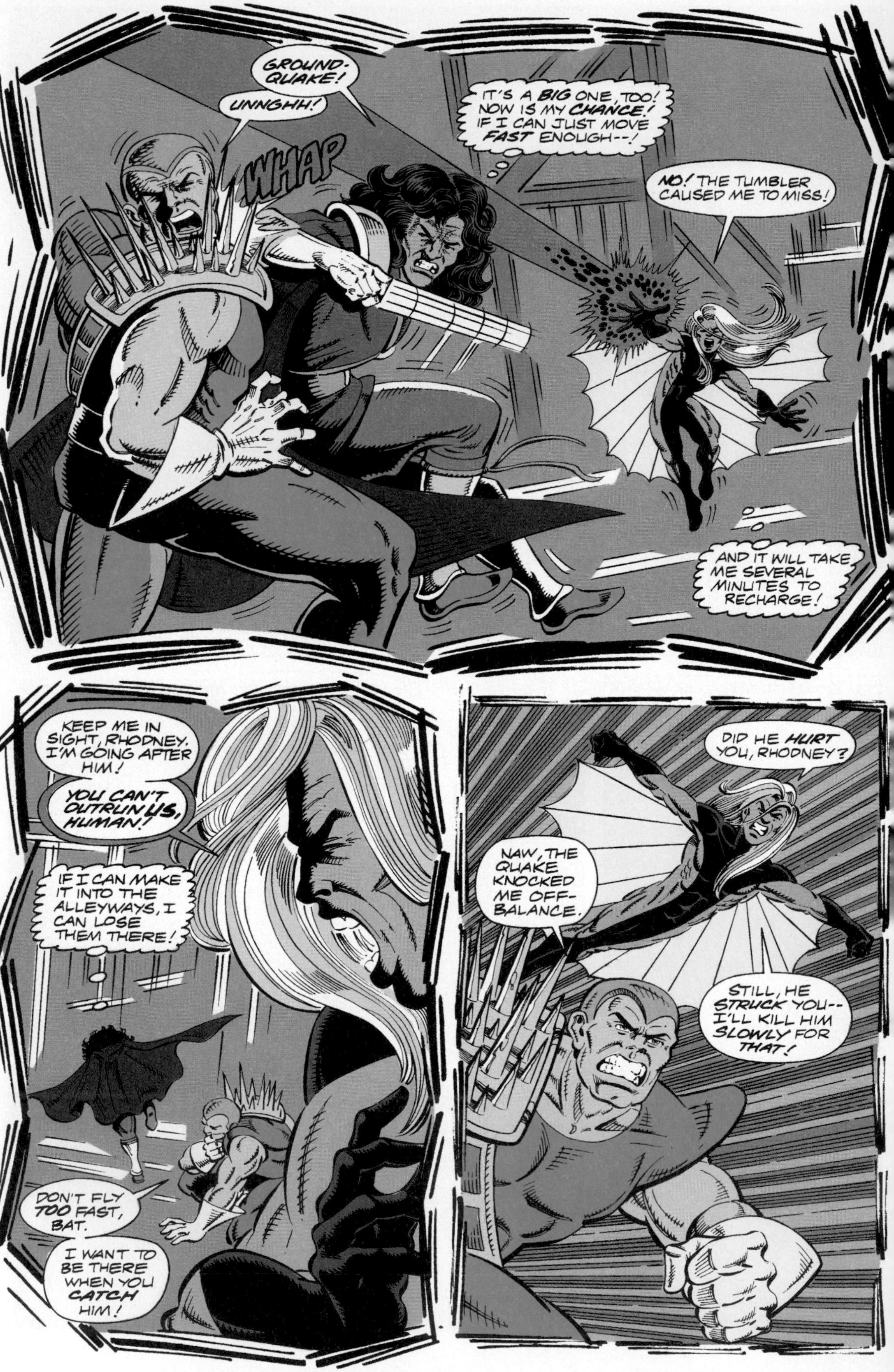
GROUND-QUAKE!
UNNGHH!
WHAP
IT'S A BIG ONE, TOO! NOW IS MY CHANCE! IF I CAN JUST MOVE FAST ENOUGH--!
NO! THE TUMBLER CAUSED ME TO MISS!
AND IT WILL TAKE ME SEVERAL MINUTES TO RECHARGE!
KEEP ME IN SIGHT, RHODNEY. I'M GOING AFTER HIM!
YOU CAN'T OUTRUN US, HUMAN!
IF I CAN MAKE IT INTO THE ALLEYWAYS, I CAN LOSE THEM THERE!
DON'T FLY TOO FAST, BAT.
I WANT TO BE THERE WHEN YOU CATCH HIM!
DID HE HURT YOU, RHODNEY?
NAW, THE QUAKE KNOCKED ME OFF-BALANCE.
STILL, HE STRUCK YOU-- I'LL KILL HIM SLOWLY FOR THAT!

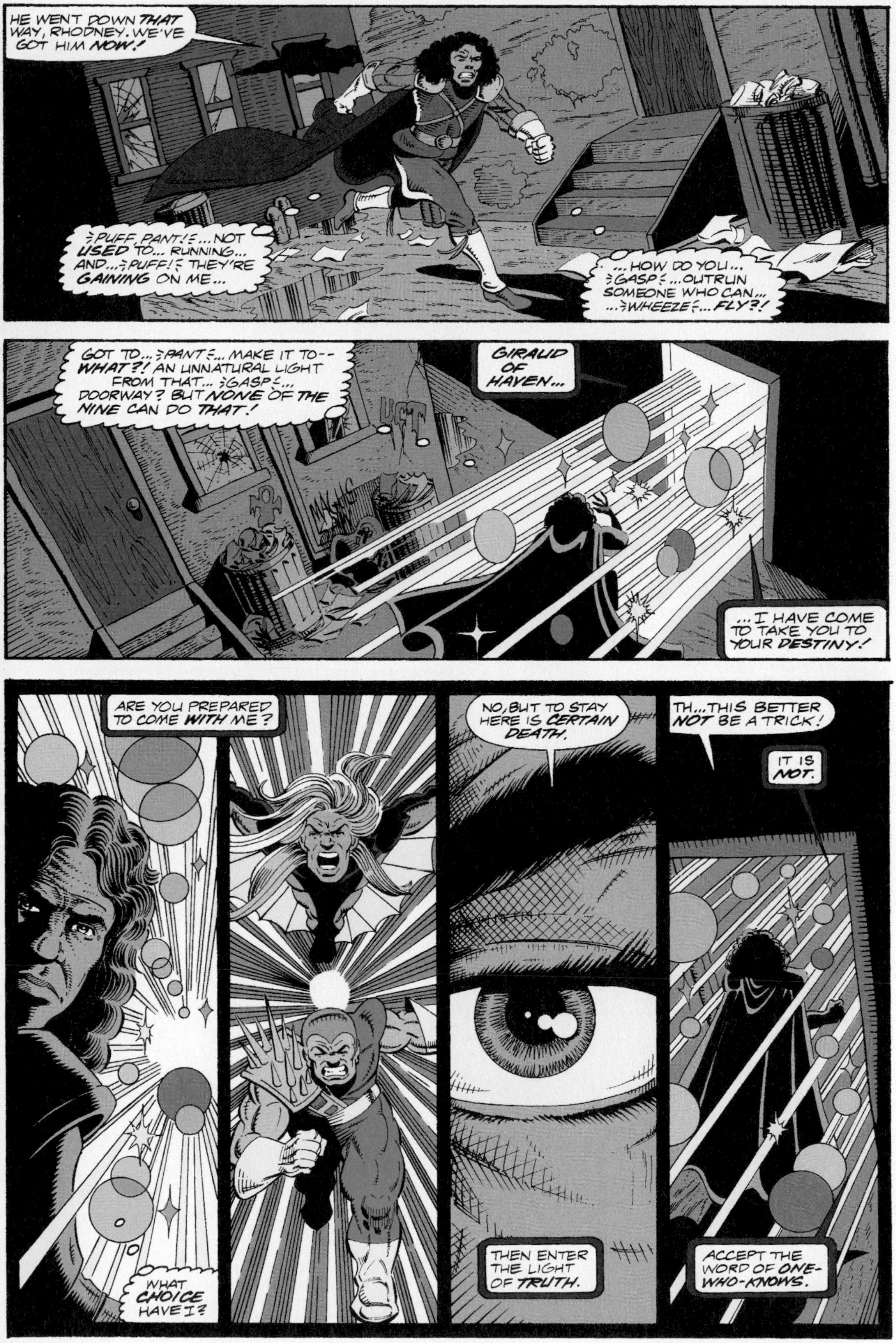

HE WENT DOWN THAT WAY, RHODNEY. WE'VE GOT HIM NOW!
PUFF, PANT! ...NOT USED TO... RUNNING... AND... PUFF! THEY'RE GAINING ON ME...
...HOW DO YOU... GASP ...OUTRUN SOMEONE WHO CAN... ...WHEEZE ...FLY?!
GOT TO... PANT ... MAKE IT TO-- WHAT?! AN UNNATURAL LIGHT FROM THAT... GASP ... DOORWAY? BUT NONE OF THE NINE CAN DO THAT!
GIRAUD OF HAVEN...
...I HAVE COME TO TAKE YOU TO YOUR DESTINY!
ARE YOU PREPARED TO COME WITH ME?
WHAT CHOICE HAVE I?
NO, BUT TO STAY HERE IS CERTAIN DEATH.
THEN ENTER THE LIGHT OF TRUTH.
TH...THIS BETTER NOT BE A TRICK!
IT IS NOT.
ACCEPT THE WORD OF ONE-WHO-KNOWS.

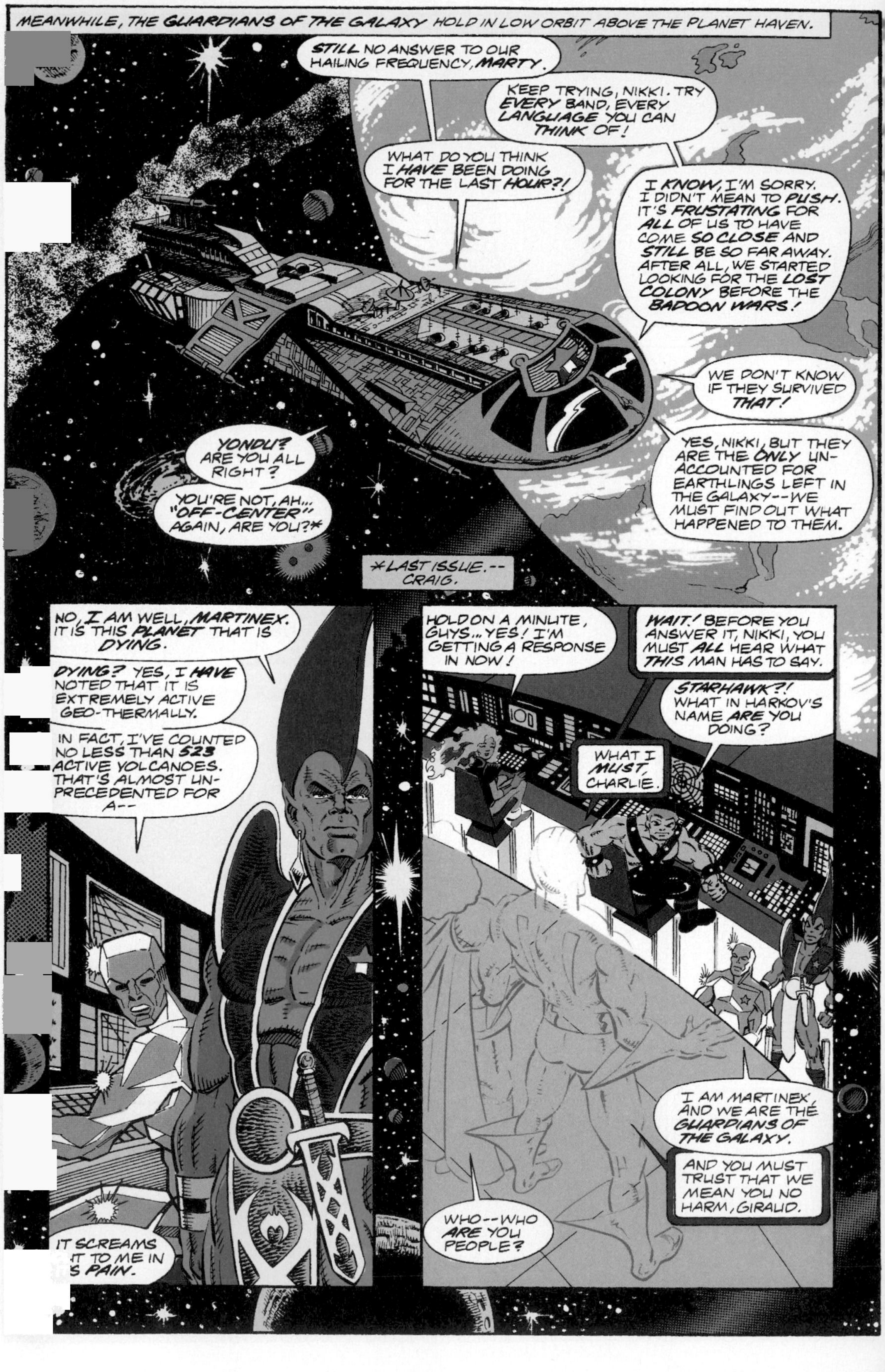
MEANWHILE, THE GUARDIANS OF THE GALAXY HOLD IN LOW ORBIT ABOVE THE PLANET HAVEN.
STILL NO ANSWER TO OUR HAILING FREQUENCY, MARTY.
KEEP TRYING, NIKKI. TRY EVERY BAND, EVERY LANGUAGE YOU CAN THINK OF!
WHAT DO YOU THINK I HAVE BEEN DOING FOR THE LAST HOUR?!
I KNOW, I'M SORRY. I DIDN'T MEAN TO PUSH. IT'S FRUSTATING FOR ALL OF US TO HAVE COME SO CLOSE AND STILL BE SO FAR AWAY. AFTER ALL, WE STARTED LOOKING FOR THE LOST COLONY BEFORE THE BADOON WARS!
WE DON'T KNOW IF THEY SURVIVED THAT!
YES, NIKKI, BUT THEY ARE THE ONLY UN-ACCOUNTED FOR EARTHLINGS LEFT IN THE GALAXY--WE MUST FIND OUT WHAT HAPPENED TO THEM.
YONDU? ARE YOU ALL RIGHT?
YOU'RE NOT, AH... "OFF-CENTER" AGAIN, ARE YOU?*
*LAST ISSUE.--CRAIG.
NO, I AM WELL, MARTINEX. IT IS THIS PLANET THAT IS DYING.
DYING? YES, I HAVE NOTED THAT IT IS EXTREMELY ACTIVE GEO-THERMALLY.
IN FACT, I'VE COUNTED NO LESS THAN 523 ACTIVE VOLCANOES. THAT'S ALMOST UN-PRECEDENTED FOR A--
IT SCREAMS
T TO ME IN
S PAIN.
HOLD ON A MINUTE, GUYS... YES! I'M GETTING A RESPONSE IN NOW!
WAIT! BEFORE YOU ANSWER IT, NIKKI, YOU MUST ALL HEAR WHAT THIS MAN HAS TO SAY.
STARHAWK?! WHAT IN HARKOV'S NAME ARE YOU DOING?
WHAT I MUST, CHARLIE.
I AM MARTINEX, AND WE ARE THE GUARDIANS OF THE GALAXY.
AND YOU MUST TRUST THAT WE MEAN YOU NO HARM, GIRAUD.
WHO--WHO ARE YOU PEOPLE?

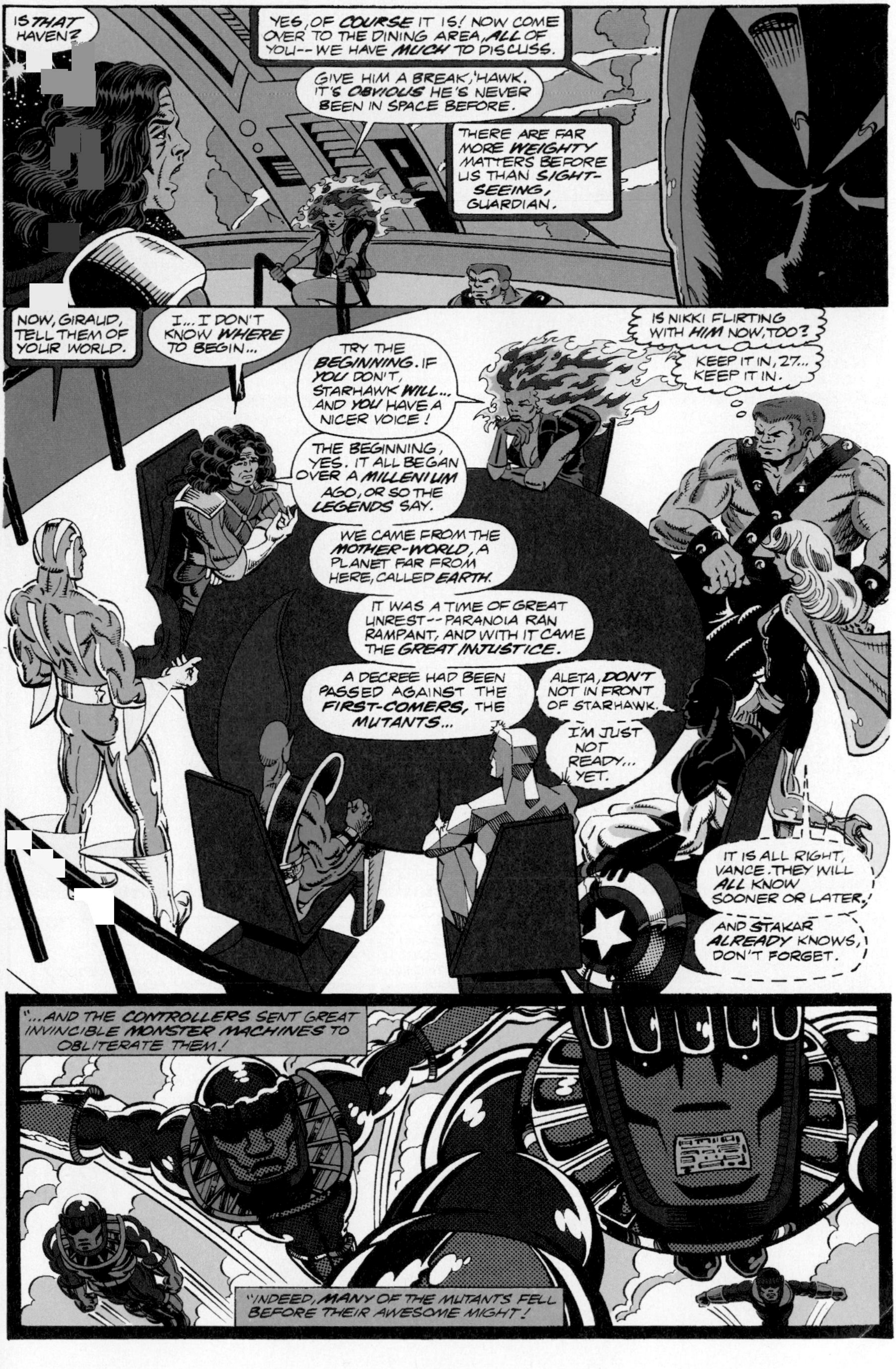
IS THAT HAVEN?
YES, OF COURSE IT IS! NOW COME OVER TO THE DINING AREA, ALL OF YOU-- WE HAVE MUCH TO DISCUSS.
GIVE HIM A BREAK, 'HAWK. IT'S OBVIOUS HE'S NEVER BEEN IN SPACE BEFORE.
THERE ARE FAR MORE WEIGHTY MATTERS BEFORE US THAN SIGHT-SEEING, GUARDIAN.
NOW, GIRAUD, TELL THEM OF YOUR WORLD.
I... I DON'T KNOW WHERE TO BEGIN...
IS NIKKI FLIRTING WITH HIM NOW, TOO?
KEEP IT IN, 27... KEEP IT IN.
TRY THE BEGINNING. IF YOU DON'T, STARHAWK WILL... AND YOU HAVE A NICER VOICE!
THE BEGINNING, YES. IT ALL BEGAN OVER A MILLENIUM AGO, OR SO THE LEGENDS SAY.
WE CAME FROM THE MOTHER-WORLD, A PLANET FAR FROM HERE, CALLED EARTH.
IT WAS A TIME OF GREAT UNREST-- PARANOIA RAN RAMPANT, AND WITH IT CAME THE GREAT INJUSTICE.
A DECREE HAD BEEN PASSED AGAINST THE FIRST-COMERS, THE MUTANTS...
ALETA, DON'T NOT IN FRONT OF STARHAWK.
I'M JUST NOT READY... YET.
IT IS ALL RIGHT, VANCE. THEY WILL ALL KNOW SOONER OR LATER.
AND STAKAR ALREADY KNOWS, DON'T FORGET.
"...AND THE CONTROLLERS SENT GREAT INVINCIBLE MONSTER MACHINES TO OBLITERATE THEM!
"INDEED, MANY OF THE MUTANTS FELL BEFORE THEIR AWESOME MIGHT!

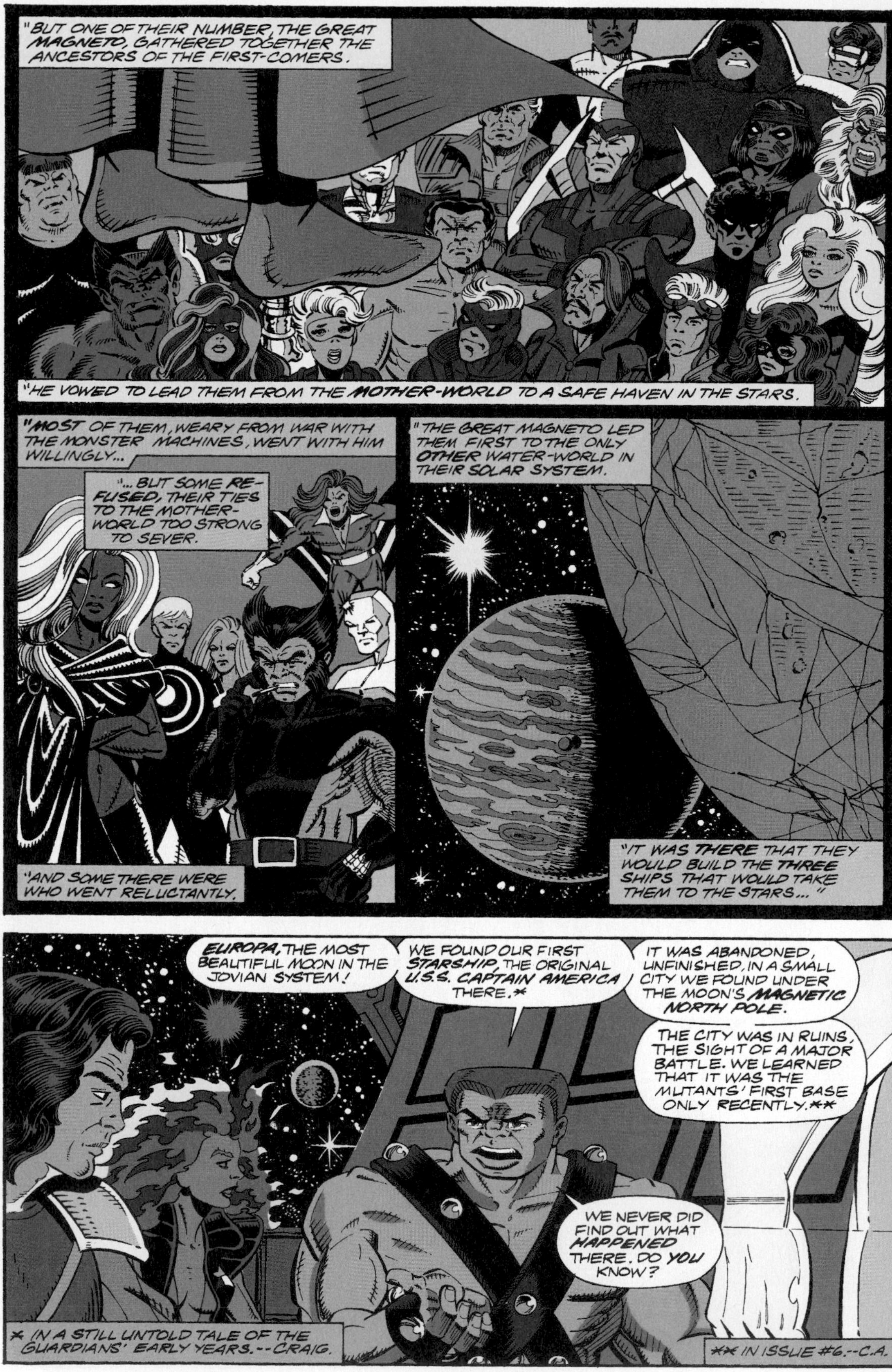
"BUT ONE OF THEIR NUMBER, THE GREAT MAGNETO, GATHERED TOGETHER THE ANCESTORS OF THE FIRST-COMERS.
"HE VOWED TO LEAD THEM FROM THE MOTHER-WORLD TO A SAFE HAVEN IN THE STARS.
"MOST OF THEM, WEARY FROM WAR WITH THE MONSTER MACHINES, WENT WITH HIM WILLINGLY...
"...BUT SOME REFUSED, THEIR TIES TO THE MOTHER-WORLD TOO STRONG TO SEVER.
"AND SOME THERE WERE WHO WENT RELUCTANTLY.
"THE GREAT MAGNETO LED THEM FIRST TO THE ONLY OTHER WATER-WORLD IN THEIR SOLAR SYSTEM.
"IT WAS THERE THAT THEY WOULD BUILD THE THREE SHIPS THAT WOULD TAKE THEM TO THE STARS..."
EUROPA, THE MOST BEAUTIFUL MOON IN THE JOVIAN SYSTEM!
WE FOUND OUR FIRST STARSHIP, THE ORIGINAL U.S.S. CAPTAIN AMERICA THERE.*
IT WAS ABANDONED, UNFINISHED, IN A SMALL CITY WE FOUND UNDER THE MOON'S MAGNETIC NORTH POLE.
THE CITY WAS IN RUINS, THE SIGHT OF A MAJOR BATTLE. WE LEARNED THAT IT WAS THE MUTANTS' FIRST BASE ONLY RECENTLY.**
WE NEVER DID FIND OUT WHAT HAPPENED THERE. DO YOU KNOW?
* IN A STILL UNTOLD TALE OF THE GUARDIANS' EARLY YEARS.--CRAIG.
** IN ISSUE #6.--C.A.

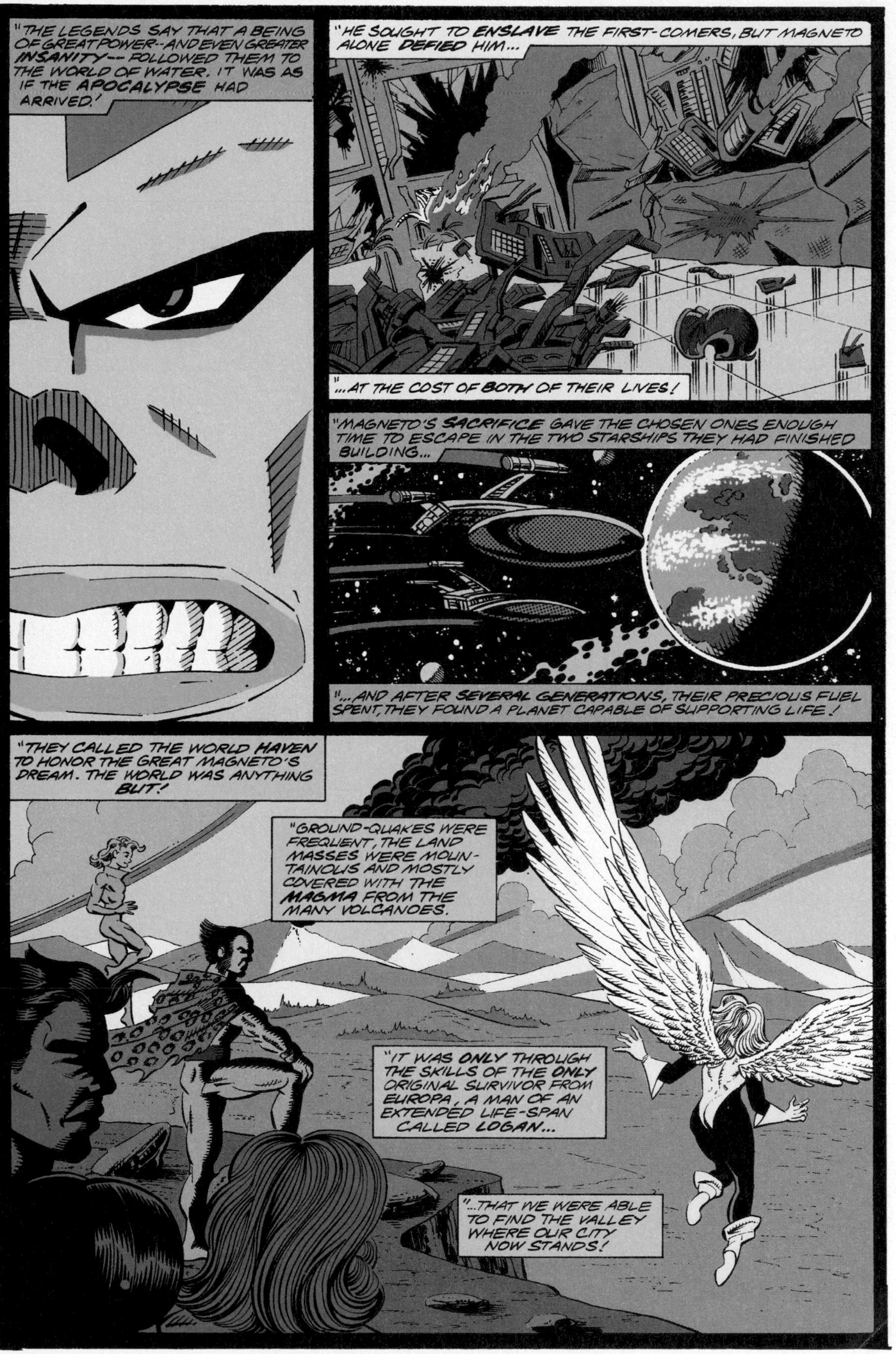
"THE LEGENDS SAY THAT A BEING OF GREAT POWER--AND EVEN GREATER INSANITY-- FOLLOWED THEM TO THE WORLD OF WATER. IT WAS AS IF THE APOCALYPSE HAD ARRIVED.'
"HE SOUGHT TO ENSLAVE THE FIRST-COMERS, BUT MAGNETO ALONE DEFIED HIM...
"...AT THE COST OF BOTH OF THEIR LIVES!
"MAGNETO'S SACRIFICE GAVE THE CHOSEN ONES ENOUGH TIME TO ESCAPE IN THE TWO STARSHIPS THEY HAD FINISHED BUILDING...
"...AND AFTER SEVERAL GENERATIONS, THEIR PRECIOUS FUEL SPENT, THEY FOUND A PLANET CAPABLE OF SUPPORTING LIFE!
"THEY CALLED THE WORLD HAVEN TO HONOR THE GREAT MAGNETO'S DREAM. THE WORLD WAS ANYTHING BUT!
"GROUND-QUAKES WERE FREQUENT, THE LAND MASSES WERE MOUNTAINOUS AND MOSTLY COVERED WITH THE MAGMA FROM THE MANY VOLCANOES.
"IT WAS ONLY THROUGH THE SKILLS OF THE ONLY ORIGINAL SURVIVOR FROM EUROPA, A MAN OF AN EXTENDED LIFE-SPAN CALLED LOGAN...
"...THAT WE WERE ABLE TO FIND THE VALLEY WHERE OUR CITY NOW STANDS!

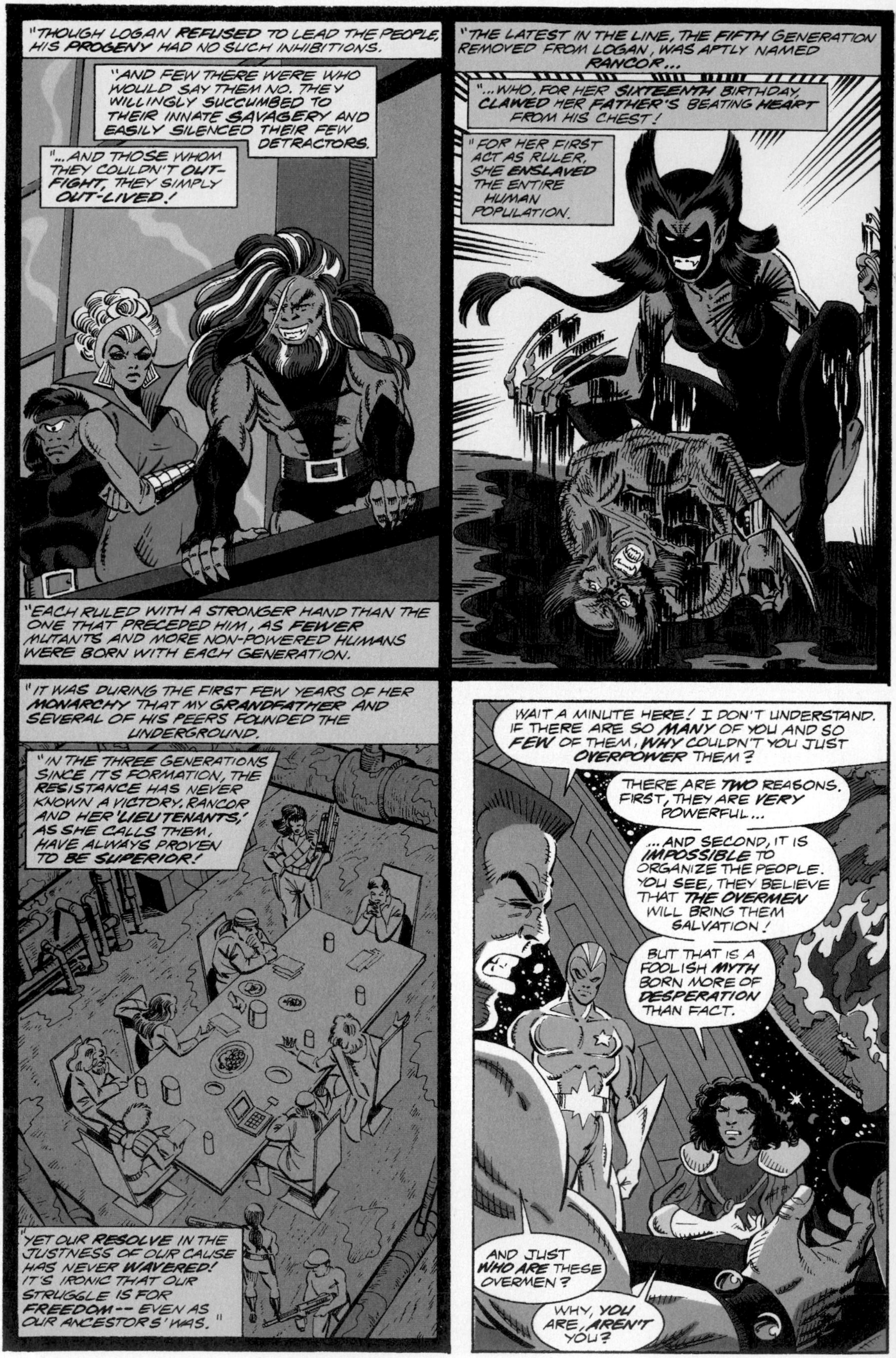
"THOUGH LOGAN REFUSED TO LEAD THE PEOPLE, HIS PROGENY HAD NO SUCH INHIBITIONS.
"AND FEW THERE WERE WHO WOULD SAY THEM NO. THEY WILLINGLY SUCCUMBED TO THEIR INNATE SAVAGERY AND EASILY SILENCED THEIR FEW DETRACTORS.
"...AND THOSE WHOM THEY COULDN'T OUT-FIGHT, THEY SIMPLY OUT-LIVED!
"EACH RULED WITH A STRONGER HAND THAN THE ONE THAT PRECEDED HIM, AS FEWER MUTANTS AND MORE NON-POWERED HUMANS WERE BORN WITH EACH GENERATION.
"THE LATEST IN THE LINE, THE FIFTH GENERATION REMOVED FROM LOGAN, WAS APTLY NAMED RANCOR...
"...WHO, FOR HER SIXTEENTH BIRTHDAY, CLAWED HER FATHER'S BEATING HEART FROM HIS CHEST!
"FOR HER FIRST ACT AS RULER, SHE ENSLAVED THE ENTIRE HUMAN POPULATION.
"IT WAS DURING THE FIRST FEW YEARS OF HER MONARCHY THAT MY GRANDFATHER AND SEVERAL OF HIS PEERS FOUNDED THE UNDERGROUND.
"IN THE THREE GENERATIONS SINCE ITS FORMATION, THE RESISTANCE HAS NEVER KNOWN A VICTORY. RANCOR AND HER 'LIEUTENANTS,' AS SHE CALLS THEM, HAVE ALWAYS PROVEN TO BE SUPERIOR!
"YET OUR RESOLVE IN THE JUSTNESS OF OUR CAUSE HAS NEVER WAVERED! IT'S IRONIC THAT OUR STRUGGLE IS FOR FREEDOM-- EVEN AS OUR ANCESTORS' WAS."
WAIT A MINUTE HERE! I DON'T UNDERSTAND. IF THERE ARE SO MANY OF YOU AND SO FEW OF THEM, WHY COULDN'T YOU JUST OVERPOWER THEM?
THERE ARE TWO REASONS. FIRST, THEY ARE VERY POWERFUL...
...AND SECOND, IT IS IMPOSSIBLE TO ORGANIZE THE PEOPLE. YOU SEE, THEY BELIEVE THAT THE OVERMEN WILL BRING THEM SALVATION!
BUT THAT IS A FOOLISH MYTH BORN MORE OF DESPERATION THAN FACT.
AND JUST WHO ARE THESE OVERMEN?
WHY, YOU ARE, AREN'T YOU?

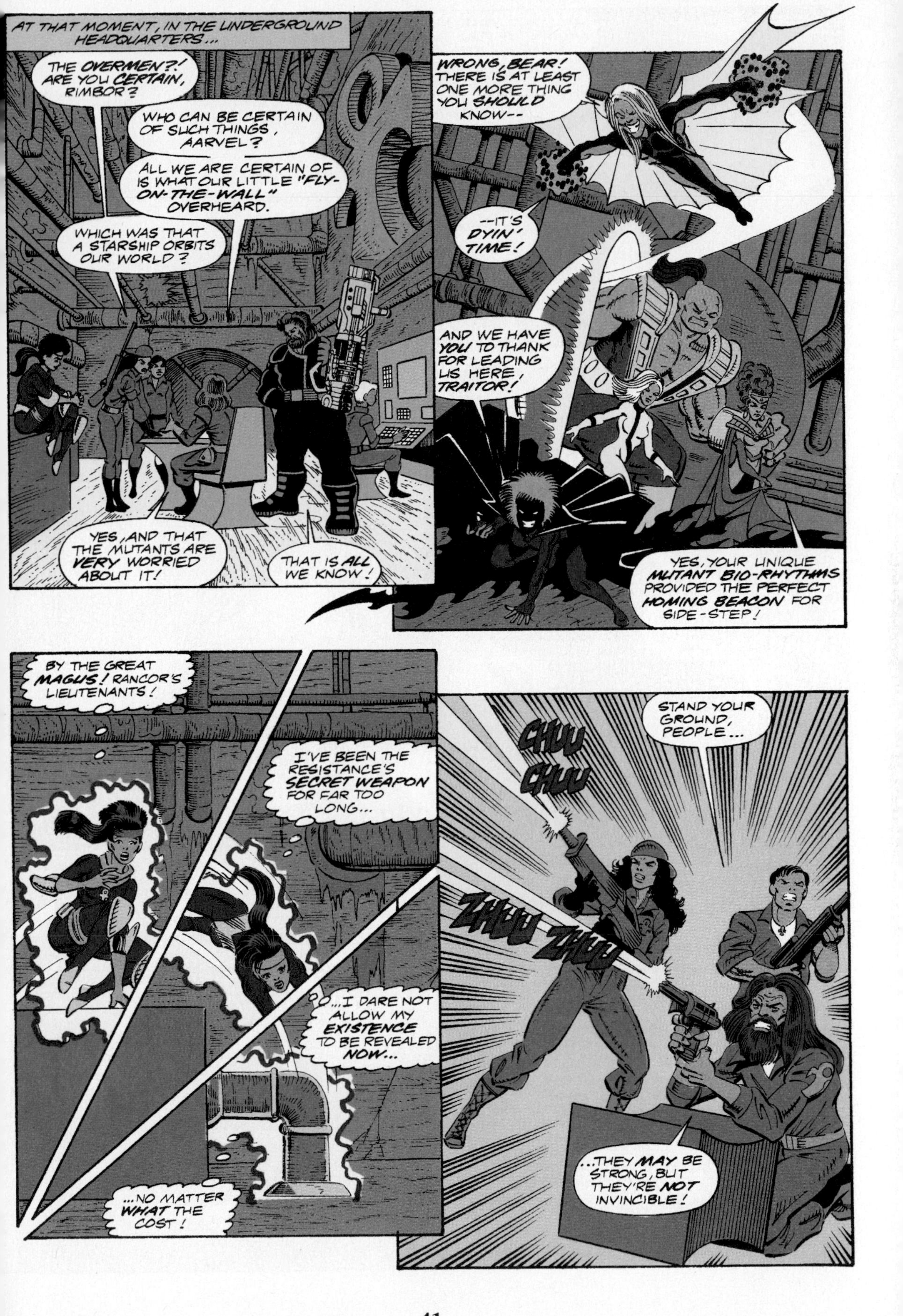
AT THAT MOMENT, IN THE UNDERGROUND HEADQUARTERS...
THE OVERMEN?! ARE YOU CERTAIN, RIMBOR?
WHO CAN BE CERTAIN OF SUCH THINGS, AARVEL?
ALL WE ARE CERTAIN OF IS WHAT OUR LITTLE "FLY-ON-THE-WALL" OVERHEARD.
WHICH WAS THAT A STARSHIP ORBITS OUR WORLD?
YES, AND THAT THE MUTANTS ARE VERY WORRIED ABOUT IT!
THAT IS ALL WE KNOW!
WRONG, BEAR! THERE IS AT LEAST ONE MORE THING YOU SHOULD KNOW--
--IT'S DYIN' TIME!
AND WE HAVE YOU TO THANK FOR LEADING US HERE, TRAITOR!
YES, YOUR UNIQUE MUTANT BIO-RHYTHMS PROVIDED THE PERFECT HOMING BEACON FOR SIDE-STEP!
BY THE GREAT MAGUS! RANCOR'S LIEUTENANTS!
I'VE BEEN THE RESISTANCE'S SECRET WEAPON FOR FAR TOO LONG...
...I DARE NOT ALLOW MY EXISTENCE TO BE REVEALED NOW...
...NO MATTER WHAT THE COST!
STAND YOUR GROUND, PEOPLE...
CHUU CHUU
ZHUU ZHUU
...THEY MAY BE STRONG, BUT THEY'RE NOT INVINCIBLE!

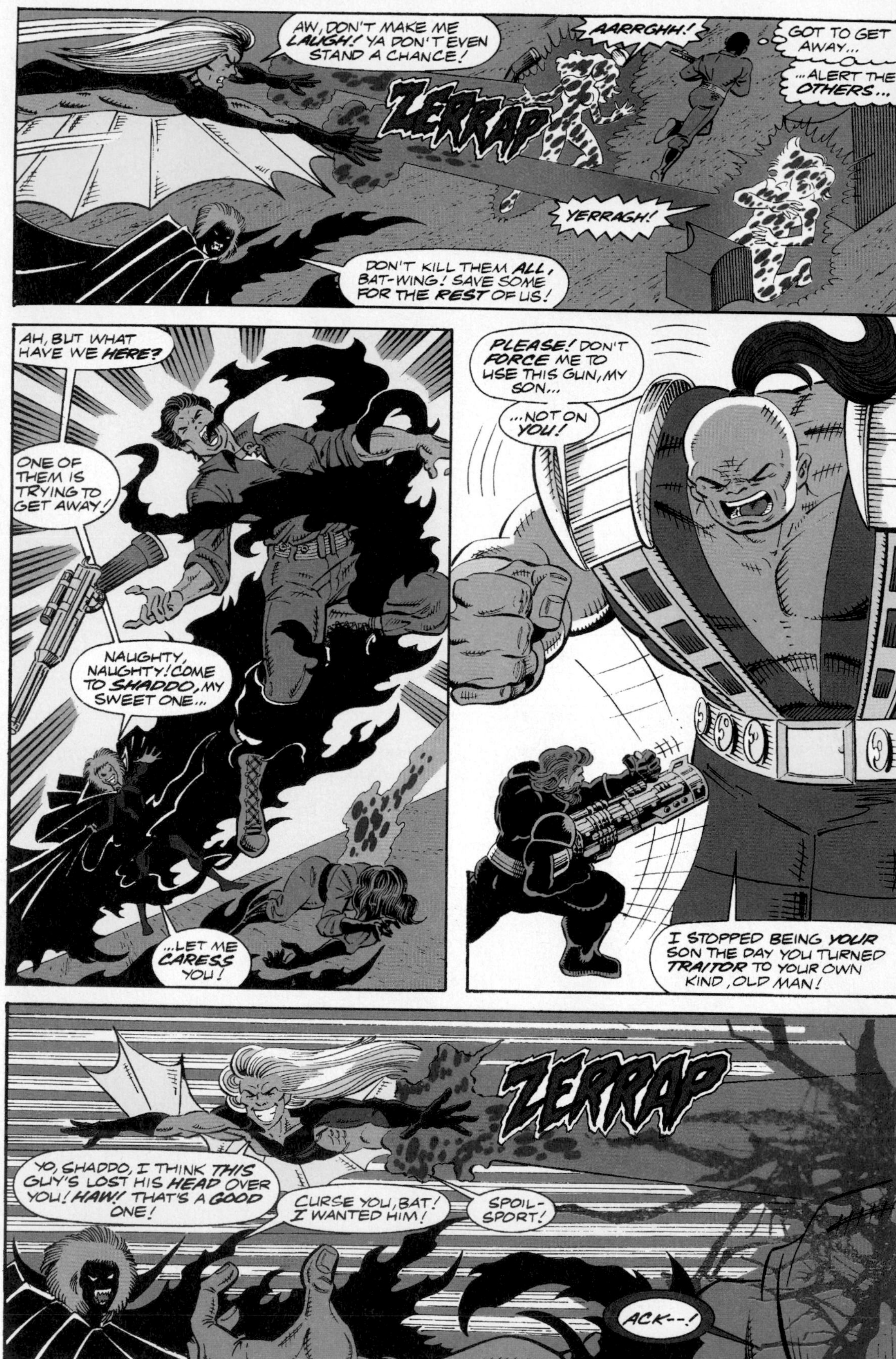
AW, DON'T MAKE ME LAUGH! YA DON'T EVEN STAND A CHANCE!
AARRGHH!
GOT TO GET AWAY...
...ALERT THE OTHERS...
ZERRAP
YERRAGH!
DON'T KILL THEM ALL, BAT-WING! SAVE SOME FOR THE REST OF US!
AH, BUT WHAT HAVE WE HERE?
ONE OF THEM IS TRYING TO GET AWAY!
NAUGHTY, NAUGHTY! COME TO SHADDO, MY SWEET ONE...
...LET ME CARESS YOU!
PLEASE! DON'T FORCE ME TO USE THIS GUN, MY SON...
...NOT ON YOU!
I STOPPED BEING YOUR SON THE DAY YOU TURNED TRAITOR TO YOUR OWN KIND, OLD MAN!
ZERRAP
YO, SHADDO, I THINK THIS GUY'S LOST HIS HEAD OVER YOU! HAW! THAT'S A GOOD ONE!
CURSE YOU, BAT! I WANTED HIM!
SPOIL-SPORT!
ACK--!

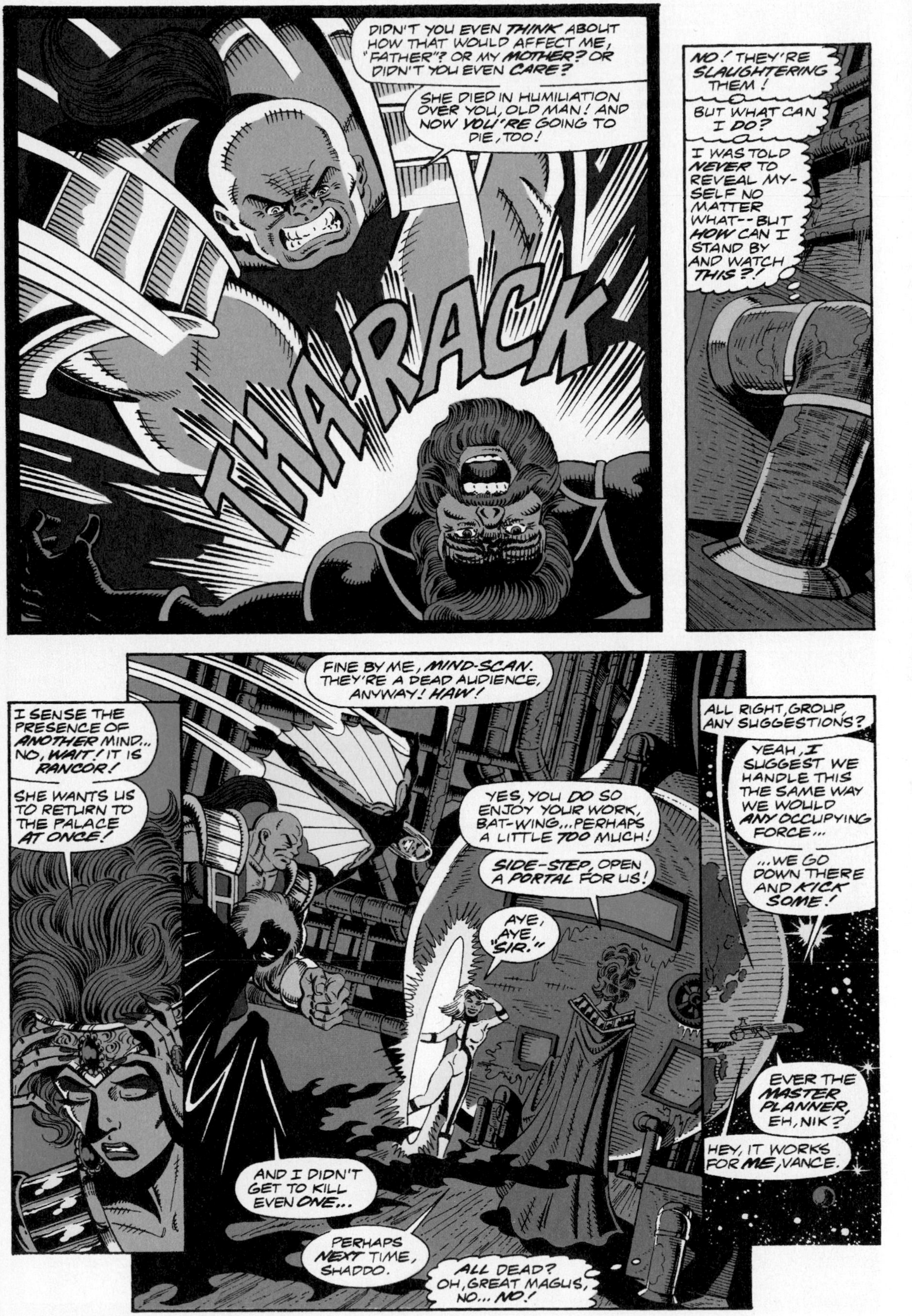
DIDN'T YOU EVEN THINK ABOUT HOW THAT WOULD AFFECT ME, "FATHER"? OR MY MOTHER? OR DIDN'T YOU EVEN CARE?
SHE DIED IN HUMILIATION OVER YOU, OLD MAN! AND NOW YOU'RE GOING TO DIE, TOO!
THA-RACK
NO! THEY'RE SLAUGHTERING THEM!
BUT WHAT CAN I DO?
I WAS TOLD NEVER TO REVEAL MY-SELF NO MATTER WHAT--BUT HOW CAN I STAND BY AND WATCH THIS?!
I SENSE THE PRESENCE OF ANOTHER MIND... NO, WAIT! IT IS RANCOR!
SHE WANTS US TO RETURN TO THE PALACE AT ONCE!
FINE BY ME, MIND-SCAN. THEY'RE A DEAD AUDIENCE, ANYWAY! HAW!
YES, YOU DO SO ENJOY YOUR WORK, BAT-WING... PERHAPS A LITTLE TOO MUCH!
SIDE-STEP, OPEN A PORTAL FOR US!
AYE, AYE, "SIR."
AND I DIDN'T GET TO KILL EVEN ONE...
PERHAPS NEXT TIME, SHADDO.
ALL DEAD? OH, GREAT MAGUS, NO... NO!
ALL RIGHT, GROUP, ANY SUGGESTIONS?
YEAH, I SUGGEST WE HANDLE THIS THE SAME WAY WE WOULD ANY OCCUPYING FORCE...
...WE GO DOWN THERE AND KICK SOME!
EVER THE MASTER PLANNER, EH, NIK?
HEY, IT WORKS FOR ME, VANCE.

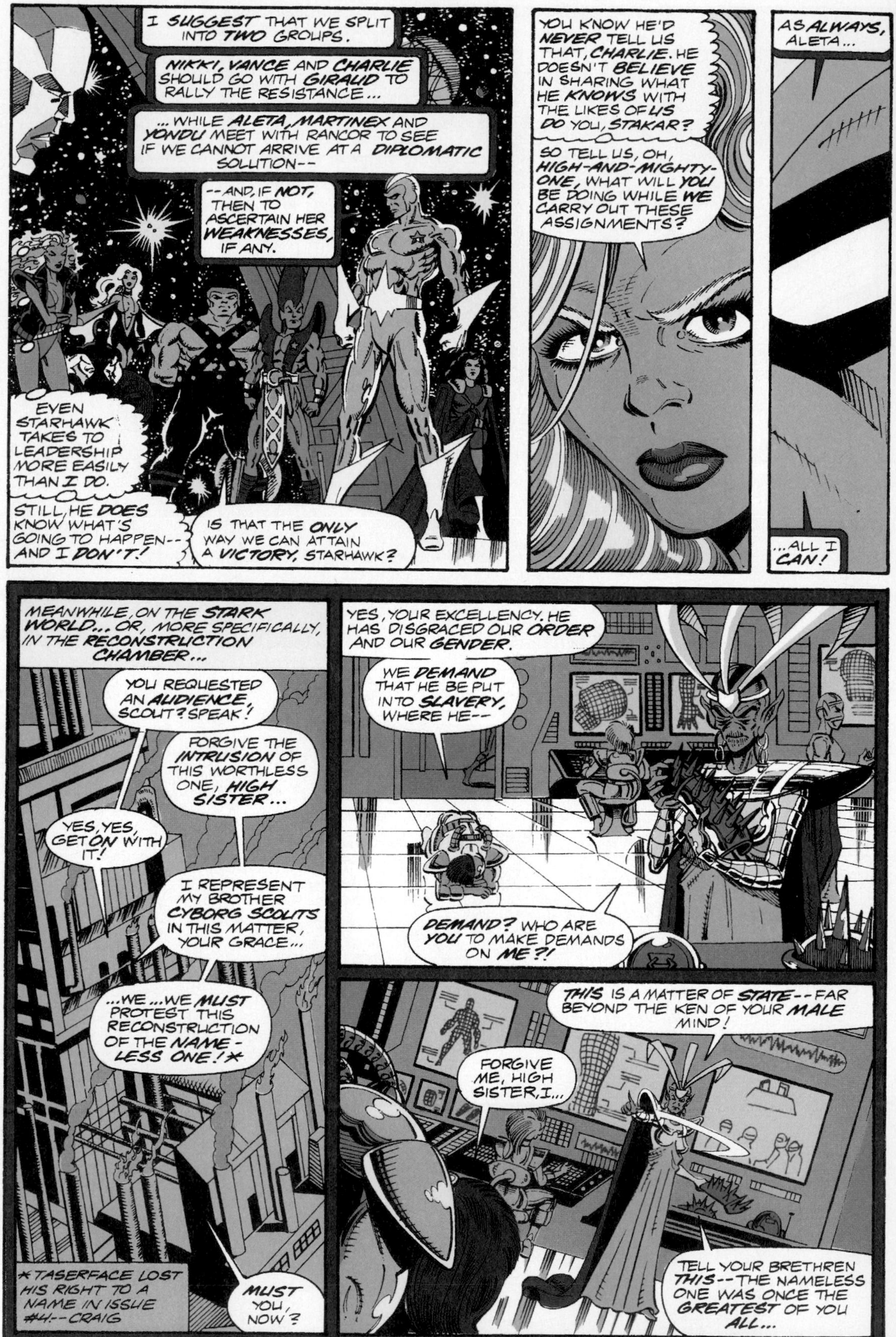
I SUGGEST THAT WE SPLIT INTO TWO GROUPS.
NIKKI, VANCE AND CHARLIE SHOULD GO WITH GIRAUD TO RALLY THE RESISTANCE...
...WHILE ALETA, MARTINEX AND YONDU MEET WITH RANCOR TO SEE IF WE CANNOT ARRIVE AT A DIPLOMATIC SOLUTION--
--AND, IF NOT, THEN TO ASCERTAIN HER WEAKNESSES, IF ANY.
EVEN STARHAWK TAKES TO LEADERSHIP MORE EASILY THAN I DO.
STILL, HE DOES KNOW WHAT'S GOING TO HAPPEN-- AND I DON'T!
IS THAT THE ONLY WAY WE CAN ATTAIN A VICTORY, STARHAWK?
YOU KNOW HE'D NEVER TELL US THAT, CHARLIE. HE DOESN'T BELIEVE IN SHARING WHAT HE KNOWS WITH THE LIKES OF US. DO YOU, STAKAR?
SO TELL US, OH, HIGH-AND-MIGHTY-ONE, WHAT WILL YOU BE DOING WHILE WE CARRY OUT THESE ASSIGNMENTS?
AS ALWAYS, ALETA...
...ALL I CAN!
MEANWHILE, ON THE STARK WORLD... OR, MORE SPECIFICALLY, IN THE RECONSTRUCTION CHAMBER...
YOU REQUESTED AN AUDIENCE, SCOUT? SPEAK!
FORGIVE THE INTRUSION OF THIS WORTHLESS ONE, HIGH SISTER...
YES, YES, GET ON WITH IT!
I REPRESENT MY BROTHER CYBORG SCOUTS IN THIS MATTER, YOUR GRACE...
...WE...WE MUST PROTEST THIS RECONSTRUCTION OF THE NAME-LESS ONE!*
*TASERFACE LOST HIS RIGHT TO A NAME IN ISSUE #4!--CRAIG
MUST YOU, NOW?
YES, YOUR EXCELLENCY. HE HAS DISGRACED OUR ORDER AND OUR GENDER.
WE DEMAND THAT HE BE PUT INTO SLAVERY, WHERE HE--
DEMAND? WHO ARE YOU TO MAKE DEMANDS ON ME?!
THIS IS A MATTER OF STATE--FAR BEYOND THE KEN OF YOUR MALE MIND!
FORGIVE ME, HIGH SISTER, I...
TELL YOUR BRETHREN THIS--THE NAMELESS ONE WAS ONCE THE GREATEST OF YOU ALL...

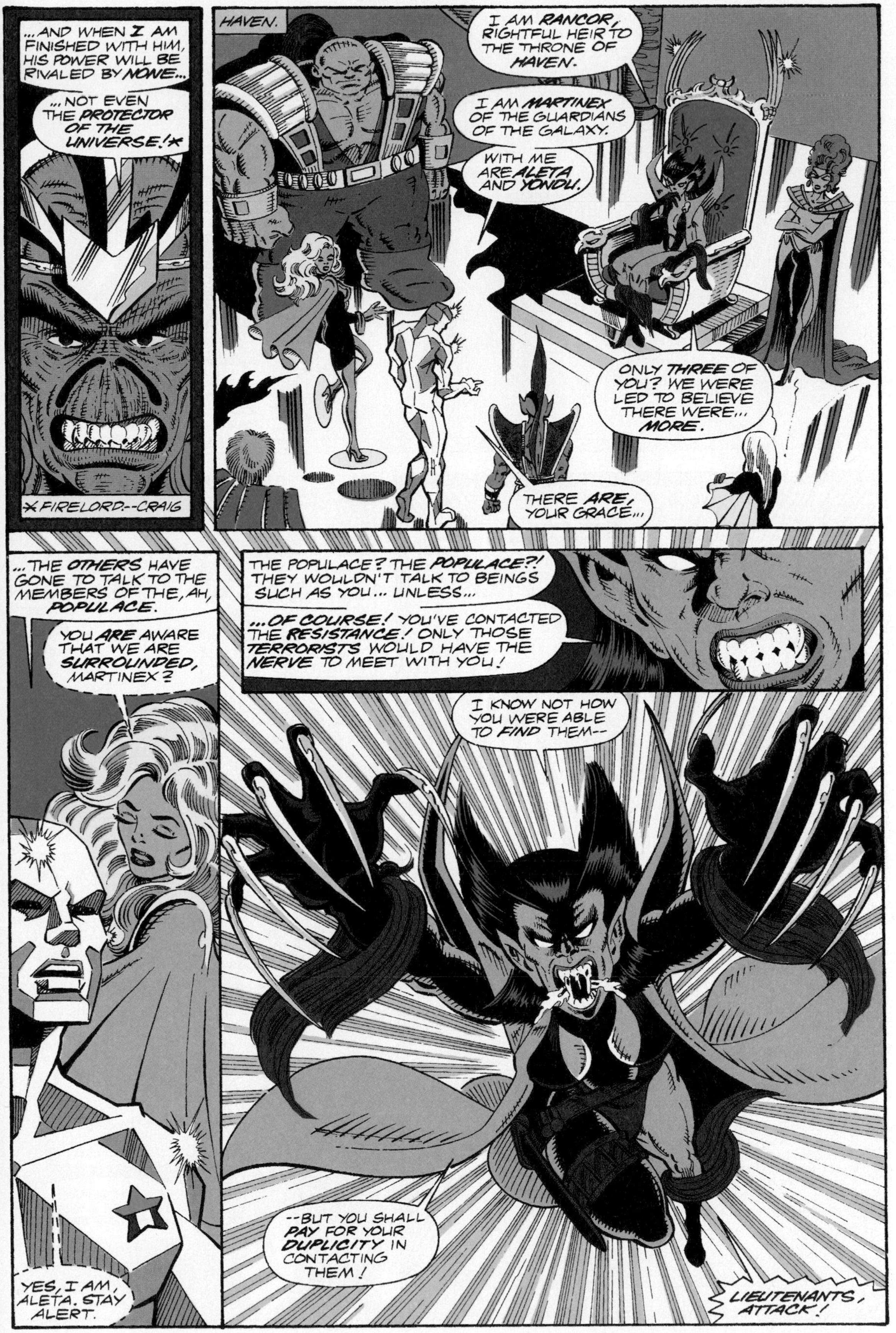
...AND WHEN I AM FINISHED WITH HIM, HIS POWER WILL BE RIVALED BY NONE...
...NOT EVEN THE PROTECTOR OF THE UNIVERSE!*
*FIRELORD.--CRAIG
HAVEN.
I AM RANCOR, RIGHTFUL HEIR TO THE THRONE OF HAVEN.
I AM MARTINEX OF THE GUARDIANS OF THE GALAXY.
WITH ME ARE ALETA AND YONDU.
ONLY THREE OF YOU? WE WERE LED TO BELIEVE THERE WERE... MORE.
THERE ARE, YOUR GRACE...
...THE OTHERS HAVE GONE TO TALK TO THE MEMBERS OF THE, AH, POPULACE.
YOU ARE AWARE THAT WE ARE SURROUNDED, MARTINEX?
THE POPULACE? THE POPULACE?! THEY WOULDN'T TALK TO BEINGS SUCH AS YOU... UNLESS...
...OF COURSE! YOU'VE CONTACTED THE RESISTANCE! ONLY THOSE TERRORISTS WOULD HAVE THE NERVE TO MEET WITH YOU!
I KNOW NOT HOW YOU WERE ABLE TO FIND THEM--
--BUT YOU SHALL PAY FOR YOUR DUPLICITY IN CONTACTING THEM!
YES, I AM, ALETA. STAY ALERT.
LIEUTENANTS, ATTACK!

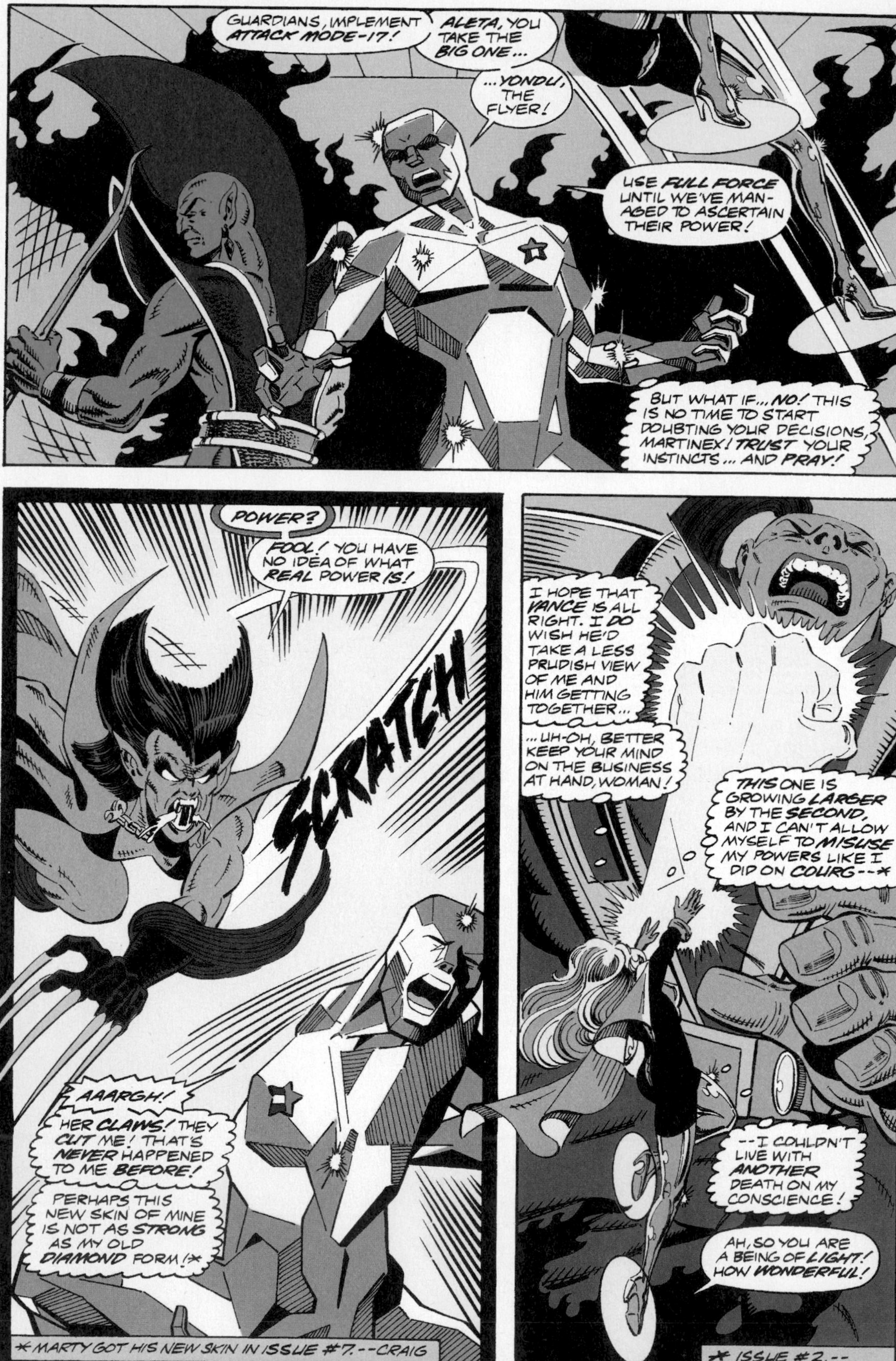
GUARDIANS, IMPLEMENT ATTACK MODE-17!
ALETA, YOU TAKE THE BIG ONE...
...YONDU, THE FLYER!
USE FULL FORCE UNTIL WE'VE MANAGED TO ASCERTAIN THEIR POWER!
BUT WHAT IF... NO! THIS IS NO TIME TO START DOUBTING YOUR DECISIONS, MARTINEX! TRUST YOUR INSTINCTS... AND PRAY!
POWER?
FOOL! YOU HAVE NO IDEA OF WHAT REAL POWER IS!
SCRATCH
AAARGH!
HER CLAWS! THEY CUT ME! THAT'S NEVER HAPPENED TO ME BEFORE!
PERHAPS THIS NEW SKIN OF MINE IS NOT AS STRONG AS MY OLD DIAMOND FORM!*
*MARTY GOT HIS NEW SKIN IN ISSUE #7.--CRAIG
I HOPE THAT VANCE IS ALL RIGHT. I DO WISH HE'D TAKE A LESS PRUDISH VIEW OF ME AND HIM GETTING TOGETHER...
...UH-OH, BETTER KEEP YOUR MIND ON THE BUSINESS AT HAND, WOMAN!
THIS ONE IS GROWING LARGER BY THE SECOND, AND I CAN'T ALLOW MYSELF TO MISUSE MY POWERS LIKE I DID ON COURG--*
--I COULDN'T LIVE WITH ANOTHER DEATH ON MY CONSCIENCE!
AH, SO YOU ARE A BEING OF LIGHT! HOW WONDERFUL!
* ISSUE #2.-- CHRONICLING CRAIG

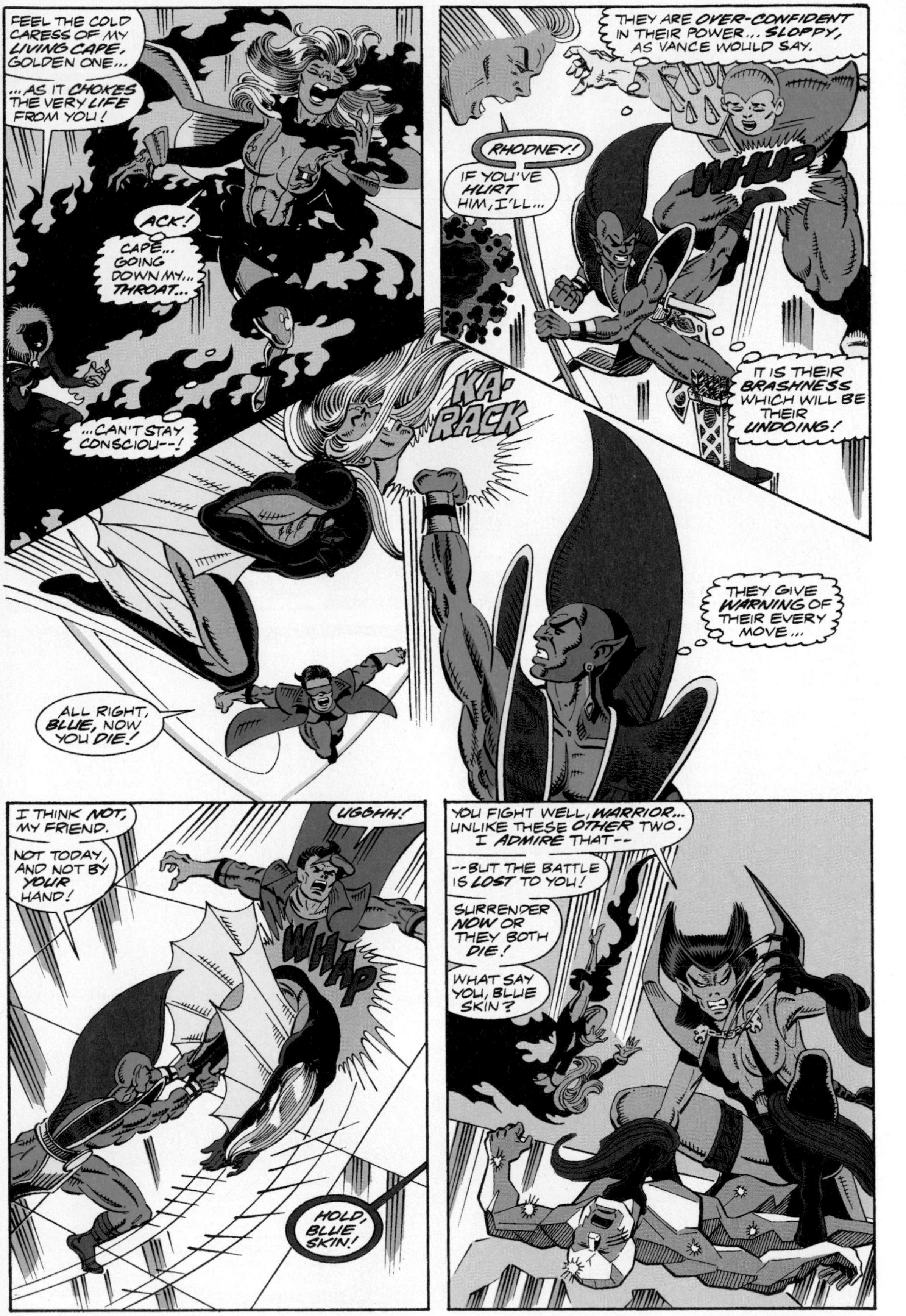

FEEL THE COLD CARESS OF MY LIVING CAPE, GOLDEN ONE...
...AS IT CHOKES THE VERY LIFE FROM YOU!
ACK!
CAPE... GOING DOWN MY... THROAT...
...CAN'T STAY CONSCIOU--!
THEY ARE OVER-CONFIDENT IN THEIR POWER... SLOPPY, AS VANCE WOULD SAY.
RHODNEY!
IF YOU'VE HURT HIM, I'LL...
WHUP
IT IS THEIR BRASHNESS WHICH WILL BE THEIR UNDOING!
KA-RACK
THEY GIVE WARNING OF THEIR EVERY MOVE...
ALL RIGHT, BLUE, NOW YOU DIE!
I THINK NOT, MY FRIEND.
NOT TODAY, AND NOT BY YOUR HAND!
UGGHH!
WHAP
HOLD, BLUE SKIN!
YOU FIGHT WELL, WARRIOR... UNLIKE THESE OTHER TWO. I ADMIRE THAT--
--BUT THE BATTLE IS LOST TO YOU!
SURRENDER NOW OR THEY BOTH DIE!
WHAT SAY YOU, BLUE SKIN?

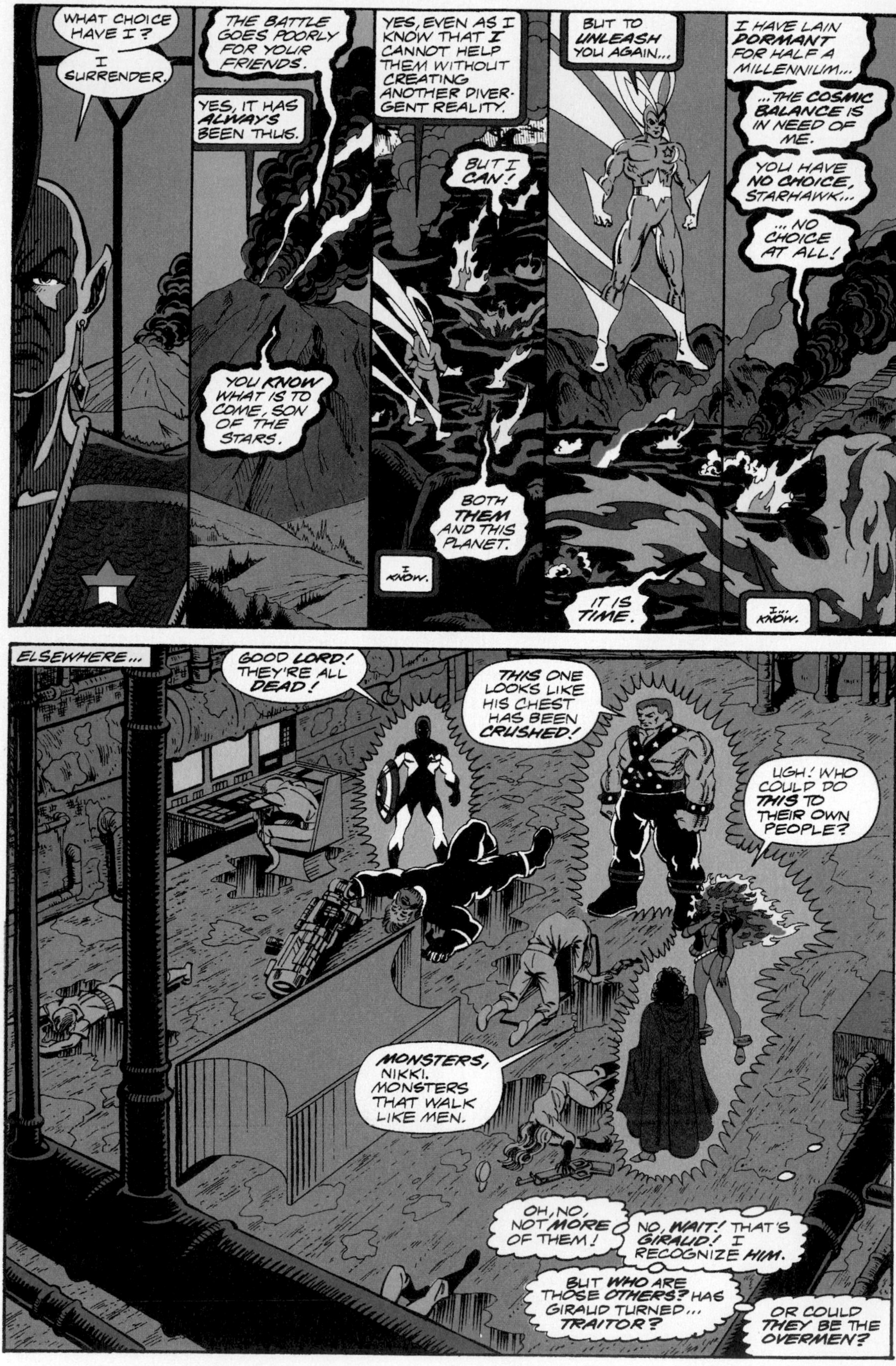
WHAT CHOICE HAVE I? I SURRENDER.
THE BATTLE GOES POORLY FOR YOUR FRIENDS.
YES, IT HAS ALWAYS BEEN THUS.
YOU KNOW WHAT IS TO COME, SON OF THE STARS.
YES, EVEN AS I KNOW THAT I CANNOT HELP THEM WITHOUT CREATING ANOTHER DIVERGENT REALITY.
BUT I CAN!
BOTH THEM AND THIS PLANET.
I KNOW.
BUT TO UNLEASH YOU AGAIN...
IT IS TIME.
I HAVE LAIN DORMANT FOR HALF A MILLENNIUM...
...THE COSMIC BALANCE IS IN NEED OF ME.
YOU HAVE NO CHOICE, STARHAWK...
...NO CHOICE AT ALL!
I... KNOW.
ELSEWHERE...
GOOD LORD! THEY'RE ALL DEAD!
THIS ONE LOOKS LIKE HIS CHEST HAS BEEN CRUSHED!
UGH! WHO COULD DO THIS TO THEIR OWN PEOPLE?
MONSTERS, NIKKI. MONSTERS THAT WALK LIKE MEN.
OH, NO, NOT MORE OF THEM!
NO, WAIT! THAT'S GIRAUD! I RECOGNIZE HIM.
BUT WHO ARE THOSE OTHERS? HAS GIRAUD TURNED... TRAITOR?
OR COULD THEY BE THE OVERMEN?

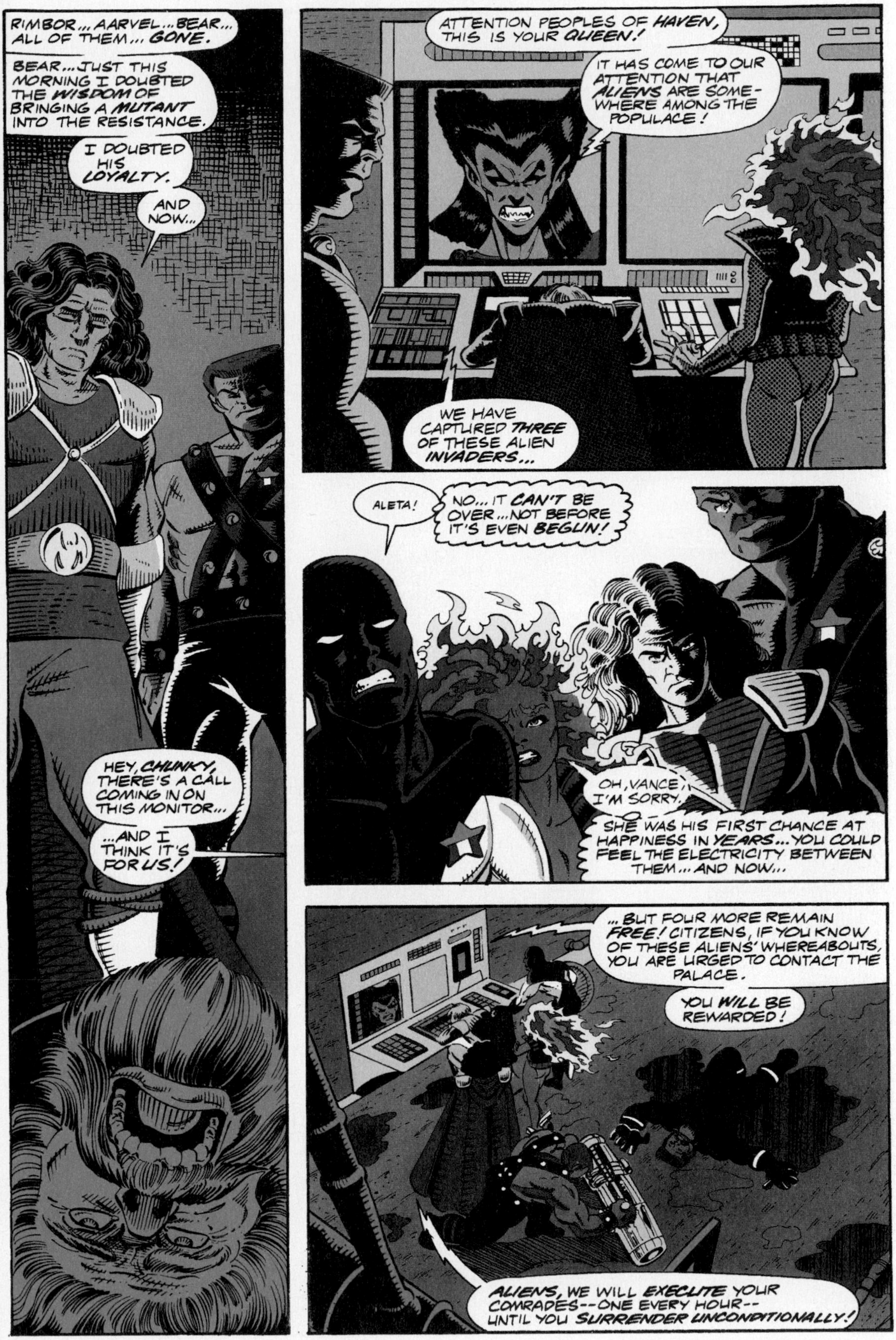
RIMBOR... AARVEL... BEAR... ALL OF THEM... GONE.
BEAR... JUST THIS MORNING I DOUBTED THE WISDOM OF BRINGING A MUTANT INTO THE RESISTANCE.
I DOUBTED HIS LOYALTY.
AND NOW...
HEY, CHUNKY, THERE'S A CALL COMING IN ON THIS MONITOR...
...AND I THINK IT'S FOR US!
ATTENTION PEOPLES OF HAVEN, THIS IS YOUR QUEEN!
IT HAS COME TO OUR ATTENTION THAT ALIENS ARE SOMEWHERE AMONG THE POPULACE!
WE HAVE CAPTURED THREE OF THESE ALIEN INVADERS...
ALETA!
NO... IT CAN'T BE OVER... NOT BEFORE IT'S EVEN BEGUN!
OH, VANCE, I'M SORRY.
SHE WAS HIS FIRST CHANCE AT HAPPINESS IN YEARS... YOU COULD FEEL THE ELECTRICITY BETWEEN THEM... AND NOW...
... BUT FOUR MORE REMAIN FREE! CITIZENS, IF YOU KNOW OF THESE ALIENS' WHEREABOUTS, YOU ARE URGED TO CONTACT THE PALACE.
YOU WILL BE REWARDED!
ALIENS, WE WILL EXECUTE YOUR COMRADES--ONE EVERY HOUR--UNTIL YOU SURRENDER UNCONDITIONALLY!

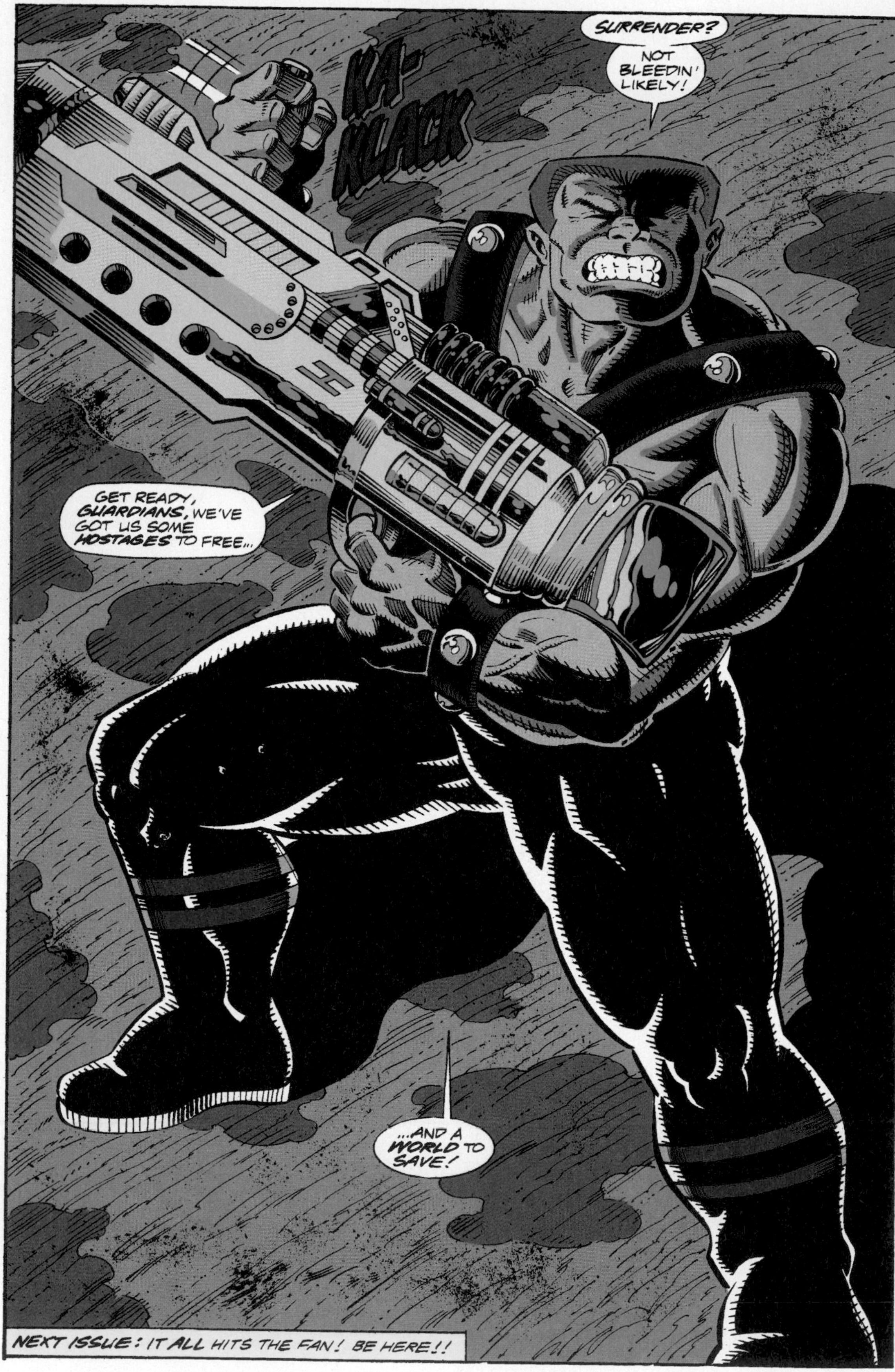
KA-KLACK
SURRENDER?
NOT BLEEDIN' LIKELY!
GET READY, GUARDIANS, WE'VE GOT US SOME HOSTAGES TO FREE...
...AND A WORLD TO SAVE!
NEXT ISSUE: IT ALL HITS THE FAN! BE HERE!!

GUARDIANS
OF THE GALAXY

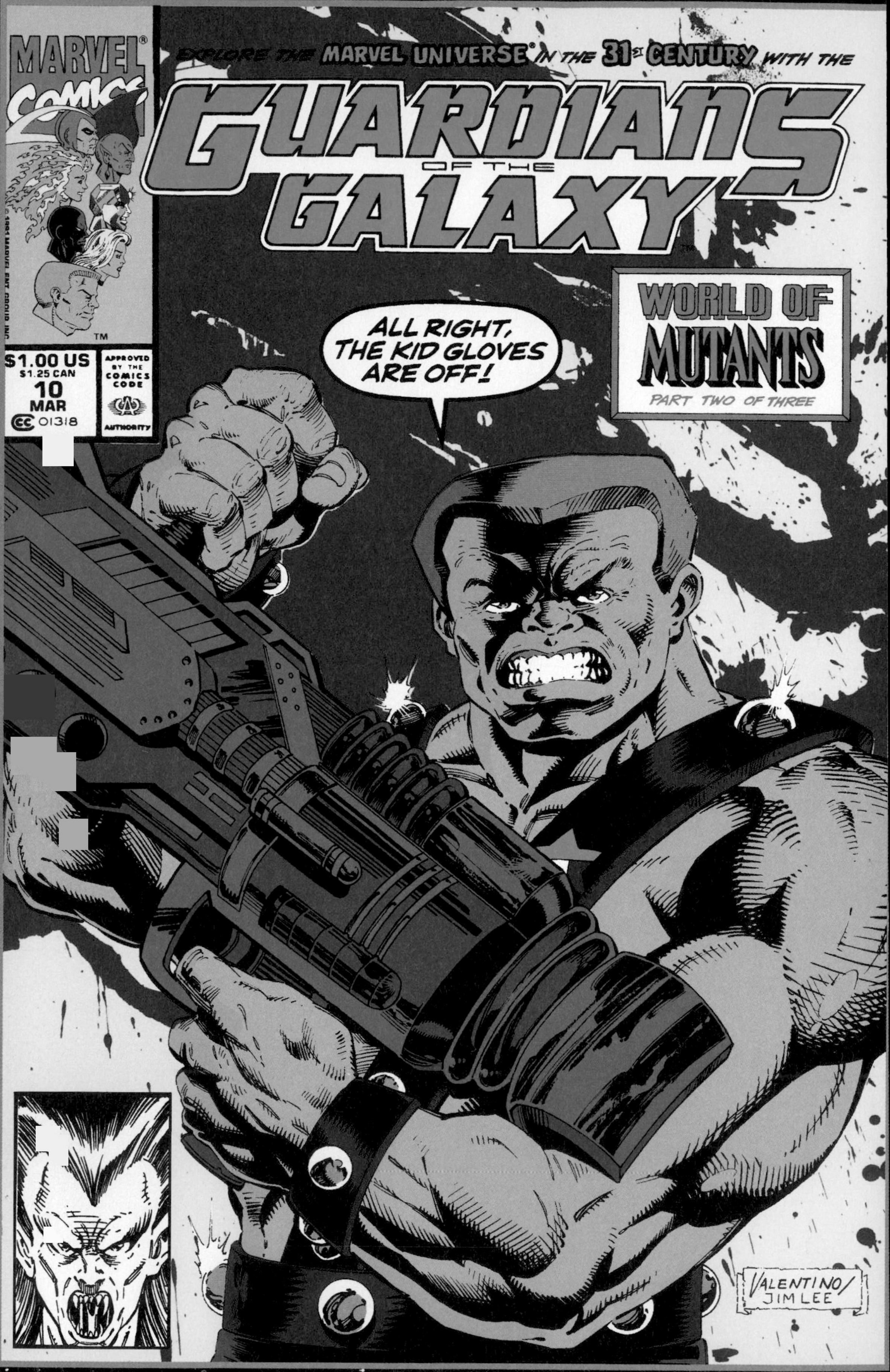
MARVEL COMICS
EXPLORE THE MARVEL UNIVERSE IN THE 31ST CENTURY WITH THE
GUARDIANS OF THE GALAXY
$1.00 US
$1.25 CAN
10
MAR
APPROVED BY THE COMICS CODE AUTHORITY
WORLD OF MUTANTS
PART TWO OF THREE
ALL RIGHT, THE KID GLOVES ARE OFF!
VALENTINO/ JIM LEE

CHARLIE 27! MARTINEX! NIKKI! VANCE ASTRO! YONDU! ALETA! STARHAWK! SEVEN EXTRAORDINARY SUPER-BEINGS, ALL SURVIVORS OF INTERSTELLAR WAR. NOW THEY ROAM THE COSMOS OF THE 31ST CENTURY ABOARD THE STARSHIP CAPTAIN AMERICA, THEIR MISSION—TO SAFEGUARD THE MILKY WAY! STAN LEE PRESENTS . . . THE GUARDIANS OF THE GALAXY!

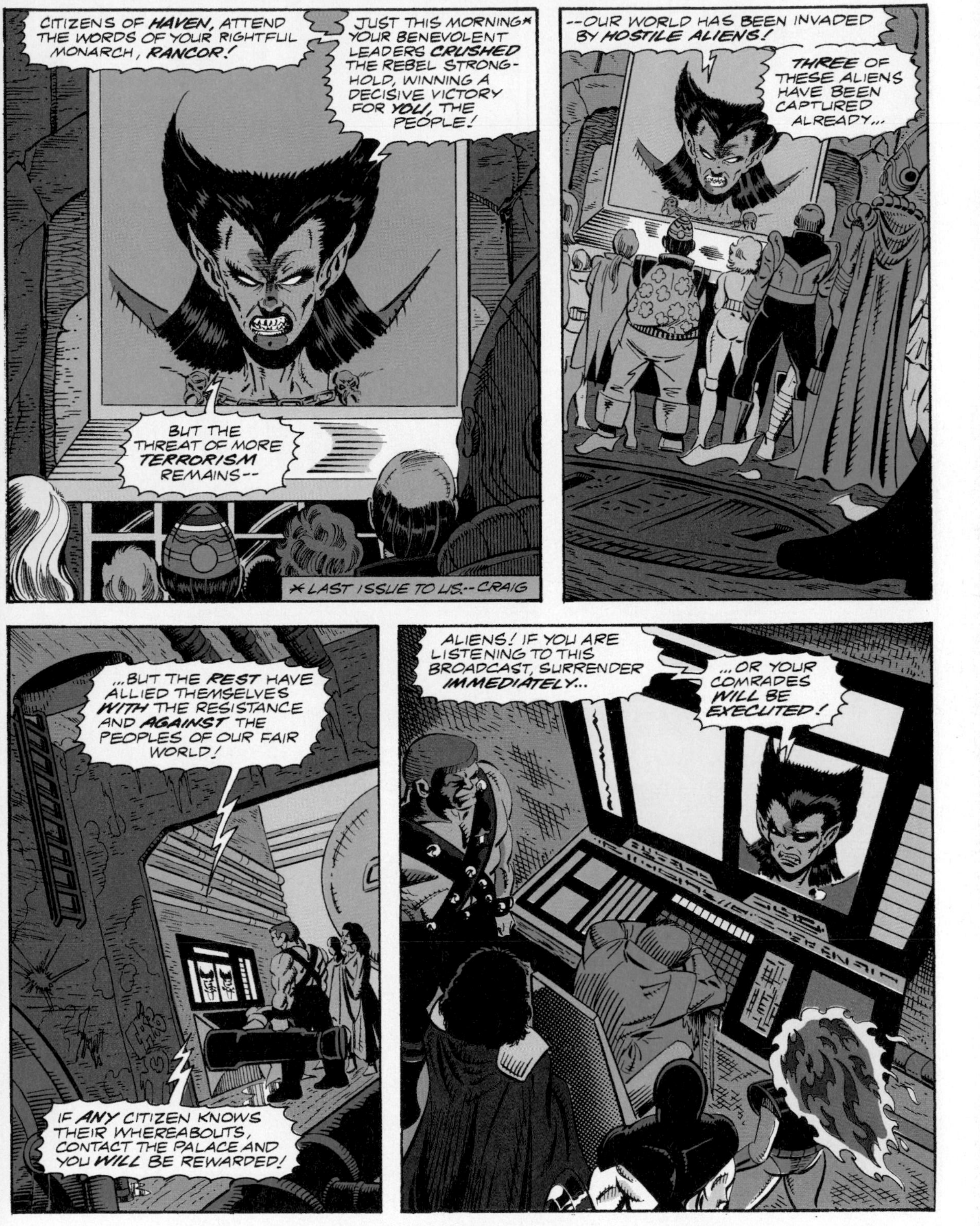

CITIZENS OF HAVEN, ATTEND THE WORDS OF YOUR RIGHTFUL MONARCH, RANCOR!
JUST THIS MORNING* YOUR BENEVOLENT LEADERS CRUSHED THE REBEL STRONGHOLD, WINNING A DECISIVE VICTORY FOR YOU, THE PEOPLE!
BUT THE THREAT OF MORE TERRORISM REMAINS--
*LAST ISSUE TO US.--CRAIG
--OUR WORLD HAS BEEN INVADED BY HOSTILE ALIENS!
THREE OF THESE ALIENS HAVE BEEN CAPTURED ALREADY...
...BUT THE REST HAVE ALLIED THEMSELVES WITH THE RESISTANCE AND AGAINST THE PEOPLES OF OUR FAIR WORLD!
IF ANY CITIZEN KNOWS THEIR WHEREABOUTS, CONTACT THE PALACE AND YOU WILL BE REWARDED!
ALIENS! IF YOU ARE LISTENING TO THIS BROADCAST, SURRENDER IMMEDIATELY...
...OR YOUR COMRADES WILL BE EXECUTED!

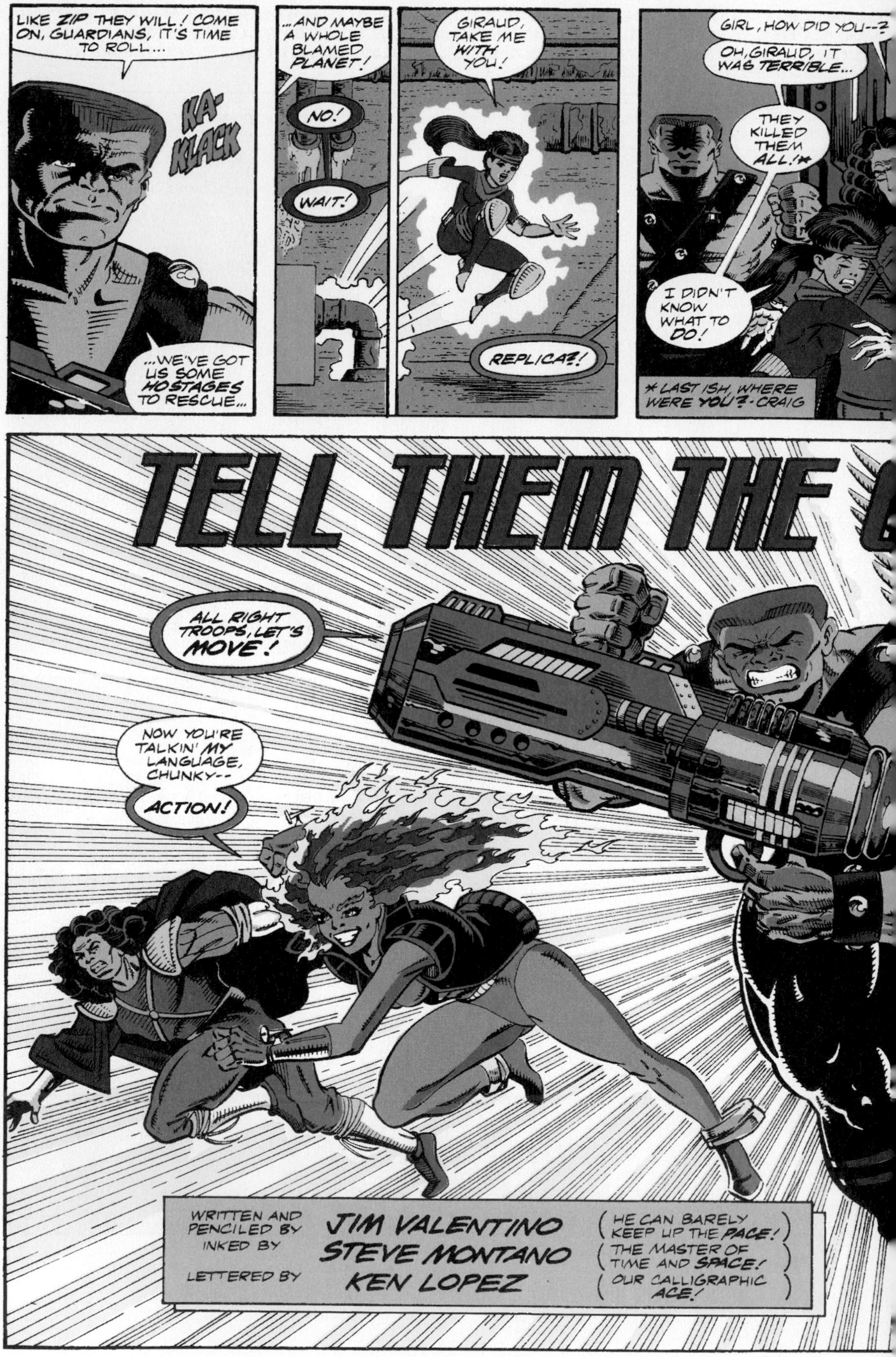
LIKE ZIP THEY WILL! COME ON, GUARDIANS, IT'S TIME TO ROLL...
KA-KLACK
...WE'VE GOT US SOME HOSTAGES TO RESCUE...
...AND MAYBE A WHOLE BLAMED PLANET!
NO!
WAIT!
GIRAUD, TAKE ME WITH YOU!
REPLICA?!
GIRL, HOW DID YOU--?
OH, GIRAUD, IT WAS TERRIBLE...
THEY KILLED THEM ALL!*
I DIDN'T KNOW WHAT TO DO!
* LAST ISH, WHERE WERE YOU? - CRAIG
TELL THEM THE G
ALL RIGHT TROOPS, LET'S MOVE!
NOW YOU'RE TALKIN' MY LANGUAGE, CHUNKY--
ACTION!
WRITTEN AND PENCILED BY JIM VALENTINO (HE CAN BARELY KEEP UP THE PACE!)
INKED BY STEVE MONTANO (THE MASTER OF TIME AND SPACE!)
LETTERED BY KEN LOPEZ (OUR CALLIGRAPHIC ACE!)

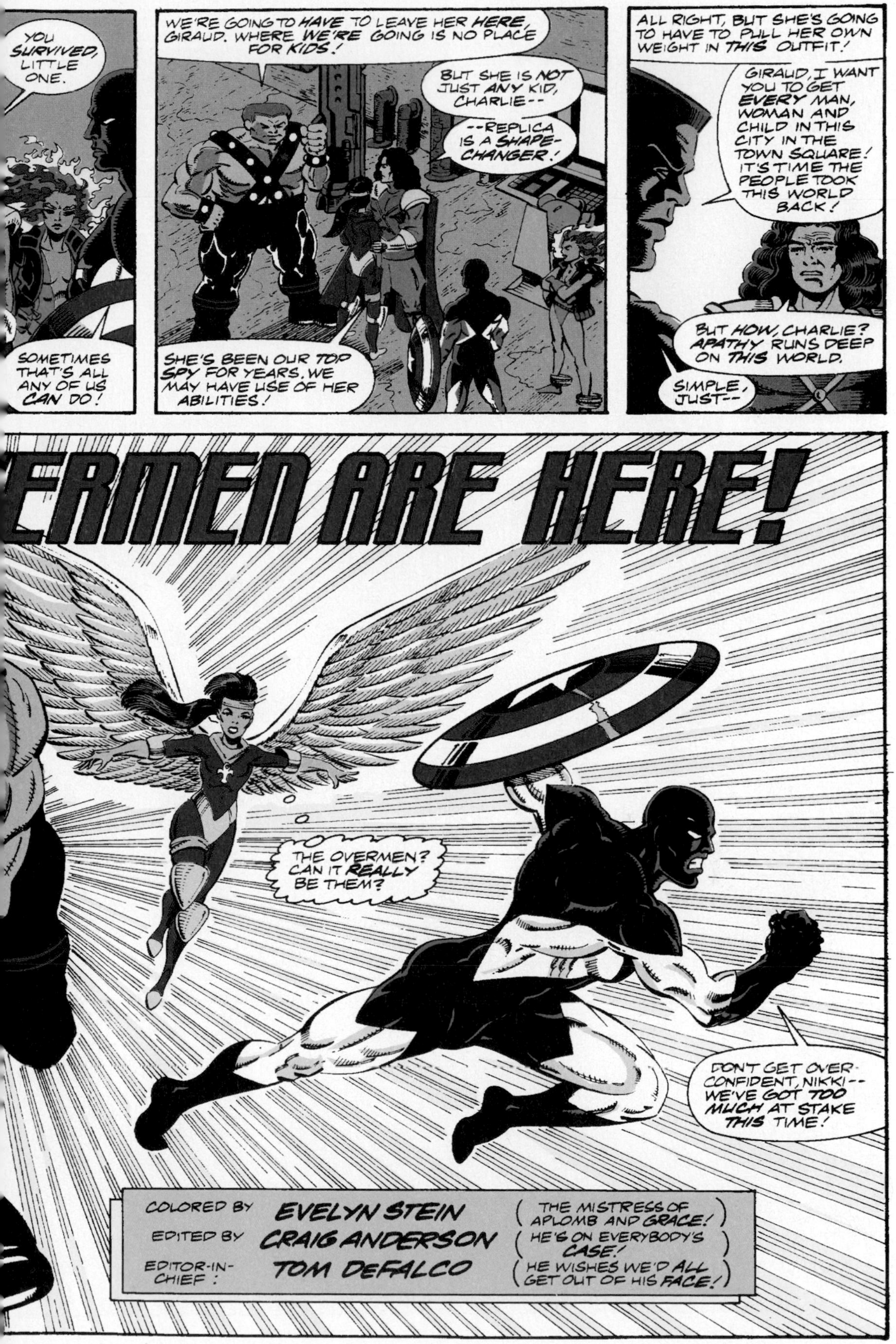
YOU SURVIVED, LITTLE ONE.
SOMETIMES THAT'S ALL ANY OF US CAN DO!
WE'RE GOING TO HAVE TO LEAVE HER HERE, GIRAUD. WHERE WE'RE GOING IS NO PLACE FOR KIDS!
BUT SHE IS NOT JUST ANY KID, CHARLIE--
--REPLICA IS A SHAPE-CHANGER!
SHE'S BEEN OUR TOP SPY FOR YEARS. WE MAY HAVE USE OF HER ABILITIES!
ALL RIGHT, BUT SHE'S GOING TO HAVE TO PULL HER OWN WEIGHT IN THIS OUTFIT!
GIRAUD, I WANT YOU TO GET EVERY MAN, WOMAN AND CHILD IN THIS CITY IN THE TOWN SQUARE! IT'S TIME THE PEOPLE TOOK THIS WORLD BACK!
BUT HOW, CHARLIE? APATHY RUNS DEEP ON THIS WORLD.
SIMPLE, JUST--
ERMEN ARE HERE!
THE OVERMEN? CAN IT REALLY BE THEM?
DON'T GET OVER-CONFIDENT, NIKKI-- WE'VE GOT TOO MUCH AT STAKE THIS TIME!
COLORED BY EVELYN STEIN (THE MISTRESS OF APLOMB AND GRACE!)
EDITED BY CRAIG ANDERSON (HE'S ON EVERYBODY'S CASE!)
EDITOR-IN-CHIEF: TOM DeFALCO (HE WISHES WE'D ALL GET OUT OF HIS FACE!)

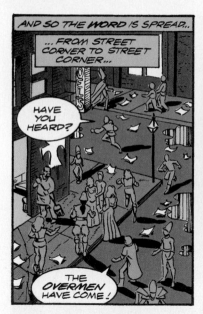

AND SO THE **WORD** IS SPREAD...

...FROM STREET CORNER TO STREET CORNER...

HAVE YOU HEARD?

THE **OVERMEN** HAVE COME!

...FROM PERSON TO PERSON...

THE OVERMEN ARE **HERE**!

PRAISE THE CHURCH!

...IN HUSHED **WHISPERS** AND IN JUBILANT **SHOUTS**!

AND WHERE ONCE **APATHY** REIGNED SUPREME...

...ACTIVISM TAKES ITS PLACE...

...AND THE PEOPLE COME TOGETHER...

...IN SMALL GROUPS, AND IN LARGE, TO **FILL** THE TOWN SQUARE!

WELL, WELL, WELL, WHAT HAVE WE **HERE**?

COMING INTO THE SQUARE WITH THEIR **TOOLS** AND THEIR **KNIVES**...

...AND THEIR **OUTLAWED** RELIGIOUS ICONS?

LOOK AT THEM **ALL**!

ARE THE PEOPLE **REVOLTING**?

OF **COURSE** THEY ARE! HAW!

OLD JOKE, **BAT**, AND A **BAD** ONE AT THAT!

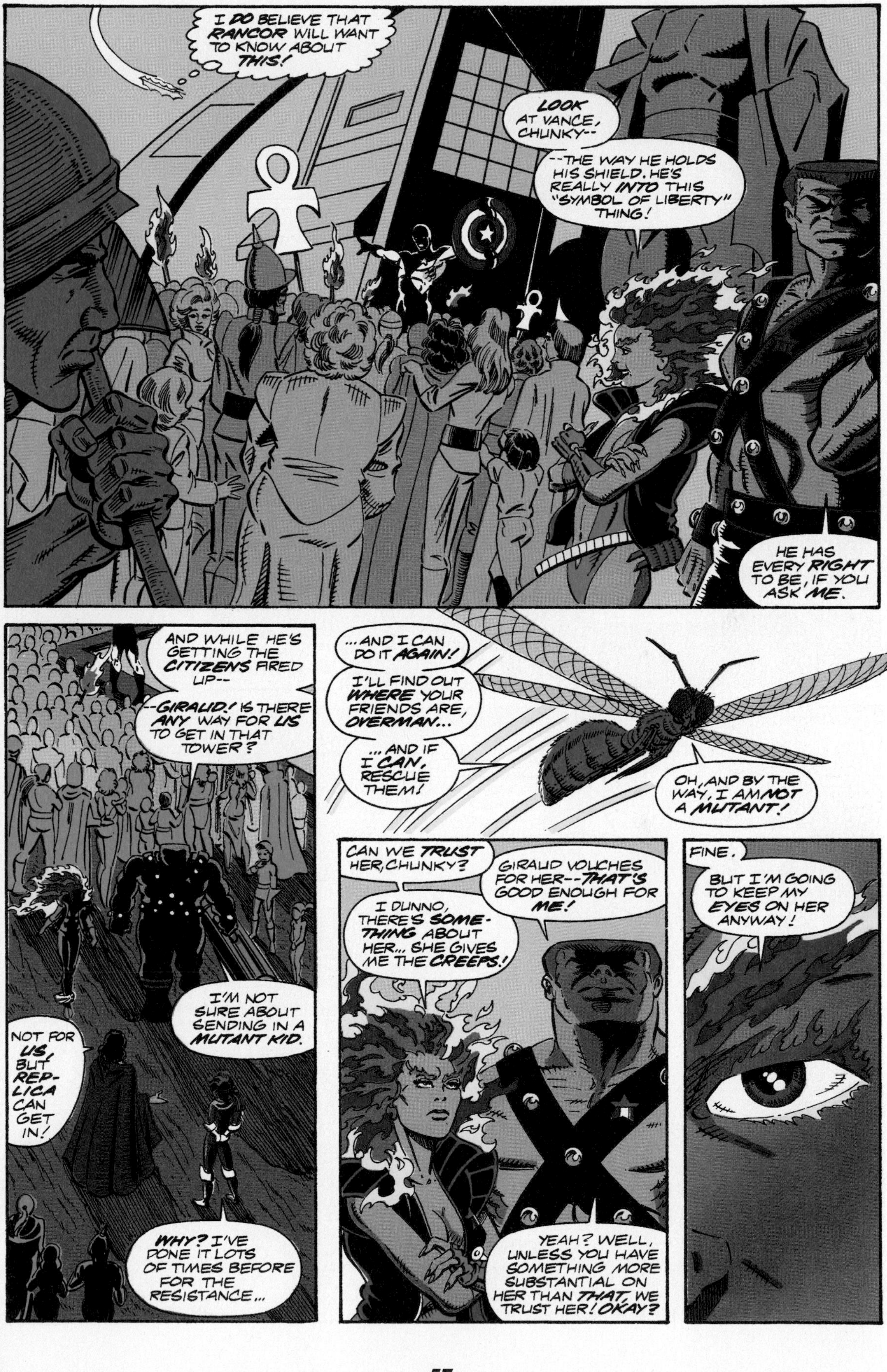

I DO BELIEVE THAT RANCOR WILL WANT TO KNOW ABOUT THIS!
LOOK AT VANCE, CHUNKY--
--THE WAY HE HOLDS HIS SHIELD. HE'S REALLY INTO THIS "SYMBOL OF LIBERTY" THING!
HE HAS EVERY RIGHT TO BE, IF YOU ASK ME.
AND WHILE HE'S GETTING THE CITIZENS FIRED UP--
--GIRAUD! IS THERE ANY WAY FOR US TO GET IN THAT TOWER?
I'M NOT SURE ABOUT SENDING IN A MUTANT KID.
NOT FOR US, BUT REPLICA CAN GET IN!
WHY? I'VE DONE IT LOTS OF TIMES BEFORE FOR THE RESISTANCE...
...AND I CAN DO IT AGAIN!
I'LL FIND OUT WHERE YOUR FRIENDS ARE, OVERMAN...
...AND IF I CAN, RESCUE THEM!
OH, AND BY THE WAY, I AM NOT A MUTANT!
CAN WE TRUST HER, CHUNKY?
GIRAUD VOUCHES FOR HER--THAT'S GOOD ENOUGH FOR ME!
I DUNNO, THERE'S SOMETHING ABOUT HER... SHE GIVES ME THE CREEPS!
YEAH? WELL, UNLESS YOU HAVE SOMETHING MORE SUBSTANTIAL ON HER THAN THAT, WE TRUST HER! OKAY?
FINE.
BUT I'M GOING TO KEEP MY EYES ON HER ANYWAY!

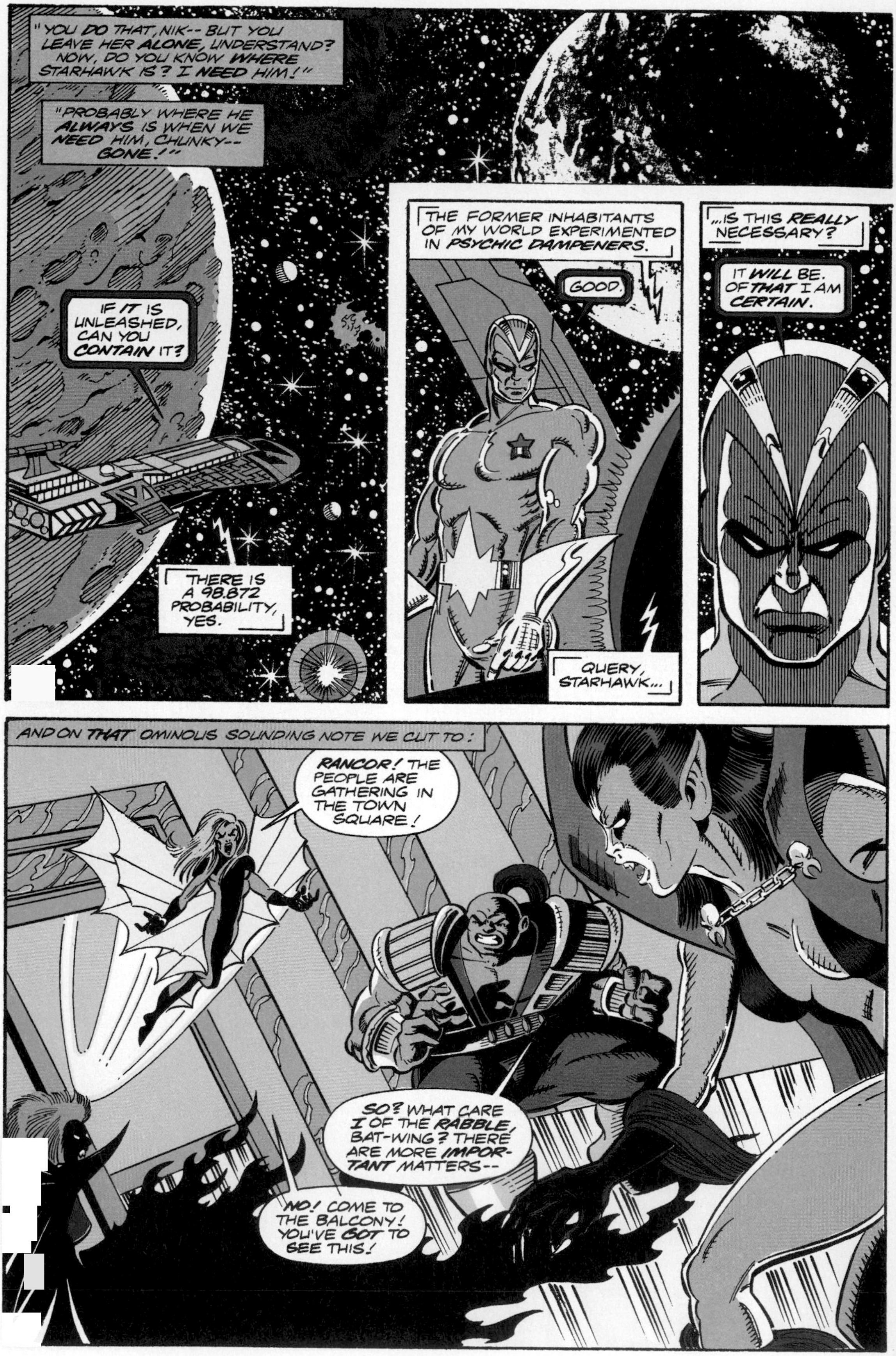
"YOU DO THAT, NIK-- BUT YOU LEAVE HER ALONE, UNDERSTAND? NOW, DO YOU KNOW WHERE STARHAWK IS? I NEED HIM!"
"PROBABLY WHERE HE ALWAYS IS WHEN WE NEED HIM, CHUNKY-- GONE!"
IF IT IS UNLEASHED, CAN YOU CONTAIN IT?
THERE IS A 98.872 PROBABILITY, YES.
THE FORMER INHABITANTS OF MY WORLD EXPERIMENTED IN PSYCHIC DAMPENERS.
GOOD.
QUERY, STARHAWK...
...IS THIS REALLY NECESSARY?
IT WILL BE. OF THAT I AM CERTAIN.
AND ON THAT OMINOUS SOUNDING NOTE WE CUT TO:
RANCOR! THE PEOPLE ARE GATHERING IN THE TOWN SQUARE!
SO? WHAT CARE I OF THE RABBLE, BAT-WING? THERE ARE MORE IMPORTANT MATTERS--
NO! COME TO THE BALCONY! YOU'VE GOT TO SEE THIS!

LOOK, COUSIN! SEE HOW THE INSECTS SWARM?

I SEE IT, 'WING.

"DO YOU SEE HOW THEY MOCK US, RANCOR, BY TEARING DOWN THE STATUE OF THE GREAT MAGNUS?"

"DO YOU SEE HOW THEY BLATANTLY DISPLAY THEIR RELIGIOUS ICONS?"

"HOW THEY BURN YOU IN EFFIGY?"

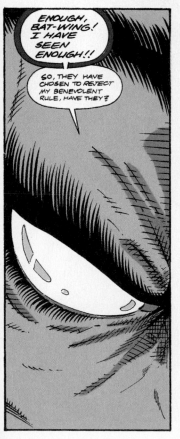

ENOUGH, BAT-WING! I HAVE SEEN ENOUGH!!

SO, THEY HAVE CHOSEN TO REJECT MY BENEVOLENT RULE, HAVE THEY?

WHEW! MADE IT JUST IN TIME! NOW, JUST KEEP THAT DOOR OPEN--!

THEN LET THE BLOOD THAT SPILLS THIS DAY...

...BE ON THEIR HANDS!

YES! I MADE IT! NOW TO FIND THE OTHER OVERMEN!

TO ME, MY LIEUTENANTS!

PREPARE THE BATTLE SPHERE--

-- WE HAVE A MASSACRE TO ATTEND TO!

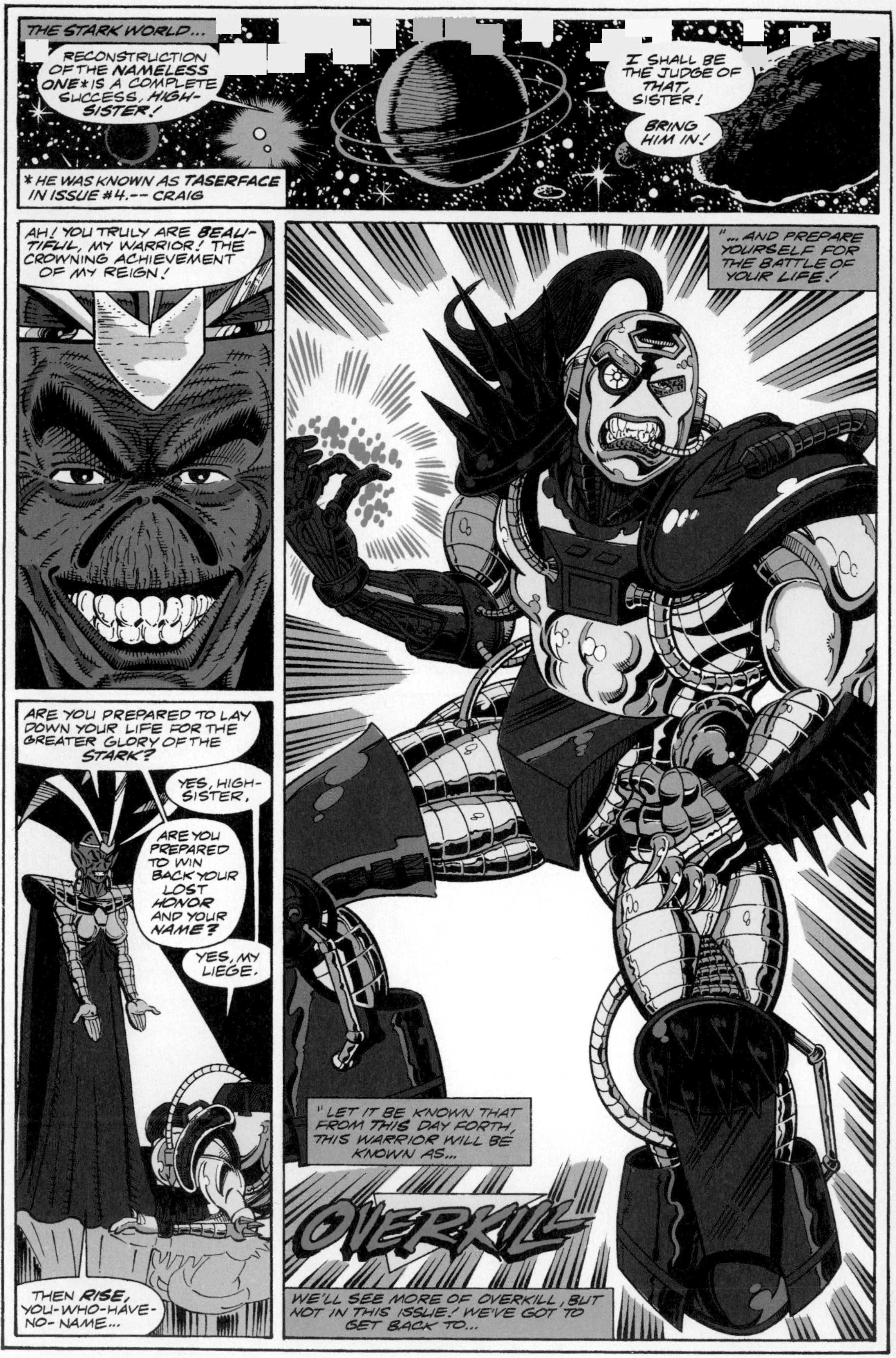
THE STARK WORLD...
RECONSTRUCTION OF THE NAMELESS ONE* IS A COMPLETE SUCCESS, HIGH-SISTER!
* HE WAS KNOWN AS TASERFACE IN ISSUE #4.-- CRAIG
I SHALL BE THE JUDGE OF THAT, SISTER!
BRING HIM IN!
AH! YOU TRULY ARE BEAUTIFUL, MY WARRIOR! THE CROWNING ACHIEVEMENT OF MY REIGN!
ARE YOU PREPARED TO LAY DOWN YOUR LIFE FOR THE GREATER GLORY OF THE STARK?
YES, HIGH-SISTER.
ARE YOU PREPARED TO WIN BACK YOUR LOST HONOR AND YOUR NAME?
YES, MY LIEGE.
THEN RISE, YOU-WHO-HAVE-NO-NAME...
"...AND PREPARE YOURSELF FOR THE BATTLE OF YOUR LIFE!
"LET IT BE KNOWN THAT FROM THIS DAY FORTH, THIS WARRIOR WILL BE KNOWN AS...
OVERKILL
WE'LL SEE MORE OF OVERKILL, BUT NOT IN THIS ISSUE! WE'VE GOT TO GET BACK TO...

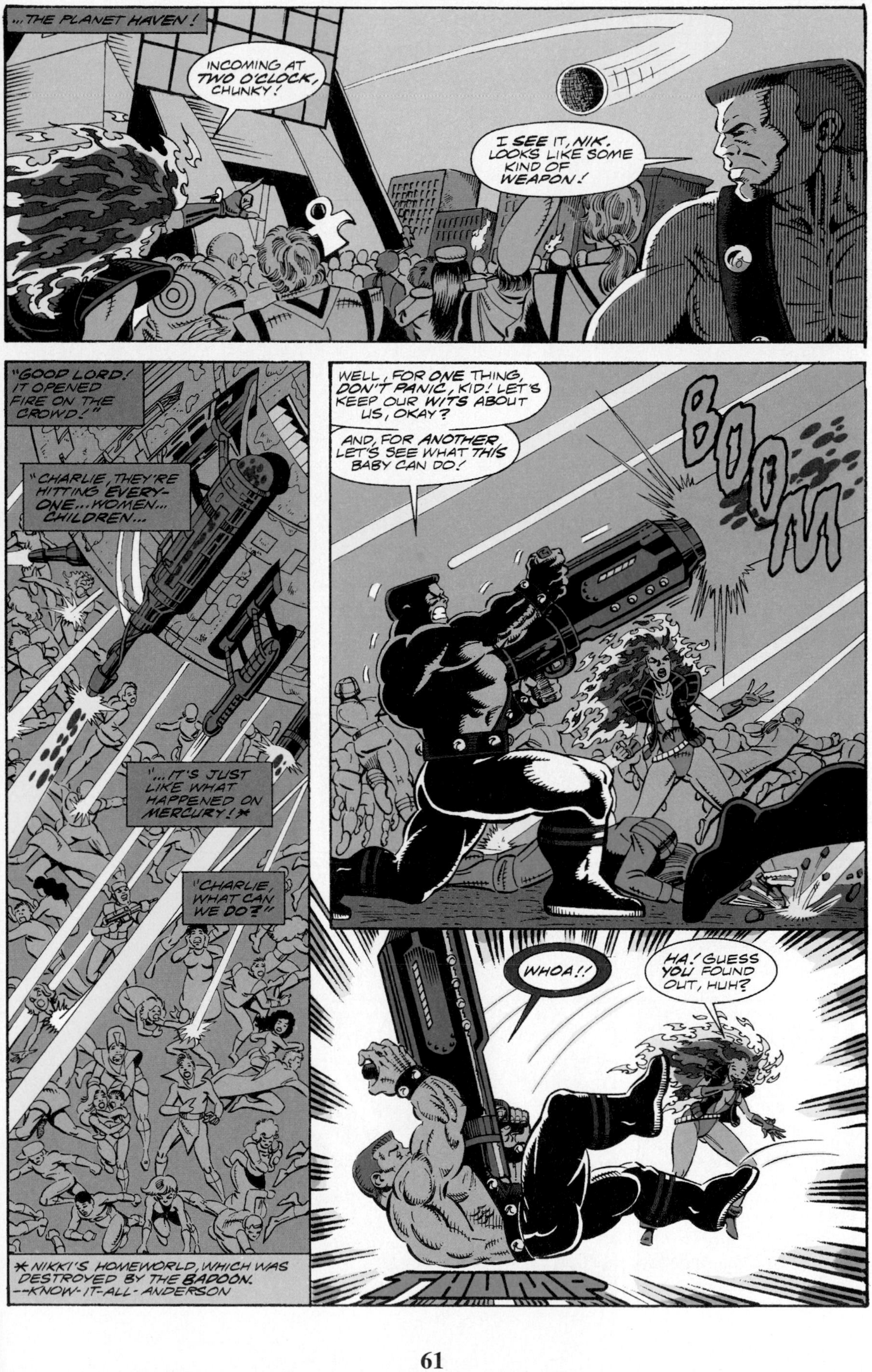
...THE PLANET HAVEN!
INCOMING AT TWO O'CLOCK, CHUNKY!
I SEE IT, NIK. LOOKS LIKE SOME KIND OF WEAPON!
"GOOD LORD! IT OPENED FIRE ON THE CROWD!"
"CHARLIE, THEY'RE HITTING EVERY-ONE...WOMEN... CHILDREN...
"...IT'S JUST LIKE WHAT HAPPENED ON MERCURY!*
"CHARLIE, WHAT CAN WE DO?"
*NIKKI'S HOMEWORLD, WHICH WAS DESTROYED BY THE BADOON. --KNOW-IT-ALL-ANDERSON
WELL, FOR ONE THING, DON'T PANIC, KID! LET'S KEEP OUR WITS ABOUT US, OKAY?
AND, FOR ANOTHER LET'S SEE WHAT THIS BABY CAN DO!
BOOM
WHOA!!
HA! GUESS YOU FOUND OUT, HUH?
THUMP

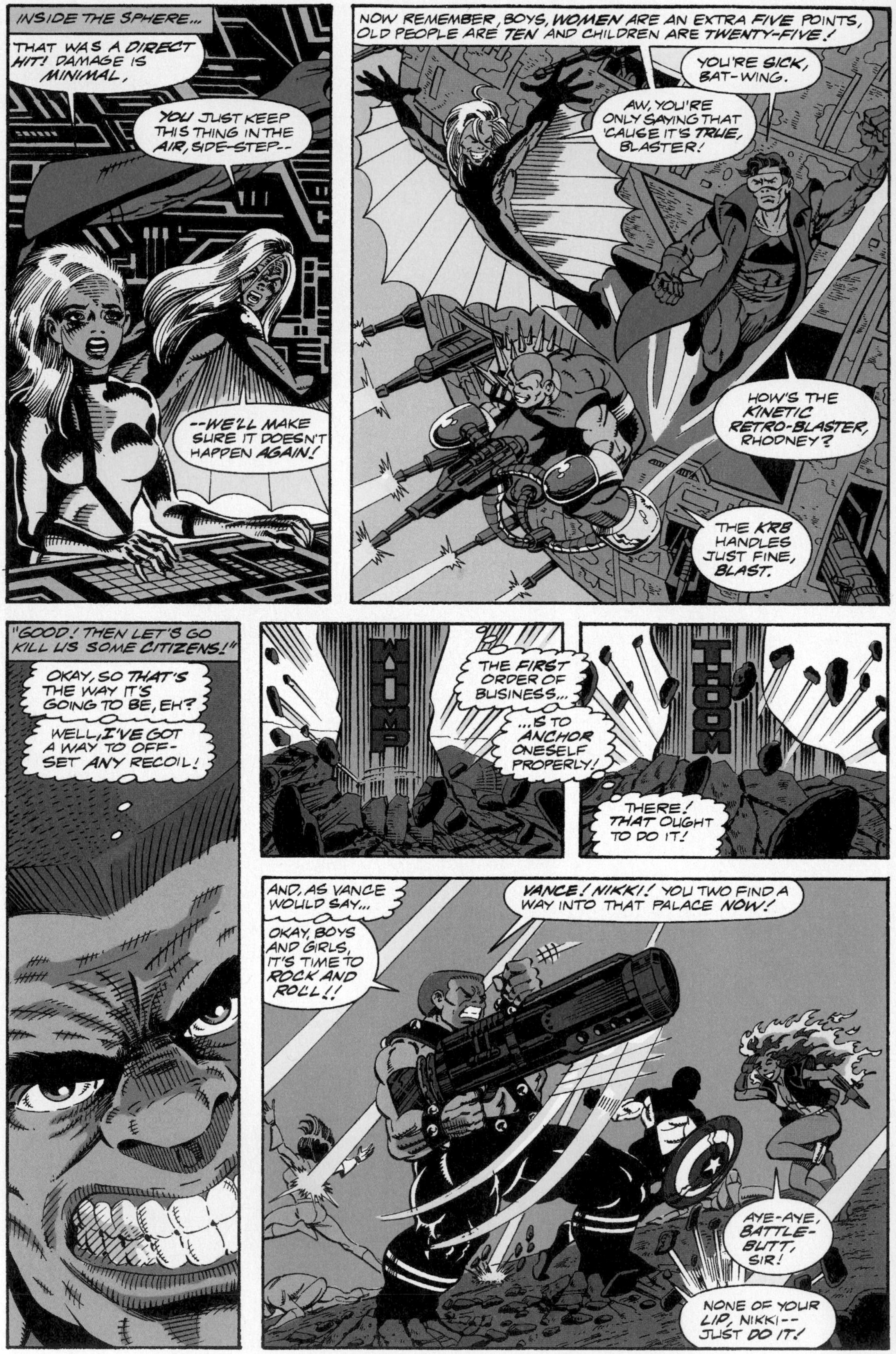
INSIDE THE SPHERE...
THAT WAS A DIRECT HIT! DAMAGE IS MINIMAL,
YOU JUST KEEP THIS THING IN THE AIR, SIDE-STEP--
--WE'LL MAKE SURE IT DOESN'T HAPPEN AGAIN!
NOW REMEMBER, BOYS, WOMEN ARE AN EXTRA FIVE POINTS, OLD PEOPLE ARE TEN AND CHILDREN ARE TWENTY-FIVE!
YOU'RE SICK, BAT-WING.
AW, YOU'RE ONLY SAYING THAT 'CAUSE IT'S TRUE, BLASTER!
HOW'S THE KINETIC RETRO-BLASTER, RHODNEY?
THE KRB HANDLES JUST FINE, BLAST.
"GOOD! THEN LET'S GO KILL US SOME CITIZENS!"
OKAY, SO THAT'S THE WAY IT'S GOING TO BE, EH?
WELL, I'VE GOT A WAY TO OFF-SET ANY RECOIL!
WHUMP
THE FIRST ORDER OF BUSINESS...
...IS TO ANCHOR ONESELF PROPERLY!
THOOM
THERE! THAT OUGHT TO DO IT!
AND, AS VANCE WOULD SAY...
OKAY, BOYS AND GIRLS, IT'S TIME TO ROCK AND ROLL!!
VANCE! NIKKI! YOU TWO FIND A WAY INTO THAT PALACE NOW!
AYE-AYE, BATTLE-BUTT, SIR!
NONE OF YOUR LIP, NIKKI-- JUST DO IT!

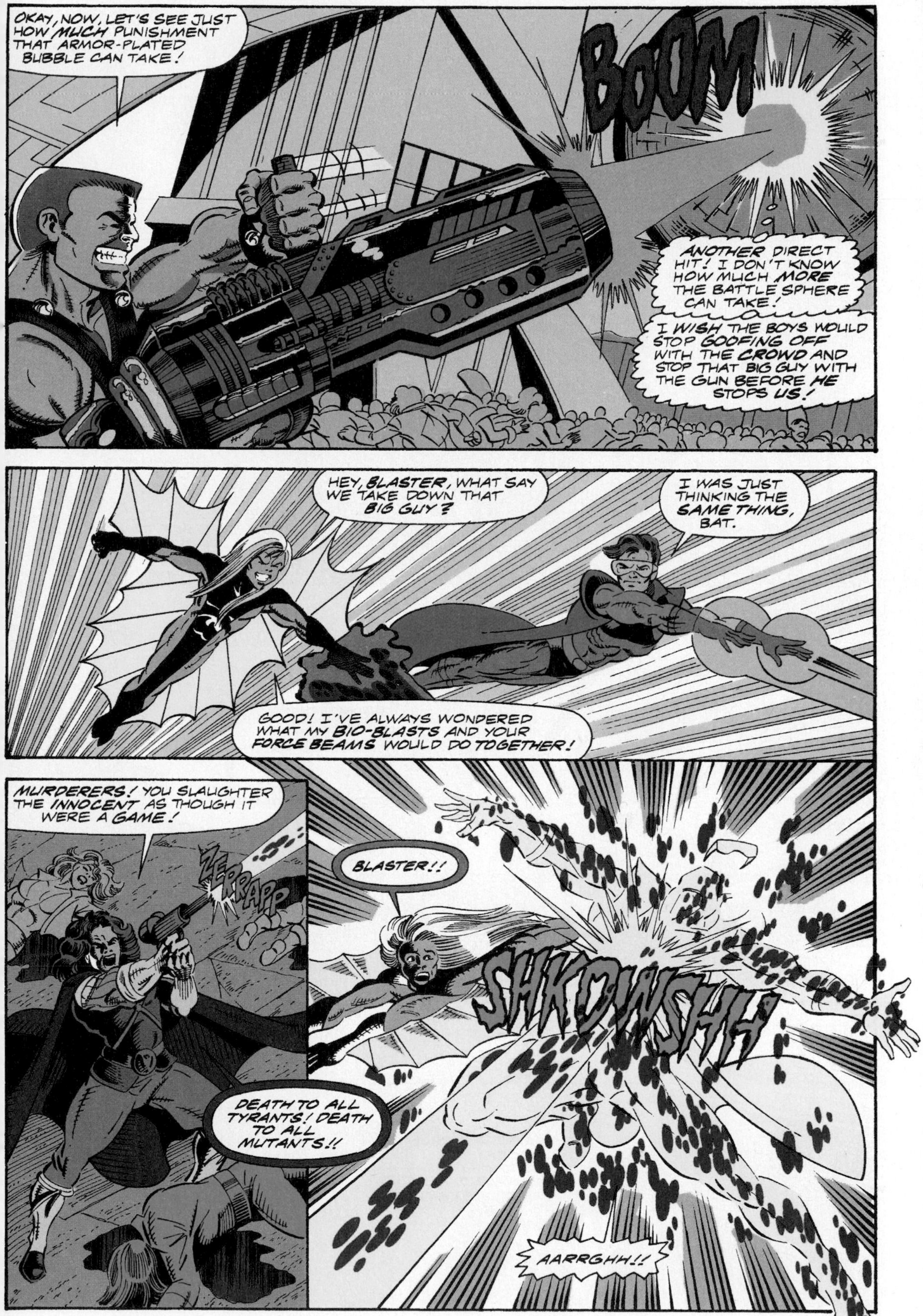
OKAY, NOW, LET'S SEE JUST HOW MUCH PUNISHMENT THAT ARMOR-PLATED BUBBLE CAN TAKE!
BOOM
ANOTHER DIRECT HIT! I DON'T KNOW HOW MUCH MORE THE BATTLE SPHERE CAN TAKE!
I WISH THE BOYS WOULD STOP GOOFING OFF WITH THE CROWD AND STOP THAT BIG GUY WITH THE GUN BEFORE HE STOPS US!
HEY, BLASTER, WHAT SAY WE TAKE DOWN THAT BIG GUY?
I WAS JUST THINKING THE SAME THING, BAT.
GOOD! I'VE ALWAYS WONDERED WHAT MY BIO-BLASTS AND YOUR FORCE BEAMS WOULD DO TOGETHER!
MURDERERS! YOU SLAUGHTER THE INNOCENT AS THOUGH IT WERE A GAME!
ZERRAPP
DEATH TO ALL TYRANTS! DEATH TO ALL MUTANTS!!
BLASTER!!
SHKOWSHH
AARRGHH!!

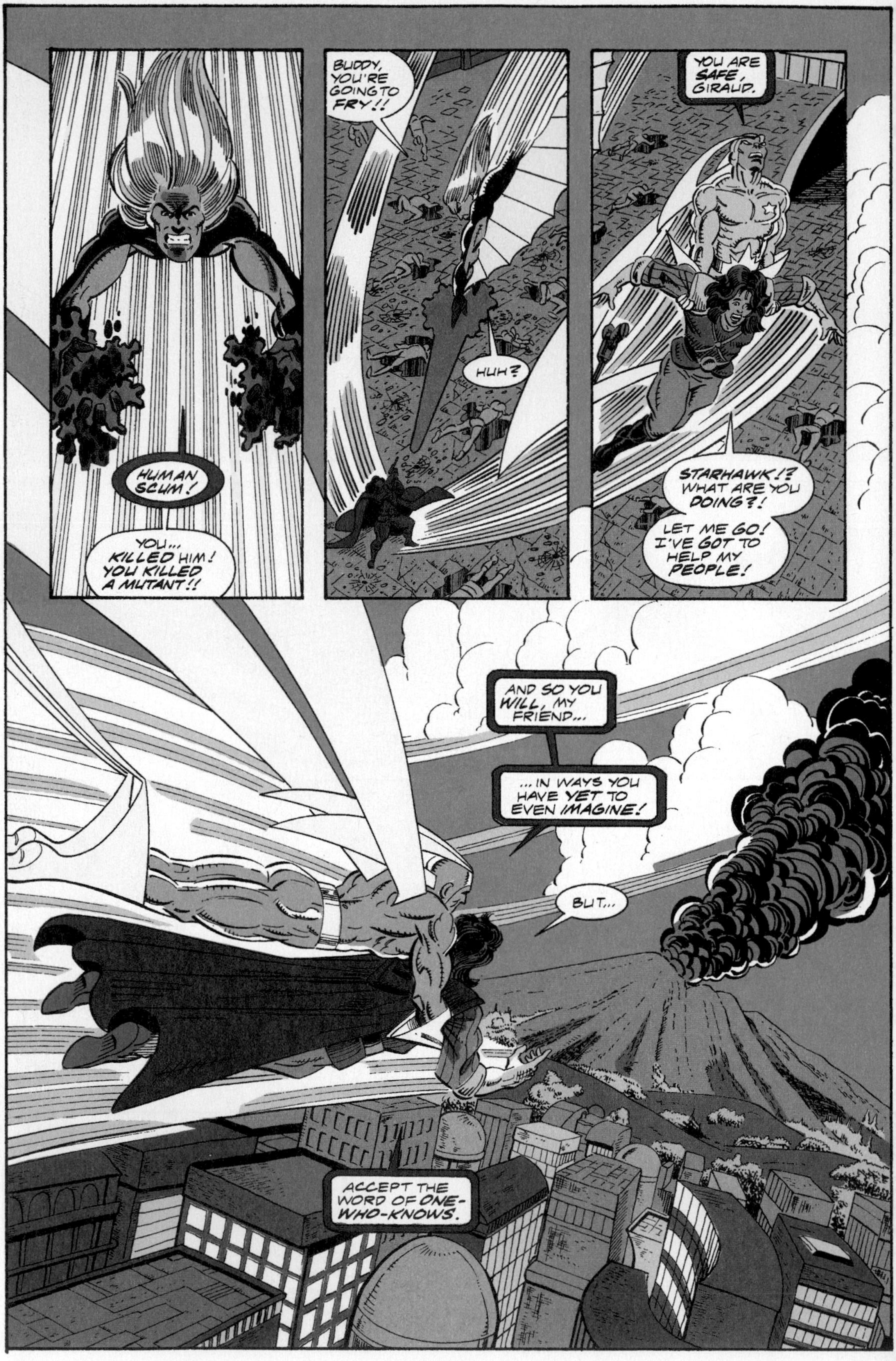
HUMAN SCUM!
YOU... KILLED HIM! YOU KILLED A MUTANT!!
BUDDY, YOU'RE GOING TO FRY!!
HUH?
YOU ARE SAFE, GIRAUD.
STARHAWK!? WHAT ARE YOU DOING?!
LET ME GO! I'VE GOT TO HELP MY PEOPLE!
AND SO YOU WILL, MY FRIEND...
...IN WAYS YOU HAVE YET TO EVEN IMAGINE!
BUT...
ACCEPT THE WORD OF ONE-WHO-KNOWS.

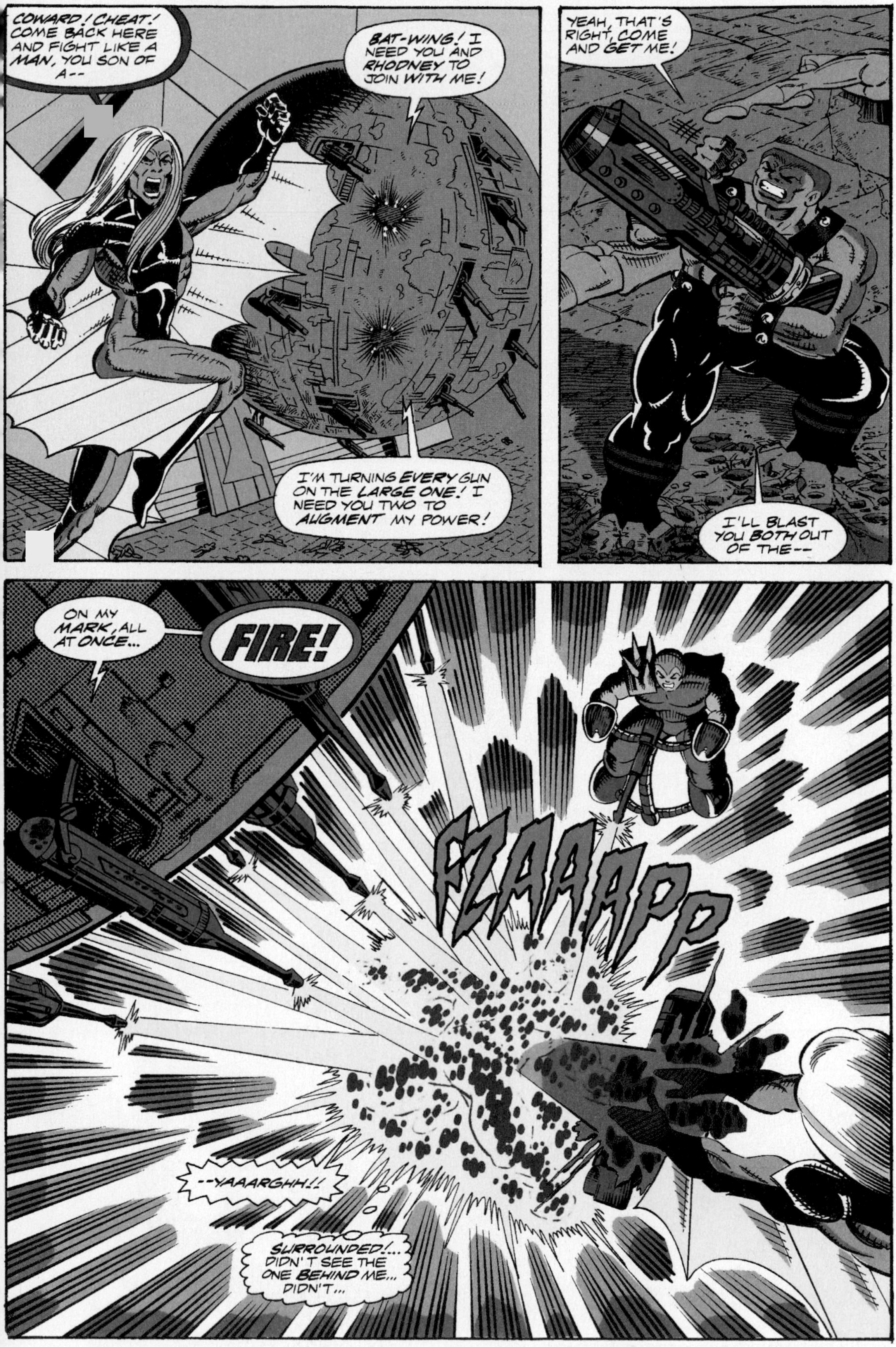
COWARD! CHEAT! COME BACK HERE AND FIGHT LIKE A MAN, YOU SON OF A--
BAT-WING! I NEED YOU AND RHODNEY TO JOIN WITH ME!
I'M TURNING EVERY GUN ON THE LARGE ONE! I NEED YOU TWO TO AUGMENT MY POWER!
YEAH, THAT'S RIGHT, COME AND GET ME!
I'LL BLAST YOU BOTH OUT OF THE--
ON MY MARK, ALL AT ONCE...
FIRE!
FZAAAPP
--YAAAARGHH!!
SURROUNDED!... DIDN'T SEE THE ONE BEHIND ME... DIDN'T...

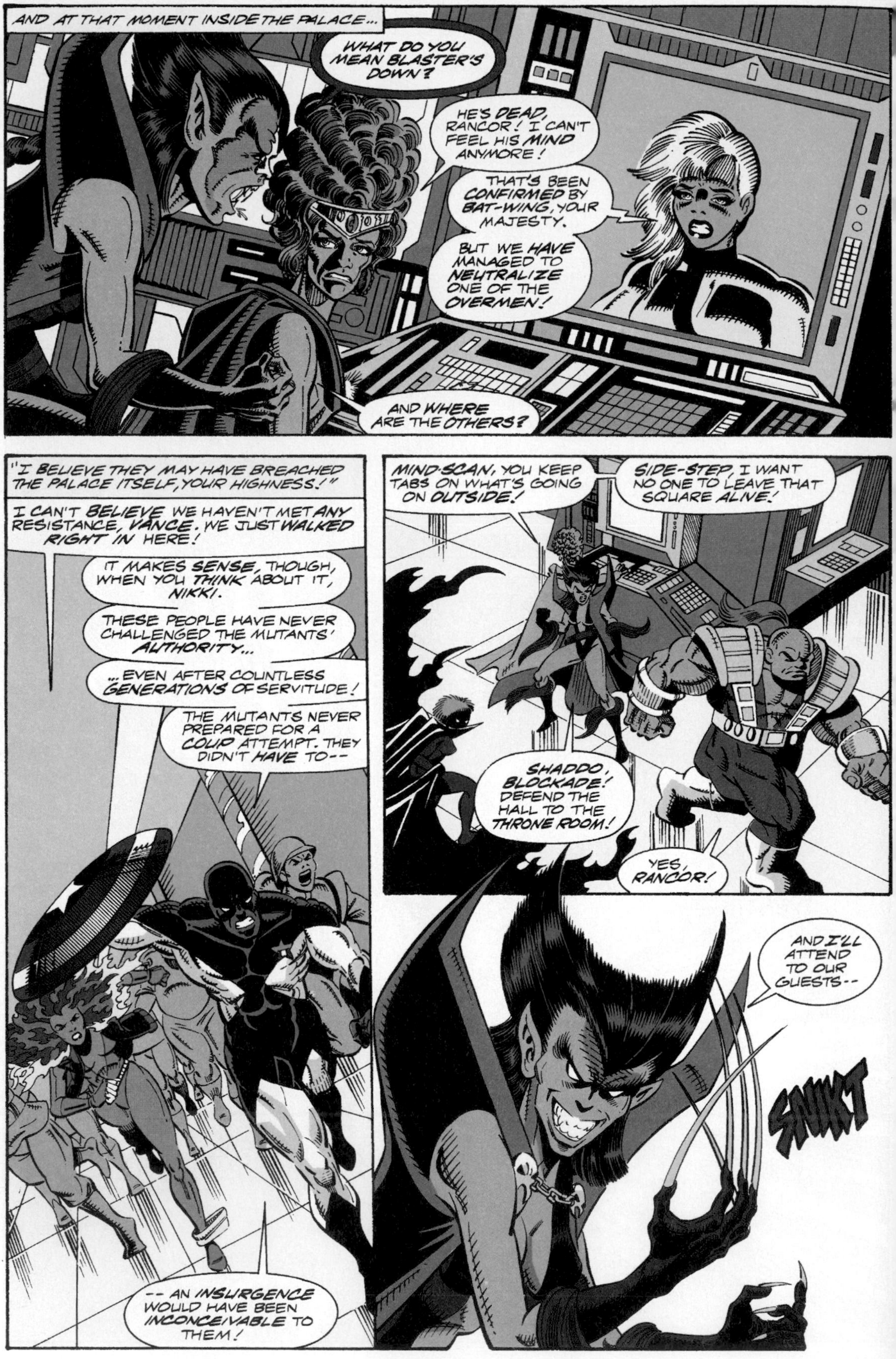
AND AT THAT MOMENT INSIDE THE PALACE...
WHAT DO YOU MEAN BLASTER'S DOWN?
HE'S DEAD, RANCOR! I CAN'T FEEL HIS MIND ANYMORE!
THAT'S BEEN CONFIRMED BY BAT-WING, YOUR MAJESTY.
BUT WE HAVE MANAGED TO NEUTRALIZE ONE OF THE OVERMEN!
AND WHERE ARE THE OTHERS?
"I BELIEVE THEY MAY HAVE BREACHED THE PALACE ITSELF, YOUR HIGHNESS!"
I CAN'T BELIEVE WE HAVEN'T MET ANY RESISTANCE, VANCE. WE JUST WALKED RIGHT IN HERE!
IT MAKES SENSE, THOUGH, WHEN YOU THINK ABOUT IT, NIKKI.
THESE PEOPLE HAVE NEVER CHALLENGED THE MUTANTS' AUTHORITY...
...EVEN AFTER COUNTLESS GENERATIONS OF SERVITUDE!
THE MUTANTS NEVER PREPARED FOR A COUP ATTEMPT. THEY DIDN'T HAVE TO--
-- AN INSURGENCE WOULD HAVE BEEN INCONCEIVABLE TO THEM!
MIND-SCAN, YOU KEEP TABS ON WHAT'S GOING ON OUTSIDE!
SIDE-STEP, I WANT NO ONE TO LEAVE THAT SQUARE ALIVE!
SHADDO, BLOCKADE! DEFEND THE HALL TO THE THRONE ROOM!
YES, RANCOR!
AND I'LL ATTEND TO OUR GUESTS--
SNIKT

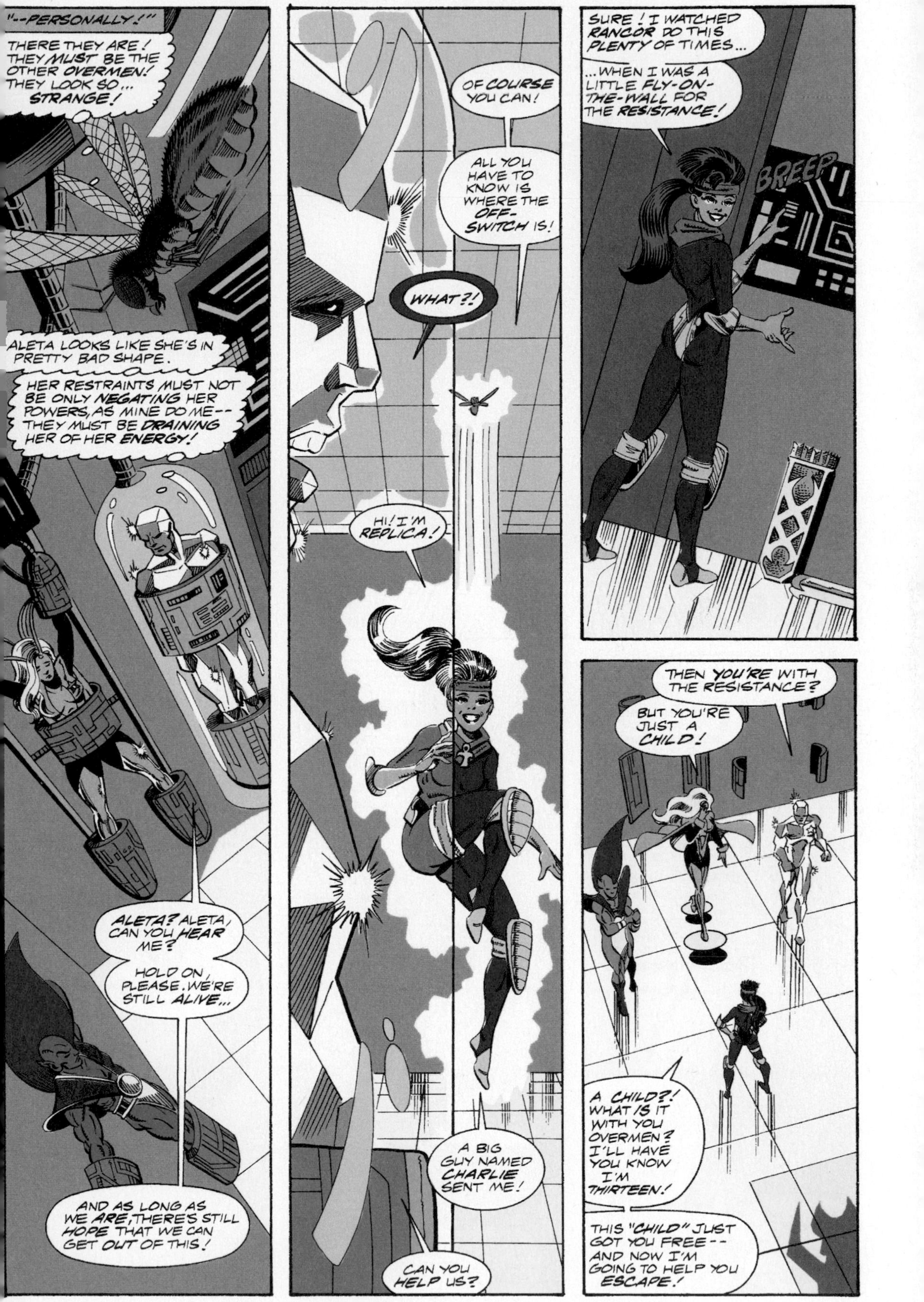

"--PERSONALLY!"
THERE THEY ARE! THEY MUST BE THE OTHER OVERMEN! THEY LOOK SO... STRANGE!
ALETA LOOKS LIKE SHE'S IN PRETTY BAD SHAPE.
HER RESTRAINTS MUST NOT BE ONLY NEGATING HER POWERS, AS MINE DO ME-- THEY MUST BE DRAINING HER OF HER ENERGY!
ALETA? ALETA, CAN YOU HEAR ME?
HOLD ON, PLEASE. WE'RE STILL ALIVE...
AND AS LONG AS WE ARE, THERE'S STILL HOPE THAT WE CAN GET OUT OF THIS!
CAN YOU HELP US?
OF COURSE YOU CAN!
ALL YOU HAVE TO KNOW IS WHERE THE OFF-SWITCH IS!
WHAT?!
HI! I'M REPLICA!
A BIG GUY NAMED CHARLIE SENT ME!
SURE! I WATCHED RANCOR DO THIS PLENTY OF TIMES...
...WHEN I WAS A LITTLE FLY-ON-THE-WALL FOR THE RESISTANCE!
BREEP
THEN YOU'RE WITH THE RESISTANCE?
BUT YOU'RE JUST A CHILD!
A CHILD?! WHAT IS IT WITH YOU OVERMEN? I'LL HAVE YOU KNOW I'M THIRTEEN!
THIS "CHILD" JUST GOT YOU FREE-- AND NOW I'M GOING TO HELP YOU ESCAPE!

NO, CHILD-- THERE IS NO ESCAPE!

UH-OH!

AND, ATOP A NEARBY VOLCANO...

DO NOT BE AFRAID OF ME, CHILD OF MAN!

BUT WHO... WHAT ARE YOU?

I AM FIRE... A FORCE OF THE UNIVERSE!

I CAN GRANT YOUR HEART'S DESIRE--

--I CAN END THE SUFFERING AND SAVE YOUR PEOPLE!

BUT I MUST HAVE FORM-- YOUR FORM!

BUT WHY ME? I HAVE NO SPECIAL GIFTS!

DO YOU NOT, GIRAUD?

IS NOT LIFE ITSELF THE GREATEST GIFT OF ALL?

LATENT WITHIN YOU IS A POWER... A POWER THAT I AM THE ZENITH OF!

TO JOIN WITH ME IS TO BE GREATER THAN THE SUM OF OUR PARTS!

AND WHAT OF ME? DO I DIE IN THIS JOINING?

AND IF YOU DO?

ARE THERE LIMITS, THEN, TO WHAT YOU ARE WILLING TO SACRIFICE FOR YOUR CAUSE?

NO... I DON'T THINK SO.

THEN YOU WILL JOIN WITH ME, GIRAUD OF HAVEN, TO SAVE THE PEOPLE OF YOUR WORLD?

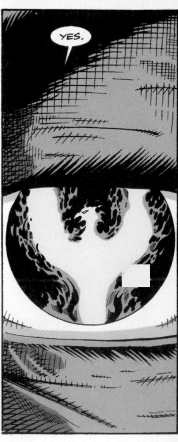

YES.

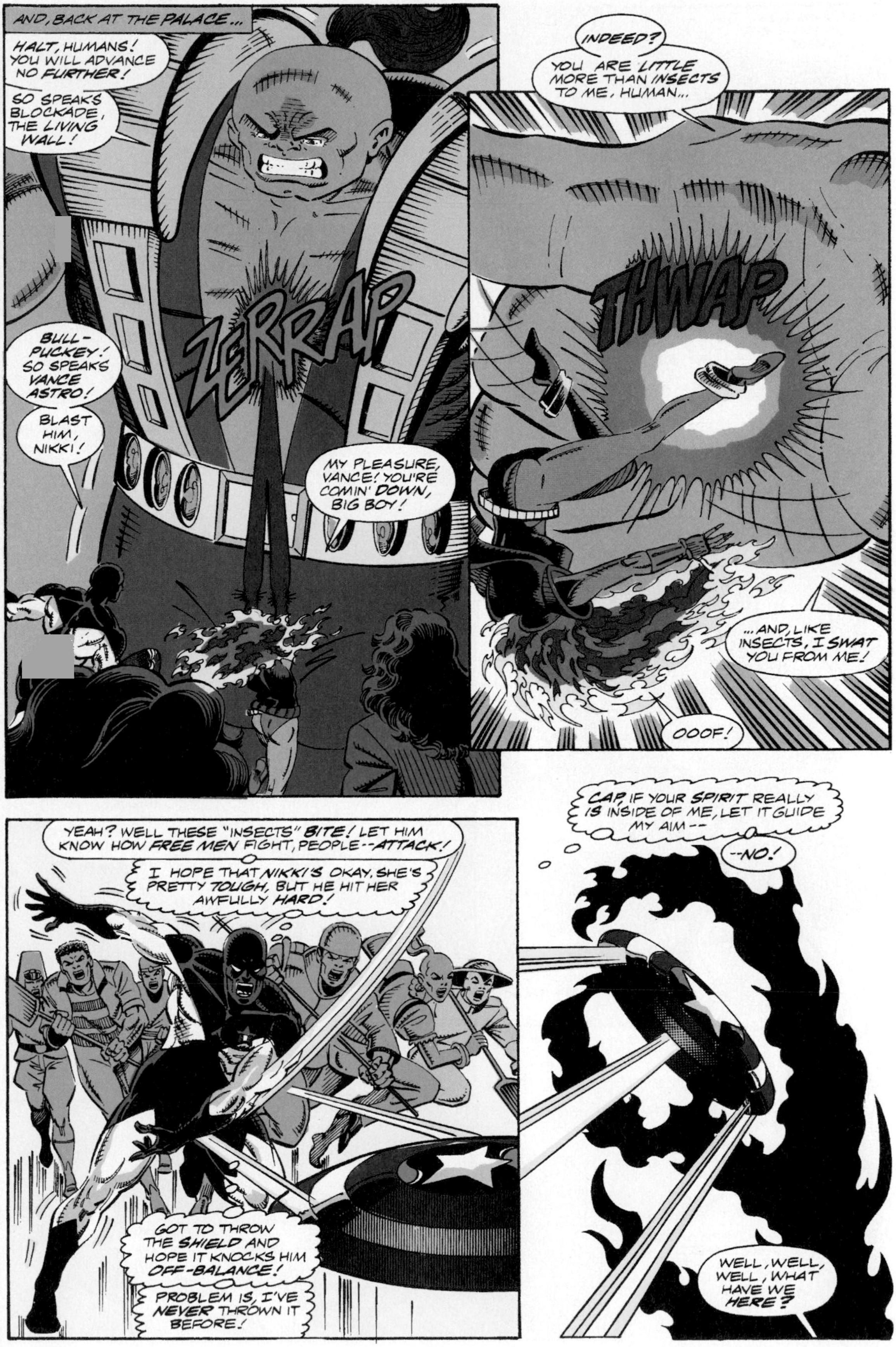
AND, BACK AT THE PALACE...
HALT, HUMANS! YOU WILL ADVANCE NO FURTHER!
SO SPEAKS BLOCKADE, THE LIVING WALL!
ZERRAP
BULL-PUCKEY! SO SPEAKS VANCE ASTRO!
BLAST HIM, NIKKI!
MY PLEASURE, VANCE! YOU'RE COMIN' DOWN, BIG BOY!
INDEED? YOU ARE LITTLE MORE THAN INSECTS TO ME, HUMAN...
THWAP
...AND, LIKE INSECTS, I SWAT YOU FROM ME!
OOOF!
YEAH? WELL THESE "INSECTS" BITE! LET HIM KNOW HOW FREE MEN FIGHT, PEOPLE--ATTACK!
I HOPE THAT NIKKI'S OKAY. SHE'S PRETTY TOUGH, BUT HE HIT HER AWFULLY HARD!
GOT TO THROW THE SHIELD AND HOPE IT KNOCKS HIM OFF-BALANCE!
PROBLEM IS, I'VE NEVER THROWN IT BEFORE!
CAP, IF YOUR SPIRIT REALLY IS INSIDE OF ME, LET IT GUIDE MY AIM --
--NO!
WELL, WELL, WELL, WHAT HAVE WE HERE?

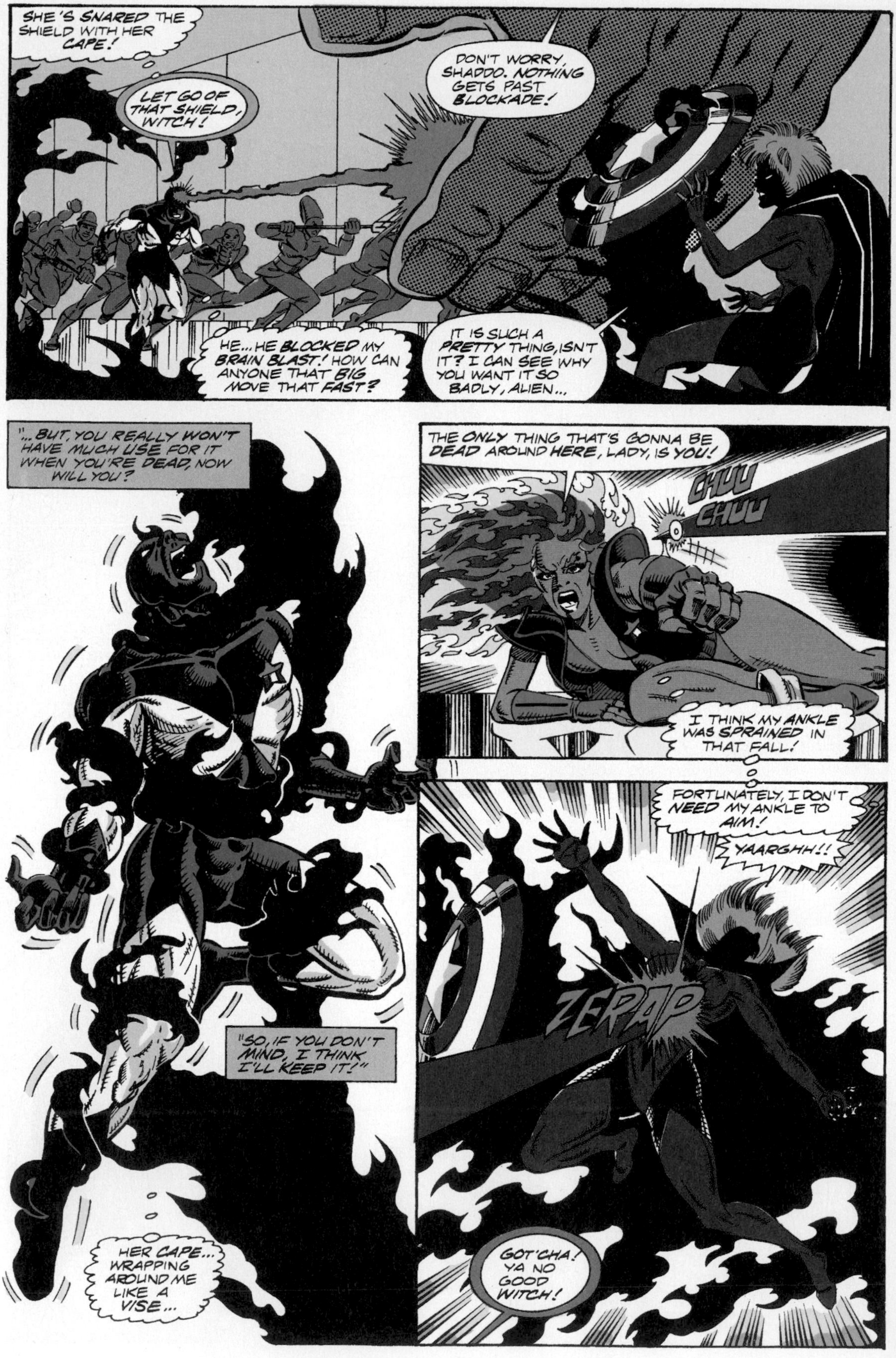
SHE'S SNARED THE SHIELD WITH HER CAPE!
LET GO OF THAT SHIELD, WITCH!
DON'T WORRY, SHADDO. NOTHING GETS PAST BLOCKADE!
HE...HE BLOCKED MY BRAIN BLAST! HOW CAN ANYONE THAT BIG MOVE THAT FAST?
IT IS SUCH A PRETTY THING, ISN'T IT? I CAN SEE WHY YOU WANT IT SO BADLY, ALIEN...
"...BUT, YOU REALLY WON'T HAVE MUCH USE FOR IT WHEN YOU'RE DEAD, NOW WILL YOU?
"SO, IF YOU DON'T MIND, I THINK I'LL KEEP IT!"
HER CAPE... WRAPPING AROUND ME LIKE A VISE...
THE ONLY THING THAT'S GONNA BE DEAD AROUND HERE, LADY, IS YOU!
CHUU CHUU
I THINK MY ANKLE WAS SPRAINED IN THAT FALL!
FORTUNATELY, I DON'T NEED MY ANKLE TO AIM!
YAARGHH!!
ZERAP
GOT'CHA! YA NO GOOD WITCH!

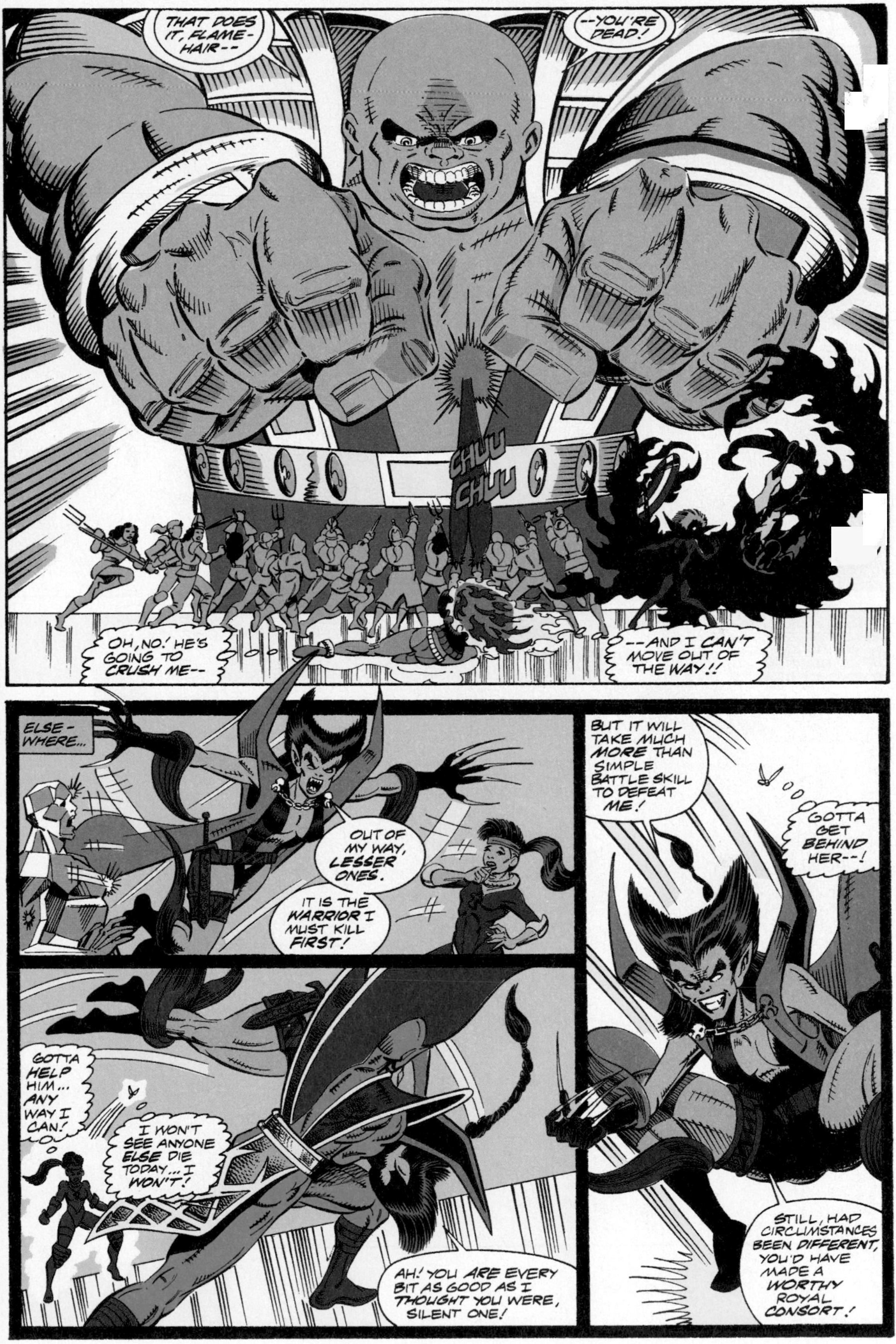
THAT DOES IT, FLAME-HAIR--
--YOU'RE DEAD!
CHUU CHUU
OH, NO! HE'S GOING TO CRUSH ME--
--AND I CAN'T MOVE OUT OF THE WAY!!
ELSE-WHERE...
OUT OF MY WAY, LESSER ONES.
IT IS THE WARRIOR I MUST KILL FIRST!
BUT IT WILL TAKE MUCH MORE THAN SIMPLE BATTLE SKILL TO DEFEAT ME!
GOTTA GET BEHIND HER--!
GOTTA HELP HIM... ANY WAY I CAN!
I WON'T SEE ANYONE ELSE DIE TODAY... I WON'T!
AH! YOU ARE EVERY BIT AS GOOD AS I THOUGHT YOU WERE, SILENT ONE!
STILL, HAD CIRCUMSTANCES BEEN DIFFERENT, YOU'D HAVE MADE A WORTHY ROYAL CONSORT!

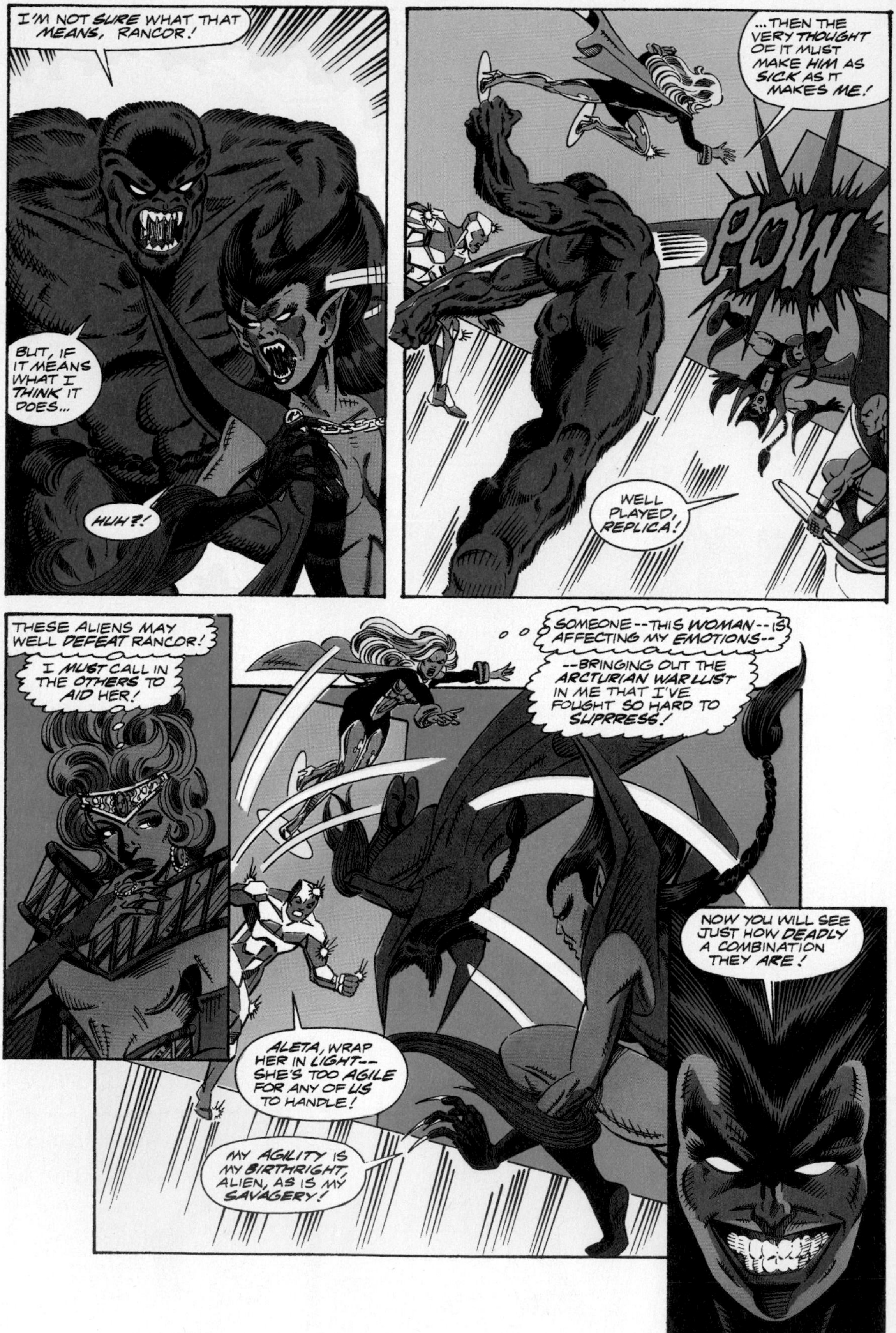
I'M NOT SURE WHAT THAT MEANS, RANCOR!
BUT, IF IT MEANS WHAT I THINK IT DOES...
HUH?!
...THEN THE VERY THOUGHT OF IT MUST MAKE HIM AS SICK AS IT MAKES ME!
POW
WELL PLAYED, REPLICA!
THESE ALIENS MAY WELL DEFEAT RANCOR!
I MUST CALL IN THE OTHERS TO AID HER!
SOMEONE--THIS WOMAN--IS AFFECTING MY EMOTIONS--
--BRINGING OUT THE ARCTURIAN WAR LUST IN ME THAT I'VE FOUGHT SO HARD TO SUPRRESS!
ALETA, WRAP HER IN LIGHT-- SHE'S TOO AGILE FOR ANY OF US TO HANDLE!
MY AGILITY IS MY BIRTHRIGHT, ALIEN, AS IS MY SAVAGERY!
NOW YOU WILL SEE JUST HOW DEADLY A COMBINATION THEY ARE!

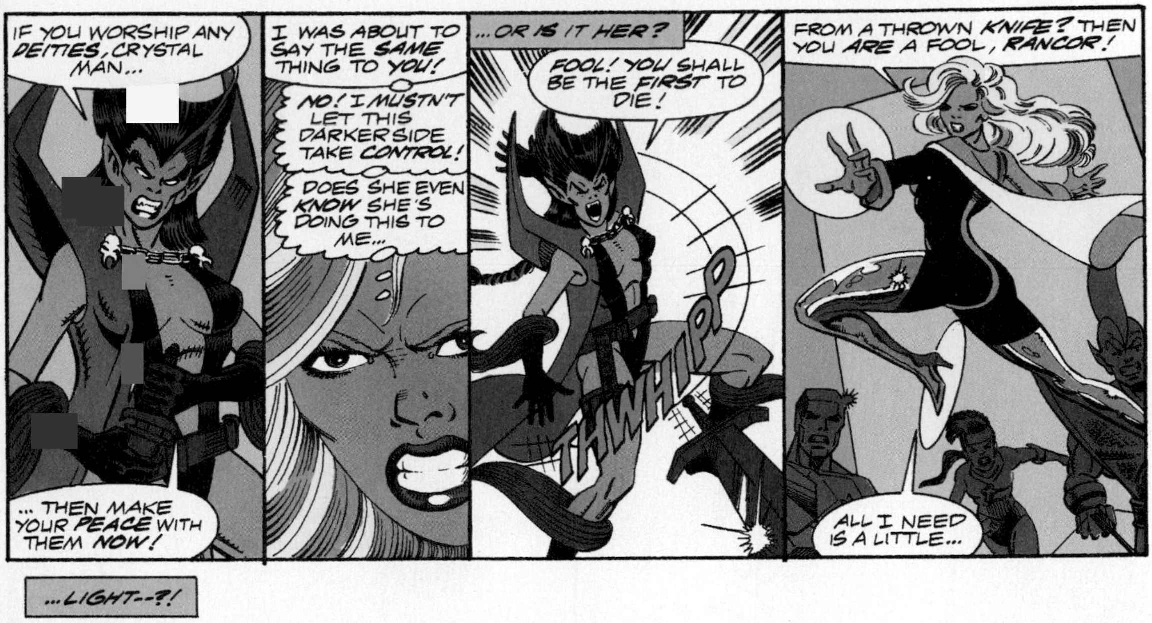
IF YOU WORSHIP ANY DEITIES, CRYSTAL MAN...
... THEN MAKE YOUR PEACE WITH THEM NOW!
I WAS ABOUT TO SAY THE SAME THING TO YOU!
NO! I MUSTN'T LET THIS DARKER SIDE TAKE CONTROL!
DOES SHE EVEN KNOW SHE'S DOING THIS TO ME...
...OR IS IT HER?
FOOL! YOU SHALL BE THE FIRST TO DIE!
THWHIPP
FROM A THROWN KNIFE? THEN YOU ARE A FOOL, RANCOR!
ALL I NEED IS A LITTLE...
...LIGHT--?!

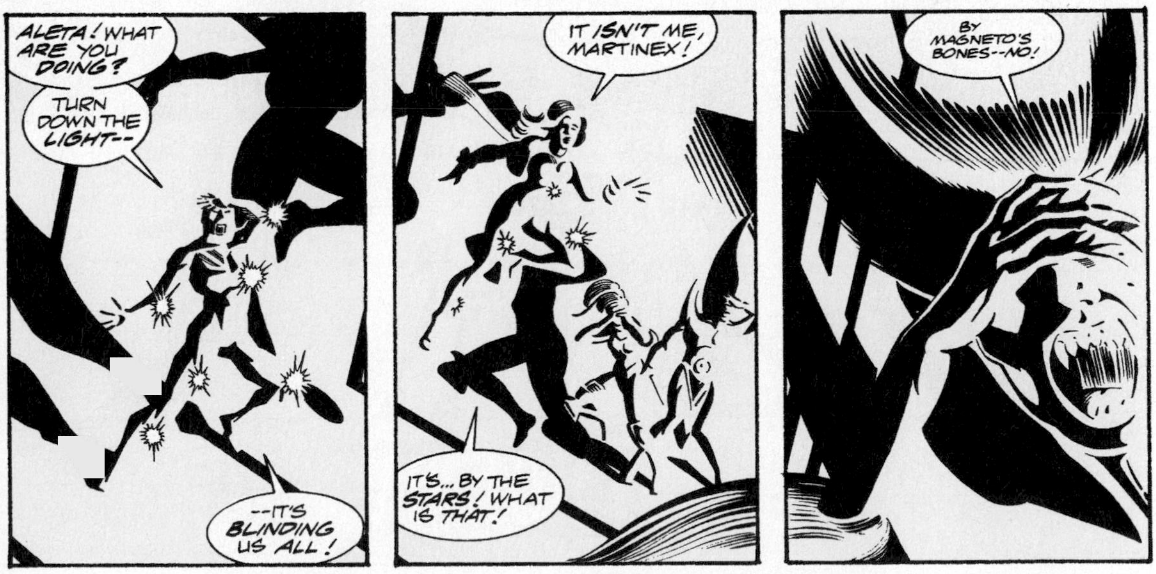
ALETA! WHAT ARE YOU DOING?
TURN DOWN THE LIGHT--
--IT'S BLINDING US ALL!
IT ISN'T ME, MARTINEX!
IT'S... BY THE STARS! WHAT IS THAT!
BY MAGNETO'S BONES--NO!

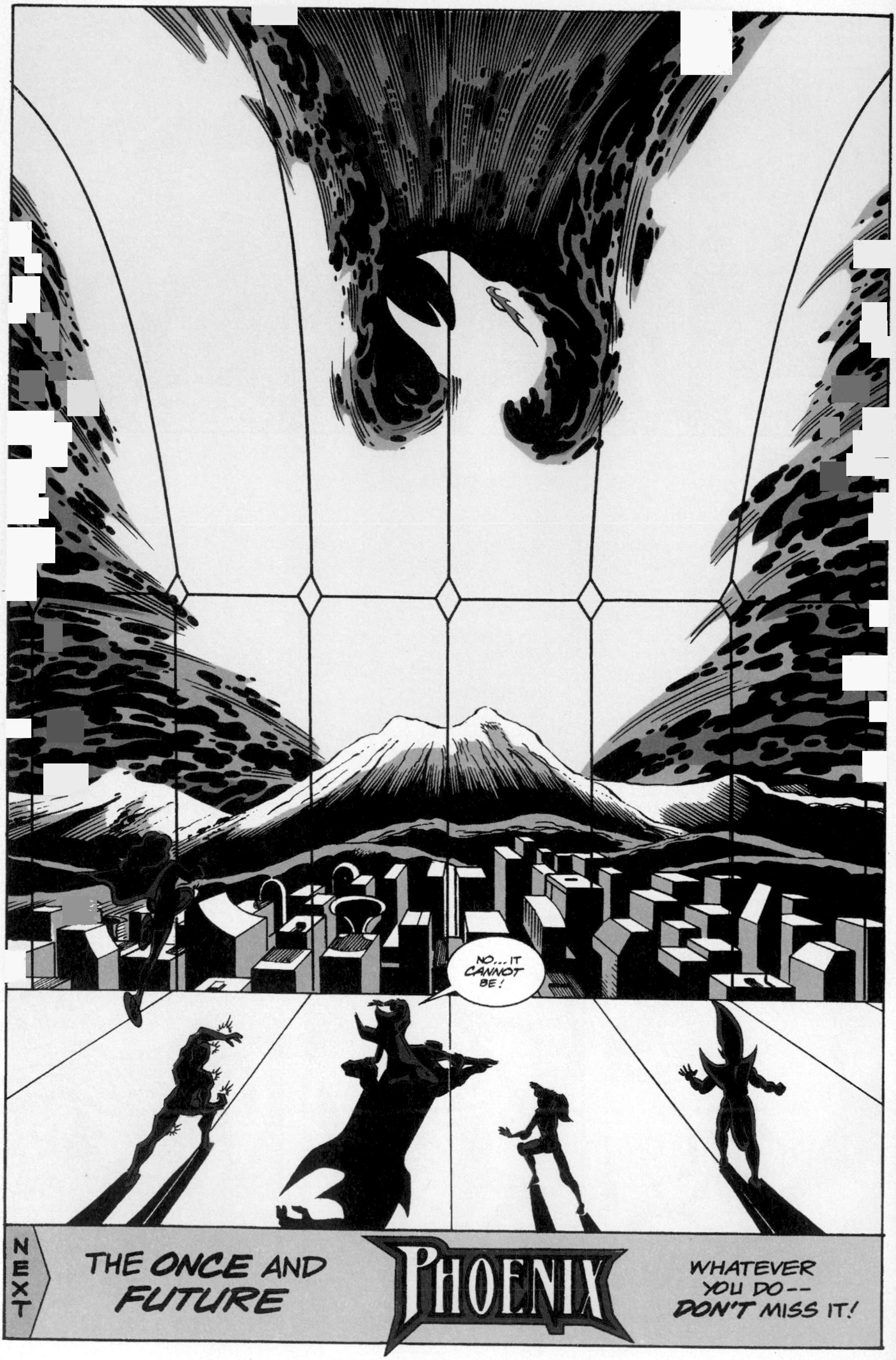
NO... IT CANNOT BE!
NEXT
THE ONCE AND FUTURE
PHOENIX
WHATEVER YOU DO-- DON'T MISS IT!

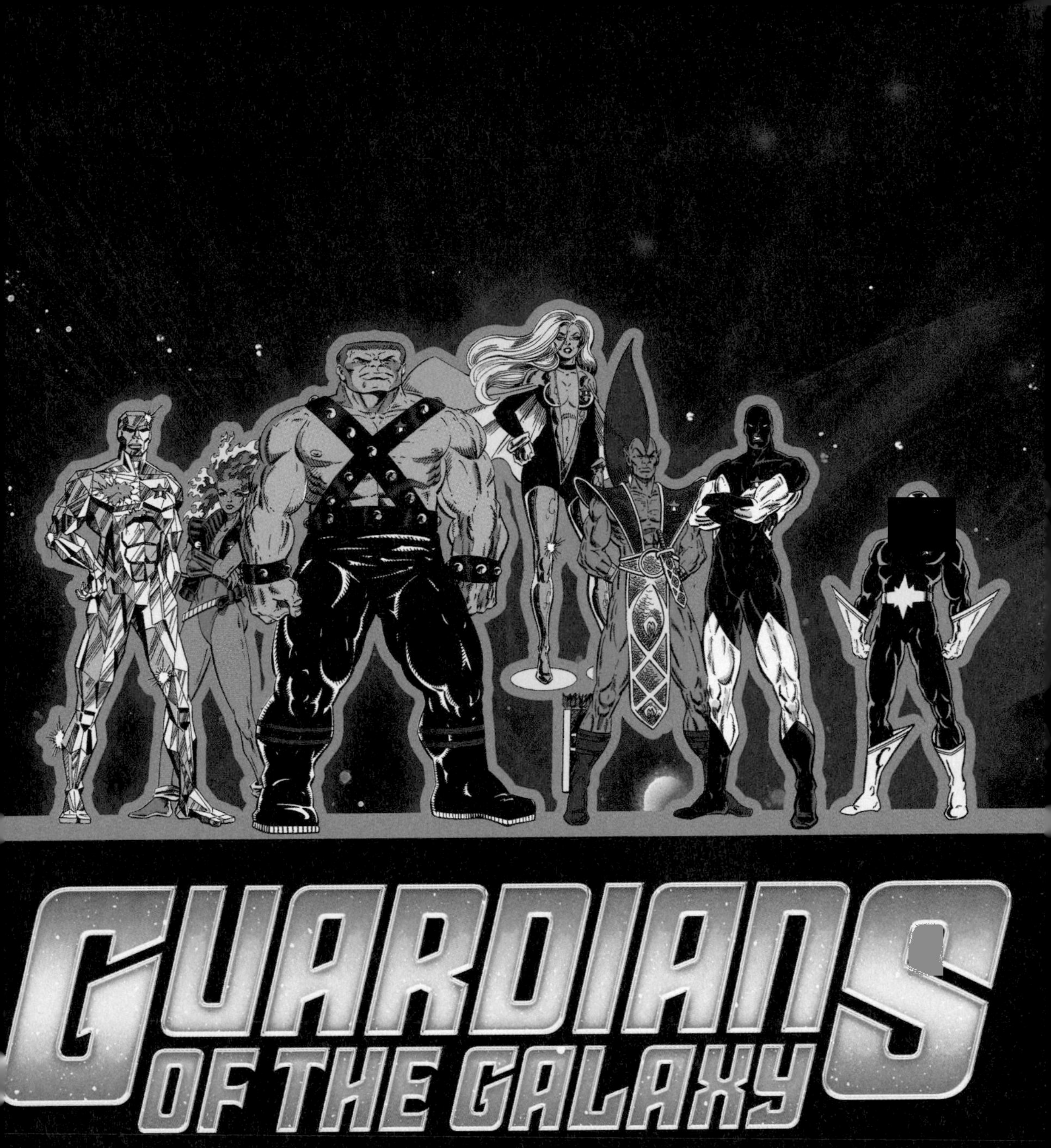
GUARDIANS
OF THE GALAXY

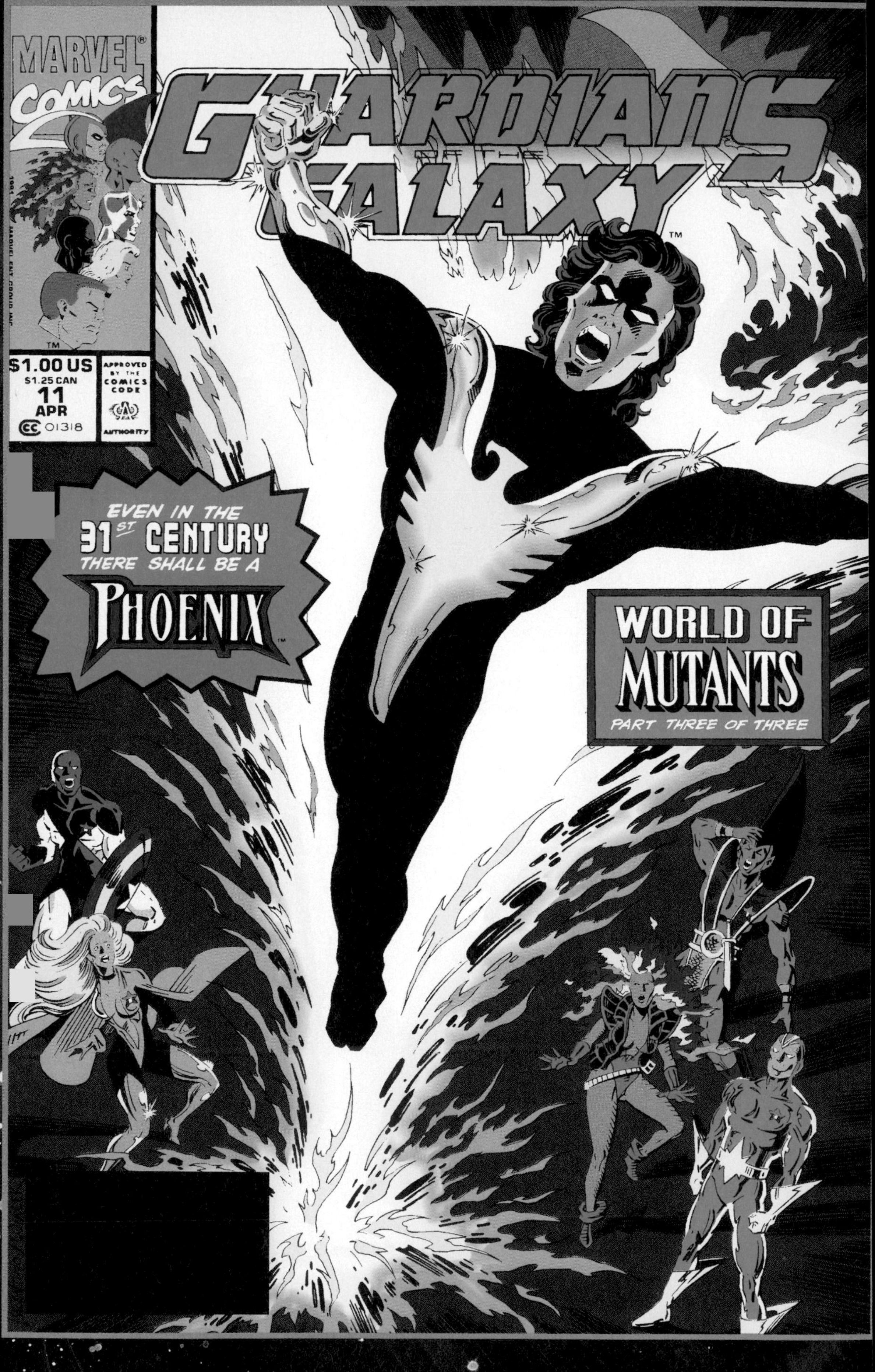
MARVEL COMICS
GUARDIANS OF THE GALAXY
$1.00 US
$1.25 CAN
11
APR
01318
APPROVED BY THE COMICS CODE AUTHORITY
EVEN IN THE 31ST CENTURY THERE SHALL BE A
PHOENIX
WORLD OF MUTANTS
PART THREE OF THREE

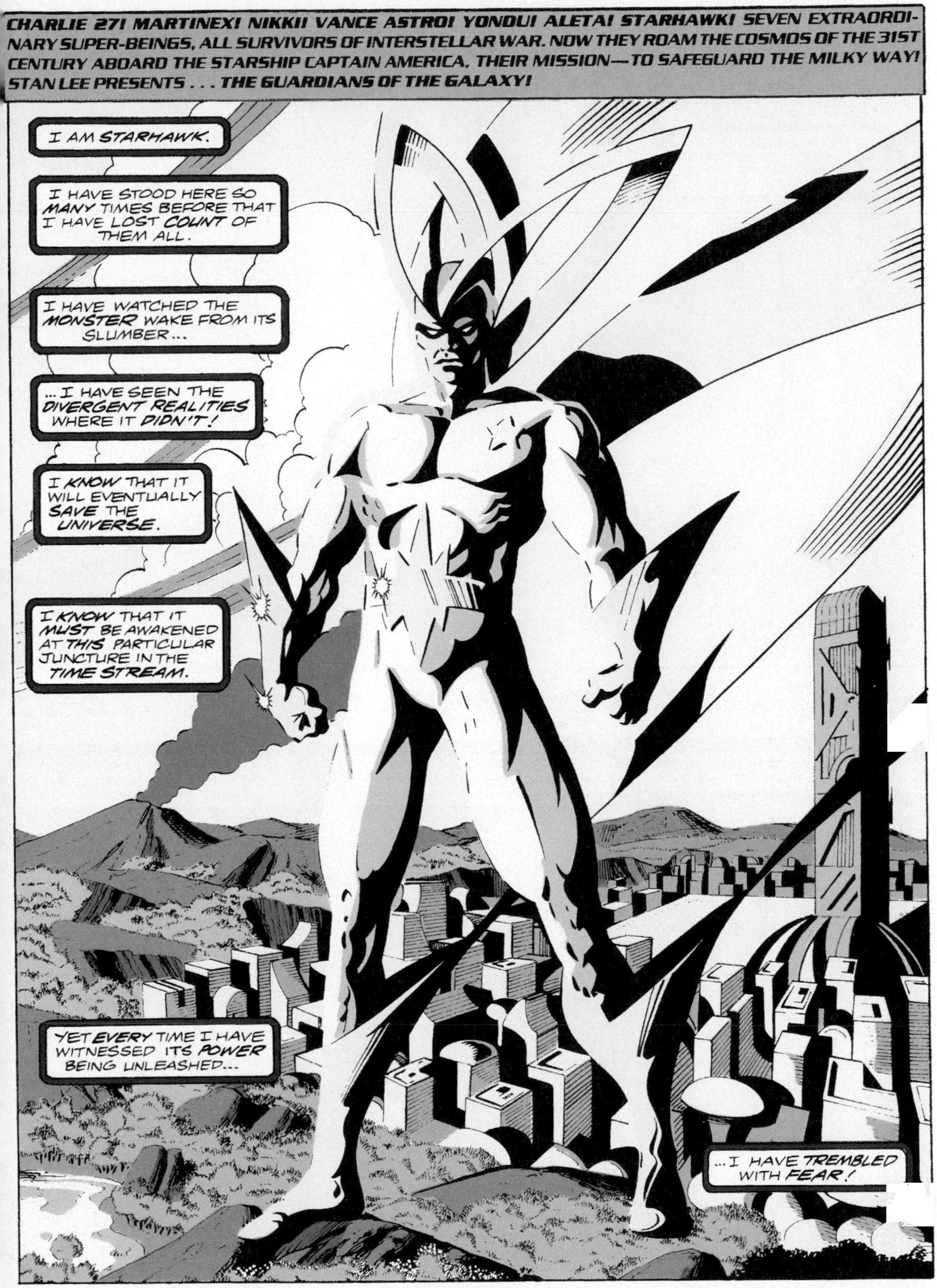
CHARLIE 27! MARTINEX! NIKKI! VANCE ASTRO! YONDU! ALETA! STARHAWK! SEVEN EXTRAORDINARY SUPER-BEINGS, ALL SURVIVORS OF INTERSTELLAR WAR. NOW THEY ROAM THE COSMOS OF THE 31ST CENTURY ABOARD THE STARSHIP CAPTAIN AMERICA, THEIR MISSION—TO SAFEGUARD THE MILKY WAY! STAN LEE PRESENTS . . . THE GUARDIANS OF THE GALAXY!
I AM STARHAWK.
I HAVE STOOD HERE SO MANY TIMES BEFORE THAT I HAVE LOST COUNT OF THEM ALL.
I HAVE WATCHED THE MONSTER WAKE FROM ITS SLUMBER...
...I HAVE SEEN THE DIVERGENT REALITIES WHERE IT DIDN'T!
I KNOW THAT IT WILL EVENTUALLY SAVE THE UNIVERSE.
I KNOW THAT IT MUST BE AWAKENED AT THIS PARTICULAR JUNCTURE IN THE TIME STREAM.
YET EVERY TIME I HAVE WITNESSED ITS POWER BEING UNLEASHED...
...I HAVE TREMBLED WITH FEAR!

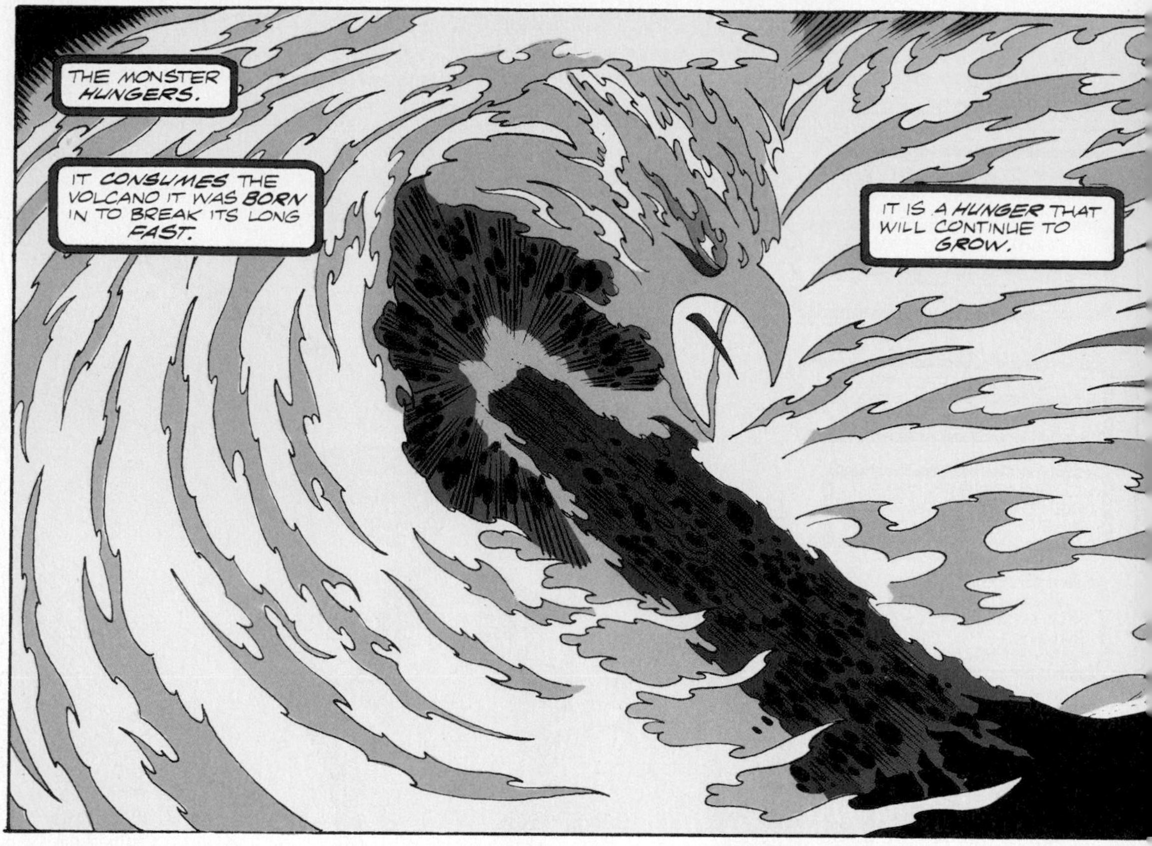
THE MONSTER HUNGERS.
IT CONSUMES THE VOLCANO IT WAS BORN IN TO BREAK ITS LONG FAST.
IT IS A HUNGER THAT WILL CONTINUE TO GROW.

ANOTHER STELLAR SPECTACULAR BROUGHT TO YOU BY:

VALENTINO WORDS/PICTURES

MONTANO BRUSHES/QUILLS

LOPEZ LETTERS/SFX

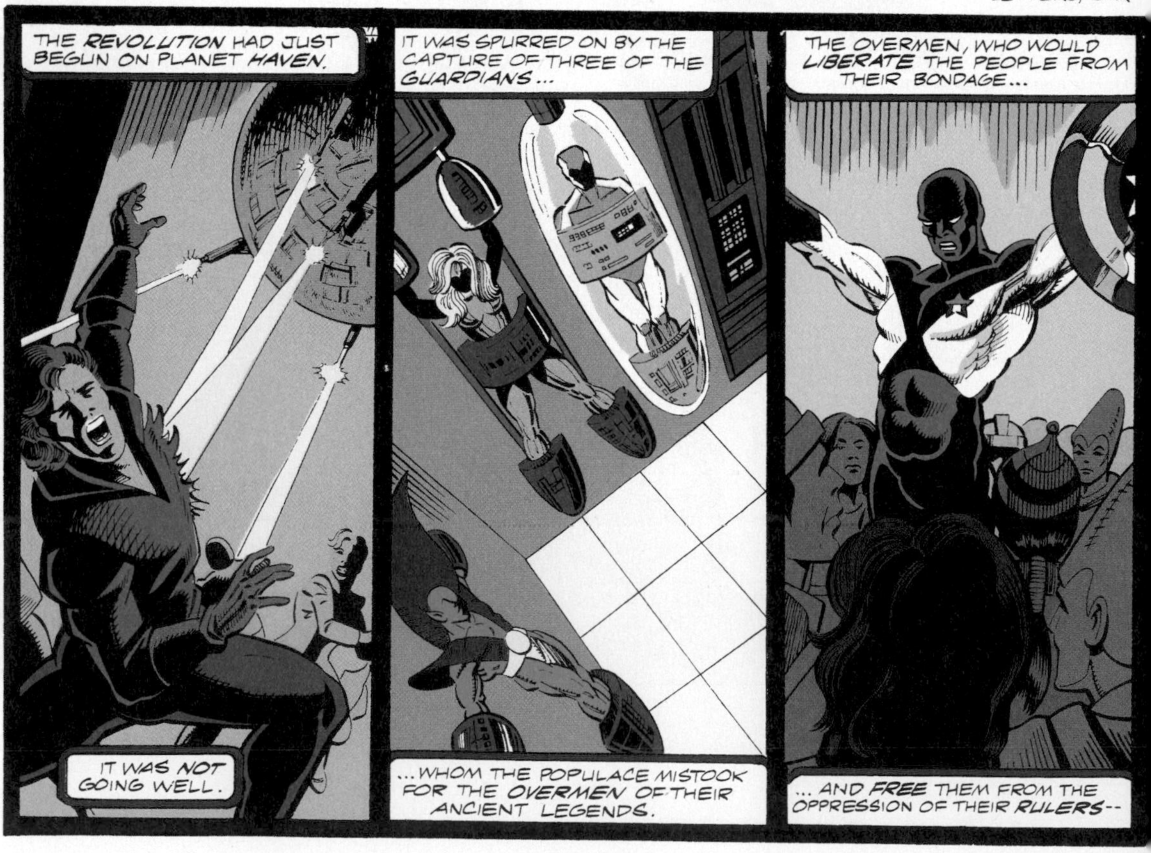
THE REVOLUTION HAD JUST BEGUN ON PLANET HAVEN.
IT WAS NOT GOING WELL.
IT WAS SPURRED ON BY THE CAPTURE OF THREE OF THE GUARDIANS...
...WHOM THE POPULACE MISTOOK FOR THE OVERMEN OF THEIR ANCIENT LEGENDS.
THE OVERMEN, WHO WOULD LIBERATE THE PEOPLE FROM THEIR BONDAGE...
... AND FREE THEM FROM THE OPPRESSION OF THEIR RULERS--

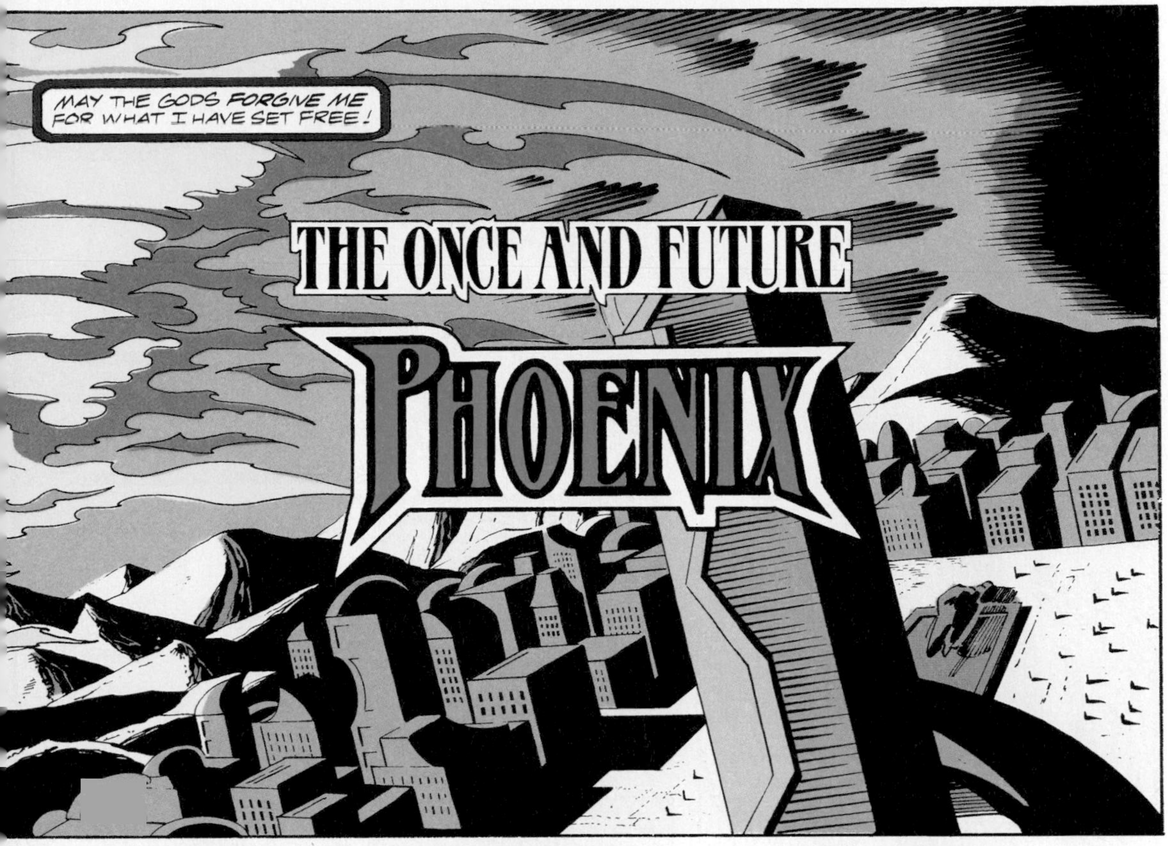
MAY THE GODS FORGIVE ME FOR WHAT I HAVE SET FREE!
THE ONCE AND FUTURE
PHOENIX

STEIN
COLORS/HUES

ANDERSON
GRIPES/COMPLAINTS

DeFALCO
GUIDANCE COUNSELOR

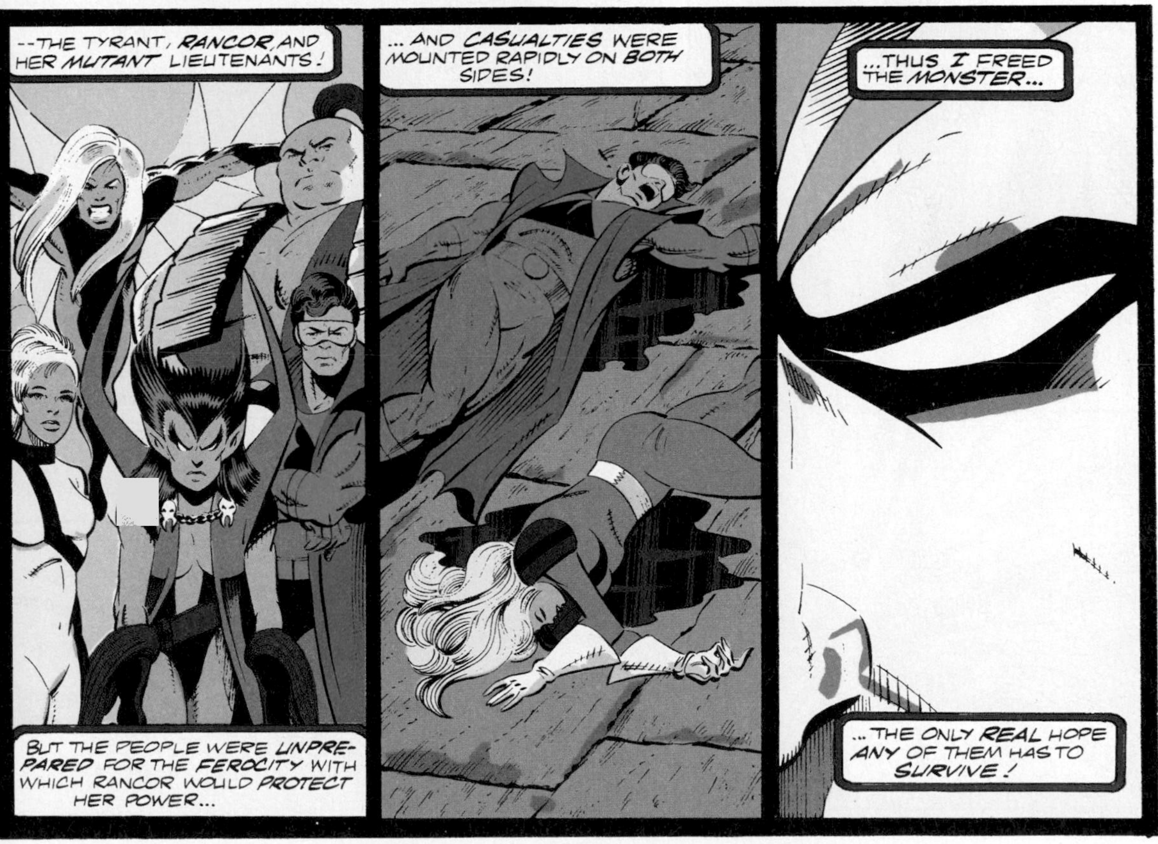
--THE TYRANT, RANCOR, AND HER MUTANT LIEUTENANTS!
BUT THE PEOPLE WERE UNPREPARED FOR THE FEROCITY WITH WHICH RANCOR WOULD PROTECT HER POWER...
...AND CASUALTIES WERE MOUNTED RAPIDLY ON BOTH SIDES!
...THUS I FREED THE MONSTER...
...THE ONLY REAL HOPE ANY OF THEM HAS TO SURVIVE!

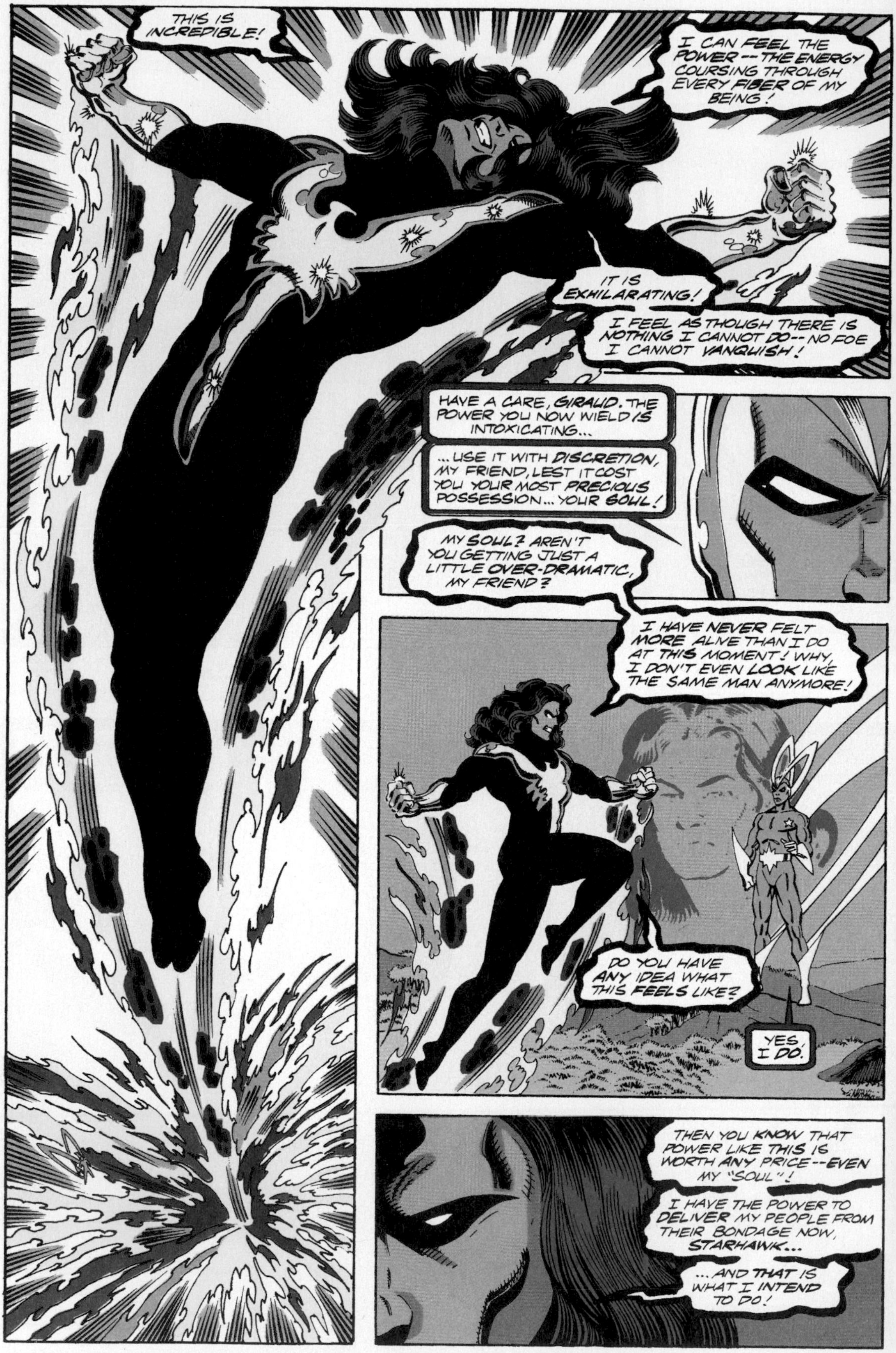
THIS IS INCREDIBLE!
I CAN FEEL THE POWER -- THE ENERGY COURSING THROUGH EVERY FIBER OF MY BEING!
IT IS EXHILARATING!
I FEEL AS THOUGH THERE IS NOTHING I CANNOT DO -- NO FOE I CANNOT VANQUISH!
HAVE A CARE, GIRAUD. THE POWER YOU NOW WIELD IS INTOXICATING...
...USE IT WITH DISCRETION, MY FRIEND, LEST IT COST YOU YOUR MOST PRECIOUS POSSESSION... YOUR SOUL!
MY SOUL? AREN'T YOU GETTING JUST A LITTLE OVER-DRAMATIC, MY FRIEND?
I HAVE NEVER FELT MORE ALIVE THAN I DO AT THIS MOMENT! WHY, I DON'T EVEN LOOK LIKE THE SAME MAN ANYMORE!
DO YOU HAVE ANY IDEA WHAT THIS FEELS LIKE?
YES, I DO.
THEN YOU KNOW THAT POWER LIKE THIS IS WORTH ANY PRICE -- EVEN MY "SOUL"!
I HAVE THE POWER TO DELIVER MY PEOPLE FROM THEIR BONDAGE NOW, STARHAWK...
...AND THAT IS WHAT I INTEND TO DO!

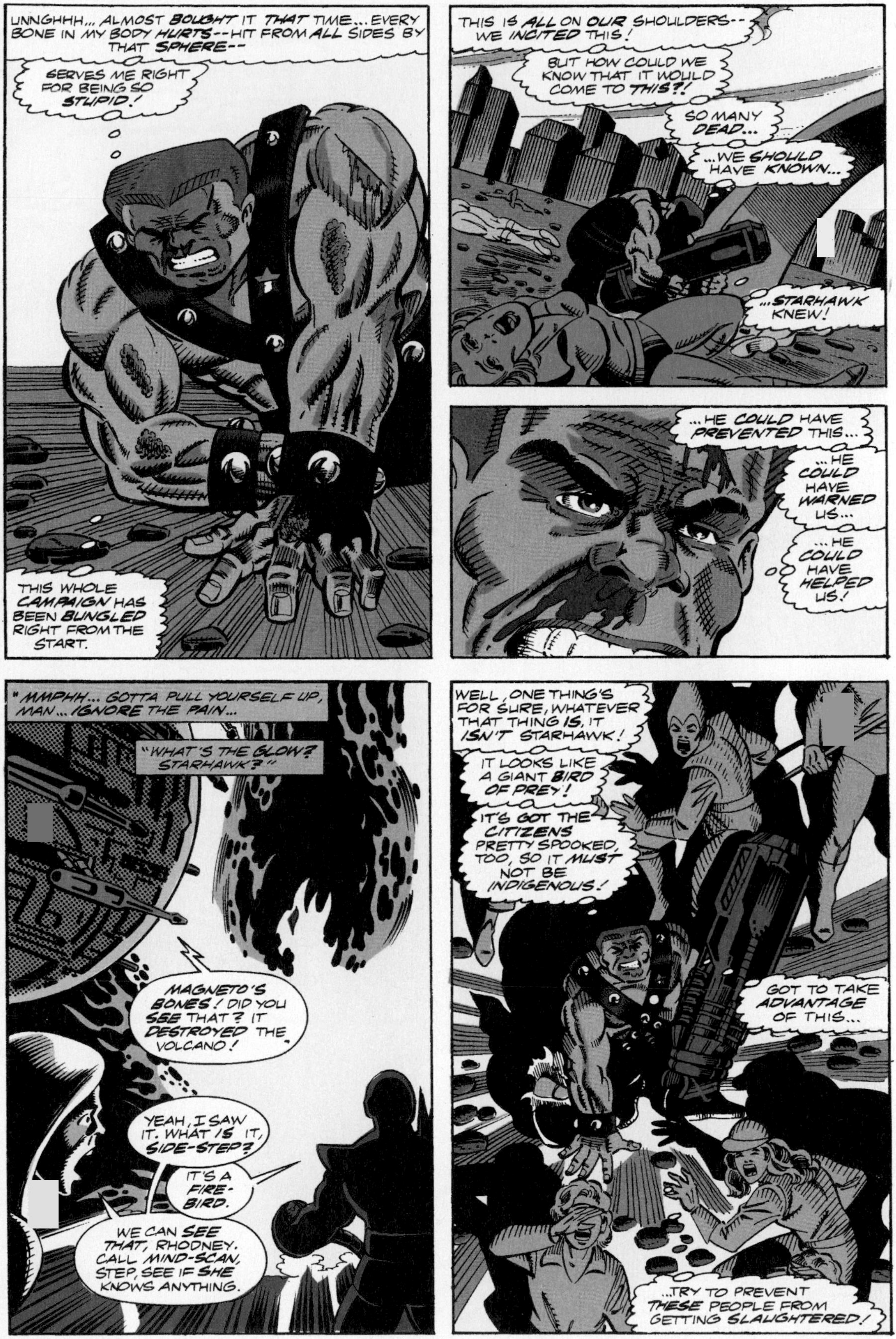
UNNGHHH... ALMOST BOUGHT IT THAT TIME... EVERY BONE IN MY BODY HURTS--HIT FROM ALL SIDES BY THAT SPHERE--
SERVES ME RIGHT FOR BEING SO STUPID!
THIS WHOLE CAMPAIGN HAS BEEN BUNGLED RIGHT FROM THE START.
THIS IS ALL ON OUR SHOULDERS-- WE INCITED THIS!
BUT HOW COULD WE KNOW THAT IT WOULD COME TO THIS?!
SO MANY DEAD...
...WE SHOULD HAVE KNOWN...
...STARHAWK KNEW!
...HE COULD HAVE PREVENTED THIS...
...HE COULD HAVE WARNED US...
...HE COULD HAVE HELPED US!
"MMPHH... GOTTA PULL YOURSELF UP, MAN... IGNORE THE PAIN...
"WHAT'S THE GLOW? STARHAWK?"
MAGNETO'S BONES! DID YOU SEE THAT? IT DESTROYED THE VOLCANO!
YEAH, I SAW IT. WHAT IS IT, SIDE-STEP?
IT'S A FIRE-BIRD.
WE CAN SEE THAT, RHODNEY. CALL MIND-SCAN, STEP, SEE IF SHE KNOWS ANYTHING.
WELL, ONE THING'S FOR SURE, WHATEVER THAT THING IS, IT ISN'T STARHAWK!
IT LOOKS LIKE A GIANT BIRD OF PREY!
IT'S GOT THE CITIZENS PRETTY SPOOKED, TOO, SO IT MUST NOT BE INDIGENOUS!
GOT TO TAKE ADVANTAGE OF THIS...
...TRY TO PREVENT THESE PEOPLE FROM GETTING SLAUGHTERED!

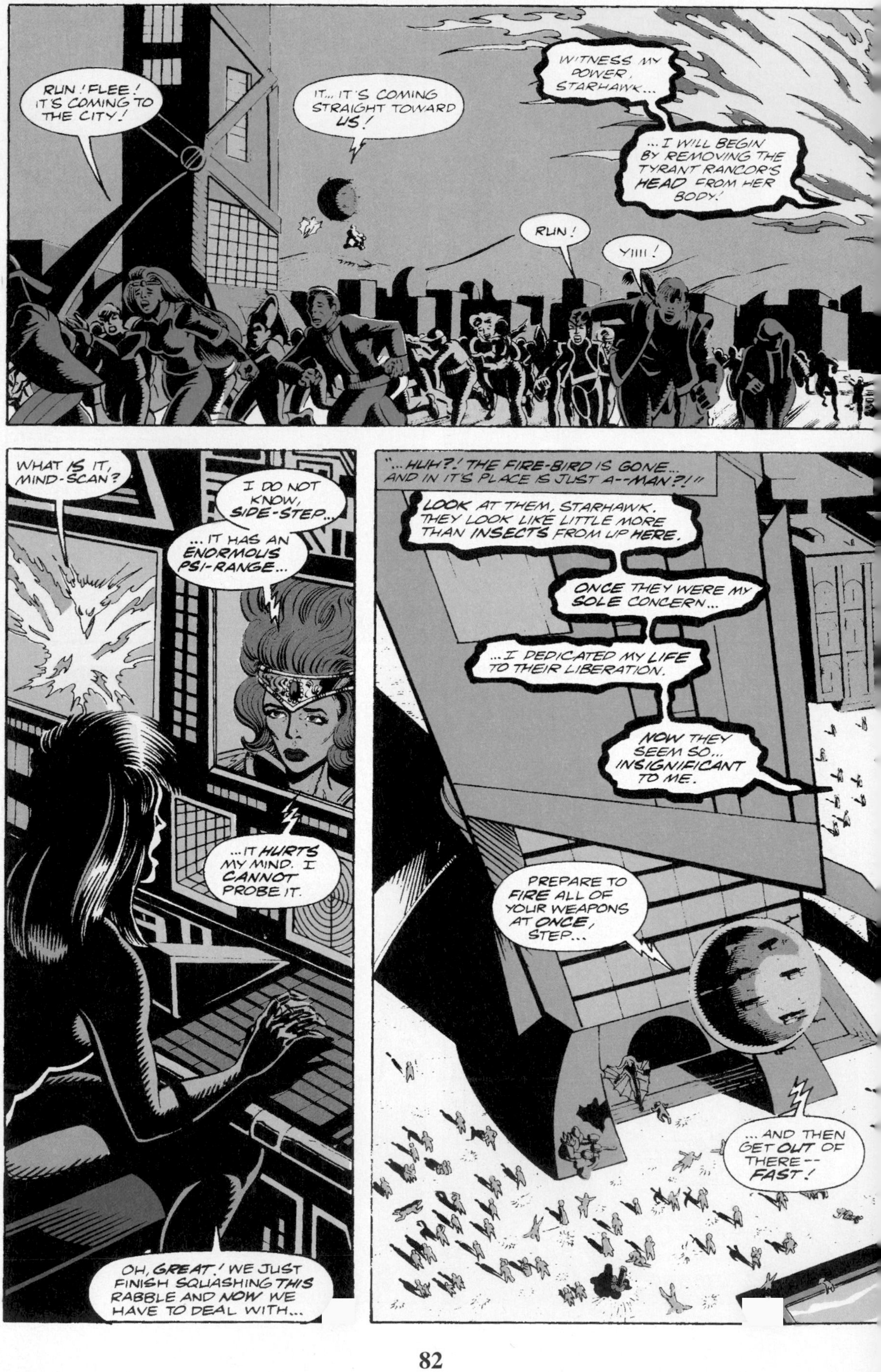
RUN! FLEE! IT'S COMING TO THE CITY!
IT... IT'S COMING STRAIGHT TOWARD US!
WITNESS MY POWER, STARHAWK...
...I WILL BEGIN BY REMOVING THE TYRANT RANCOR'S HEAD FROM HER BODY!
RUN!
YIIII!
WHAT IS IT, MIND-SCAN?
I DO NOT KNOW, SIDE-STEP...
...IT HAS AN ENORMOUS PSI-RANGE...
...IT HURTS MY MIND. I CANNOT PROBE IT.
OH, GREAT! WE JUST FINISH SQUASHING THIS RABBLE AND NOW WE HAVE TO DEAL WITH...
"...HUH?! THE FIRE-BIRD IS GONE... AND IN IT'S PLACE IS JUST A--MAN?!"
LOOK AT THEM, STARHAWK. THEY LOOK LIKE LITTLE MORE THAN INSECTS FROM UP HERE.
ONCE THEY WERE MY SOLE CONCERN...
...I DEDICATED MY LIFE TO THEIR LIBERATION.
NOW THEY SEEM SO... INSIGNIFICANT TO ME.
PREPARE TO FIRE ALL OF YOUR WEAPONS AT ONCE, STEP...
...AND THEN GET OUT OF THERE--FAST!

THE BIRD OF FIRE ATTACKS!

IT WILL KILL US ALL!

YOU MUST *FIGHT* THOSE PERCEPTIONS, GIRAUD...

...THAT IS THE *PHOENIX'S* WORLD-VIEW NOT *YOURS.*

PREPARING TO FIRE ALL GUNS--NOW!

BUT, STARHAWK...

...I AM THE *PHOENIX!*

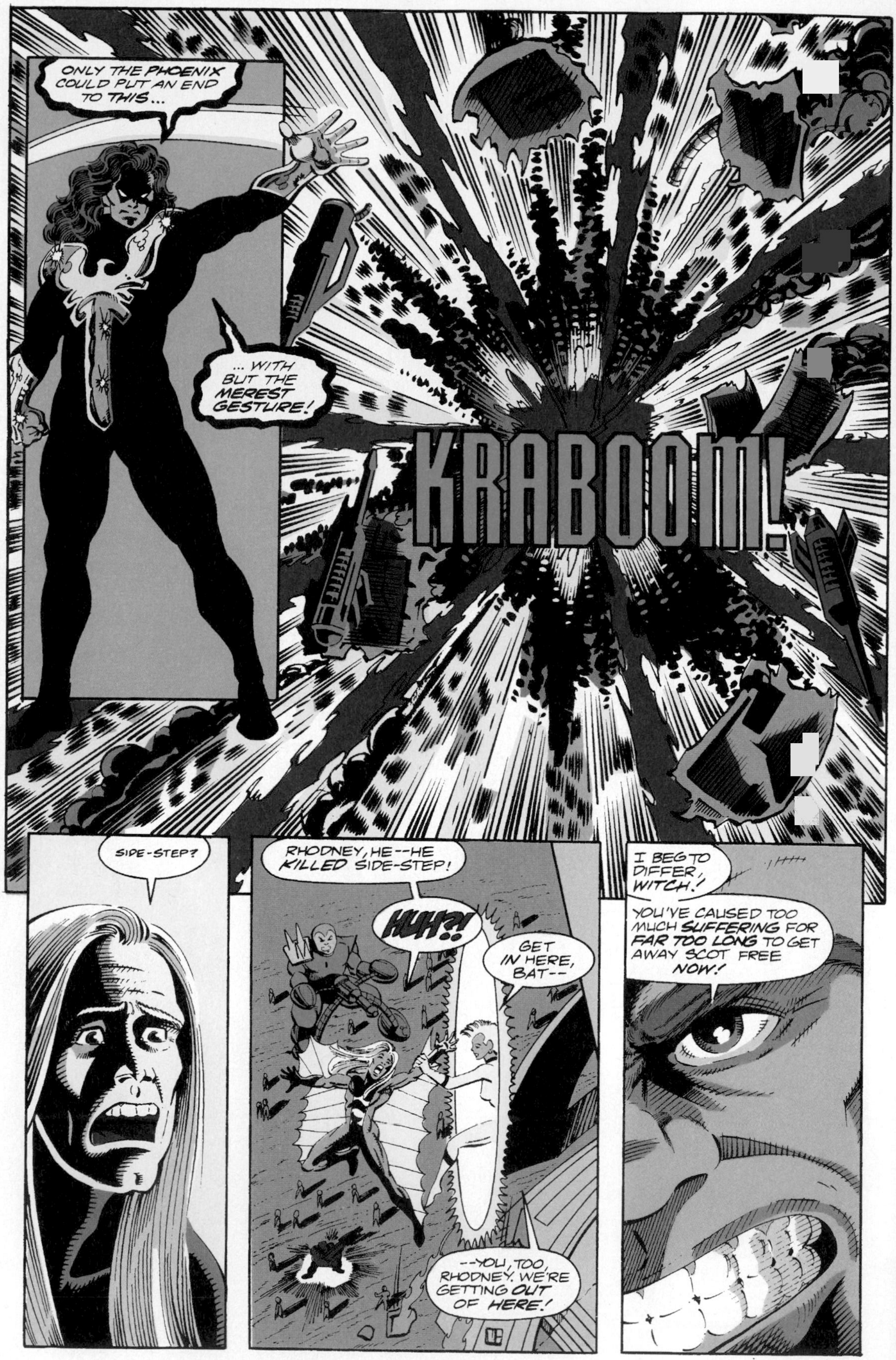

ONLY THE PHOENIX COULD PUT AN END TO THIS...
... WITH BUT THE MEREST GESTURE!
KRABOOM!
SIDE-STEP?
RHODNEY, HE--HE KILLED SIDE-STEP!
HUH?!
GET IN HERE, BAT--
--YOU, TOO, RHODNEY. WE'RE GETTING OUT OF HERE!
I BEG TO DIFFER, WITCH!
YOU'VE CAUSED TOO MUCH SUFFERING FOR FAR TOO LONG TO GET AWAY SCOT FREE NOW!

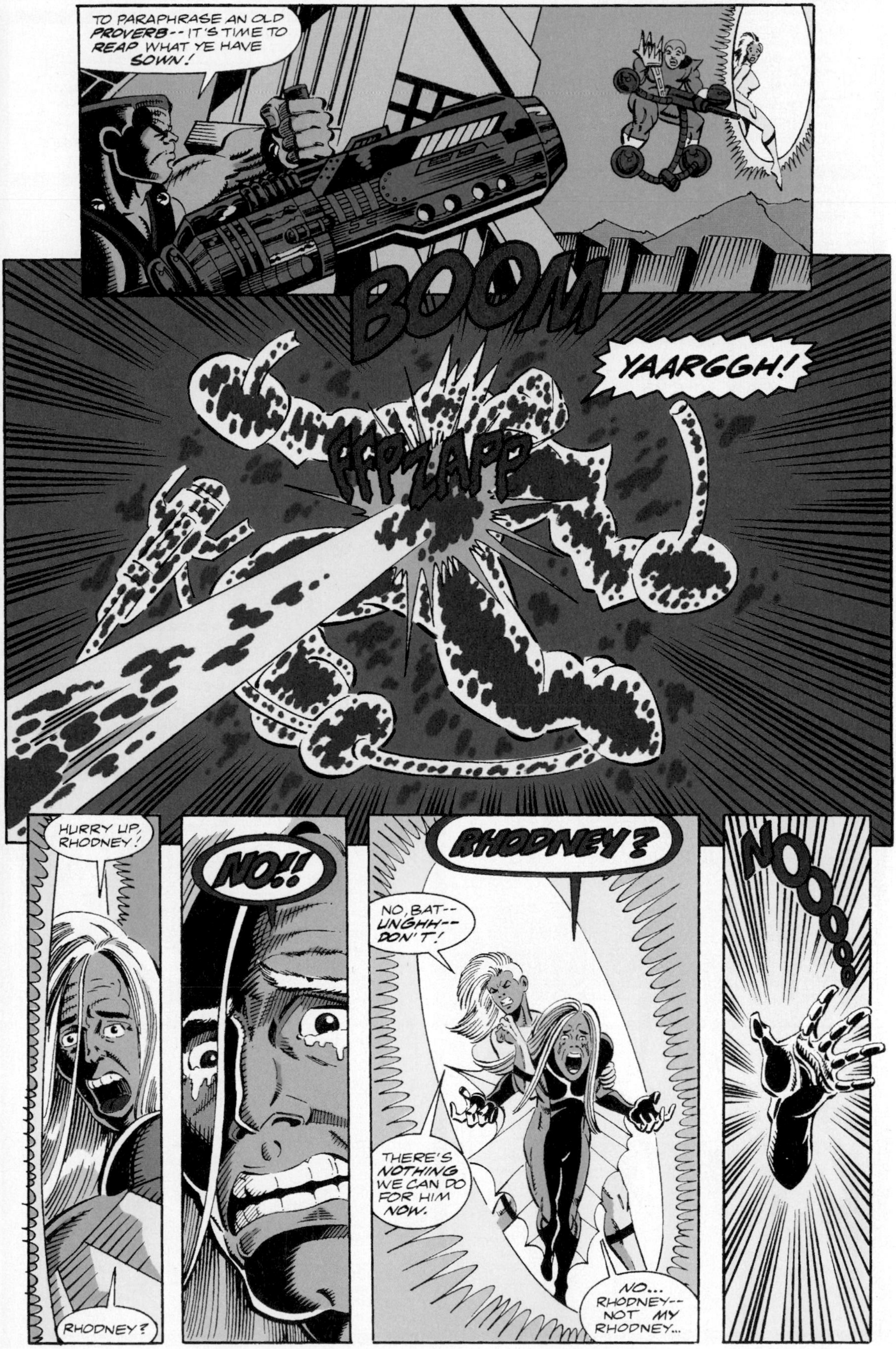

TO PARAPHRASE AN OLD PROVERB-- IT'S TIME TO REAP WHAT YE HAVE SOWN!
BOOM
YAARGGH!
FFPZAPP
HURRY UP, RHODNEY!
RHODNEY?
NO!!
RHODNEY?
NO, BAT-- UNGHH-- DON'T!
THERE'S NOTHING WE CAN DO FOR HIM NOW.
NO... RHODNEY-- NOT MY RHODNEY...
NOOOOOO

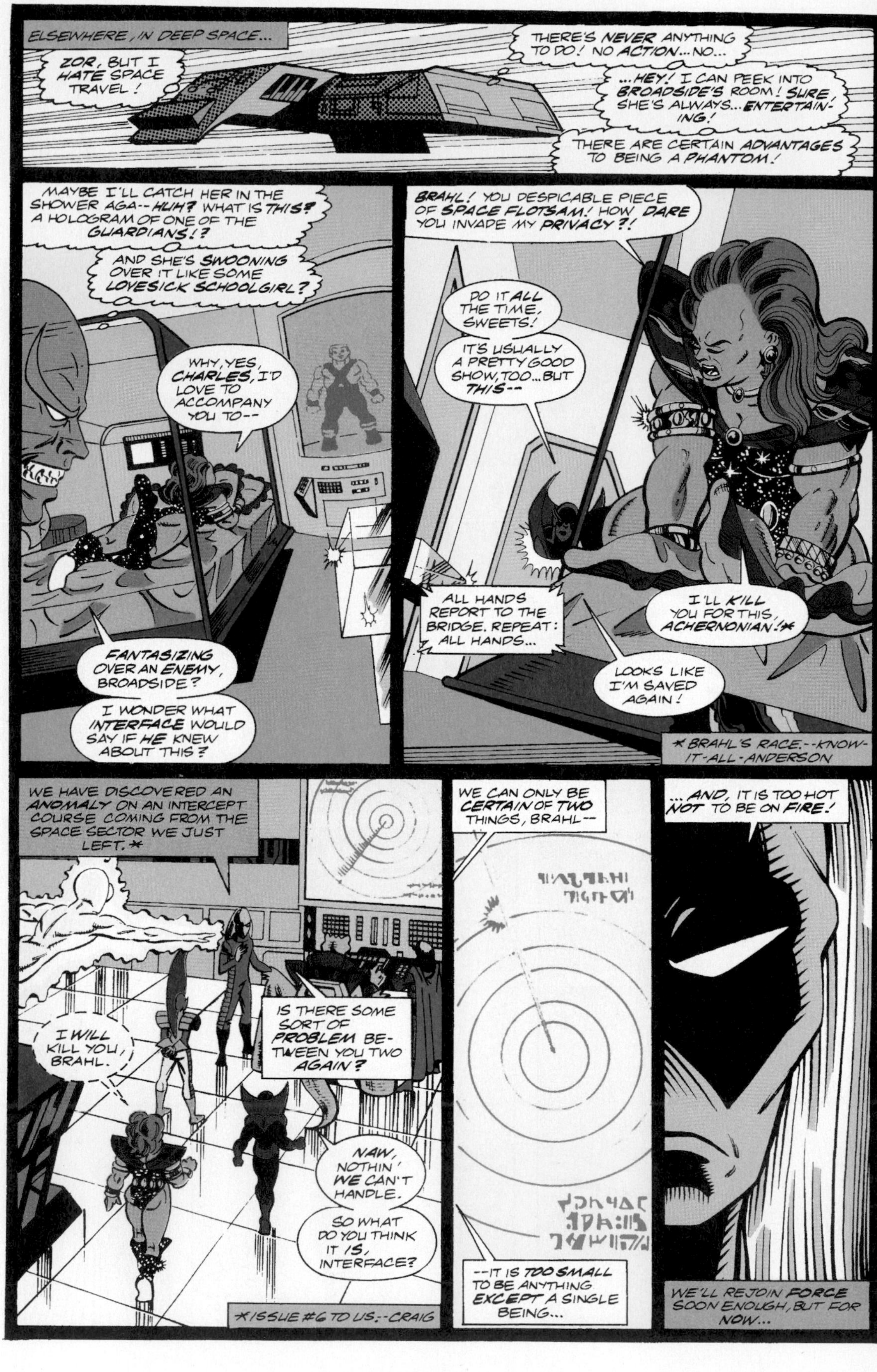
ELSEWHERE, IN DEEP SPACE...
ZOR, BUT I HATE SPACE TRAVEL!
THERE'S NEVER ANYTHING TO DO! NO ACTION...NO...
...HEY! I CAN PEEK INTO BROADSIDE'S ROOM! SURE, SHE'S ALWAYS...ENTERTAINING!
THERE ARE CERTAIN ADVANTAGES TO BEING A PHANTOM!
MAYBE I'LL CATCH HER IN THE SHOWER AGA-- HUH? WHAT IS THIS? A HOLOGRAM OF ONE OF THE GUARDIANS!?
AND SHE'S SWOONING OVER IT LIKE SOME LOVESICK SCHOOLGIRL?
WHY, YES, CHARLES, I'D LOVE TO ACCOMPANY YOU TO--
FANTASIZING OVER AN ENEMY, BROADSIDE?
I WONDER WHAT INTERFACE WOULD SAY IF HE KNEW ABOUT THIS?
BRAHL! YOU DESPICABLE PIECE OF SPACE FLOTSAM! HOW DARE YOU INVADE MY PRIVACY?!
DO IT ALL THE TIME, SWEETS!
IT'S USUALLY A PRETTY GOOD SHOW, TOO...BUT THIS--
ALL HANDS REPORT TO THE BRIDGE. REPEAT: ALL HANDS...
I'LL KILL YOU FOR THIS, ACHERNONIAN!*
LOOKS LIKE I'M SAVED AGAIN!
*BRAHL'S RACE.--KNOW-IT-ALL-ANDERSON
WE HAVE DISCOVERED AN ANOMALY ON AN INTERCEPT COURSE COMING FROM THE SPACE SECTOR WE JUST LEFT.*
I WILL KILL YOU, BRAHL.
IS THERE SOME SORT OF PROBLEM BETWEEN YOU TWO AGAIN?
NAW, NOTHIN' WE CAN'T HANDLE.
SO WHAT DO YOU THINK IT IS, INTERFACE?
*ISSUE #6 TO US.-CRAIG
WE CAN ONLY BE CERTAIN OF TWO THINGS, BRAHL--
--IT IS TOO SMALL TO BE ANYTHING EXCEPT A SINGLE BEING...
...AND, IT IS TOO HOT NOT TO BE ON FIRE!
WE'LL REJOIN FORCE SOON ENOUGH, BUT FOR NOW...

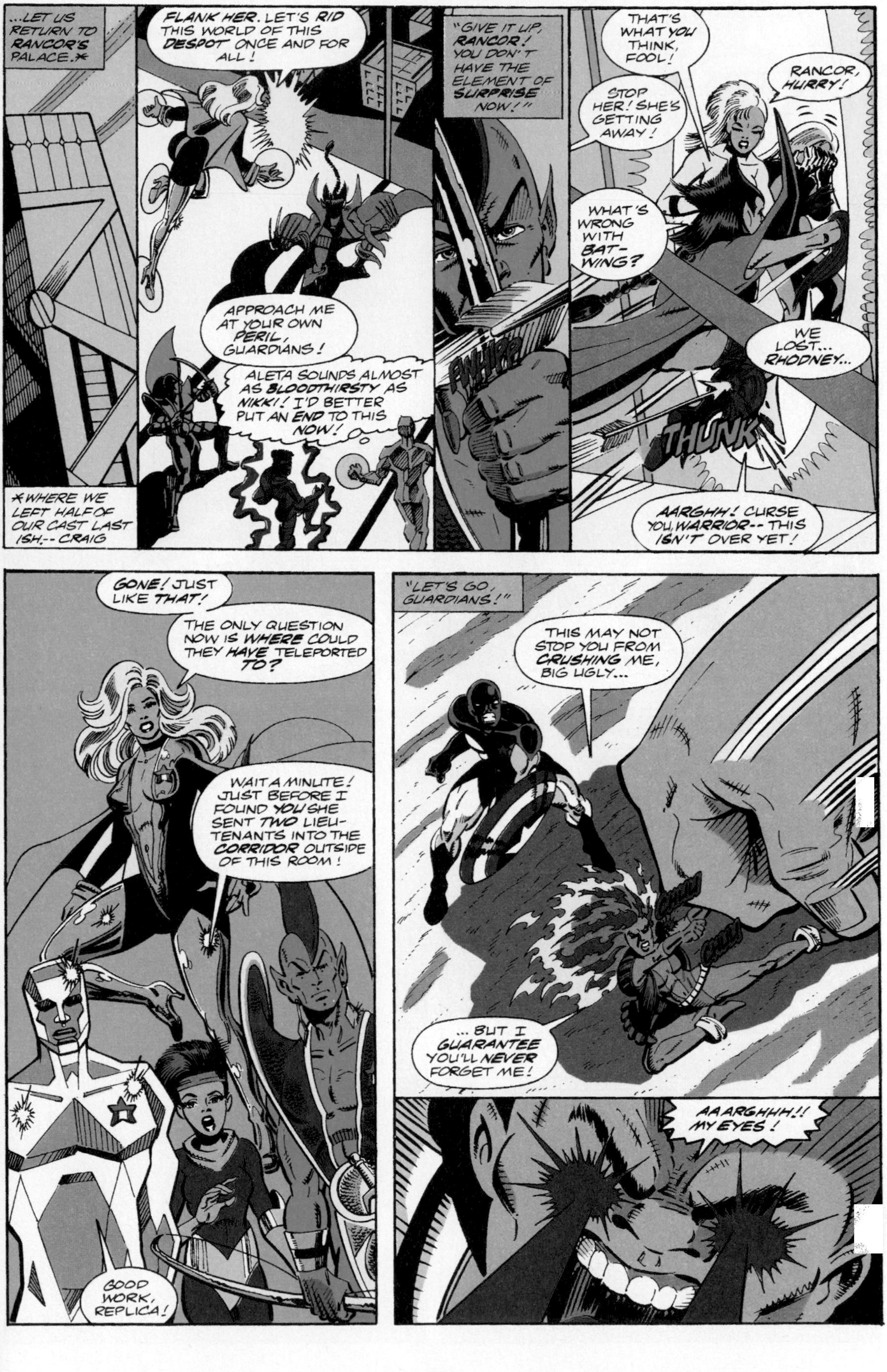

...LET US RETURN TO RANCOR'S PALACE.*
FLANK HER. LET'S RID THIS WORLD OF THIS DESPOT ONCE AND FOR ALL!
APPROACH ME AT YOUR OWN PERIL, GUARDIANS!
ALETA SOUNDS ALMOST AS BLOODTHIRSTY AS NIKKI! I'D BETTER PUT AN END TO THIS NOW!
*WHERE WE LEFT HALF OF OUR CAST LAST ISH.-- CRAIG
"GIVE IT UP, RANCOR! YOU DON'T HAVE THE ELEMENT OF SURPRISE NOW!"
PWHIPP
THAT'S WHAT YOU THINK, FOOL!
STOP HER! SHE'S GETTING AWAY!
RANCOR, HURRY!
WHAT'S WRONG WITH BAT-WING?
WE LOST... RHODNEY...
THUNK
AARGHH! CURSE YOU, WARRIOR-- THIS ISN'T OVER YET!
GONE! JUST LIKE THAT!
THE ONLY QUESTION NOW IS WHERE COULD THEY HAVE TELEPORTED TO?
WAIT A MINUTE! JUST BEFORE I FOUND YOU SHE SENT TWO LIEU-TENANTS INTO THE CORRIDOR OUTSIDE OF THIS ROOM!
GOOD WORK, REPLICA!
"LET'S GO, GUARDIANS!"
THIS MAY NOT STOP YOU FROM CRUSHING ME, BIG UGLY...
...BUT I GUARANTEE YOU'LL NEVER FORGET ME!
AAARGHHH!! MY EYES!

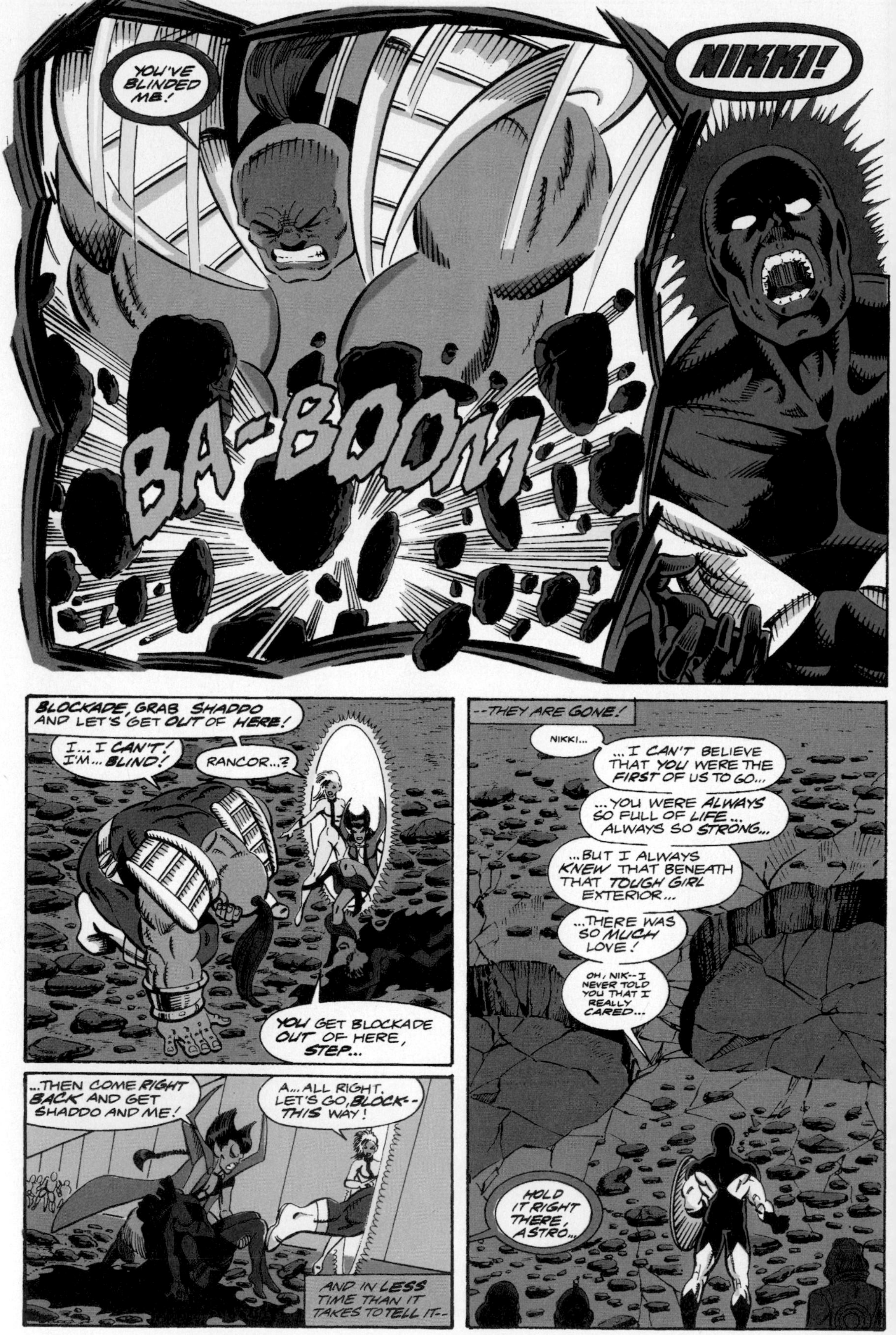
YOU'VE BLINDED ME!
NIKKI!
BA-BOOM
BLOCKADE, GRAB SHADDO AND LET'S GET OUT OF HERE!
I... I CAN'T! I'M... BLIND!
RANCOR...?
YOU GET BLOCKADE OUT OF HERE, STEP...
...THEN COME RIGHT BACK AND GET SHADDO AND ME!
A... ALL RIGHT. LET'S GO, BLOCK-- THIS WAY!
AND IN LESS TIME THAN IT TAKES TO TELL IT--
--THEY ARE GONE!
NIKKI...
...I CAN'T BELIEVE THAT YOU WERE THE FIRST OF US TO GO...
...YOU WERE ALWAYS SO FULL OF LIFE... ALWAYS SO STRONG...
...BUT I ALWAYS KNEW THAT BENEATH THAT TOUGH GIRL EXTERIOR...
...THERE WAS SO MUCH LOVE!
OH, NIK--I NEVER TOLD YOU THAT I REALLY CARED...
HOLD IT RIGHT THERE, ASTRO...

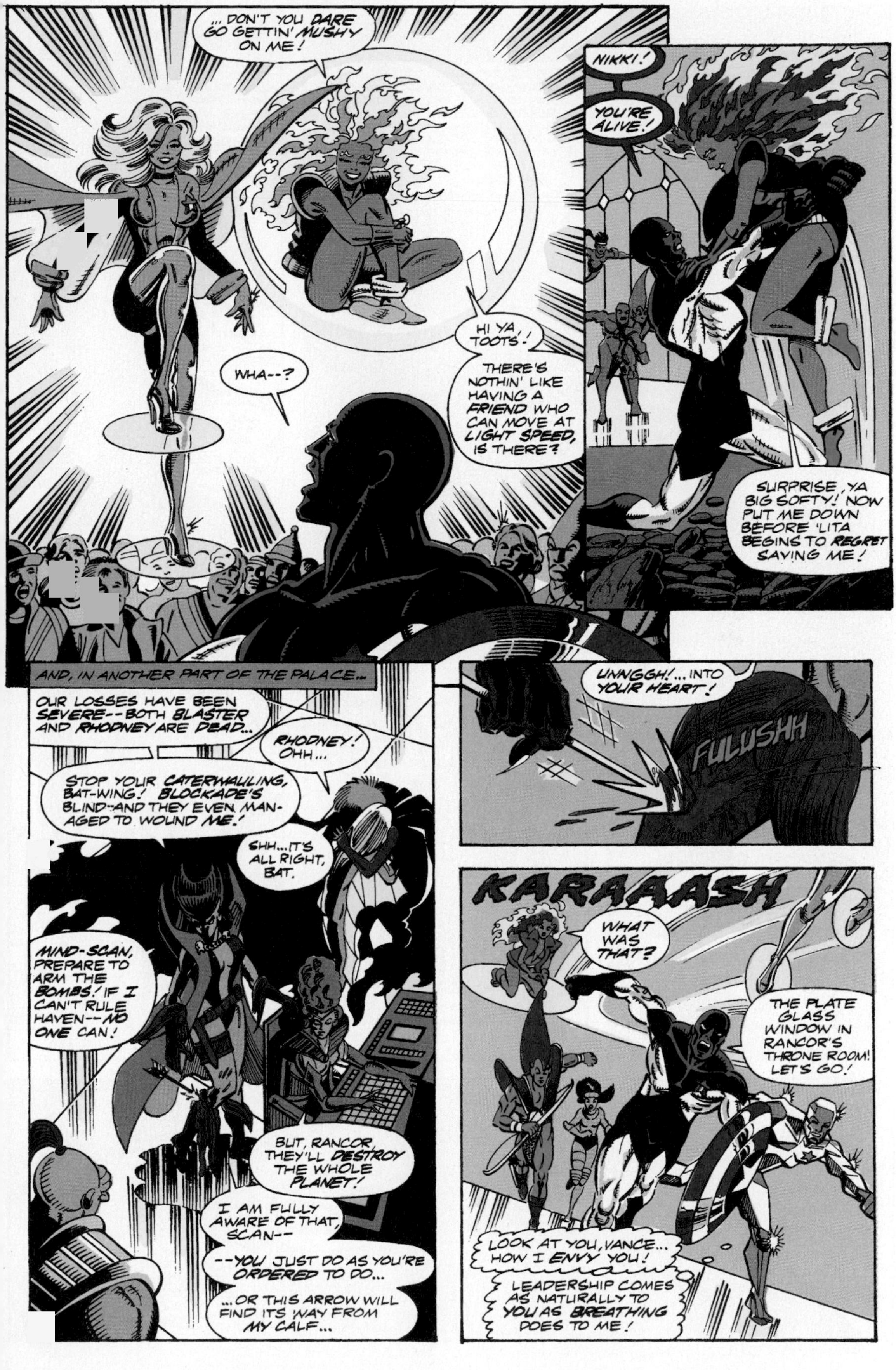
...DON'T YOU DARE GO GETTIN' MUSHY ON ME!
WHA--?
HI YA, TOOTS!
THERE'S NOTHIN' LIKE HAVING A FRIEND WHO CAN MOVE AT LIGHT SPEED, IS THERE?
NIKKI!
YOU'RE ALIVE!
SURPRISE, YA BIG SOFTY! NOW PUT ME DOWN BEFORE 'LITA BEGINS TO REGRET SAVING ME!
AND, IN ANOTHER PART OF THE PALACE...
OUR LOSSES HAVE BEEN SEVERE--BOTH BLASTER AND RHODNEY ARE DEAD...
RHODNEY! OHH...
STOP YOUR CATERWAULING, BAT-WING! BLOCKADE'S BLIND--AND THEY EVEN MANAGED TO WOUND ME!
SHH...IT'S ALL RIGHT, BAT.
MIND-SCAN, PREPARE TO ARM THE BOMBS! IF I CAN'T RULE HAVEN--NO ONE CAN!
BUT, RANCOR, THEY'LL DESTROY THE WHOLE PLANET!
I AM FULLY AWARE OF THAT, SCAN--
--YOU JUST DO AS YOU'RE ORDERED TO DO...
...OR THIS ARROW WILL FIND ITS WAY FROM MY CALF...
UNNGGH!...INTO YOUR HEART!
FULUSHH
KARAAASH
WHAT WAS THAT?
THE PLATE GLASS WINDOW IN RANCOR'S THRONE ROOM! LET'S GO!
LOOK AT YOU, VANCE... HOW I ENVY YOU!
LEADERSHIP COMES AS NATURALLY TO YOU AS BREATHING DOES TO ME!

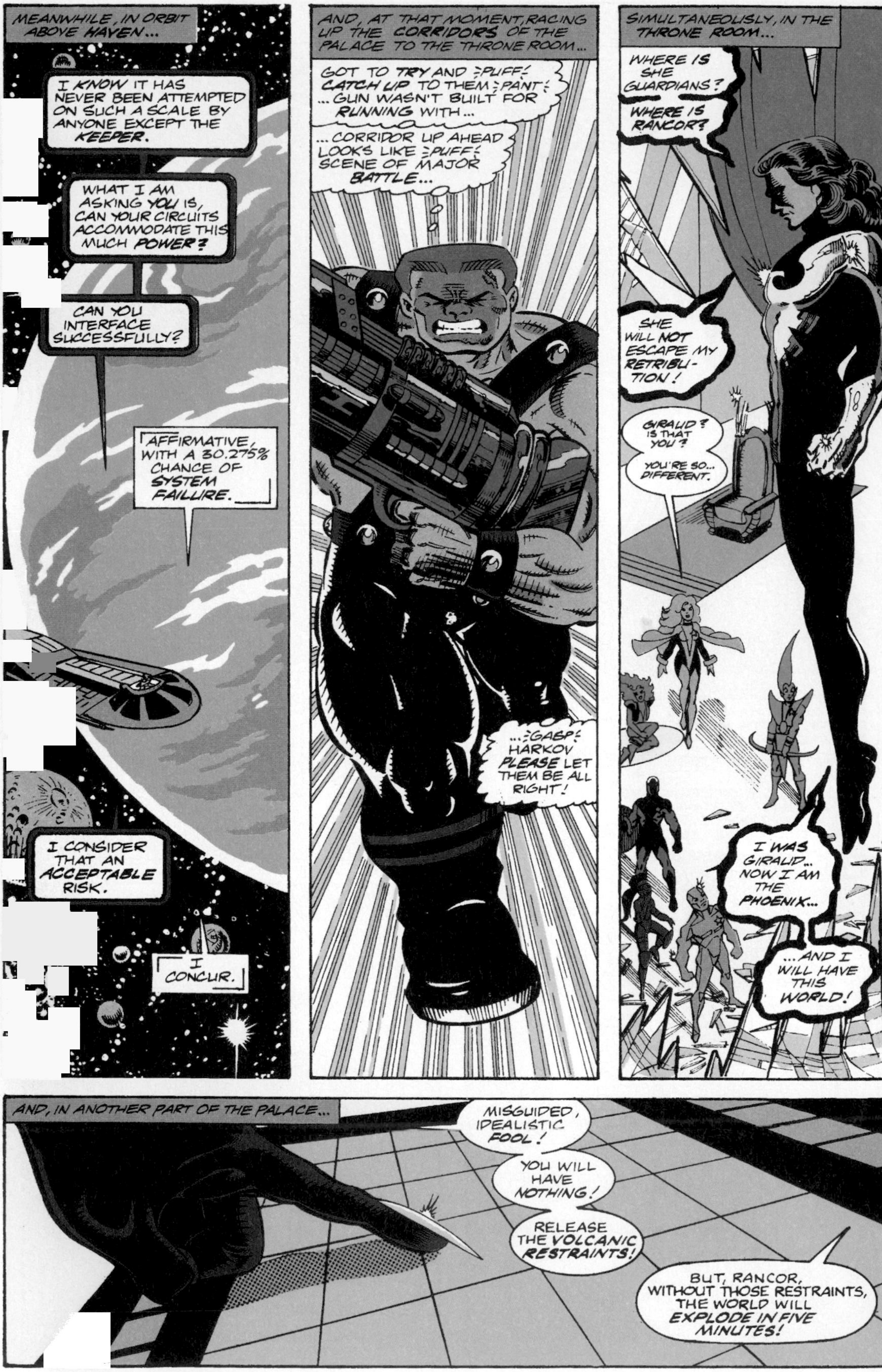
MEANWHILE, IN ORBIT ABOVE HAVEN...
I KNOW IT HAS NEVER BEEN ATTEMPTED ON SUCH A SCALE BY ANYONE EXCEPT THE KEEPER.
WHAT I AM ASKING YOU IS, CAN YOUR CIRCUITS ACCOMMODATE THIS MUCH POWER?
CAN YOU INTERFACE SUCCESSFULLY?
AFFIRMATIVE, WITH A 30.275% CHANCE OF SYSTEM FAILURE.
I CONSIDER THAT AN ACCEPTABLE RISK.
I CONCUR.
AND, AT THAT MOMENT, RACING UP THE CORRIDORS OF THE PALACE TO THE THRONE ROOM...
GOT TO TRY AND :PUFF: CATCH UP TO THEM :PANT: ...GUN WASN'T BUILT FOR RUNNING WITH...
...CORRIDOR UP AHEAD LOOKS LIKE :PUFF: SCENE OF MAJOR BATTLE...
...:GASP: HARKOV PLEASE LET THEM BE ALL RIGHT!
SIMULTANEOUSLY, IN THE THRONE ROOM...
WHERE IS SHE GUARDIANS?
WHERE IS RANCOR?
SHE WILL NOT ESCAPE MY RETRIBUTION!
GIRAUD? IS THAT YOU?
YOU'RE SO... DIFFERENT.
I WAS GIRAUD... NOW I AM THE PHOENIX...
...AND I WILL HAVE THIS WORLD!
AND, IN ANOTHER PART OF THE PALACE...
MISGUIDED, IDEALISTIC FOOL!
YOU WILL HAVE NOTHING!
RELEASE THE VOLCANIC RESTRAINTS!
BUT, RANCOR, WITHOUT THOSE RESTRAINTS, THE WORLD WILL EXPLODE IN FIVE MINUTES!

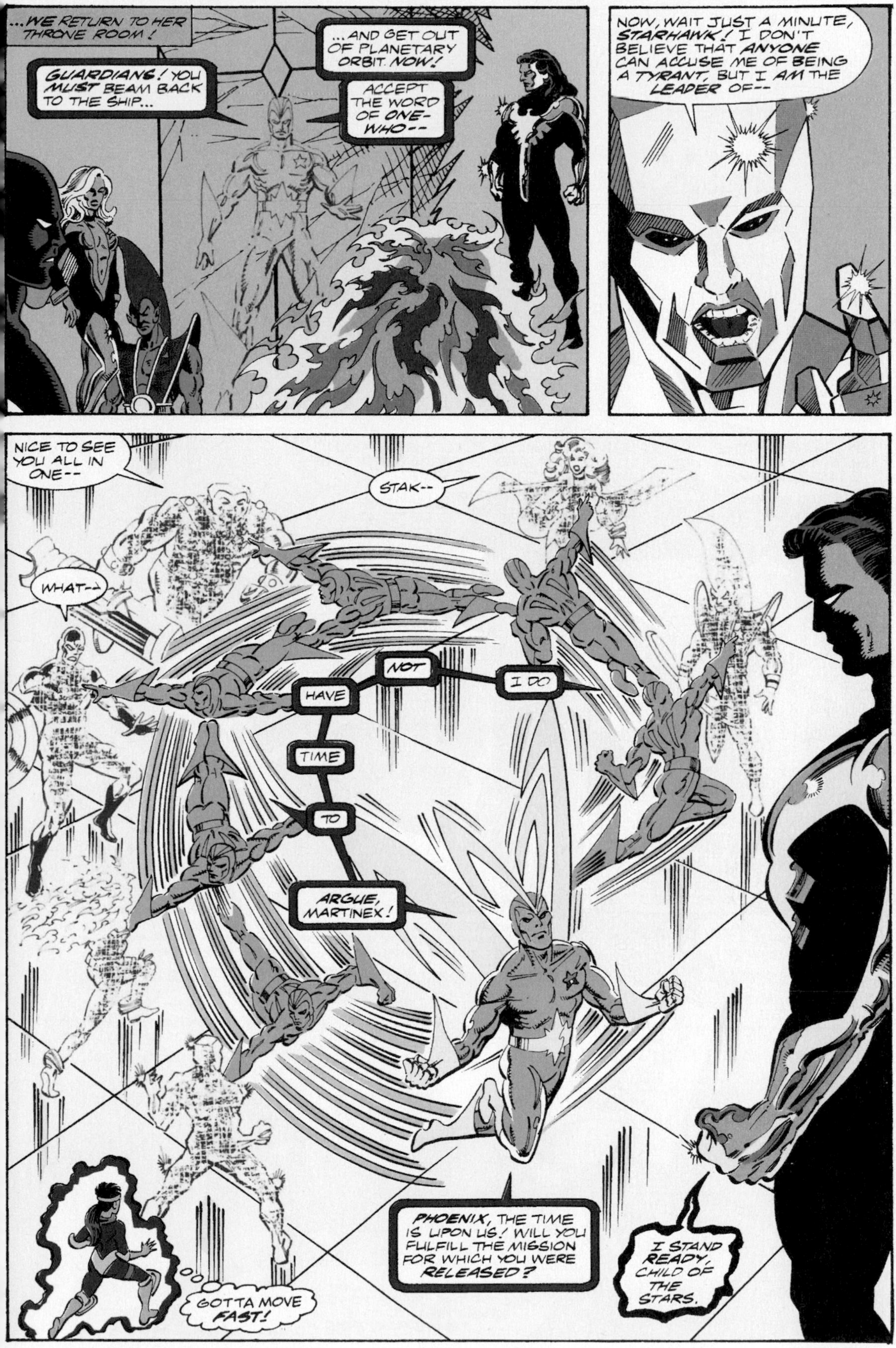
...WE RETURN TO HER THRONE ROOM!
GUARDIANS! YOU MUST BEAM BACK TO THE SHIP...
...AND GET OUT OF PLANETARY ORBIT. NOW!
ACCEPT THE WORD OF ONE-WHO--
NOW, WAIT JUST A MINUTE, STARHAWK! I DON'T BELIEVE THAT ANYONE CAN ACCUSE ME OF BEING A TYRANT, BUT I AM THE LEADER OF--
NICE TO SEE YOU ALL IN ONE--
STAK--
WHAT--
I DO
NOT
HAVE
TIME
TO
ARGUE, MARTINEX!
PHOENIX, THE TIME IS UPON US! WILL YOU FULFILL THE MISSION FOR WHICH YOU WERE RELEASED?
I STAND READY, CHILD OF THE STARS.
GOTTA MOVE FAST!

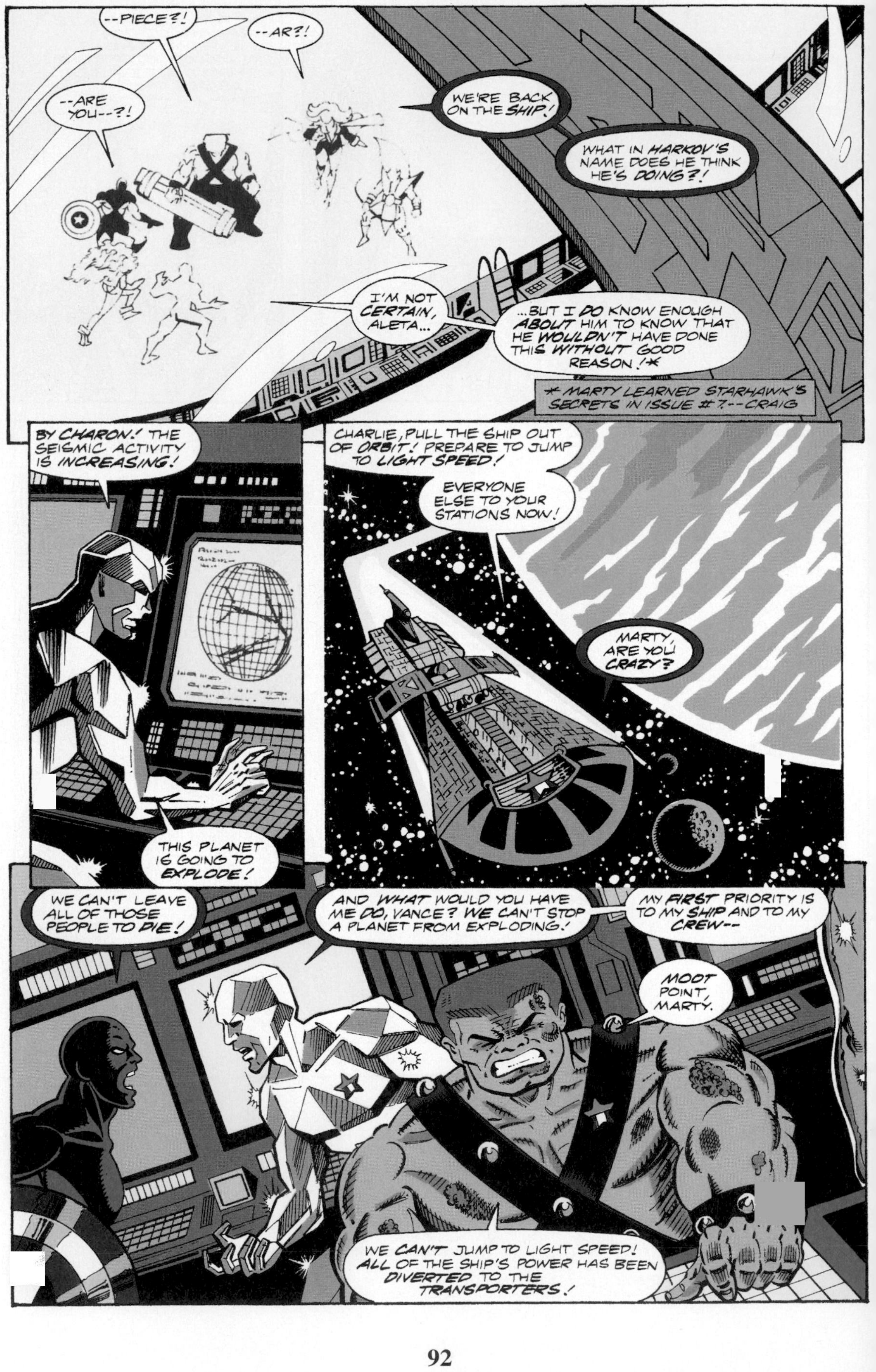
--PIECE?!
--AR?!
--ARE YOU--?!
WE'RE BACK ON THE SHIP!
WHAT IN HARKOV'S NAME DOES HE THINK HE'S DOING?!
I'M NOT CERTAIN, ALETA...
...BUT I DO KNOW ENOUGH ABOUT HIM TO KNOW THAT HE WOULDN'T HAVE DONE THIS WITHOUT GOOD REASON!*
* MARTY LEARNED STARHAWK'S SECRETS IN ISSUE #7.--CRAIG
BY CHARON! THE SEISMIC ACTIVITY IS INCREASING!
THIS PLANET IS GOING TO EXPLODE!
CHARLIE, PULL THE SHIP OUT OF ORBIT! PREPARE TO JUMP TO LIGHT SPEED!
EVERYONE ELSE TO YOUR STATIONS NOW!
MARTY, ARE YOU CRAZY?
WE CAN'T LEAVE ALL OF THOSE PEOPLE TO DIE!
AND WHAT WOULD YOU HAVE ME DO, VANCE? WE CAN'T STOP A PLANET FROM EXPLODING!
MY FIRST PRIORITY IS TO MY SHIP AND TO MY CREW--
MOOT POINT, MARTY.
WE CAN'T JUMP TO LIGHT SPEED! ALL OF THE SHIP'S POWER HAS BEEN DIVERTED TO THE TRANSPORTERS!

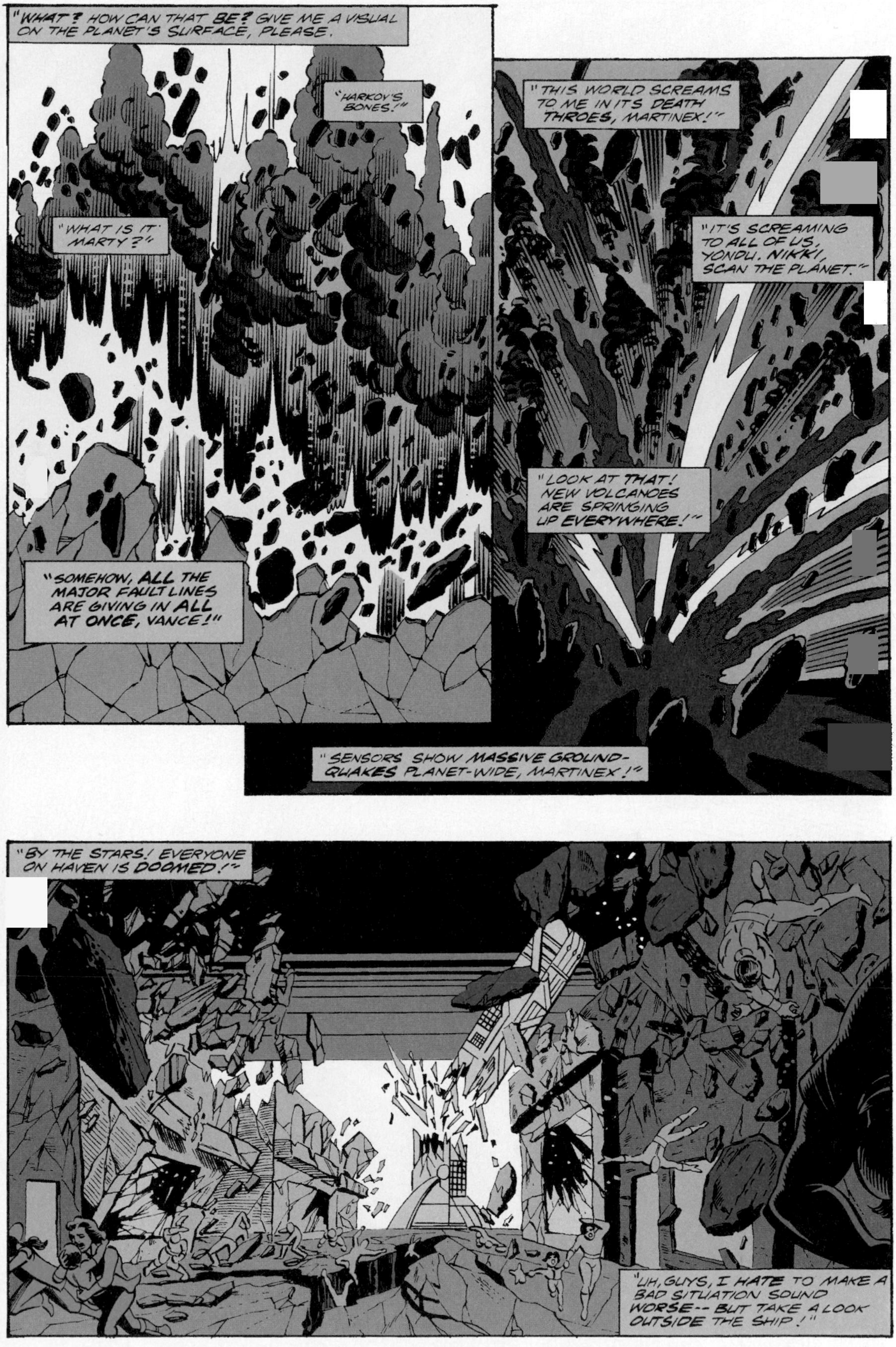
"WHAT? HOW CAN THAT BE? GIVE ME A VISUAL ON THE PLANET'S SURFACE, PLEASE.
"HARKOV'S BONES!"
"WHAT IS IT MARTY?"
"SOMEHOW, ALL THE MAJOR FAULT LINES ARE GIVING IN ALL AT ONCE, VANCE!"
"THIS WORLD SCREAMS TO ME IN ITS DEATH THROES, MARTINEX!"
"IT'S SCREAMING TO ALL OF US, YONDU. NIKKI, SCAN THE PLANET."
"LOOK AT THAT! NEW VOLCANOES ARE SPRINGING UP EVERYWHERE!"
"SENSORS SHOW MASSIVE GROUND-QUAKES PLANET-WIDE, MARTINEX!"
"BY THE STARS! EVERYONE ON HAVEN IS DOOMED!"
"UH, GUYS, I HATE TO MAKE A BAD SITUATION SOUND WORSE-- BUT TAKE A LOOK OUTSIDE THE SHIP!"

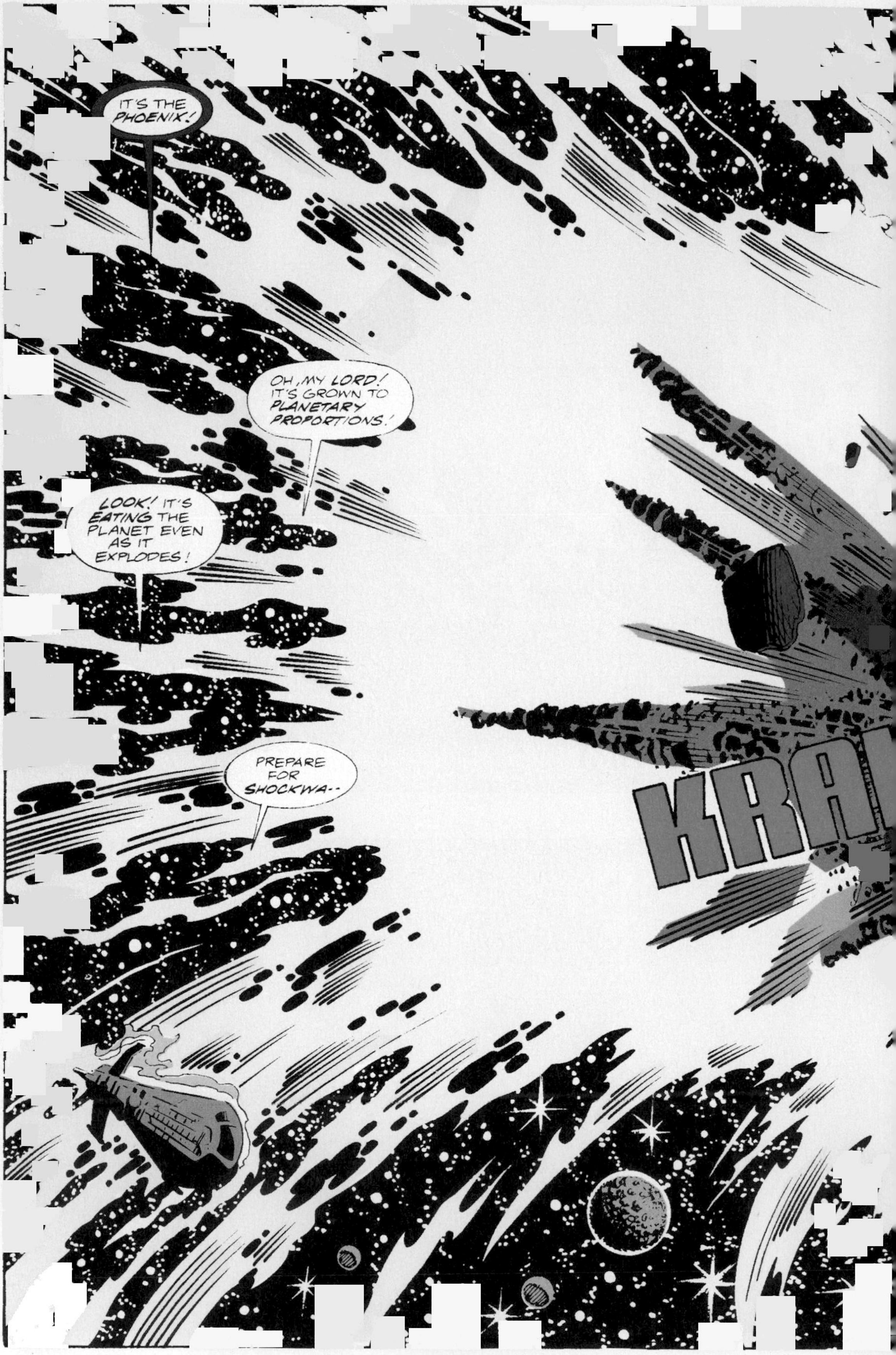

IT'S THE PHOENIX!
OH, MY LORD! IT'S GROWN TO PLANETARY PROPORTIONS!
LOOK! IT'S EATING THE PLANET EVEN AS IT EXPLODES!
PREPARE FOR SHOCKWA--
KRA

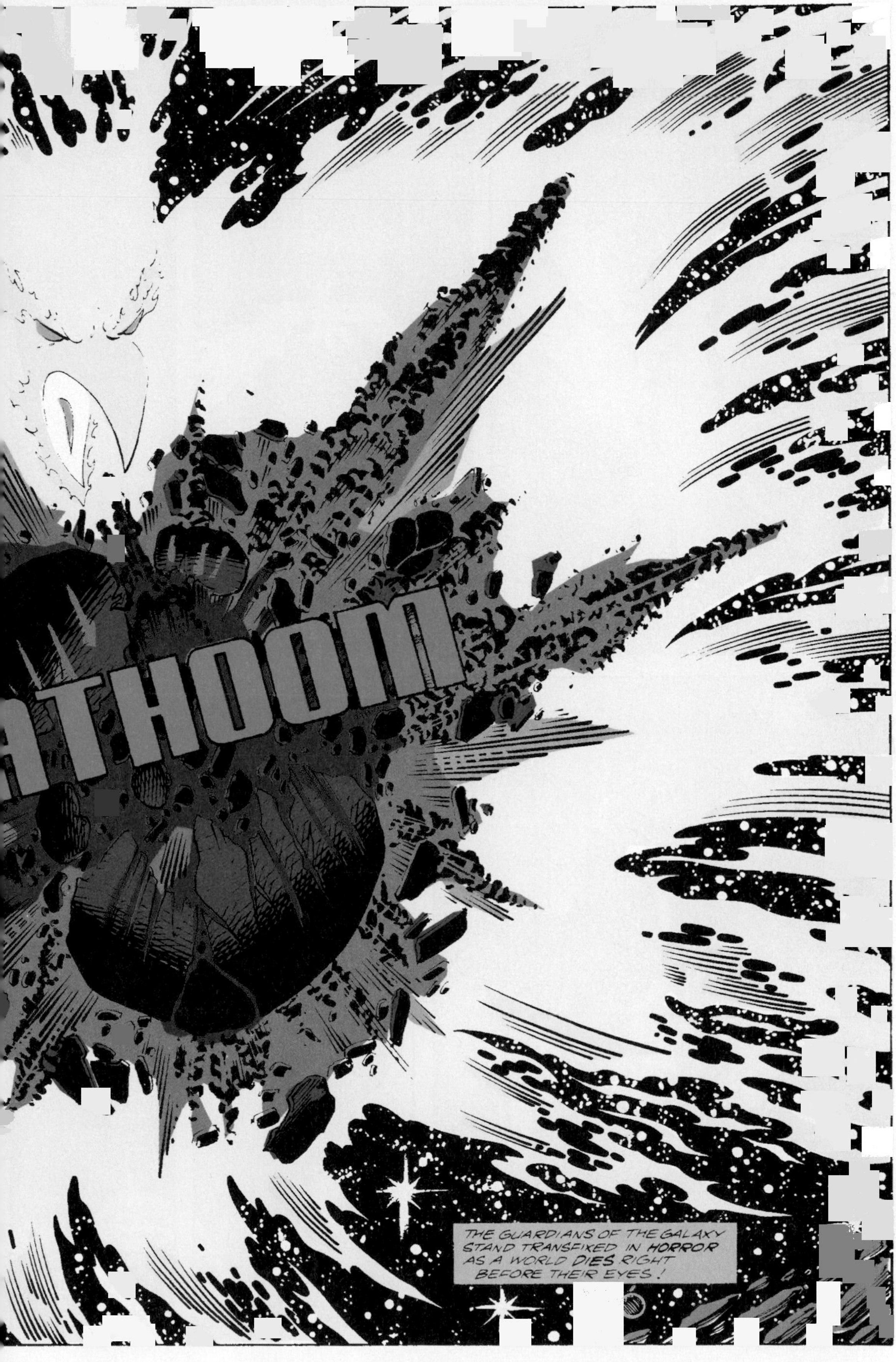
ATHOOM
THE GUARDIANS OF THE GALAXY STAND TRANSFIXED IN HORROR AS A WORLD DIES RIGHT BEFORE THEIR EYES!

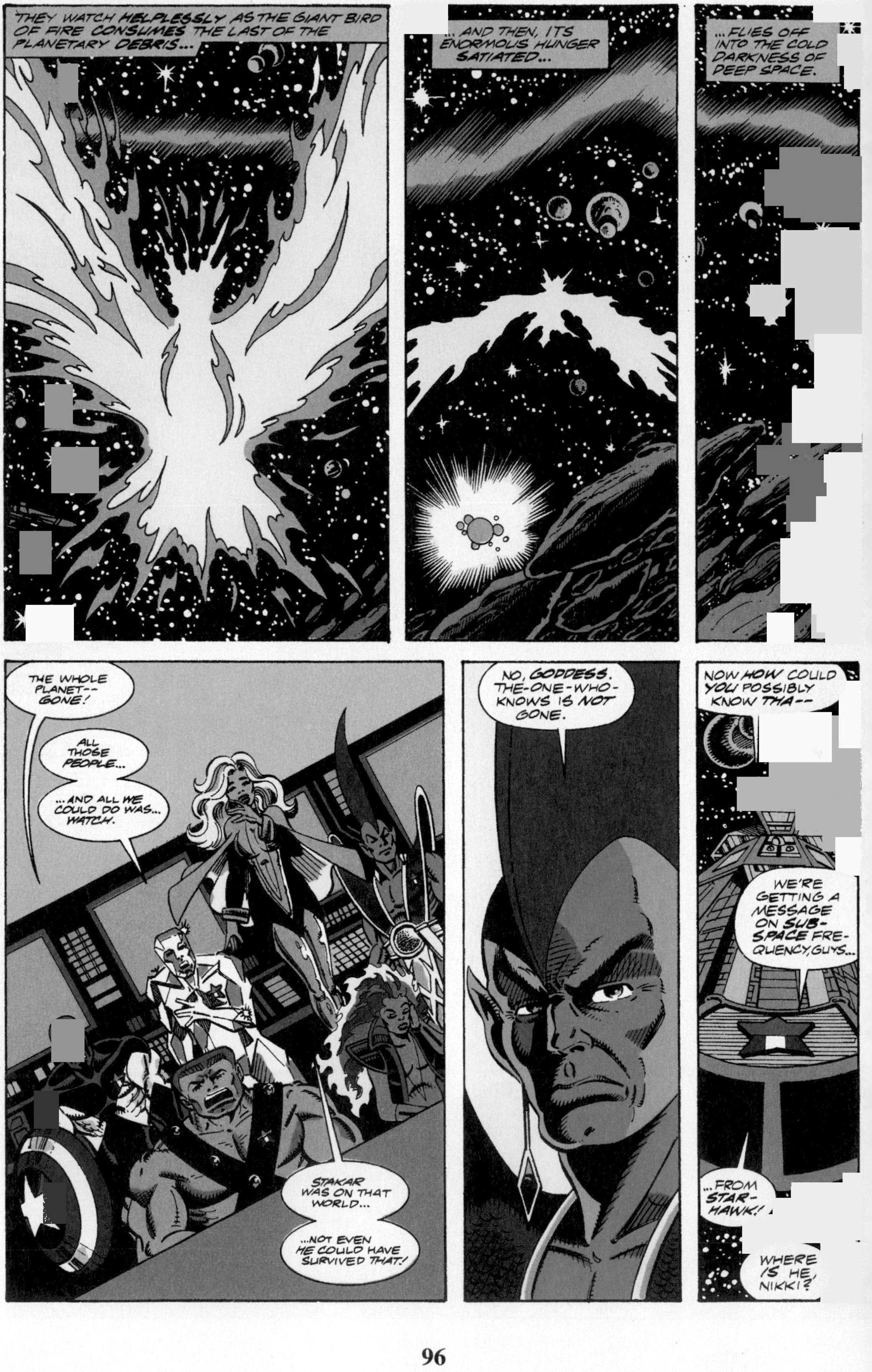
THEY WATCH HELPLESSLY AS THE GIANT BIRD OF FIRE CONSUMES THE LAST OF THE PLANETARY DEBRIS...
...AND THEN, ITS ENORMOUS HUNGER SATIATED...
...FLIES OFF INTO THE COLD DARKNESS OF DEEP SPACE.
THE WHOLE PLANET--GONE!
ALL THOSE PEOPLE...
...AND ALL WE COULD DO WAS... WATCH.
STAKAR WAS ON THAT WORLD...
...NOT EVEN HE COULD HAVE SURVIVED THAT!
NO, GODDESS. THE-ONE-WHO-KNOWS IS NOT GONE.
NOW HOW COULD YOU POSSIBLY KNOW THA--
WE'RE GETTING A MESSAGE ON SUB-SPACE FRE-QUENCY, GUYS...
...FROM STAR-HAWK!
WHERE IS HE, NIKKI?

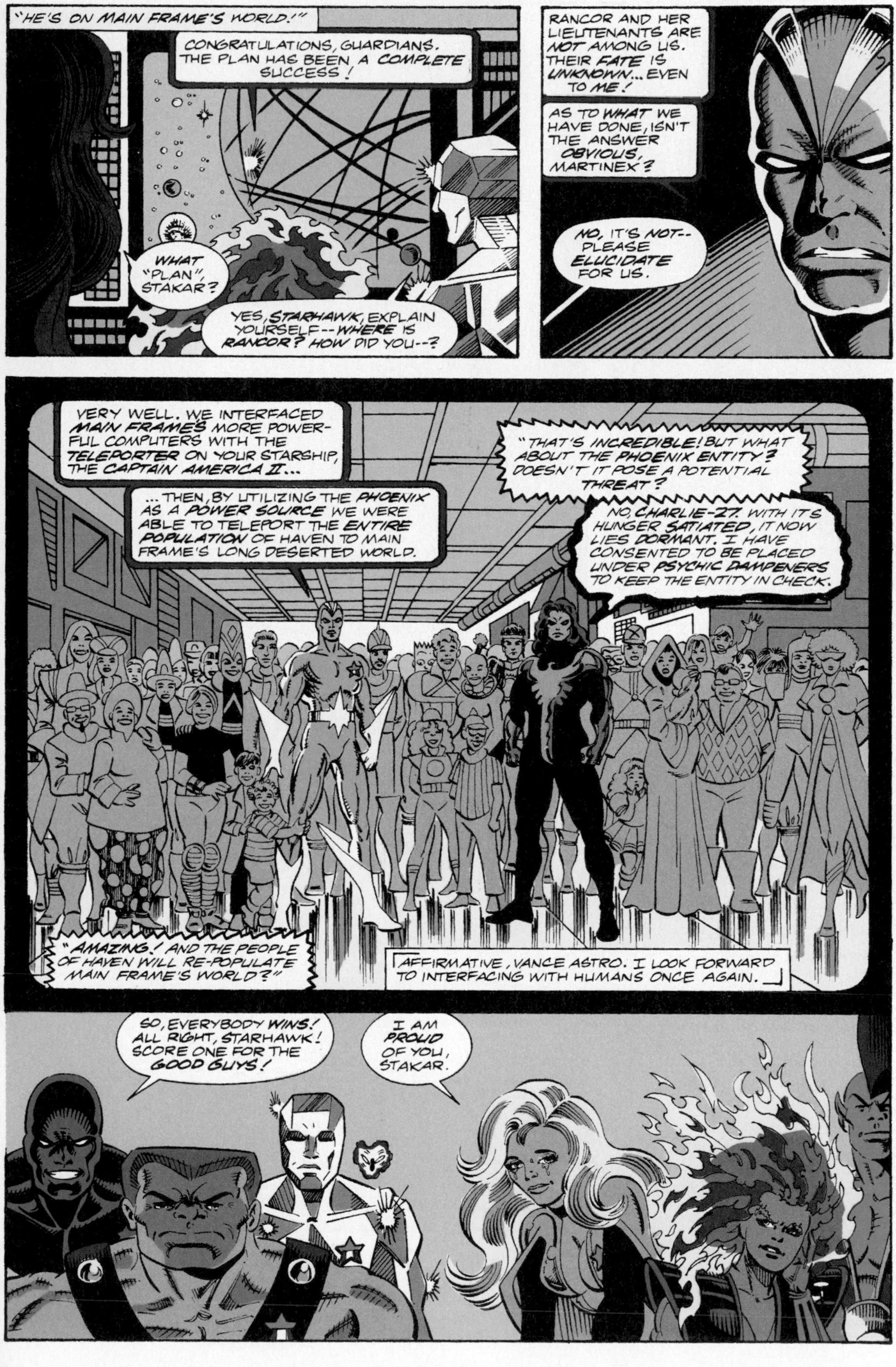
"HE'S ON MAIN FRAME'S WORLD!"
CONGRATULATIONS, GUARDIANS. THE PLAN HAS BEEN A COMPLETE SUCCESS!
WHAT "PLAN", STAKAR?
YES, STARHAWK, EXPLAIN YOURSELF--WHERE IS RANCOR? HOW DID YOU--?
RANCOR AND HER LIEUTENANTS ARE NOT AMONG US. THEIR FATE IS UNKNOWN... EVEN TO ME!
AS TO WHAT WE HAVE DONE, ISN'T THE ANSWER OBVIOUS, MARTINEX?
NO, IT'S NOT-- PLEASE ELUCIDATE FOR US.
VERY WELL. WE INTERFACED MAIN FRAME'S MORE POWERFUL COMPUTERS WITH THE TELEPORTER ON YOUR STARSHIP, THE CAPTAIN AMERICA II...
...THEN, BY UTILIZING THE PHOENIX AS A POWER SOURCE WE WERE ABLE TO TELEPORT THE ENTIRE POPULATION OF HAVEN TO MAIN FRAME'S LONG DESERTED WORLD.
"THAT'S INCREDIBLE! BUT WHAT ABOUT THE PHOENIX ENTITY? DOESN'T IT POSE A POTENTIAL THREAT?
NO, CHARLIE-27. WITH IT'S HUNGER SATIATED, IT NOW LIES DORMANT. I HAVE CONSENTED TO BE PLACED UNDER PSYCHIC DAMPENERS TO KEEP THE ENTITY IN CHECK.
"AMAZING! AND THE PEOPLE OF HAVEN WILL RE-POPULATE MAIN FRAME'S WORLD?"
AFFIRMATIVE, VANCE ASTRO. I LOOK FORWARD TO INTERFACING WITH HUMANS ONCE AGAIN.
SO, EVERYBODY WINS! ALL RIGHT, STARHAWK! SCORE ONE FOR THE GOOD GUYS!
I AM PROUD OF YOU, STAKAR.

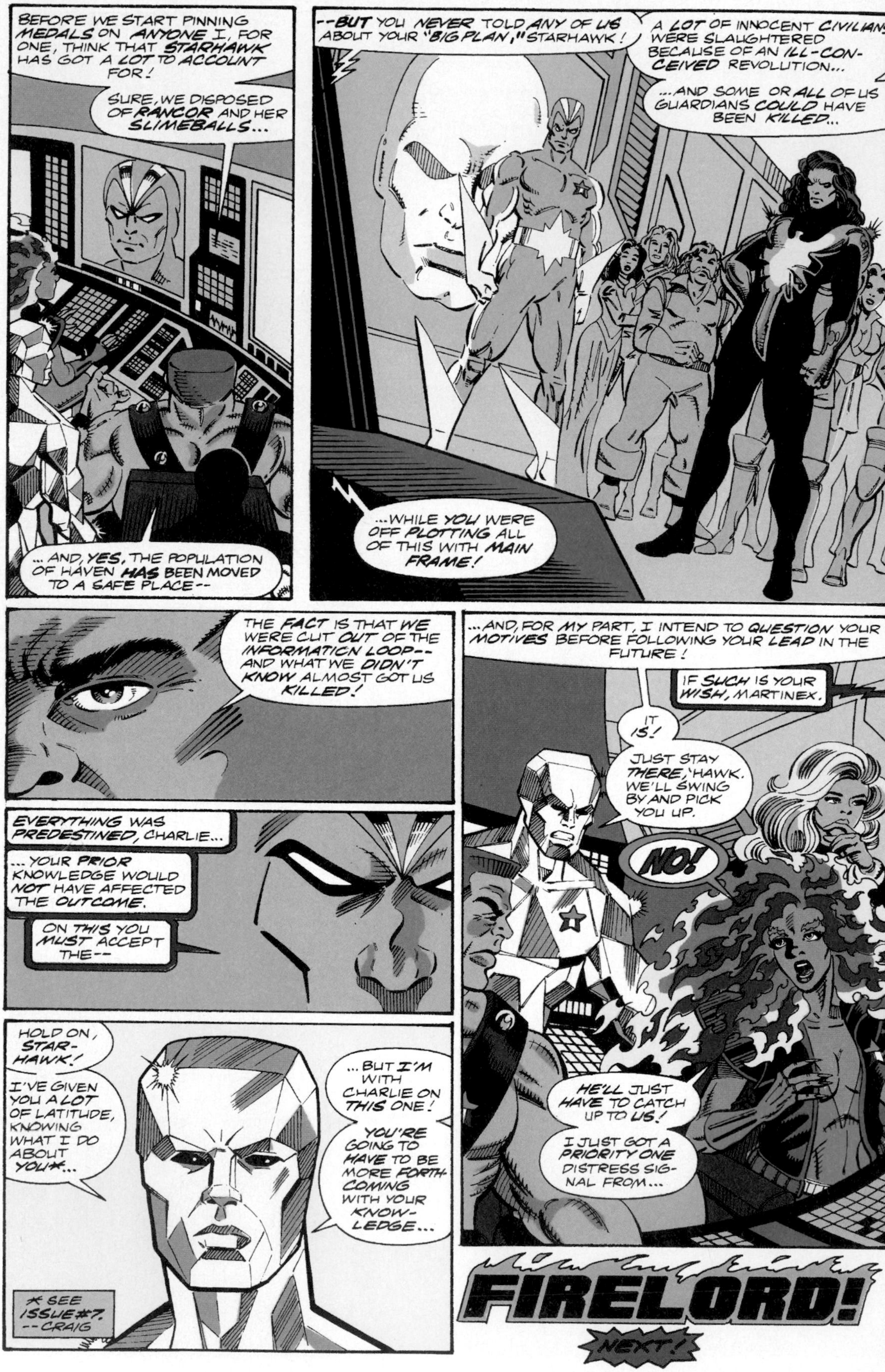
BEFORE WE START PINNING MEDALS ON ANYONE I, FOR ONE, THINK THAT STARHAWK HAS GOT A LOT TO ACCOUNT FOR!
SURE, WE DISPOSED OF RANCOR AND HER SLIMEBALLS...
...AND, YES, THE POPULATION OF HAVEN HAS BEEN MOVED TO A SAFE PLACE--
--BUT YOU NEVER TOLD ANY OF US ABOUT YOUR "BIG PLAN," STARHAWK!
A LOT OF INNOCENT CIVILIANS WERE SLAUGHTERED BECAUSE OF AN ILL-CONCEIVED REVOLUTION...
...AND SOME OR ALL OF US GUARDIANS COULD HAVE BEEN KILLED...
...WHILE YOU WERE OFF PLOTTING ALL OF THIS WITH MAIN FRAME!
THE FACT IS THAT WE WERE CUT OUT OF THE INFORMATION LOOP--AND WHAT WE DIDN'T KNOW ALMOST GOT US KILLED!
EVERYTHING WAS PREDESTINED, CHARLIE...
...YOUR PRIOR KNOWLEDGE WOULD NOT HAVE AFFECTED THE OUTCOME.
ON THIS YOU MUST ACCEPT THE--
HOLD ON, STAR-HAWK!
I'VE GIVEN YOU A LOT OF LATITUDE, KNOWING WHAT I DO ABOUT YOU*...
...BUT I'M WITH CHARLIE ON THIS ONE!
YOU'RE GOING TO HAVE TO BE MORE FORTHCOMING WITH YOUR KNOWLEDGE...
* SEE ISSUE #7. --CRAIG
...AND, FOR MY PART, I INTEND TO QUESTION YOUR MOTIVES BEFORE FOLLOWING YOUR LEAD IN THE FUTURE!
IF SUCH IS YOUR WISH, MARTINEX.
IT IS!
JUST STAY THERE, 'HAWK. WE'LL SWING BY AND PICK YOU UP.
NO!
HE'LL JUST HAVE TO CATCH UP TO US!
I JUST GOT A PRIORITY ONE DISTRESS SIGNAL FROM...
FIRELORD!
NEXT!

GUARDIANS
OF THE GALAXY

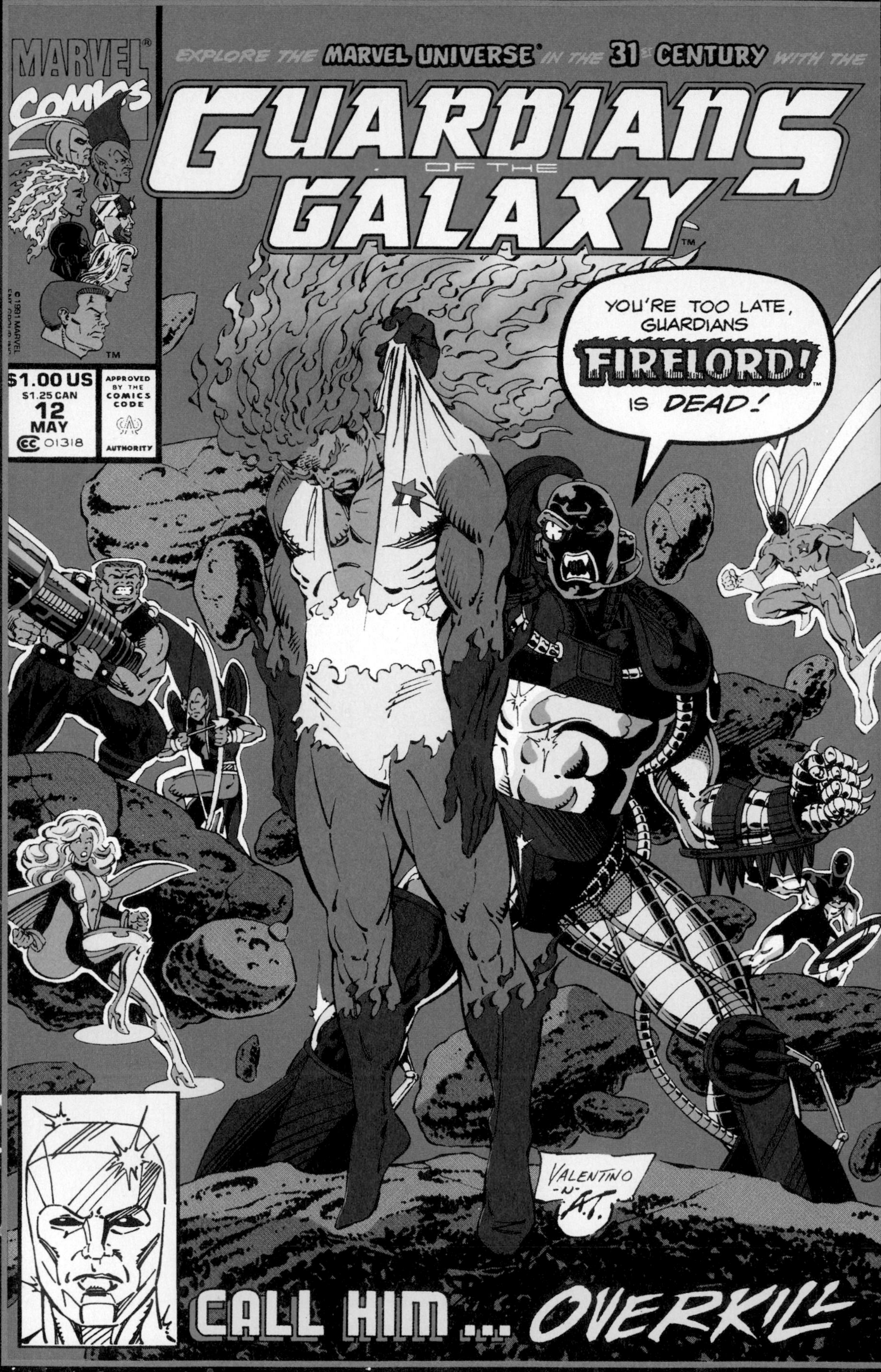
MARVEL COMICS
EXPLORE THE MARVEL UNIVERSE IN THE 31st CENTURY WITH THE
GUARDIANS OF THE GALAXY
$1.00 US
$1.25 CAN
12
MAY
01318
APPROVED BY THE COMICS CODE AUTHORITY
YOU'RE TOO LATE, GUARDIANS
FIRELORD! IS DEAD!
VALENTINO -N- A.T.
CALL HIM ... OVERKILL

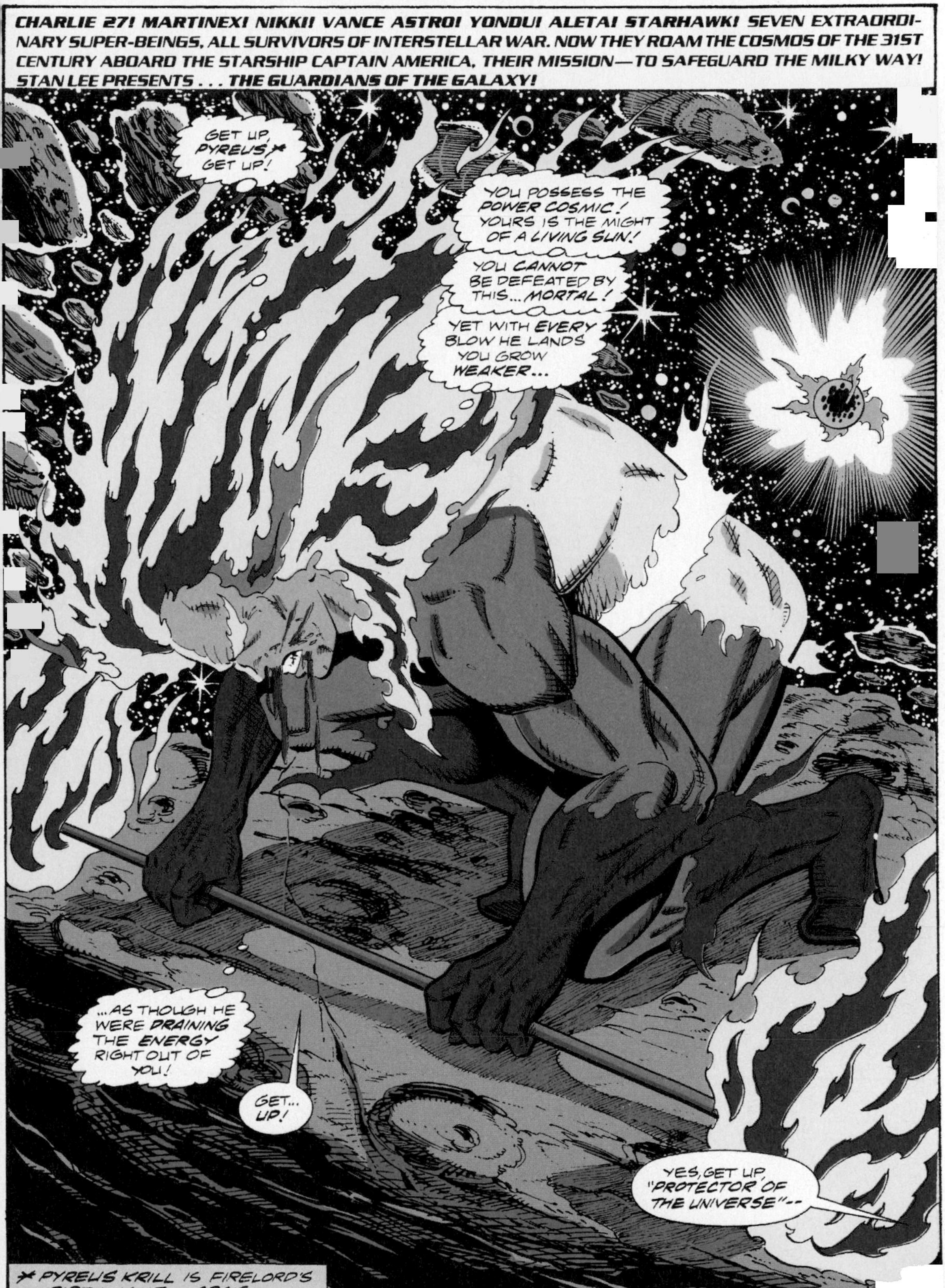
CHARLIE 27! MARTINEX! NIKKI! VANCE ASTRO! YONDU! ALETA! STARHAWK! SEVEN EXTRAORDINARY SUPER-BEINGS, ALL SURVIVORS OF INTERSTELLAR WAR. NOW THEY ROAM THE COSMOS OF THE 31ST CENTURY ABOARD THE STARSHIP CAPTAIN AMERICA, THEIR MISSION—TO SAFEGUARD THE MILKY WAY! STAN LEE PRESENTS . . . THE GUARDIANS OF THE GALAXY!
GET UP, PYREUS,* GET UP!
YOU POSSESS THE POWER COSMIC! YOURS IS THE MIGHT OF A LIVING SUN!
YOU CANNOT BE DEFEATED BY THIS... MORTAL!
YET WITH EVERY BLOW HE LANDS YOU GROW WEAKER...
...AS THOUGH HE WERE DRAINING THE ENERGY RIGHT OUT OF YOU!
GET... UP!
YES, GET UP, "PROTECTOR OF THE UNIVERSE"--
* PYREUS KRILL IS FIRELORD'S BIRTH NAME.-- CRAIG

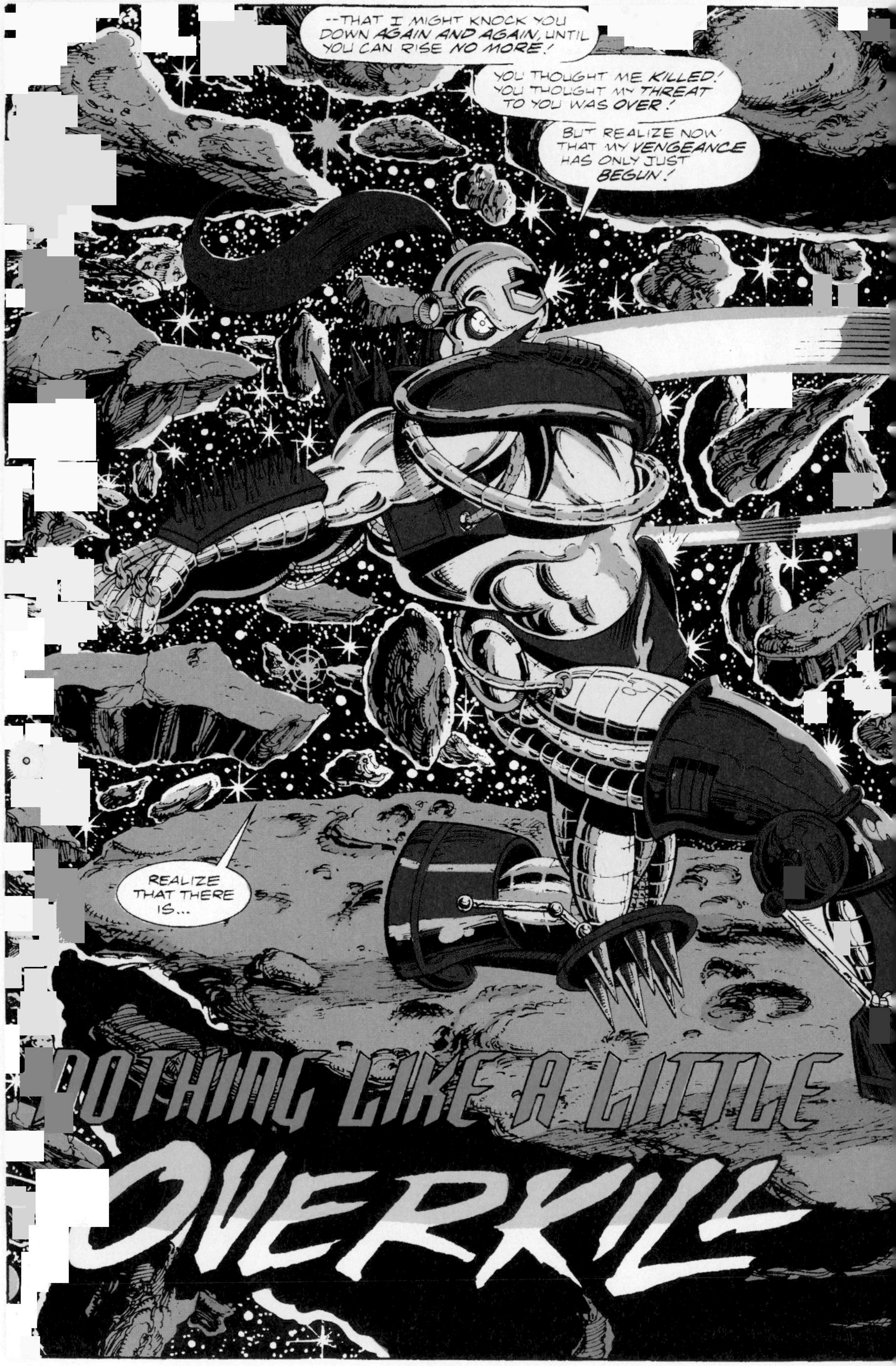
--THAT I MIGHT KNOCK YOU DOWN AGAIN AND AGAIN, UNTIL YOU CAN RISE NO MORE!
YOU THOUGHT ME KILLED! YOU THOUGHT MY THREAT TO YOU WAS OVER!
BUT REALIZE NOW THAT MY VENGEANCE HAS ONLY JUST BEGUN!
REALIZE THAT THERE IS...
NOTHING LIKE A LITTLE
OVERKILL

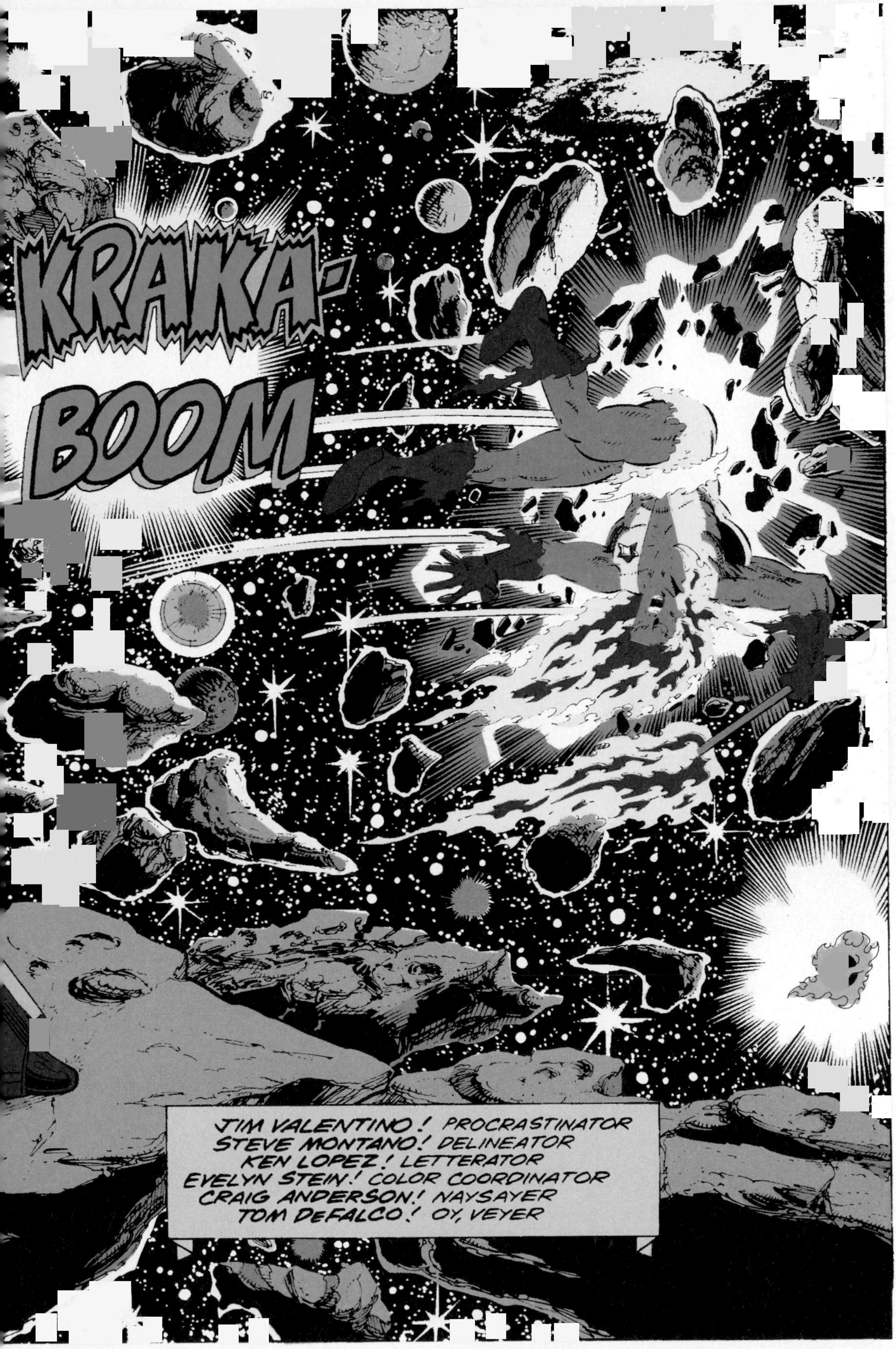
KRAKA-BOOM
JIM VALENTINO! PROCRASTINATOR
STEVE MONTANO! DELINEATOR
KEN LOPEZ! LETTERATOR
EVELYN STEIN! COLOR COORDINATOR
CRAIG ANDERSON! NAYSAYER
TOM DEFALCO! OY, VEYER

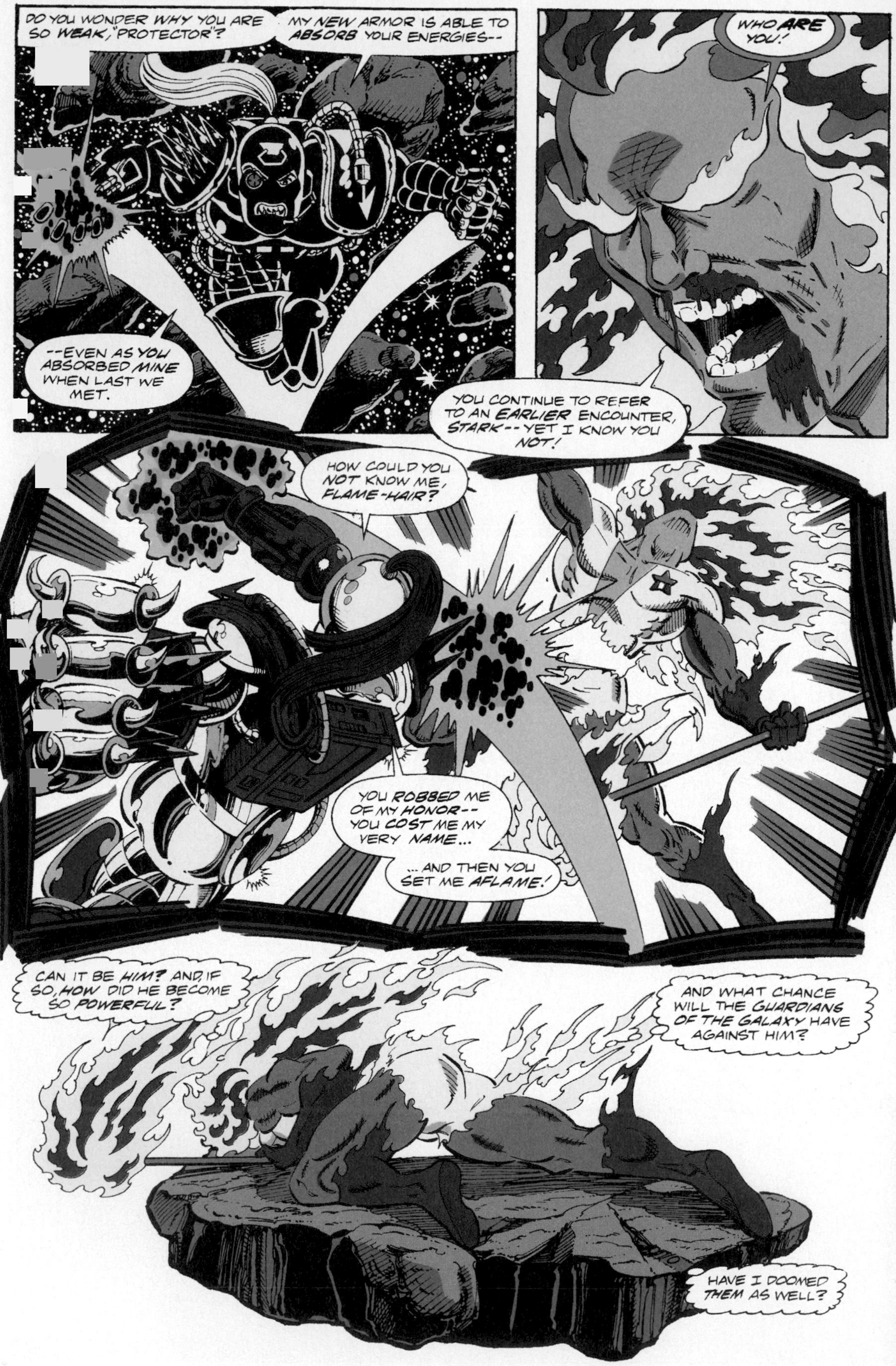
DO YOU WONDER WHY YOU ARE SO WEAK, "PROTECTOR"?
MY NEW ARMOR IS ABLE TO ABSORB YOUR ENERGIES--
--EVEN AS YOU ABSORBED MINE WHEN LAST WE MET.
WHO ARE YOU!
YOU CONTINUE TO REFER TO AN EARLIER ENCOUNTER, STARK--YET I KNOW YOU NOT!
HOW COULD YOU NOT KNOW ME, FLAME-HAIR?
YOU ROBBED ME OF MY HONOR--YOU COST ME MY VERY NAME...
...AND THEN YOU SET ME AFLAME!
CAN IT BE HIM? AND, IF SO, HOW DID HE BECOME SO POWERFUL?
AND WHAT CHANCE WILL THE GUARDIANS OF THE GALAXY HAVE AGAINST HIM?
HAVE I DOOMED THEM AS WELL?

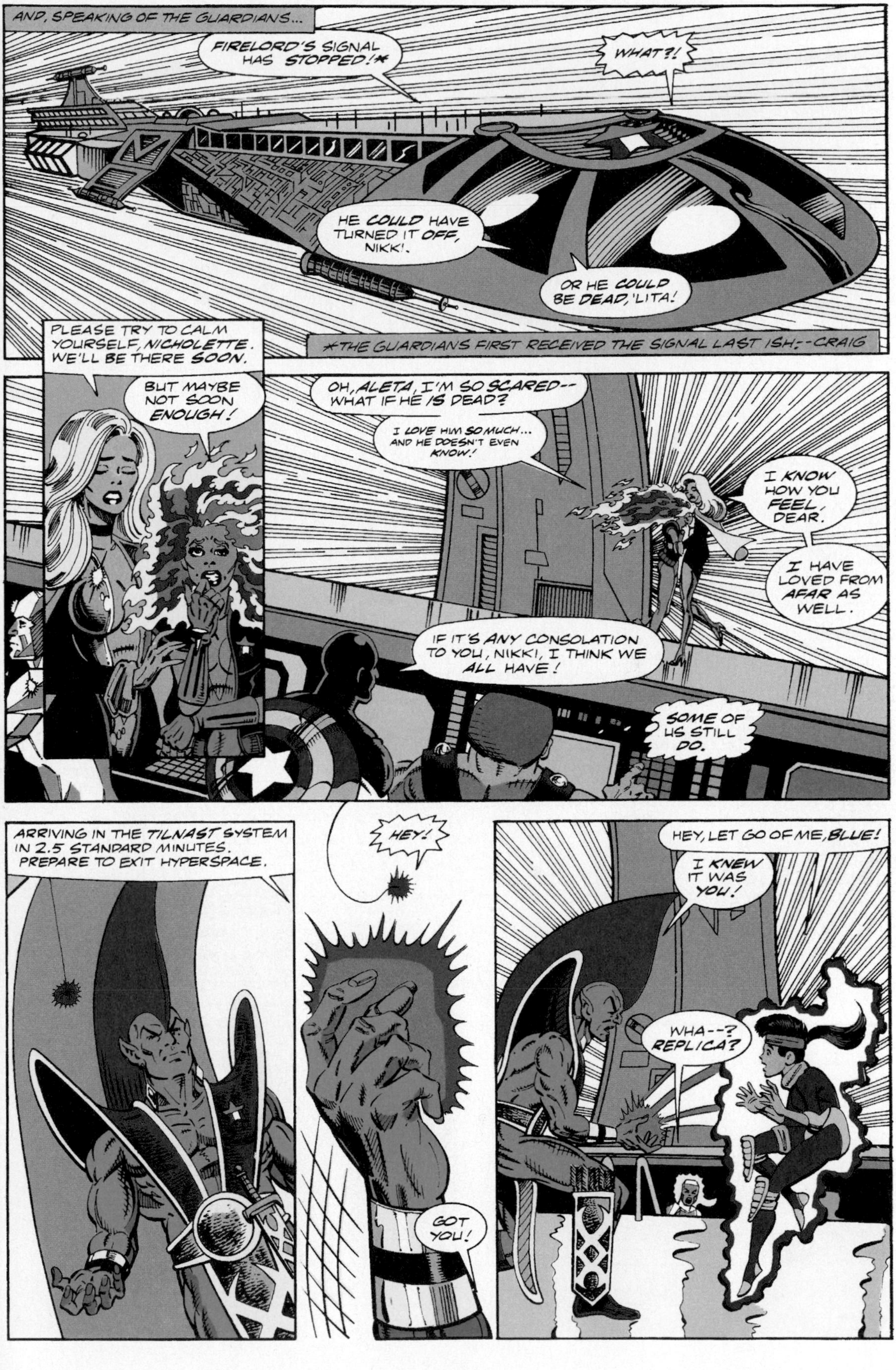
AND, SPEAKING OF THE GUARDIANS...
FIRELORD'S SIGNAL HAS STOPPED! *
WHAT?!
HE COULD HAVE TURNED IT OFF, NIKK!.
OR HE COULD BE DEAD, 'LITA!
*THE GUARDIANS FIRST RECEIVED THE SIGNAL LAST ISH.--CRAIG
PLEASE TRY TO CALM YOURSELF, NICHOLETTE. WE'LL BE THERE SOON.
BUT MAYBE NOT SOON ENOUGH!
OH, ALETA, I'M SO SCARED-- WHAT IF HE IS DEAD?
I LOVE HIM SO MUCH... AND HE DOESN'T EVEN KNOW!
I KNOW HOW YOU FEEL, DEAR.
I HAVE LOVED FROM AFAR AS WELL.
IF IT'S ANY CONSOLATION TO YOU, NIKK!, I THINK WE ALL HAVE!
SOME OF US STILL DO.
ARRIVING IN THE TILNAST SYSTEM IN 2.5 STANDARD MINUTES. PREPARE TO EXIT HYPERSPACE.
HEY!
GOT YOU!
HEY, LET GO OF ME, BLUE!
I KNEW IT WAS YOU!
WHA--? REPLICA?

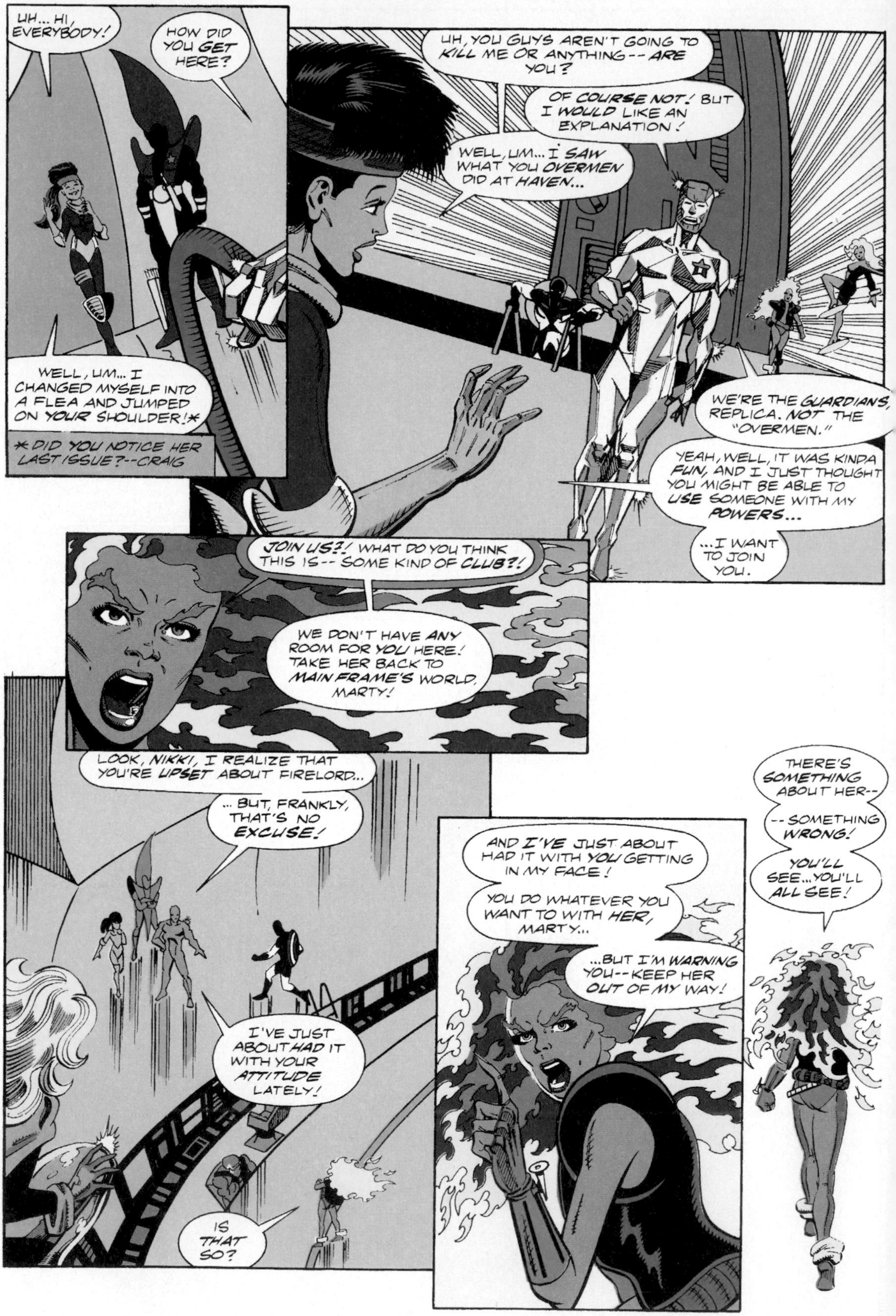
UH... HI, EVERYBODY!
HOW DID YOU GET HERE?
WELL, UM... I CHANGED MYSELF INTO A FLEA AND JUMPED ON YOUR SHOULDER!*
*DID YOU NOTICE HER LAST ISSUE?--CRAIG
UH, YOU GUYS AREN'T GOING TO KILL ME OR ANYTHING-- ARE YOU?
OF COURSE NOT! BUT I WOULD LIKE AN EXPLANATION!
WELL, UM... I SAW WHAT YOU OVERMEN DID AT HAVEN...
WE'RE THE GUARDIANS, REPLICA. NOT THE "OVERMEN."
YEAH, WELL, IT WAS KINDA FUN, AND I JUST THOUGHT YOU MIGHT BE ABLE TO USE SOMEONE WITH MY POWERS...
...I WANT TO JOIN YOU.
JOIN US?! WHAT DO YOU THINK THIS IS-- SOME KIND OF CLUB?!
WE DON'T HAVE ANY ROOM FOR YOU HERE! TAKE HER BACK TO MAINFRAME'S WORLD, MARTY!
LOOK, NIKKI, I REALIZE THAT YOU'RE UPSET ABOUT FIRELORD...
... BUT, FRANKLY, THAT'S NO EXCUSE!
I'VE JUST ABOUT HAD IT WITH YOUR ATTITUDE LATELY!
IS THAT SO?
AND I'VE JUST ABOUT HAD IT WITH YOU GETTING IN MY FACE!
YOU DO WHATEVER YOU WANT TO WITH HER, MARTY...
...BUT I'M WARNING YOU-- KEEP HER OUT OF MY WAY!
THERE'S SOMETHING ABOUT HER--
--SOMETHING WRONG!
YOU'LL SEE...YOU'LL ALL SEE!

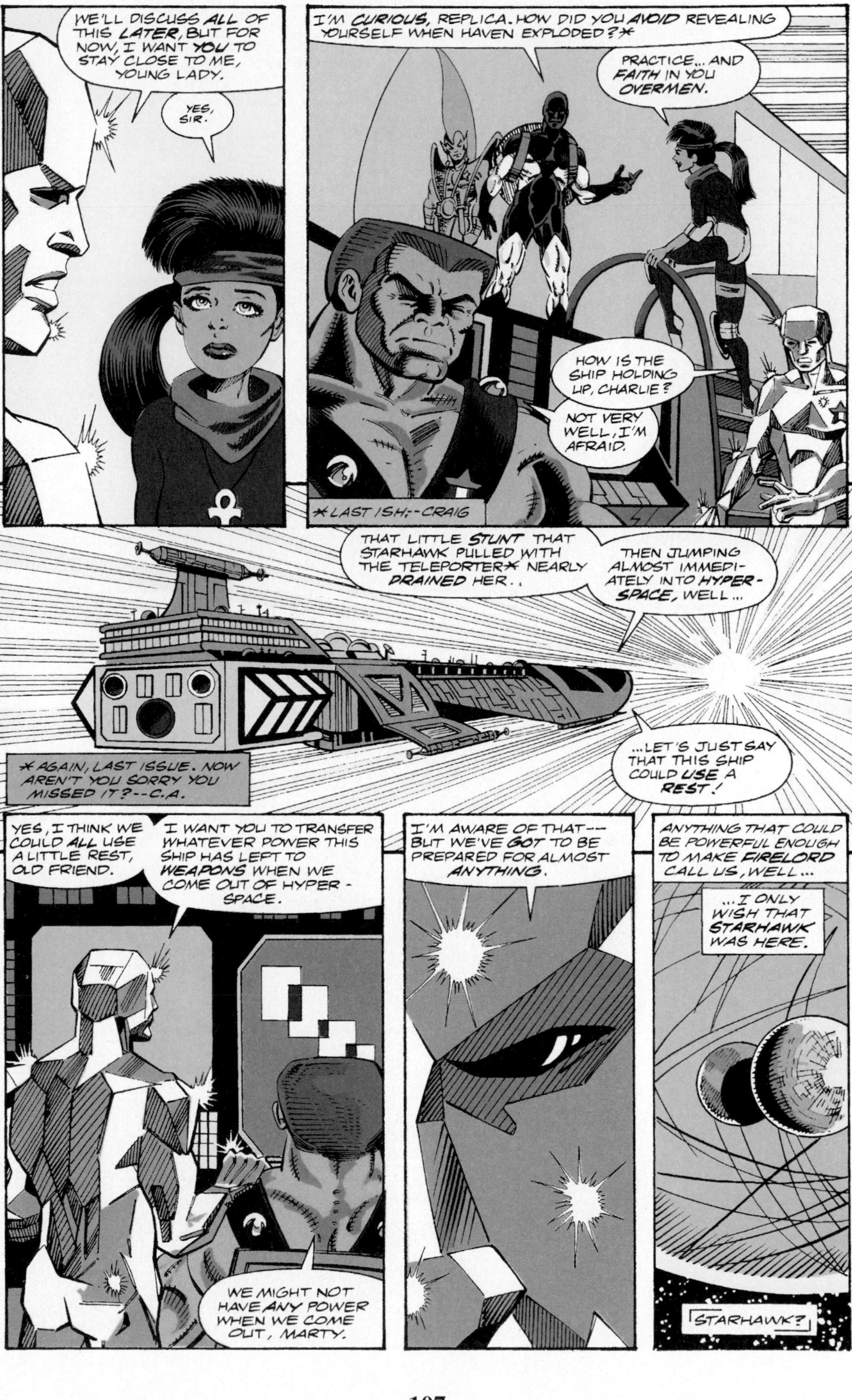
WE'LL DISCUSS ALL OF THIS LATER, BUT FOR NOW, I WANT YOU TO STAY CLOSE TO ME, YOUNG LADY.
YES, SIR.
I'M CURIOUS, REPLICA. HOW DID YOU AVOID REVEALING YOURSELF WHEN HAVEN EXPLODED?*
PRACTICE... AND FAITH IN YOU OVERMEN.
HOW IS THE SHIP HOLDING UP, CHARLIE?
NOT VERY WELL, I'M AFRAID.
*LAST ISH.--CRAIG
THAT LITTLE STUNT THAT STARHAWK PULLED WITH THE TELEPORTER* NEARLY DRAINED HER..
THEN JUMPING ALMOST IMMEDIATELY INTO HYPER-SPACE, WELL...
...LET'S JUST SAY THAT THIS SHIP COULD USE A REST!
*AGAIN, LAST ISSUE. NOW AREN'T YOU SORRY YOU MISSED IT?--C.A.
YES, I THINK WE COULD ALL USE A LITTLE REST, OLD FRIEND.
I WANT YOU TO TRANSFER WHATEVER POWER THIS SHIP HAS LEFT TO WEAPONS WHEN WE COME OUT OF HYPER-SPACE.
WE MIGHT NOT HAVE ANY POWER WHEN WE COME OUT, MARTY.
I'M AWARE OF THAT--BUT WE'VE GOT TO BE PREPARED FOR ALMOST ANYTHING.
ANYTHING THAT COULD BE POWERFUL ENOUGH TO MAKE FIRELORD CALL US, WELL...
...I ONLY WISH THAT STARHAWK WAS HERE.
STARHAWK?

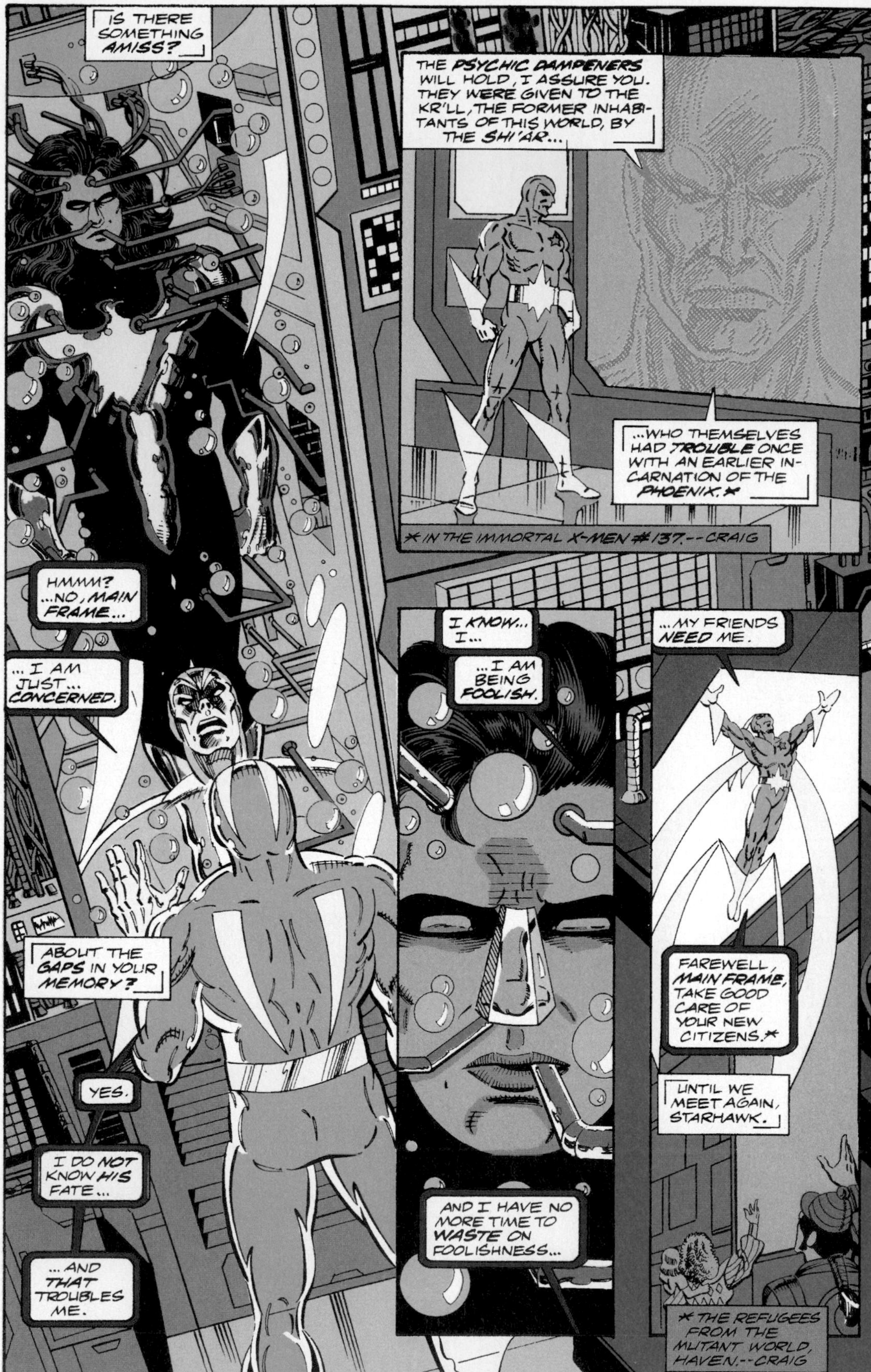
IS THERE SOMETHING AMISS?
THE PSYCHIC DAMPENERS WILL HOLD, I ASSURE YOU. THEY WERE GIVEN TO THE KR'LL, THE FORMER INHABITANTS OF THIS WORLD, BY THE SHI'AR...
...WHO THEMSELVES HAD TROUBLE ONCE WITH AN EARLIER INCARNATION OF THE PHOENIX.*
* IN THE IMMORTAL X-MEN #137.--CRAIG
HMMM? ...NO, MAIN FRAME...
...I AM JUST... CONCERNED.
ABOUT THE GAPS IN YOUR MEMORY?
YES.
I DO NOT KNOW HIS FATE...
...AND THAT TROUBLES ME.
I KNOW... I...
...I AM BEING FOOLISH.
AND I HAVE NO MORE TIME TO WASTE ON FOOLISHNESS...
...MY FRIENDS NEED ME.
FAREWELL, MAIN FRAME. TAKE GOOD CARE OF YOUR NEW CITIZENS.*
UNTIL WE MEET AGAIN, STARHAWK.
* THE REFUGEES FROM THE MUTANT WORLD, HAVEN.--CRAIG

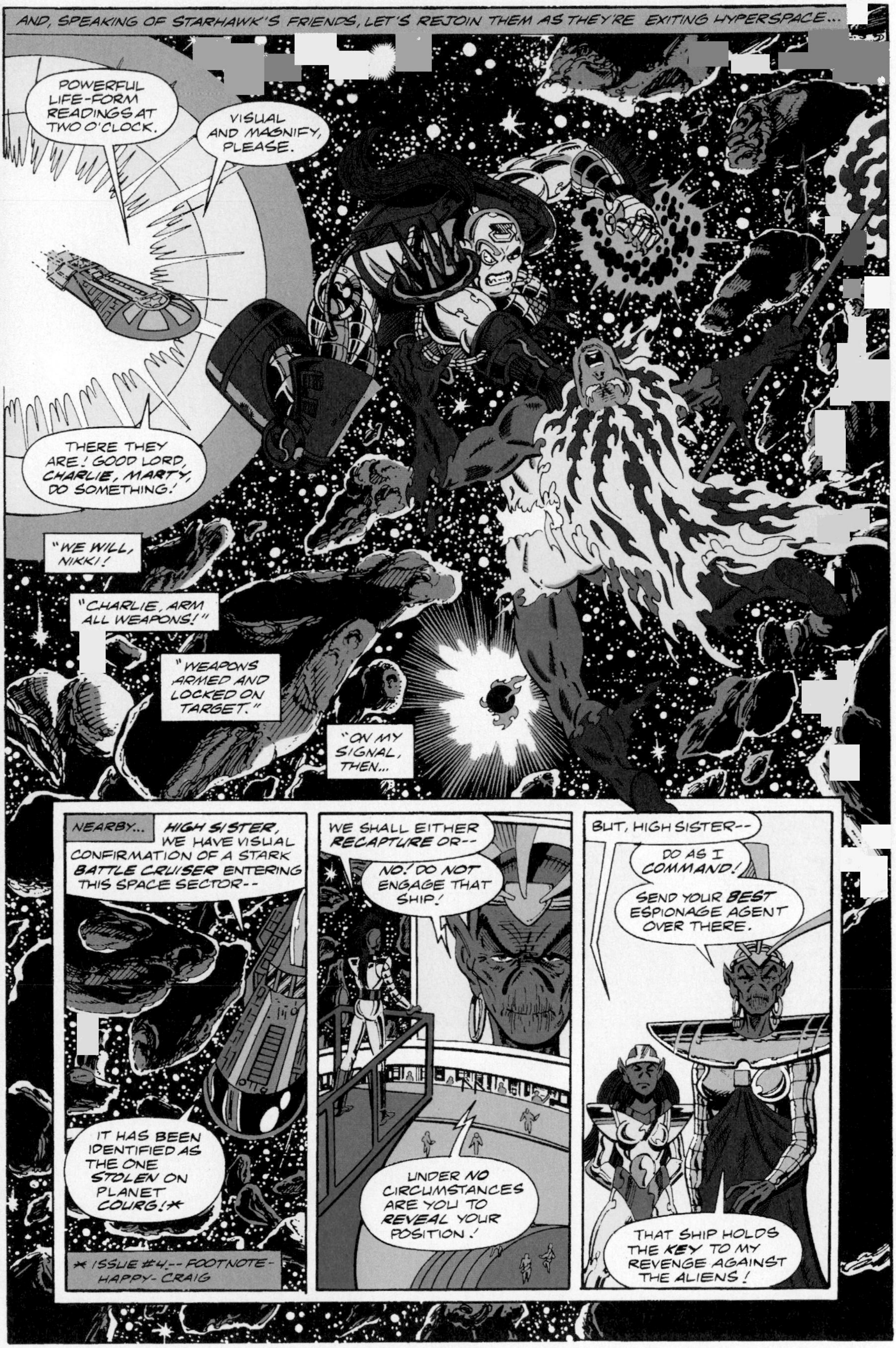
AND, SPEAKING OF STARHAWK'S FRIENDS, LET'S REJOIN THEM AS THEY'RE EXITING HYPERSPACE...
POWERFUL LIFE-FORM READINGS AT TWO O'CLOCK.
VISUAL AND MAGNIFY, PLEASE.
THERE THEY ARE! GOOD LORD, CHARLIE, MARTY, DO SOMETHING!
"WE WILL, NIKKI!
"CHARLIE, ARM ALL WEAPONS!"
"WEAPONS ARMED AND LOCKED ON TARGET."
"ON MY SIGNAL, THEN...
NEARBY...
HIGH SISTER, WE HAVE VISUAL CONFIRMATION OF A STARK BATTLE CRUISER ENTERING THIS SPACE SECTOR--
IT HAS BEEN IDENTIFIED AS THE ONE STOLEN ON PLANET COURG!*
* ISSUE #4 -- FOOTNOTE-HAPPY-CRAIG
WE SHALL EITHER RECAPTURE OR--
NO! DO NOT ENGAGE THAT SHIP!
UNDER NO CIRCUMSTANCES ARE YOU TO REVEAL YOUR POSITION!
BUT, HIGH SISTER--
DO AS I COMMAND!
SEND YOUR BEST ESPIONAGE AGENT OVER THERE.
THAT SHIP HOLDS THE KEY TO MY REVENGE AGAINST THE ALIENS!

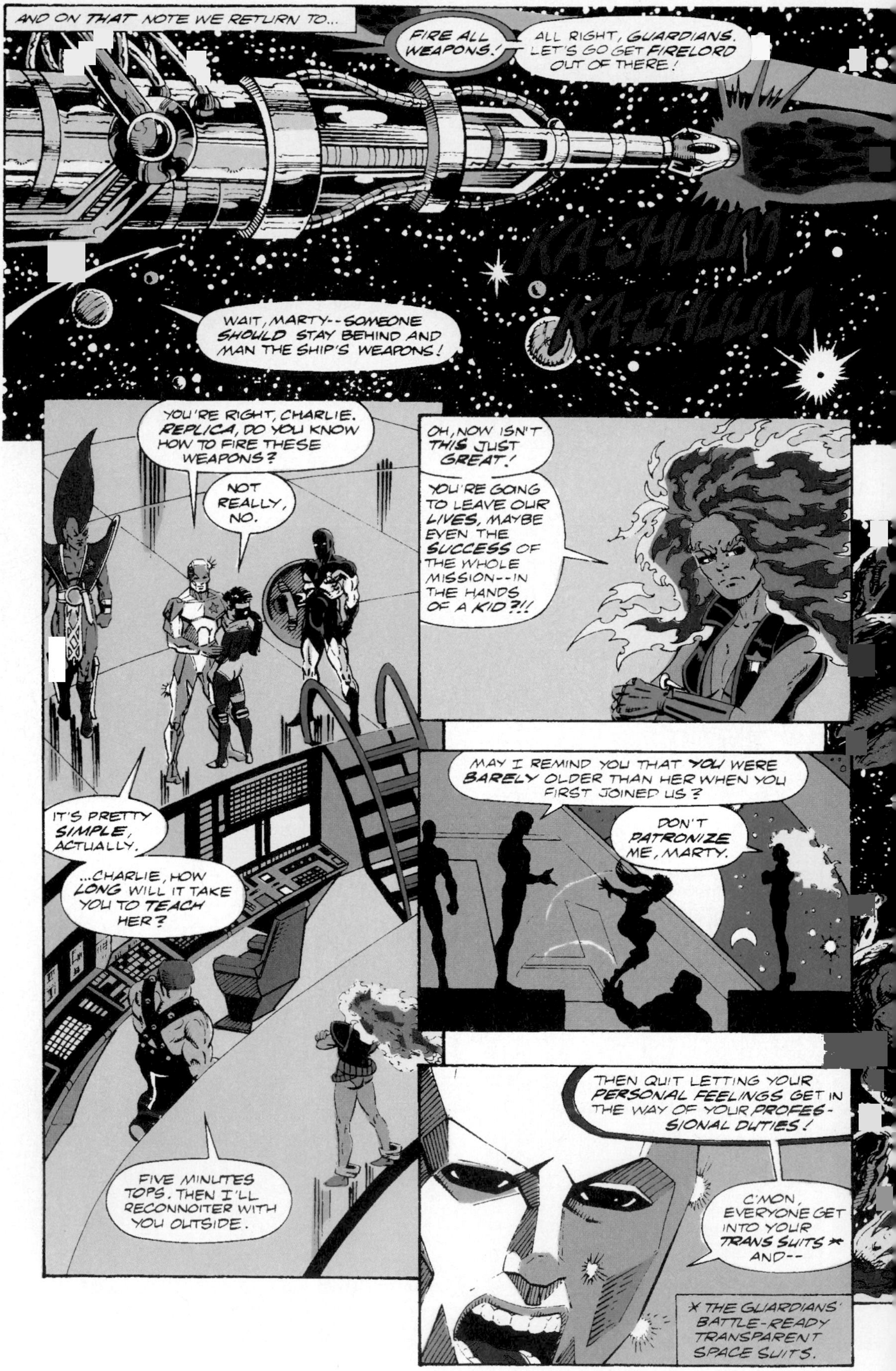
AND ON THAT NOTE WE RETURN TO...
FIRE ALL WEAPONS!
ALL RIGHT, GUARDIANS. LET'S GO GET FIRELORD OUT OF THERE!
KA-SHUUM
KA-CHUUM
WAIT, MARTY--SOMEONE SHOULD STAY BEHIND AND MAN THE SHIP'S WEAPONS!
YOU'RE RIGHT, CHARLIE. REPLICA, DO YOU KNOW HOW TO FIRE THESE WEAPONS?
NOT REALLY, NO.
OH, NOW ISN'T THIS JUST GREAT!
YOU'RE GOING TO LEAVE OUR LIVES, MAYBE EVEN THE SUCCESS OF THE WHOLE MISSION--IN THE HANDS OF A KID?!!
IT'S PRETTY SIMPLE, ACTUALLY.
...CHARLIE, HOW LONG WILL IT TAKE YOU TO TEACH HER?
FIVE MINUTES TOPS. THEN I'LL RECONNOITER WITH YOU OUTSIDE.
MAY I REMIND YOU THAT YOU WERE BARELY OLDER THAN HER WHEN YOU FIRST JOINED US?
DON'T PATRONIZE ME, MARTY.
THEN QUIT LETTING YOUR PERSONAL FEELINGS GET IN THE WAY OF YOUR PROFES-SIONAL DUTIES!
C'MON, EVERYONE GET INTO YOUR TRANS SUITS* AND--
* THE GUARDIANS' BATTLE-READY TRANSPARENT SPACE SUITS.

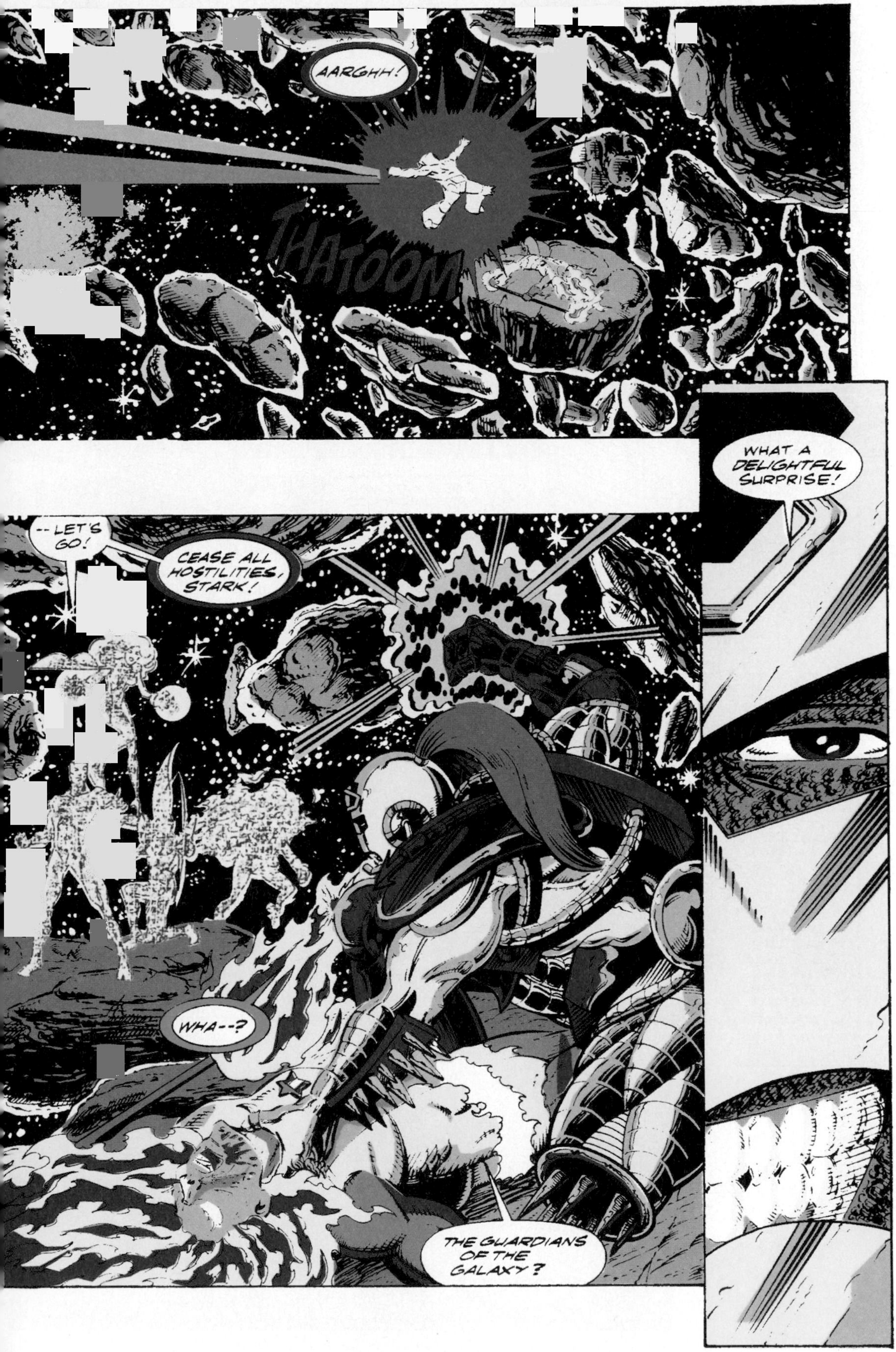
AARGHH!
THATOOM
WHAT A DELIGHTFUL SURPRISE!
--LET'S GO!
CEASE ALL HOSTILITIES, STARK!
WHA--?
THE GUARDIANS OF THE GALAXY?

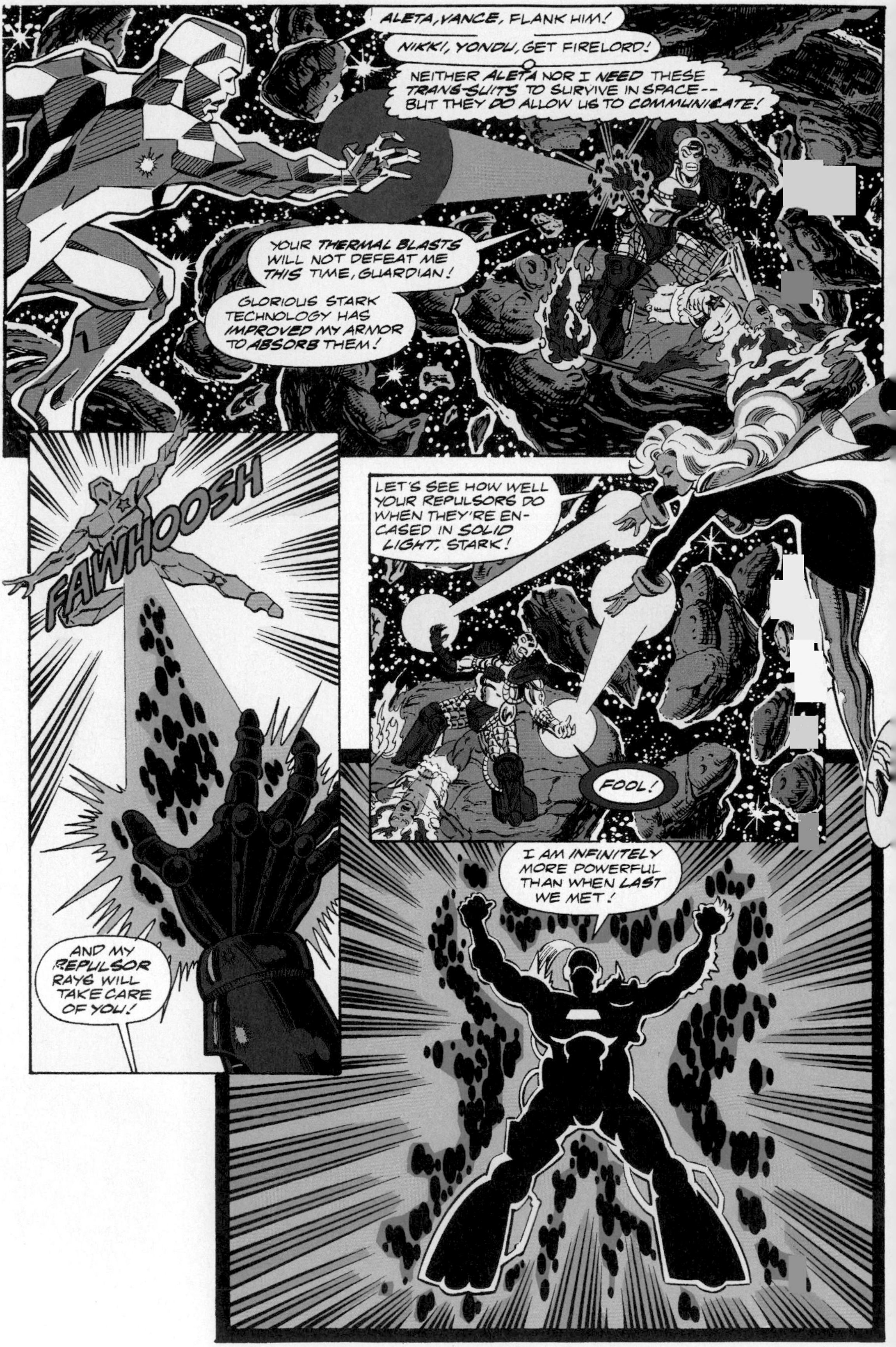
ALETA, VANCE, FLANK HIM!
NIKKI, YONDU, GET FIRELORD!
NEITHER ALETA NOR I NEED THESE TRANS-SUITS TO SURVIVE IN SPACE-- BUT THEY DO ALLOW US TO COMMUNICATE!
YOUR THERMAL BLASTS WILL NOT DEFEAT ME THIS TIME, GUARDIAN!
GLORIOUS STARK TECHNOLOGY HAS IMPROVED MY ARMOR TO ABSORB THEM!
FAWHOOSH
AND MY REPULSOR RAYS WILL TAKE CARE OF YOU!
LET'S SEE HOW WELL YOUR REPULSORS DO WHEN THEY'RE ENCASED IN SOLID LIGHT, STARK!
FOOL!
I AM INFINITELY MORE POWERFUL THAN WHEN LAST WE MET!

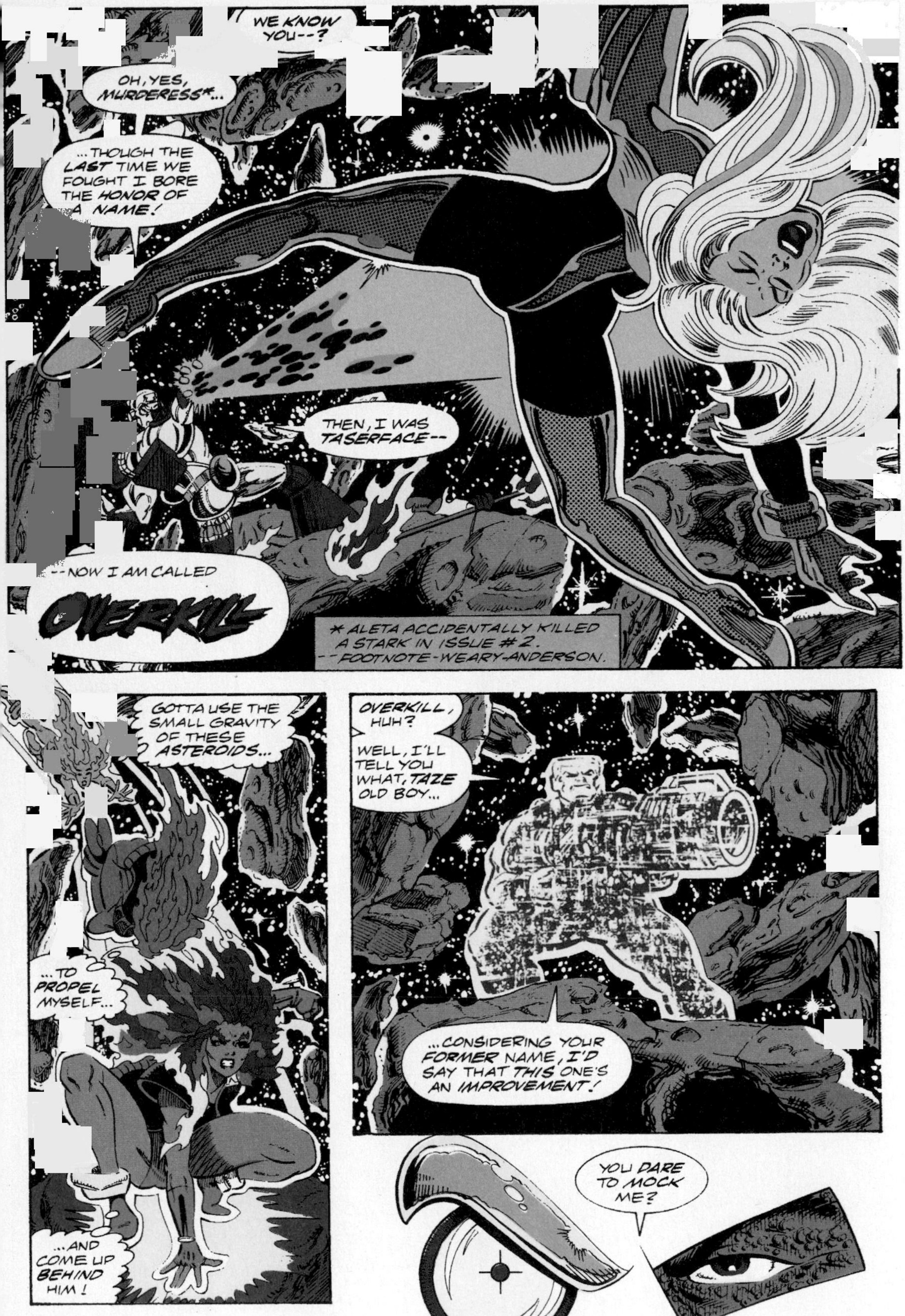
WE KNOW YOU--?
OH, YES, MURDERESS*...
...THOUGH THE LAST TIME WE FOUGHT I BORE THE HONOR OF A NAME!
THEN, I WAS TASERFACE--
--NOW I AM CALLED
OVERKILL
* ALETA ACCIDENTALLY KILLED A STARK IN ISSUE #2. --FOOTNOTE-WEARY-ANDERSON.
GOTTA USE THE SMALL GRAVITY OF THESE ASTEROIDS...
...TO PROPEL MYSELF...
...AND COME UP BEHIND HIM!
OVERKILL, HUH?
WELL, I'LL TELL YOU WHAT, TAZE OLD BOY...
...CONSIDERING YOUR FORMER NAME, I'D SAY THAT THIS ONE'S AN IMPROVEMENT!
YOU DARE TO MOCK ME?

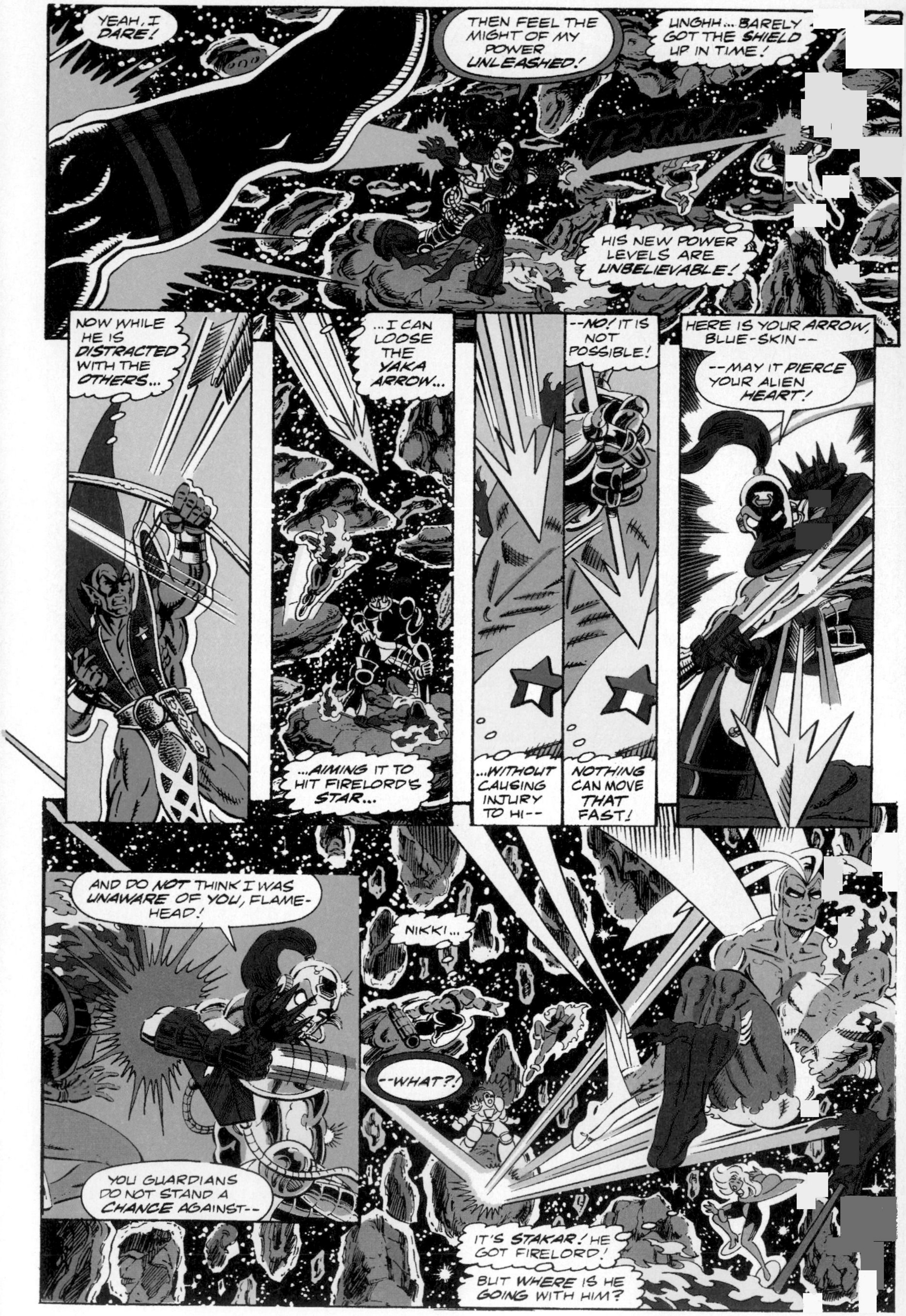

YEAH, I DARE!
THEN FEEL THE MIGHT OF MY POWER UNLEASHED!
UNGHH... BARELY GOT THE SHIELD UP IN TIME!
HIS NEW POWER LEVELS ARE UNBELIEVABLE!
NOW WHILE HE IS DISTRACTED WITH THE OTHERS...
...I CAN LOOSE THE YAKA ARROW...
...AIMING IT TO HIT FIRELORD'S STAR...
...WITHOUT CAUSING INJURY TO HI--
--NO! IT IS NOT POSSIBLE!
NOTHING CAN MOVE THAT FAST!
HERE IS YOUR ARROW, BLUE-SKIN--
--MAY IT PIERCE YOUR ALIEN HEART!
AND DO NOT THINK I WAS UNAWARE OF YOU, FLAME-HEAD!
YOU GUARDIANS DO NOT STAND A CHANCE AGAINST--
NIKKI...
--WHAT?!
IT'S STAKAR! HE GOT FIRELORD!
BUT WHERE IS HE GOING WITH HIM?

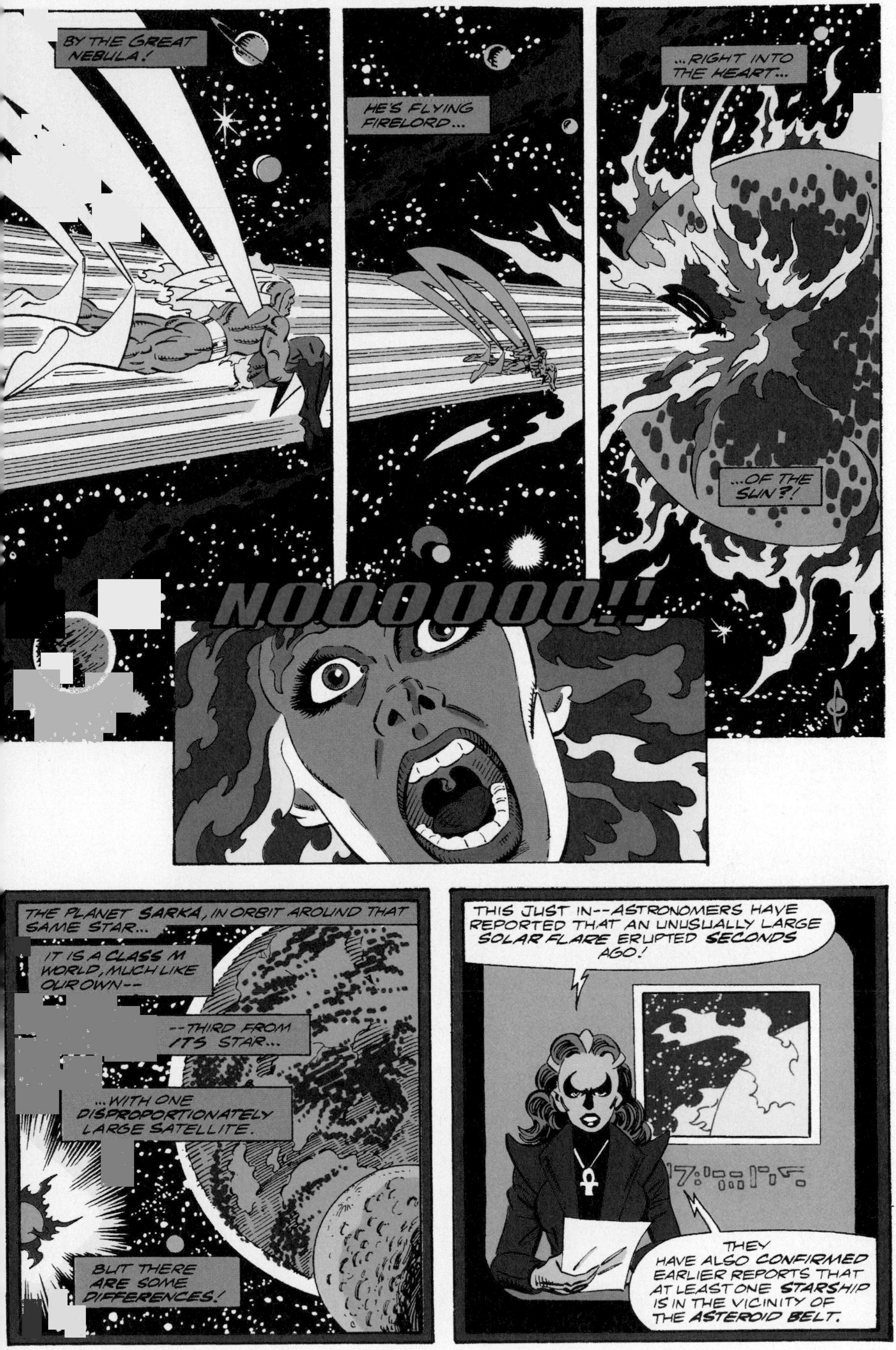
BY THE GREAT NEBULA!
HE'S FLYING FIRELORD...
...RIGHT INTO THE HEART...
...OF THE SUN?!
NOOOOOOO!!
THE PLANET SARKA, IN ORBIT AROUND THAT SAME STAR...
IT IS A CLASS M WORLD, MUCH LIKE OUR OWN--
--THIRD FROM ITS STAR...
...WITH ONE DISPROPORTIONATELY LARGE SATELLITE.
BUT THERE ARE SOME DIFFERENCES!
THIS JUST IN--ASTRONOMERS HAVE REPORTED THAT AN UNUSUALLY LARGE SOLAR FLARE ERUPTED SECONDS AGO!
THEY HAVE ALSO CONFIRMED EARLIER REPORTS THAT AT LEAST ONE STARSHIP IS IN THE VICINITY OF THE ASTEROID BELT.

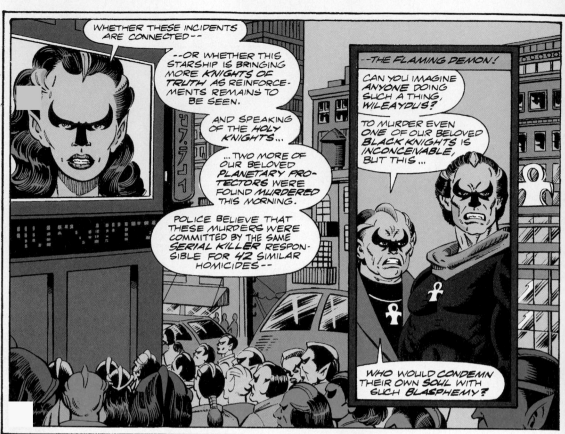

WHETHER THESE INCIDENTS ARE CONNECTED--

--OR WHETHER THIS STARSHIP IS BRINGING MORE *KNIGHTS OF TRUTH* AS REINFORCEMENTS REMAINS TO BE SEEN.

AND SPEAKING OF THE *HOLY KNIGHTS*...

...TWO MORE OF OUR BELOVED *PLANETARY PROTECTORS* WERE FOUND *MURDERED* THIS MORNING.

POLICE BELIEVE THAT THESE MURDERS WERE COMMITTED BY THE SAME *SERIAL KILLER* RESPONSIBLE FOR *42* SIMILAR HOMICIDES--

--THE *FLAMING DEMON!*

CAN YOU IMAGINE *ANYONE* DOING SUCH A THING, WILEAYDUS?

TO MURDER EVEN ONE OF OUR BELOVED *BLACK KNIGHTS* IS INCONCEIVABLE, BUT THIS...

WHO WOULD *CONDEMN* THEIR OWN *SOUL* WITH SUCH *BLASPHEMY?*

ONLY A *MADMAN*, CARINTHUS--THAT OR A *DEMON!*

EXCUSE ME, MY FRIEND, I MUST RETURN TO MY *WORK.*

SURE, SEE YOU LATER, OKAY?

HE SURE HAS BEEN ACTING *STRANGE* LATELY ...I WONDER...?

I MUST FIND OUT MORE ABOUT THAT SHIP!

AND, SPEAKING ABOUT "THAT SHIP," LET'S RETURN TO IT NOW...

AS A *YOUNG GIRL* ON HER *FIRST ASSIGNMENT* GETS AN *UNEXPECTED VISITOR...*

HUH?! WHERE'D SHE COME FROM?

SHE'S *NOT* ONE OF THE *OVER--* ER, *GUARDIANS!*

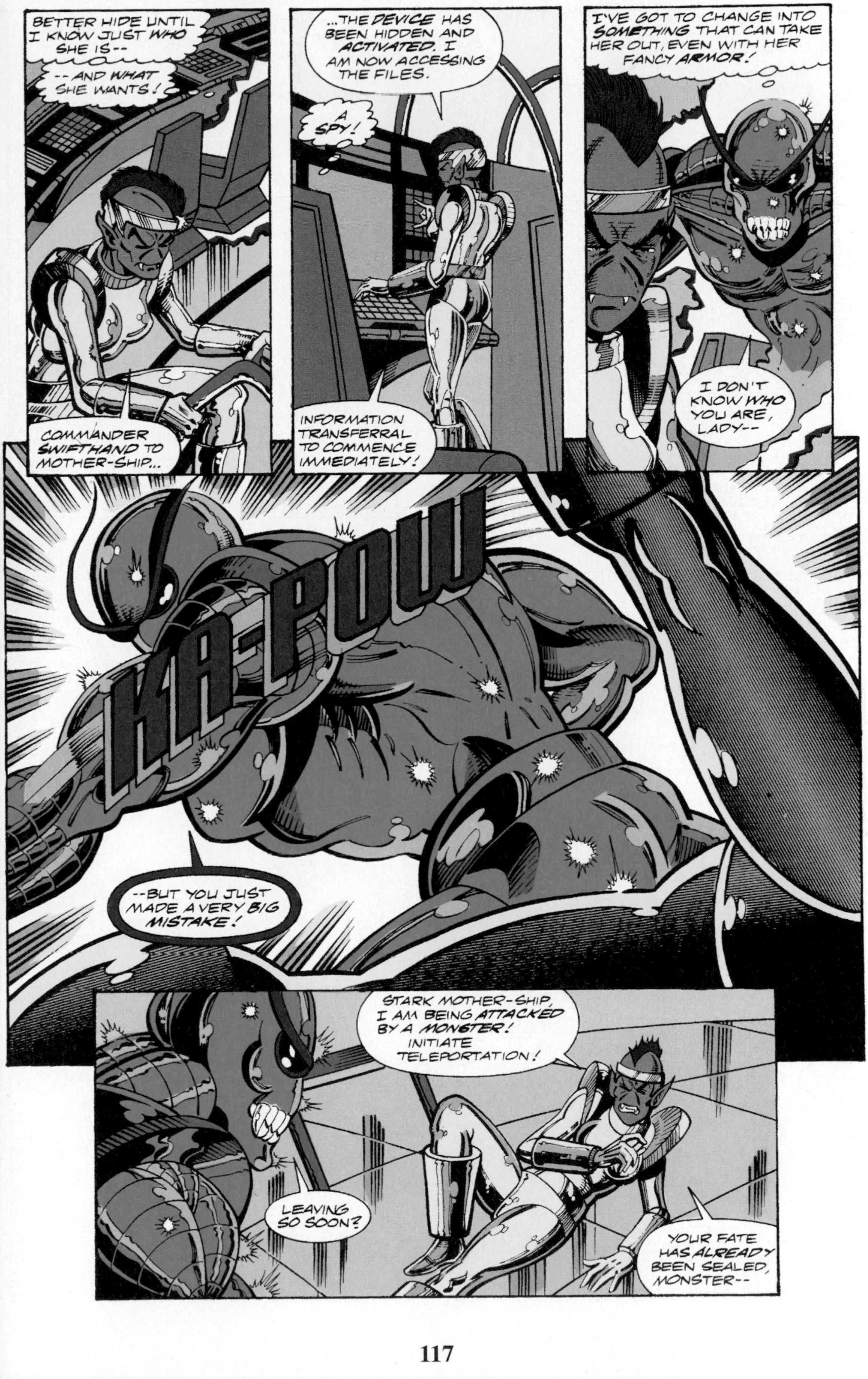
BETTER HIDE UNTIL I KNOW JUST WHO SHE IS--
--AND WHAT SHE WANTS!
COMMANDER SWIFTHAND TO MOTHER-SHIP...
...THE DEVICE HAS BEEN HIDDEN AND ACTIVATED. I AM NOW ACCESSING THE FILES.
A SPY!
INFORMATION TRANSFERRAL TO COMMENCE IMMEDIATELY!
I'VE GOT TO CHANGE INTO SOMETHING THAT CAN TAKE HER OUT, EVEN WITH HER FANCY ARMOR!
I DON'T KNOW WHO YOU ARE, LADY--
KA-POW
--BUT YOU JUST MADE A VERY BIG MISTAKE!
STARK MOTHER-SHIP, I AM BEING ATTACKED BY A MONSTER! INITIATE TELEPORTATION!
LEAVING SO SOON?
YOUR FATE HAS ALREADY BEEN SEALED, MONSTER--

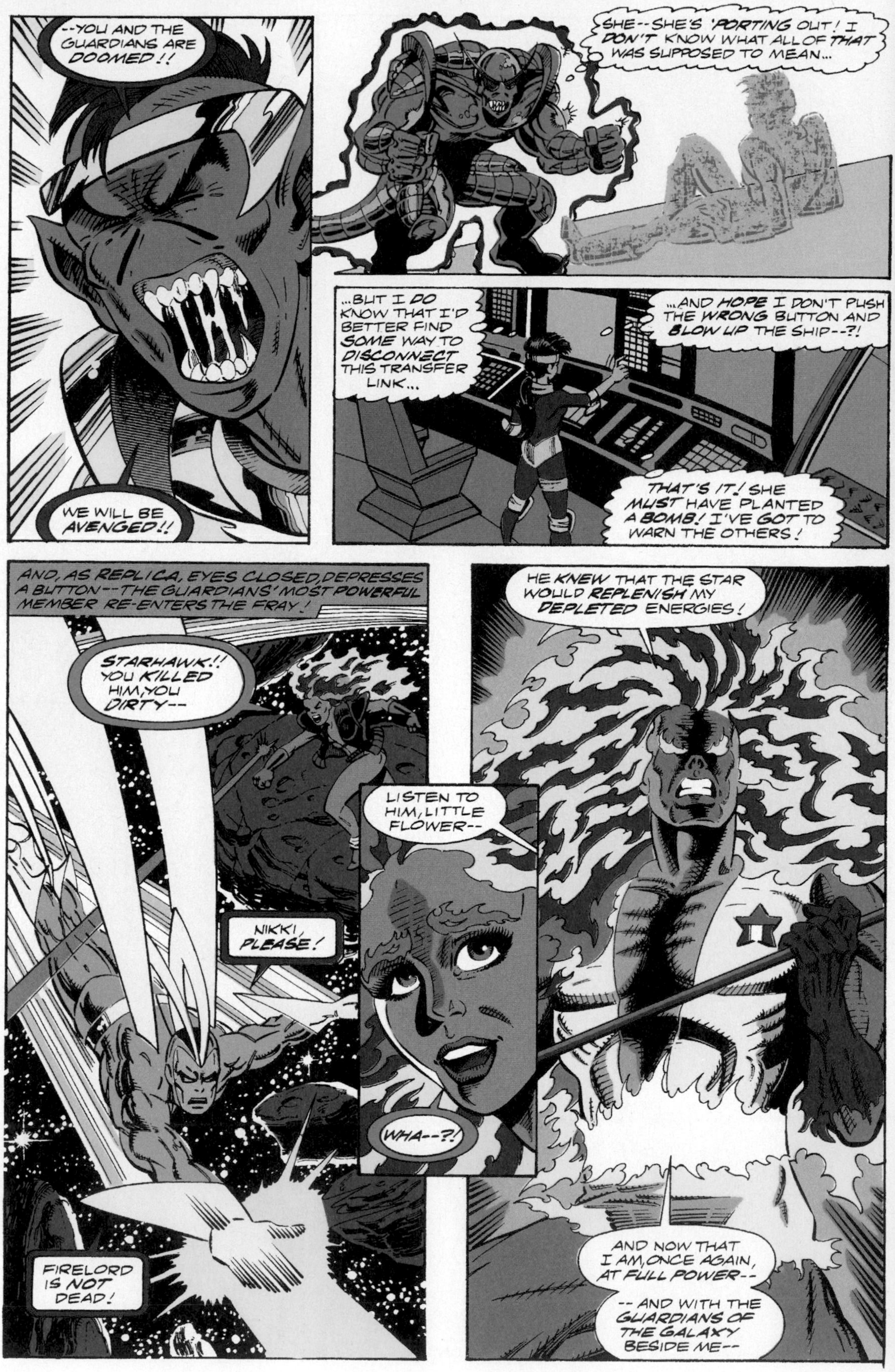
--YOU AND THE GUARDIANS ARE DOOMED!!
WE WILL BE AVENGED!!
SHE--SHE'S 'PORTING OUT! I DON'T KNOW WHAT ALL OF THAT WAS SUPPOSED TO MEAN...
...BUT I DO KNOW THAT I'D BETTER FIND SOME WAY TO DISCONNECT THIS TRANSFER LINK...
...AND HOPE I DON'T PUSH THE WRONG BUTTON AND BLOW UP THE SHIP--?!
THAT'S IT! SHE MUST HAVE PLANTED A BOMB! I'VE GOT TO WARN THE OTHERS!
AND, AS REPLICA, EYES CLOSED, DEPRESSES A BUTTON--THE GUARDIANS' MOST POWERFUL MEMBER RE-ENTERS THE FRAY!
STARHAWK!! YOU KILLED HIM, YOU DIRTY--
NIKKI, PLEASE!
FIRELORD IS NOT DEAD!
LISTEN TO HIM, LITTLE FLOWER--
WHA--?!
HE KNEW THAT THE STAR WOULD REPLENISH MY DEPLETED ENERGIES!
AND NOW THAT I AM, ONCE AGAIN, AT FULL POWER--
--AND WITH THE GUARDIANS OF THE GALAXY BESIDE ME--

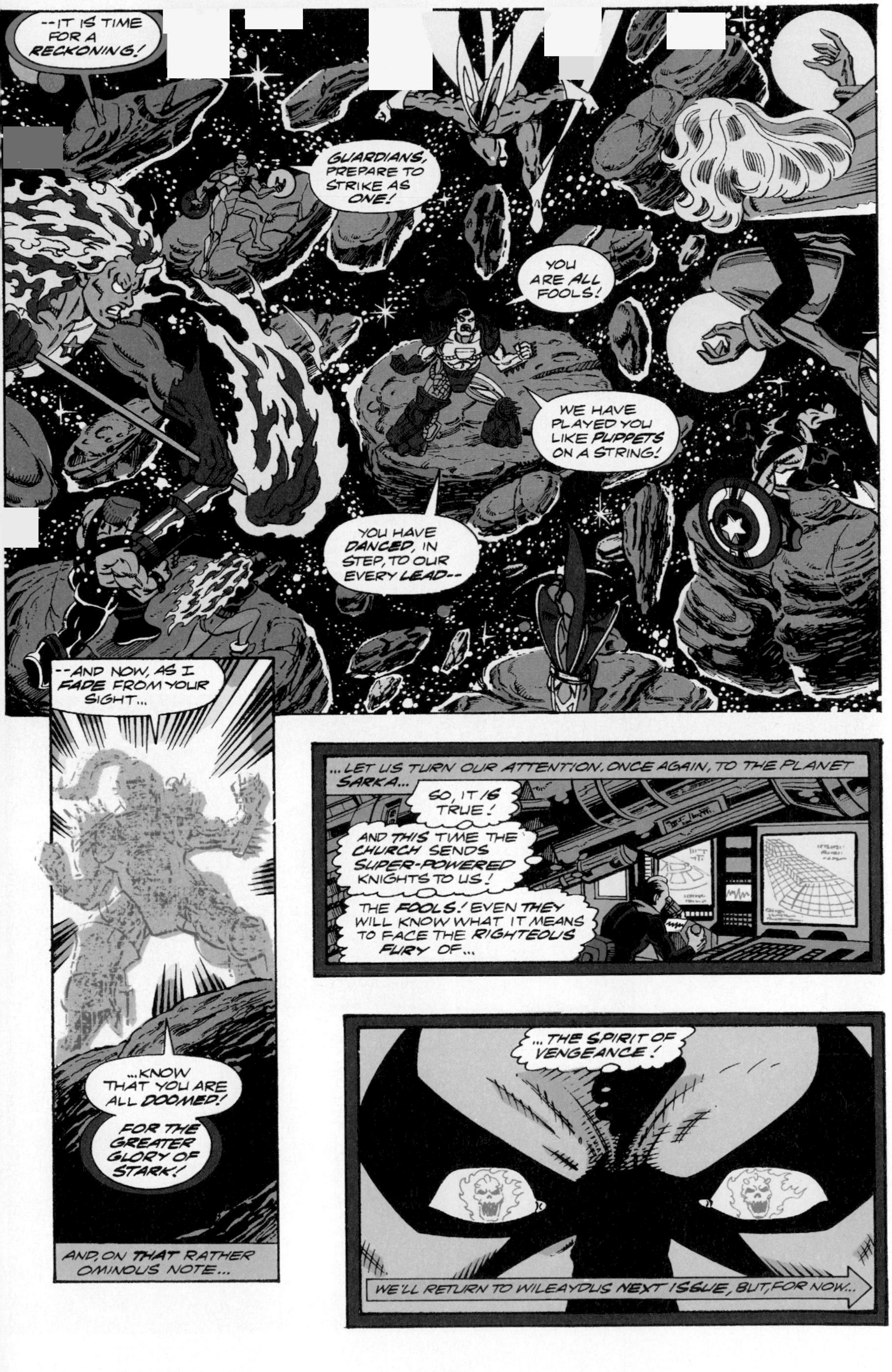
--IT IS TIME FOR A RECKONING!
GUARDIANS, PREPARE TO STRIKE AS ONE!
YOU ARE ALL FOOLS!
WE HAVE PLAYED YOU LIKE PUPPETS ON A STRING!
YOU HAVE DANCED, IN STEP, TO OUR EVERY LEAD--
--AND NOW, AS I FADE FROM YOUR SIGHT...
...KNOW THAT YOU ARE ALL DOOMED!
FOR THE GREATER GLORY OF STARK!
AND, ON THAT RATHER OMINOUS NOTE...
...LET US TURN OUR ATTENTION, ONCE AGAIN, TO THE PLANET SARKA...
SO, IT IS TRUE!
AND THIS TIME THE CHURCH SENDS SUPER-POWERED KNIGHTS TO US!
THE FOOLS! EVEN THEY WILL KNOW WHAT IT MEANS TO FACE THE RIGHTEOUS FURY OF...
...THE SPIRIT OF VENGEANCE!
WE'LL RETURN TO WILEAYDUS NEXT ISSUE, BUT, FOR NOW...

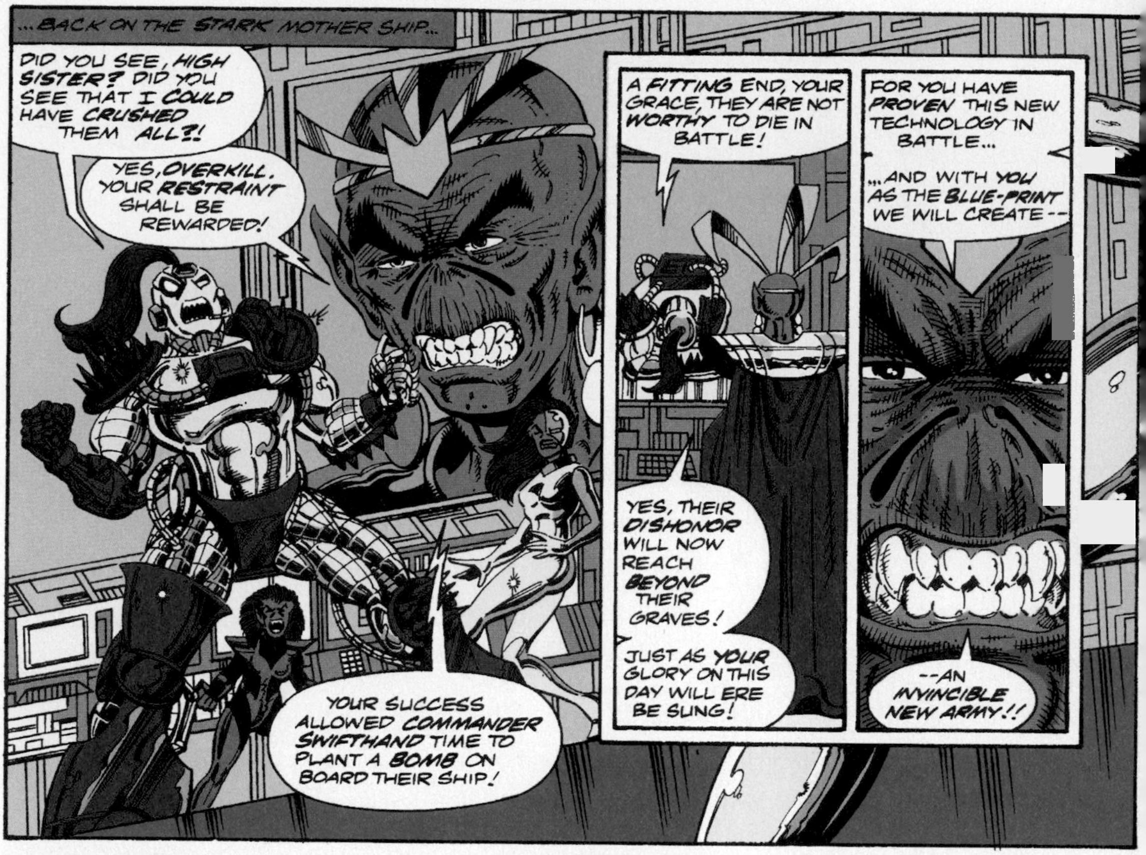
...BACK ON THE STARK MOTHER SHIP...
DID YOU SEE, HIGH SISTER? DID YOU SEE THAT I COULD HAVE CRUSHED THEM ALL?!
YES, OVERKILL. YOUR RESTRAINT SHALL BE REWARDED!
YOUR SUCCESS ALLOWED COMMANDER SWIFTHAND TIME TO PLANT A BOMB ON BOARD THEIR SHIP!
A FITTING END, YOUR GRACE, THEY ARE NOT WORTHY TO DIE IN BATTLE!
YES, THEIR DISHONOR WILL NOW REACH BEYOND THEIR GRAVES!
JUST AS YOUR GLORY ON THIS DAY WILL ERE BE SUNG!
FOR YOU HAVE PROVEN THIS NEW TECHNOLOGY IN BATTLE...
...AND WITH YOU AS THE BLUE-PRINT WE WILL CREATE--
--AN INVINCIBLE NEW ARMY!!

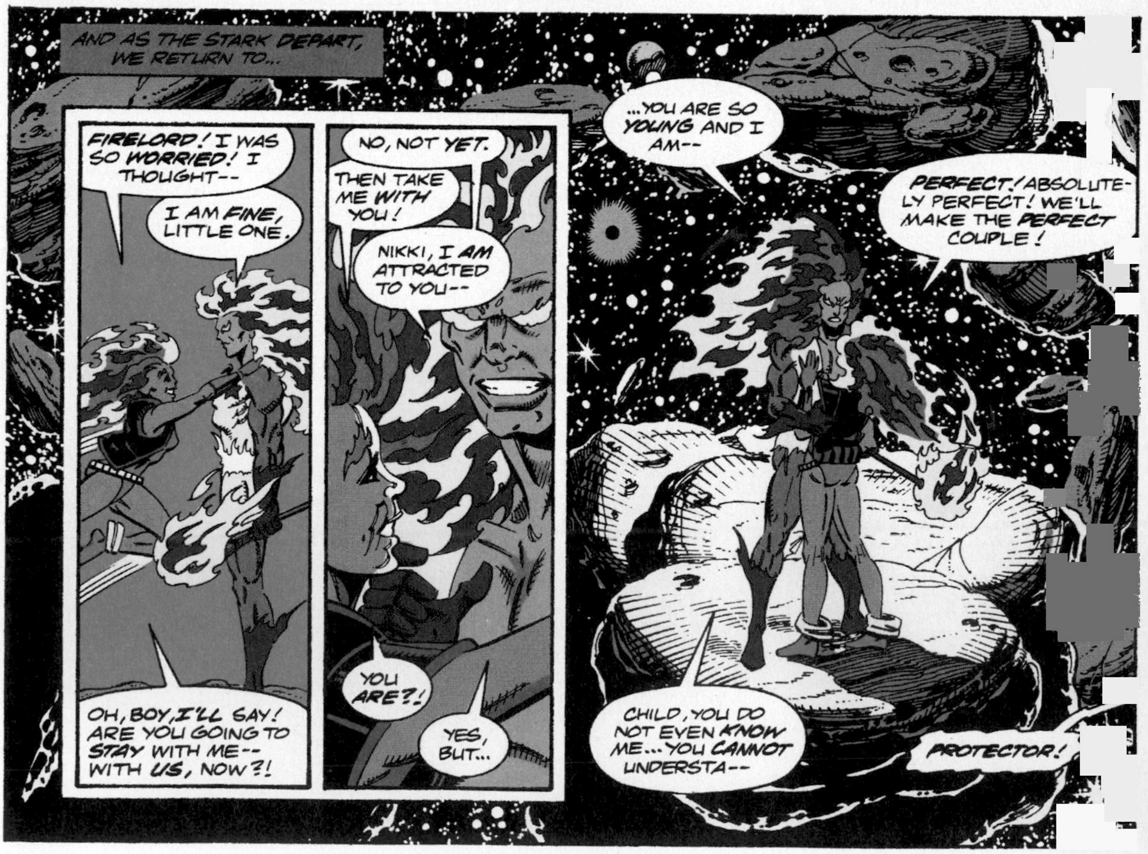
AND AS THE STARK DEPART, WE RETURN TO...
FIRELORD! I WAS SO WORRIED! I THOUGHT--
I AM FINE, LITTLE ONE.
OH, BOY, I'LL SAY! ARE YOU GOING TO STAY WITH ME-- WITH US, NOW?!
NO, NOT YET.
THEN TAKE ME WITH YOU!
NIKKI, I AM ATTRACTED TO YOU--
YOU ARE?!
YES, BUT...
...YOU ARE SO YOUNG AND I AM--
PERFECT! ABSOLUTE-LY PERFECT! WE'LL MAKE THE PERFECT COUPLE!
CHILD, YOU DO NOT EVEN KNOW ME... YOU CANNOT UNDERSTA--
PROTECTOR!

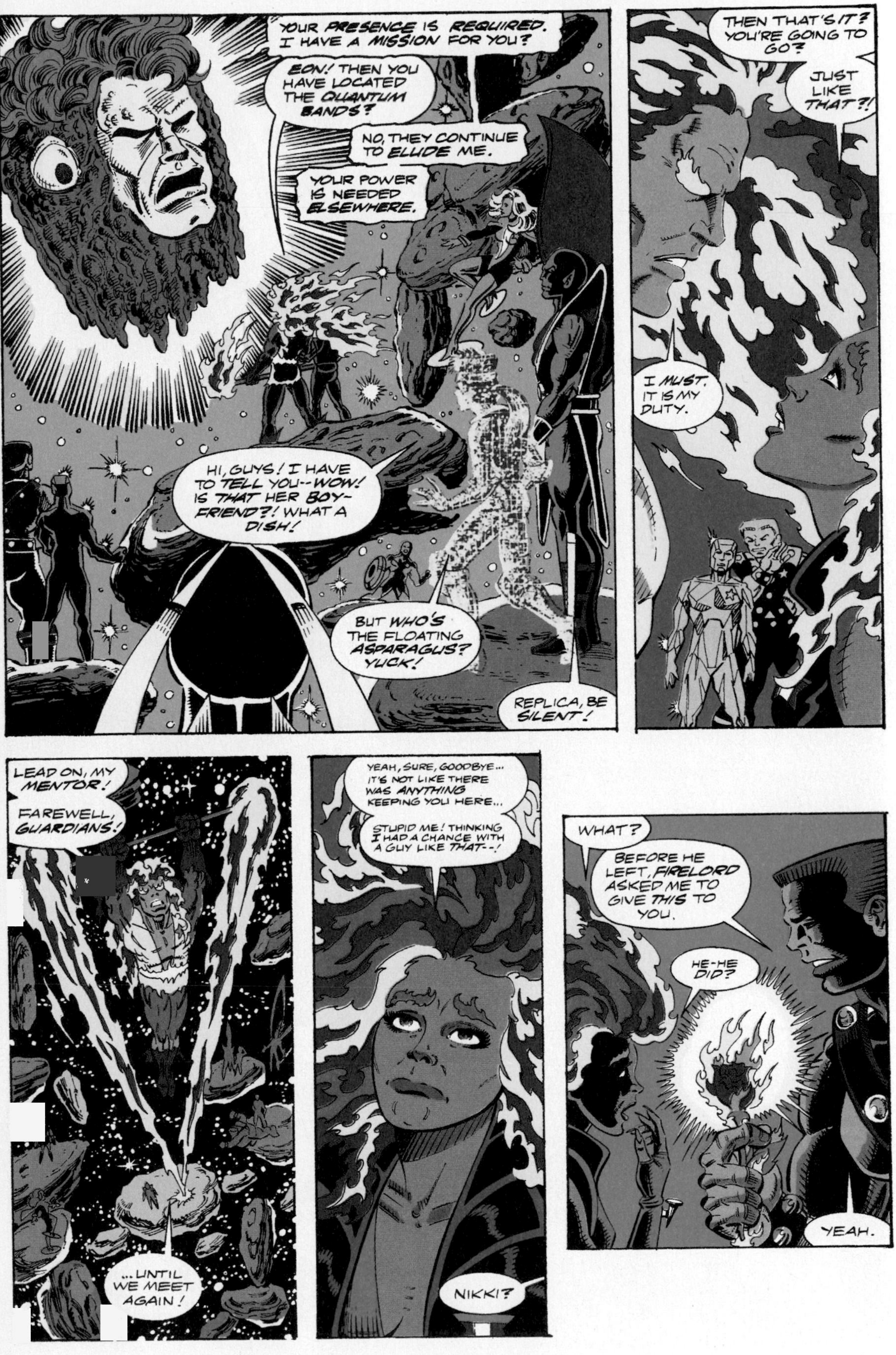
YOUR PRESENCE IS REQUIRED. I HAVE A MISSION FOR YOU?
EON! THEN YOU HAVE LOCATED THE QUANTUM BANDS?
NO, THEY CONTINUE TO ELUDE ME.
YOUR POWER IS NEEDED ELSEWHERE.
HI, GUYS! I HAVE TO TELL YOU--WOW! IS THAT HER BOY-FRIEND?! WHAT A DISH!
BUT WHO'S THE FLOATING ASPARAGUS? YUCK!
REPLICA, BE SILENT!
THEN THAT'S IT? YOU'RE GOING TO GO?
JUST LIKE THAT?!
I MUST. IT IS MY DUTY.
LEAD ON, MY MENTOR!
FAREWELL, GUARDIANS!
...UNTIL WE MEET AGAIN!
YEAH, SURE, GOODBYE... IT'S NOT LIKE THERE WAS ANYTHING KEEPING YOU HERE...
STUPID ME! THINKING I HAD A CHANCE WITH A GUY LIKE THAT--!
NIKKI?
WHAT?
BEFORE HE LEFT, FIRELORD ASKED ME TO GIVE THIS TO YOU.
HE-HE DID?
YEAH.

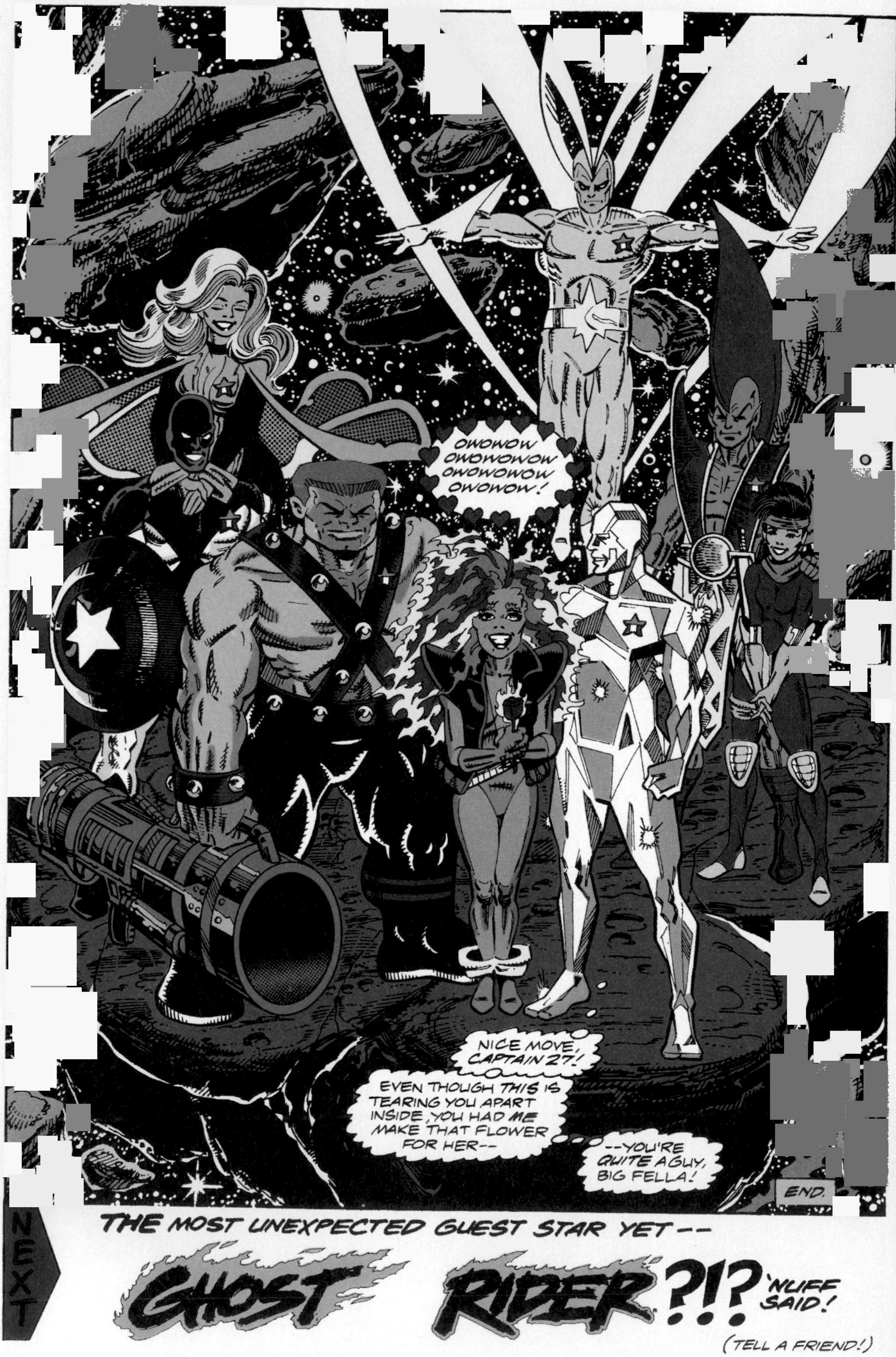
OWOWOW OWOWOWOW OWOWOWOW OWOWOW!
NICE MOVE, CAPTAIN 27!
EVEN THOUGH THIS IS TEARING YOU APART INSIDE, YOU HAD ME MAKE THAT FLOWER FOR HER--
--YOU'RE QUITE A GUY, BIG FELLA!
END.
NEXT
THE MOST UNEXPECTED GUEST STAR YET--
GHOST RIDER?!?
'NUFF SAID!
(TELL A FRIEND!)

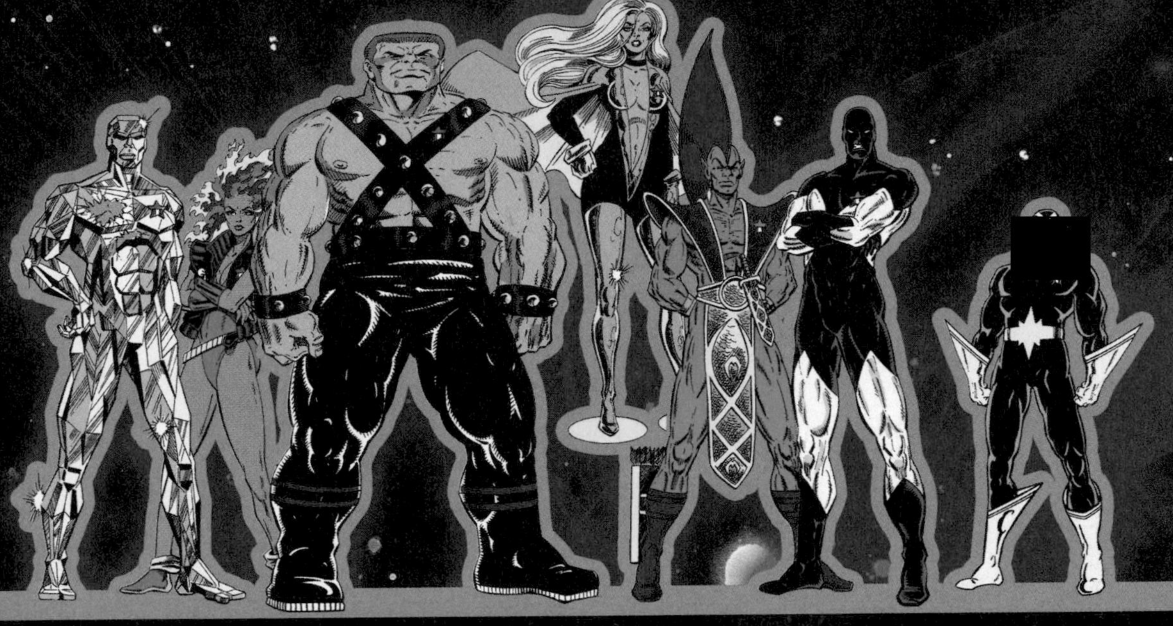

GUARDIANS OF THE GALAXY

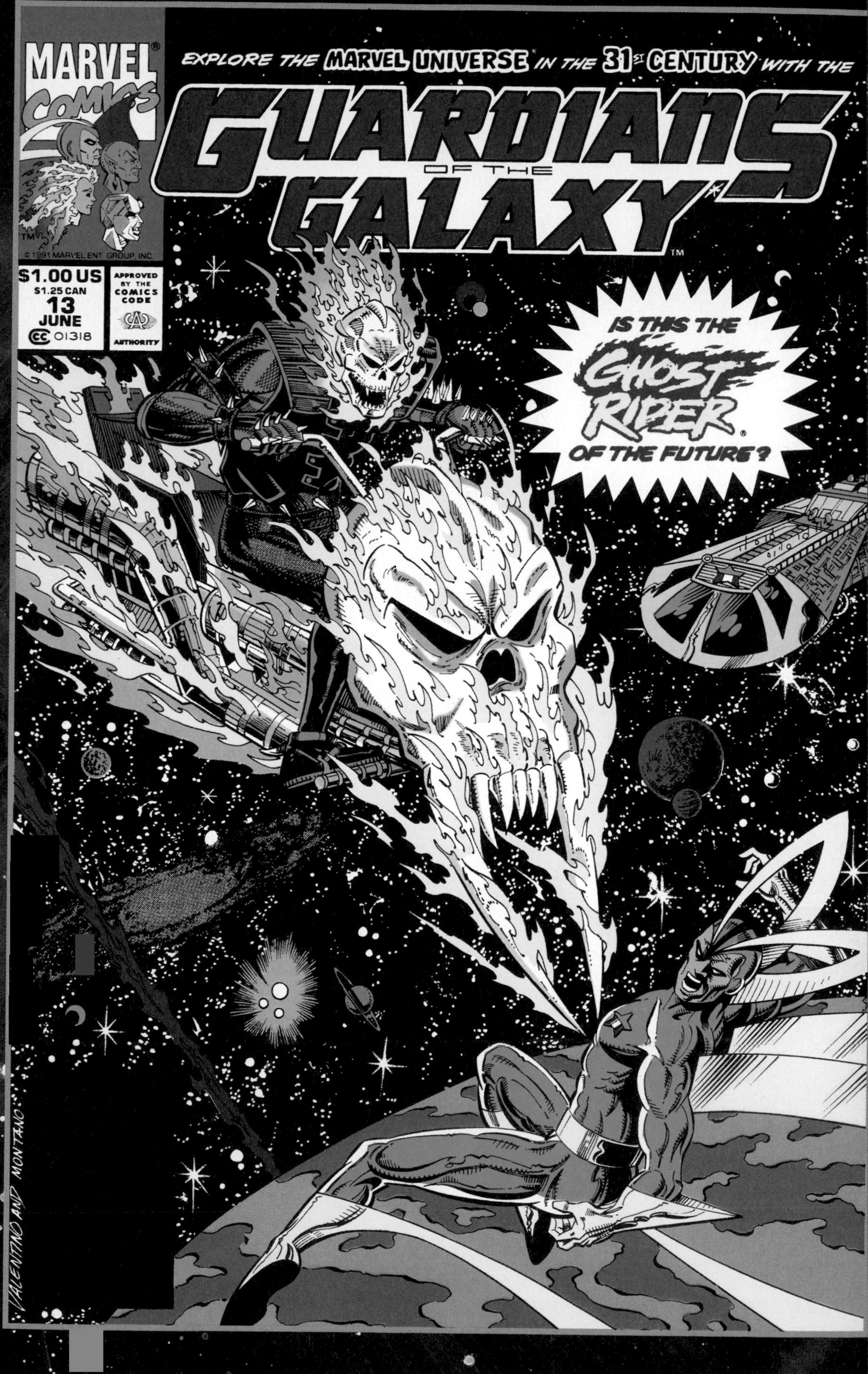
MARVEL COMICS
EXPLORE THE MARVEL UNIVERSE IN THE 31ST CENTURY WITH THE
GUARDIANS OF THE GALAXY
© 1991 MARVEL ENT. GROUP, INC.
$1.00 US
$1.25 CAN
13
JUNE
01318
APPROVED BY THE COMICS CODE AUTHORITY
IS THIS THE GHOST RIDER OF THE FUTURE?
VALENTINO AND MONTANO

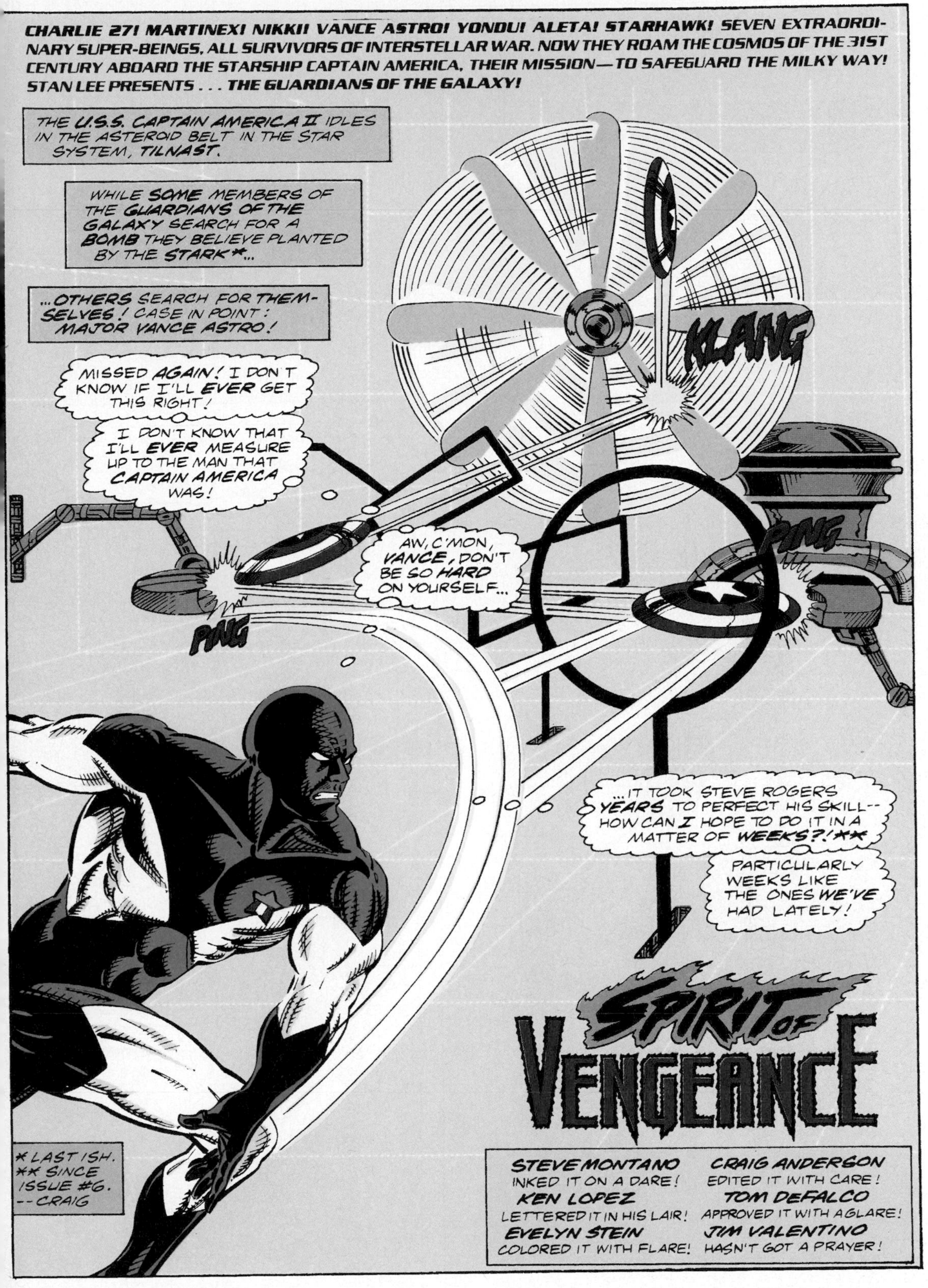
CHARLIE 27! MARTINEX! NIKKI! VANCE ASTRO! YONDU! ALETA! STARHAWK! SEVEN EXTRAORDINARY SUPER-BEINGS, ALL SURVIVORS OF INTERSTELLAR WAR. NOW THEY ROAM THE COSMOS OF THE 31ST CENTURY ABOARD THE STARSHIP CAPTAIN AMERICA, THEIR MISSION—TO SAFEGUARD THE MILKY WAY! STAN LEE PRESENTS . . . THE GUARDIANS OF THE GALAXY!
THE U.S.S. CAPTAIN AMERICA II IDLES IN THE ASTEROID BELT IN THE STAR SYSTEM, TILNAST.
WHILE SOME MEMBERS OF THE GUARDIANS OF THE GALAXY SEARCH FOR A BOMB THEY BELIEVE PLANTED BY THE STARK*...
...OTHERS SEARCH FOR THEMSELVES! CASE IN POINT: MAJOR VANCE ASTRO!
KLANG
MISSED AGAIN! I DON'T KNOW IF I'LL EVER GET THIS RIGHT!
I DON'T KNOW THAT I'LL EVER MEASURE UP TO THE MAN THAT CAPTAIN AMERICA WAS!
PING
AW, C'MON, VANCE, DON'T BE SO HARD ON YOURSELF...
PING
...IT TOOK STEVE ROGERS YEARS TO PERFECT HIS SKILL-- HOW CAN I HOPE TO DO IT IN A MATTER OF WEEKS?!**
PARTICULARLY WEEKS LIKE THE ONES WE'VE HAD LATELY!
SPIRIT OF VENGEANCE
* LAST ISH. ** SINCE ISSUE #6. --CRAIG
STEVE MONTANO INKED IT ON A DARE!
KEN LOPEZ LETTERED IT IN HIS LAIR!
EVELYN STEIN COLORED IT WITH FLARE!
CRAIG ANDERSON EDITED IT WITH CARE!
TOM DEFALCO APPROVED IT WITH A GLARE!
JIM VALENTINO HASN'T GOT A PRAYER!

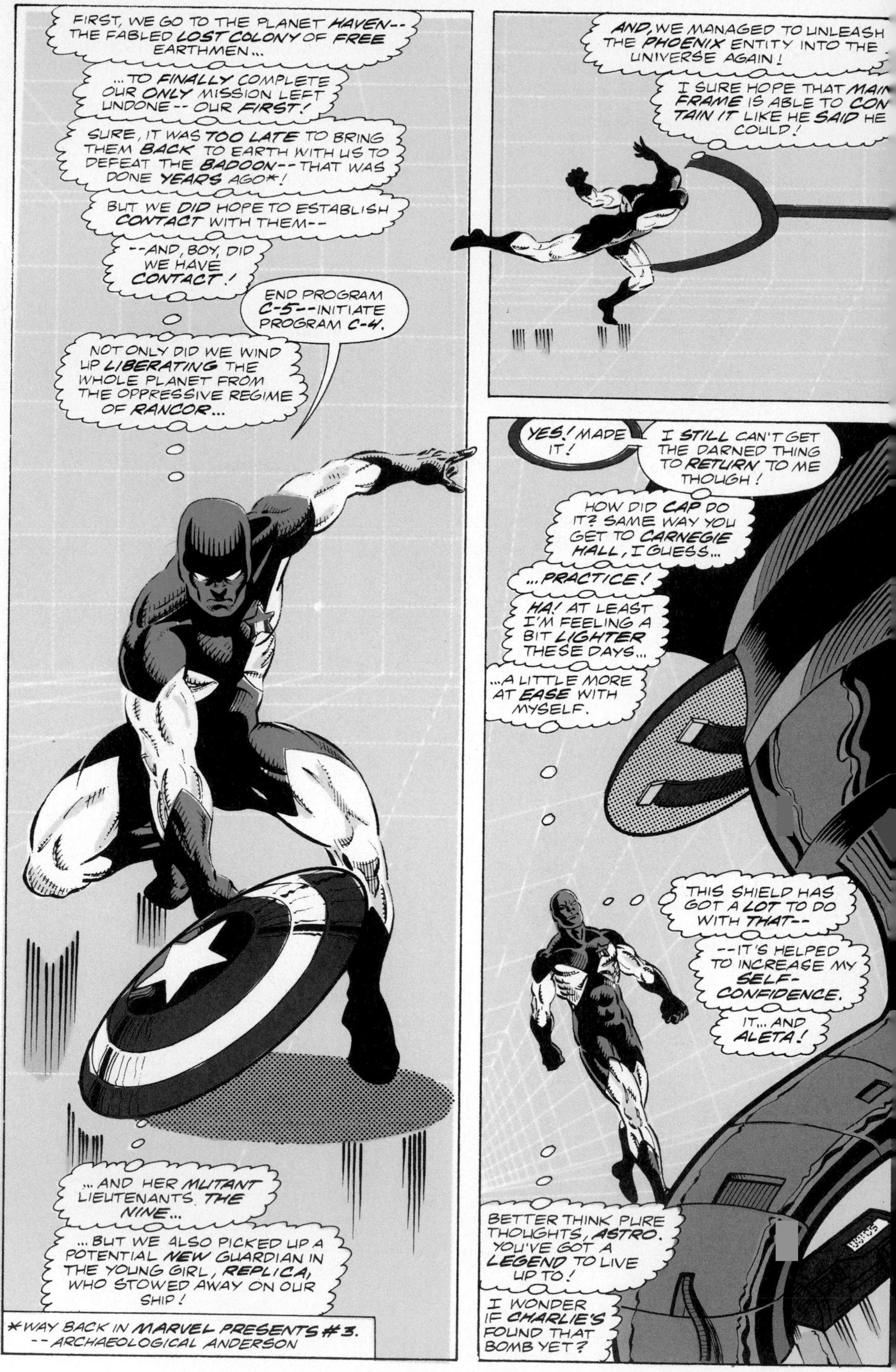
FIRST, WE GO TO THE PLANET HAVEN-- THE FABLED LOST COLONY OF FREE EARTHMEN...
...TO FINALLY COMPLETE OUR ONLY MISSION LEFT UNDONE-- OUR FIRST!
SURE, IT WAS TOO LATE TO BRING THEM BACK TO EARTH WITH US TO DEFEAT THE BADOON--THAT WAS DONE YEARS AGO*!
BUT WE DID HOPE TO ESTABLISH CONTACT WITH THEM--
--AND, BOY, DID WE HAVE CONTACT!
END PROGRAM C-5--INITIATE PROGRAM C-4.
NOT ONLY DID WE WIND UP LIBERATING THE WHOLE PLANET FROM THE OPPRESSIVE REGIME OF RANCOR...
...AND HER MUTANT LIEUTENANTS, THE NINE...
...BUT WE ALSO PICKED UP A POTENTIAL NEW GUARDIAN IN THE YOUNG GIRL, REPLICA, WHO STOWED AWAY ON OUR SHIP!
*WAY BACK IN MARVEL PRESENTS #3. --ARCHAEOLOGICAL ANDERSON
AND, WE MANAGED TO UNLEASH THE PHOENIX ENTITY INTO THE UNIVERSE AGAIN!
I SURE HOPE THAT MAIN FRAME IS ABLE TO CON TAIN IT LIKE HE SAID HE COULD!
YES! MADE IT!
I STILL CAN'T GET THE DARNED THING TO RETURN TO ME THOUGH!
HOW DID CAP DO IT? SAME WAY YOU GET TO CARNEGIE HALL, I GUESS...
...PRACTICE!
HA! AT LEAST I'M FEELING A BIT LIGHTER THESE DAYS...
...A LITTLE MORE AT EASE WITH MYSELF.
THIS SHIELD HAS GOT A LOT TO DO WITH THAT--
--IT'S HELPED TO INCREASE MY SELF-CONFIDENCE.
IT... AND ALETA!
BETTER THINK PURE THOUGHTS, ASTRO. YOU'VE GOT A LEGEND TO LIVE UP TO!
I WONDER IF CHARLIE'S FOUND THAT BOMB YET?

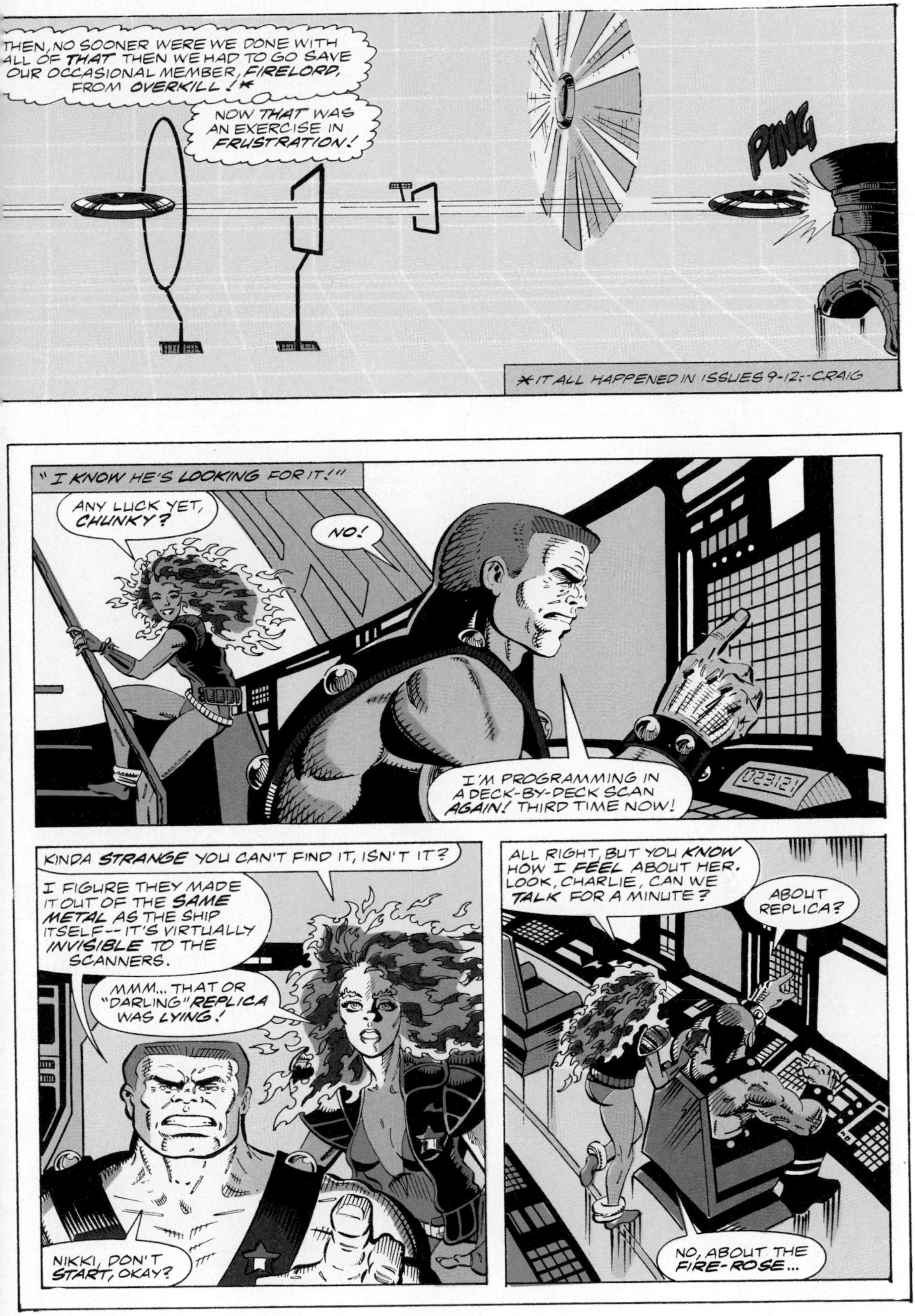
THEN, NO SOONER WERE WE DONE WITH ALL OF THAT THEN WE HAD TO GO SAVE OUR OCCASIONAL MEMBER, FIRELORD, FROM OVERKILL!*
NOW THAT WAS AN EXERCISE IN FRUSTRATION!
PING
*IT ALL HAPPENED IN ISSUES 9-12:-CRAIG
"I KNOW HE'S LOOKING FOR IT!"
ANY LUCK YET, CHUNKY?
NO!
I'M PROGRAMMING IN A DECK-BY-DECK SCAN AGAIN! THIRD TIME NOW!
KINDA STRANGE YOU CAN'T FIND IT, ISN'T IT?
I FIGURE THEY MADE IT OUT OF THE SAME METAL AS THE SHIP ITSELF-- IT'S VIRTUALLY INVISIBLE TO THE SCANNERS.
MMM... THAT OR "DARLING" REPLICA WAS LYING!
NIKKI, DON'T START, OKAY?
ALL RIGHT, BUT YOU KNOW HOW I FEEL ABOUT HER. LOOK, CHARLIE, CAN WE TALK FOR A MINUTE?
ABOUT REPLICA?
NO, ABOUT THE FIRE-ROSE...

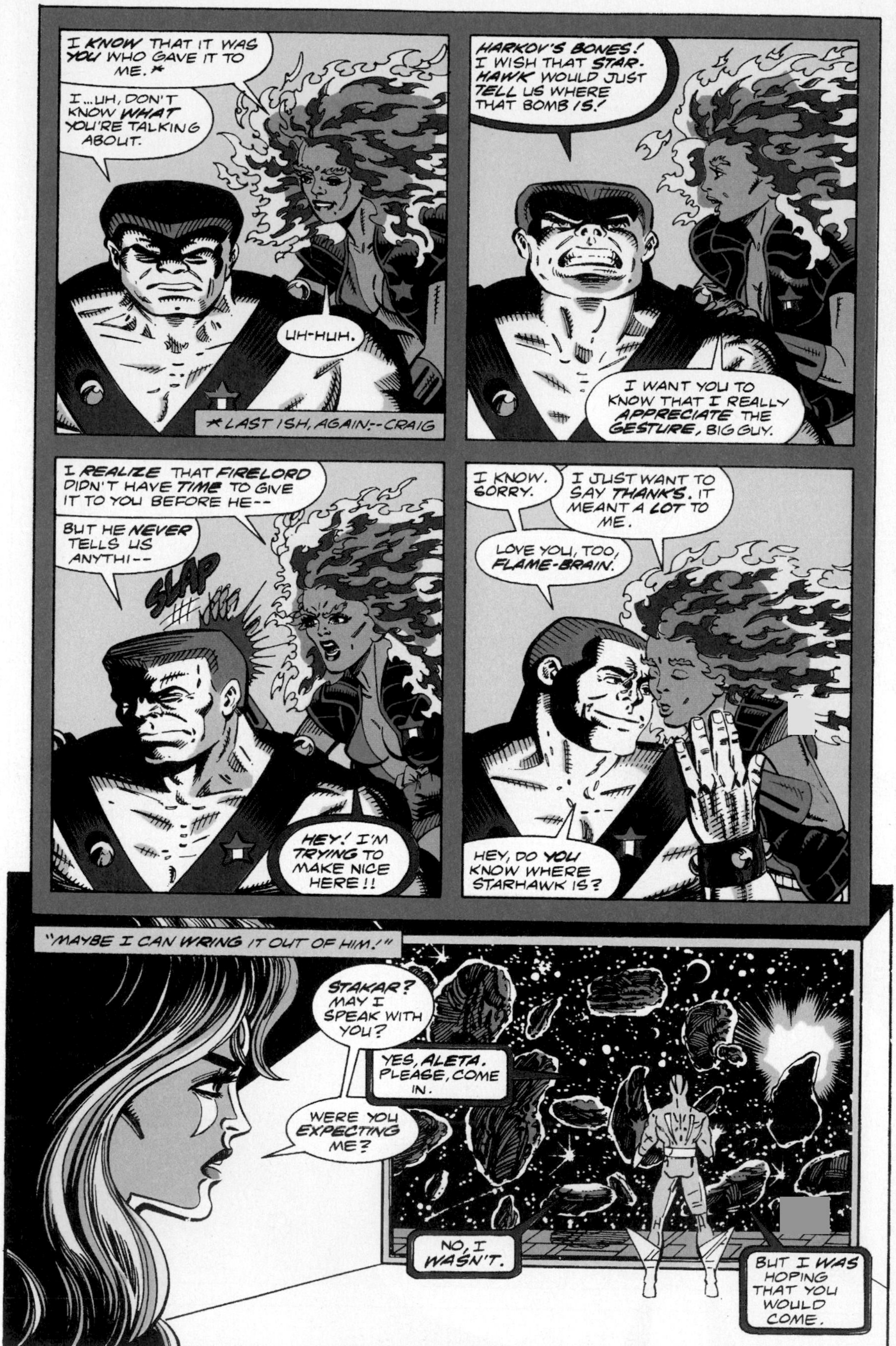

I KNOW THAT IT WAS YOU WHO GAVE IT TO ME.*
I...UH, DON'T KNOW WHAT YOU'RE TALKING ABOUT.
UH-HUH.
*LAST ISH, AGAIN.--CRAIG
HARKOV'S BONES! I WISH THAT STAR-HAWK WOULD JUST TELL US WHERE THAT BOMB IS!
I WANT YOU TO KNOW THAT I REALLY APPRECIATE THE GESTURE, BIG GUY.
I REALIZE THAT FIRELORD DIDN'T HAVE TIME TO GIVE IT TO YOU BEFORE HE--
BUT HE NEVER TELLS US ANYTHI--
SLAP
HEY! I'M TRYING TO MAKE NICE HERE!!
I KNOW. SORRY.
I JUST WANT TO SAY THANKS. IT MEANT A LOT TO ME.
LOVE YOU, TOO, FLAME-BRAIN.
HEY, DO YOU KNOW WHERE STARHAWK IS?
"MAYBE I CAN WRING IT OUT OF HIM!"
STAKAR? MAY I SPEAK WITH YOU?
YES, ALETA. PLEASE, COME IN.
WERE YOU EXPECTING ME?
NO, I WASN'T.
BUT I WAS HOPING THAT YOU WOULD COME.

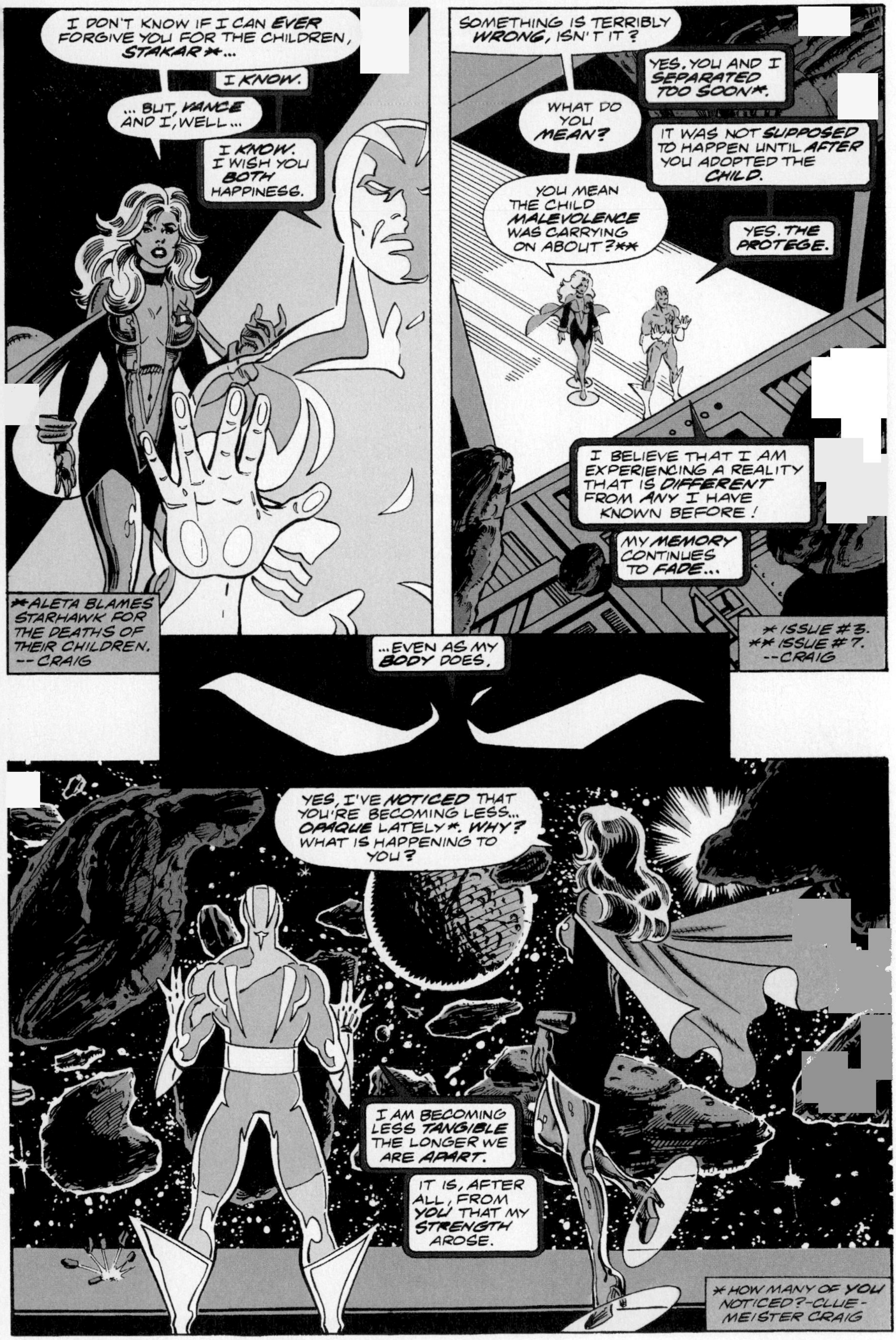
I DON'T KNOW IF I CAN EVER FORGIVE YOU FOR THE CHILDREN, STAKAR*...
I KNOW.
... BUT, VANCE AND I, WELL...
I KNOW. I WISH YOU BOTH HAPPINESS.
*ALETA BLAMES STARHAWK FOR THE DEATHS OF THEIR CHILDREN. --CRAIG
SOMETHING IS TERRIBLY WRONG, ISN'T IT?
YES. YOU AND I SEPARATED TOO SOON*.
WHAT DO YOU MEAN?
IT WAS NOT SUPPOSED TO HAPPEN UNTIL AFTER YOU ADOPTED THE CHILD.
YOU MEAN THE CHILD MALEVOLENCE WAS CARRYING ON ABOUT?**
YES. THE PROTEGE.
I BELIEVE THAT I AM EXPERIENCING A REALITY THAT IS DIFFERENT FROM ANY I HAVE KNOWN BEFORE!
MY MEMORY CONTINUES TO FADE...
*ISSUE #3. **ISSUE #7. --CRAIG
...EVEN AS MY BODY DOES.
YES, I'VE NOTICED THAT YOU'RE BECOMING LESS... OPAQUE LATELY*. WHY? WHAT IS HAPPENING TO YOU?
I AM BECOMING LESS TANGIBLE THE LONGER WE ARE APART.
IT IS, AFTER ALL, FROM YOU THAT MY STRENGTH AROSE.
*HOW MANY OF YOU NOTICED?-CLUE-MEISTER CRAIG

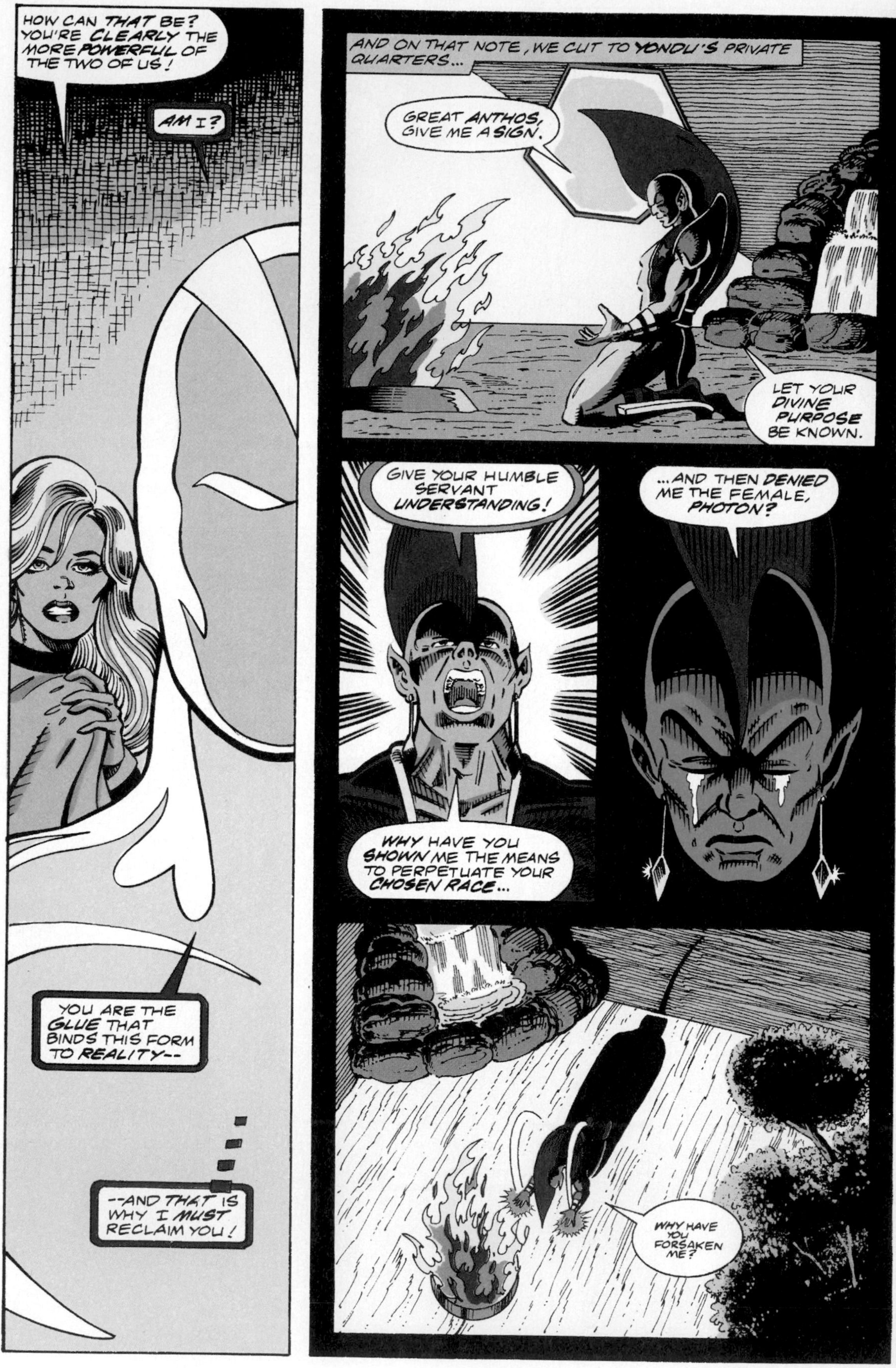
HOW CAN THAT BE? YOU'RE CLEARLY THE MORE POWERFUL OF THE TWO OF US!
AM I?
YOU ARE THE GLUE THAT BINDS THIS FORM TO REALITY--
--AND THAT IS WHY I MUST RECLAIM YOU!
AND ON THAT NOTE, WE CUT TO YONDU'S PRIVATE QUARTERS...
GREAT ANTHOS, GIVE ME A SIGN.
LET YOUR DIVINE PURPOSE BE KNOWN.
GIVE YOUR HUMBLE SERVANT UNDERSTANDING!
WHY HAVE YOU SHOWN ME THE MEANS TO PERPETUATE YOUR CHOSEN RACE...
...AND THEN DENIED ME THE FEMALE, PHOTON?
WHY HAVE YOU FORSAKEN ME?

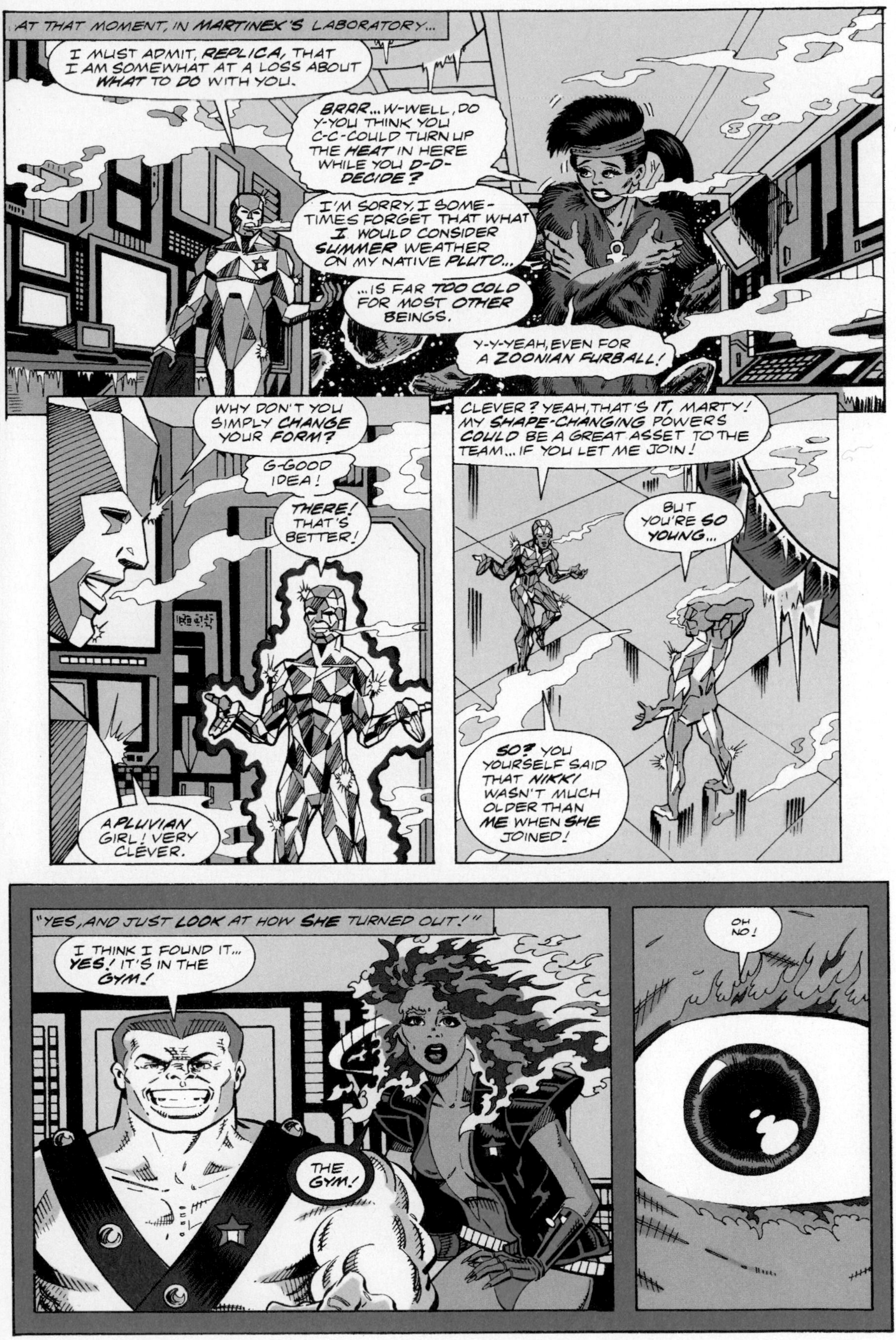

AT THAT MOMENT, IN MARTINEX'S LABORATORY...
I MUST ADMIT, REPLICA, THAT I AM SOMEWHAT AT A LOSS ABOUT WHAT TO DO WITH YOU.
BRRR... W-WELL, DO Y-YOU THINK YOU C-C-COULD TURN UP THE HEAT IN HERE WHILE YOU D-D-DECIDE?
I'M SORRY, I SOMETIMES FORGET THAT WHAT I WOULD CONSIDER SUMMER WEATHER ON MY NATIVE PLUTO...
...IS FAR TOO COLD FOR MOST OTHER BEINGS.
Y-Y-YEAH, EVEN FOR A ZOONIAN FURBALL!
WHY DON'T YOU SIMPLY CHANGE YOUR FORM?
G-GOOD IDEA!
THERE! THAT'S BETTER!
A PLUVIAN GIRL! VERY CLEVER.
CLEVER? YEAH, THAT'S IT, MARTY! MY SHAPE-CHANGING POWERS COULD BE A GREAT ASSET TO THE TEAM... IF YOU LET ME JOIN!
BUT YOU'RE SO YOUNG...
SO? YOU YOURSELF SAID THAT NIKKI WASN'T MUCH OLDER THAN ME WHEN SHE JOINED!
"YES, AND JUST LOOK AT HOW SHE TURNED OUT!"
I THINK I FOUND IT... YES! IT'S IN THE GYM!
THE GYM!
OH NO!

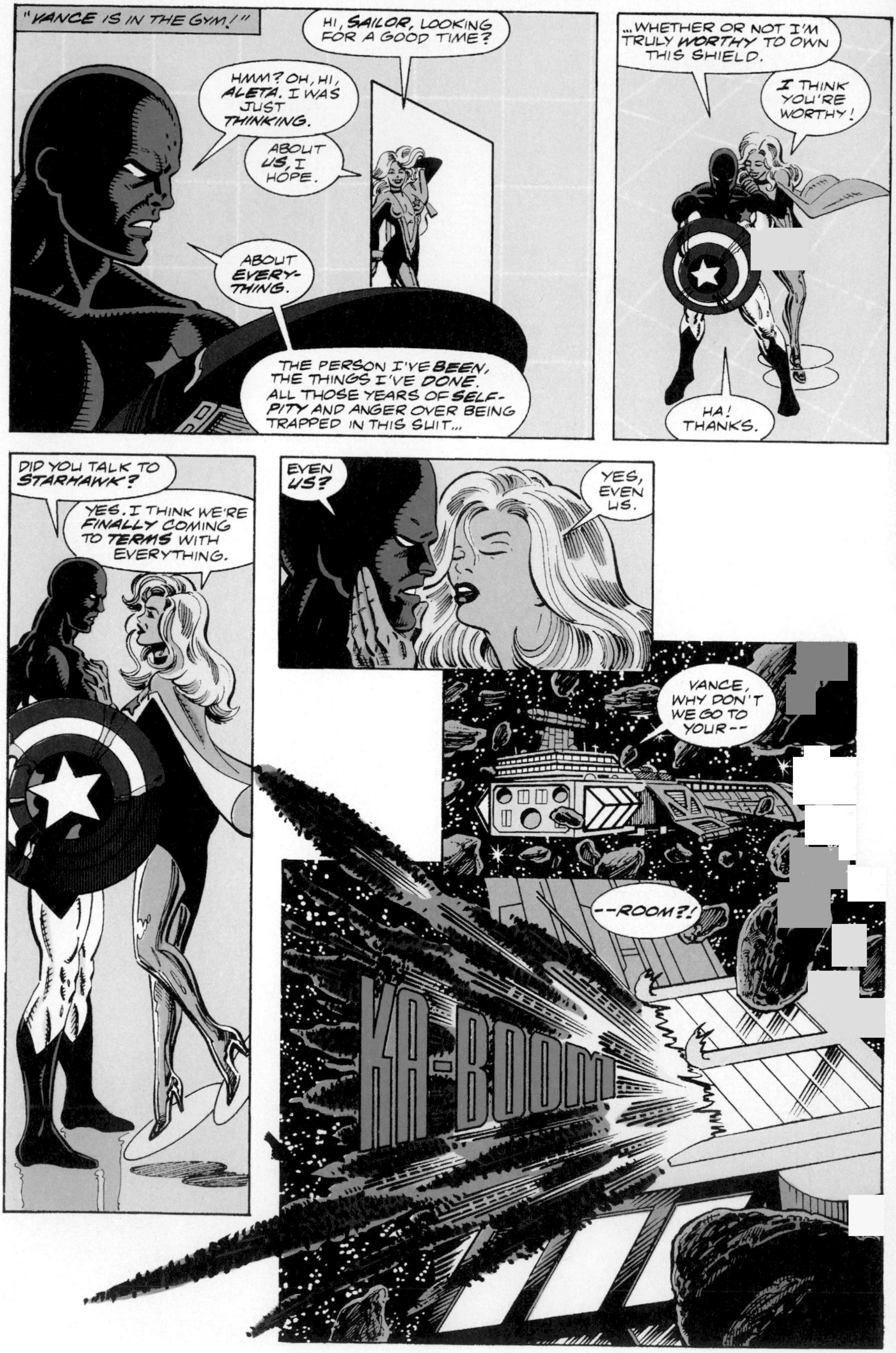
"VANCE IS IN THE GYM!"
HI, SAILOR, LOOKING FOR A GOOD TIME?
HMM? OH, HI, ALETA. I WAS JUST THINKING.
ABOUT US, I HOPE.
ABOUT EVERY-THING.
THE PERSON I'VE BEEN, THE THINGS I'VE DONE. ALL THOSE YEARS OF SELF-PITY AND ANGER OVER BEING TRAPPED IN THIS SUIT...
...WHETHER OR NOT I'M TRULY WORTHY TO OWN THIS SHIELD.
I THINK YOU'RE WORTHY!
HA! THANKS.
DID YOU TALK TO STARHAWK?
YES. I THINK WE'RE FINALLY COMING TO TERMS WITH EVERYTHING.
EVEN US?
YES, EVEN US.
VANCE, WHY DON'T WE GO TO YOUR--
--ROOM?!
KA-BOOM

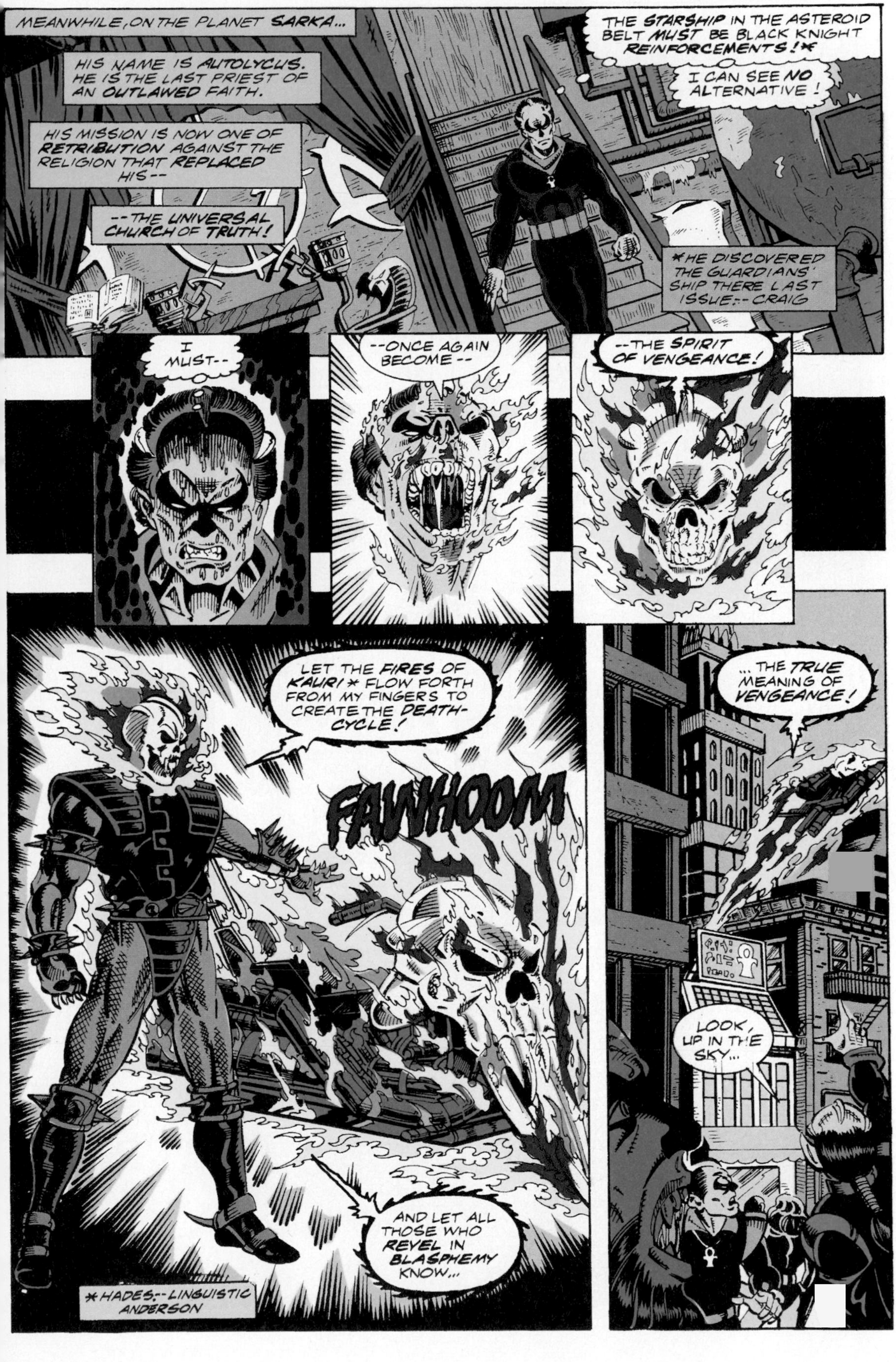
MEANWHILE, ON THE PLANET SARKA...
HIS NAME IS AUTOLYCUS. HE IS THE LAST PRIEST OF AN OUTLAWED FAITH.
HIS MISSION IS NOW ONE OF RETRIBUTION AGAINST THE RELIGION THAT REPLACED HIS--
--THE UNIVERSAL CHURCH OF TRUTH!
THE STARSHIP IN THE ASTEROID BELT MUST BE BLACK KNIGHT REINFORCEMENTS!*
I CAN SEE NO ALTERNATIVE!
*HE DISCOVERED THE GUARDIANS' SHIP THERE LAST ISSUE.--CRAIG
I MUST--
--ONCE AGAIN BECOME--
--THE SPIRIT OF VENGEANCE!
LET THE FIRES OF KAURI* FLOW FORTH FROM MY FINGERS TO CREATE THE DEATH-CYCLE!
FAWHOOM
AND LET ALL THOSE WHO REVEL IN BLASPHEMY KNOW...
*HADES.--LINGUISTIC ANDERSON
...THE TRUE MEANING OF VENGEANCE!
LOOK, UP IN THE SKY...

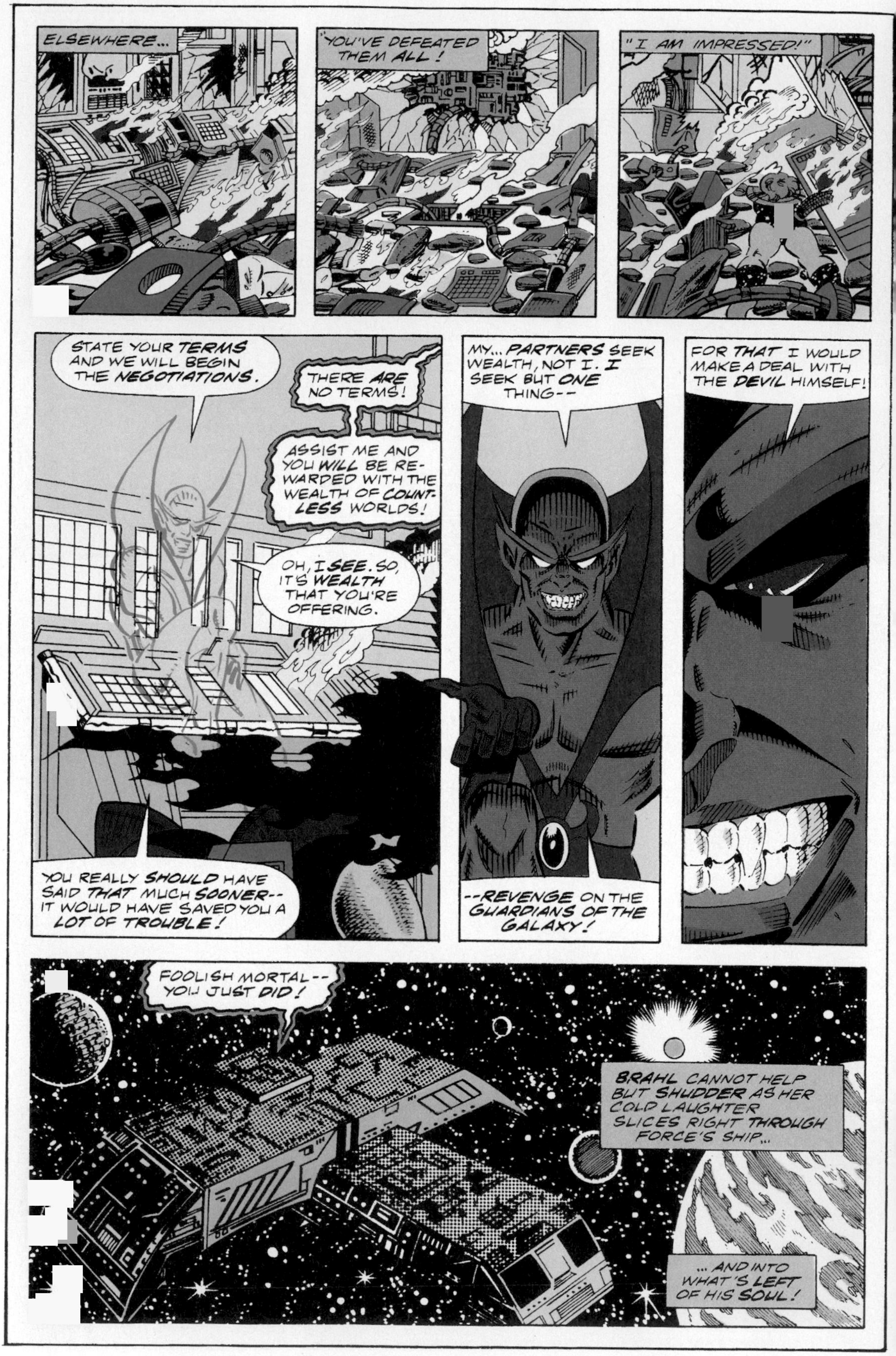
ELSEWHERE...
"YOU'VE DEFEATED THEM ALL!
"I AM IMPRESSED!"
STATE YOUR TERMS AND WE WILL BEGIN THE NEGOTIATIONS.
THERE ARE NO TERMS!
ASSIST ME AND YOU WILL BE RE-WARDED WITH THE WEALTH OF COUNT-LESS WORLDS!
OH, I SEE. SO, IT'S WEALTH THAT YOU'RE OFFERING.
YOU REALLY SHOULD HAVE SAID THAT MUCH SOONER-- IT WOULD HAVE SAVED YOU A LOT OF TROUBLE!
MY... PARTNERS SEEK WEALTH, NOT I. I SEEK BUT ONE THING--
--REVENGE ON THE GUARDIANS OF THE GALAXY!
FOR THAT I WOULD MAKE A DEAL WITH THE DEVIL HIMSELF!
FOOLISH MORTAL-- YOU JUST DID!
BRAHL CANNOT HELP BUT SHUDDER AS HER COLD LAUGHTER SLICES RIGHT THROUGH FORCE'S SHIP...
...AND INTO WHAT'S LEFT OF HIS SOUL!

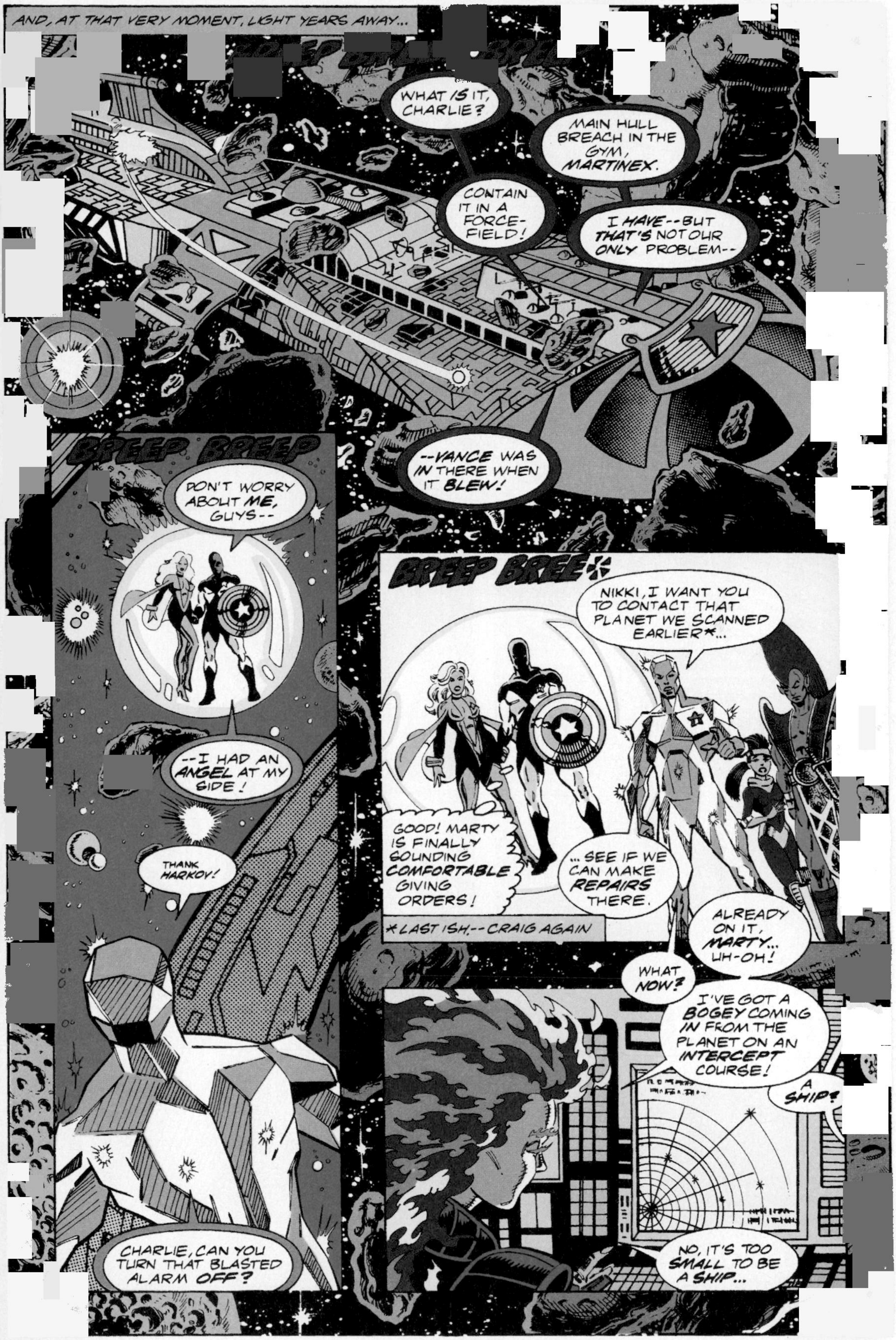
AND, AT THAT VERY MOMENT, LIGHT YEARS AWAY...
WHAT IS IT, CHARLIE?
MAIN HULL BREACH IN THE GYM, MARTINEX.
CONTAIN IT IN A FORCE-FIELD!
I HAVE--BUT THAT'S NOT OUR ONLY PROBLEM--
--VANCE WAS IN THERE WHEN IT BLEW!
BREEP BREEP
DON'T WORRY ABOUT ME, GUYS--
--I HAD AN ANGEL AT MY SIDE!
THANK HARKOV!
CHARLIE, CAN YOU TURN THAT BLASTED ALARM OFF?
BREEP BREE
NIKKI, I WANT YOU TO CONTACT THAT PLANET WE SCANNED EARLIER*...
GOOD! MARTY IS FINALLY SOUNDING COMFORTABLE GIVING ORDERS!
... SEE IF WE CAN MAKE REPAIRS THERE.
*LAST ISH.--CRAIG AGAIN
ALREADY ON IT, MARTY... UH-OH!
WHAT NOW?
I'VE GOT A BOGEY COMING IN FROM THE PLANET ON AN INTERCEPT COURSE!
A SHIP?
NO, IT'S TOO SMALL TO BE A SHIP...

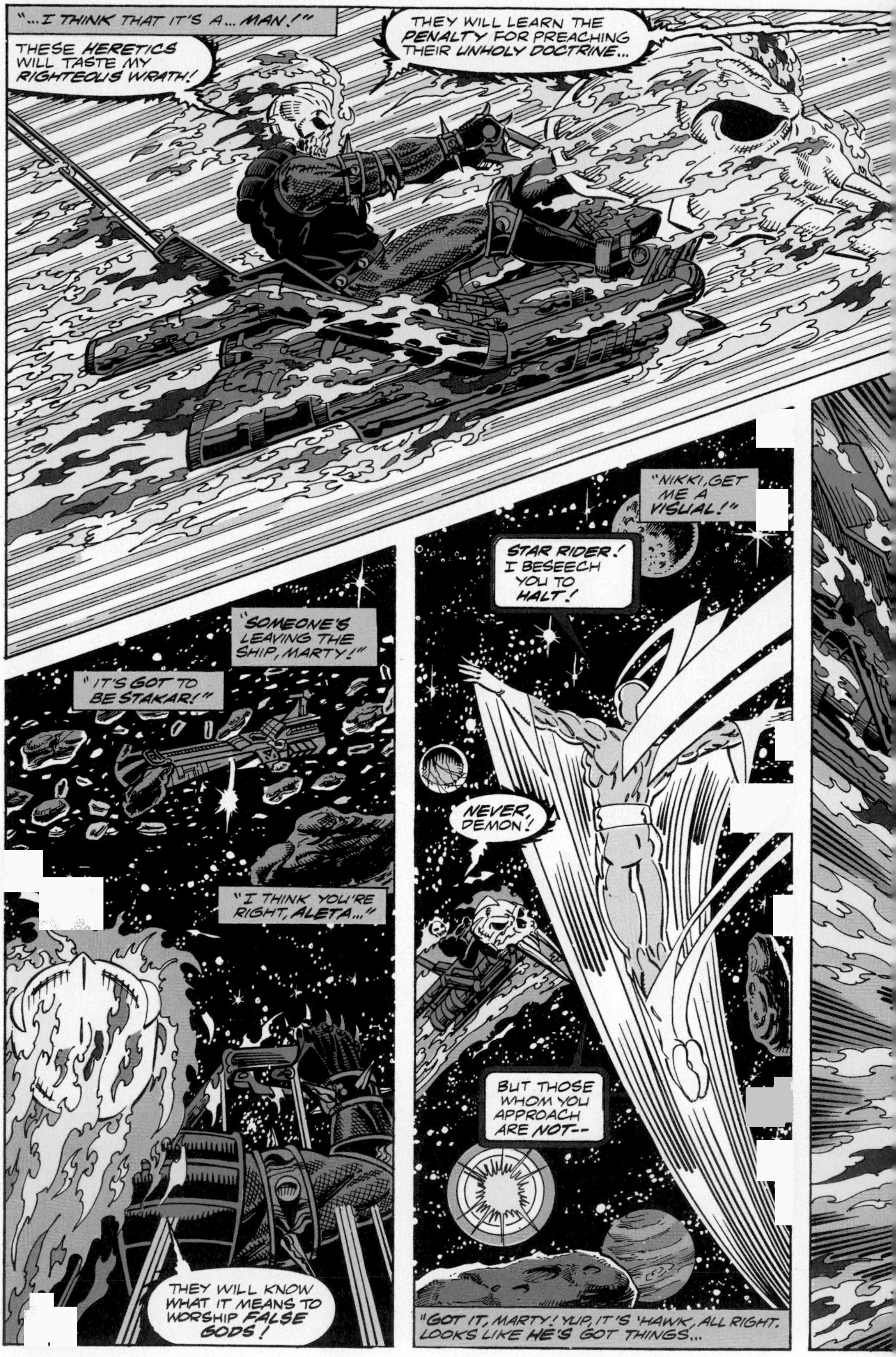
"...I THINK THAT IT'S A... MAN!"
THESE HERETICS WILL TASTE MY RIGHTEOUS WRATH!
THEY WILL LEARN THE PENALTY FOR PREACHING THEIR UNHOLY DOCTRINE...
"SOMEONE'S LEAVING THE SHIP, MARTY!"
"IT'S GOT TO BE STAKAR!"
"I THINK YOU'RE RIGHT, ALETA..."
THEY WILL KNOW WHAT IT MEANS TO WORSHIP FALSE GODS!
"NIKKI, GET ME A VISUAL!"
STAR RIDER! I BESEECH YOU TO HALT!
NEVER, DEMON!
BUT THOSE WHOM YOU APPROACH ARE NOT--
"GOT IT, MARTY! YUP, IT'S 'HAWK, ALL RIGHT. LOOKS LIKE HE'S GOT THINGS...

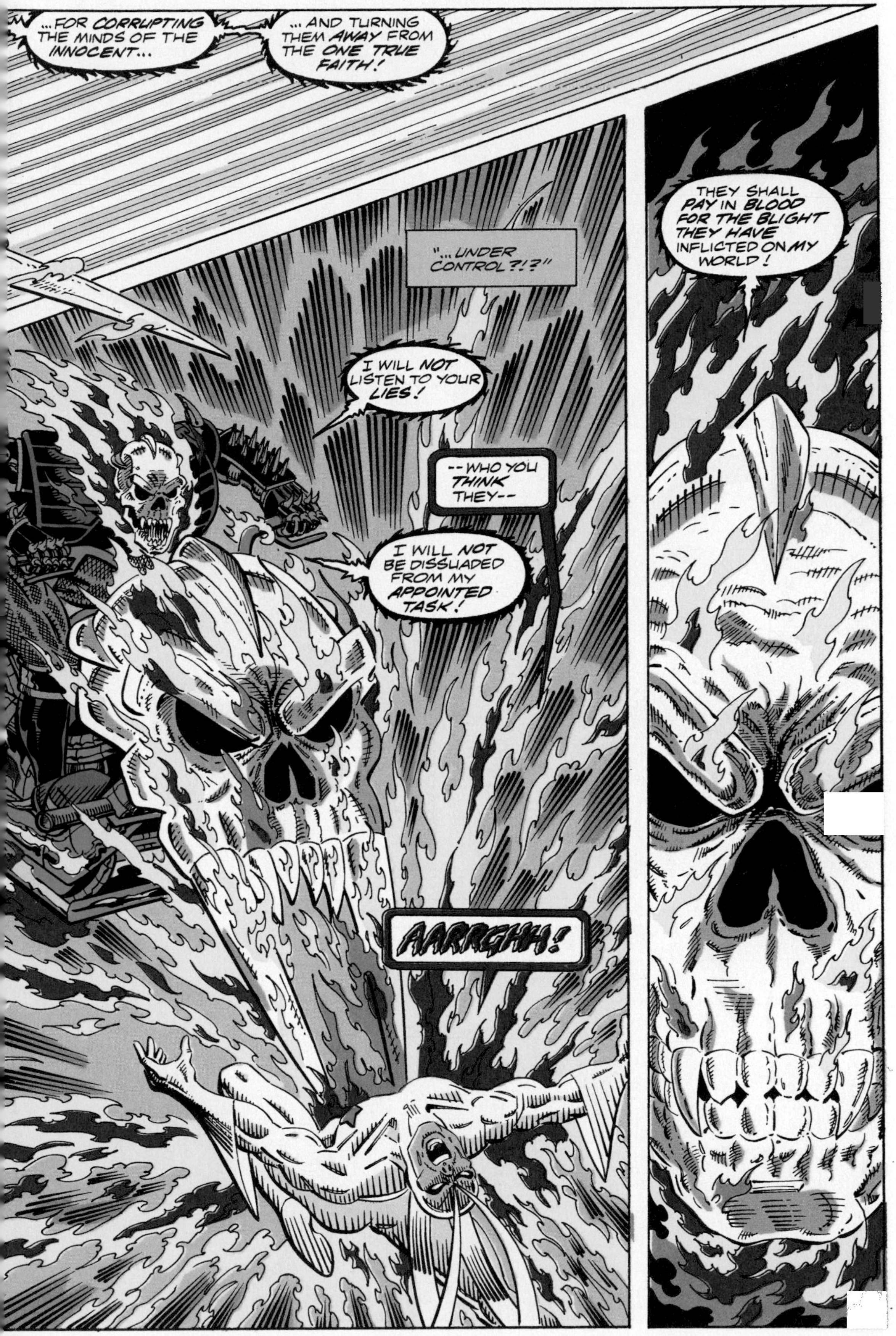
...FOR CORRUPTING THE MINDS OF THE INNOCENT...
...AND TURNING THEM AWAY FROM THE ONE TRUE FAITH!
"...UNDER CONTROL?!?"
I WILL NOT LISTEN TO YOUR LIES!
--WHO YOU THINK THEY--
I WILL NOT BE DISSUADED FROM MY APPOINTED TASK!
AARRGHH!
THEY SHALL PAY IN BLOOD FOR THE BLIGHT THEY HAVE INFLICTED ON MY WORLD!

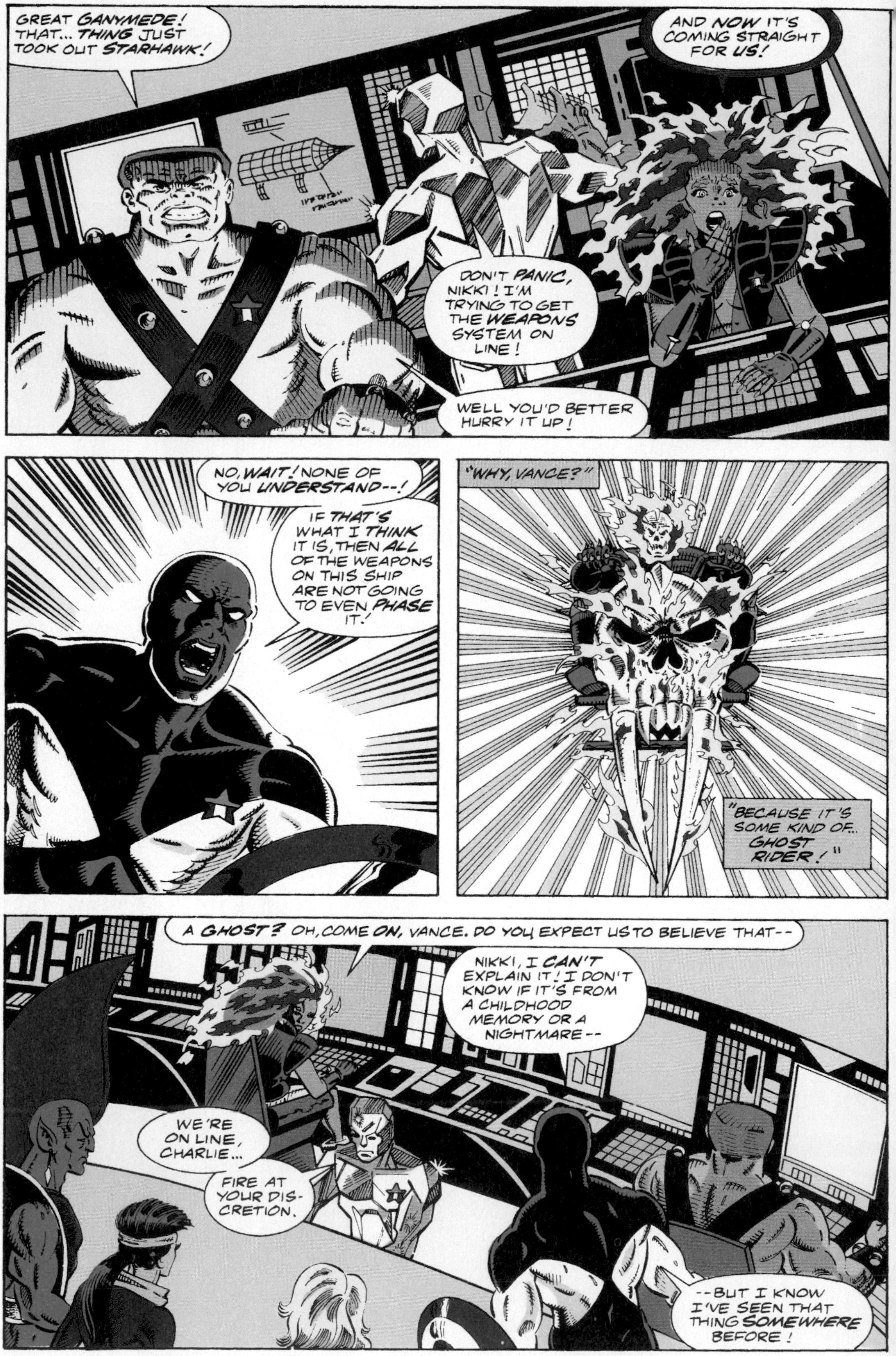
GREAT GANYMEDE! THAT... THING JUST TOOK OUT STARHAWK!
AND NOW IT'S COMING STRAIGHT FOR US!
DON'T PANIC, NIKKI! I'M TRYING TO GET THE WEAPONS SYSTEM ON LINE!
WELL YOU'D BETTER HURRY IT UP!
NO, WAIT! NONE OF YOU UNDERSTAND--!
IF THAT'S WHAT I THINK IT IS, THEN ALL OF THE WEAPONS ON THIS SHIP ARE NOT GOING TO EVEN PHASE IT!
"WHY, VANCE?"
"BECAUSE IT'S SOME KIND OF.. GHOST RIDER!"
A GHOST? OH, COME ON, VANCE. DO YOU EXPECT US TO BELIEVE THAT--
NIKKI, I CAN'T EXPLAIN IT! I DON'T KNOW IF IT'S FROM A CHILDHOOD MEMORY OR A NIGHTMARE--
WE'RE ON LINE, CHARLIE...
FIRE AT YOUR DIS-CRETION.
--BUT I KNOW I'VE SEEN THAT THING SOMEWHERE BEFORE!

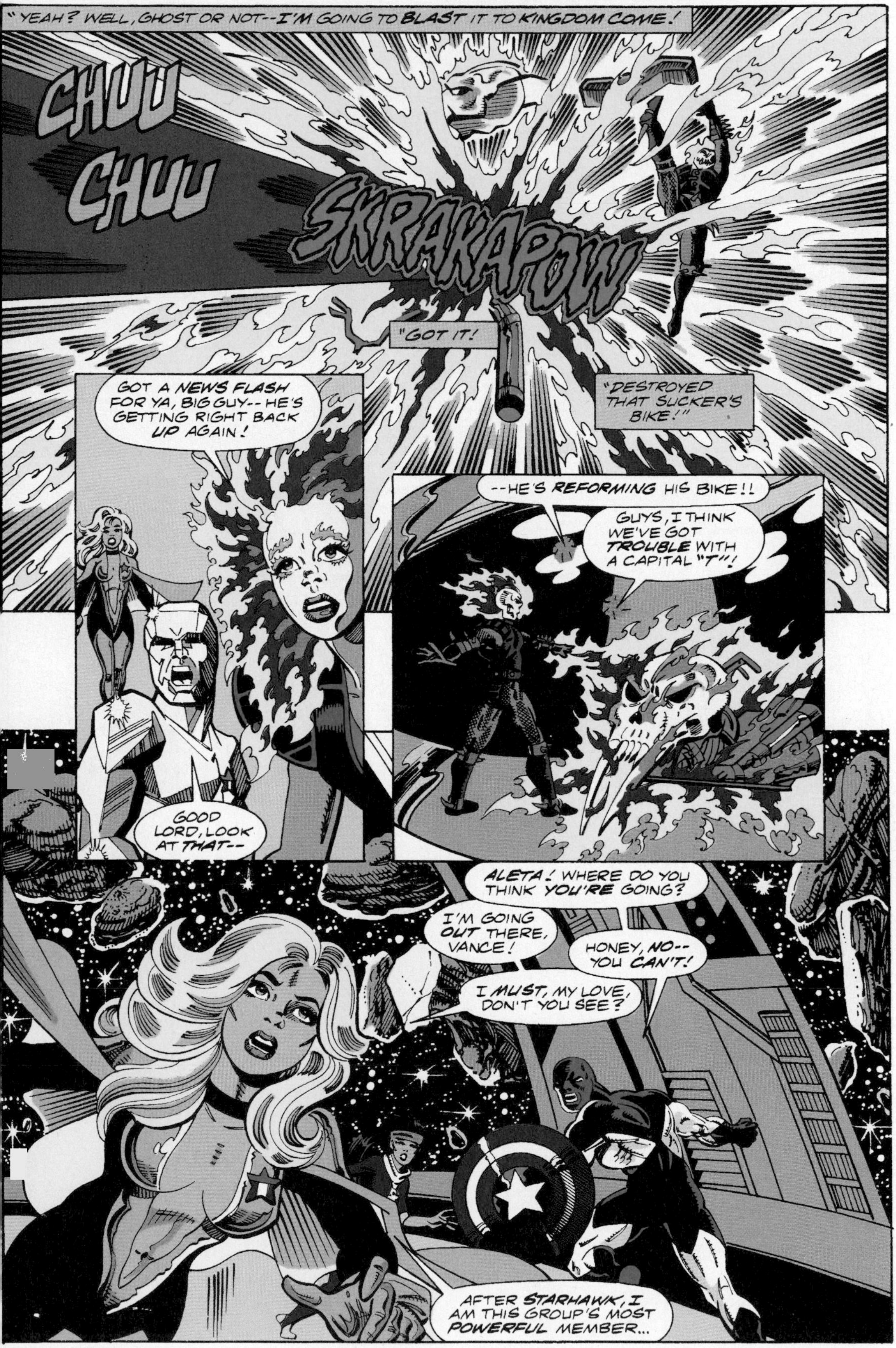
"YEAH? WELL, GHOST OR NOT--I'M GOING TO BLAST IT TO KINGDOM COME!
CHUU CHUU
SKRAKAPOW
"GOT IT!
"DESTROYED THAT SUCKER'S BIKE!"
GOT A NEWS FLASH FOR YA, BIG GUY-- HE'S GETTING RIGHT BACK UP AGAIN!
GOOD LORD, LOOK AT THAT--
--HE'S REFORMING HIS BIKE!!
GUYS, I THINK WE'VE GOT TROUBLE WITH A CAPITAL "T"!
ALETA! WHERE DO YOU THINK YOU'RE GOING?
I'M GOING OUT THERE, VANCE!
HONEY, NO-- YOU CAN'T!
I MUST, MY LOVE, DON'T YOU SEE?
AFTER STARHAWK, I AM THIS GROUP'S MOST POWERFUL MEMBER...

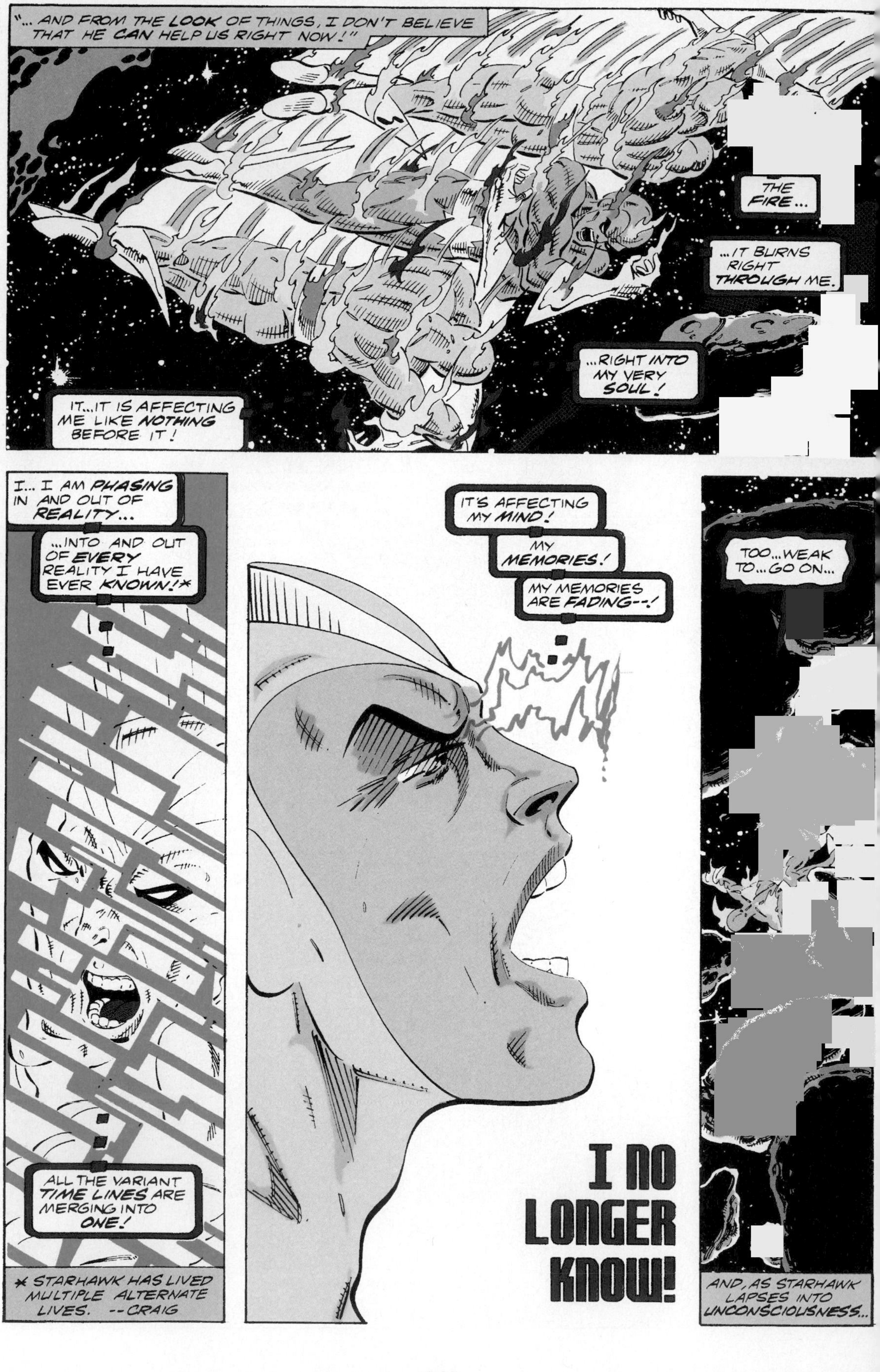
"...AND FROM THE LOOK OF THINGS, I DON'T BELIEVE THAT HE CAN HELP US RIGHT NOW!"
THE FIRE...
...IT BURNS RIGHT THROUGH ME.
...RIGHT INTO MY VERY SOUL!
IT...IT IS AFFECTING ME LIKE NOTHING BEFORE IT!
I... I AM PHASING IN AND OUT OF REALITY...
...INTO AND OUT OF EVERY REALITY I HAVE EVER KNOWN!*
ALL THE VARIANT TIME LINES ARE MERGING INTO ONE!
* STARHAWK HAS LIVED MULTIPLE ALTERNATE LIVES. --CRAIG
IT'S AFFECTING MY MIND!
MY MEMORIES!
MY MEMORIES ARE FADING--!
I NO LONGER KNOW!
TOO...WEAK TO...GO ON...
AND, AS STARHAWK LAPSES INTO UNCONSCIOUSNESS...

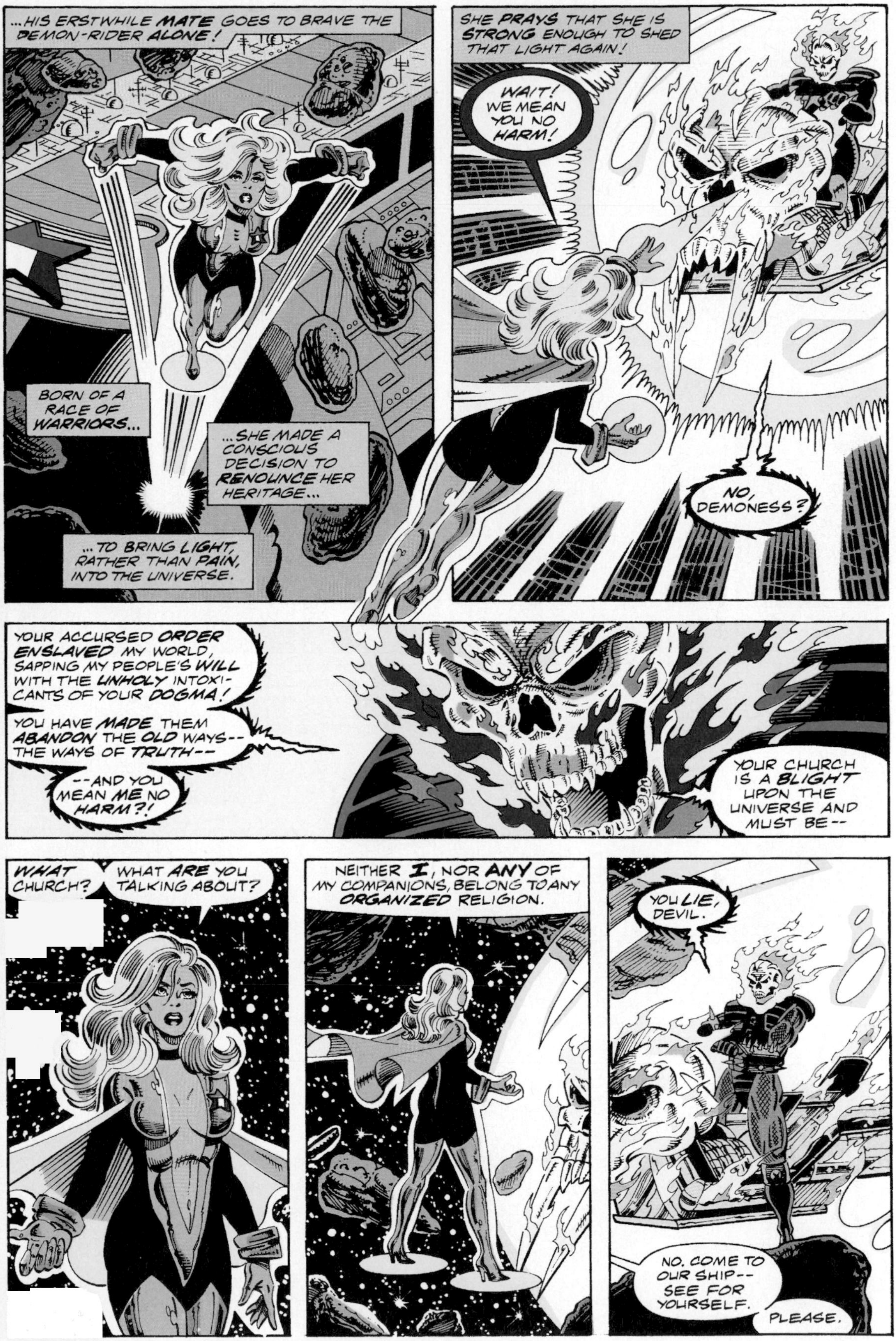
...HIS ERSTWHILE MATE GOES TO BRAVE THE DEMON-RIDER ALONE!
BORN OF A RACE OF WARRIORS...
...SHE MADE A CONSCIOUS DECISION TO RENOUNCE HER HERITAGE...
...TO BRING LIGHT, RATHER THAN PAIN, INTO THE UNIVERSE.
SHE PRAYS THAT SHE IS STRONG ENOUGH TO SHED THAT LIGHT AGAIN!
WAIT! WE MEAN YOU NO HARM!
NO, DEMONESS?
YOUR ACCURSED ORDER ENSLAVED MY WORLD, SAPPING MY PEOPLE'S WILL WITH THE UNHOLY INTOXI-CANTS OF YOUR DOGMA!
YOU HAVE MADE THEM ABANDON THE OLD WAYS-- THE WAYS OF TRUTH--
--AND YOU MEAN ME NO HARM?!
YOUR CHURCH IS A BLIGHT UPON THE UNIVERSE AND MUST BE--
WHAT CHURCH?
WHAT ARE YOU TALKING ABOUT?
NEITHER I, NOR ANY OF MY COMPANIONS, BELONG TO ANY ORGANIZED RELIGION.
YOU LIE, DEVIL.
NO. COME TO OUR SHIP-- SEE FOR YOURSELF.
PLEASE.

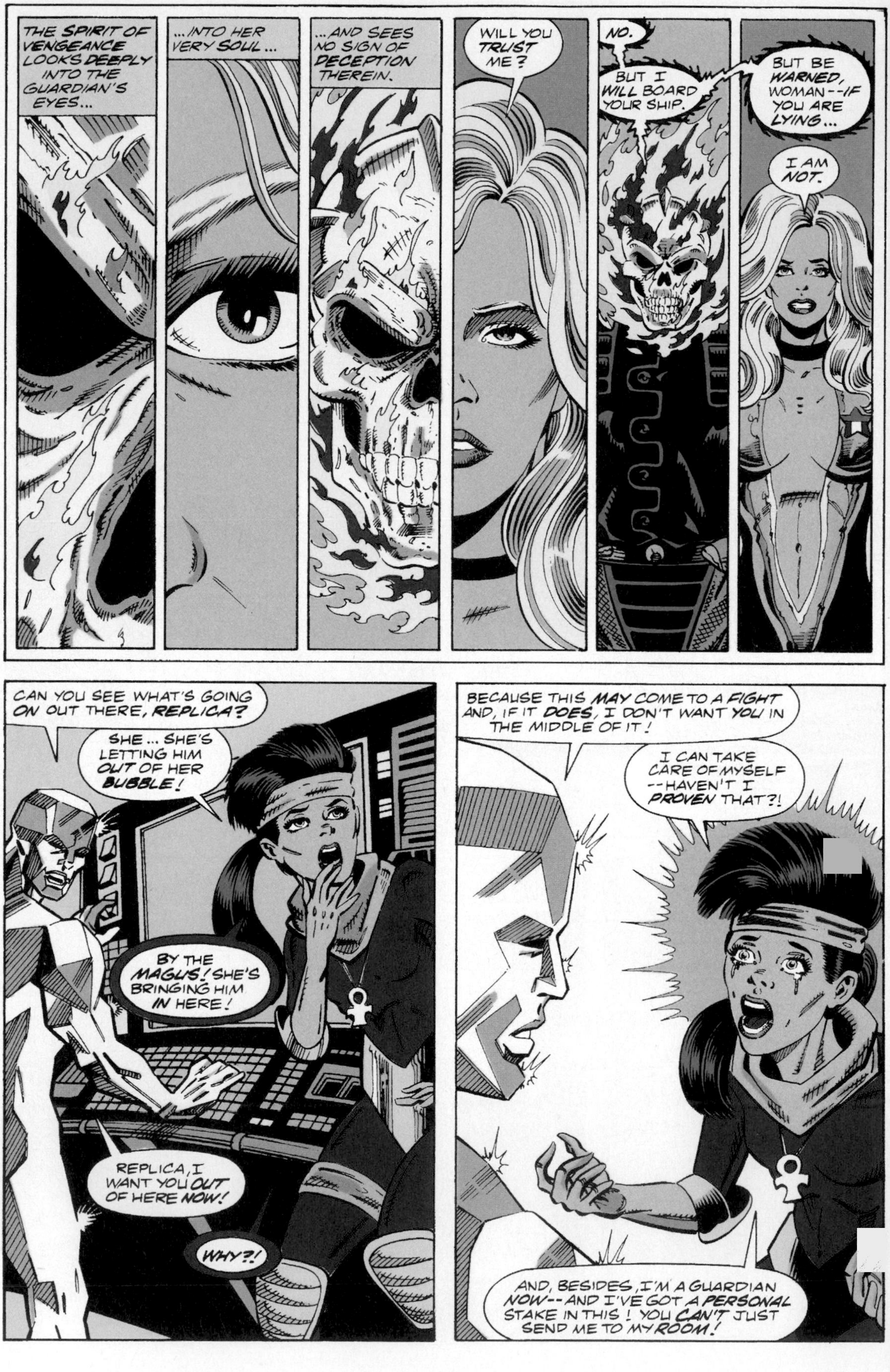
THE SPIRIT OF VENGEANCE LOOKS DEEPLY INTO THE GUARDIAN'S EYES...
...INTO HER VERY SOUL...
...AND SEES NO SIGN OF DECEPTION THEREIN.
WILL YOU TRUST ME?
NO.
BUT I WILL BOARD YOUR SHIP.
BUT BE WARNED, WOMAN--IF YOU ARE LYING...
I AM NOT.
CAN YOU SEE WHAT'S GOING ON OUT THERE, REPLICA?
SHE... SHE'S LETTING HIM OUT OF HER BUBBLE!
BY THE MAGUS! SHE'S BRINGING HIM IN HERE!
REPLICA, I WANT YOU OUT OF HERE NOW!
WHY?!
BECAUSE THIS MAY COME TO A FIGHT AND, IF IT DOES, I DON'T WANT YOU IN THE MIDDLE OF IT!
I CAN TAKE CARE OF MYSELF --HAVEN'T I PROVEN THAT?!
AND, BESIDES, I'M A GUARDIAN NOW-- AND I'VE GOT A PERSONAL STAKE IN THIS! YOU CAN'T JUST SEND ME TO MY ROOM!

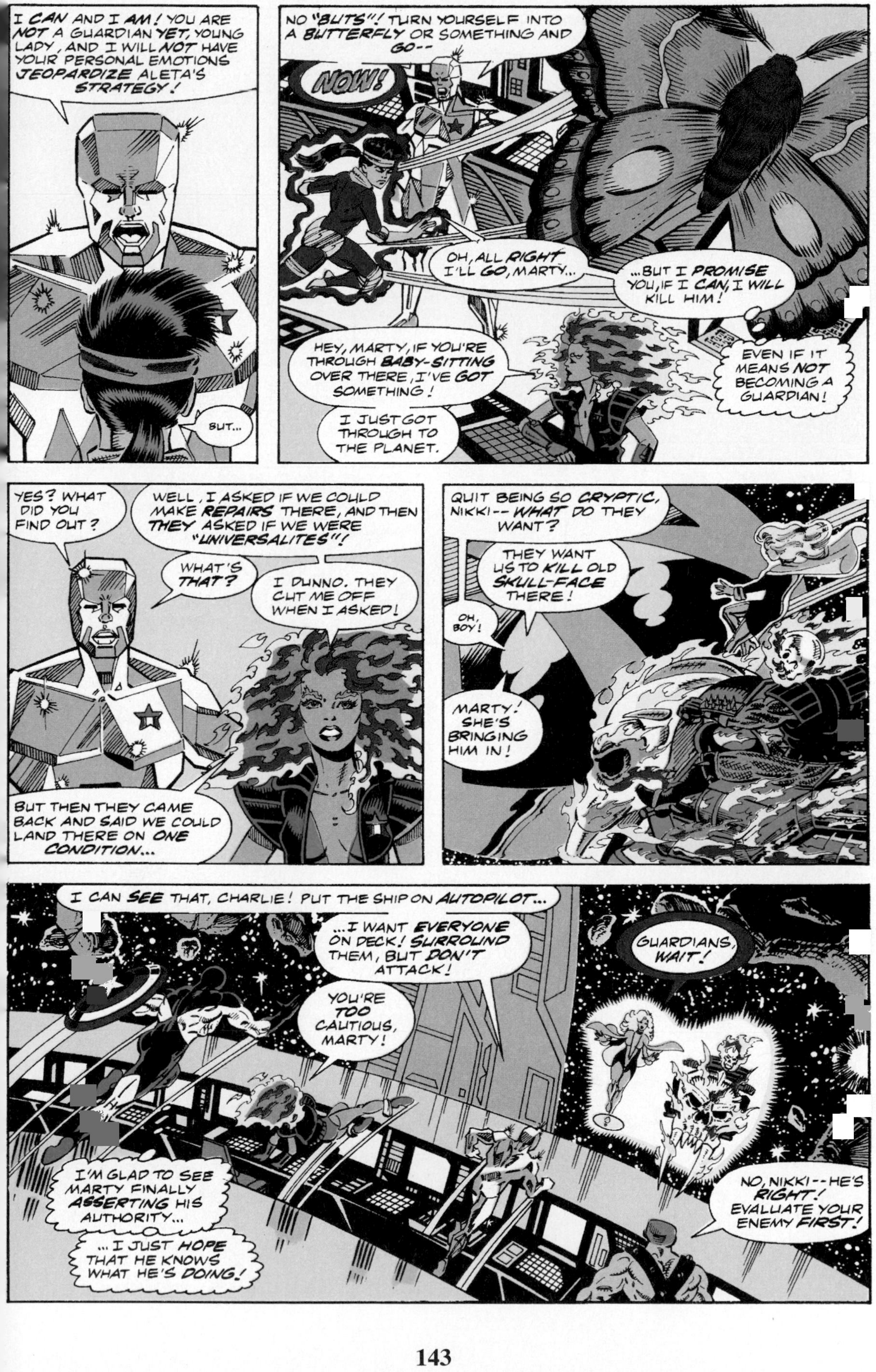
I CAN AND I AM! YOU ARE NOT A GUARDIAN YET, YOUNG LADY, AND I WILL NOT HAVE YOUR PERSONAL EMOTIONS JEOPARDIZE ALETA'S STRATEGY!
BUT...
NO "BUTS"! TURN YOURSELF INTO A BUTTERFLY OR SOMETHING AND GO--
NOW!
OH, ALL RIGHT I'LL GO, MARTY...
...BUT I PROMISE YOU, IF I CAN, I WILL KILL HIM!
EVEN IF IT MEANS NOT BECOMING A GUARDIAN!
HEY, MARTY, IF YOU'RE THROUGH BABY-SITTING OVER THERE, I'VE GOT SOMETHING!
I JUST GOT THROUGH TO THE PLANET.
YES? WHAT DID YOU FIND OUT?
WELL, I ASKED IF WE COULD MAKE REPAIRS THERE, AND THEN THEY ASKED IF WE WERE "UNIVERSALITES"!
WHAT'S THAT?
I DUNNO. THEY CUT ME OFF WHEN I ASKED!
BUT THEN THEY CAME BACK AND SAID WE COULD LAND THERE ON ONE CONDITION...
QUIT BEING SO CRYPTIC, NIKKI-- WHAT DO THEY WANT?
THEY WANT US TO KILL OLD SKULL-FACE THERE!
OH, BOY!
MARTY! SHE'S BRINGING HIM IN!
I CAN SEE THAT, CHARLIE! PUT THE SHIP ON AUTOPILOT...
...I WANT EVERYONE ON DECK! SURROUND THEM, BUT DON'T ATTACK!
YOU'RE TOO CAUTIOUS, MARTY!
GUARDIANS, WAIT!
I'M GLAD TO SEE MARTY FINALLY ASSERTING HIS AUTHORITY...
...I JUST HOPE THAT HE KNOWS WHAT HE'S DOING!
NO, NIKKI--HE'S RIGHT! EVALUATE YOUR ENEMY FIRST!

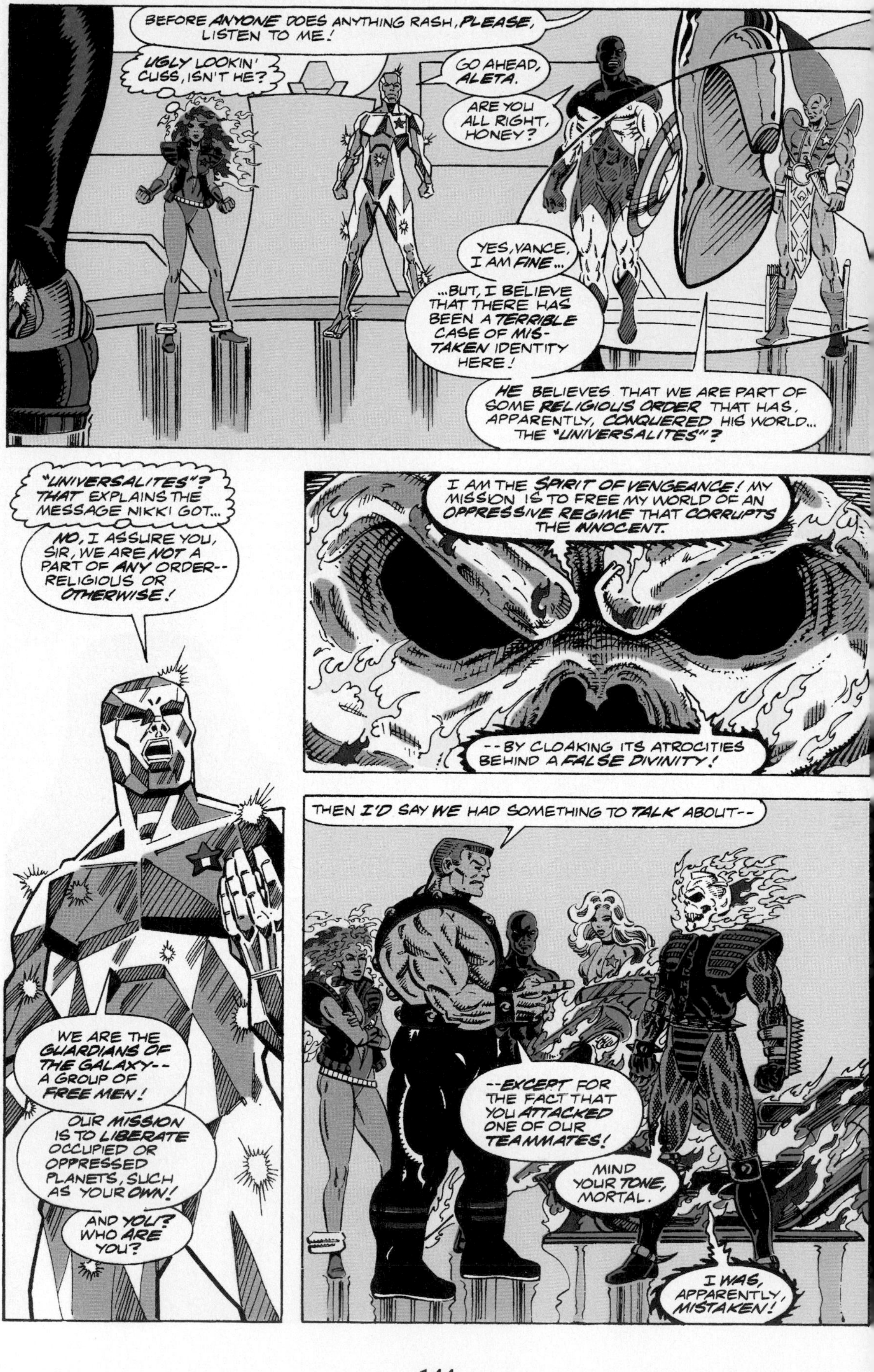
BEFORE ANYONE DOES ANYTHING RASH, PLEASE, LISTEN TO ME!
UGLY LOOKIN' CUSS, ISN'T HE?
GO AHEAD, ALETA.
ARE YOU ALL RIGHT, HONEY?
YES, VANCE, I AM FINE...
...BUT, I BELIEVE THAT THERE HAS BEEN A TERRIBLE CASE OF MIS-TAKEN IDENTITY HERE!
HE BELIEVES THAT WE ARE PART OF SOME RELIGIOUS ORDER THAT HAS, APPARENTLY, CONQUERED HIS WORLD... THE "UNIVERSALITES"?
"UNIVERSALITES"? THAT EXPLAINS THE MESSAGE NIKKI GOT...
NO, I ASSURE YOU, SIR, WE ARE NOT A PART OF ANY ORDER-- RELIGIOUS OR OTHERWISE!
I AM THE SPIRIT OF VENGEANCE! MY MISSION IS TO FREE MY WORLD OF AN OPPRESSIVE REGIME THAT CORRUPTS THE INNOCENT.
--BY CLOAKING ITS ATROCITIES BEHIND A FALSE DIVINITY!
WE ARE THE GUARDIANS OF THE GALAXY-- A GROUP OF FREE MEN!
OUR MISSION IS TO LIBERATE OCCUPIED OR OPPRESSED PLANETS, SUCH AS YOUR OWN!
AND YOU? WHO ARE YOU?
THEN I'D SAY WE HAD SOMETHING TO TALK ABOUT--
--EXCEPT FOR THE FACT THAT YOU ATTACKED ONE OF OUR TEAMMATES!
MIND YOUR TONE, MORTAL.
I WAS, APPARENTLY, MISTAKEN!

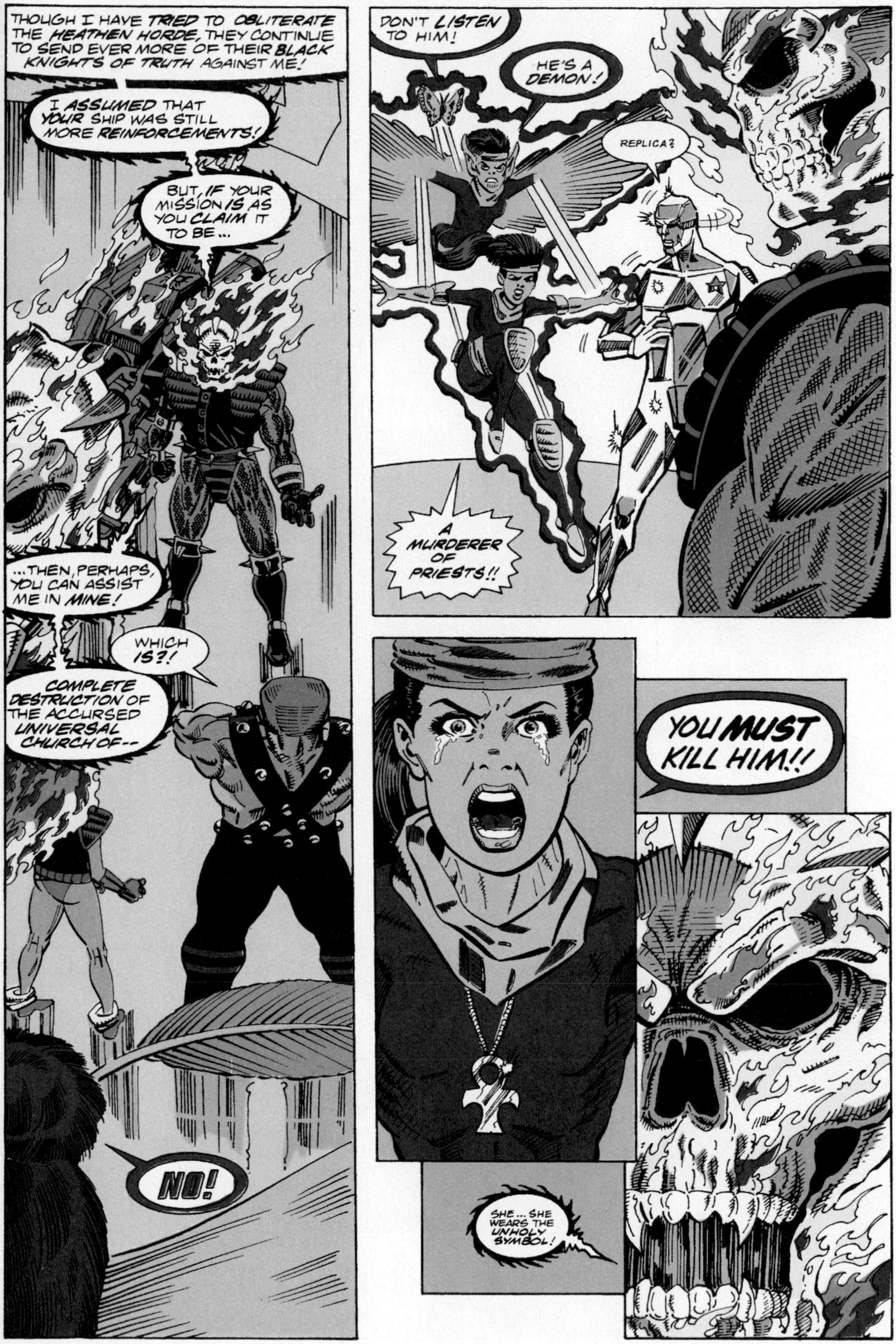
THOUGH I HAVE TRIED TO OBLITERATE THE HEATHEN HORDE, THEY CONTINUE TO SEND EVER MORE OF THEIR BLACK KNIGHTS OF TRUTH AGAINST ME!
I ASSUMED THAT YOUR SHIP WAS STILL MORE REINFORCEMENTS!
BUT, IF YOUR MISSION IS AS YOU CLAIM IT TO BE...
...THEN, PERHAPS, YOU CAN ASSIST ME IN MINE!
WHICH IS?!
COMPLETE DESTRUCTION OF THE ACCURSED UNIVERSAL CHURCH OF--
NO!
DON'T LISTEN TO HIM!
HE'S A DEMON!
REPLICA?
A MURDERER OF PRIESTS!!
YOU MUST KILL HIM!!
SHE... SHE WEARS THE UNHOLY SYMBOL!

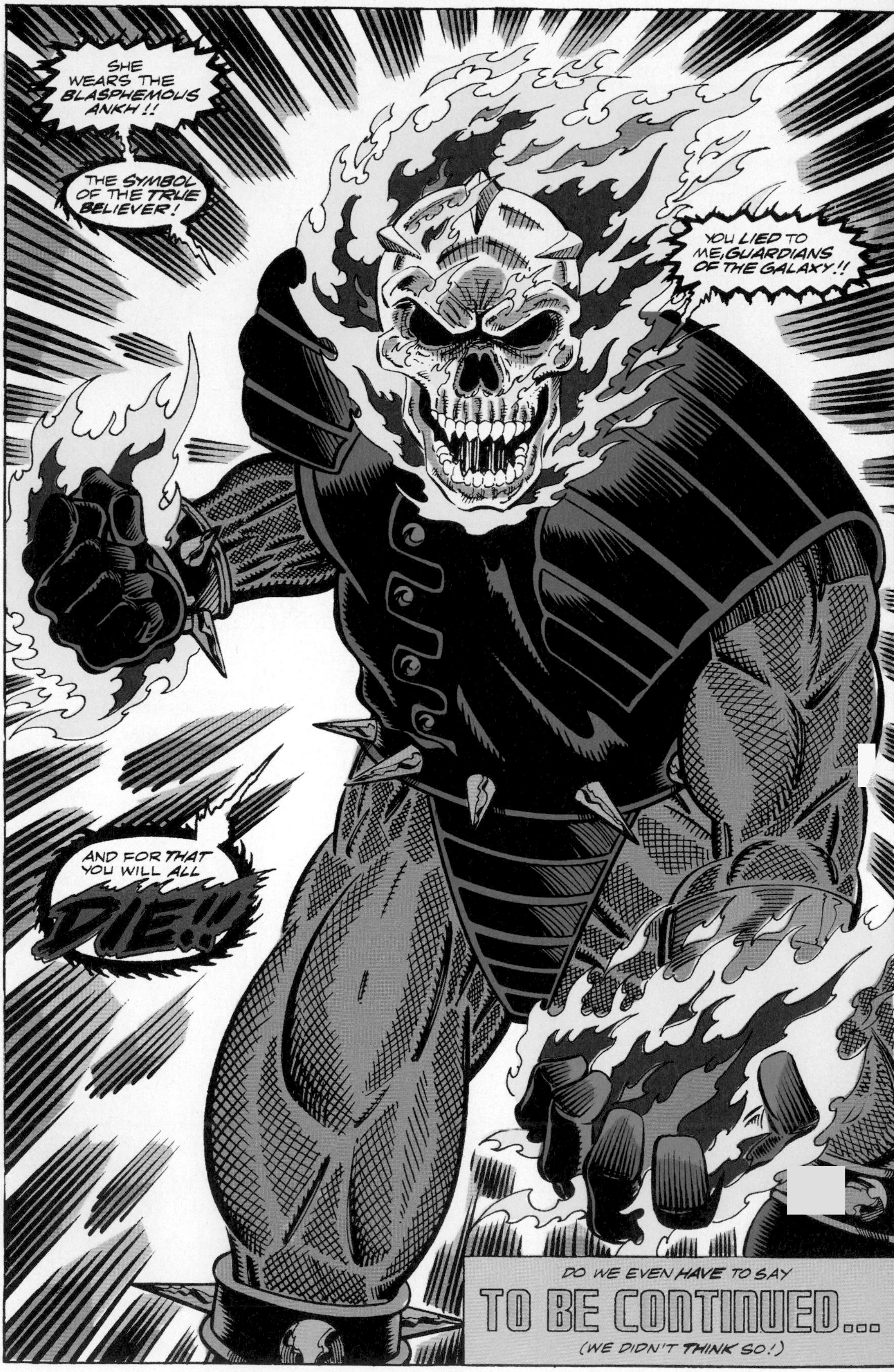
SHE WEARS THE BLASPHEMOUS ANKH!!
THE SYMBOL OF THE TRUE BELIEVER!
YOU LIED TO ME, GUARDIANS OF THE GALAXY!!
AND FOR THAT YOU WILL ALL
DIE!!
DO WE EVEN HAVE TO SAY
TO BE CONTINUED...
(WE DIDN'T THINK SO!)

GUARDIANS
OF THE GALAXY

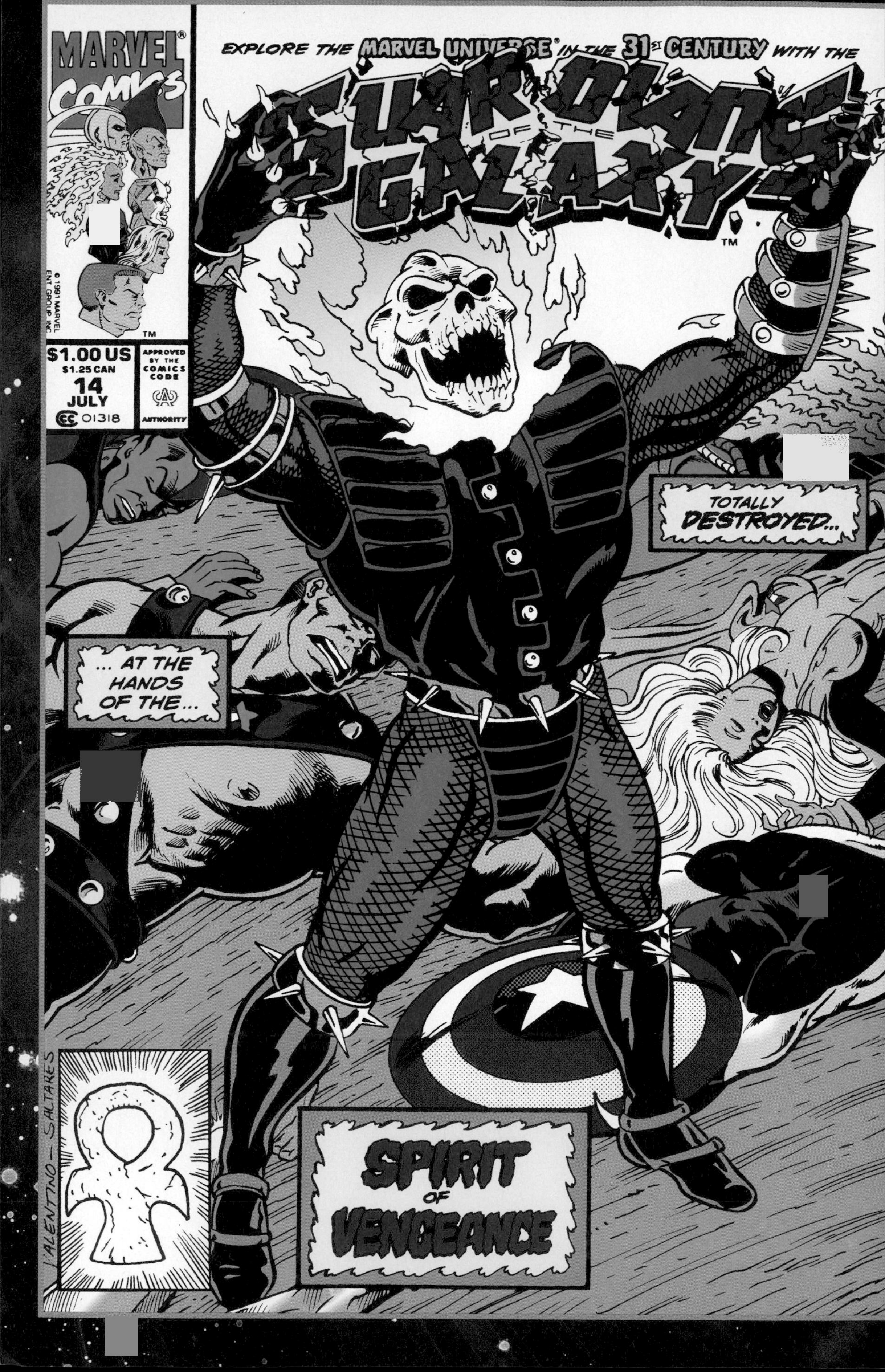
MARVEL COMICS
EXPLORE THE MARVEL UNIVERSE® IN THE 31st CENTURY WITH THE
GUARDIANS OF THE GALAXY
TM
© 1991 MARVEL ENT. GROUP, INC.
$1.00 US
$1.25 CAN
14
JULY
01318
APPROVED BY THE COMICS CODE AUTHORITY
TOTALLY DESTROYED...
... AT THE HANDS OF THE...
SPIRIT OF VENGEANCE
VALENTINO-SALTARES

CHARLIE 27! MARTINEX! NIKKI! VANCE ASTRO! YONDU! ALETA! STARHAWK! SEVEN EXTRAORDINARY SUPER-BEINGS, ALL SURVIVORS OF INTERSTELLAR WAR. NOW THEY ROAM THE COSMOS OF THE 31ST CENTURY ABOARD THE STARSHIP CAPTAIN AMERICA, THEIR MISSION—TO SAFEGUARD THE MILKY WAY! STAN LEE PRESENTS . . . THE GUARDIANS OF THE GALAXY!

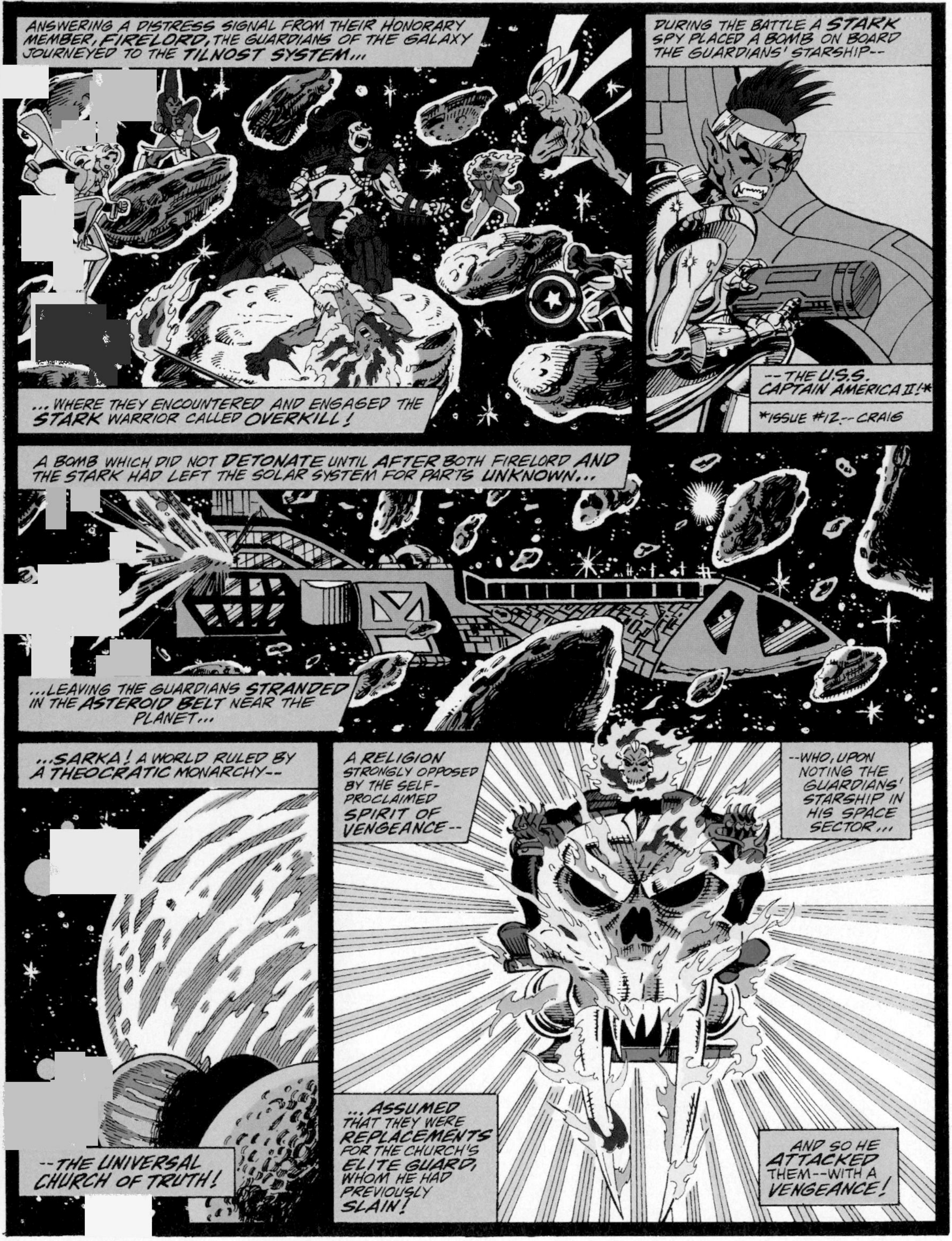

ANSWERING A DISTRESS SIGNAL FROM THEIR HONORARY MEMBER, FIRELORD, THE GUARDIANS OF THE GALAXY JOURNEYED TO THE TILNOST SYSTEM...
...WHERE THEY ENCOUNTERED AND ENGAGED THE STARK WARRIOR CALLED OVERKILL!
DURING THE BATTLE A STARK SPY PLACED A BOMB ON BOARD THE GUARDIANS' STARSHIP--
--THE U.S.S. CAPTAIN AMERICA II!*
*ISSUE #12.--CRAIG
A BOMB WHICH DID NOT DETONATE UNTIL AFTER BOTH FIRELORD AND THE STARK HAD LEFT THE SOLAR SYSTEM FOR PARTS UNKNOWN...
...LEAVING THE GUARDIANS STRANDED IN THE ASTEROID BELT NEAR THE PLANET...
...SARKA! A WORLD RULED BY A THEOCRATIC MONARCHY--
--THE UNIVERSAL CHURCH OF TRUTH!
A RELIGION STRONGLY OPPOSED BY THE SELF-PROCLAIMED SPIRIT OF VENGEANCE--
--WHO, UPON NOTING THE GUARDIANS' STARSHIP IN HIS SPACE SECTOR...
...ASSUMED THAT THEY WERE REPLACEMENTS FOR THE CHURCH'S ELITE GUARD, WHOM HE HAD PREVIOUSLY SLAIN!
AND SO HE ATTACKED THEM--WITH A VENGEANCE!

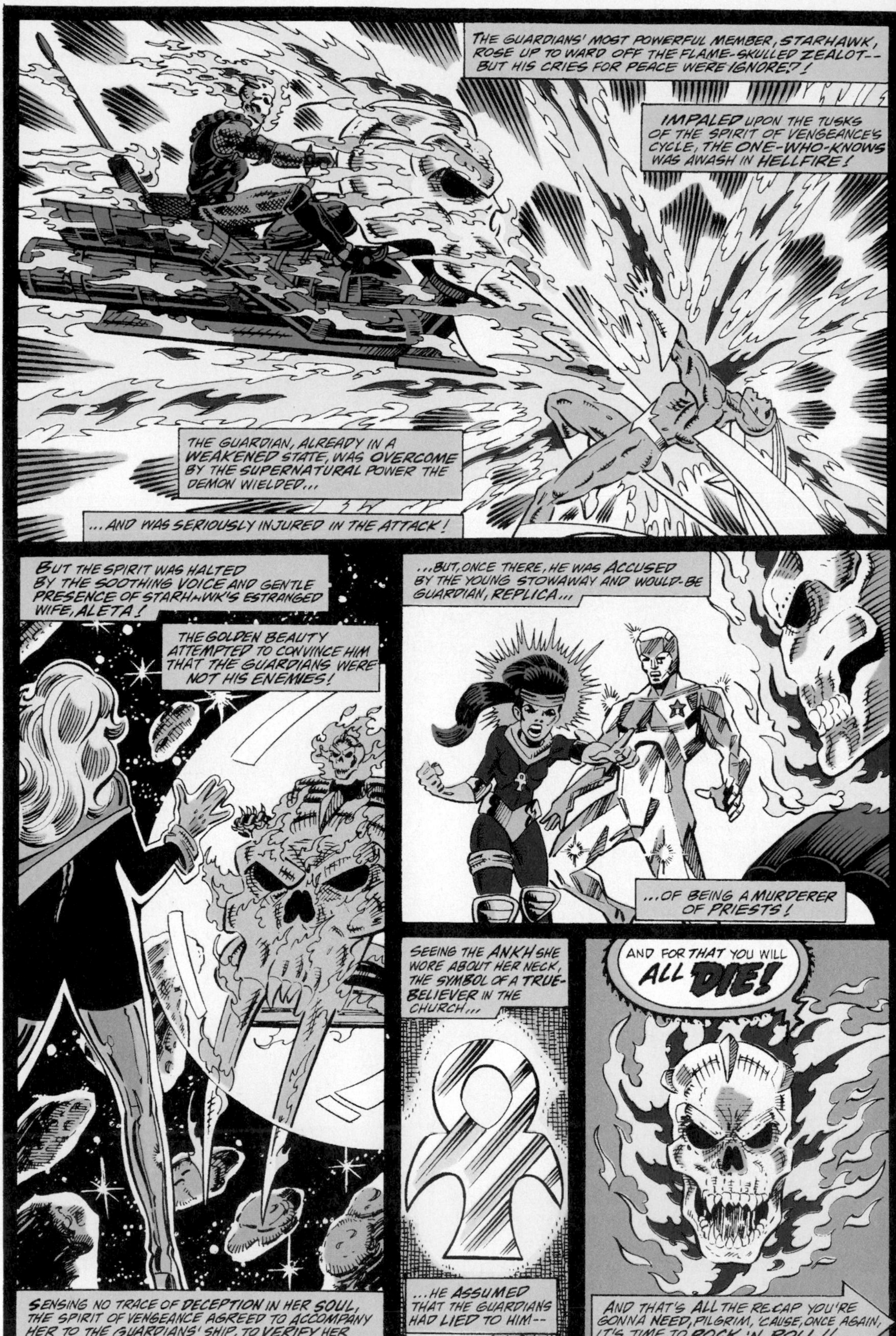
THE GUARDIANS' MOST POWERFUL MEMBER, STARHAWK, ROSE UP TO WARD OFF THE FLAME-SKULLED ZEALOT-- BUT HIS CRIES FOR PEACE WERE IGNORED!
IMPALED UPON THE TUSKS OF THE SPIRIT OF VENGEANCE'S CYCLE, THE ONE-WHO-KNOWS WAS AWASH IN HELLFIRE!
THE GUARDIAN, ALREADY IN A WEAKENED STATE, WAS OVERCOME BY THE SUPERNATURAL POWER THE DEMON WIELDED...
...AND WAS SERIOUSLY INJURED IN THE ATTACK!
BUT THE SPIRIT WAS HALTED BY THE SOOTHING VOICE AND GENTLE PRESENCE OF STARHAWK'S ESTRANGED WIFE, ALETA!
THE GOLDEN BEAUTY ATTEMPTED TO CONVINCE HIM THAT THE GUARDIANS WERE NOT HIS ENEMIES!
SENSING NO TRACE OF DECEPTION IN HER SOUL, THE SPIRIT OF VENGEANCE AGREED TO ACCOMPANY HER TO THE GUARDIANS' SHIP, TO VERIFY HER CLAIM FOR HIMSELF...
...BUT, ONCE THERE, HE WAS ACCUSED BY THE YOUNG STOWAWAY AND WOULD-BE GUARDIAN, REPLICA...
...OF BEING A MURDERER OF PRIESTS!
SEEING THE ANKH SHE WORE ABOUT HER NECK, THE SYMBOL OF A TRUE-BELIEVER IN THE CHURCH...
...HE ASSUMED THAT THE GUARDIANS HAD LIED TO HIM--
AND FOR THAT YOU WILL ALL DIE!
AND THAT'S ALL THE RE-CAP YOU'RE GONNA NEED, PILGRIM, 'CAUSE, ONCE AGAIN, IT'S TIME TO ROCK 'N ROLL!!

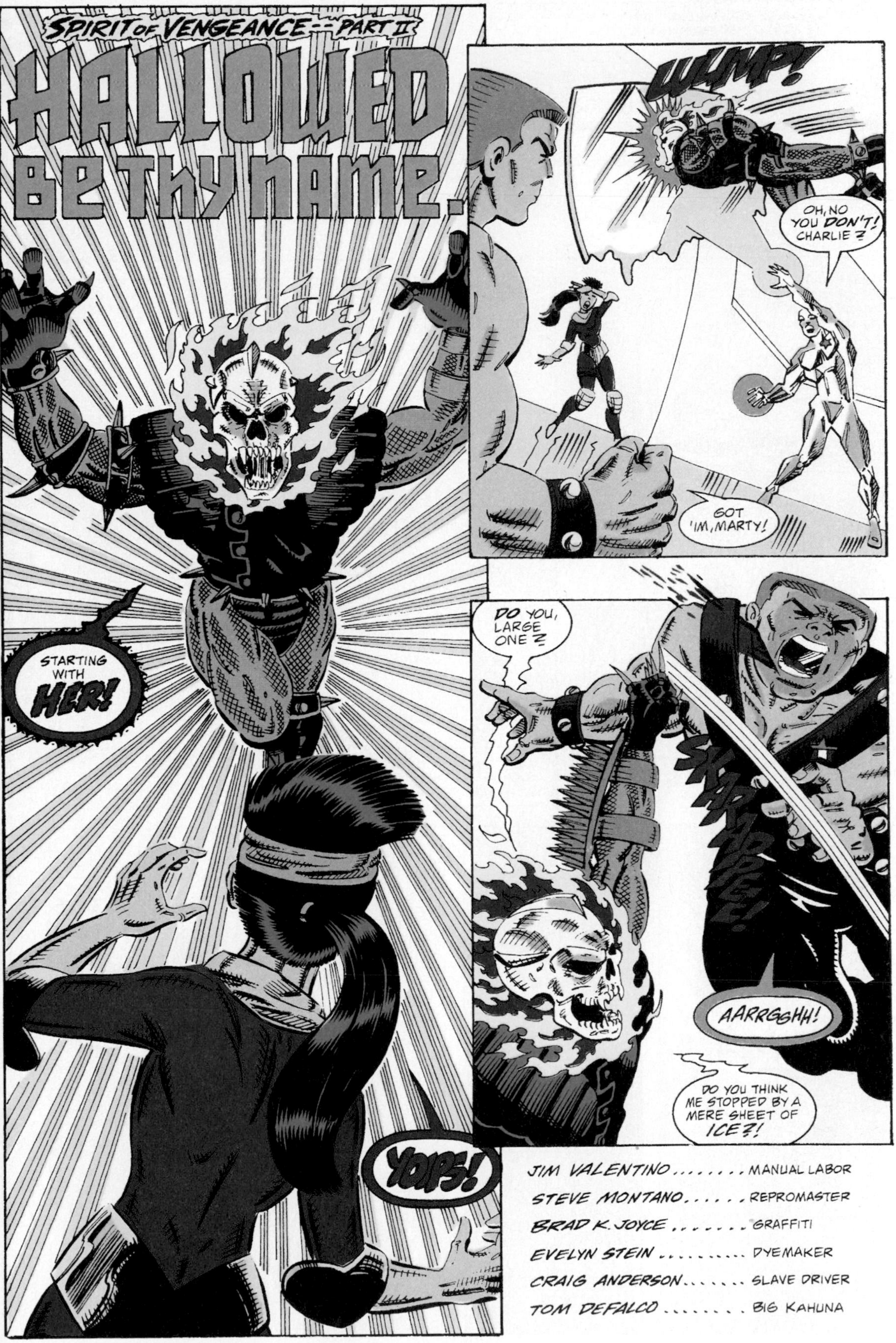
SPIRIT OF VENGEANCE--PART II
HALLOWED BE THY NAME.
STARTING WITH HER!
YOIPS!
WUMP!
OH, NO YOU DON'T! CHARLIE?!
GOT 'IM, MARTY!
DO YOU, LARGE ONE?
AARRGGHH!
DO YOU THINK ME STOPPED BY A MERE SHEET OF ICE?!

JIM VALENTINO........ MANUAL LABOR
STEVE MONTANO...... REPROMASTER
BRAD K. JOYCE....... GRAFFITI
EVELYN STEIN.......... DYEMAKER
CRAIG ANDERSON........ SLAVE DRIVER
TOM DEFALCO........ BIG KAHUNA

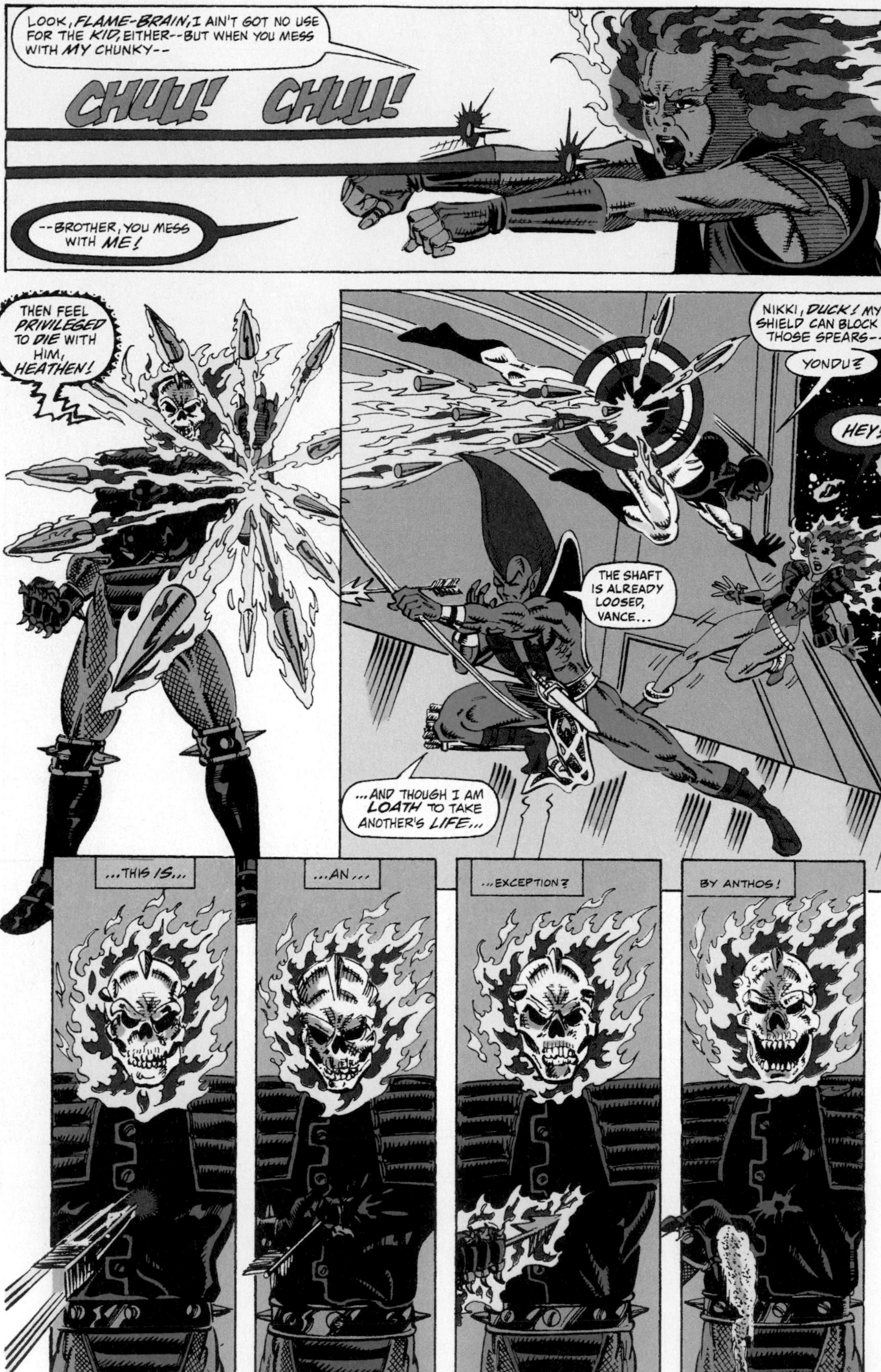
LOOK, FLAME-BRAIN, I AIN'T GOT NO USE FOR THE KID, EITHER--BUT WHEN YOU MESS WITH MY CHUNKY--
CHUU! CHUU!
--BROTHER, YOU MESS WITH ME!
THEN FEEL PRIVILEGED TO DIE WITH HIM, HEATHEN!
NIKKI, DUCK! MY SHIELD CAN BLOCK THOSE SPEARS--
YONDU?
HEY!
THE SHAFT IS ALREADY LOOSED, VANCE...
...AND THOUGH I AM LOATH TO TAKE ANOTHER'S LIFE...
...THIS IS...
...AN...
...EXCEPTION?
BY ANTHOS!

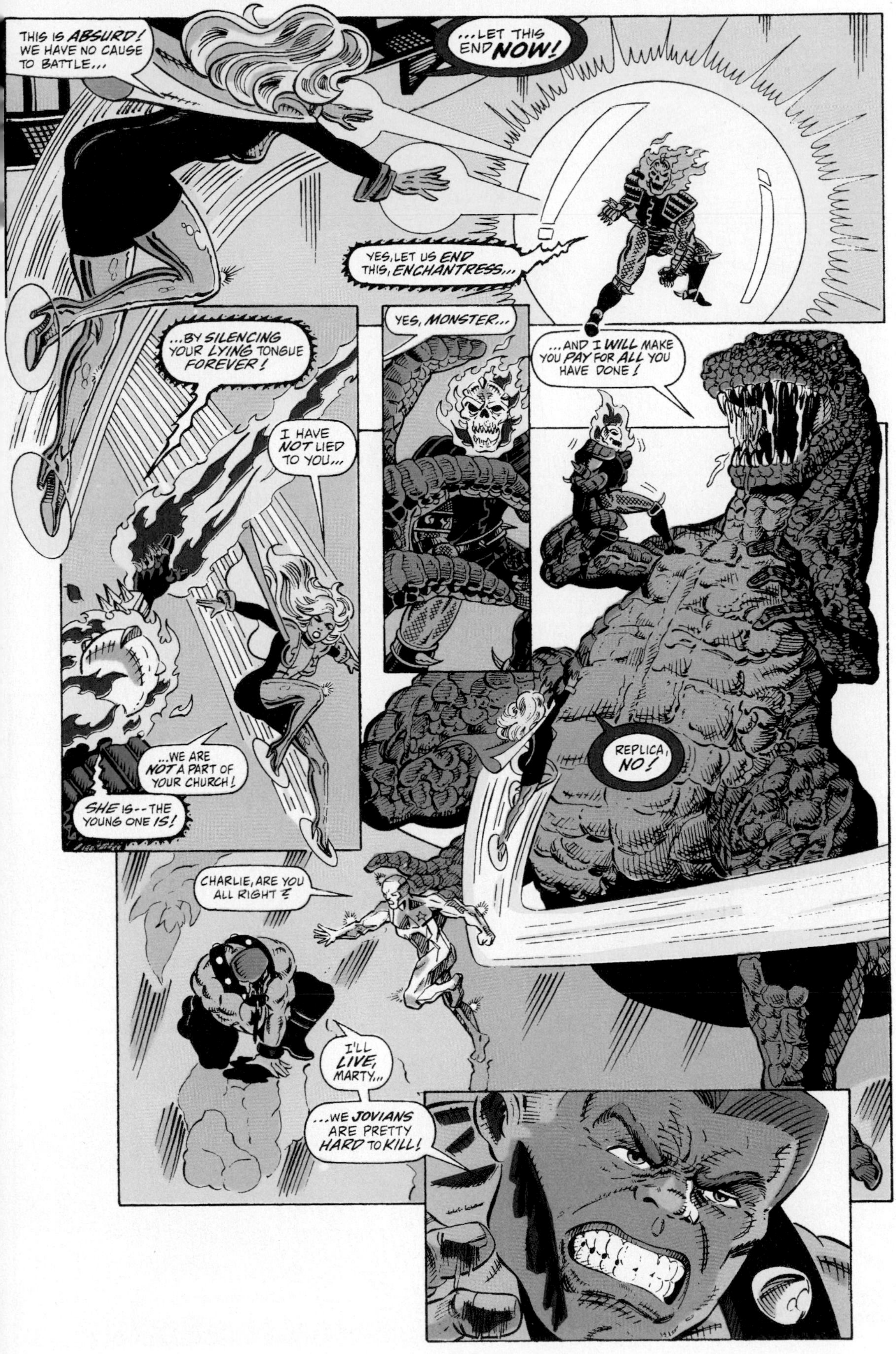

THIS IS ABSURD! WE HAVE NO CAUSE TO BATTLE...
...LET THIS END NOW!
YES, LET US END THIS, ENCHANTRESS...
...BY SILENCING YOUR LYING TONGUE FOREVER!
I HAVE NOT LIED TO YOU...
...WE ARE NOT A PART OF YOUR CHURCH!
SHE IS--THE YOUNG ONE IS!
YES, MONSTER...
...AND I WILL MAKE YOU PAY FOR ALL YOU HAVE DONE!
REPLICA, NO!
CHARLIE, ARE YOU ALL RIGHT?
I'LL LIVE, MARTY...
...WE JOVIANS ARE PRETTY HARD TO KILL!

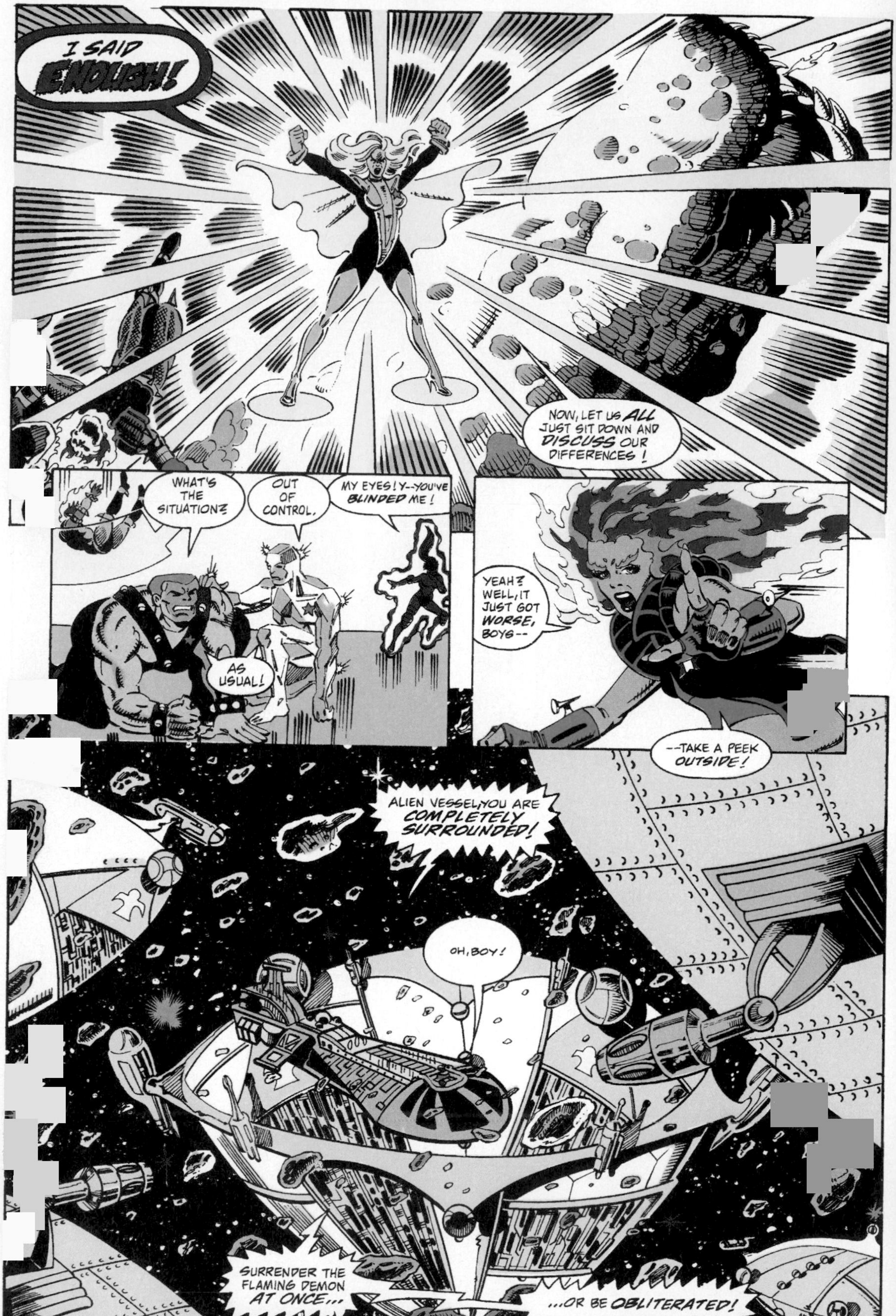
I SAID ENOUGH!
NOW, LET US ALL JUST SIT DOWN AND DISCUSS OUR DIFFERENCES!
WHAT'S THE SITUATION?
OUT OF CONTROL.
MY EYES! Y--YOU'VE BLINDED ME!
AS USUAL!
YEAH? WELL, IT JUST GOT WORSE, BOYS--
--TAKE A PEEK OUTSIDE!
ALIEN VESSEL, YOU ARE COMPLETELY SURROUNDED!
OH, BOY!
SURRENDER THE FLAMING DEMON AT ONCE...
...OR BE OBLITERATED!

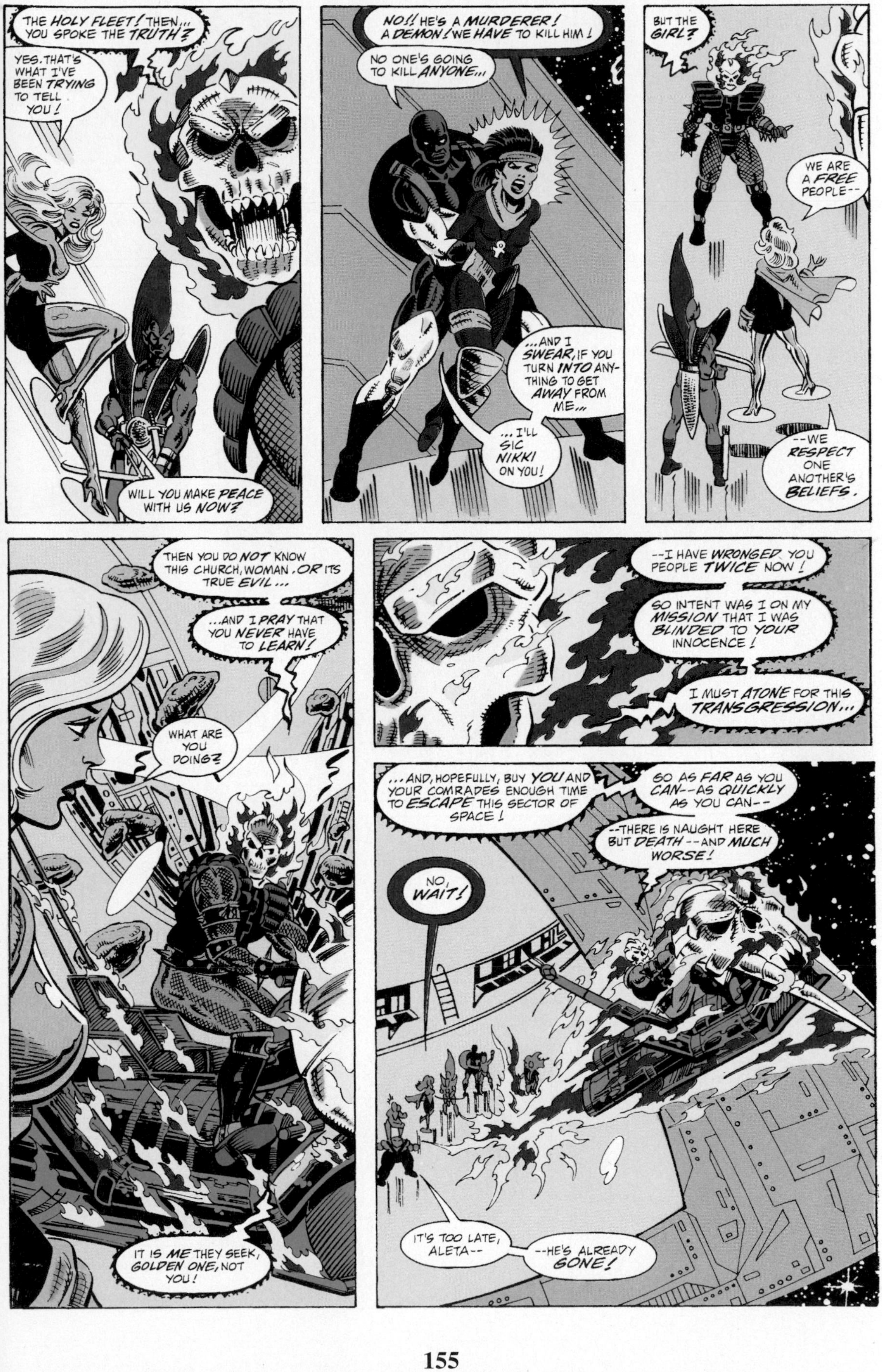
THE HOLY FLEET! THEN... YOU SPOKE THE TRUTH?
YES. THAT'S WHAT I'VE BEEN TRYING TO TELL YOU!
WILL YOU MAKE PEACE WITH US NOW?
NO!! HE'S A MURDERER! A DEMON! WE HAVE TO KILL HIM!
NO ONE'S GOING TO KILL ANYONE...
...AND I SWEAR, IF YOU TURN INTO ANYTHING TO GET AWAY FROM ME...
...I'LL SIC NIKKI ON YOU!
BUT THE GIRL?
WE ARE A FREE PEOPLE--
--WE RESPECT ONE ANOTHER'S BELIEFS.
THEN YOU DO NOT KNOW THIS CHURCH, WOMAN, OR ITS TRUE EVIL...
...AND I PRAY THAT YOU NEVER HAVE TO LEARN!
WHAT ARE YOU DOING?
IT IS ME THEY SEEK, GOLDEN ONE, NOT YOU!
--I HAVE WRONGED YOU PEOPLE TWICE NOW!
SO INTENT WAS I ON MY MISSION THAT I WAS BLINDED TO YOUR INNOCENCE!
I MUST ATONE FOR THIS TRANSGRESSION...
...AND, HOPEFULLY, BUY YOU AND YOUR COMRADES ENOUGH TIME TO ESCAPE THIS SECTOR OF SPACE!
GO AS FAR AS YOU CAN--AS QUICKLY AS YOU CAN--
--THERE IS NAUGHT HERE BUT DEATH--AND MUCH WORSE!
NO, WAIT!
IT'S TOO LATE, ALETA--
--HE'S ALREADY GONE!

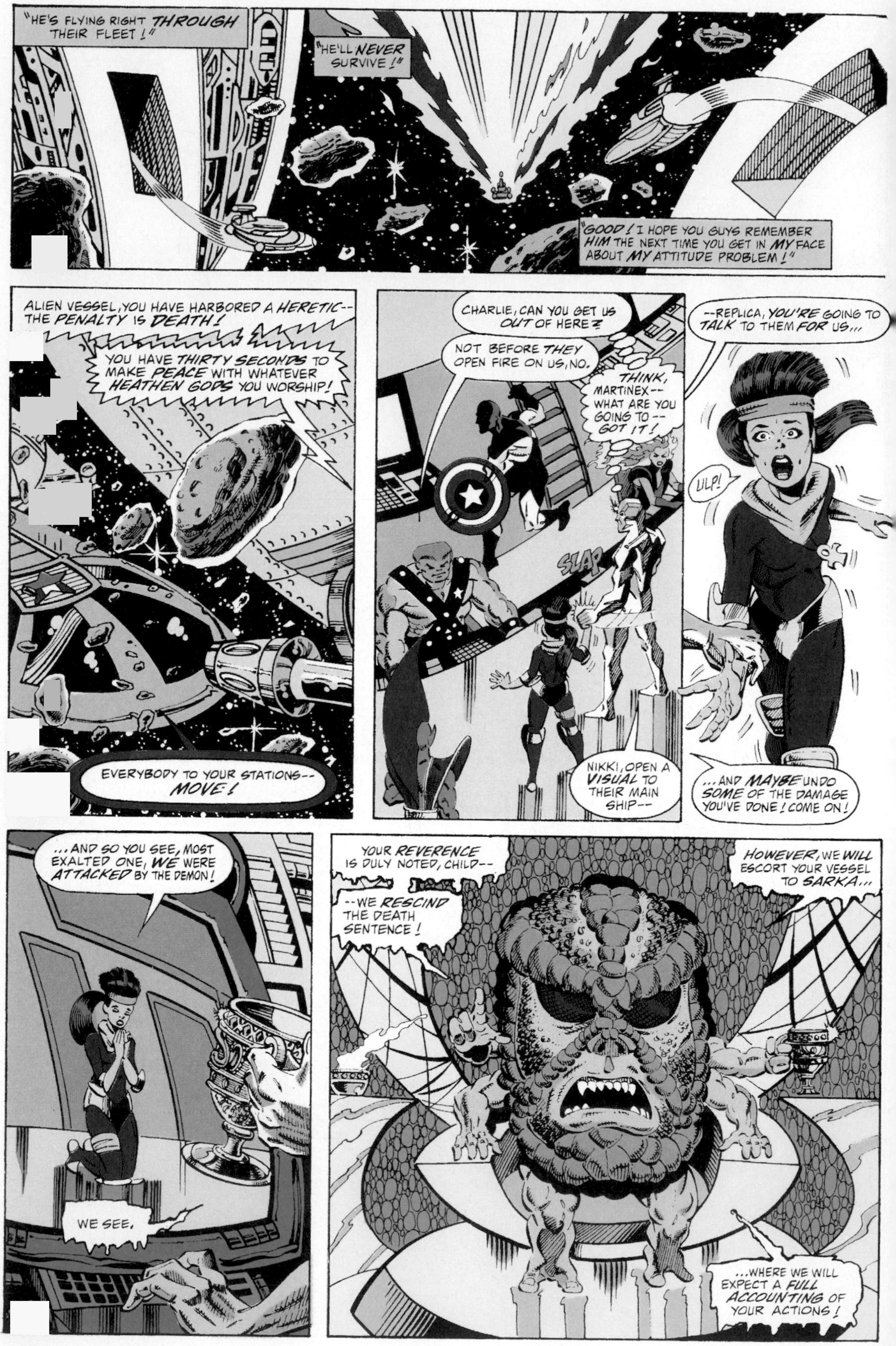
"HE'S FLYING RIGHT THROUGH THEIR FLEET!"
"HE'LL NEVER SURVIVE!"
"GOOD! I HOPE YOU GUYS REMEMBER HIM THE NEXT TIME YOU GET IN MY FACE ABOUT MY ATTITUDE PROBLEM!"
ALIEN VESSEL, YOU HAVE HARBORED A HERETIC-- THE PENALTY IS DEATH!
YOU HAVE THIRTY SECONDS TO MAKE PEACE WITH WHATEVER HEATHEN GODS YOU WORSHIP!
EVERYBODY TO YOUR STATIONS-- MOVE!
CHARLIE, CAN YOU GET US OUT OF HERE?
NOT BEFORE THEY OPEN FIRE ON US, NO.
THINK, MARTINEX-- WHAT ARE YOU GOING TO-- GOT IT!
SLAP
NIKKI, OPEN A VISUAL TO THEIR MAIN SHIP--
--REPLICA, YOU'RE GOING TO TALK TO THEM FOR US...
ULP!
...AND MAYBE UNDO SOME OF THE DAMAGE YOU'VE DONE! COME ON!
...AND SO YOU SEE, MOST EXALTED ONE, WE WERE ATTACKED BY THE DEMON!
WE SEE.
YOUR REVERENCE IS DULY NOTED, CHILD--
--WE RESCIND THE DEATH SENTENCE!
HOWEVER, WE WILL ESCORT YOUR VESSEL TO SARKA...
...WHERE WE WILL EXPECT A FULL ACCOUNTING OF YOUR ACTIONS!

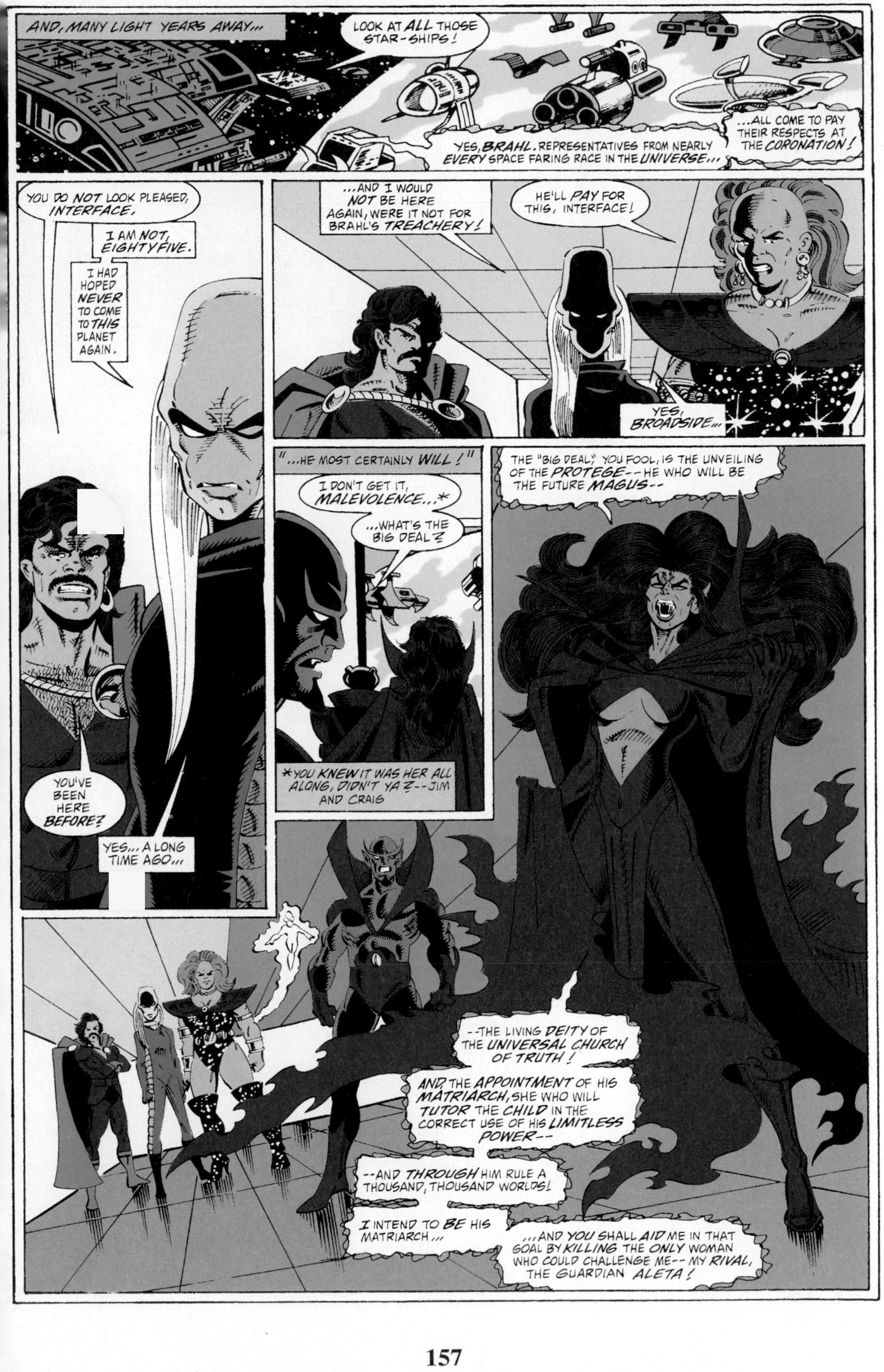
AND, MANY LIGHT YEARS AWAY...
LOOK AT ALL THOSE STAR-SHIPS!
YES, BRAHL. REPRESENTATIVES FROM NEARLY EVERY SPACE FARING RACE IN THE UNIVERSE...
...ALL COME TO PAY THEIR RESPECTS AT THE CORONATION!
YOU DO NOT LOOK PLEASED, INTERFACE.
I AM NOT, EIGHTYFIVE.
I HAD HOPED NEVER TO COME TO THIS PLANET AGAIN.
YOU'VE BEEN HERE BEFORE?
YES... A LONG TIME AGO...
...AND I WOULD NOT BE HERE AGAIN, WERE IT NOT FOR BRAHL'S TREACHERY!
HE'LL PAY FOR THIS, INTERFACE!
YES, BROADSIDE...
"...HE MOST CERTAINLY WILL!"
I DON'T GET IT, MALEVOLENCE...*
...WHAT'S THE BIG DEAL?
*YOU KNEW IT WAS HER ALL ALONG, DIDN'T YA?--JIM AND CRAIG
THE "BIG DEAL," YOU FOOL, IS THE UNVEILING OF THE PROTEGE--HE WHO WILL BE THE FUTURE MAGUS--
--THE LIVING DEITY OF THE UNIVERSAL CHURCH OF TRUTH!
AND, THE APPOINTMENT OF HIS MATRIARCH, SHE WHO WILL TUTOR THE CHILD IN THE CORRECT USE OF HIS LIMITLESS POWER--
--AND THROUGH HIM RULE A THOUSAND, THOUSAND WORLDS!
I INTEND TO BE HIS MATRIARCH...
...AND YOU SHALL AID ME IN THAT GOAL BY KILLING THE ONLY WOMAN WHO COULD CHALLENGE ME-- MY RIVAL, THE GUARDIAN ALETA!

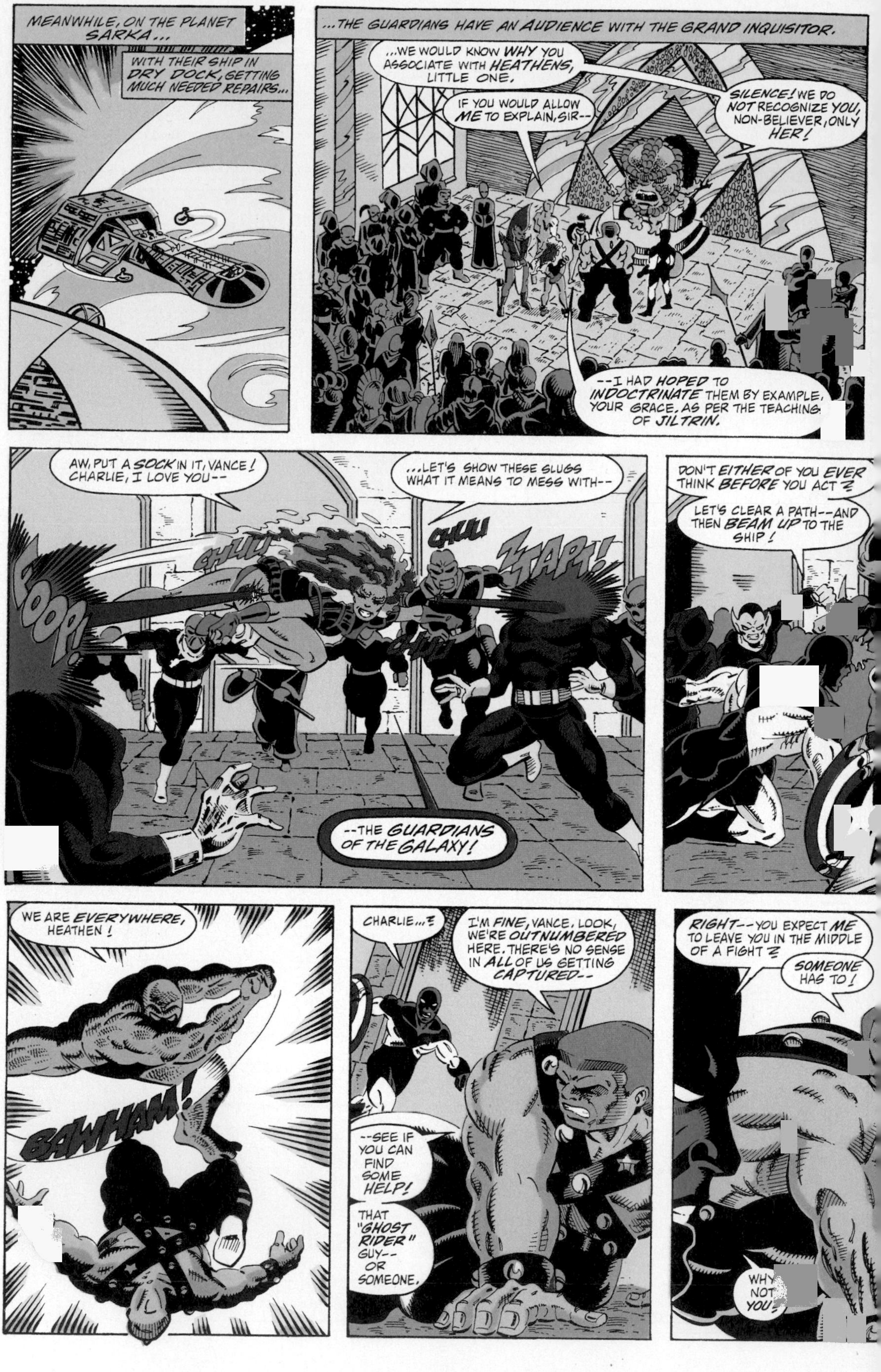
MEANWHILE, ON THE PLANET SARKA...
WITH THEIR SHIP IN DRY DOCK, GETTING MUCH NEEDED REPAIRS...
...THE GUARDIANS HAVE AN AUDIENCE WITH THE GRAND INQUISITOR.
...WE WOULD KNOW WHY YOU ASSOCIATE WITH HEATHENS, LITTLE ONE.
IF YOU WOULD ALLOW ME TO EXPLAIN, SIR--
SILENCE! WE DO NOT RECOGNIZE YOU, NON-BELIEVER, ONLY HER!
--I HAD HOPED TO INDOCTRINATE THEM BY EXAMPLE, YOUR GRACE. AS PER THE TEACHINGS OF JILTRIN.
AW, PUT A SOCK IN IT, VANCE! CHARLIE, I LOVE YOU--
...LET'S SHOW THESE SLUGS WHAT IT MEANS TO MESS WITH--
WOOP!
CHUU
CHUU
ZZTAP!
CHUU
--THE GUARDIANS OF THE GALAXY!
DON'T EITHER OF YOU EVER THINK BEFORE YOU ACT?
LET'S CLEAR A PATH--AND THEN BEAM UP TO THE SHIP!
WE ARE EVERYWHERE, HEATHEN!
BAWHAM!
CHARLIE...?
I'M FINE, VANCE. LOOK, WE'RE OUTNUMBERED HERE. THERE'S NO SENSE IN ALL OF US GETTING CAPTURED--
--SEE IF YOU CAN FIND SOME HELP!
THAT "GHOST RIDER" GUY--OR SOMEONE.
RIGHT--YOU EXPECT ME TO LEAVE YOU IN THE MIDDLE OF A FIGHT?
SOMEONE HAS TO!
WHY NOT YOU?

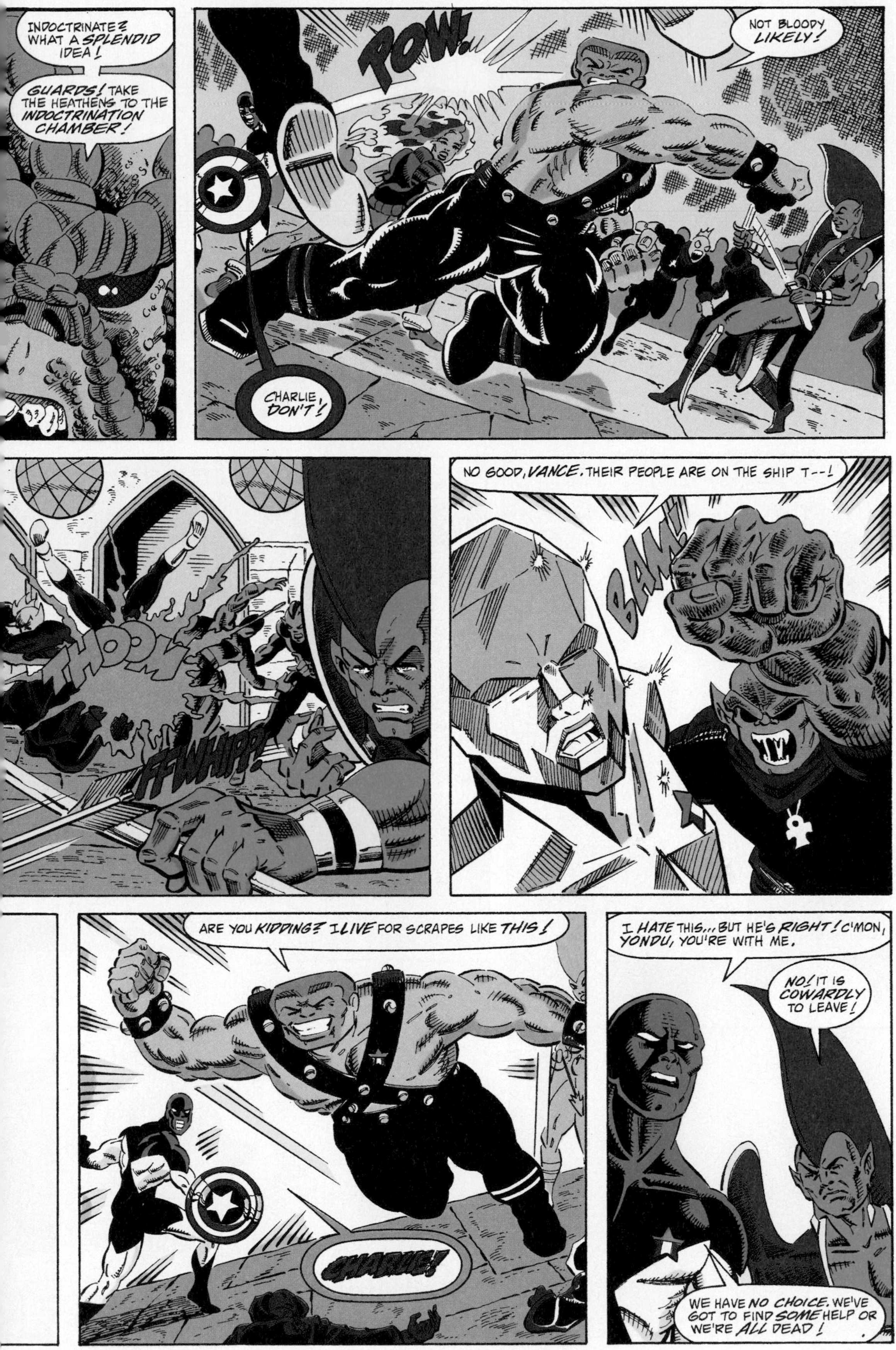
INDOCTRINATE? WHAT A SPLENDID IDEA!
GUARDS! TAKE THE HEATHENS TO THE INDOCTRINATION CHAMBER!
POW!
NOT BLOODY LIKELY!
CHARLIE DON'T!
THOOM
FFWHIPP!
NO GOOD, VANCE. THEIR PEOPLE ARE ON THE SHIP T--!
BAM!
ARE YOU KIDDING? I LIVE FOR SCRAPES LIKE THIS!
CHARLIE!
I HATE THIS... BUT HE'S RIGHT! C'MON, YONDU, YOU'RE WITH ME.
NO! IT IS COWARDLY TO LEAVE!
WE HAVE NO CHOICE. WE'VE GOT TO FIND SOME HELP OR WE'RE ALL DEAD!

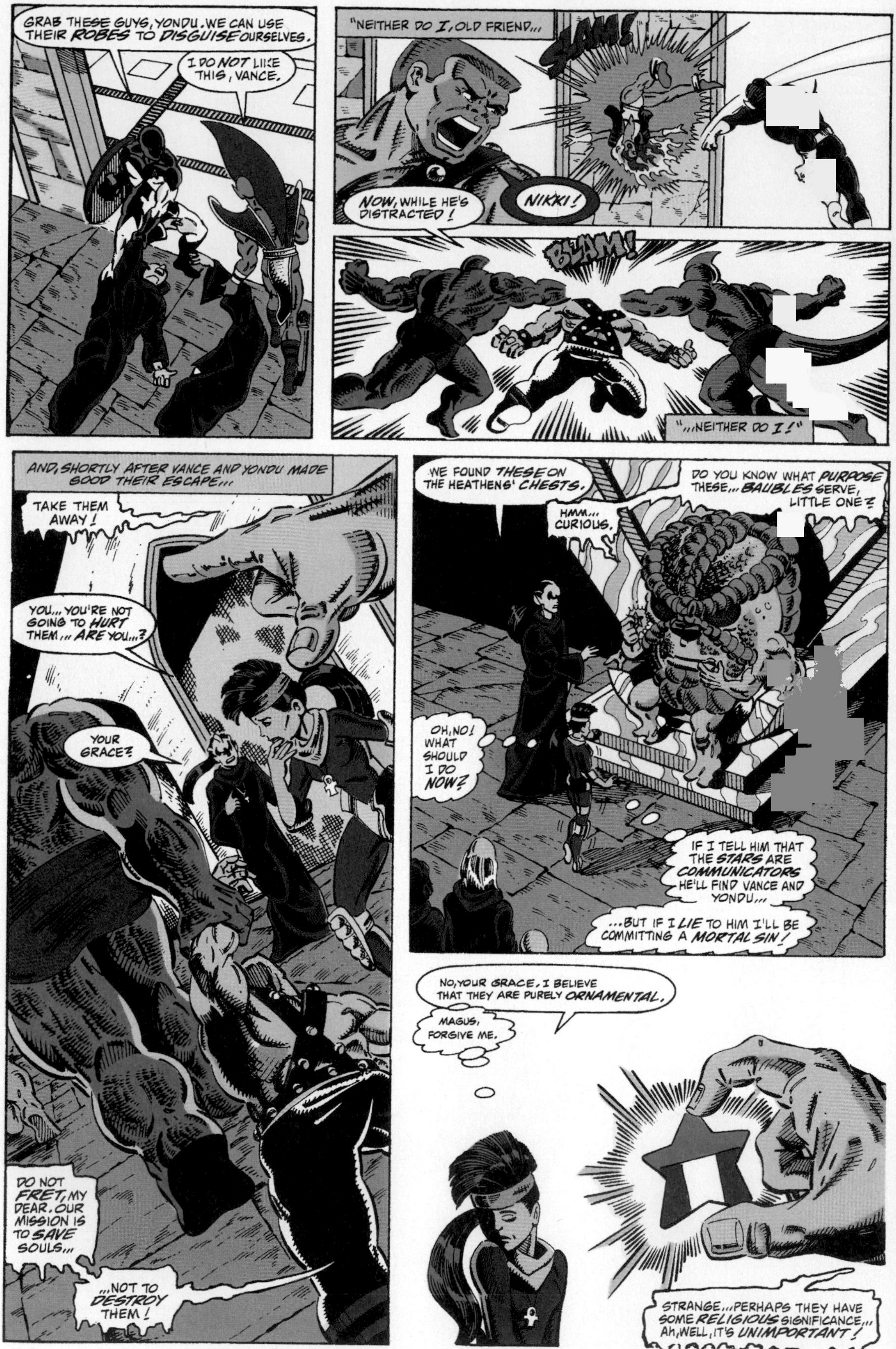

GRAB THESE GUYS, YONDU. WE CAN USE THEIR ROBES TO DISGUISE OURSELVES.
I DO NOT LIKE THIS, VANCE.
"NEITHER DO I, OLD FRIEND...
SLAM!
NOW, WHILE HE'S DISTRACTED!
NIKKI!
BLAM!
"...NEITHER DO I!"
AND, SHORTLY AFTER VANCE AND YONDU MADE GOOD THEIR ESCAPE...
TAKE THEM AWAY!
YOU... YOU'RE NOT GOING TO HURT THEM... ARE YOU...?
YOUR GRACE?
DO NOT FRET, MY DEAR. OUR MISSION IS TO SAVE SOULS...
...NOT TO DESTROY THEM!
WE FOUND THESE ON THE HEATHENS' CHESTS.
HMM... CURIOUS.
DO YOU KNOW WHAT PURPOSE THESE... BAUBLES SERVE, LITTLE ONE?
OH, NO! WHAT SHOULD I DO NOW?
IF I TELL HIM THAT THE STARS ARE COMMUNICATORS HE'LL FIND VANCE AND YONDU...
...BUT IF I LIE TO HIM I'LL BE COMMITTING A MORTAL SIN!
NO, YOUR GRACE. I BELIEVE THAT THEY ARE PURELY ORNAMENTAL.
MAGUS, FORGIVE ME.
STRANGE... PERHAPS THEY HAVE SOME RELIGIOUS SIGNIFICANCE... AH, WELL, IT'S UNIMPORTANT!

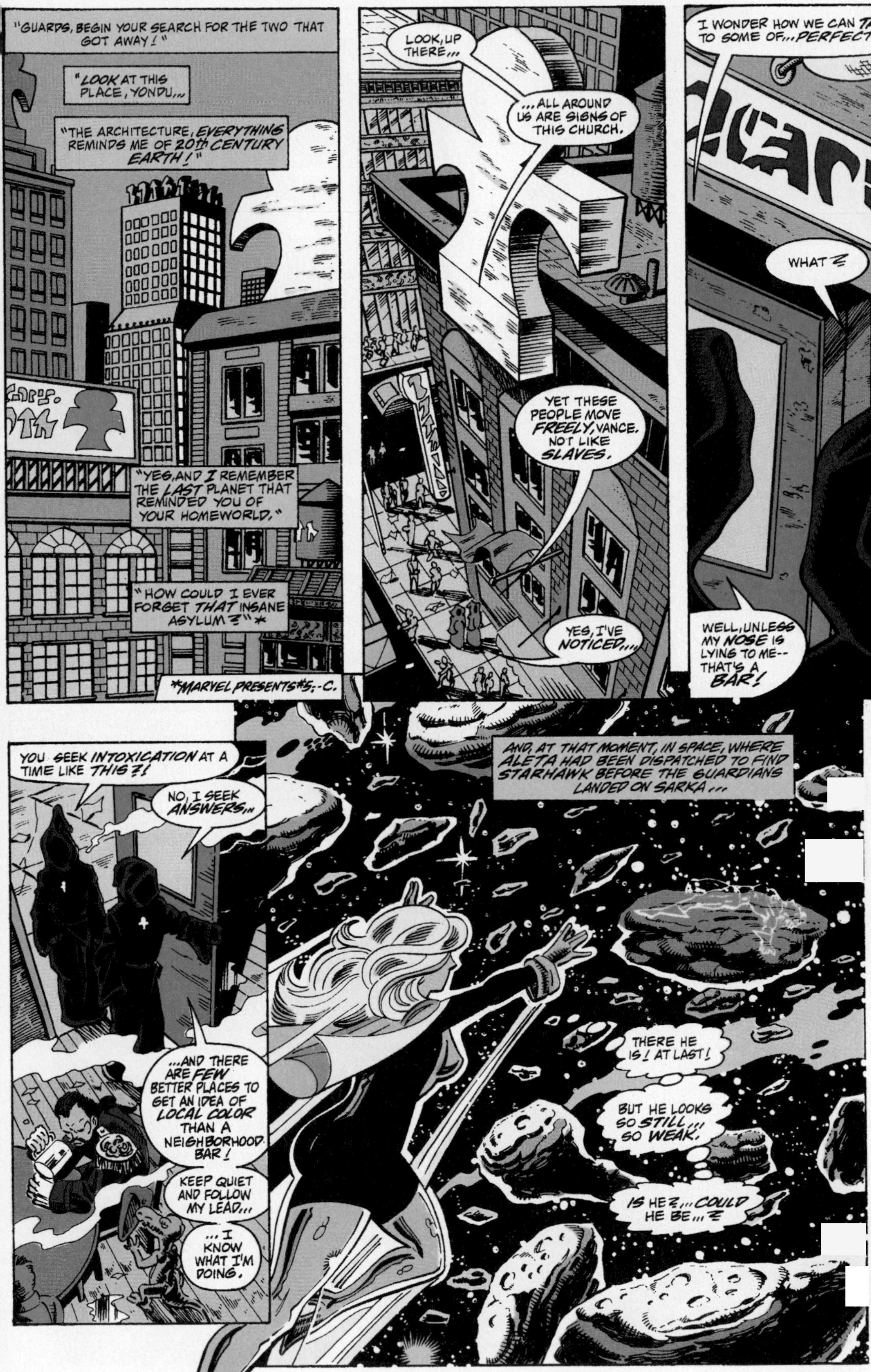
"GUARDS, BEGIN YOUR SEARCH FOR THE TWO THAT GOT AWAY!"
"LOOK AT THIS PLACE, YONDU...
"THE ARCHITECTURE, EVERYTHING REMINDS ME OF 20TH CENTURY EARTH!"
"YES, AND I REMEMBER THE LAST PLANET THAT REMINDED YOU OF YOUR HOMEWORLD."
"HOW COULD I EVER FORGET THAT INSANE ASYLUM?"*
*MARVEL PRESENTS #5.--C.
LOOK, UP THERE...
...ALL AROUND US ARE SIGNS OF THIS CHURCH.
YET THESE PEOPLE MOVE FREELY, VANCE. NOT LIKE SLAVES.
YES, I'VE NOTICED...
I WONDER HOW WE CAN TALK TO SOME OF...PERFECT!
WHAT?
WELL, UNLESS MY NOSE IS LYING TO ME-- THAT'S A BAR!
YOU SEEK INTOXICATION AT A TIME LIKE THIS?!
NO, I SEEK ANSWERS...
...AND THERE ARE FEW BETTER PLACES TO GET AN IDEA OF LOCAL COLOR THAN A NEIGHBORHOOD BAR!
KEEP QUIET AND FOLLOW MY LEAD...
...I KNOW WHAT I'M DOING.
AND, AT THAT MOMENT, IN SPACE, WHERE ALETA HAD BEEN DISPATCHED TO FIND STARHAWK BEFORE THE GUARDIANS LANDED ON SARKA...
THERE HE IS! AT LAST!
BUT HE LOOKS SO STILL, SO WEAK.
IS HE?...COULD HE BE...?

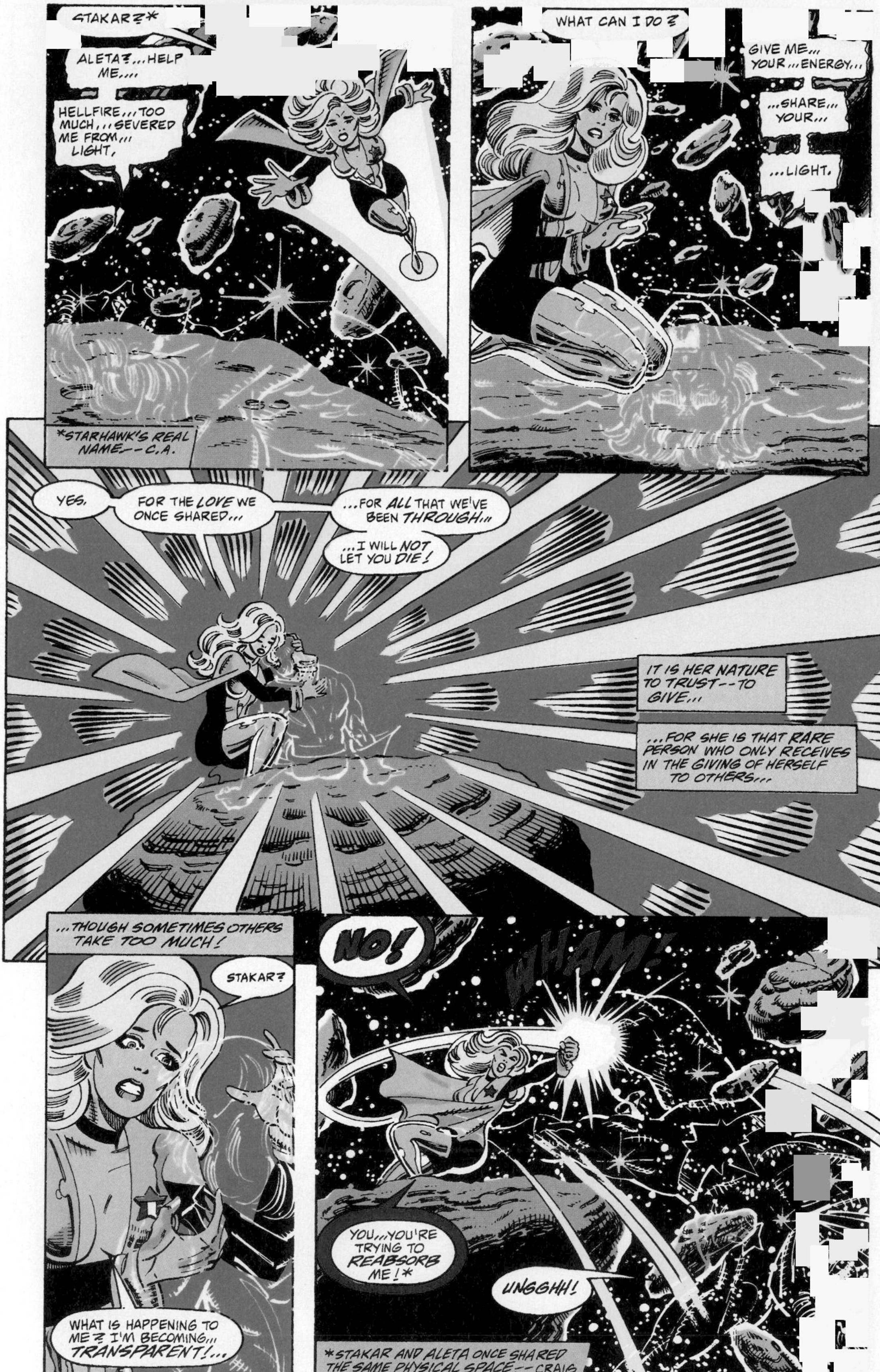
STAKAR?*
ALETA?... HELP ME....
HELLFIRE... TOO MUCH... SEVERED ME FROM... LIGHT.
*STARHAWK'S REAL NAME.--C.A.
WHAT CAN I DO?
GIVE ME... YOUR... ENERGY...
...SHARE... YOUR...
...LIGHT.
YES.
FOR THE LOVE WE ONCE SHARED...
...FOR ALL THAT WE'VE BEEN THROUGH...
...I WILL NOT LET YOU DIE!
IT IS HER NATURE TO TRUST--TO GIVE...
...FOR SHE IS THAT RARE PERSON WHO ONLY RECEIVES IN THE GIVING OF HERSELF TO OTHERS...
...THOUGH SOMETIMES OTHERS TAKE TOO MUCH!
STAKAR?
WHAT IS HAPPENING TO ME? I'M BECOMING... TRANSPARENT!...
NO!
WHAM!
YOU... YOU'RE TRYING TO REABSORB ME!*
UNGGHH!
*STAKAR AND ALETA ONCE SHARED THE SAME PHYSICAL SPACE.--CRAIG

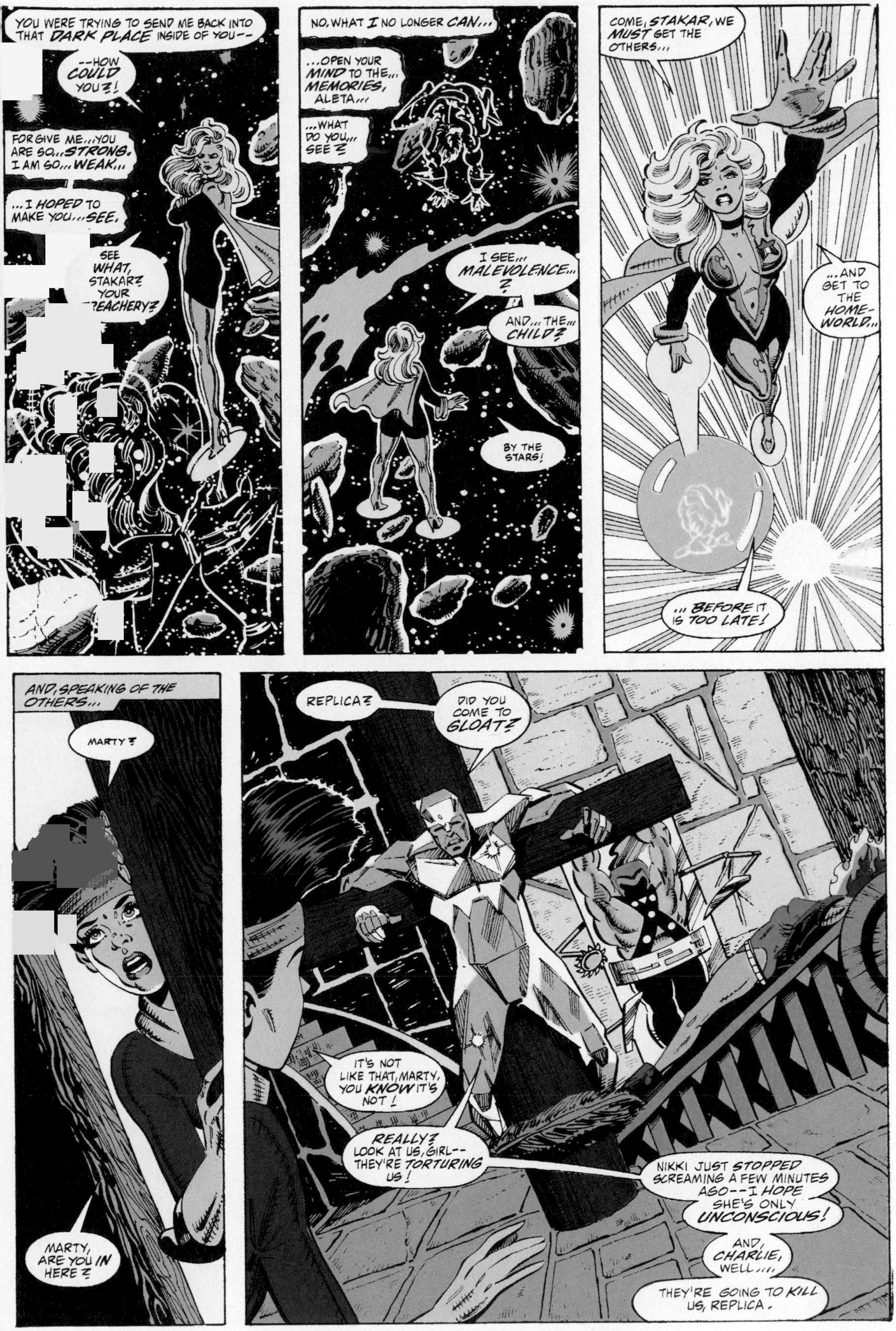
YOU WERE TRYING TO SEND ME BACK INTO THAT DARK PLACE INSIDE OF YOU--
--HOW COULD YOU?!
FORGIVE ME...YOU ARE SO...STRONG. I AM SO...WEAK...
...I HOPED TO MAKE YOU...SEE.
SEE WHAT, STAKAR? YOUR TREACHERY?
NO, WHAT I NO LONGER CAN...
...OPEN YOUR MIND TO THE... MEMORIES, ALETA...
...WHAT DO YOU... SEE?
I SEE... MALEVOLENCE...?
AND... THE CHILD?
BY THE STARS!
COME, STAKAR, WE MUST GET THE OTHERS...
...AND GET TO THE HOME-WORLD...
...BEFORE IT IS TOO LATE!
AND, SPEAKING OF THE OTHERS...
MARTY?
MARTY, ARE YOU IN HERE?
REPLICA?
DID YOU COME TO GLOAT?
IT'S NOT LIKE THAT, MARTY, YOU KNOW IT'S NOT!
REALLY? LOOK AT US, GIRL-- THEY'RE TORTURING US!
NIKKI JUST STOPPED SCREAMING A FEW MINUTES AGO--I HOPE SHE'S ONLY UNCONSCIOUS!
AND, CHARLIE, WELL....
THEY'RE GOING TO KILL US, REPLICA.

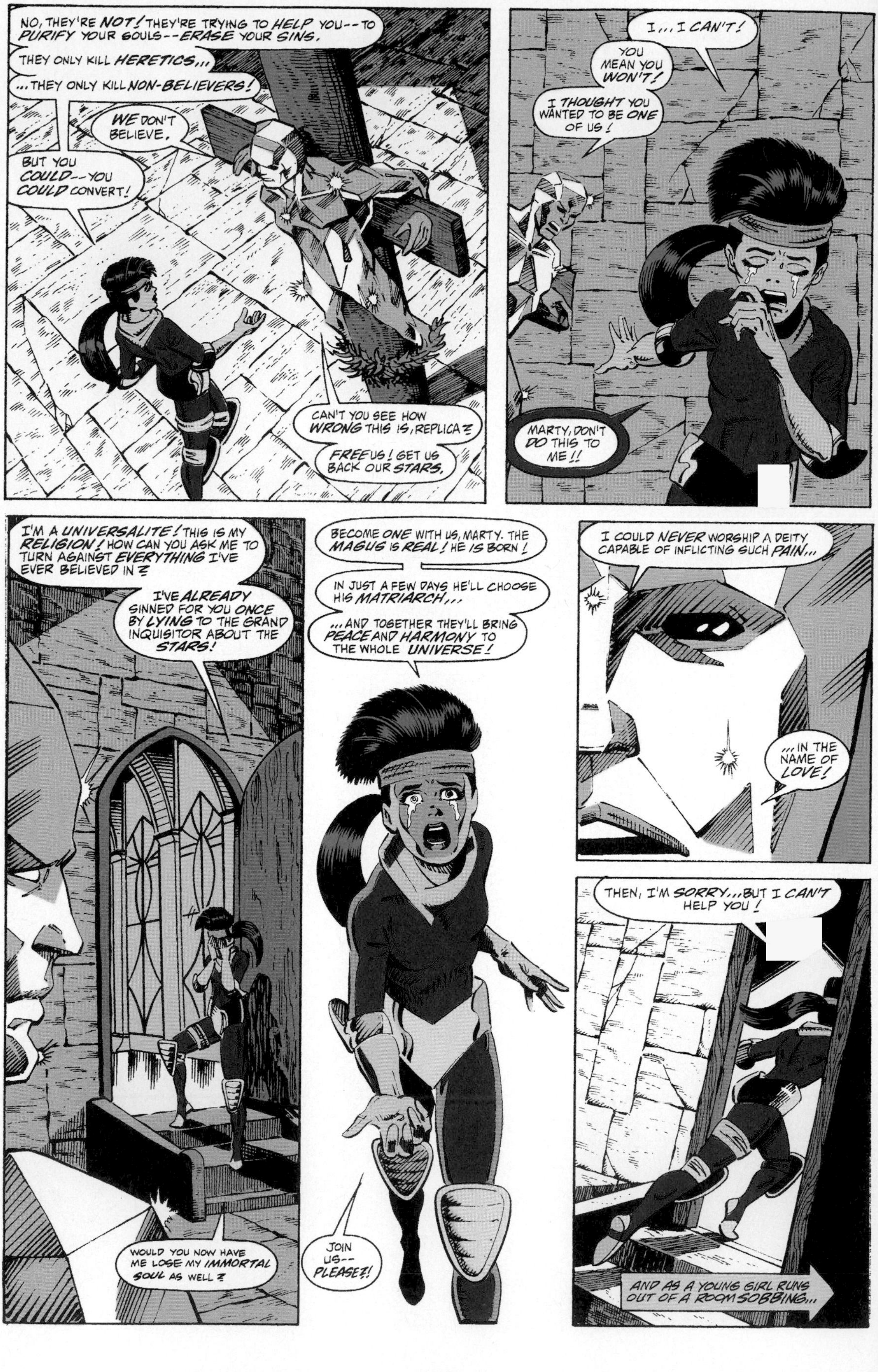
NO, THEY'RE NOT! THEY'RE TRYING TO HELP YOU--TO PURIFY YOUR SOULS--ERASE YOUR SINS.
THEY ONLY KILL HERETICS...
...THEY ONLY KILL NON-BELIEVERS!
WE DON'T BELIEVE.
BUT YOU COULD--YOU COULD CONVERT!
CAN'T YOU SEE HOW WRONG THIS IS, REPLICA?
FREE US! GET US BACK OUR STARS.
I... I CAN'T!
YOU MEAN YOU WON'T!
I THOUGHT YOU WANTED TO BE ONE OF US!
MARTY, DON'T DO THIS TO ME!!
I'M A UNIVERSALITE! THIS IS MY RELIGION! HOW CAN YOU ASK ME TO TURN AGAINST EVERYTHING I'VE EVER BELIEVED IN?
I'VE ALREADY SINNED FOR YOU ONCE BY LYING TO THE GRAND INQUISITOR ABOUT THE STARS!
WOULD YOU NOW HAVE ME LOSE MY IMMORTAL SOUL AS WELL?
BECOME ONE WITH US, MARTY. THE MAGUS IS REAL! HE IS BORN!
IN JUST A FEW DAYS HE'LL CHOOSE HIS MATRIARCH...
...AND TOGETHER THEY'LL BRING PEACE AND HARMONY TO THE WHOLE UNIVERSE!
JOIN US--PLEASE?!
I COULD NEVER WORSHIP A DEITY CAPABLE OF INFLICTING SUCH PAIN...
...IN THE NAME OF LOVE!
THEN, I'M SORRY... BUT I CAN'T HELP YOU!
AND AS A YOUNG GIRL RUNS OUT OF A ROOM SOBBING...

...TWO MEN EXIT A DOWNTOWN BAR...

WELL, THAT CERTAINLY WAS *ENLIGHTENING!*

WHAT WAS, VANCE? I DO *NOT* SEE HOW DISCUSSING *LOCAL POLITICS* AND *TELEVISED SPORTS* COULD BE *ENLIGHTENING!*

YES, YOU *WOULDN'T,* YONDU.

BUT *I* LEARNED *ALL* I NEEDED TO KNOW--

--THEIR *CHURCH* IS *EVERYWHERE,* THEIR ENTIRE *CULTURE* REVOLVES AROUND IT!

IT'S A *POSITIVE* FORCE IN THEIR LIVES--

--THEY DRAW THEIR *STRENGTH* FROM IT...

...EVEN AS YOU DO IN *YOUR* FAITH!

BUT IS *THAT* NOT THE *PURPOSE* OF FAITH?

YES, I SUPPOSE SO. BUT FROM WHAT THE *SPIRIT OF VENGEANCE* SAID--

HE IS A *FANATIC...*

"...WHO HAS LOST *THE WAY TO--"*

OUT OF THE WAY!

HEY!

INFIDELS, *HALT!*

THEY WERE *WARNED!*

BLAST 'EM!

MAY THE *MAGUS* HAVE *MERCY* ON THEIR HEATHEN SOULS!

AARRGGHH!

YEAAHH!

ZERRAP!

FTCHU

FTCHU

ZTOT

GOOD LORD!

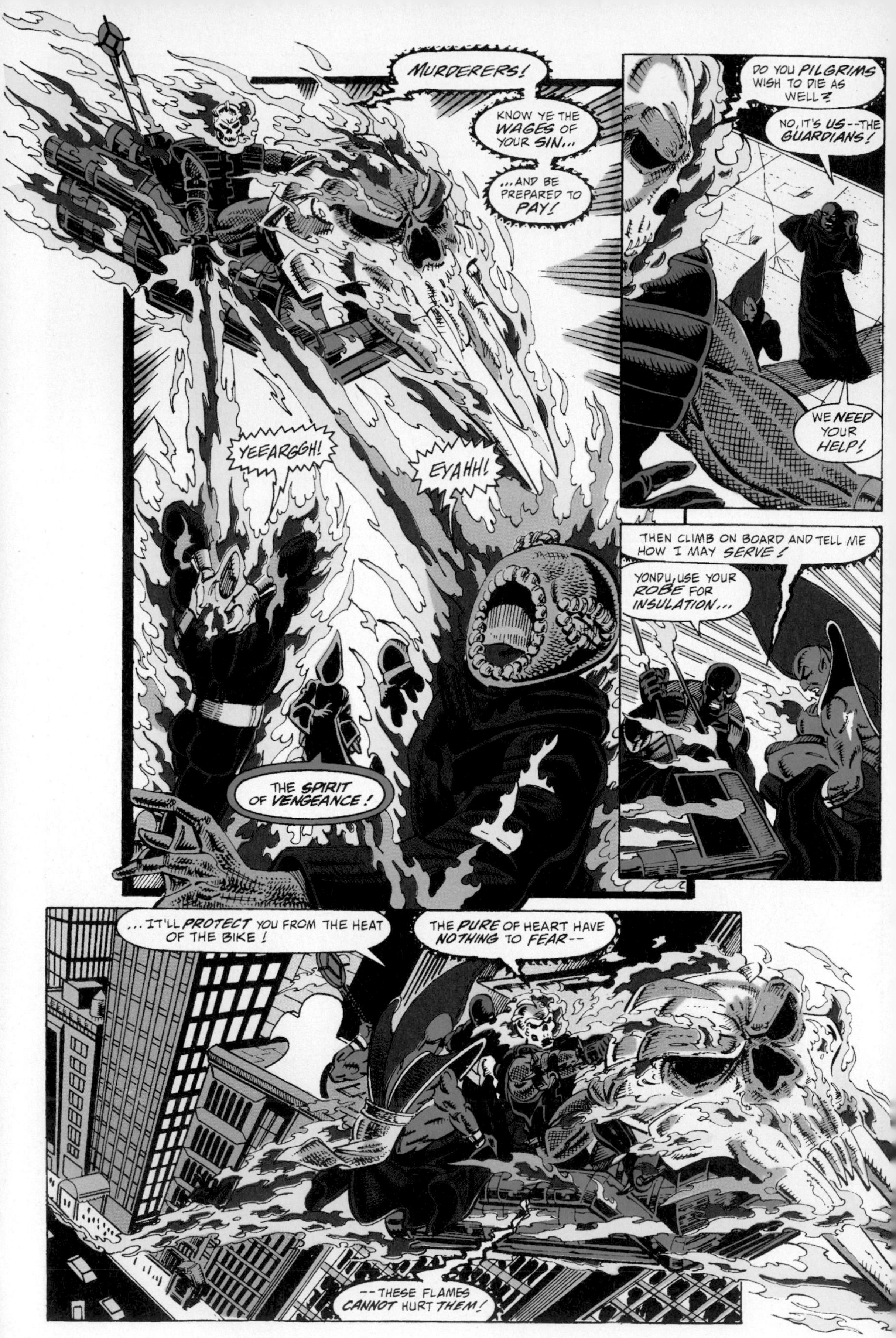
MURDERERS!
KNOW YE THE WAGES OF YOUR SIN...
...AND BE PREPARED TO PAY!
YEEARGGH!
EYAHH!
THE SPIRIT OF VENGEANCE!
DO YOU PILGRIMS WISH TO DIE AS WELL?
NO, IT'S US--THE GUARDIANS!
WE NEED YOUR HELP!
THEN CLIMB ON BOARD AND TELL ME HOW I MAY SERVE!
YONDU, USE YOUR ROBE FOR INSULATION...
...IT'LL PROTECT YOU FROM THE HEAT OF THE BIKE!
THE PURE OF HEART HAVE NOTHING TO FEAR--
--THESE FLAMES CANNOT HURT THEM!

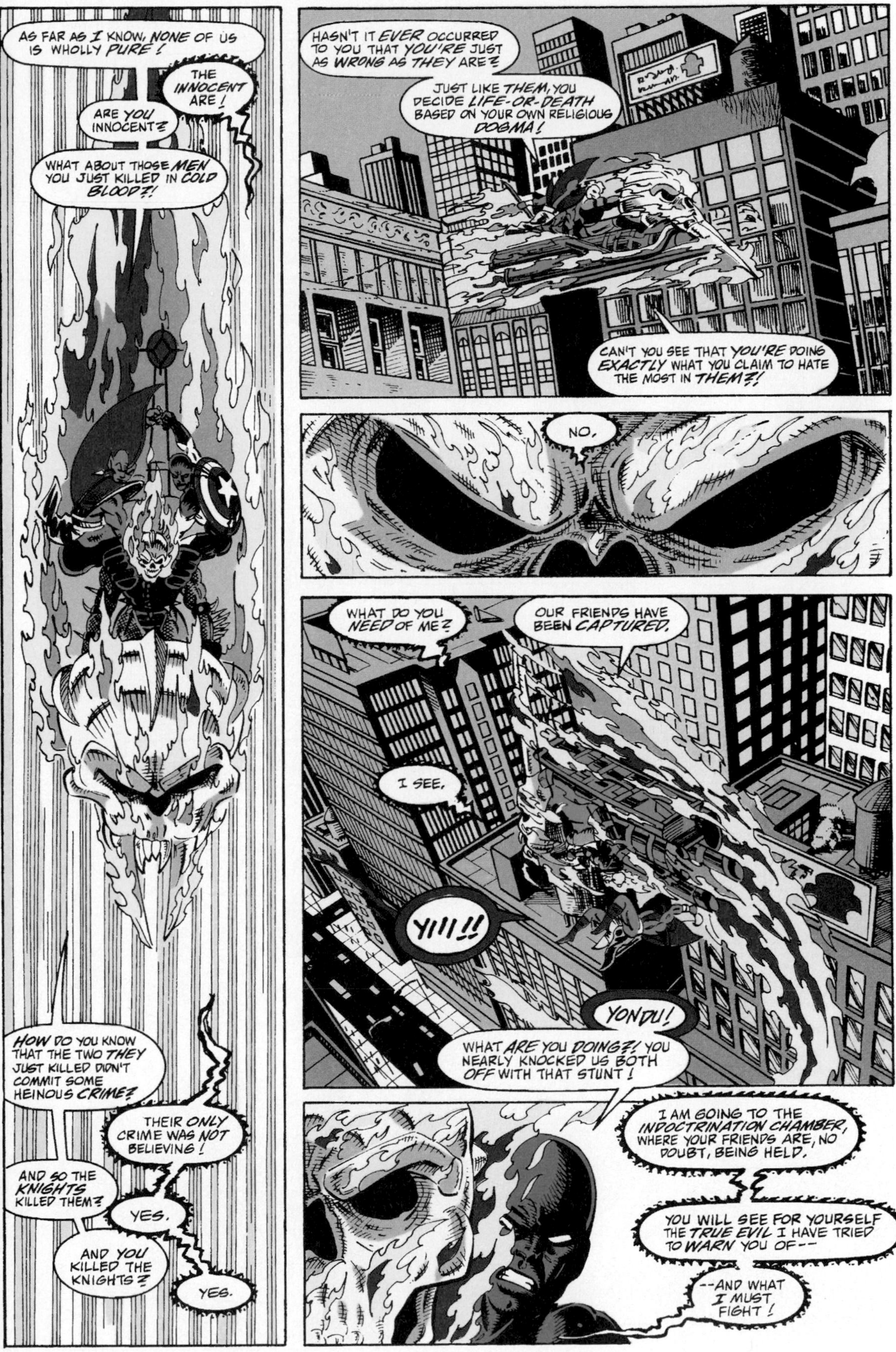
AS FAR AS I KNOW, NONE OF US IS WHOLLY PURE!
THE INNOCENT ARE!
ARE YOU INNOCENT?
WHAT ABOUT THOSE MEN YOU JUST KILLED IN COLD BLOOD?!
HOW DO YOU KNOW THAT THE TWO THEY JUST KILLED DIDN'T COMMIT SOME HEINOUS CRIME?
THEIR ONLY CRIME WAS NOT BELIEVING!
AND SO THE KNIGHTS KILLED THEM?
YES.
AND YOU KILLED THE KNIGHTS?
YES.
HASN'T IT EVER OCCURRED TO YOU THAT YOU'RE JUST AS WRONG AS THEY ARE?
JUST LIKE THEM, YOU DECIDE LIFE-OR-DEATH BASED ON YOUR OWN RELIGIOUS DOGMA!
CAN'T YOU SEE THAT YOU'RE DOING EXACTLY WHAT YOU CLAIM TO HATE THE MOST IN THEM?!
NO.
WHAT DO YOU NEED OF ME?
OUR FRIENDS HAVE BEEN CAPTURED.
I SEE.
YIII!!
YONDU!
WHAT ARE YOU DOING?! YOU NEARLY KNOCKED US BOTH OFF WITH THAT STUNT!
I AM GOING TO THE INDOCTRINATION CHAMBER, WHERE YOUR FRIENDS ARE, NO DOUBT, BEING HELD.
YOU WILL SEE FOR YOURSELF THE TRUE EVIL I HAVE TRIED TO WARN YOU OF--
--AND WHAT I MUST FIGHT!

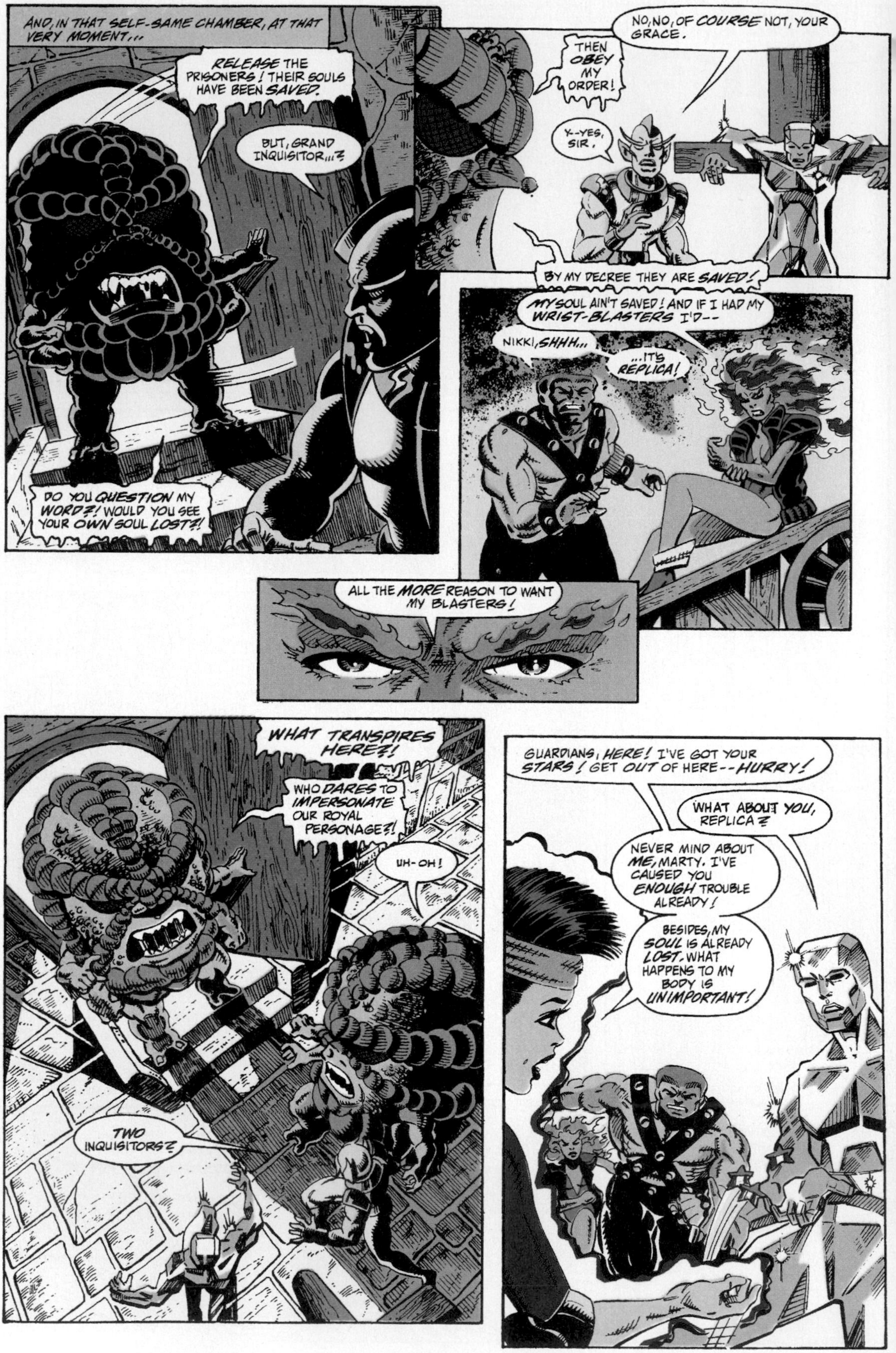

AND, IN THAT SELF-SAME CHAMBER, AT THAT VERY MOMENT...
RELEASE THE PRISONERS! THEIR SOULS HAVE BEEN SAVED.
BUT, GRAND INQUISITOR...?
DO YOU QUESTION MY WORD?! WOULD YOU SEE YOUR OWN SOUL LOST?!
NO, NO, OF COURSE NOT, YOUR GRACE.
THEN OBEY MY ORDER!
Y--YES, SIR.
BY MY DECREE THEY ARE SAVED!
MY SOUL AIN'T SAVED! AND IF I HAD MY WRIST-BLASTERS I'D--
NIKKI, SHHH...
...IT'S REPLICA!
ALL THE MORE REASON TO WANT MY BLASTERS!
WHAT TRANSPIRES HERE?!
WHO DARES TO IMPERSONATE OUR ROYAL PERSONAGE?!
UH-OH!
TWO INQUISITORS?
GUARDIANS, HERE! I'VE GOT YOUR STARS! GET OUT OF HERE--HURRY!
WHAT ABOUT YOU, REPLICA?
NEVER MIND ABOUT ME, MARTY. I'VE CAUSED YOU ENOUGH TROUBLE ALREADY!
BESIDES, MY SOUL IS ALREADY LOST. WHAT HAPPENS TO MY BODY IS UNIMPORTANT!

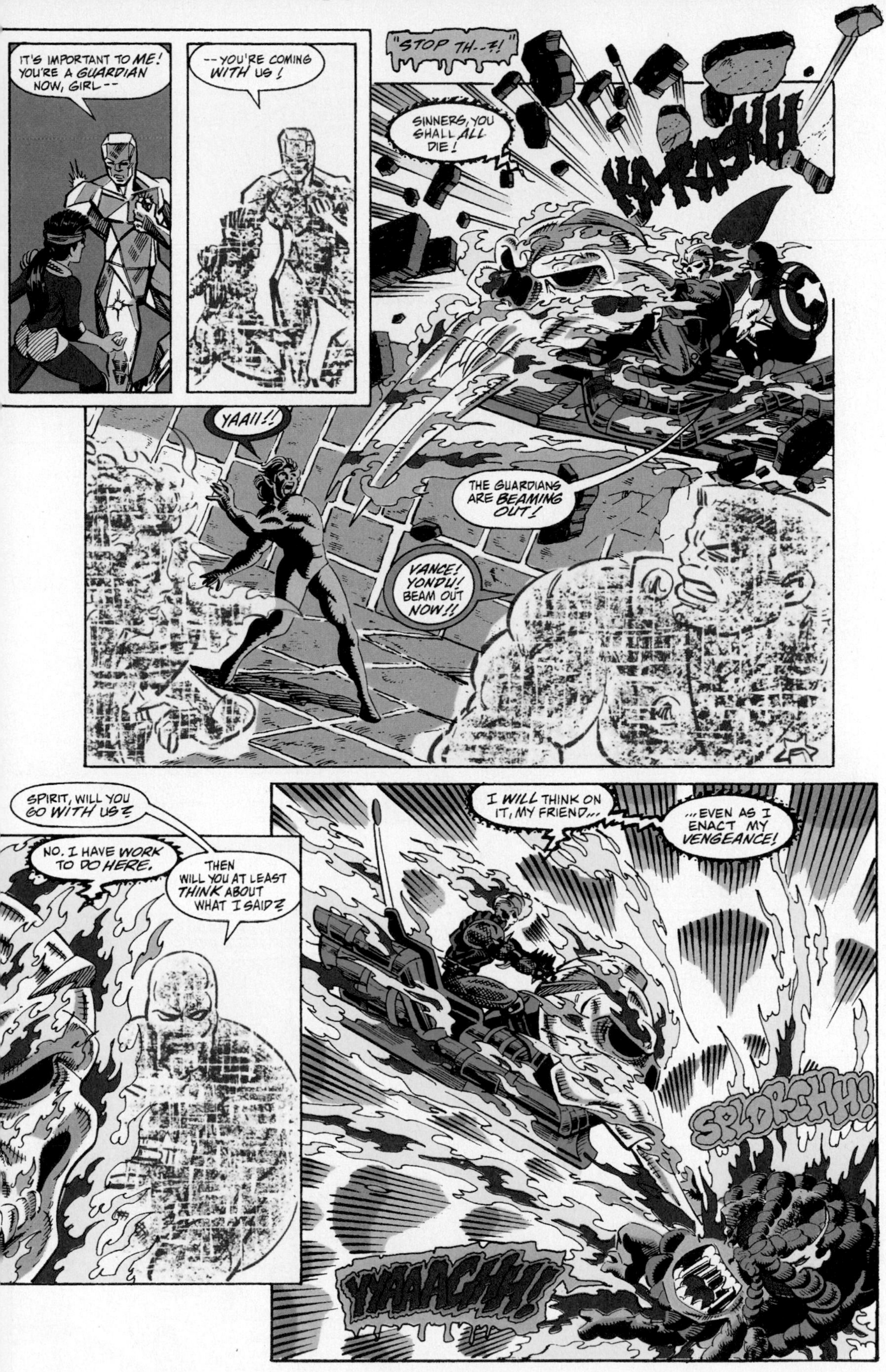
IT'S IMPORTANT TO ME! YOU'RE A GUARDIAN NOW, GIRL --
-- YOU'RE COMING WITH US!
"STOP TH--?!"
SINNERS, YOU SHALL ALL DIE!
KA-RASHH
YAAII!!
THE GUARDIANS ARE BEAMING OUT!
VANCE! YONDU! BEAM OUT NOW!!
SPIRIT, WILL YOU GO WITH US?
NO. I HAVE WORK TO DO HERE.
THEN WILL YOU AT LEAST THINK ABOUT WHAT I SAID?
I WILL THINK ON IT, MY FRIEND...
...EVEN AS I ENACT MY VENGEANCE!
SPLORCHH!
YAAACHH!

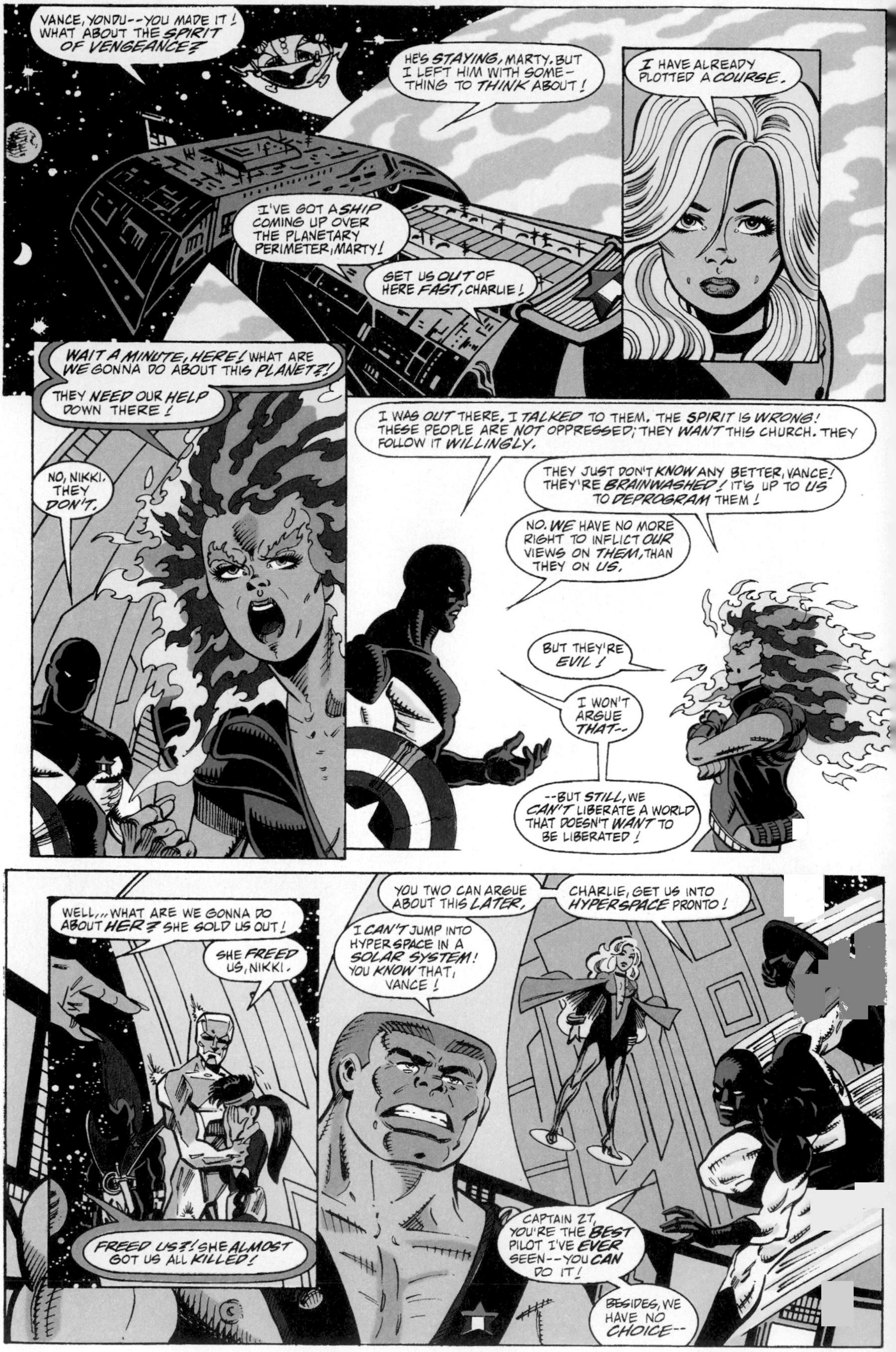
VANCE, YONDU--YOU MADE IT! WHAT ABOUT THE SPIRIT OF VENGEANCE?
HE'S STAYING, MARTY. BUT I LEFT HIM WITH SOMETHING TO THINK ABOUT!
I HAVE ALREADY PLOTTED A COURSE.
I'VE GOT A SHIP COMING UP OVER THE PLANETARY PERIMETER, MARTY!
GET US OUT OF HERE FAST, CHARLIE!
WAIT A MINUTE, HERE! WHAT ARE WE GONNA DO ABOUT THIS PLANET?!
THEY NEED OUR HELP DOWN THERE!
NO, NIKKI. THEY DON'T.
I WAS OUT THERE. I TALKED TO THEM. THE SPIRIT IS WRONG! THESE PEOPLE ARE NOT OPPRESSED; THEY WANT THIS CHURCH. THEY FOLLOW IT WILLINGLY.
THEY JUST DON'T KNOW ANY BETTER, VANCE! THEY'RE BRAINWASHED! IT'S UP TO US TO DEPROGRAM THEM!
NO. WE HAVE NO MORE RIGHT TO INFLICT OUR VIEWS ON THEM, THAN THEY ON US.
BUT THEY'RE EVIL!
I WON'T ARGUE THAT--
--BUT STILL, WE CAN'T LIBERATE A WORLD THAT DOESN'T WANT TO BE LIBERATED!
WELL... WHAT ARE WE GONNA DO ABOUT HER? SHE SOLD US OUT!
SHE FREED US, NIKKI.
FREED US?! SHE ALMOST GOT US ALL KILLED!
YOU TWO CAN ARGUE ABOUT THIS LATER.
CHARLIE, GET US INTO HYPERSPACE PRONTO!
I CAN'T JUMP INTO HYPERSPACE IN A SOLAR SYSTEM! YOU KNOW THAT, VANCE!
CAPTAIN 27, YOU'RE THE BEST PILOT I'VE EVER SEEN--YOU CAN DO IT!
BESIDES, WE HAVE NO CHOICE--

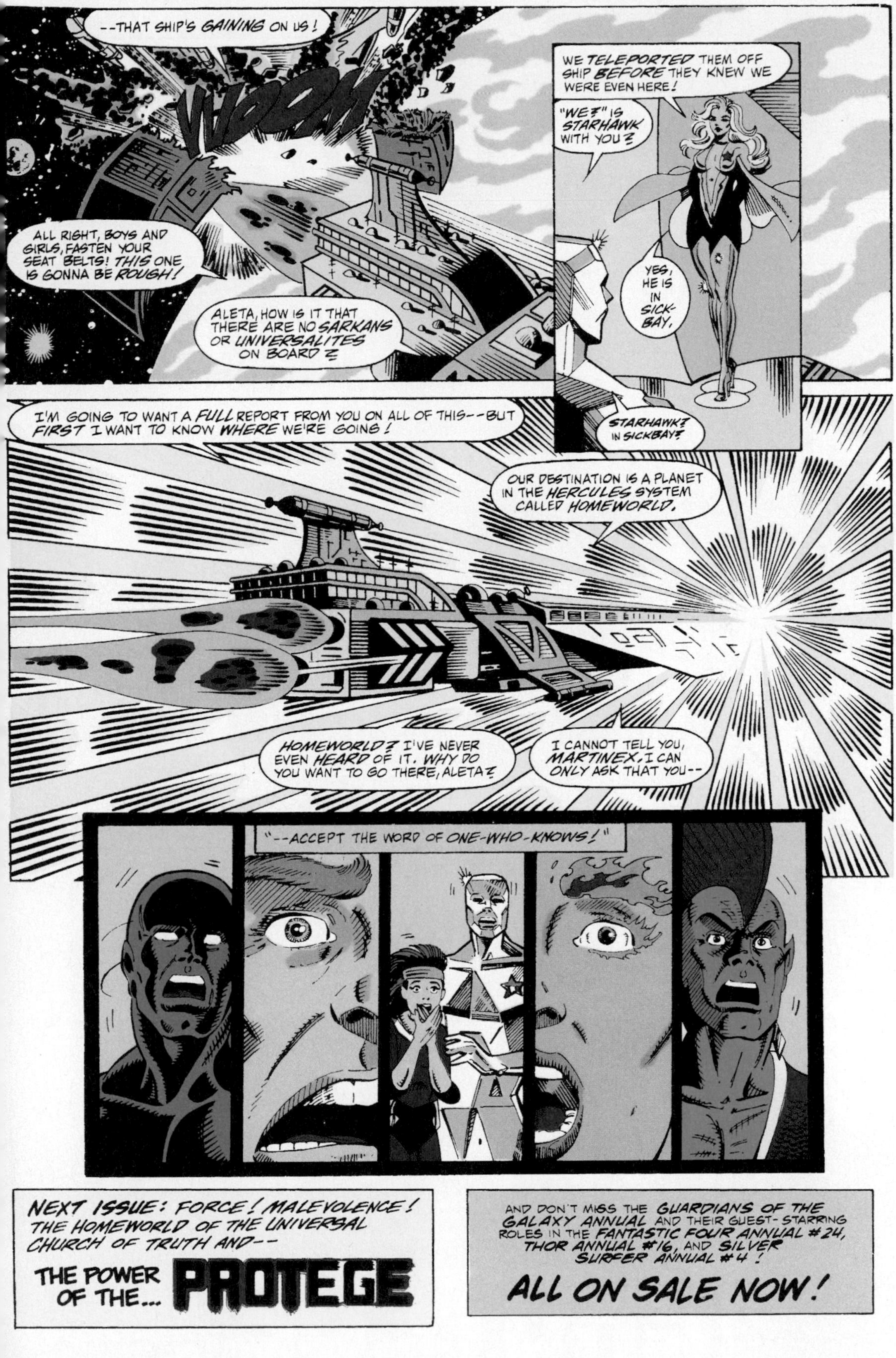
--THAT SHIP'S GAINING ON US!
WOOM
ALL RIGHT, BOYS AND GIRLS, FASTEN YOUR SEAT BELTS! THIS ONE IS GONNA BE ROUGH!
ALETA, HOW IS IT THAT THERE ARE NO SARKANS OR UNIVERSALITES ON BOARD?
WE TELEPORTED THEM OFF SHIP BEFORE THEY KNEW WE WERE EVEN HERE!
"WE?" IS STARHAWK WITH YOU?
YES, HE IS IN SICK-BAY.
STARHAWK? IN SICKBAY?
I'M GOING TO WANT A FULL REPORT FROM YOU ON ALL OF THIS--BUT FIRST I WANT TO KNOW WHERE WE'RE GOING!
OUR DESTINATION IS A PLANET IN THE HERCULES SYSTEM CALLED HOMEWORLD.
HOMEWORLD? I'VE NEVER EVEN HEARD OF IT. WHY DO YOU WANT TO GO THERE, ALETA?
I CANNOT TELL YOU, MARTINEX. I CAN ONLY ASK THAT YOU--
"--ACCEPT THE WORD OF ONE-WHO-KNOWS!"
NEXT ISSUE: FORCE! MALEVOLENCE! THE HOMEWORLD OF THE UNIVERSAL CHURCH OF TRUTH AND--
THE POWER OF THE... PROTEGE
AND DON'T MISS THE GUARDIANS OF THE GALAXY ANNUAL AND THEIR GUEST-STARRING ROLES IN THE FANTASTIC FOUR ANNUAL #24, THOR ANNUAL #16, AND SILVER SURFER ANNUAL #4!
ALL ON SALE NOW!

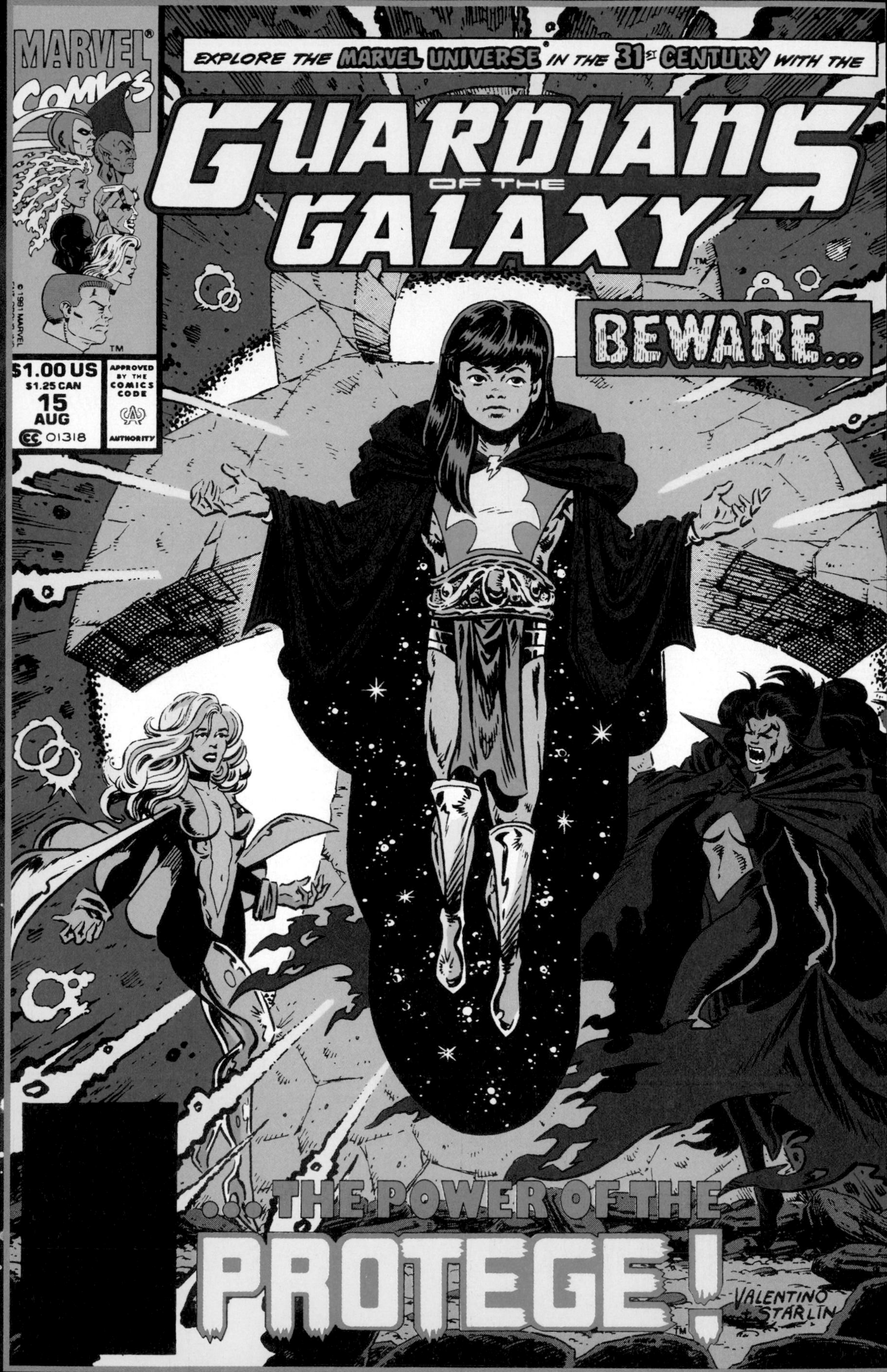
MARVEL COMICS
EXPLORE THE MARVEL UNIVERSE IN THE 31ST CENTURY WITH THE
GUARDIANS OF THE GALAXY
BEWARE...
$1.00 US
$1.25 CAN
15
AUG
01318
APPROVED BY THE COMICS CODE AUTHORITY
...THE POWER OF THE
PROTEGE!
VALENTINO + STARLIN

CHARLIE 27! MARTINEX! NIKKI! VANCE ASTRO! YONDU! ALETA! STARHAWK! SEVEN EXTRAORDINARY SUPER-BEINGS, ALL SURVIVORS OF INTERSTELLAR WAR. NOW THEY ROAM THE COSMOS OF THE 31ST CENTURY ABOARD THE STARSHIP CAPTAIN AMERICA, THEIR MISSION—TO SAFEGUARD THE MILKY WAY! STAN LEE PRESENTS . . . THE GUARDIANS OF THE GALAXY!

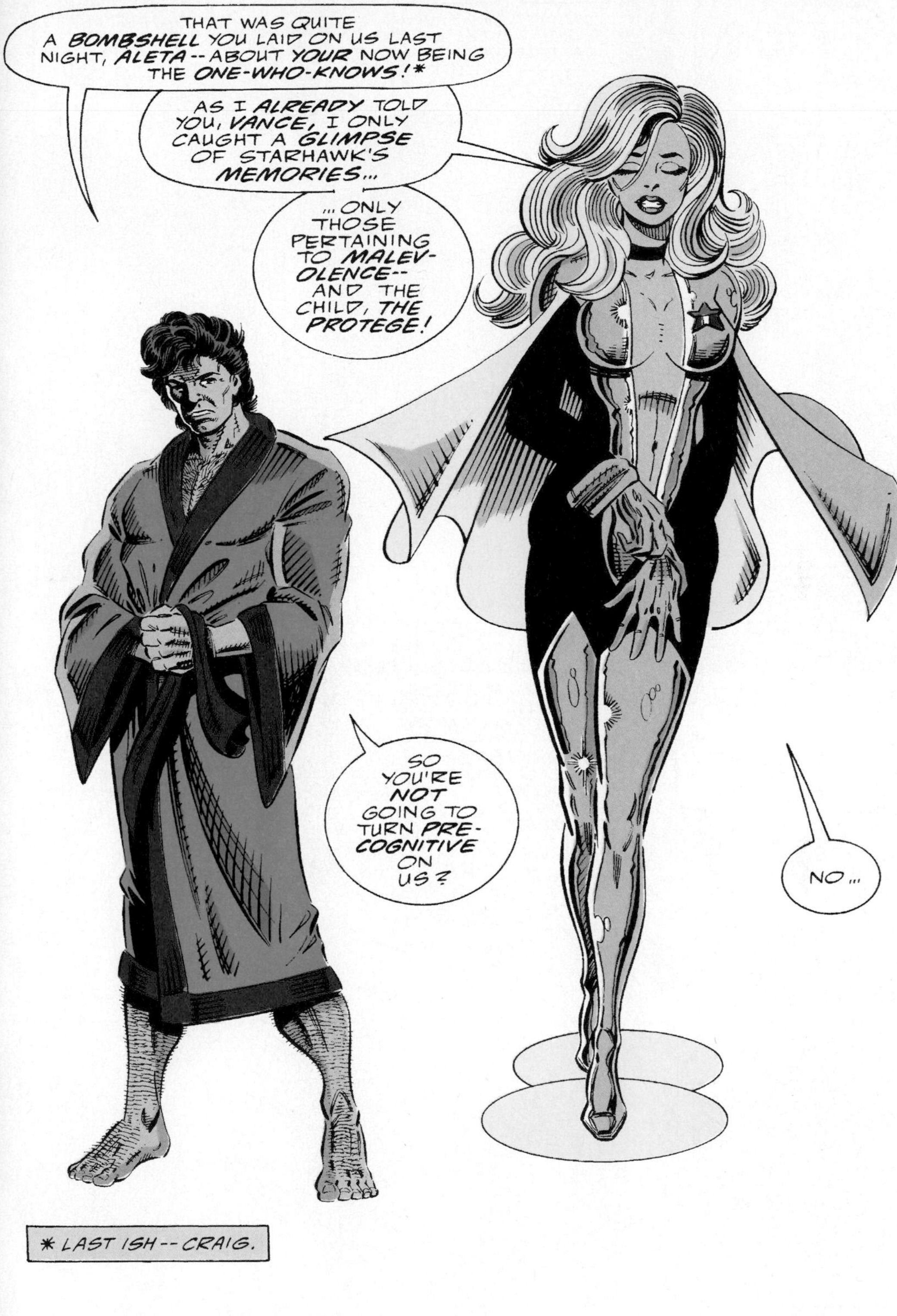
THAT WAS QUITE A BOMBSHELL YOU LAID ON US LAST NIGHT, ALETA--ABOUT YOUR NOW BEING THE ONE-WHO-KNOWS!*
AS I ALREADY TOLD YOU, VANCE, I ONLY CAUGHT A GLIMPSE OF STARHAWK'S MEMORIES...
...ONLY THOSE PERTAINING TO MALEVOLENCE--AND THE CHILD, THE PROTEGE!
SO YOU'RE NOT GOING TO TURN PRECOGNITIVE ON US?
NO...
* LAST ISH--CRAIG.

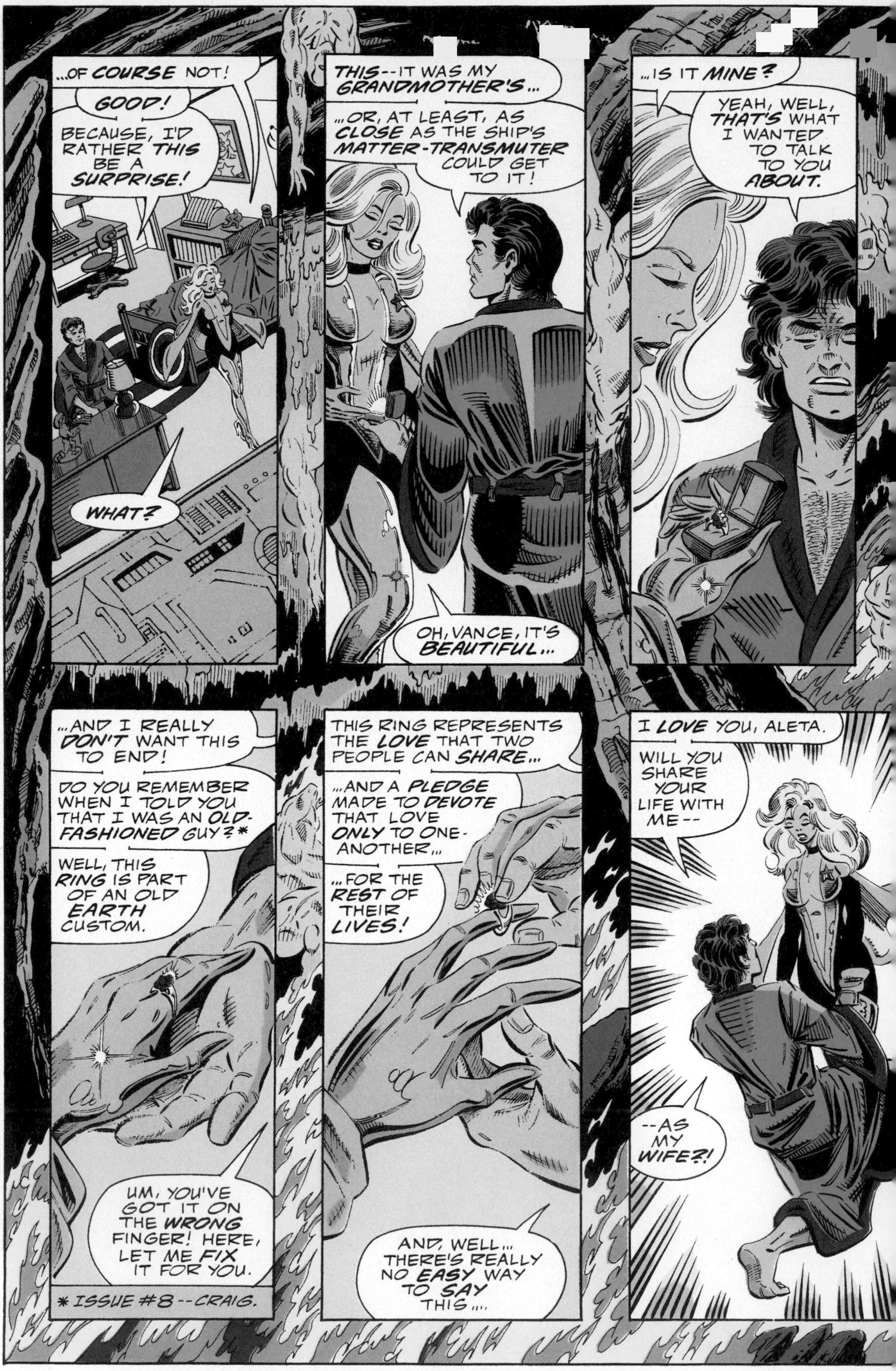
...OF COURSE NOT!
GOOD!
BECAUSE, I'D RATHER THIS BE A SURPRISE!
WHAT?
THIS--IT WAS MY GRANDMOTHER'S...
...OR, AT LEAST, AS CLOSE AS THE SHIP'S MATTER-TRANSMUTER COULD GET TO IT!
OH, VANCE, IT'S BEAUTIFUL...
...IS IT MINE?
YEAH, WELL, THAT'S WHAT I WANTED TO TALK TO YOU ABOUT.
...AND I REALLY DON'T WANT THIS TO END!
DO YOU REMEMBER WHEN I TOLD YOU THAT I WAS AN OLD-FASHIONED GUY?*
WELL, THIS RING IS PART OF AN OLD EARTH CUSTOM.
UM, YOU'VE GOT IT ON THE WRONG FINGER! HERE, LET ME FIX IT FOR YOU.
*ISSUE #8--CRAIG.
THIS RING REPRESENTS THE LOVE THAT TWO PEOPLE CAN SHARE...
...AND A PLEDGE MADE TO DEVOTE THAT LOVE ONLY TO ONE-ANOTHER...
...FOR THE REST OF THEIR LIVES!
AND, WELL... THERE'S REALLY NO EASY WAY TO SAY THIS....
I LOVE YOU, ALETA.
WILL YOU SHARE YOUR LIFE WITH ME--
--AS MY WIFE?!

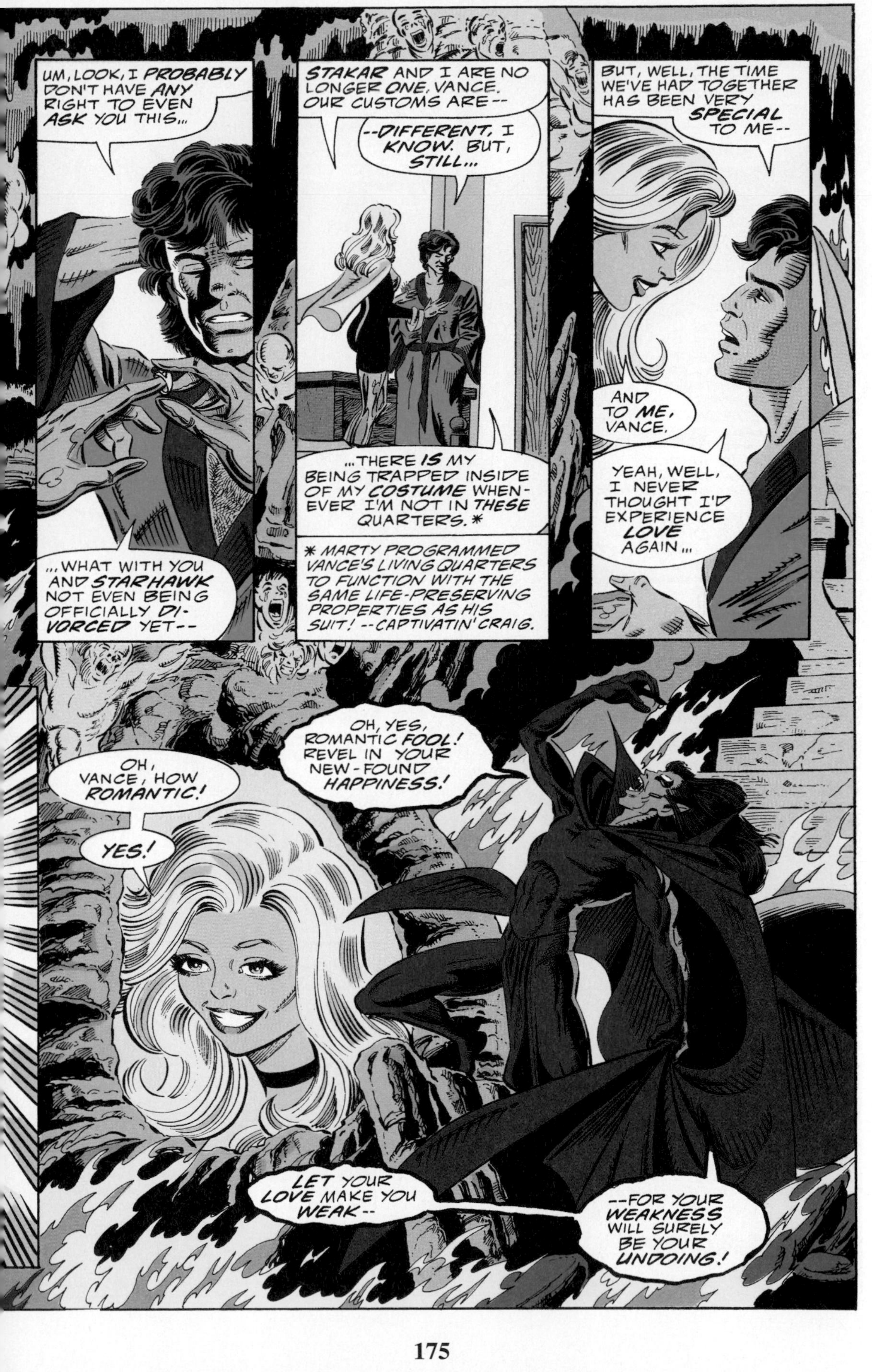
UM, LOOK, I PROBABLY DON'T HAVE ANY RIGHT TO EVEN ASK YOU THIS...
...WHAT WITH YOU AND STARHAWK NOT EVEN BEING OFFICIALLY DI-VORCED YET--
STAKAR AND I ARE NO LONGER ONE, VANCE. OUR CUSTOMS ARE--
--DIFFERENT, I KNOW. BUT, STILL...
...THERE IS MY BEING TRAPPED INSIDE OF MY COSTUME WHEN-EVER I'M NOT IN THESE QUARTERS.*
* MARTY PROGRAMMED VANCE'S LIVING QUARTERS TO FUNCTION WITH THE SAME LIFE-PRESERVING PROPERTIES AS HIS SUIT! --CAPTIVATIN' CRAIG.
BUT, WELL, THE TIME WE'VE HAD TOGETHER HAS BEEN VERY SPECIAL TO ME--
AND TO ME, VANCE.
YEAH, WELL, I NEVER THOUGHT I'D EXPERIENCE LOVE AGAIN...
OH, VANCE, HOW ROMANTIC!
YES!
OH, YES, ROMANTIC FOOL! REVEL IN YOUR NEW-FOUND HAPPINESS!
LET YOUR LOVE MAKE YOU WEAK--
--FOR YOUR WEAKNESS WILL SURELY BE YOUR UNDOING!

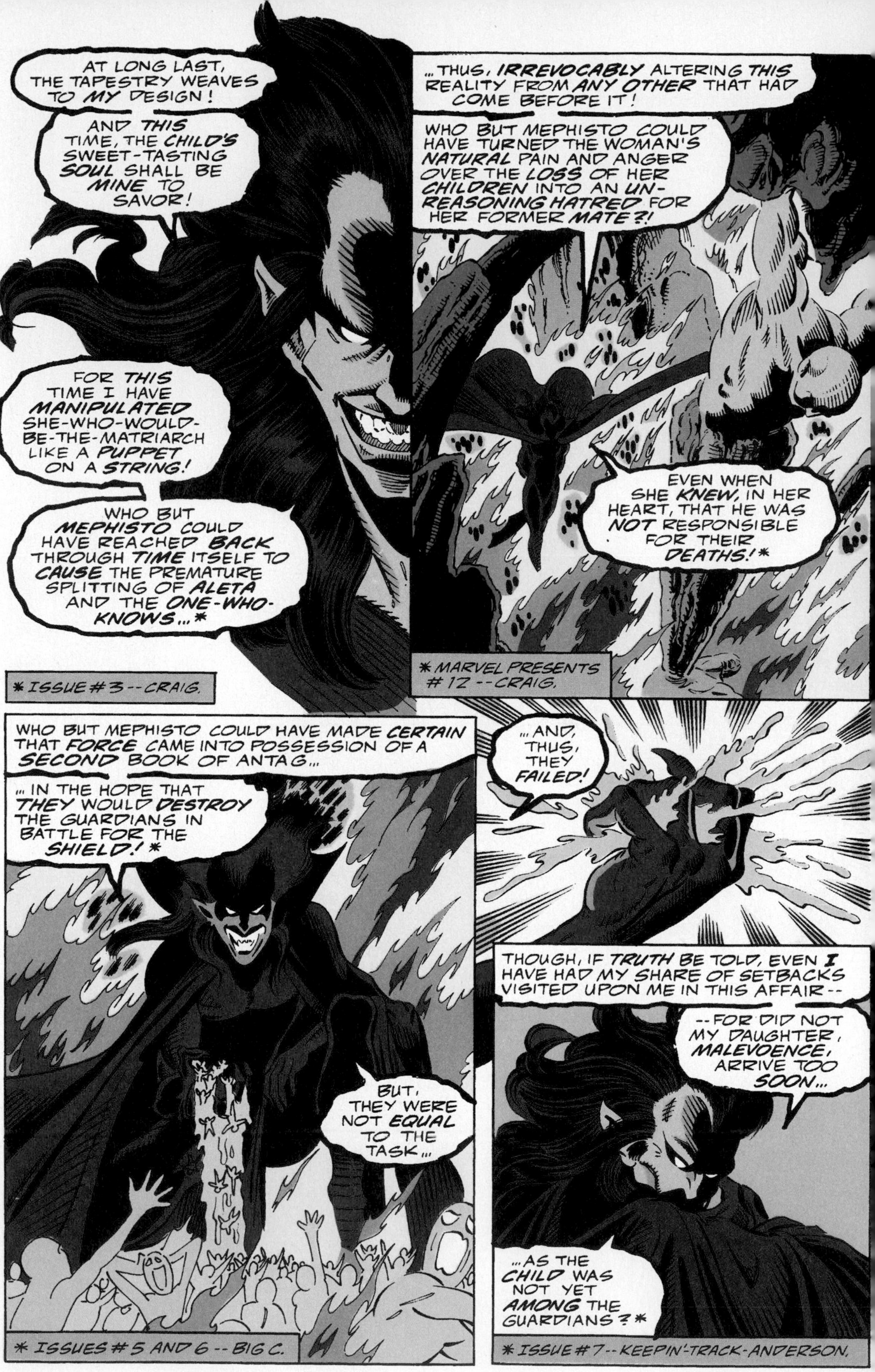

AT LONG LAST, THE TAPESTRY WEAVES TO MY DESIGN!
AND THIS TIME, THE CHILD'S SWEET-TASTING SOUL SHALL BE MINE TO SAVOR!
FOR THIS TIME I HAVE MANIPULATED SHE-WHO-WOULD-BE-THE-MATRIARCH LIKE A PUPPET ON A STRING!
WHO BUT MEPHISTO COULD HAVE REACHED BACK THROUGH TIME ITSELF TO CAUSE THE PREMATURE SPLITTING OF ALETA AND THE ONE-WHO-KNOWS...*
* ISSUE #3 -- CRAIG.
...THUS, IRREVOCABLY ALTERING THIS REALITY FROM ANY OTHER THAT HAD COME BEFORE IT!
WHO BUT MEPHISTO COULD HAVE TURNED THE WOMAN'S NATURAL PAIN AND ANGER OVER THE LOSS OF HER CHILDREN INTO AN UNREASONING HATRED FOR HER FORMER MATE?!
EVEN WHEN SHE KNEW, IN HER HEART, THAT HE WAS NOT RESPONSIBLE FOR THEIR DEATHS!*
* MARVEL PRESENTS #12 -- CRAIG.
WHO BUT MEPHISTO COULD HAVE MADE CERTAIN THAT FORCE CAME INTO POSSESSION OF A SECOND BOOK OF ANTAG...
... IN THE HOPE THAT THEY WOULD DESTROY THE GUARDIANS IN BATTLE FOR THE SHIELD! *
BUT, THEY WERE NOT EQUAL TO THE TASK...
* ISSUES #5 AND 6 -- BIG C.
...AND, THUS, THEY FAILED!
THOUGH, IF TRUTH BE TOLD, EVEN I HAVE HAD MY SHARE OF SETBACKS VISITED UPON ME IN THIS AFFAIR --
-- FOR DID NOT MY DAUGHTER, MALEVOENCE, ARRIVE TOO SOON...
...AS THE CHILD WAS NOT YET AMONG THE GUARDIANS? *
* ISSUE #7 -- KEEPIN'-TRACK-ANDERSON.

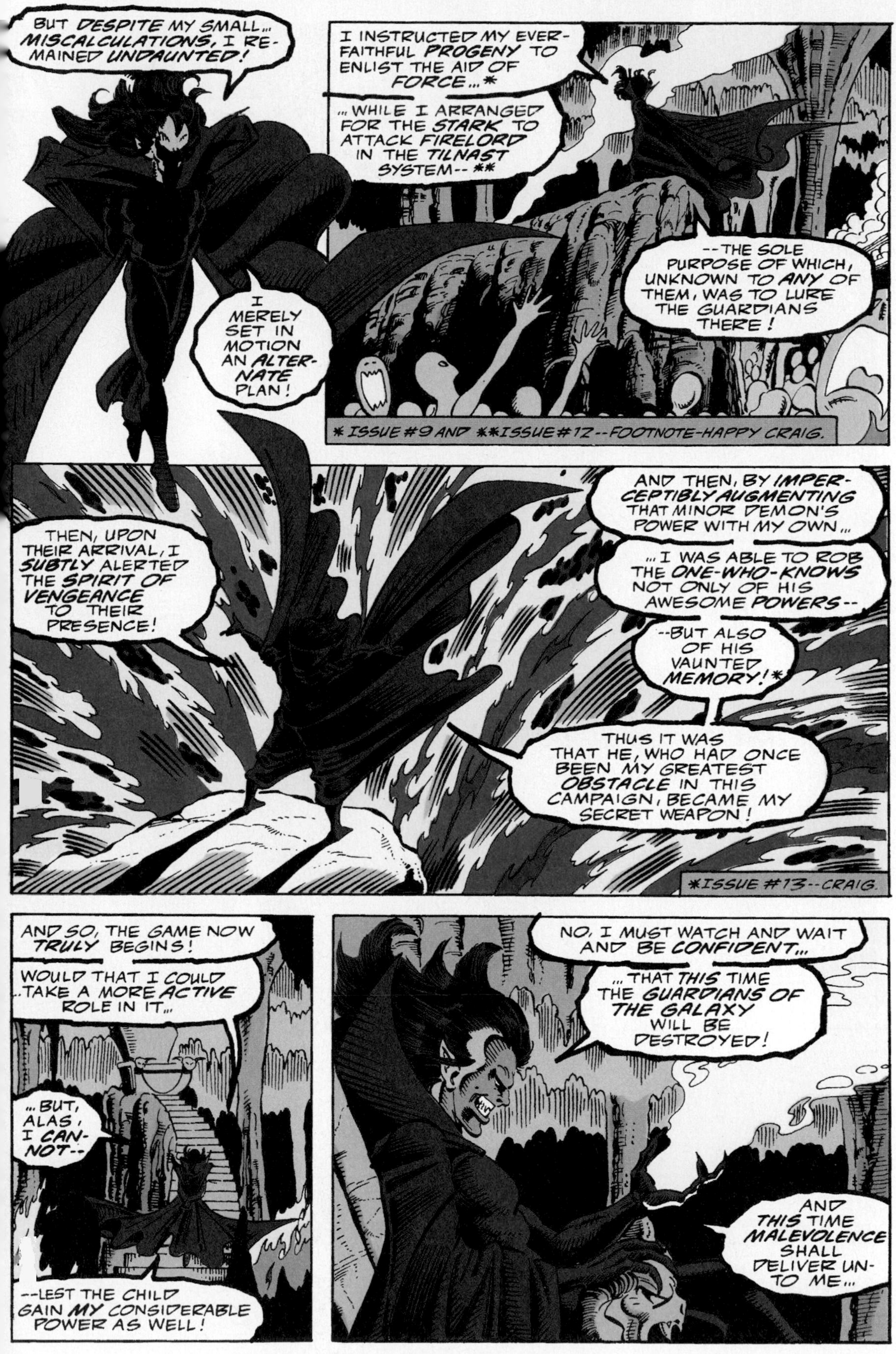

BUT DESPITE MY SMALL... MISCALCULATIONS, I REMAINED UNDAUNTED!
I MERELY SET IN MOTION AN ALTERNATE PLAN!
I INSTRUCTED MY EVER-FAITHFUL PROGENY TO ENLIST THE AID OF FORCE...*
...WHILE I ARRANGED FOR THE STARK TO ATTACK FIRELORD IN THE TILNAST SYSTEM--**
--THE SOLE PURPOSE OF WHICH, UNKNOWN TO ANY OF THEM, WAS TO LURE THE GUARDIANS THERE!
*ISSUE #9 AND **ISSUE #12--FOOTNOTE-HAPPY CRAIG.
THEN, UPON THEIR ARRIVAL, I SUBTLY ALERTED THE SPIRIT OF VENGEANCE TO THEIR PRESENCE!
AND THEN, BY IMPERCEPTIBLY AUGMENTING THAT MINOR DEMON'S POWER WITH MY OWN...
...I WAS ABLE TO ROB THE ONE-WHO-KNOWS NOT ONLY OF HIS AWESOME POWERS--
--BUT ALSO OF HIS VAUNTED MEMORY!*
THUS IT WAS THAT HE, WHO HAD ONCE BEEN MY GREATEST OBSTACLE IN THIS CAMPAIGN, BECAME MY SECRET WEAPON!
*ISSUE #13--CRAIG.
AND SO, THE GAME NOW TRULY BEGINS!
WOULD THAT I COULD ..TAKE A MORE ACTIVE ROLE IN IT...
...BUT, ALAS, I CAN-NOT--
--LEST THE CHILD GAIN MY CONSIDERABLE POWER AS WELL!
NO, I MUST WATCH AND WAIT AND BE CONFIDENT...
...THAT THIS TIME THE GUARDIANS OF THE GALAXY WILL BE DESTROYED!
AND THIS TIME MALEVOLENCE SHALL DELIVER UNTO ME...

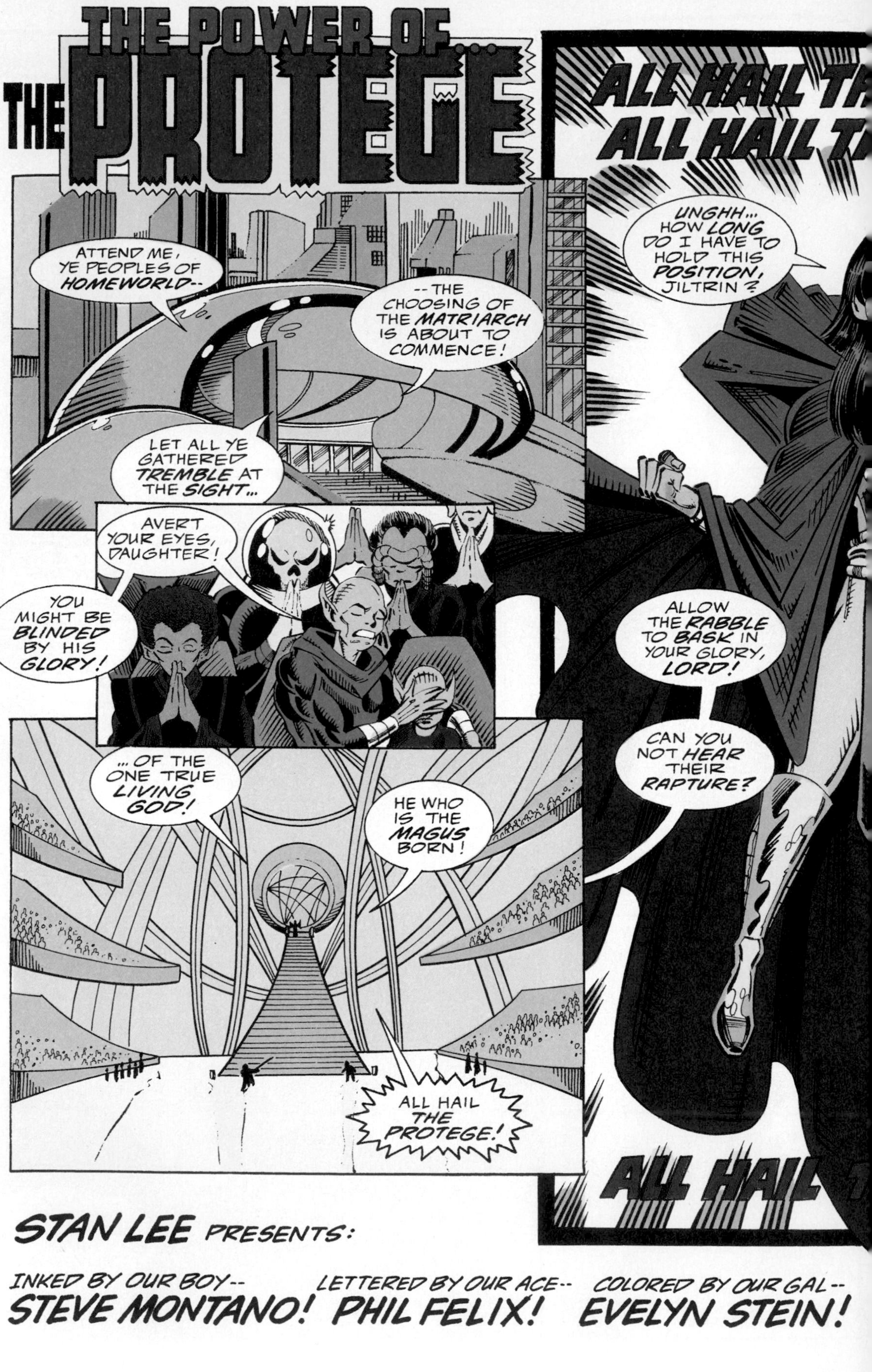
THE POWER OF...
THE PROTEGE
ALL HAIL
ALL HAIL
ATTEND ME, YE PEOPLES OF HOMEWORLD--
--THE CHOOSING OF THE MATRIARCH IS ABOUT TO COMMENCE!
LET ALL YE GATHERED TREMBLE AT THE SIGHT...
AVERT YOUR EYES, DAUGHTER!
YOU MIGHT BE BLINDED BY HIS GLORY!
...OF THE ONE TRUE LIVING GOD!
HE WHO IS THE MAGUS BORN!
ALL HAIL THE PROTEGE!
UNGHH... HOW LONG DO I HAVE TO HOLD THIS POSITION, JILTRIN?
ALLOW THE RABBLE TO BASK IN YOUR GLORY, LORD!
CAN YOU NOT HEAR THEIR RAPTURE?
ALL HAIL
STAN LEE PRESENTS:
INKED BY OUR BOY-- STEVE MONTANO!
LETTERED BY OUR ACE-- PHIL FELIX!
COLORED BY OUR GAL-- EVELYN STEIN!

PROTEGE!
PROTEGE!

;SIGH; VERY WELL, MOST HOLY.

FINAL ELIMINATIONS ARE ABOUT TO COMMENCE!

ARE THE CONTESTANTS PREPARED TO DIE?!

WE ARE, YOUR GRACE!

YES, YES, JUST HAVE THEM HURRY--THIS HURTS!

YOU CAN CONCEDE NOW WITH NO DISHONOR, STARK!

A STARK NEVER CONCEDES!

THEN YOU MUST DIE!!

PROTEGE!

BASED LOOSELY ON CONCEPTS CREATED BY OUR IDOL--JIM STARLIN!

EDITED BY OUR BOSS-- CRAIG ANDERSON!

CHIEFED BY OUR HERO-- TOM DeFALCO!

THE MESS BY OUR PINHEAD-- JIM VALENTINO!

GUARDIANS
OF THE GALAXY

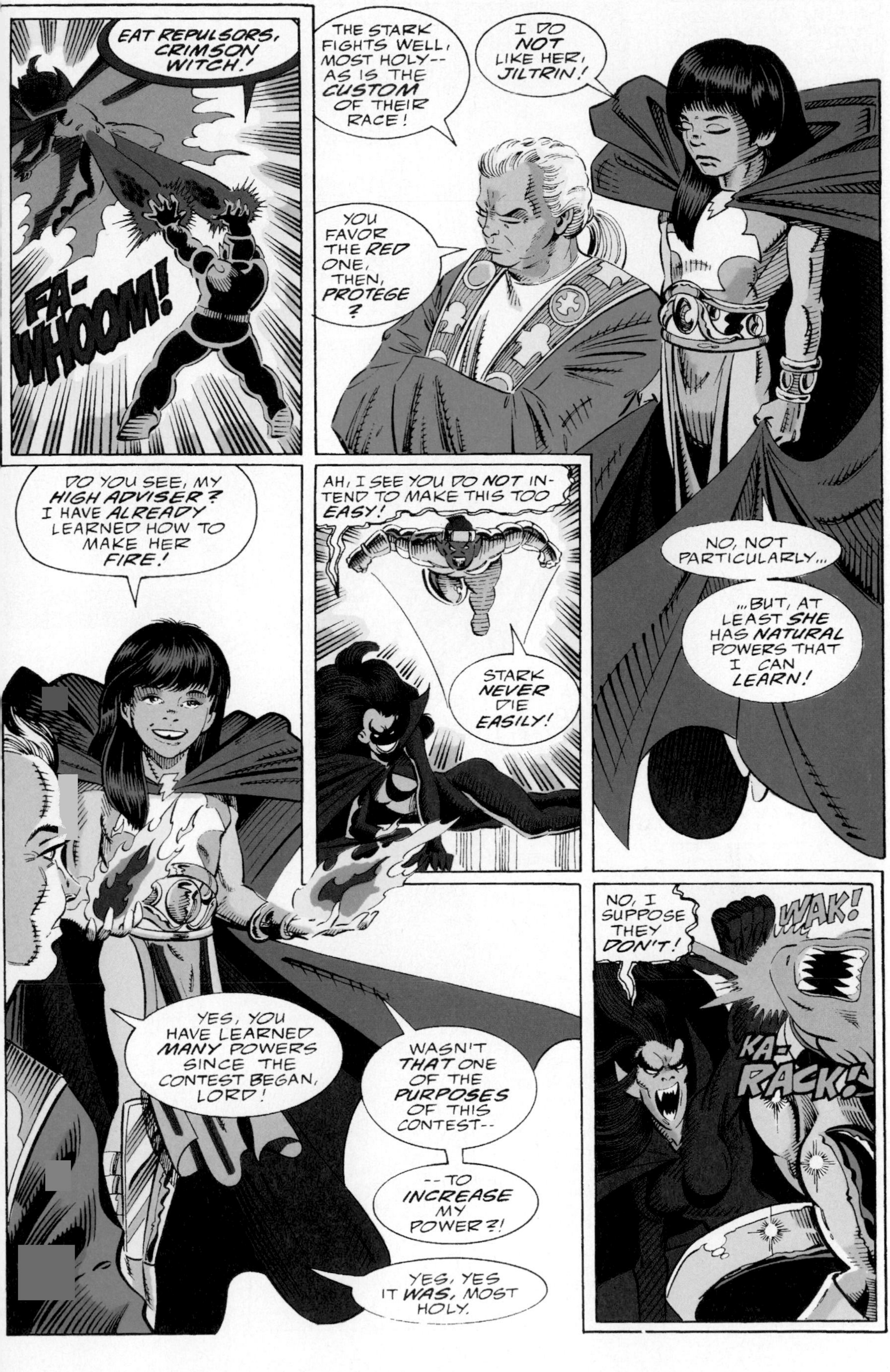
EAT REPULSORS, CRIMSON WITCH!
FA-WHOOM!
THE STARK FIGHTS WELL, MOST HOLY-- AS IS THE CUSTOM OF THEIR RACE!
I DO NOT LIKE HER, JILTRIN!
YOU FAVOR THE RED ONE, THEN, PROTEGE?
NO, NOT PARTICULARLY...
...BUT, AT LEAST SHE HAS NATURAL POWERS THAT I CAN LEARN!
AH, I SEE YOU DO NOT INTEND TO MAKE THIS TOO EASY!
STARK NEVER DIE EASILY!
DO YOU SEE, MY HIGH ADVISER? I HAVE ALREADY LEARNED HOW TO MAKE HER FIRE!
YES, YOU HAVE LEARNED MANY POWERS SINCE THE CONTEST BEGAN, LORD!
WASN'T THAT ONE OF THE PURPOSES OF THIS CONTEST--
--TO INCREASE MY POWER?!
YES, YES IT WAS, MOST HOLY.
NO, I SUPPOSE THEY DON'T!
WAK!
KA-RACK!

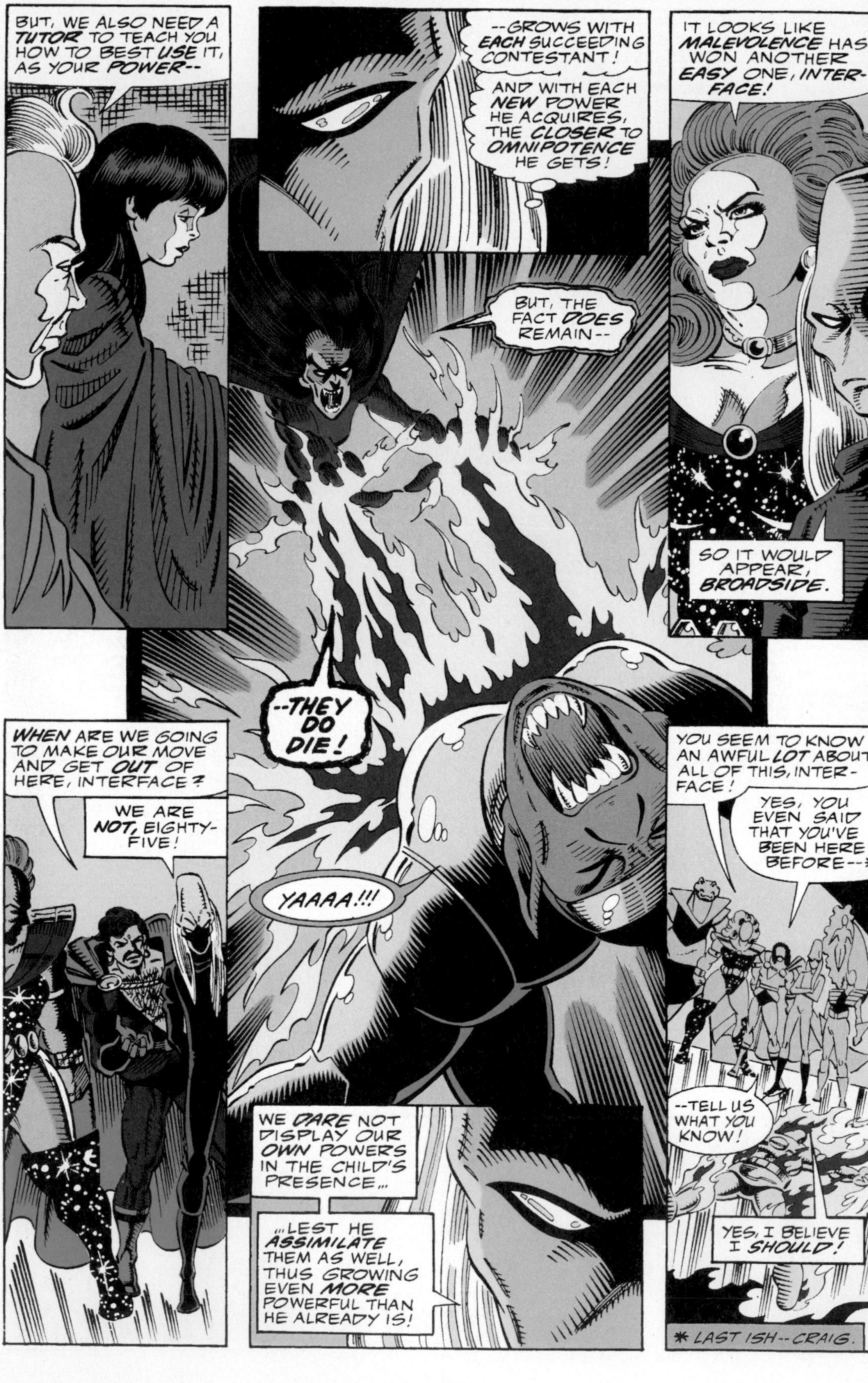
BUT, WE ALSO NEED A TUTOR TO TEACH YOU HOW TO BEST USE IT, AS YOUR POWER--
--GROWS WITH EACH SUCCEEDING CONTESTANT!
AND WITH EACH NEW POWER HE ACQUIRES, THE CLOSER TO OMNIPOTENCE HE GETS!
IT LOOKS LIKE MALEVOLENCE HAS WON ANOTHER EASY ONE, INTER-FACE!
BUT, THE FACT DOES REMAIN--
SO IT WOULD APPEAR, BROADSIDE.
--THEY DO DIE!
WHEN ARE WE GOING TO MAKE OUR MOVE AND GET OUT OF HERE, INTERFACE?
WE ARE NOT, EIGHTY-FIVE!
YAAAA!!!
WE DARE NOT DISPLAY OUR OWN POWERS IN THE CHILD'S PRESENCE...
...LEST HE ASSIMILATE THEM AS WELL, THUS GROWING EVEN MORE POWERFUL THAN HE ALREADY IS!
YOU SEEM TO KNOW AN AWFUL LOT ABOUT ALL OF THIS, INTER-FACE!
YES, YOU EVEN SAID THAT YOU'VE BEEN HERE BEFORE--*
--TELL US WHAT YOU KNOW!
YES, I BELIEVE I SHOULD!
* LAST ISH--CRAIG.

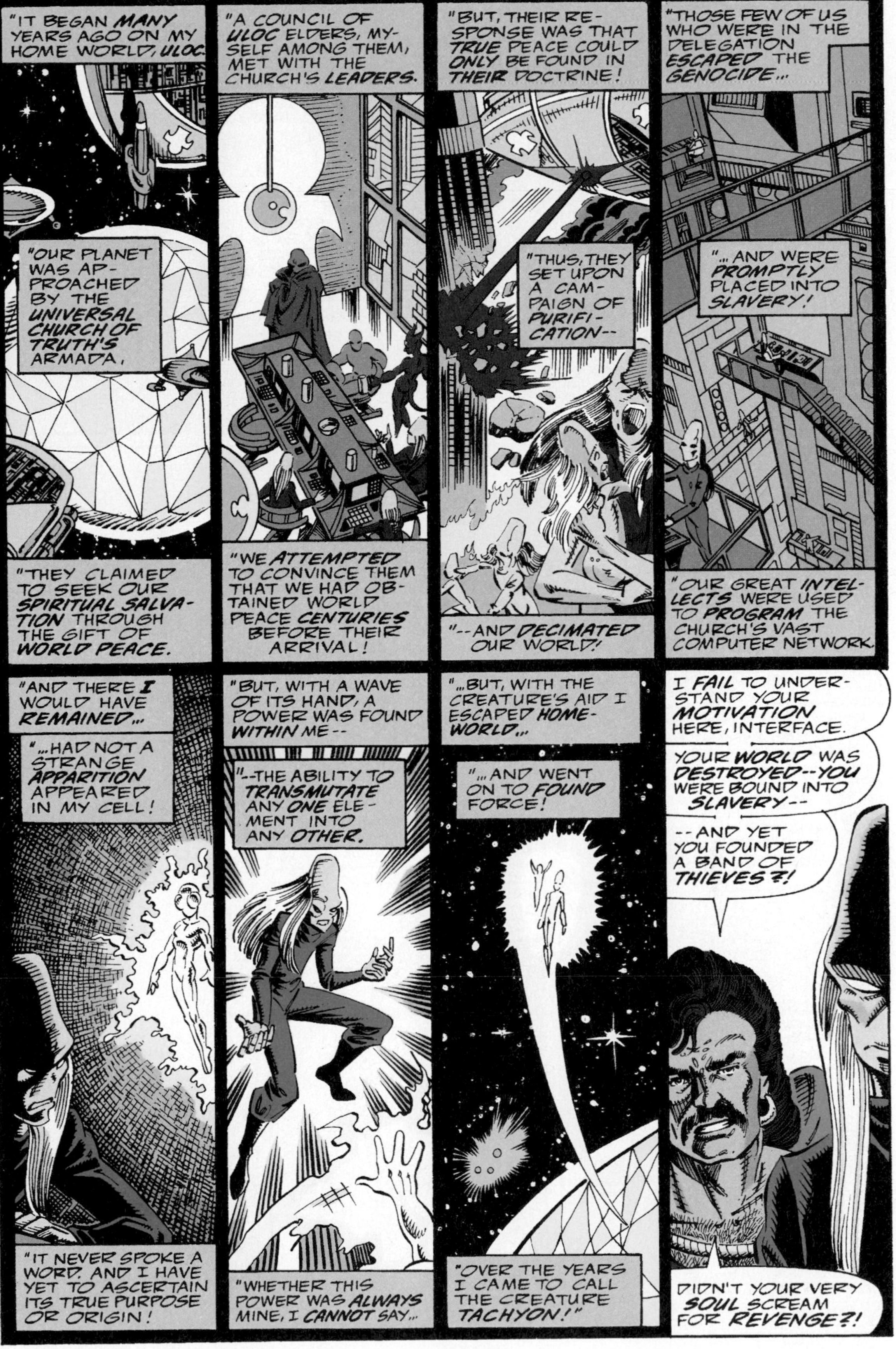
"IT BEGAN MANY YEARS AGO ON MY HOME WORLD, ULOC.
"OUR PLANET WAS APPROACHED BY THE UNIVERSAL CHURCH OF TRUTH'S ARMADA.
"THEY CLAIMED TO SEEK OUR SPIRITUAL SALVATION THROUGH THE GIFT OF WORLD PEACE.
"A COUNCIL OF ULOC ELDERS, MYSELF AMONG THEM, MET WITH THE CHURCH'S LEADERS.
"WE ATTEMPTED TO CONVINCE THEM THAT WE HAD OBTAINED WORLD PEACE CENTURIES BEFORE THEIR ARRIVAL!
"BUT, THEIR RESPONSE WAS THAT TRUE PEACE COULD ONLY BE FOUND IN THEIR DOCTRINE!
"THUS, THEY SET UPON A CAMPAIGN OF PURIFICATION--
"--AND DECIMATED OUR WORLD!
"THOSE FEW OF US WHO WERE IN THE DELEGATION ESCAPED THE GENOCIDE...
"...AND WERE PROMPTLY PLACED INTO SLAVERY!
"OUR GREAT INTELLECTS WERE USED TO PROGRAM THE CHURCH'S VAST COMPUTER NETWORK.
"AND THERE I WOULD HAVE REMAINED...
"...HAD NOT A STRANGE APPARITION APPEARED IN MY CELL!
"IT NEVER SPOKE A WORD, AND I HAVE YET TO ASCERTAIN ITS TRUE PURPOSE OR ORIGIN!
"BUT, WITH A WAVE OF ITS HAND, A POWER WAS FOUND WITHIN ME--
"--THE ABILITY TO TRANSMUTATE ANY ONE ELEMENT INTO ANY OTHER.
"WHETHER THIS POWER WAS ALWAYS MINE, I CANNOT SAY...
"...BUT, WITH THE CREATURE'S AID I ESCAPED HOMEWORLD...
"...AND WENT ON TO FOUND FORCE!
"OVER THE YEARS I CAME TO CALL THE CREATURE TACHYON!"
I FAIL TO UNDERSTAND YOUR MOTIVATION HERE, INTERFACE.
YOUR WORLD WAS DESTROYED--YOU WERE BOUND INTO SLAVERY--
--AND YET YOU FOUNDED A BAND OF THIEVES?!
DIDN'T YOUR VERY SOUL SCREAM FOR REVENGE?!

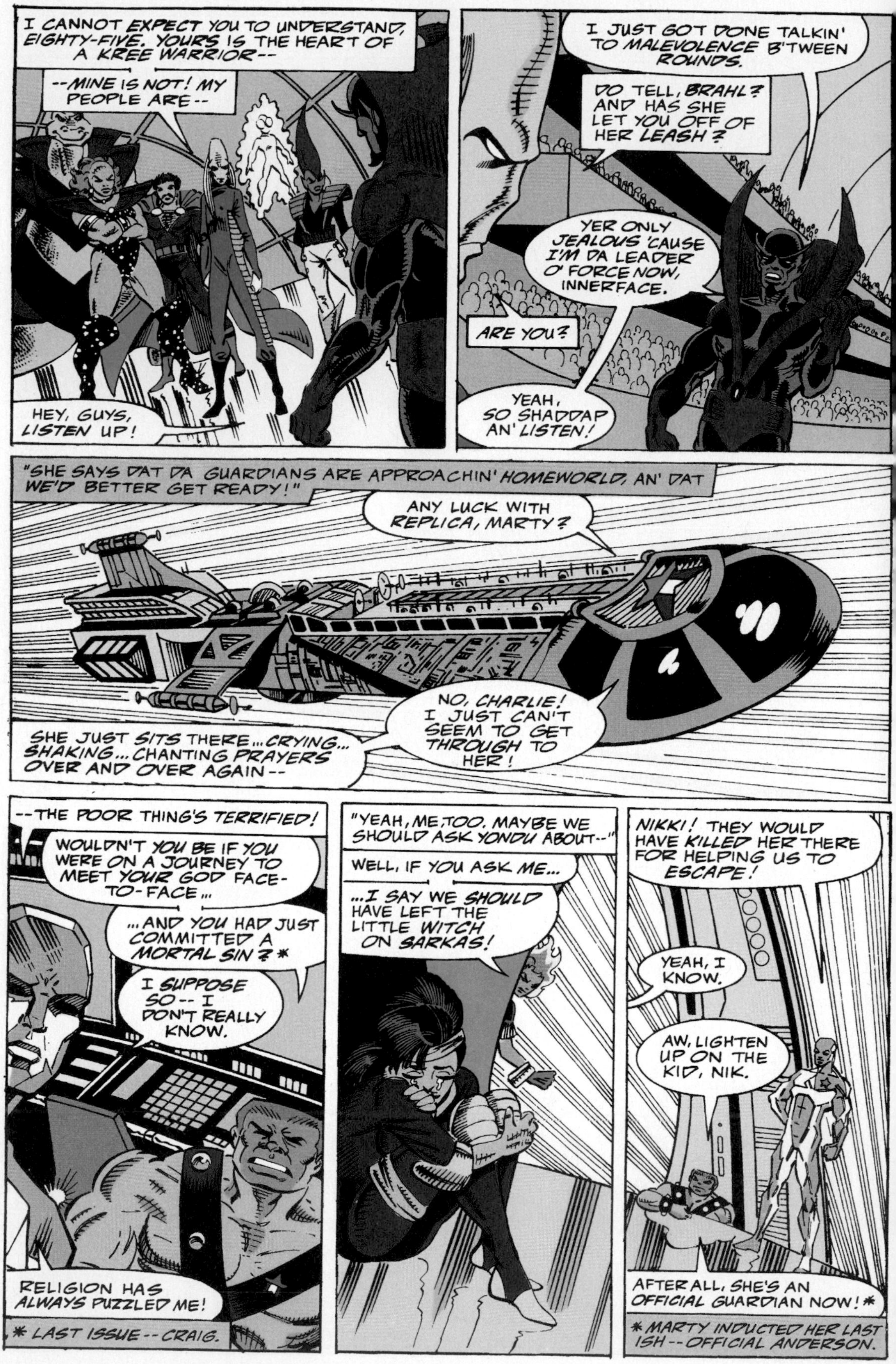
I CANNOT EXPECT YOU TO UNDERSTAND, EIGHTY-FIVE. YOURS IS THE HEART OF A KREE WARRIOR--
--MINE IS NOT! MY PEOPLE ARE--
HEY, GUYS, LISTEN UP!
I JUST GOT DONE TALKIN' TO MALEVOLENCE B'TWEEN ROUNDS.
DO TELL, BRAHL? AND HAS SHE LET YOU OFF OF HER LEASH?
YER ONLY JEALOUS 'CAUSE I'M DA LEADER O' FORCE NOW, INNERFACE.
ARE YOU?
YEAH, SO SHADDAP AN' LISTEN!
"SHE SAYS DAT DA GUARDIANS ARE APPROACHIN' HOMEWORLD, AN' DAT WE'D BETTER GET READY!"
ANY LUCK WITH REPLICA, MARTY?
NO, CHARLIE! I JUST CAN'T SEEM TO GET THROUGH TO HER!
SHE JUST SITS THERE... CRYING... SHAKING... CHANTING PRAYERS OVER AND OVER AGAIN--
--THE POOR THING'S TERRIFIED!
WOULDN'T YOU BE IF YOU WERE ON A JOURNEY TO MEET YOUR GOD FACE-TO-FACE...
...AND YOU HAD JUST COMMITTED A MORTAL SIN? *
I SUPPOSE SO-- I DON'T REALLY KNOW.
RELIGION HAS ALWAYS PUZZLED ME!
* LAST ISSUE--CRAIG.
"YEAH, ME, TOO. MAYBE WE SHOULD ASK YONDU ABOUT--"
WELL, IF YOU ASK ME...
...I SAY WE SHOULD HAVE LEFT THE LITTLE WITCH ON SARKAS!
NIKKI! THEY WOULD HAVE KILLED HER THERE FOR HELPING US TO ESCAPE!
YEAH, I KNOW.
AW, LIGHTEN UP ON THE KID, NIK.
AFTER ALL, SHE'S AN OFFICIAL GUARDIAN NOW! *
* MARTY INDUCTED HER LAST ISH--OFFICIAL ANDERSON.

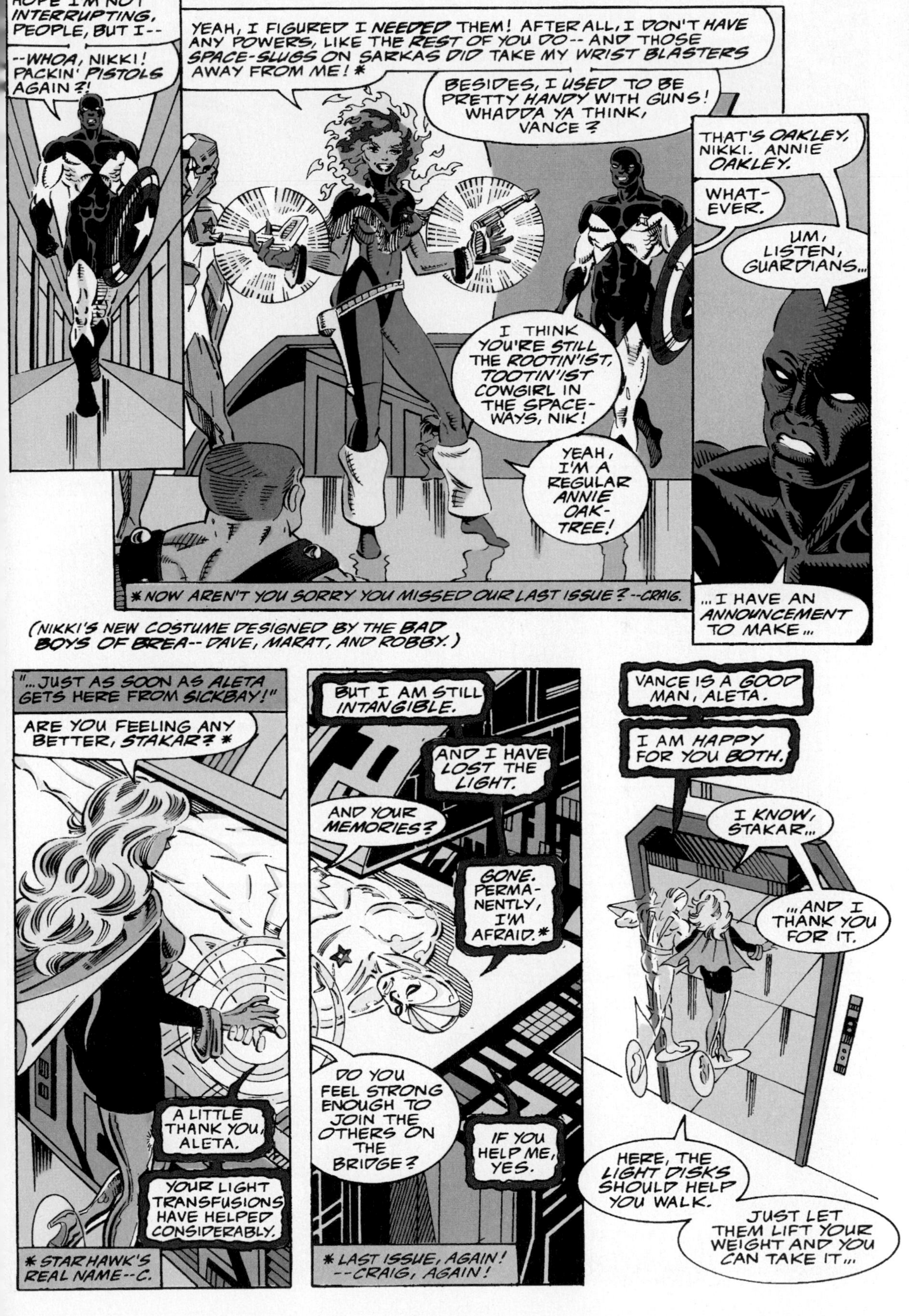
HOPE I'M NOT INTERRUPTING, PEOPLE, BUT I--
--WHOA, NIKKI! PACKIN' PISTOLS AGAIN?!
YEAH, I FIGURED I NEEDED THEM! AFTER ALL, I DON'T HAVE ANY POWERS, LIKE THE REST OF YOU DO-- AND THOSE SPACE-SLUGS ON SARKAS DID TAKE MY WRIST BLASTERS AWAY FROM ME! *
BESIDES, I USED TO BE PRETTY HANDY WITH GUNS! WHADDA YA THINK, VANCE?
I THINK YOU'RE STILL THE ROOTIN'IST, TOOTIN'IST COWGIRL IN THE SPACE-WAYS, NIK!
YEAH, I'M A REGULAR ANNIE OAK-TREE!
* NOW AREN'T YOU SORRY YOU MISSED OUR LAST ISSUE? --CRAIG.
THAT'S OAKLEY, NIKKI. ANNIE OAKLEY.
WHAT-EVER.
UM, LISTEN, GUARDIANS...
...I HAVE AN ANNOUNCEMENT TO MAKE...
(NIKKI'S NEW COSTUME DESIGNED BY THE BAD BOYS OF BREA-- DAVE, MARAT, AND ROBBY.)
"...JUST AS SOON AS ALETA GETS HERE FROM SICKBAY!"
ARE YOU FEELING ANY BETTER, STAKAR? *
A LITTLE THANK YOU, ALETA.
YOUR LIGHT TRANSFUSIONS HAVE HELPED CONSIDERABLY.
* STARHAWK'S REAL NAME --C.
BUT I AM STILL INTANGIBLE.
AND I HAVE LOST THE LIGHT.
AND YOUR MEMORIES?
GONE. PERMANENTLY, I'M AFRAID.*
DO YOU FEEL STRONG ENOUGH TO JOIN THE OTHERS ON THE BRIDGE?
IF YOU HELP ME, YES.
* LAST ISSUE, AGAIN! --CRAIG, AGAIN!
VANCE IS A GOOD MAN, ALETA.
I AM HAPPY FOR YOU BOTH.
I KNOW, STAKAR...
...AND I THANK YOU FOR IT.
HERE, THE LIGHT DISKS SHOULD HELP YOU WALK.
JUST LET THEM LIFT YOUR WEIGHT AND YOU CAN TAKE IT...

...EASY!

YOU MAKE THIS TOO EASY FOR ME!

IS THERE NONE HERE TO TRULY CHALLENGE ME?!

I MUST ADMIT, SIRE, I AM IMPRESSED BY HER!

HER CONFIDENCE-- HER POWER--

YES... BUT, STILL, JILTRIN...

...THERE IS SOMETHING ABOUT HER...

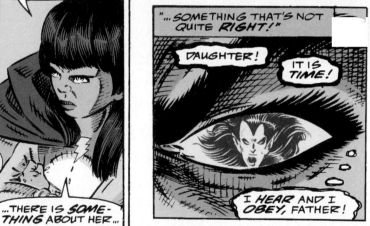

"...SOMETHING THAT'S NOT QUITE RIGHT!"

DAUGHTER!

IT IS TIME!

I HEAR AND I OBEY, FATHER!

FORCE! THE TIME IS AT HAND! GO NOW AND DO AS YOU WERE BID, LEST YOU FORFEIT WHAT'S LEFT OF YOUR IMMORTAL SOULS!

AND, AS FORCE DISAPPEARS...

...THE U.S.S. CAPTAIN AMERICA II RE-ENTERS REAL SPACE...

...JOINING THE MULTITUDE OF SHIPS ALREADY IN ORBIT ABOUT HOMEWORLD!

STARHAWK! AM I GLAD TO SEE YOU--

--I NEED YOUR HELP!

186

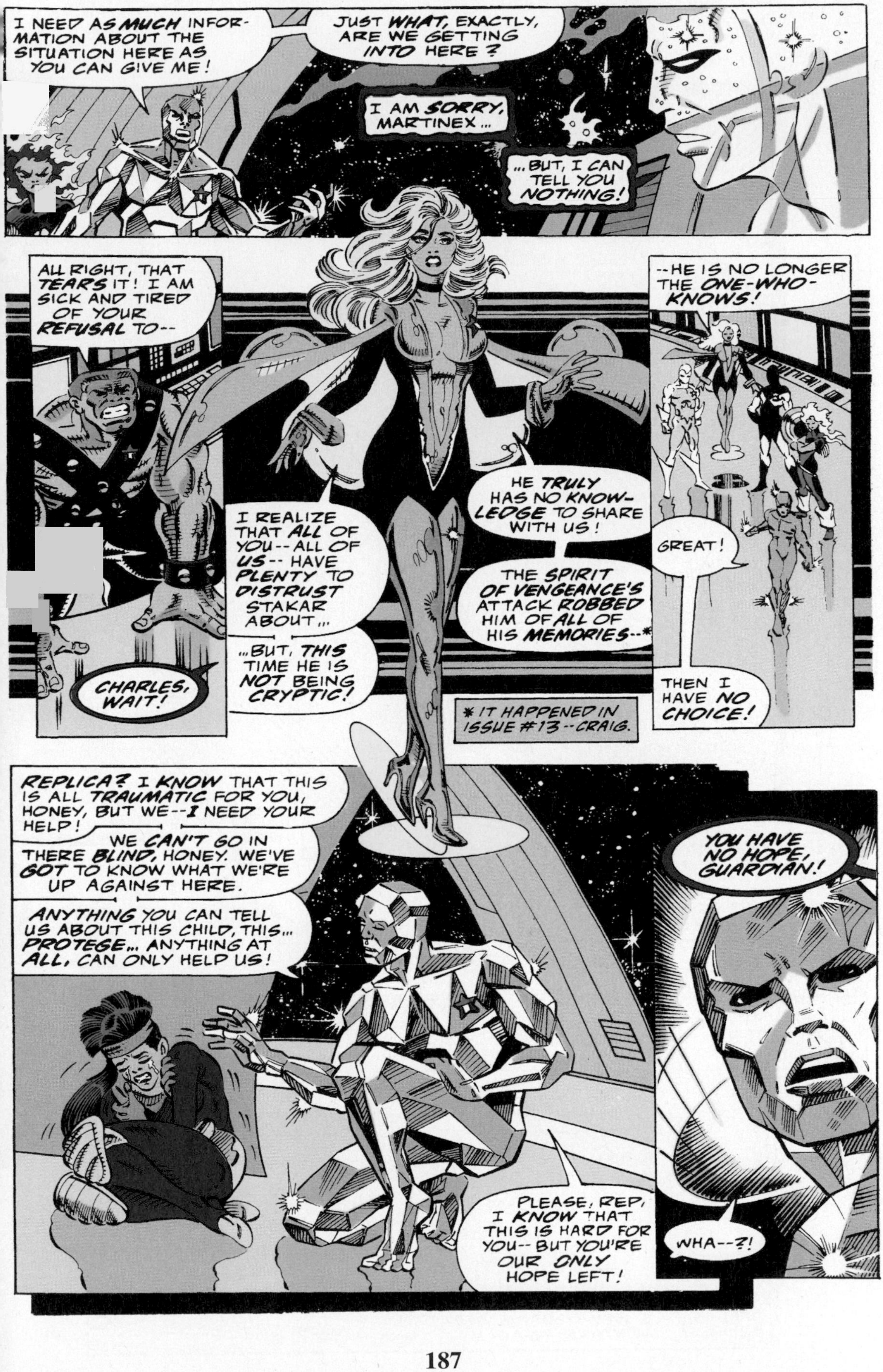

I NEED AS MUCH INFORMATION ABOUT THE SITUATION HERE AS YOU CAN GIVE ME!
JUST WHAT, EXACTLY, ARE WE GETTING INTO HERE?
I AM SORRY, MARTINEX...
...BUT, I CAN TELL YOU NOTHING!
ALL RIGHT, THAT TEARS IT! I AM SICK AND TIRED OF YOUR REFUSAL TO--
CHARLES, WAIT!
I REALIZE THAT ALL OF YOU--ALL OF US--HAVE PLENTY TO DISTRUST STAKAR ABOUT...
...BUT, THIS TIME HE IS NOT BEING CRYPTIC!
HE TRULY HAS NO KNOWLEDGE TO SHARE WITH US!
THE SPIRIT OF VENGEANCE'S ATTACK ROBBED HIM OF ALL OF HIS MEMORIES--*
--HE IS NO LONGER THE ONE-WHO-KNOWS!
GREAT!
THEN I HAVE NO CHOICE!
*IT HAPPENED IN ISSUE #13--CRAIG.
REPLICA? I KNOW THAT THIS IS ALL TRAUMATIC FOR YOU, HONEY, BUT WE--I NEED YOUR HELP!
WE CAN'T GO IN THERE BLIND, HONEY. WE'VE GOT TO KNOW WHAT WE'RE UP AGAINST HERE.
ANYTHING YOU CAN TELL US ABOUT THIS CHILD, THIS... PROTEGE... ANYTHING AT ALL, CAN ONLY HELP US!
PLEASE, REP, I KNOW THAT THIS IS HARD FOR YOU--BUT YOU'RE OUR ONLY HOPE LEFT!
YOU HAVE NO HOPE, GUARDIAN!
WHA--?!

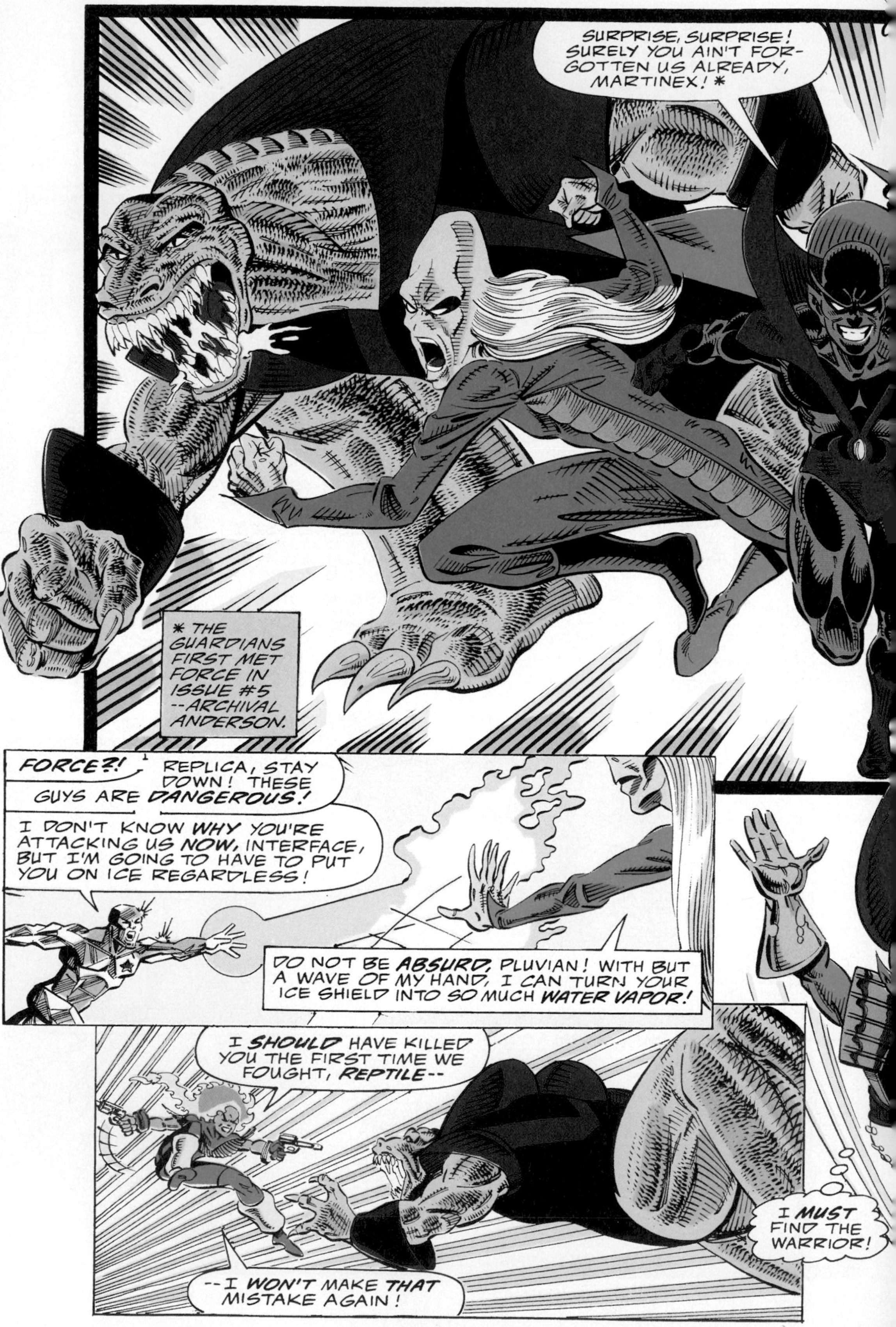
SURPRISE, SURPRISE! SURELY YOU AIN'T FOR-GOTTEN US ALREADY, MARTINEX! *
* THE GUARDIANS FIRST MET FORCE IN ISSUE #5 --ARCHIVAL ANDERSON.
FORCE?!
REPLICA, STAY DOWN! THESE GUYS ARE DANGEROUS!
I DON'T KNOW WHY YOU'RE ATTACKING US NOW, INTERFACE, BUT I'M GOING TO HAVE TO PUT YOU ON ICE REGARDLESS!
DO NOT BE ABSURD, PLUVIAN! WITH BUT A WAVE OF MY HAND, I CAN TURN YOUR ICE SHIELD INTO SO MUCH WATER VAPOR!
I SHOULD HAVE KILLED YOU THE FIRST TIME WE FOUGHT, REPTILE--
--I WON'T MAKE THAT MISTAKE AGAIN!
I MUST FIND THE WARRIOR!

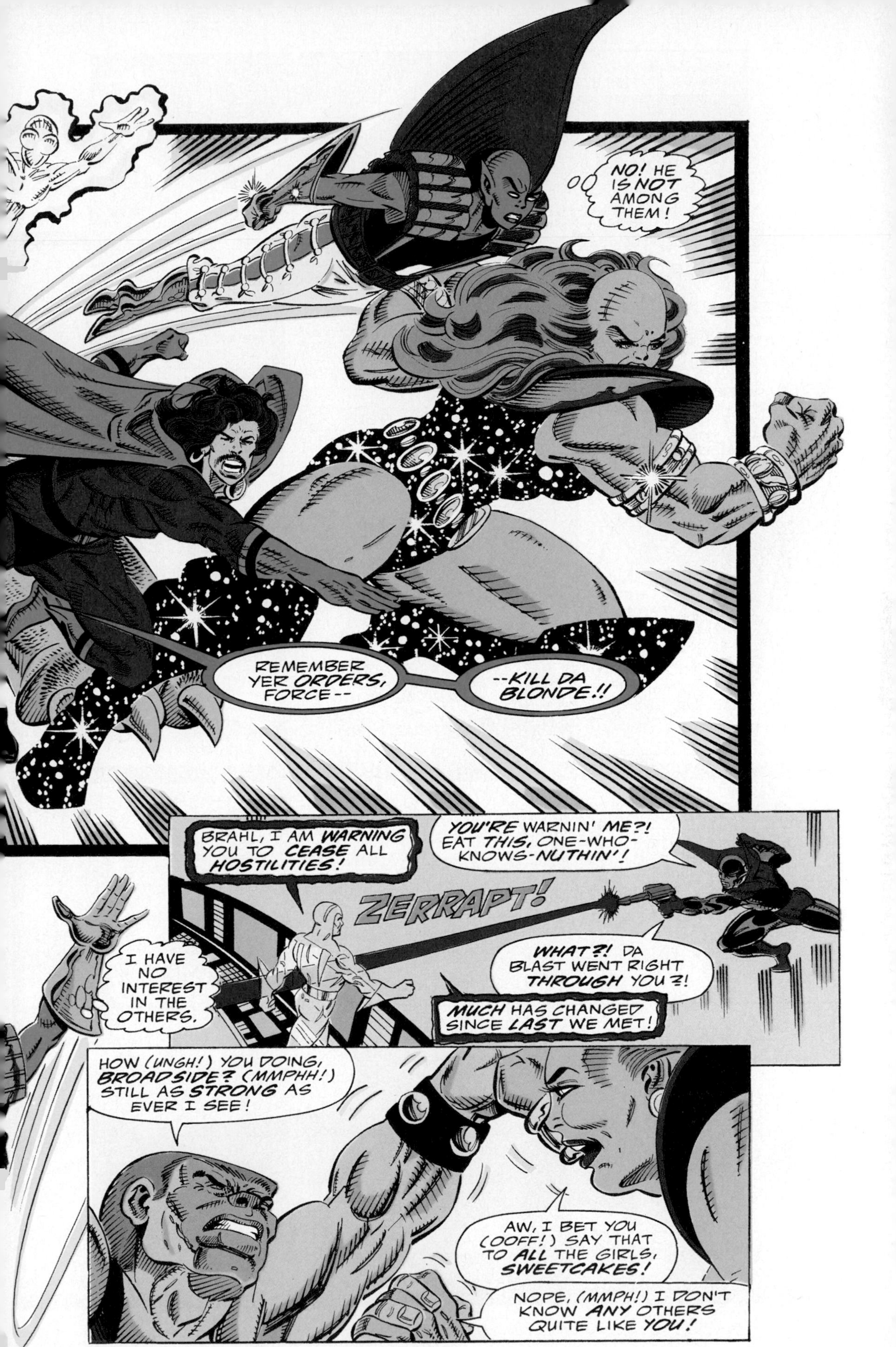
NO! HE IS NOT AMONG THEM!
REMEMBER YER ORDERS, FORCE--
--KILL DA BLONDE!!
BRAHL, I AM WARNING YOU TO CEASE ALL HOSTILITIES!
YOU'RE WARNIN' ME?! EAT THIS, ONE-WHO-KNOWS-NUTHIN'!
ZERRAPT!
I HAVE NO INTEREST IN THE OTHERS.
WHAT?! DA BLAST WENT RIGHT THROUGH YOU?!
MUCH HAS CHANGED SINCE LAST WE MET!
HOW (UNGH!) YOU DOING, BROADSIDE? (MMPHH!) STILL AS STRONG AS EVER I SEE!
AW, I BET YOU (OOFF!) SAY THAT TO ALL THE GIRLS, SWEETCAKES!
NOPE, (MMPH!) I DON'T KNOW ANY OTHERS QUITE LIKE YOU!

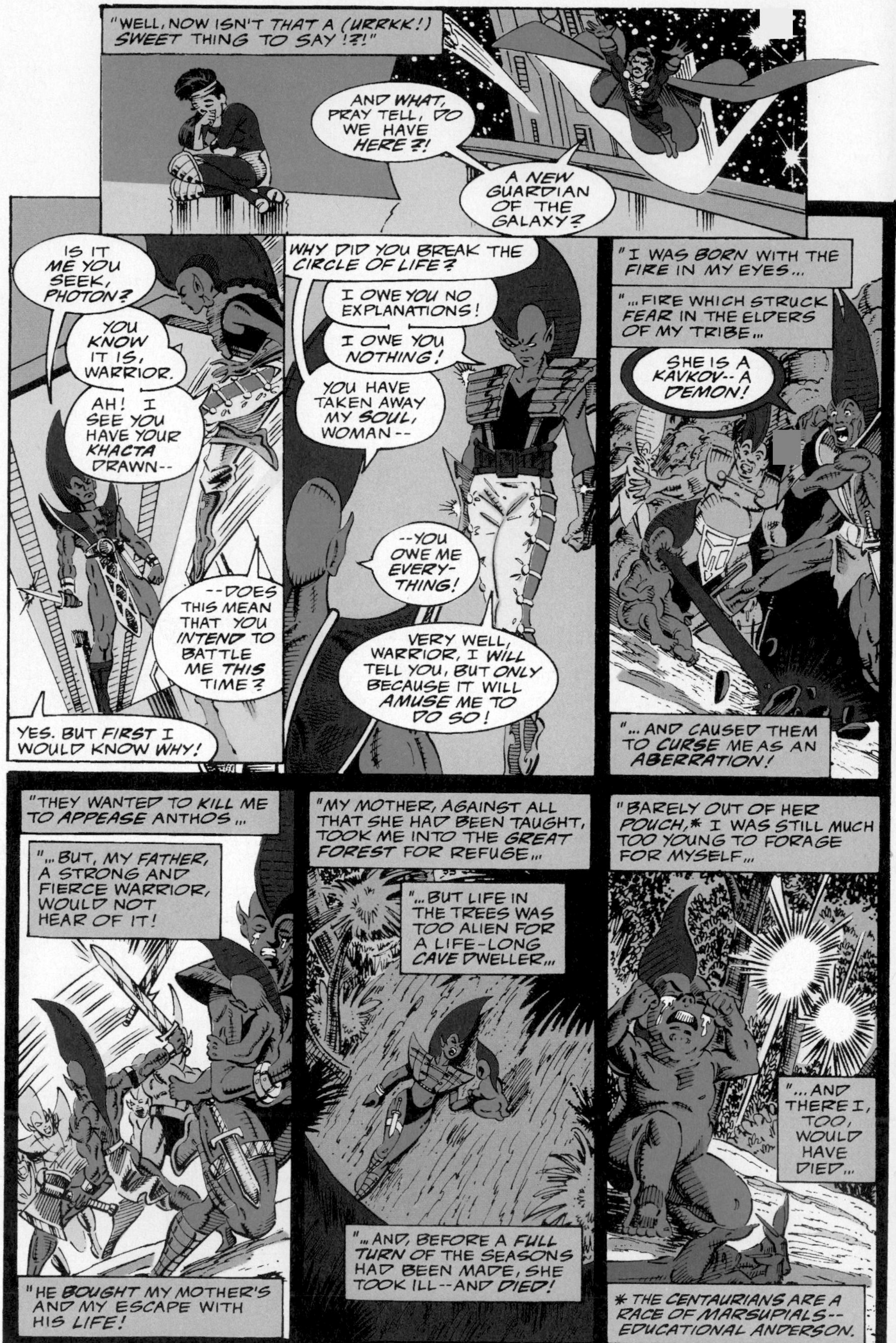
"WELL, NOW ISN'T THAT A (URRKK!) SWEET THING TO SAY!?!"
AND WHAT, PRAY TELL, DO WE HAVE HERE?!
A NEW GUARDIAN OF THE GALAXY?
IS IT ME YOU SEEK, PHOTON?
YOU KNOW IT IS, WARRIOR.
AH! I SEE YOU HAVE YOUR KHACTA DRAWN--
--DOES THIS MEAN THAT YOU INTEND TO BATTLE ME THIS TIME?
YES. BUT FIRST I WOULD KNOW WHY!
WHY DID YOU BREAK THE CIRCLE OF LIFE?
I OWE YOU NO EXPLANATIONS!
I OWE YOU NOTHING!
YOU HAVE TAKEN AWAY MY SOUL, WOMAN--
--YOU OWE ME EVERY-THING!
VERY WELL, WARRIOR, I WILL TELL YOU, BUT ONLY BECAUSE IT WILL AMUSE ME TO DO SO!
"I WAS BORN WITH THE FIRE IN MY EYES...
"...FIRE WHICH STRUCK FEAR IN THE ELDERS OF MY TRIBE...
SHE IS A KAVKOV--A DEMON!
"...AND CAUSED THEM TO CURSE ME AS AN ABERRATION!
"THEY WANTED TO KILL ME TO APPEASE ANTHOS...
"...BUT, MY FATHER, A STRONG AND FIERCE WARRIOR, WOULD NOT HEAR OF IT!
"HE BOUGHT MY MOTHER'S AND MY ESCAPE WITH HIS LIFE!
"MY MOTHER, AGAINST ALL THAT SHE HAD BEEN TAUGHT, TOOK ME INTO THE GREAT FOREST FOR REFUGE...
"...BUT LIFE IN THE TREES WAS TOO ALIEN FOR A LIFE-LONG CAVE DWELLER...
"...AND, BEFORE A FULL TURN OF THE SEASONS HAD BEEN MADE, SHE TOOK ILL--AND DIED!
"BARELY OUT OF HER POUCH,* I WAS STILL MUCH TOO YOUNG TO FORAGE FOR MYSELF...
"...AND THERE I, TOO, WOULD HAVE DIED...
* THE CENTAURIANS ARE A RACE OF MARSUPIALS--EDUCATIONAL ANDERSON.

"...WERE IT NOT FOR THE ARRIVAL OF *INTERFACE!*

"HE TOOK ME AWAY FROM *CENTAURI IV...*

"...AND MADE ME HIS NEW DAUGHTER, TO REPLACE THE ONE HE HAD *LOST* TO THE *UNIVERSALITES!*

"AS I GREW, HE TAUGHT ME MANY THINGS...

"...NOT THE *LEAST* OF WHICH WAS THE FACT THAT RE-LIGION HAD TORN US *BOTH* FROM OUR FAMILIES!

"THUS, I REJECTED THE CIRCLE OF LIFE AND CLOSED MY HEART TO IT..."

"...AND WHEN I LEARNED THAT THE *BADOON* HAD COMMITTED *GENOCIDE* ON CENTAURI IV --

--I RE-JOICED!

UNTIL I MET *YOU,* WARRIOR! AND THEN MY REJOICING...

"...STOPPED RIGHT IN FRONT OF ME!

VANCE, WAIT! IF WHAT *STAR-HAWK* SAID ABOUT HIM IS *TRUE...*

...*TACHYON* WILL ONLY ACT IF *ACTED* UPON!

AND WHAT IF IT *ISN'T* TRUE?

THEN, MY LOVE...

...YOU WILL FIND OUT *ALONE!*

SKREEEE

WHAT?!

FORGIVE ME, PLEASE, VANCE...

...BUT I MUST GO *NOW!*

ALETA, WAIT! WHERE ARE YOU GOING--?!!

NO! THE *BLONDE* HAS *ESCAPED!!*

YOU *FOOLS* LET HER *GO!!*

BRAHL--

POW!

--SHUT UP!

NO! THIS IS NOT A NEW GUARDIAN, BUT ONLY A *CHILD!*

A POOR, FRIGHTENED, *DEFENSELESS* CHILD!

TAKE *MY* SOUL IF YOU WILL, MALEVOLENCE--

--THE *KREE* DO NOT WAGE WAR ON *CHILDREN!*

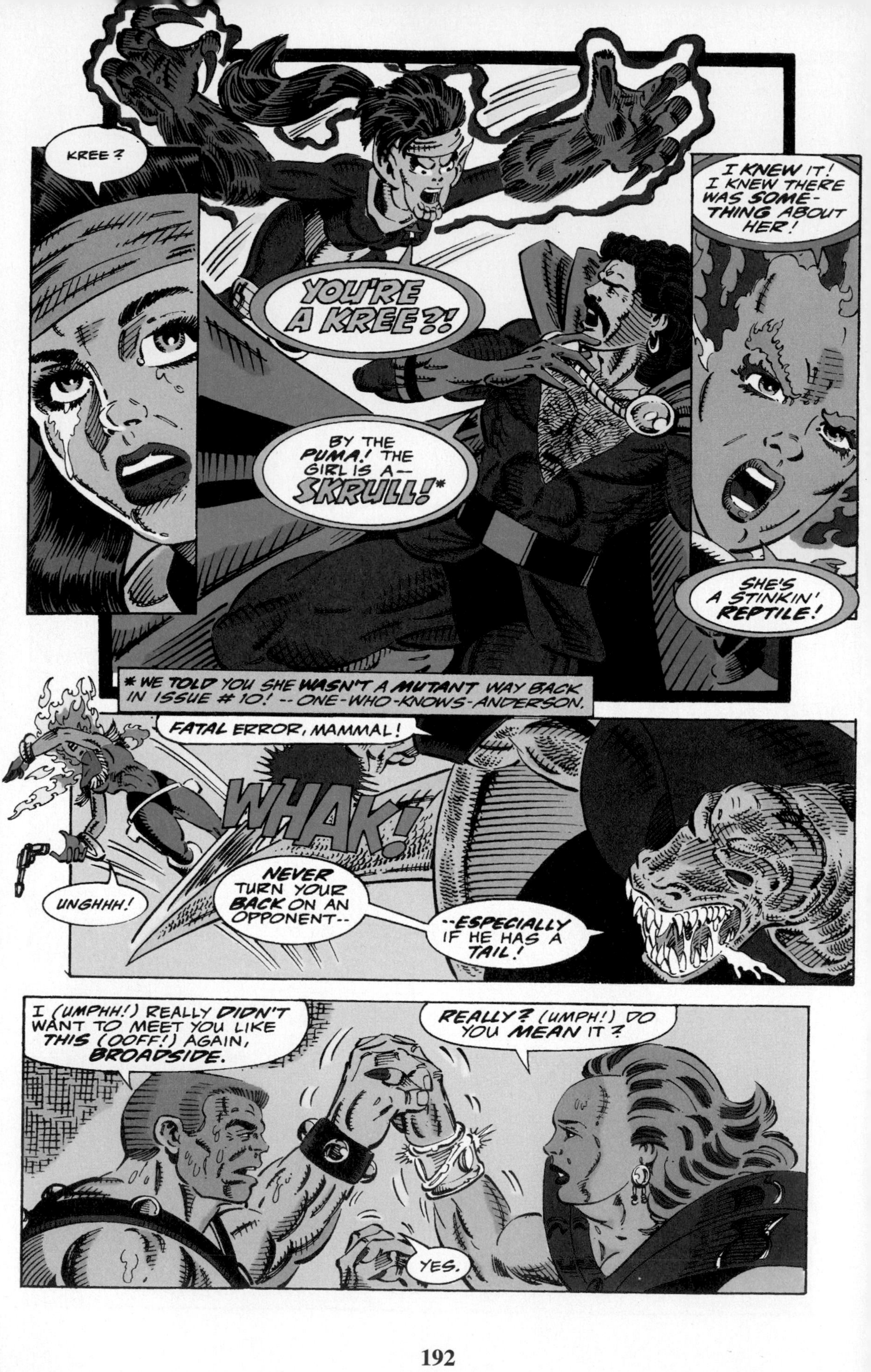
KREE?
YOU'RE A KREE?!
I KNEW IT! I KNEW THERE WAS SOME-THING ABOUT HER!
BY THE PUMA! THE GIRL IS A-- SKRULL!*
SHE'S A STINKIN' REPTILE!
* WE TOLD YOU SHE WASN'T A MUTANT WAY BACK IN ISSUE #10! --ONE-WHO-KNOWS-ANDERSON.
FATAL ERROR, MAMMAL!
WHAK!
UNGHHH!
NEVER TURN YOUR BACK ON AN OPPONENT--
--ESPECIALLY IF HE HAS A TAIL!
I (UMPHH!) REALLY DIDN'T WANT TO MEET YOU LIKE THIS (OOFF!) AGAIN, BROADSIDE.
REALLY? (UMPH!) DO YOU MEAN IT?
YES.

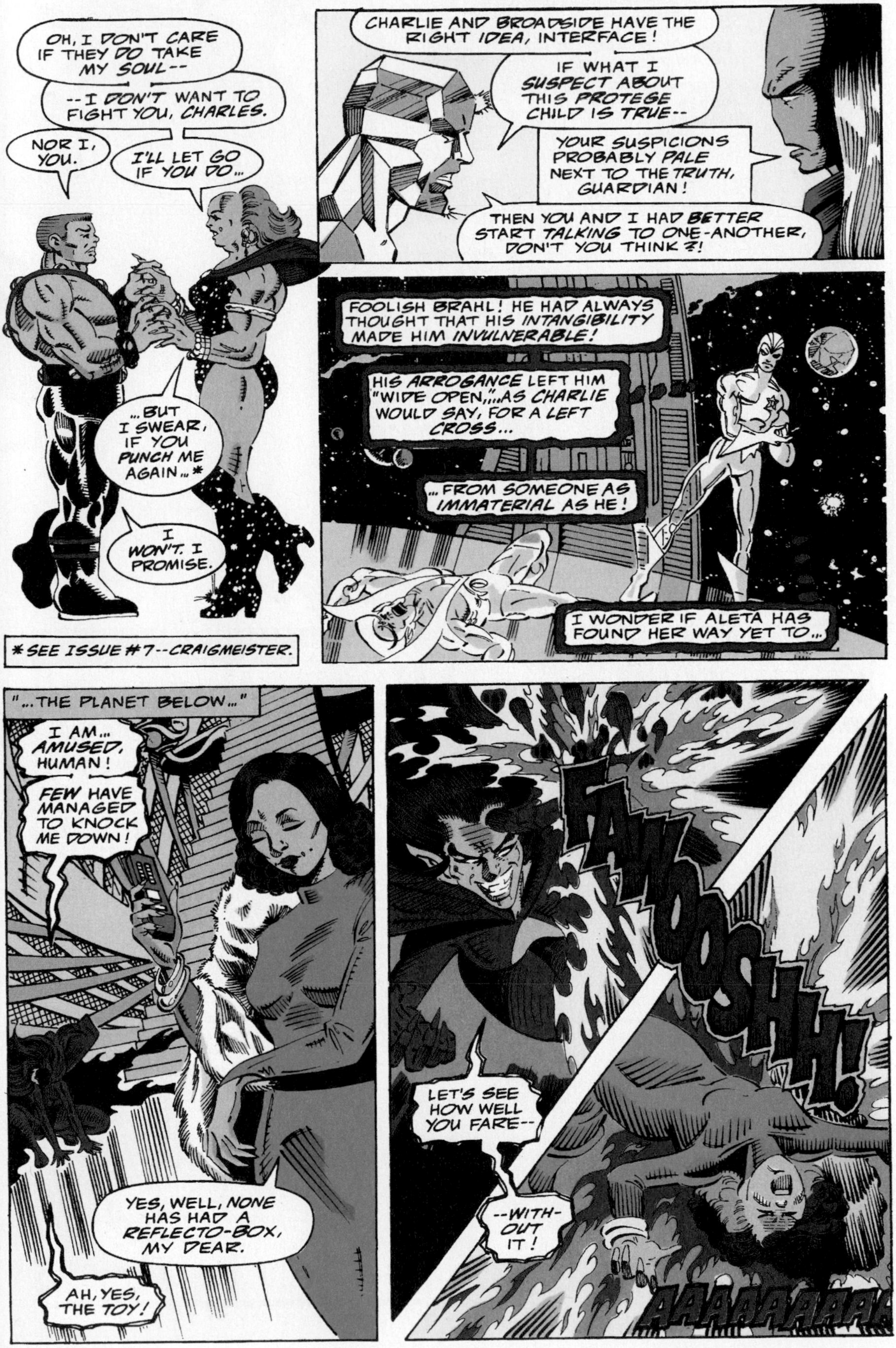
OH, I DON'T CARE IF THEY DO TAKE MY SOUL--
--I DON'T WANT TO FIGHT YOU, CHARLES.
NOR I, YOU.
I'LL LET GO IF YOU DO...
...BUT I SWEAR, IF YOU PUNCH ME AGAIN...*
I WON'T. I PROMISE.
* SEE ISSUE #7--CRAIGMEISTER.
CHARLIE AND BROADSIDE HAVE THE RIGHT IDEA, INTERFACE!
IF WHAT I SUSPECT ABOUT THIS PROTEGE CHILD IS TRUE--
YOUR SUSPICIONS PROBABLY PALE NEXT TO THE TRUTH, GUARDIAN!
THEN YOU AND I HAD BETTER START TALKING TO ONE-ANOTHER, DON'T YOU THINK?!
FOOLISH BRAHL! HE HAD ALWAYS THOUGHT THAT HIS INTANGIBILITY MADE HIM INVULNERABLE!
HIS ARROGANCE LEFT HIM "WIDE OPEN,"...AS CHARLIE WOULD SAY, FOR A LEFT CROSS...
...FROM SOMEONE AS IMMATERIAL AS HE!
I WONDER IF ALETA HAS FOUND HER WAY YET TO...
"...THE PLANET BELOW..."
I AM... AMUSED, HUMAN!
FEW HAVE MANAGED TO KNOCK ME DOWN!
YES, WELL, NONE HAS HAD A REFLECTO-BOX, MY DEAR.
AH, YES, THE TOY!
FAWOOSHH!
LET'S SEE HOW WELL YOU FARE--
--WITH-OUT IT!
AAAAAAAAA

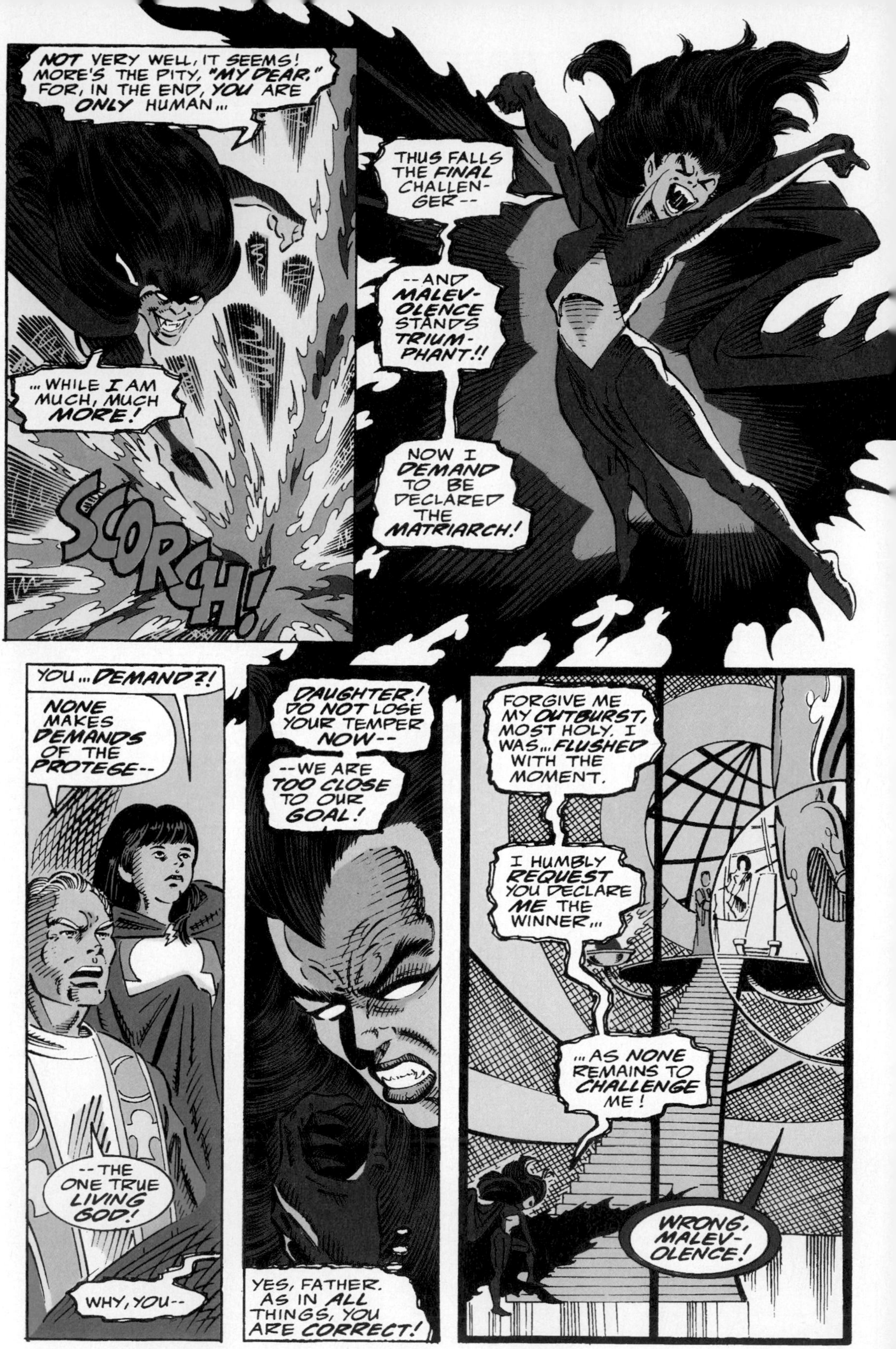
NOT VERY WELL, IT SEEMS! MORE'S THE PITY, "MY DEAR," FOR, IN THE END, YOU ARE ONLY HUMAN...
...WHILE I AM MUCH, MUCH MORE!
SCORCH!
THUS FALLS THE FINAL CHALLENGER--
--AND MALEVOLENCE STANDS TRIUMPHANT!!
NOW I DEMAND TO BE DECLARED THE MATRIARCH!
YOU...DEMAND?!
NONE MAKES DEMANDS OF THE PROTEGE--
--THE ONE TRUE LIVING GOD!
WHY, YOU--
DAUGHTER! DO NOT LOSE YOUR TEMPER NOW--
--WE ARE TOO CLOSE TO OUR GOAL!
YES, FATHER. AS IN ALL THINGS, YOU ARE CORRECT!
FORGIVE ME MY OUTBURST, MOST HOLY. I WAS...FLUSHED WITH THE MOMENT.
I HUMBLY REQUEST YOU DECLARE ME THE WINNER...
...AS NONE REMAINS TO CHALLENGE ME!
WRONG, MALEVOLENCE!

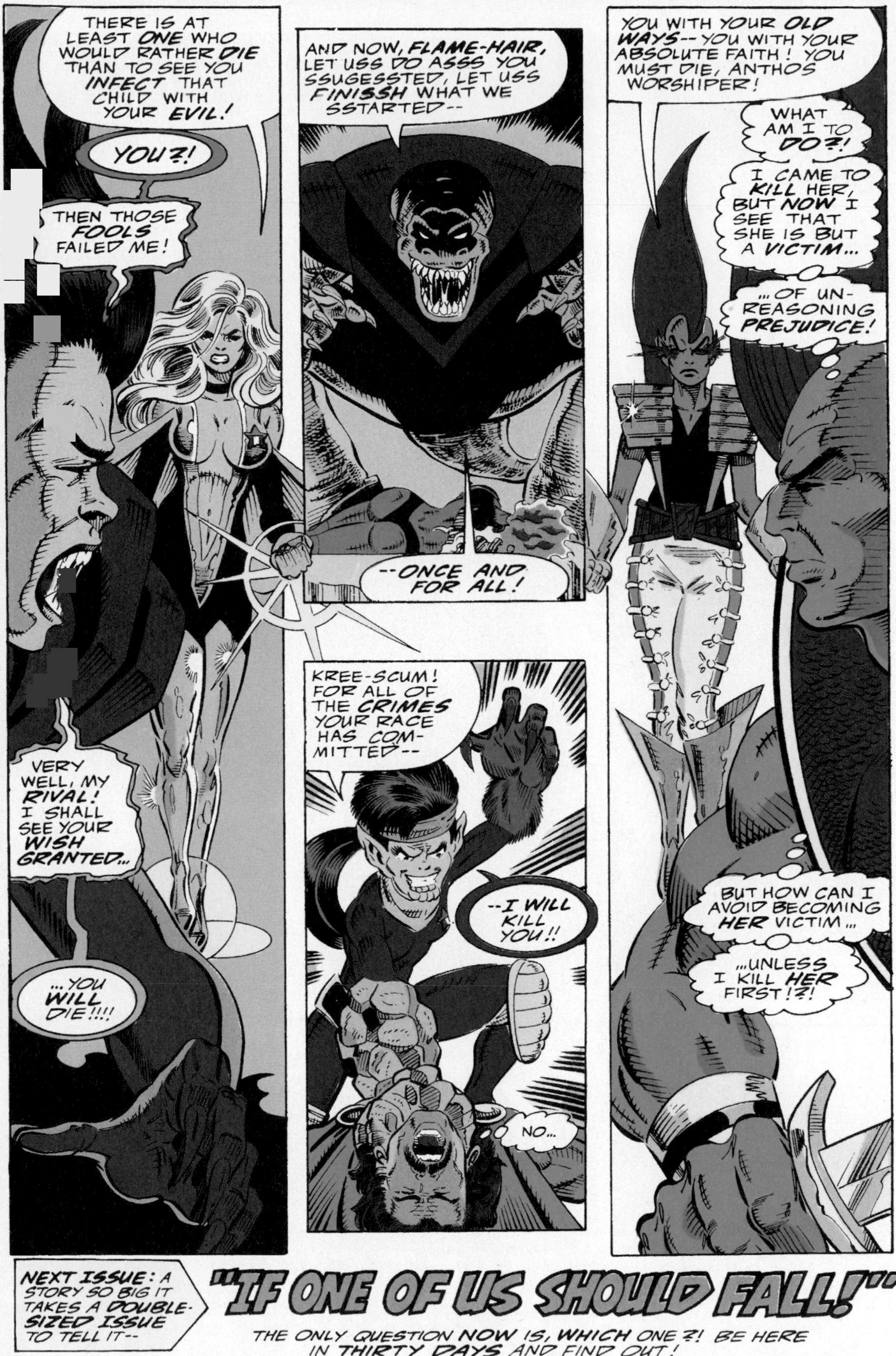
THERE IS AT LEAST ONE WHO WOULD RATHER DIE THAN TO SEE YOU INFECT THAT CHILD WITH YOUR EVIL!
YOU?!
THEN THOSE FOOLS FAILED ME!
VERY WELL, MY RIVAL! I SHALL SEE YOUR WISH GRANTED...
...YOU WILL DIE!!!!
AND NOW, FLAME-HAIR, LET USS DO ASSS YOU SSUGESSTED, LET USS FINISSH WHAT WE SSTARTED--
--ONCE AND FOR ALL!
KREE-SCUM! FOR ALL OF THE CRIMES YOUR RACE HAS COM-MITTED--
--I WILL KILL YOU!!
NO...
YOU WITH YOUR OLD WAYS-- YOU WITH YOUR ABSOLUTE FAITH! YOU MUST DIE, ANTHOS WORSHIPER!
WHAT AM I TO DO?!
I CAME TO KILL HER, BUT NOW I SEE THAT SHE IS BUT A VICTIM...
...OF UN-REASONING PREJUDICE!
BUT HOW CAN I AVOID BECOMING HER VICTIM...
...UNLESS I KILL HER FIRST!?!

NEXT ISSUE: A STORY SO BIG IT TAKES A DOUBLE-SIZED ISSUE TO TELL IT--

"IF ONE OF US SHOULD FALL!"

THE ONLY QUESTION NOW IS, WHICH ONE?! BE HERE IN THIRTY DAYS AND FIND OUT!

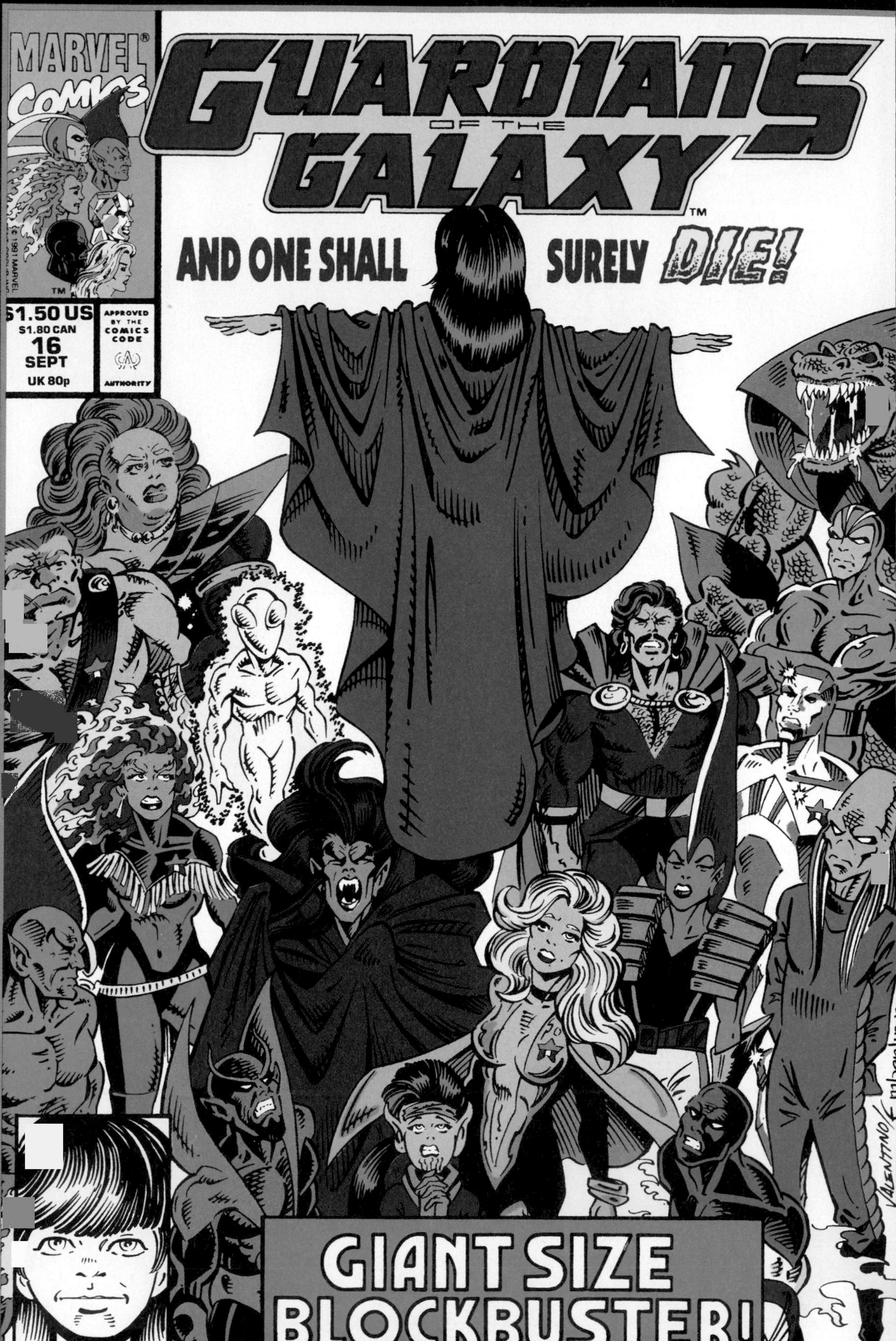
MARVEL® COMICS
GUARDIANS OF THE GALAXY™
AND ONE SHALL SURELY DIE!
$1.50 US
$1.80 CAN
16
SEPT
UK 80p
APPROVED BY THE COMICS CODE AUTHORITY
GIANT SIZE BLOCKBUSTER!

CHARLIE 27! MARTINEX! NIKKI! VANCE ASTRO! YONDU! ALETA! STARHAWK! SEVEN EXTRAORDINARY SUPER-BEINGS, ALL SURVIVORS OF INTERSTELLAR WAR. NOW THEY ROAM THE COSMOS OF THE 31ST CENTURY ABOARD THE STARSHIP CAPTAIN AMERICA, THEIR MISSION—TO SAFEGUARD THE MILKY WAY! STAN LEE PRESENTS . . . THE GUARDIANS OF THE GALAXY!

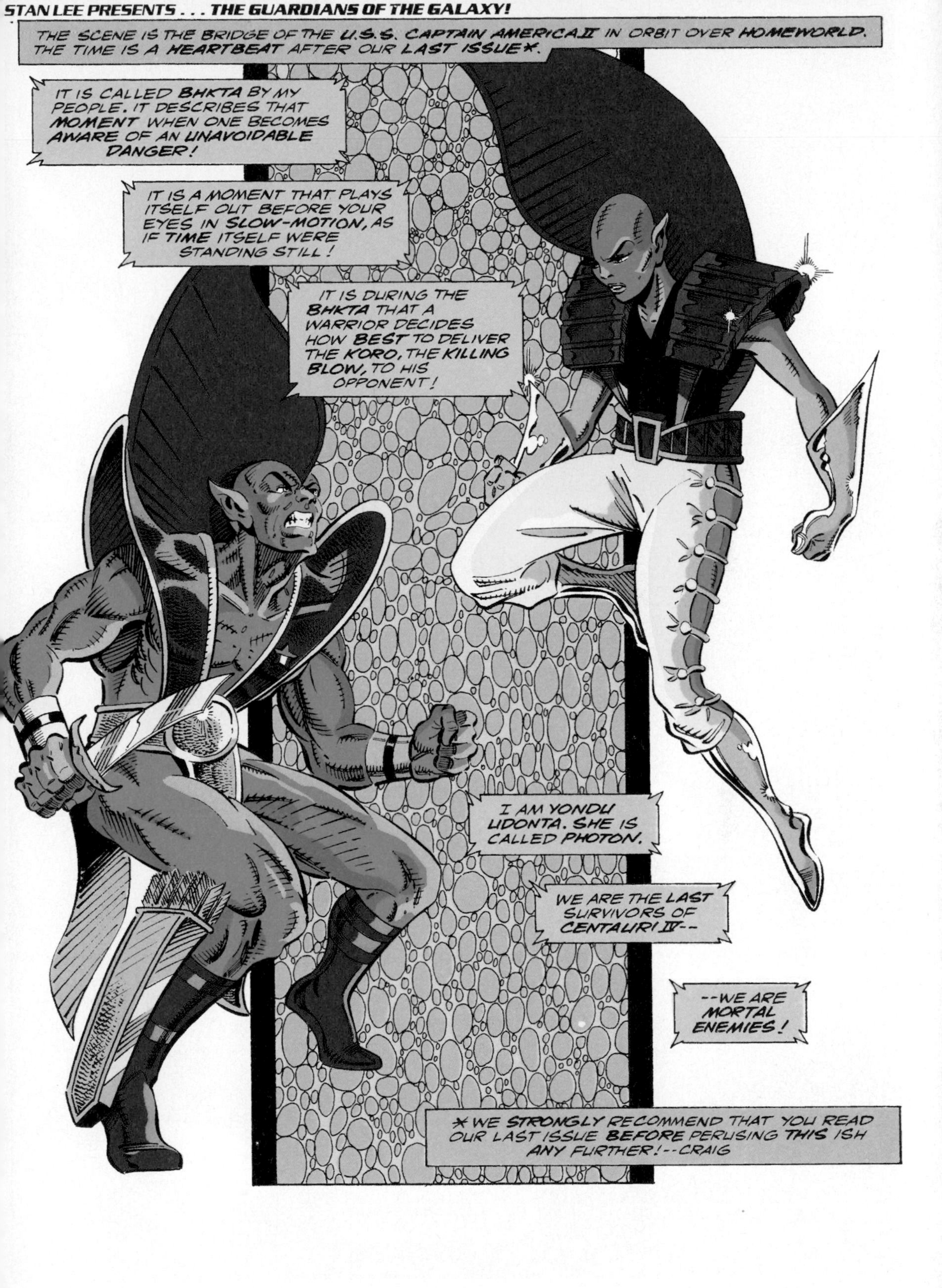

THE SCENE IS THE BRIDGE OF THE U.S.S. CAPTAIN AMERICA II IN ORBIT OVER HOMEWORLD. THE TIME IS A HEARTBEAT AFTER OUR LAST ISSUE*.
IT IS CALLED BHKTA BY MY PEOPLE. IT DESCRIBES THAT MOMENT WHEN ONE BECOMES AWARE OF AN UNAVOIDABLE DANGER!
IT IS A MOMENT THAT PLAYS ITSELF OUT BEFORE YOUR EYES IN SLOW-MOTION, AS IF TIME ITSELF WERE STANDING STILL!
IT IS DURING THE BHKTA THAT A WARRIOR DECIDES HOW BEST TO DELIVER THE KORO, THE KILLING BLOW, TO HIS OPPONENT!
I AM YONDU UDONTA. SHE IS CALLED PHOTON.
WE ARE THE LAST SURVIVORS OF CENTAURI IV--
--WE ARE MORTAL ENEMIES!
*WE STRONGLY RECOMMEND THAT YOU READ OUR LAST ISSUE BEFORE PERUSING THIS ISH ANY FURTHER!--CRAIG

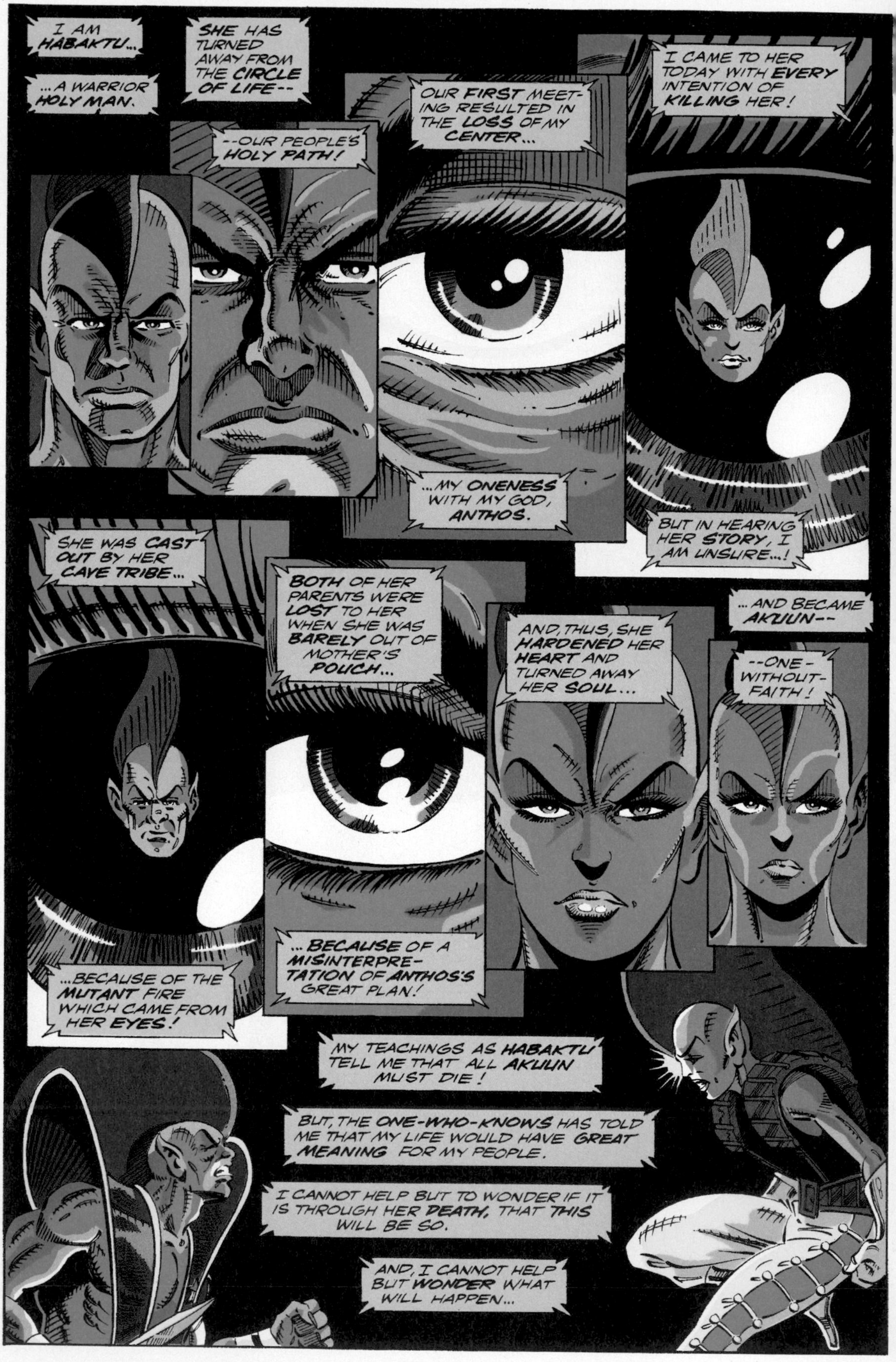
I AM HABAKTU...
...A WARRIOR HOLY MAN.
SHE HAS TURNED AWAY FROM THE CIRCLE OF LIFE--
--OUR PEOPLE'S HOLY PATH!
OUR FIRST MEETING RESULTED IN THE LOSS OF MY CENTER...
...MY ONENESS WITH MY GOD, ANTHOS.
I CAME TO HER TODAY WITH EVERY INTENTION OF KILLING HER!
BUT IN HEARING HER STORY, I AM UNSURE...!
SHE WAS CAST OUT BY HER CAVE TRIBE...
...BECAUSE OF THE MUTANT FIRE WHICH CAME FROM HER EYES!
BOTH OF HER PARENTS WERE LOST TO HER WHEN SHE WAS BARELY OUT OF MOTHER'S POUCH...
...BECAUSE OF A MISINTERPRETATION OF ANTHOS'S GREAT PLAN!
AND, THUS, SHE HARDENED HER HEART AND TURNED AWAY HER SOUL...
...AND BECAME AKUUN--
--ONE-WITHOUT-FAITH!
MY TEACHINGS AS HABAKTU TELL ME THAT ALL AKUUN MUST DIE!
BUT, THE ONE-WHO-KNOWS HAS TOLD ME THAT MY LIFE WOULD HAVE GREAT MEANING FOR MY PEOPLE.
I CANNOT HELP BUT TO WONDER IF IT IS THROUGH HER DEATH, THAT THIS WILL BE SO.
AND, I CANNOT HELP BUT WONDER WHAT WILL HAPPEN...

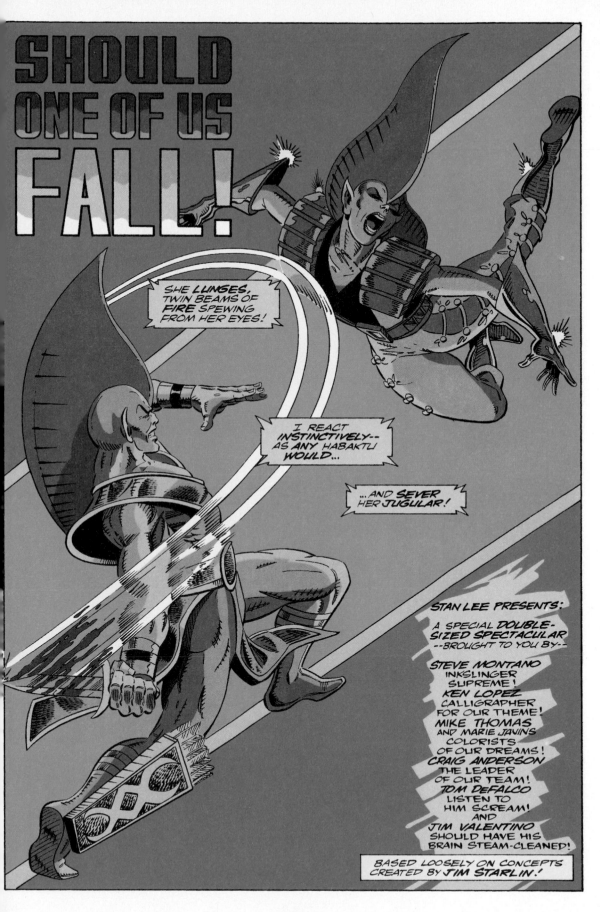

SHOULD ONE OF US FALL!

SHE *LUNGES,* TWIN BEAMS OF *FIRE* SPEWING FROM HER EYES!

I REACT INSTINCTIVELY-- AS ANY HABAKTU WOULD...

...AND SEVER HER JUGULAR!

STAN LEE PRESENTS:

A SPECIAL *DOUBLE-SIZED SPECTACULAR* --BROUGHT TO YOU BY--

STEVE MONTANO INKSLINGER SUPREME! KEN LOPEZ CALLIGRAPHER FOR OUR THEME! MIKE THOMAS AND MARIE JAVINS COLORISTS OF OUR DREAMS! CRAIG ANDERSON THE LEADER OF OUR TEAM! TOM DEFALCO LISTEN TO HIM SCREAM! AND JIM VALENTINO SHOULD HAVE HIS BRAIN STEAM-CLEANED!

BASED LOOSELY ON CONCEPTS CREATED BY *JIM STARLIN!*

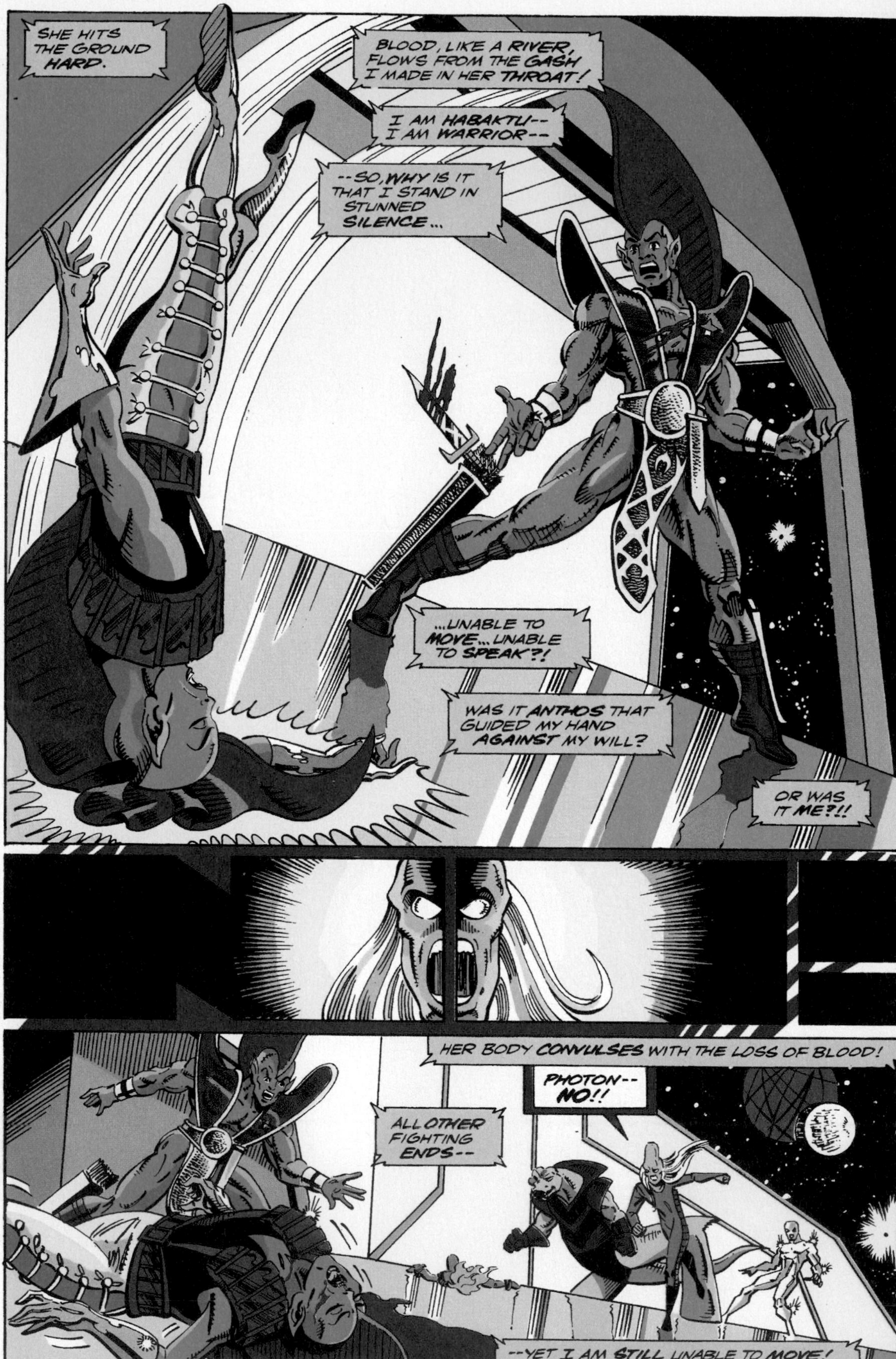
SHE HITS THE GROUND HARD.
BLOOD, LIKE A RIVER, FLOWS FROM THE GASH I MADE IN HER THROAT!
I AM HABAKTU-- I AM WARRIOR--
--SO, WHY IS IT THAT I STAND IN STUNNED SILENCE...
...UNABLE TO MOVE... UNABLE TO SPEAK?!
WAS IT ANTHOS THAT GUIDED MY HAND AGAINST MY WILL?
OR WAS IT ME?!!
HER BODY CONVULSES WITH THE LOSS OF BLOOD!
PHOTON-- NO!!
ALL OTHER FIGHTING ENDS--
--YET I AM STILL UNABLE TO MOVE!

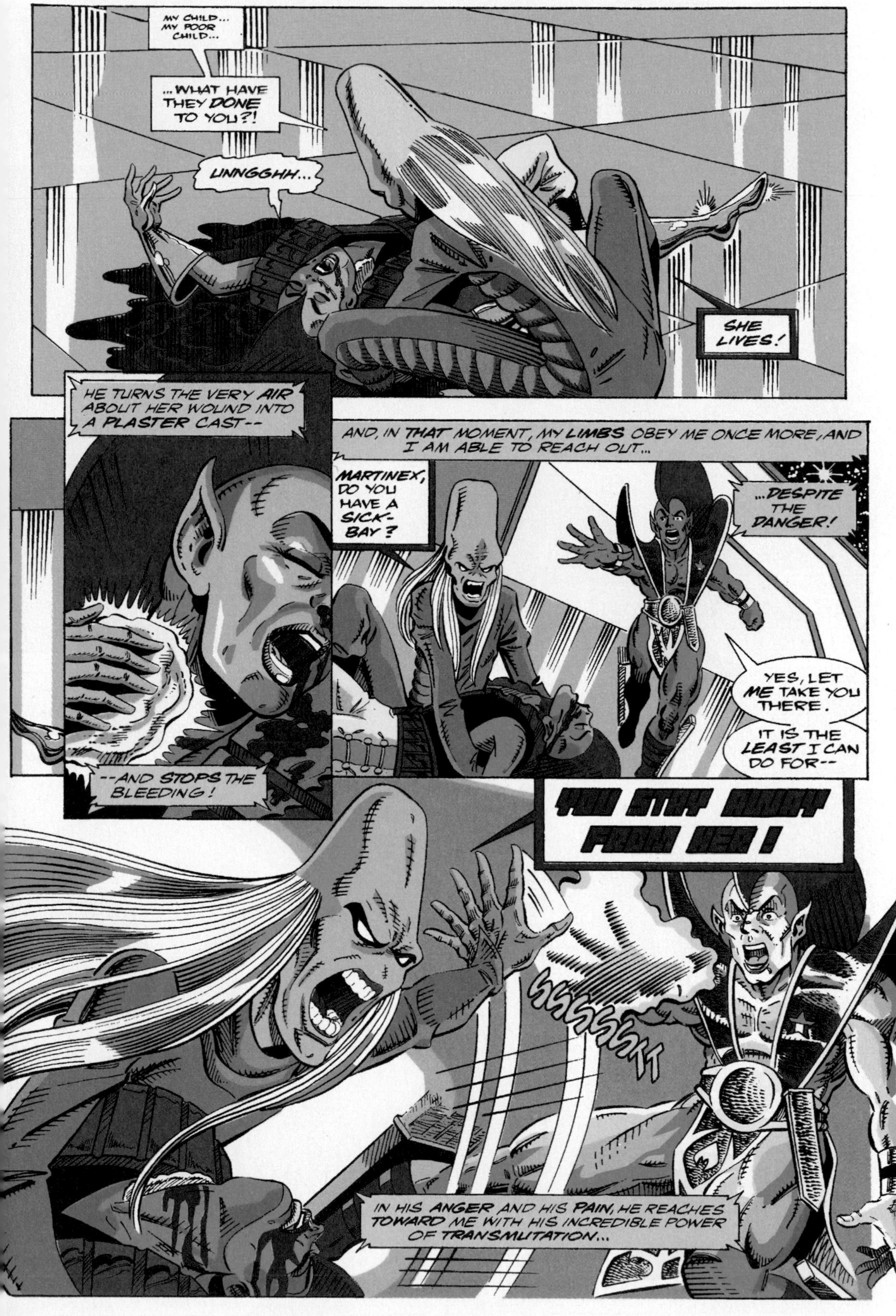
MY CHILD... MY POOR CHILD...
...WHAT HAVE THEY DONE TO YOU?!
UNNGGHH...
SHE LIVES!
HE TURNS THE VERY AIR ABOUT HER WOUND INTO A PLASTER CAST--
--AND STOPS THE BLEEDING!
AND, IN THAT MOMENT, MY LIMBS OBEY ME ONCE MORE, AND I AM ABLE TO REACH OUT...
...DESPITE THE DANGER!
MARTINEX, DO YOU HAVE A SICK-BAY?
YES, LET ME TAKE YOU THERE.
IT IS THE LEAST I CAN DO FOR--
YOU STAY AWAY FROM HER!
SSSSSSTT
IN HIS ANGER AND HIS PAIN, HE REACHES TOWARD ME WITH HIS INCREDIBLE POWER OF TRANSMUTATION...

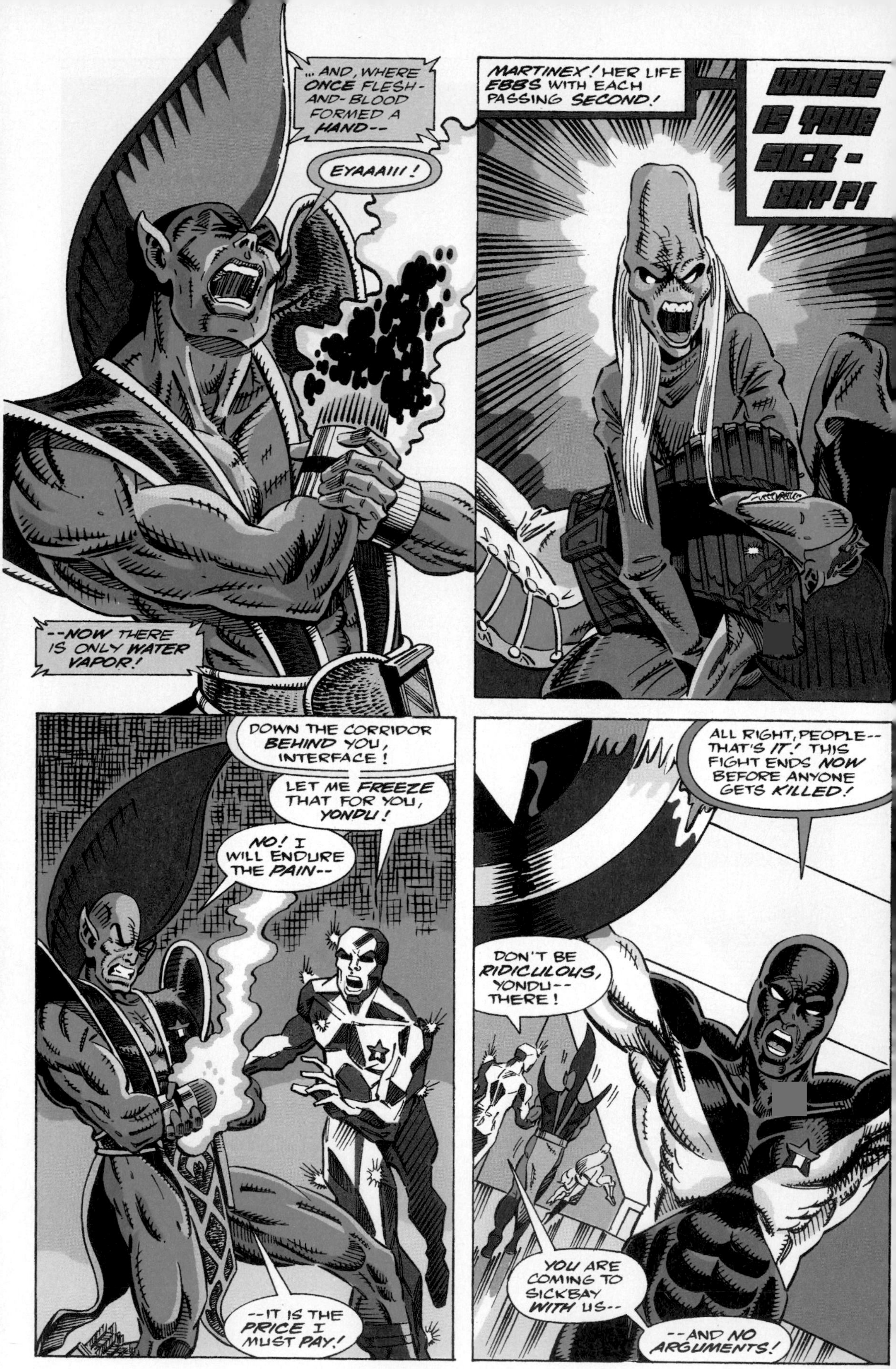
...AND, WHERE ONCE FLESH-AND-BLOOD FORMED A HAND--
EYAAAIII!
--NOW THERE IS ONLY WATER VAPOR!
MARTINEX! HER LIFE EBBS WITH EACH PASSING SECOND!
WHERE IS YOUR SICK-BAY?!
DOWN THE CORRIDOR BEHIND YOU, INTERFACE!
LET ME FREEZE THAT FOR YOU, YONDU!
NO! I WILL ENDURE THE PAIN--
--IT IS THE PRICE I MUST PAY!
ALL RIGHT, PEOPLE--THAT'S IT! THIS FIGHT ENDS NOW BEFORE ANYONE GETS KILLED!
DON'T BE RIDICULOUS, YONDU--THERE!
YOU ARE COMING TO SICKBAY WITH US--
--AND NO ARGUMENTS!

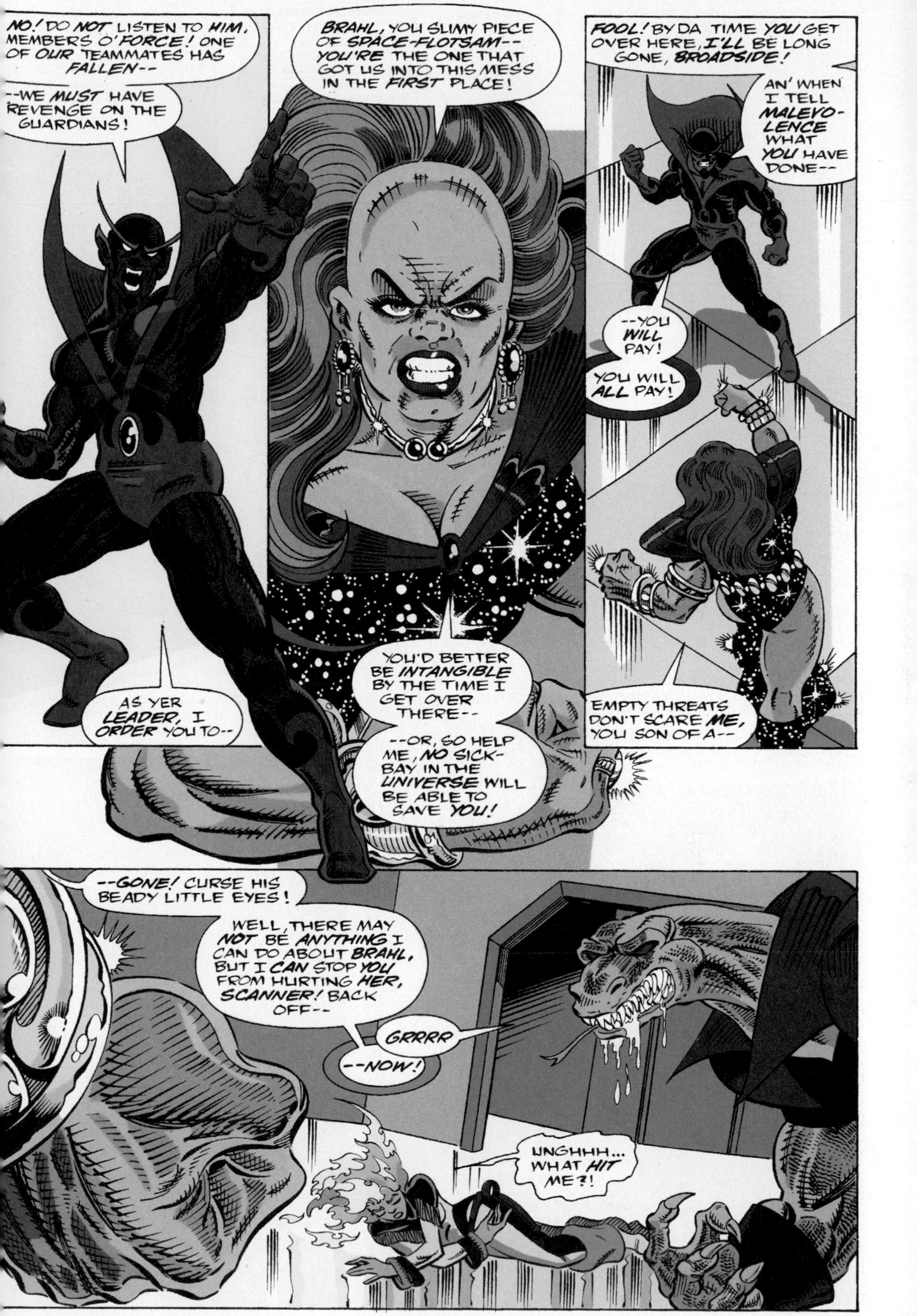
NO! DO NOT LISTEN TO HIM, MEMBERS O' FORCE! ONE OF OUR TEAMMATES HAS FALLEN--
--WE MUST HAVE REVENGE ON THE GUARDIANS!
AS YER LEADER, I ORDER YOU TO--
BRAHL, YOU SLIMY PIECE OF SPACE-FLOTSAM-- YOU'RE THE ONE THAT GOT US INTO THIS MESS IN THE FIRST PLACE!
YOU'D BETTER BE INTANGIBLE BY THE TIME I GET OVER THERE--
--OR, SO HELP ME, NO SICK-BAY IN THE UNIVERSE WILL BE ABLE TO SAVE YOU!
FOOL! BY DA TIME YOU GET OVER HERE, I'LL BE LONG GONE, BROADSIDE!
AN' WHEN I TELL MALEVO-LENCE WHAT YOU HAVE DONE--
--YOU WILL PAY!
YOU WILL ALL PAY!
EMPTY THREATS DON'T SCARE ME, YOU SON OF A--
--GONE! CURSE HIS BEADY LITTLE EYES!
WELL, THERE MAY NOT BE ANYTHING I CAN DO ABOUT BRAHL, BUT I CAN STOP YOU FROM HURTING HER, SCANNER! BACK OFF--
GRRRR
--NOW!
UNGHHH... WHAT HIT ME?!

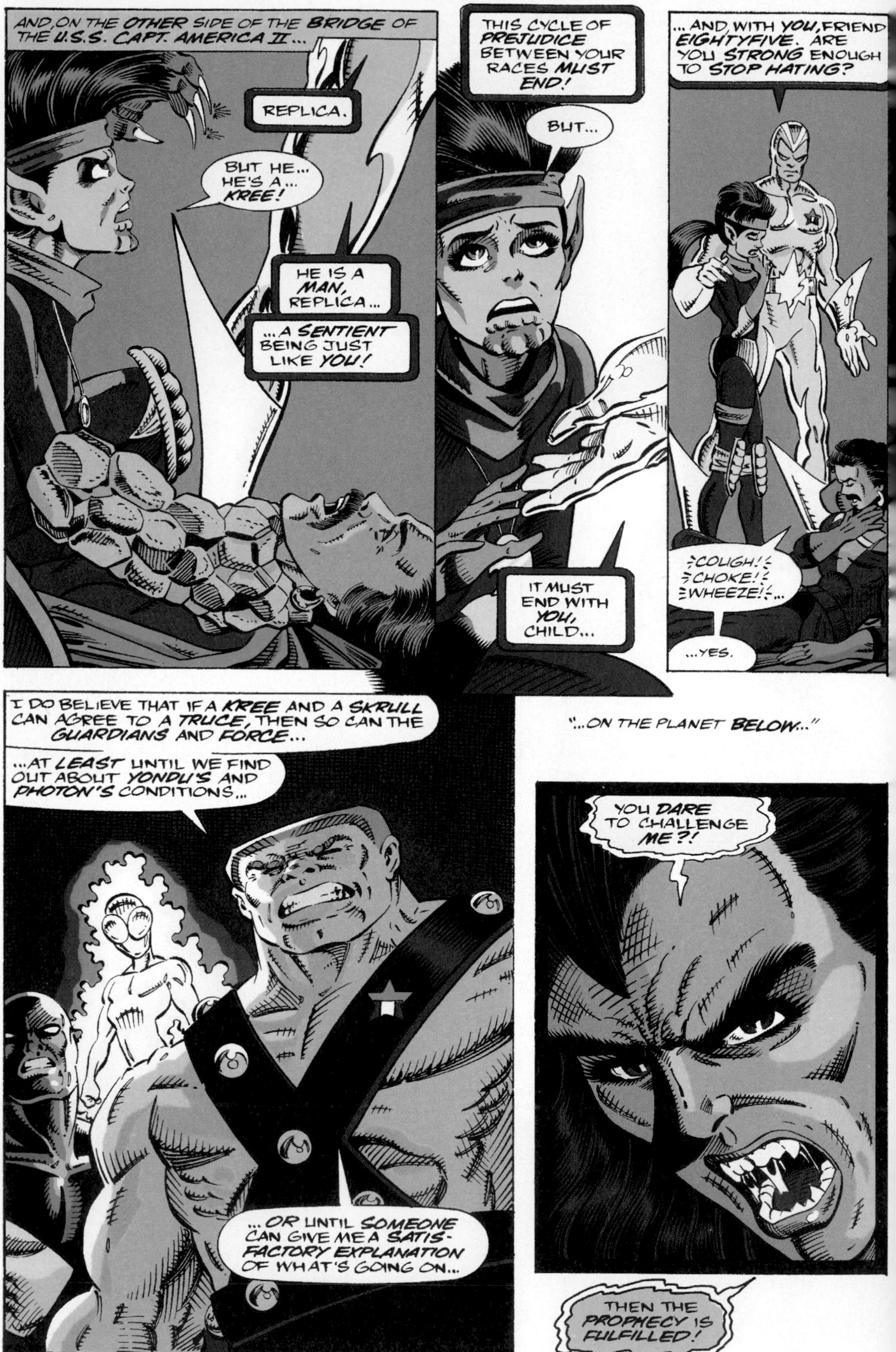

AND, ON THE OTHER SIDE OF THE BRIDGE OF THE U.S.S. CAPT. AMERICA II ...
REPLICA.
BUT HE... HE'S A... KREE!
HE IS A MAN, REPLICA...
...A SENTIENT BEING JUST LIKE YOU!
THIS CYCLE OF PREJUDICE BETWEEN YOUR RACES MUST END!
BUT...
IT MUST END WITH YOU, CHILD...
... AND, WITH YOU, FRIEND EIGHTYFIVE. ARE YOU STRONG ENOUGH TO STOP HATING?
COUGH! CHOKE! WHEEZE!...
...YES.
I DO BELIEVE THAT IF A KREE AND A SKRULL CAN AGREE TO A TRUCE, THEN SO CAN THE GUARDIANS AND FORCE...
...AT LEAST UNTIL WE FIND OUT ABOUT YONDU'S AND PHOTON'S CONDITIONS...
... OR UNTIL SOMEONE CAN GIVE ME A SATIS-FACTORY EXPLANATION OF WHAT'S GOING ON...
"...ON THE PLANET BELOW..."
YOU DARE TO CHALLENGE ME?!
THEN THE PROPHECY IS FULFILLED!

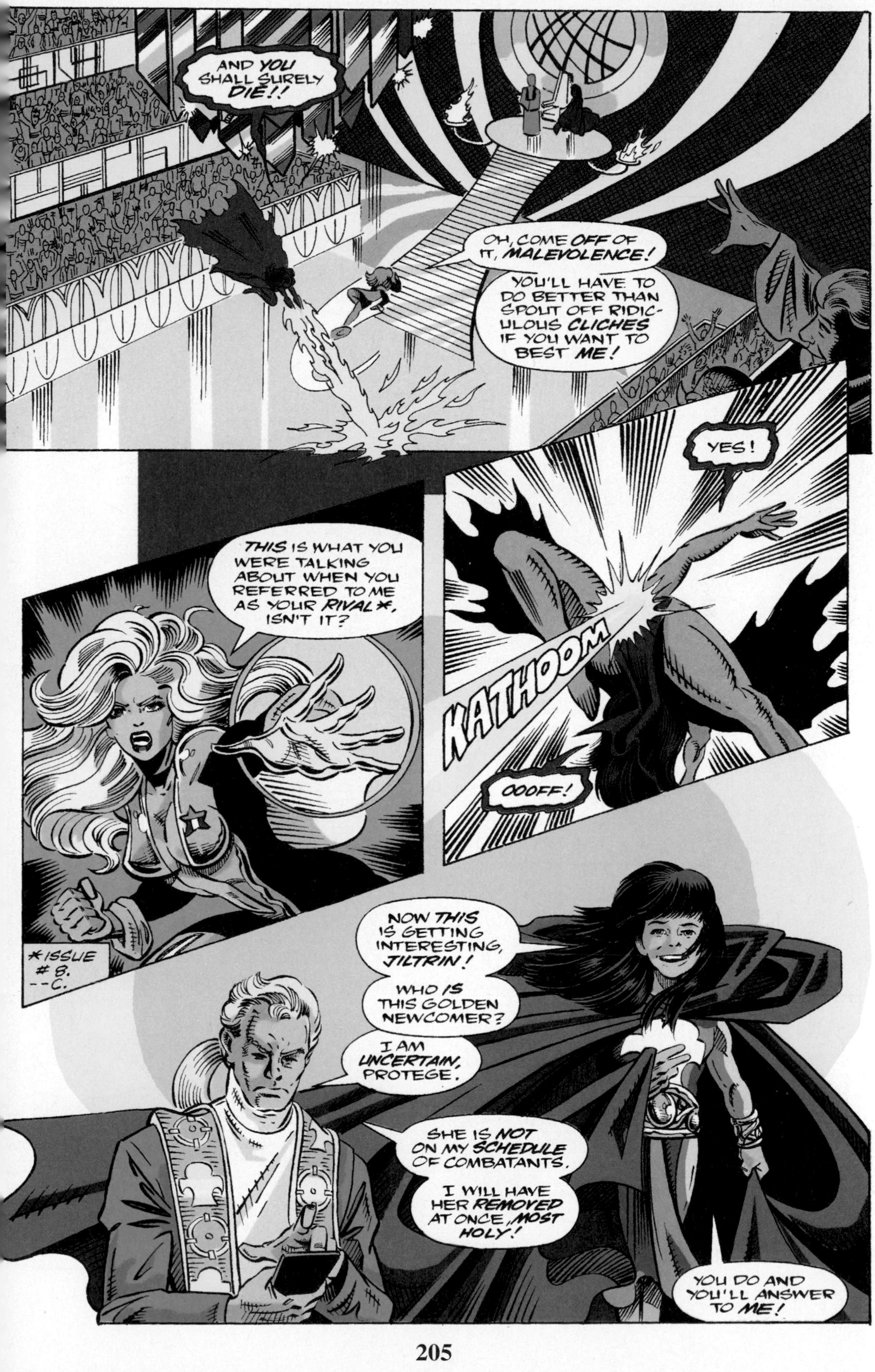
AND YOU SHALL SURELY DIE!!
OH, COME OFF OF IT, MALEVOLENCE!
YOU'LL HAVE TO DO BETTER THAN SPOUT OFF RIDICULOUS CLICHES IF YOU WANT TO BEST ME!
THIS IS WHAT YOU WERE TALKING ABOUT WHEN YOU REFERRED TO ME AS YOUR RIVAL*, ISN'T IT?
*ISSUE #8. --C.
YES!
KATHOOM
OOOFF!
NOW THIS IS GETTING INTERESTING, JILTRIN!
WHO IS THIS GOLDEN NEWCOMER?
I AM UNCERTAIN, PROTEGE.
SHE IS NOT ON MY SCHEDULE OF COMBATANTS.
I WILL HAVE HER REMOVED AT ONCE, MOST HOLY!
YOU DO AND YOU'LL ANSWER TO ME!

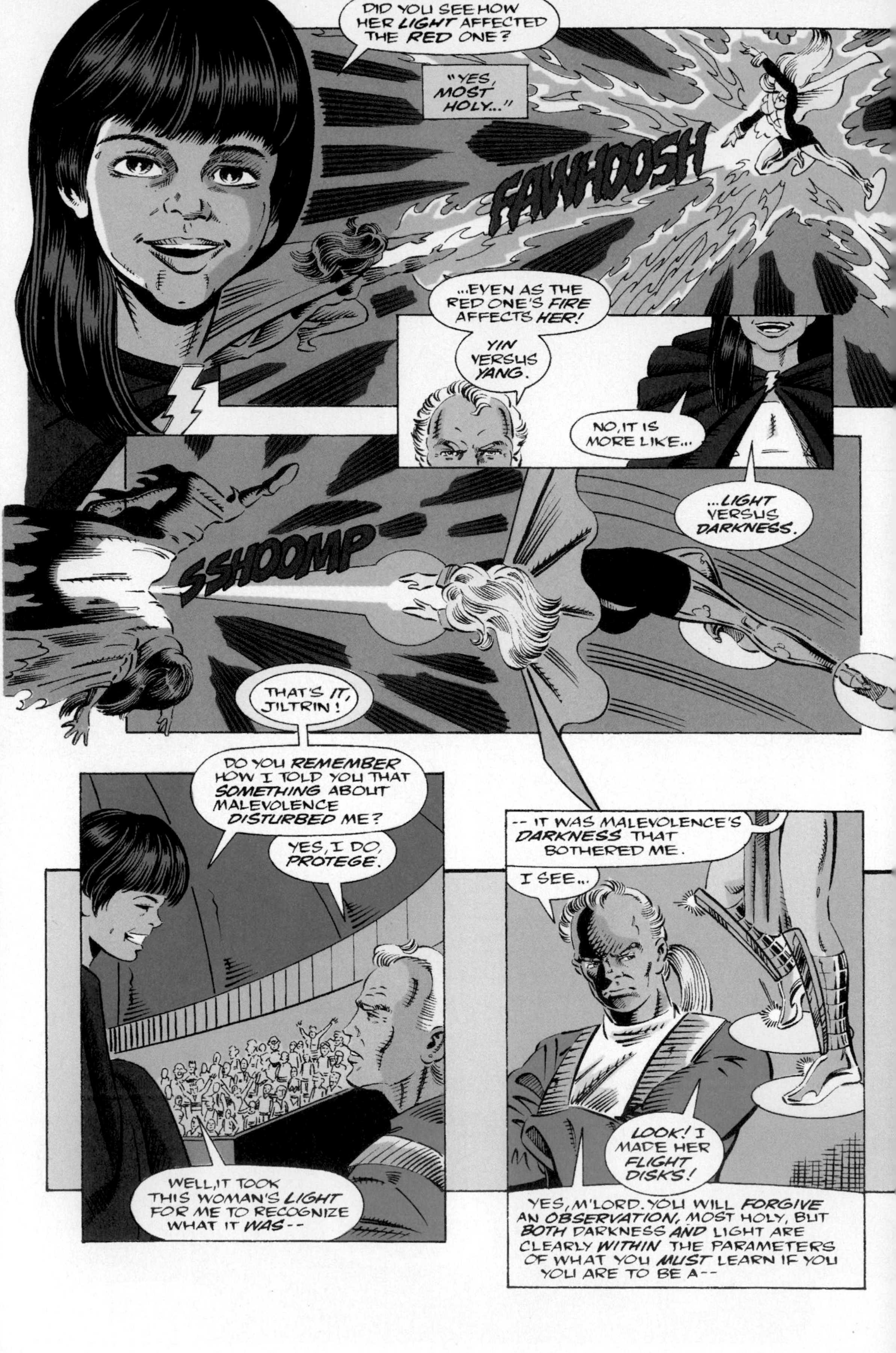
DID YOU SEE HOW HER LIGHT AFFECTED THE RED ONE?
"YES, MOST HOLY..."
FAWHOOSH
...EVEN AS THE RED ONE'S FIRE AFFECTS HER!
YIN VERSUS YANG.
NO, IT IS MORE LIKE...
...LIGHT VERSUS DARKNESS.
SSHOOMP
THAT'S IT, JILTRIN!
DO YOU REMEMBER HOW I TOLD YOU THAT SOMETHING ABOUT MALEVOLENCE DISTURBED ME?
YES, I DO, PROTEGE.
WELL, IT TOOK THIS WOMAN'S LIGHT FOR ME TO RECOGNIZE WHAT IT WAS--
-- IT WAS MALEVOLENCE'S DARKNESS THAT BOTHERED ME.
I SEE...
LOOK! I MADE HER FLIGHT DISKS!
YES, M'LORD. YOU WILL FORGIVE AN OBSERVATION, MOST HOLY, BUT BOTH DARKNESS AND LIGHT ARE CLEARLY WITHIN THE PARAMETERS OF WHAT YOU MUST LEARN IF YOU YOU ARE TO BE A--

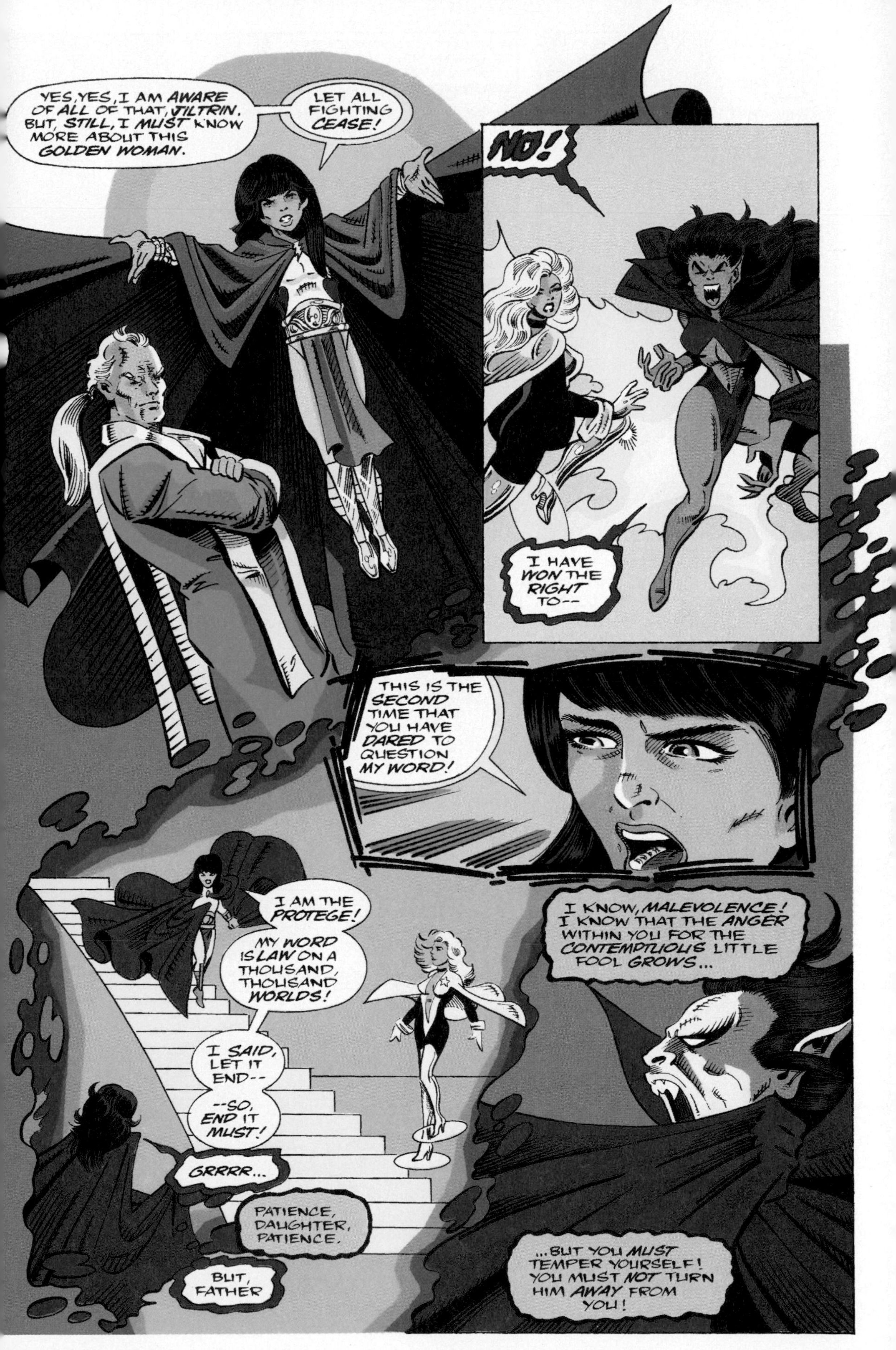
YES, YES, I AM AWARE OF ALL OF THAT, JILTRIN. BUT, STILL, I MUST KNOW MORE ABOUT THIS GOLDEN WOMAN.
LET ALL FIGHTING CEASE!
NO!
I HAVE WON THE RIGHT TO--
THIS IS THE SECOND TIME THAT YOU HAVE DARED TO QUESTION MY WORD!
I AM THE PROTEGE!
MY WORD IS LAW ON A THOUSAND, THOUSAND WORLDS!
I SAID, LET IT END--
--SO, END IT MUST!
GRRRR...
PATIENCE, DAUGHTER, PATIENCE.
BUT, FATHER
I KNOW, MALEVOLENCE! I KNOW THAT THE ANGER WITHIN YOU FOR THE CONTEMPTUOUS LITTLE FOOL GROWS...
...BUT YOU MUST TEMPER YOURSELF! YOU MUST NOT TURN HIM AWAY FROM YOU!

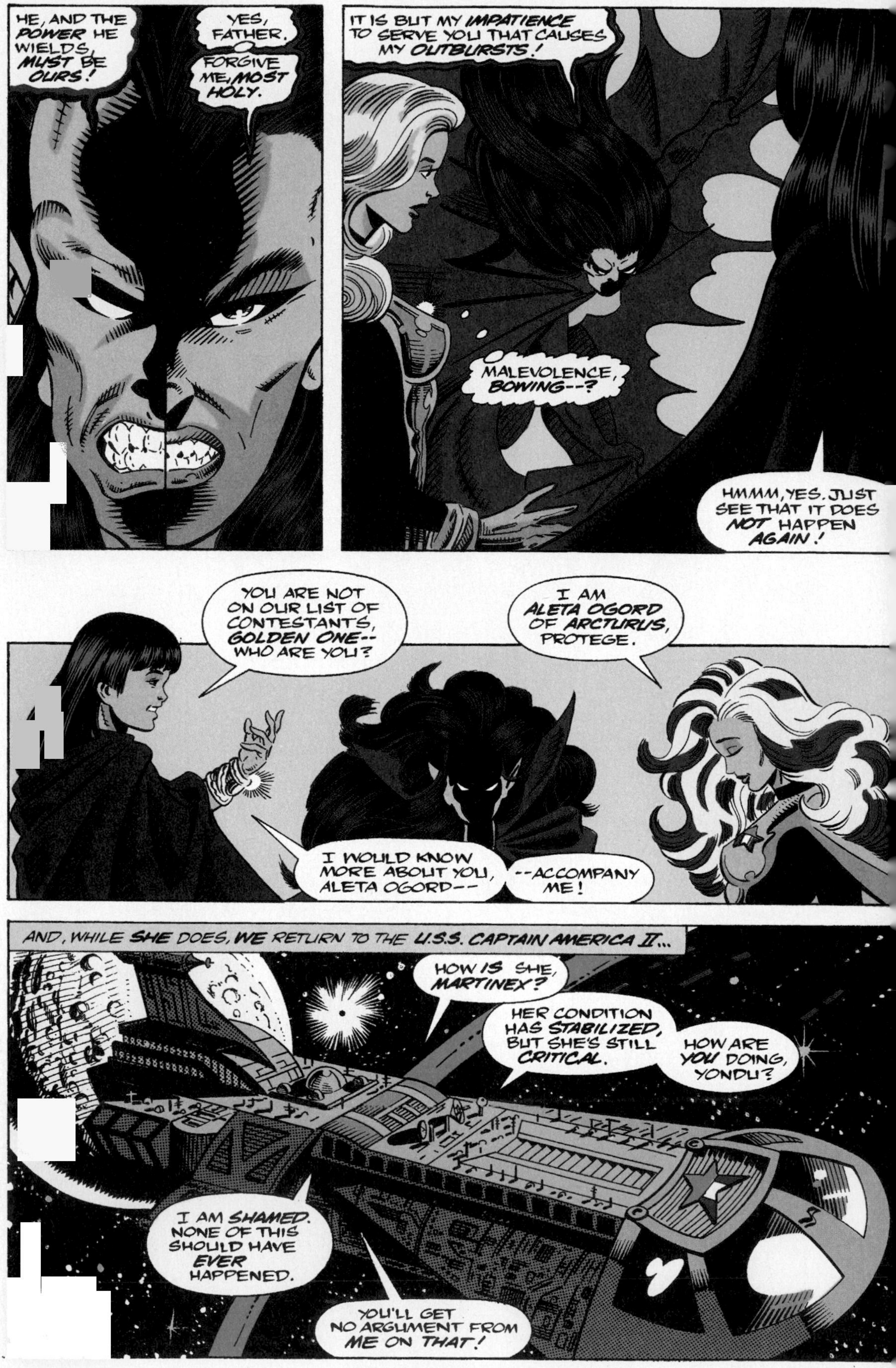

HE, AND THE POWER HE WIELDS, MUST BE OURS!
YES, FATHER.
FORGIVE ME, MOST HOLY.
IT IS BUT MY IMPATIENCE TO SERVE YOU THAT CAUSES MY OUTBURSTS!
MALEVOLENCE, BOWING--?
HMMM, YES. JUST SEE THAT IT DOES NOT HAPPEN AGAIN!
YOU ARE NOT ON OUR LIST OF CONTESTANTS, GOLDEN ONE-- WHO ARE YOU?
I AM ALETA OGORD OF ARCTURUS, PROTEGE.
I WOULD KNOW MORE ABOUT YOU, ALETA OGORD--
--ACCOMPANY ME!
AND, WHILE SHE DOES, WE RETURN TO THE U.S.S. CAPTAIN AMERICA II...
HOW IS SHE, MARTINEX?
HER CONDITION HAS STABILIZED, BUT SHE'S STILL CRITICAL.
HOW ARE YOU DOING, YONDU?
I AM SHAMED. NONE OF THIS SHOULD HAVE EVER HAPPENED.
YOU'LL GET NO ARGUMENT FROM ME ON THAT!

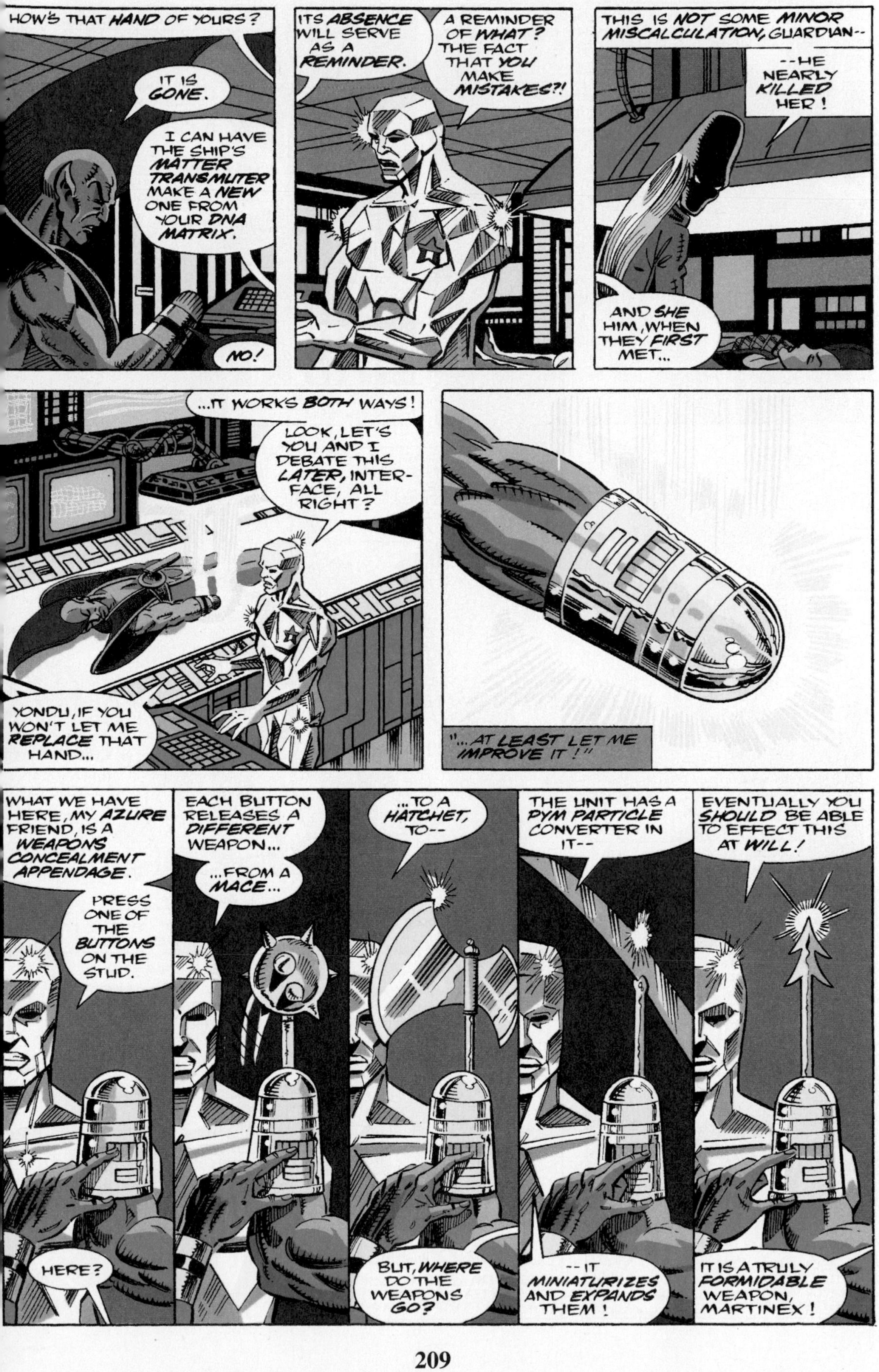
HOW'S THAT HAND OF YOURS?
IT IS GONE.
I CAN HAVE THE SHIP'S MATTER TRANSMUTER MAKE A NEW ONE FROM YOUR DNA MATRIX.
NO!
ITS ABSENCE WILL SERVE AS A REMINDER.
A REMINDER OF WHAT? THE FACT THAT YOU MAKE MISTAKES?!
THIS IS NOT SOME MINOR MISCALCULATION, GUARDIAN--
--HE NEARLY KILLED HER!
AND SHE HIM, WHEN THEY FIRST MET...
...IT WORKS BOTH WAYS!
LOOK, LET'S YOU AND I DEBATE THIS LATER, INTERFACE, ALL RIGHT?
YONDU, IF YOU WON'T LET ME REPLACE THAT HAND...
"...AT LEAST LET ME IMPROVE IT!"
WHAT WE HAVE HERE, MY AZURE FRIEND, IS A WEAPONS CONCEALMENT APPENDAGE.
PRESS ONE OF THE BUTTONS ON THE STUD.
HERE?
EACH BUTTON RELEASES A DIFFERENT WEAPON...
...FROM A MACE...
...TO A HATCHET, TO--
BUT, WHERE DO THE WEAPONS GO?
THE UNIT HAS A PYM PARTICLE CONVERTER IN IT--
--IT MINIATURIZES AND EXPANDS THEM!
EVENTUALLY YOU SHOULD BE ABLE TO EFFECT THIS AT WILL!
IT IS A TRULY FORMIDABLE WEAPON, MARTINEX!

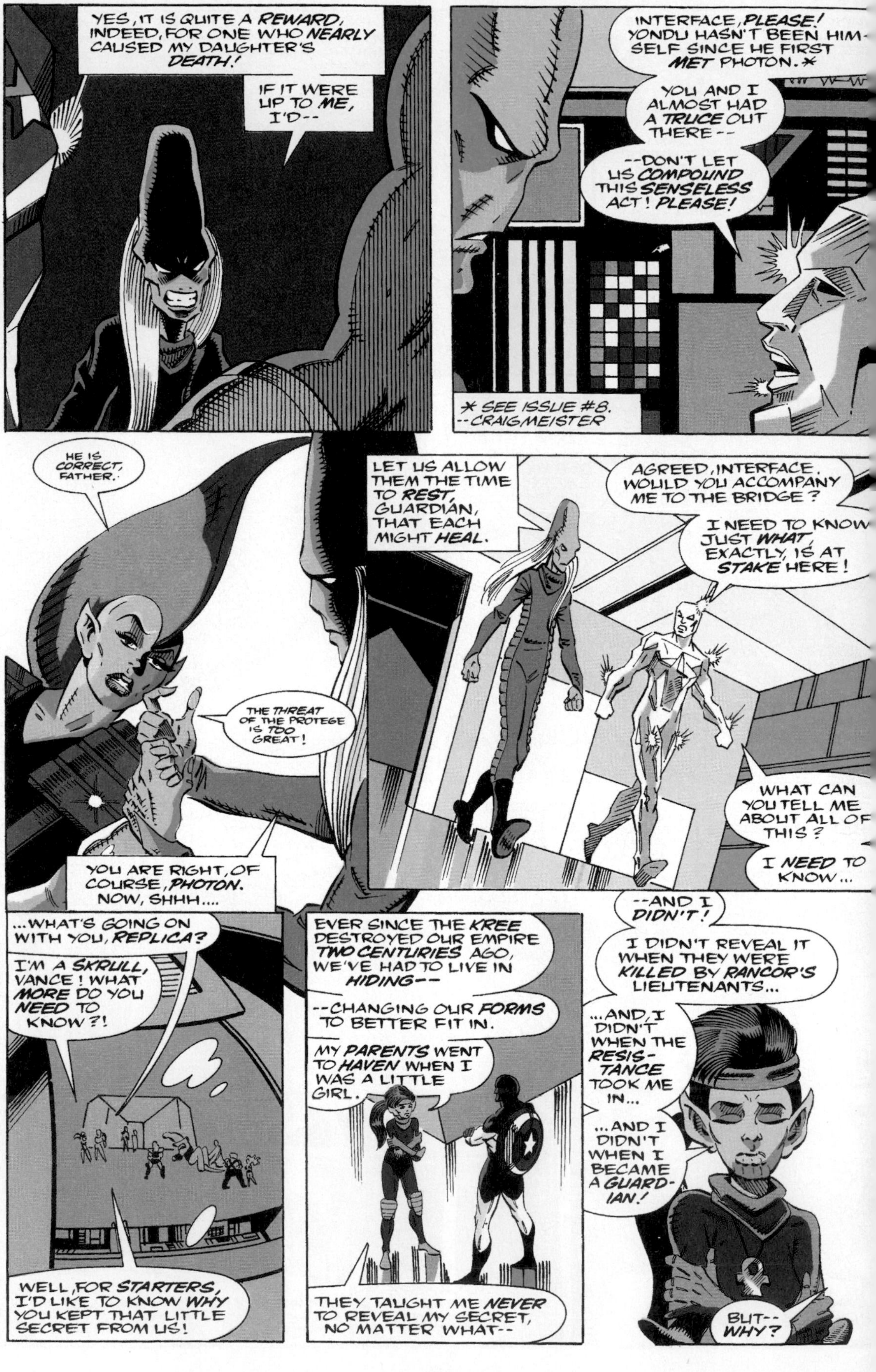
YES, IT IS QUITE A REWARD, INDEED, FOR ONE WHO NEARLY CAUSED MY DAUGHTER'S DEATH!
IF IT WERE UP TO ME, I'D--
INTERFACE, PLEASE! YONDU HASN'T BEEN HIMSELF SINCE HE FIRST MET PHOTON.*
YOU AND I ALMOST HAD A TRUCE OUT THERE--
--DON'T LET US COMPOUND THIS SENSELESS ACT! PLEASE!
* SEE ISSUE #8. --CRAIGMEISTER
HE IS CORRECT, FATHER.
THE THREAT OF THE PROTEGE IS TOO GREAT!
YOU ARE RIGHT, OF COURSE, PHOTON. NOW, SHHH....
LET US ALLOW THEM THE TIME TO REST, GUARDIAN, THAT EACH MIGHT HEAL.
AGREED, INTERFACE. WOULD YOU ACCOMPANY ME TO THE BRIDGE?
I NEED TO KNOW JUST WHAT, EXACTLY, IS AT STAKE HERE!
WHAT CAN YOU TELL ME ABOUT ALL OF THIS?
I NEED TO KNOW...
...WHAT'S GOING ON WITH YOU, REPLICA?
I'M A SKRULL, VANCE! WHAT MORE DO YOU NEED TO KNOW?!
WELL, FOR STARTERS, I'D LIKE TO KNOW WHY YOU KEPT THAT LITTLE SECRET FROM US!
EVER SINCE THE KREE DESTROYED OUR EMPIRE TWO CENTURIES AGO, WE'VE HAD TO LIVE IN HIDING--
--CHANGING OUR FORMS TO BETTER FIT IN.
MY PARENTS WENT TO HAVEN WHEN I WAS A LITTLE GIRL.
THEY TAUGHT ME NEVER TO REVEAL MY SECRET, NO MATTER WHAT--
--AND I DIDN'T!
I DIDN'T REVEAL IT WHEN THEY WERE KILLED BY RANCOR'S LIEUTENANTS...
...AND, I DIDN'T WHEN THE RESIS-TANCE TOOK ME IN...
...AND I DIDN'T WHEN I BECAME A GUARD-IAN!
BUT-- WHY?

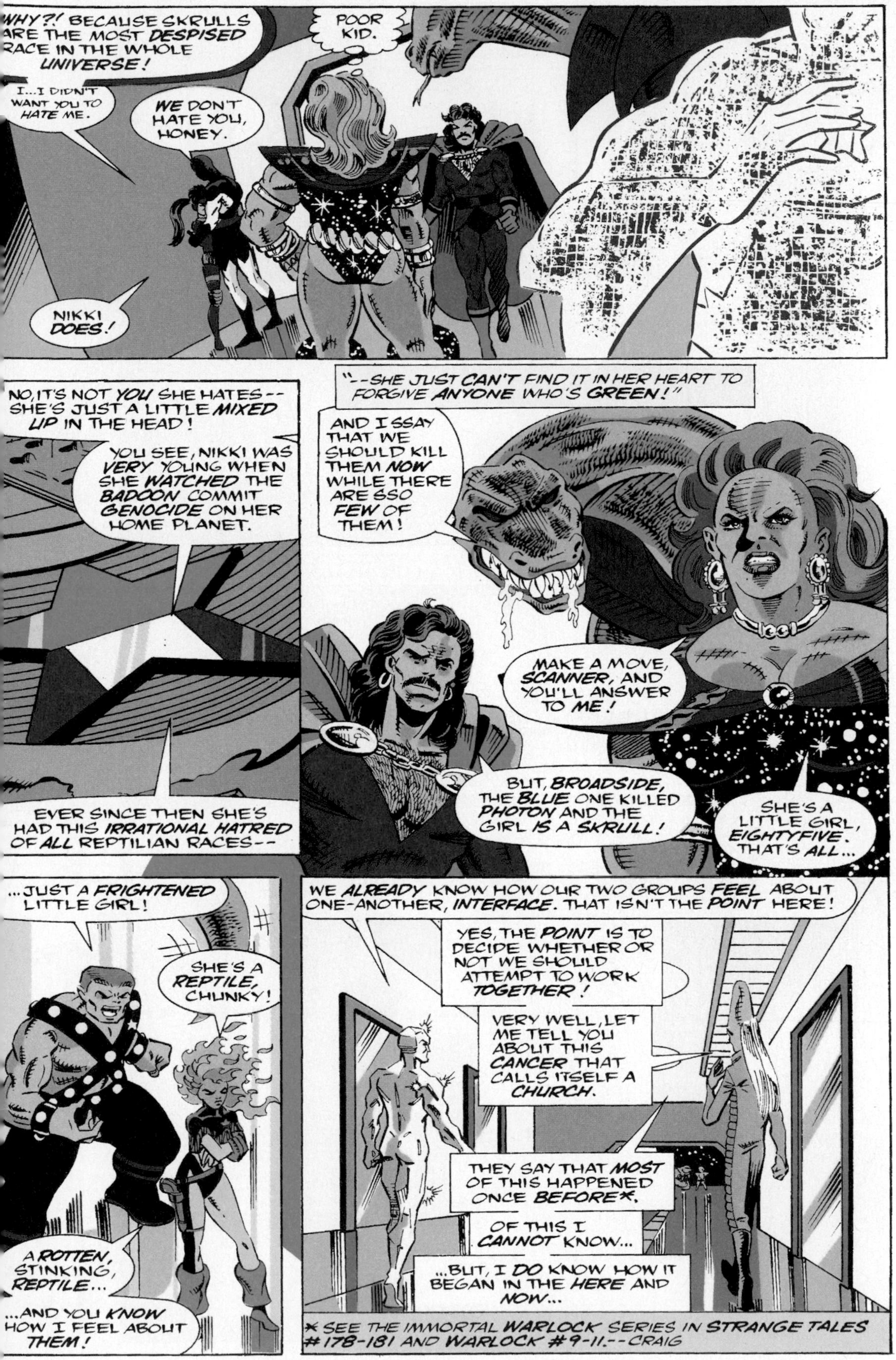
WHY?! BECAUSE SKRULLS ARE THE MOST DESPISED RACE IN THE WHOLE UNIVERSE!
POOR KID.
I...I DIDN'T WANT YOU TO HATE ME.
WE DON'T HATE YOU, HONEY.
NIKKI DOES!
NO, IT'S NOT YOU SHE HATES-- SHE'S JUST A LITTLE MIXED UP IN THE HEAD!
YOU SEE, NIKKI WAS VERY YOUNG WHEN SHE WATCHED THE BADOON COMMIT GENOCIDE ON HER HOME PLANET.
EVER SINCE THEN SHE'S HAD THIS IRRATIONAL HATRED OF ALL REPTILIAN RACES--
"--SHE JUST CAN'T FIND IT IN HER HEART TO FORGIVE ANYONE WHO'S GREEN!"
AND I SSAY THAT WE SHOULD KILL THEM NOW WHILE THERE ARE SSO FEW OF THEM!
MAKE A MOVE, SCANNER, AND YOU'LL ANSWER TO ME!
BUT, BROADSIDE, THE BLUE ONE KILLED PHOTON AND THE GIRL IS A SKRULL!
SHE'S A LITTLE GIRL, EIGHTYFIVE. THAT'S ALL...
...JUST A FRIGHTENED LITTLE GIRL!
SHE'S A REPTILE, CHUNKY!
A ROTTEN, STINKING REPTILE...
...AND YOU KNOW HOW I FEEL ABOUT THEM!
WE ALREADY KNOW HOW OUR TWO GROUPS FEEL ABOUT ONE-ANOTHER, INTERFACE. THAT ISN'T THE POINT HERE!
YES, THE POINT IS TO DECIDE WHETHER OR NOT WE SHOULD ATTEMPT TO WORK TOGETHER!
VERY WELL, LET ME TELL YOU ABOUT THIS CANCER THAT CALLS ITSELF A CHURCH.
THEY SAY THAT MOST OF THIS HAPPENED ONCE BEFORE*.
OF THIS I CANNOT KNOW...
...BUT, I DO KNOW HOW IT BEGAN IN THE HERE AND NOW...
* SEE THE IMMORTAL WARLOCK SERIES IN STRANGE TALES #178-181 AND WARLOCK #9-11.--CRAIG

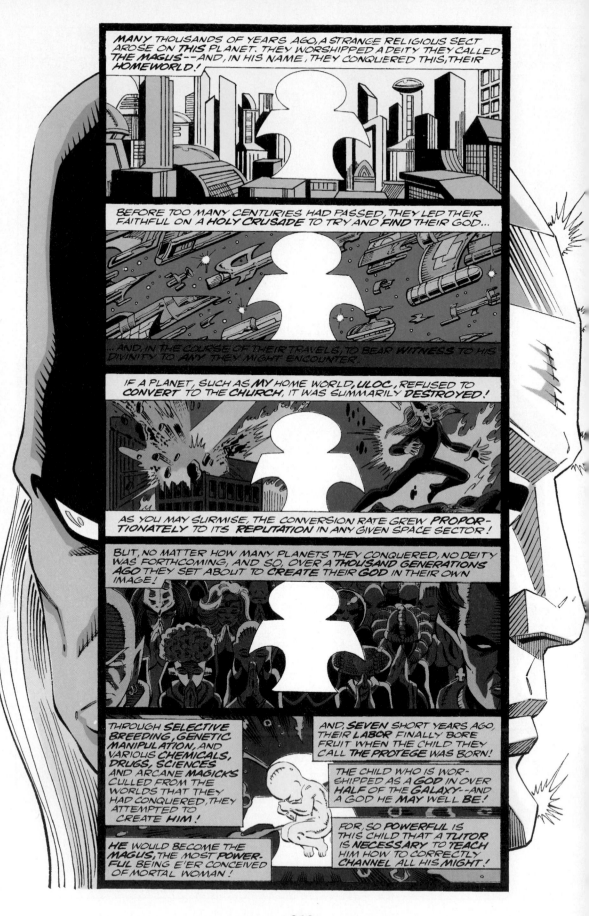

MANY THOUSANDS OF YEARS AGO, A STRANGE RELIGIOUS SECT AROSE ON *THIS* PLANET. THEY WORSHIPPED A DEITY THEY CALLED *THE MAGUS*--AND, IN HIS NAME, THEY CONQUERED *THIS*, THEIR HOMEWORLD!

BEFORE TOO MANY CENTURIES HAD PASSED, THEY LED THEIR FAITHFUL ON A *HOLY CRUSADE* TO TRY AND *FIND* THEIR GOD...

...AND, IN THE COURSE OF THEIR TRAVELS, TO BEAR *WITNESS* TO HIS DIVINITY TO *ANY* THEY MIGHT ENCOUNTER.

IF A PLANET, SUCH AS *MY* HOME WORLD, *ULOC,* REFUSED TO *CONVERT* TO THE *CHURCH,* IT WAS SUMMARILY *DESTROYED!*

AS YOU MAY SURMISE, THE CONVERSION RATE GREW *PROPOR-TIONATELY* TO ITS *REPUTATION* IN ANY GIVEN SPACE SECTOR!

BUT, NO MATTER HOW MANY PLANETS THEY CONQUERED, NO DEITY WAS FORTHCOMING, AND SO, OVER A *THOUSAND GENERATIONS AGO* THEY SET ABOUT TO *CREATE* THEIR *GOD* IN THEIR OWN IMAGE!

THROUGH *SELECTIVE BREEDING, GENETIC MANIPULATION,* AND VARIOUS *CHEMICALS, DRUGS, SCIENCES* AND ARCANE *MAGICKS* CULLED FROM THE WORLDS THAT THEY HAD CONQUERED, THEY ATTEMPTED TO *CREATE HIM!*

AND, *SEVEN SHORT YEARS AGO,* THEIR *LABOR* FINALLY BORE FRUIT WHEN THE CHILD THEY CALL *THE PROTEGE* WAS BORN!

THE CHILD WHO IS WOR-SHIPPED AS A *GOD* IN OVER *HALF* OF THE *GALAXY*--AND A GOD HE *MAY WELL BE!*

HE WOULD BECOME THE *MAGUS,* THE MOST *POWER-FUL* BEING E'ER CONCEIVED OF MORTAL WOMAN!

FOR, *SO POWERFUL* IS THIS CHILD THAT A *TUTOR* IS *NECESSARY* TO TEACH HIM HOW TO CORRECTLY *CHANNEL* ALL HIS *MIGHT!*

I'M STILL NOT CERTAIN THAT I UNDERSTAND, INTERFACE. ARE *YOU* CLAIMING THAT THIS CHILD IS ACTUALLY A--*GOD*?!

THAT *PURELY* DEPENDS ON WHAT YOUR DEFINITION OF A GOD *IS*, MARTINEX.

WELL, FOR MYSELF, I SEE IT IN THE *ABSTRACT*...

YES, WELL, CONSIDER THE FACT THAT THE BOY POSSESSES THE ABILITY TO *INSTANTLY ACQUIRE ANY NATURAL POWER* OR *ABILITY* UPON *OBSERVING* IT IN USE!

AND, ONCE ACQUIRED, IT IS HIS *PERMANENTLY*!

FOR EXAMPLE, HE CAN JUST AS EASILY *LEARN* HOW TO FIRE A *WEAPON* UPON WATCHING *CHARLIE* DO SO...

...AS HE CAN *LEARN* TO EMIT *THERMAL* BEAMS FROM WATCHING *YOU*!

OR, *SUPER-STRENGTH* FROM *BROADSIDE*!

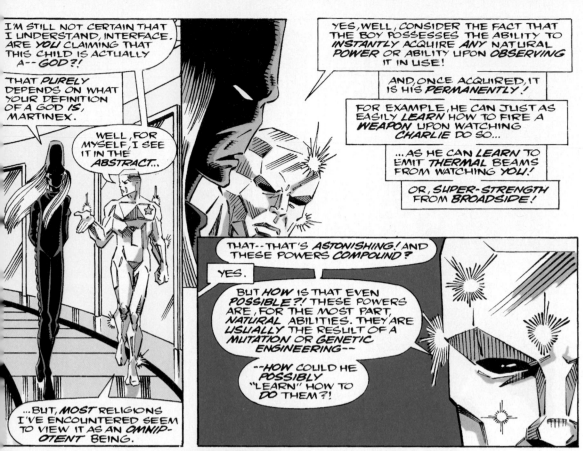

...BUT, *MOST* RELIGIONS I'VE ENCOUNTERED SEEM TO VIEW IT AS AN *OMNIPOTENT* BEING.

THAT--THAT'S *ASTONISHING*! AND THESE POWERS *COMPOUND*?

YES.

BUT *HOW* IS THAT EVEN *POSSIBLE*?! THESE POWERS ARE, FOR THE MOST PART, *NATURAL* ABILITIES. THEY ARE USUALLY THE RESULT OF A *MUTATION* OR *GENETIC ENGINEERING*--

--HOW COULD HE POSSIBLY "LEARN" HOW TO *DO* THEM?!

I AM *UNCERTAIN*.

THERE IS, AS WELL YOU KNOW, VERY LITTLE HARD *DATA* ON PARANORMAL *POWER SOURCES*.

ONE THEORY SUGGESTS THAT THESE *POWER SOURCES* THEMSELVES ARE *INTRA-DIMENSIONAL* IN NATURE--

--AND *HE'S* ABLE TO TAP *INTO* THESE *SOURCES*?

YES, EVEN AS THE *PARA-HUMAN* WITH THE POWER WOULD!

HMMM, WELL THAT WOULD EXPLAIN *QUITE A BIT*--

--BUT *NOT ALL*!

NO, THERE ARE THE *LEARNED SKILLS*, THOSE THAT COME FROM *PRAC-TICE* AND HARD WORK, NOT THEORETIC "POWER SOURCES!"

TRUE ENOUGH, MARTINEX. AS I SAID, I *DO NOT* UNDERSTAND HIS POWER-- BUT THE *FACT* THAT HE *HAS* IT IS *IRREFUTABLE*!

I FIND THIS INFORMATION *ALARMING* INTERFACE.

AS WELL YOU *SHOULD*, GUARDIAN.

IF WHAT YOU SAY IS *TRUE*...

"...THIS PROTEGE MAY BE THE MOST *POWERFUL* PERSON *EVER BORN*!"

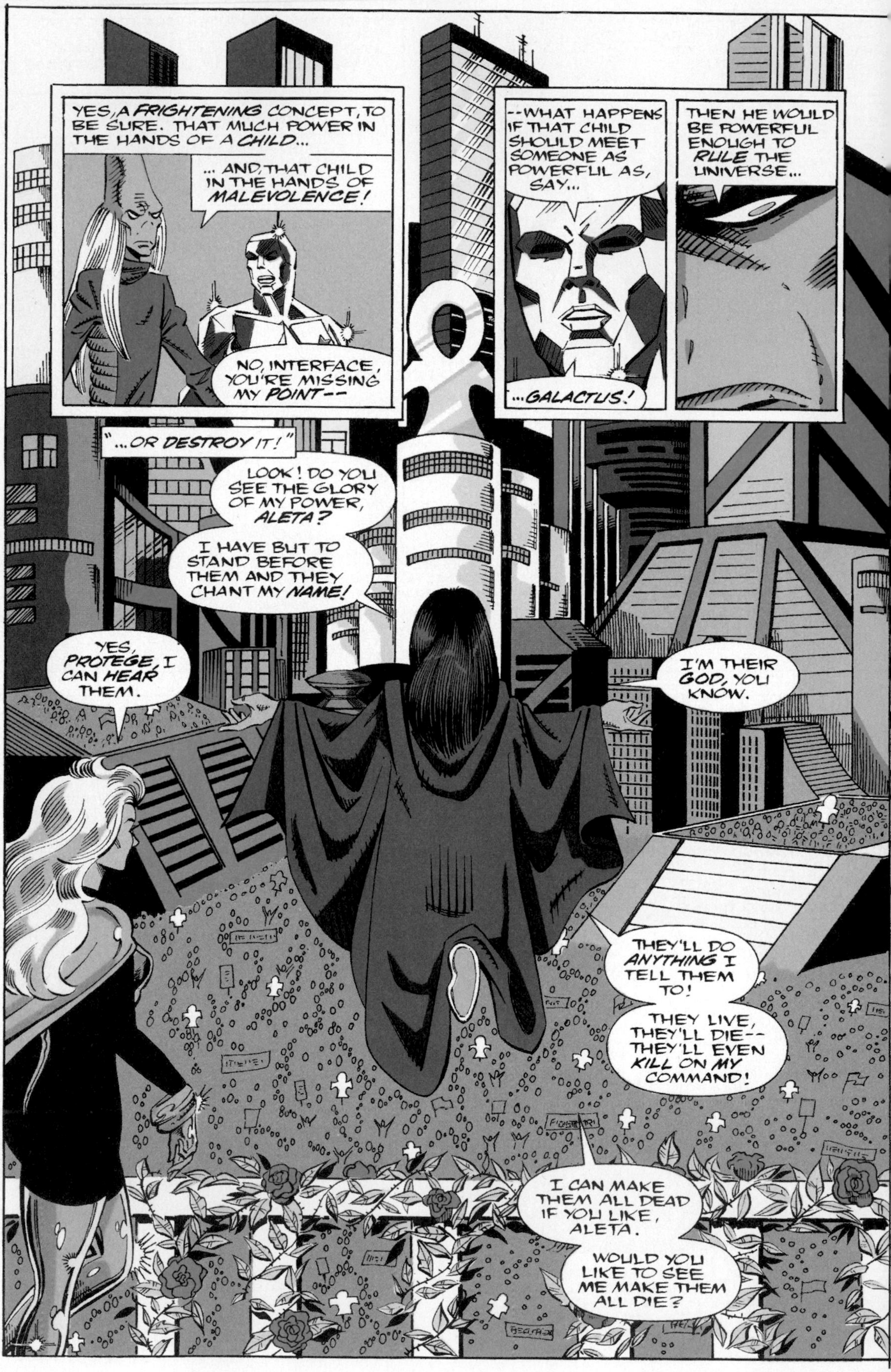
YES, A FRIGHTENING CONCEPT, TO BE SURE. THAT MUCH POWER IN THE HANDS OF A CHILD...
... AND, THAT CHILD IN THE HANDS OF MALEVOLENCE!
NO, INTERFACE, YOU'RE MISSING MY POINT--
--WHAT HAPPENS IF THAT CHILD SHOULD MEET SOMEONE AS POWERFUL AS, SAY...
...GALACTUS!
THEN HE WOULD BE POWERFUL ENOUGH TO RULE THE UNIVERSE...
"...OR DESTROY IT!"
LOOK! DO YOU SEE THE GLORY OF MY POWER, ALETA?
I HAVE BUT TO STAND BEFORE THEM AND THEY CHANT MY NAME!
YES, PROTEGE, I CAN HEAR THEM.
I'M THEIR GOD, YOU KNOW.
THEY'LL DO ANYTHING I TELL THEM TO!
THEY LIVE, THEY'LL DIE-- THEY'LL EVEN KILL ON MY COMMAND!
I CAN MAKE THEM ALL DEAD IF YOU LIKE, ALETA.
WOULD YOU LIKE TO SEE ME MAKE THEM ALL DIE?

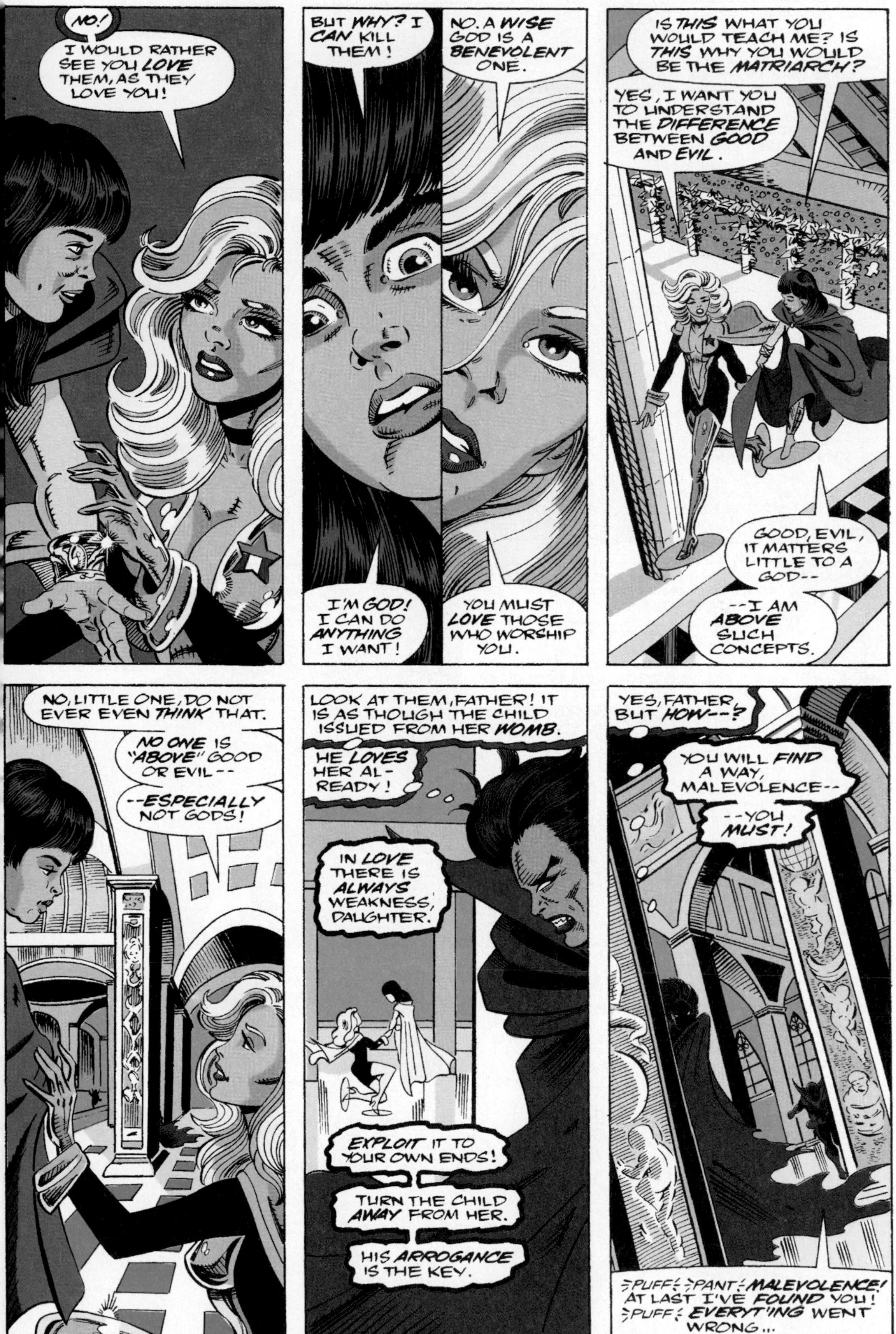
NO!
I WOULD RATHER SEE YOU LOVE THEM, AS THEY LOVE YOU!
BUT WHY? I CAN KILL THEM!
NO. A WISE GOD IS A BENEVOLENT ONE.
I'M GOD! I CAN DO ANYTHING I WANT!
YOU MUST LOVE THOSE WHO WORSHIP YOU.
IS THIS WHAT YOU WOULD TEACH ME? IS THIS WHY YOU WOULD BE THE MATRIARCH?
YES, I WANT YOU TO UNDERSTAND THE DIFFERENCE BETWEEN GOOD AND EVIL.
GOOD, EVIL, IT MATTERS LITTLE TO A GOD--
--I AM ABOVE SUCH CONCEPTS.
NO, LITTLE ONE, DO NOT EVER EVEN THINK THAT.
NO ONE IS "ABOVE" GOOD OR EVIL--
--ESPECIALLY NOT GODS!
LOOK AT THEM, FATHER! IT IS AS THOUGH THE CHILD ISSUED FROM HER WOMB.
HE LOVES HER AL-READY!
IN LOVE THERE IS ALWAYS WEAKNESS, DAUGHTER.
EXPLOIT IT TO YOUR OWN ENDS!
TURN THE CHILD AWAY FROM HER.
HIS ARROGANCE IS THE KEY.
YES, FATHER, BUT HOW--?
YOU WILL FIND A WAY, MALEVOLENCE--
--YOU MUST!
-PUFF- -PANT- MALEVOLENCE! AT LAST I'VE FOUND YOU! -PUFF- EVERYT'ING WENT WRONG...

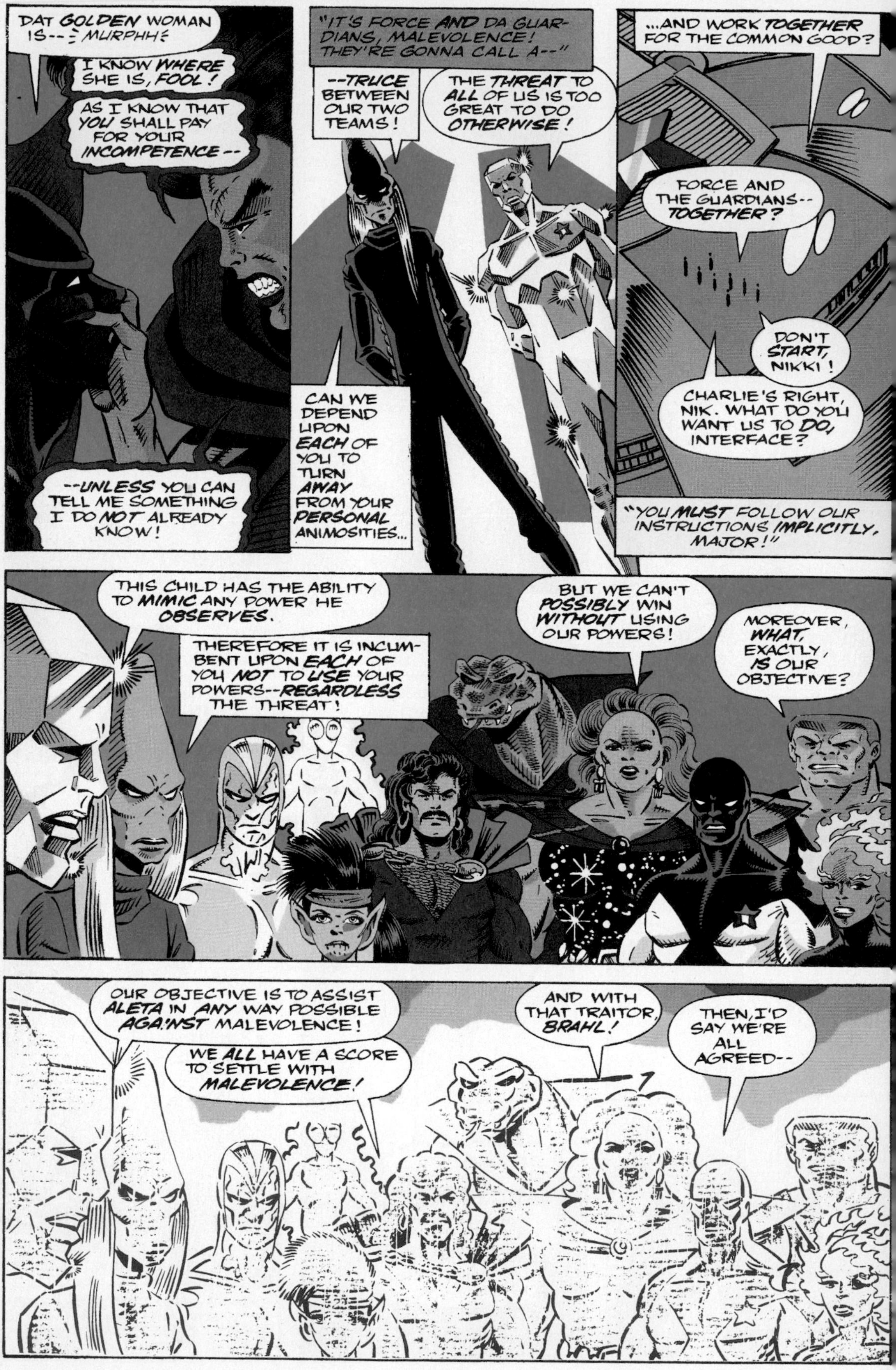
DAT GOLDEN WOMAN IS-- MURPHH
I KNOW WHERE SHE IS, FOOL!
AS I KNOW THAT YOU SHALL PAY FOR YOUR INCOMPETENCE--
--UNLESS YOU CAN TELL ME SOMETHING I DO NOT ALREADY KNOW!
"IT'S FORCE AND DA GUARDIANS, MALEVOLENCE! THEY'RE GONNA CALL A--"
--TRUCE BETWEEN OUR TWO TEAMS!
THE THREAT TO ALL OF US IS TOO GREAT TO DO OTHERWISE!
CAN WE DEPEND UPON EACH OF YOU TO TURN AWAY FROM YOUR PERSONAL ANIMOSITIES...
...AND WORK TOGETHER FOR THE COMMON GOOD?
FORCE AND THE GUARDIANS--TOGETHER?
DON'T START, NIKKI!
CHARLIE'S RIGHT, NIK. WHAT DO YOU WANT US TO DO, INTERFACE?
"YOU MUST FOLLOW OUR INSTRUCTIONS IMPLICITLY, MAJOR!"
THIS CHILD HAS THE ABILITY TO MIMIC ANY POWER HE OBSERVES.
THEREFORE IT IS INCUMBENT UPON EACH OF YOU NOT TO USE YOUR POWERS--REGARDLESS THE THREAT!
BUT WE CAN'T POSSIBLY WIN WITHOUT USING OUR POWERS!
MOREOVER, WHAT, EXACTLY, IS OUR OBJECTIVE?
OUR OBJECTIVE IS TO ASSIST ALETA IN ANY WAY POSSIBLE AGAINST MALEVOLENCE!
WE ALL HAVE A SCORE TO SETTLE WITH MALEVOLENCE!
AND WITH THAT TRAITOR, BRAHL!
THEN, I'D SAY WE'RE ALL AGREED--

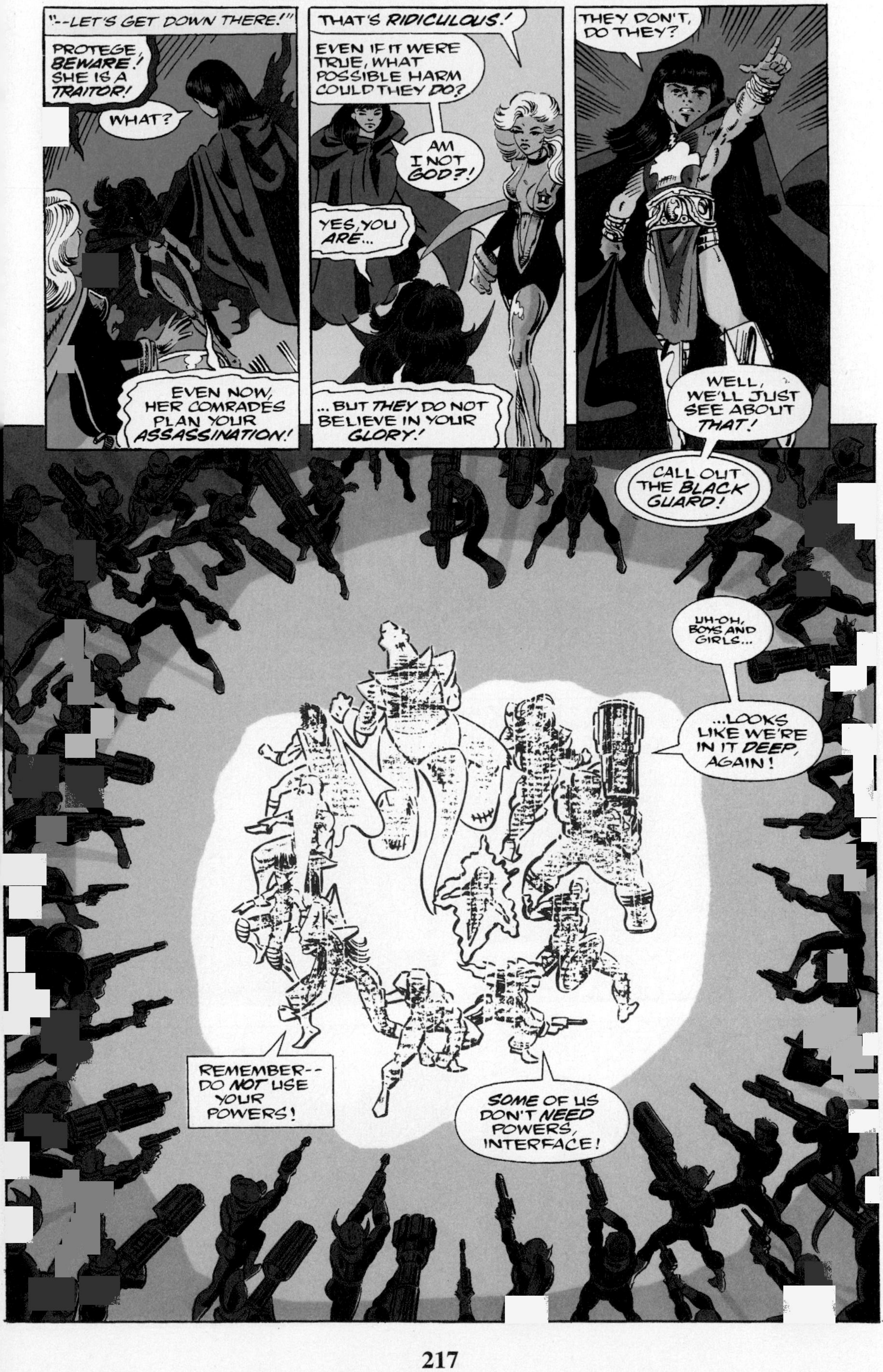
"--LET'S GET DOWN THERE!"
PROTEGE, BEWARE! SHE IS A TRAITOR!
WHAT?
EVEN NOW, HER COMRADES PLAN YOUR ASSASSINATION!
THAT'S RIDICULOUS!
EVEN IF IT WERE TRUE, WHAT POSSIBLE HARM COULD THEY DO?
AM I NOT GOD?!
YES, YOU ARE...
...BUT THEY DO NOT BELIEVE IN YOUR GLORY!
THEY DON'T, DO THEY?
WELL, WE'LL JUST SEE ABOUT THAT!
CALL OUT THE BLACK GUARD!
UH-OH, BOYS AND GIRLS...
...LOOKS LIKE WE'RE IN IT DEEP, AGAIN!
REMEMBER-- DO NOT USE YOUR POWERS!
SOME OF US DON'T NEED POWERS, INTERFACE!

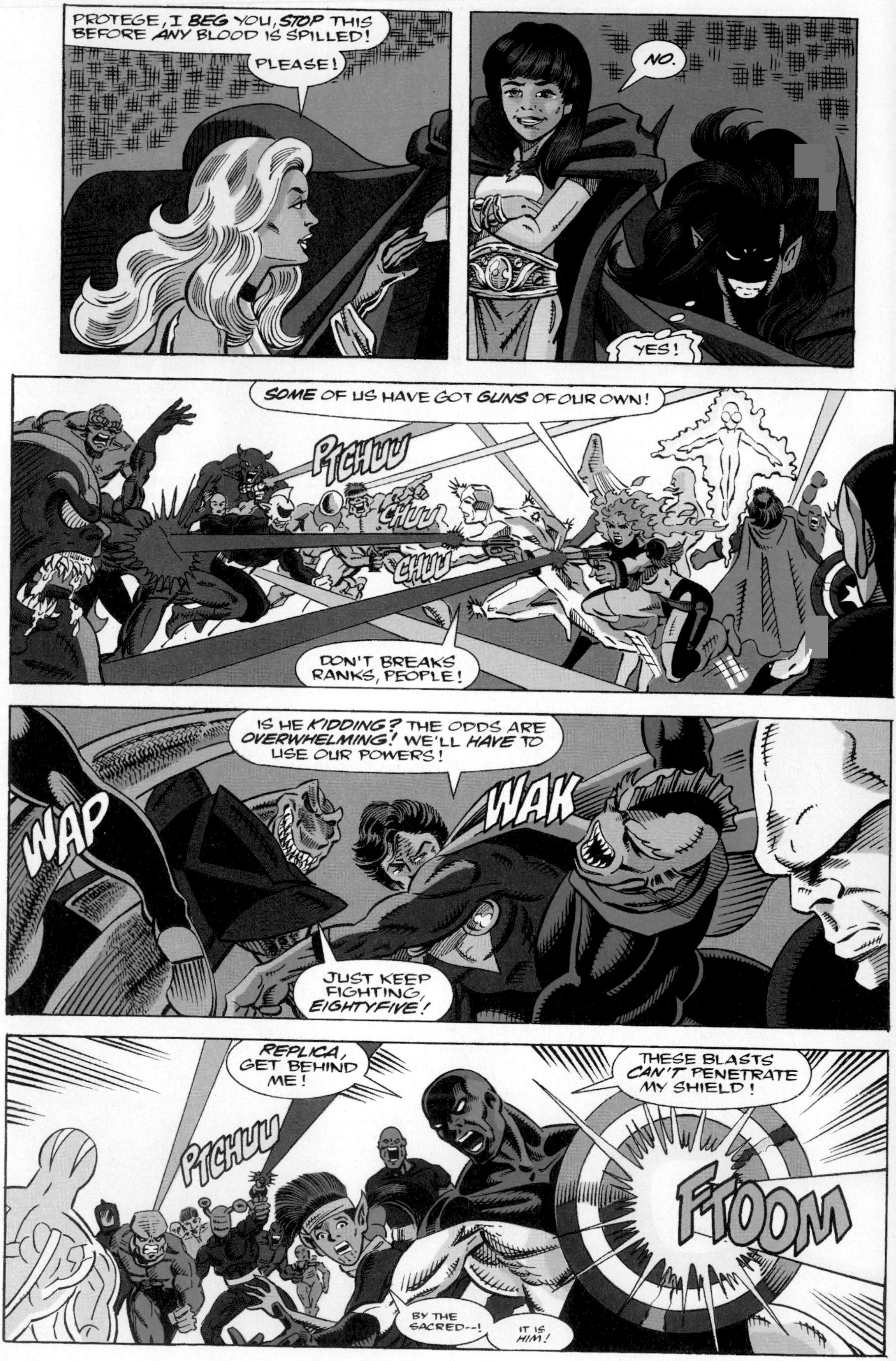
PROTEGE, I BEG YOU, STOP THIS BEFORE ANY BLOOD IS SPILLED!
PLEASE!
NO.
YES!
SOME OF US HAVE GOT GUNS OF OUR OWN!
PTCHUU
CHUU
CHUU
DON'T BREAKS RANKS, PEOPLE!
IS HE KIDDING? THE ODDS ARE OVERWHELMING! WE'LL HAVE TO USE OUR POWERS!
WAP
WAK
JUST KEEP FIGHTING, EIGHTYFIVE!
REPLICA, GET BEHIND ME!
THESE BLASTS CAN'T PENETRATE MY SHIELD!
PTCHUU
FTOOM
BY THE SACRED--!
IT IS HIM!

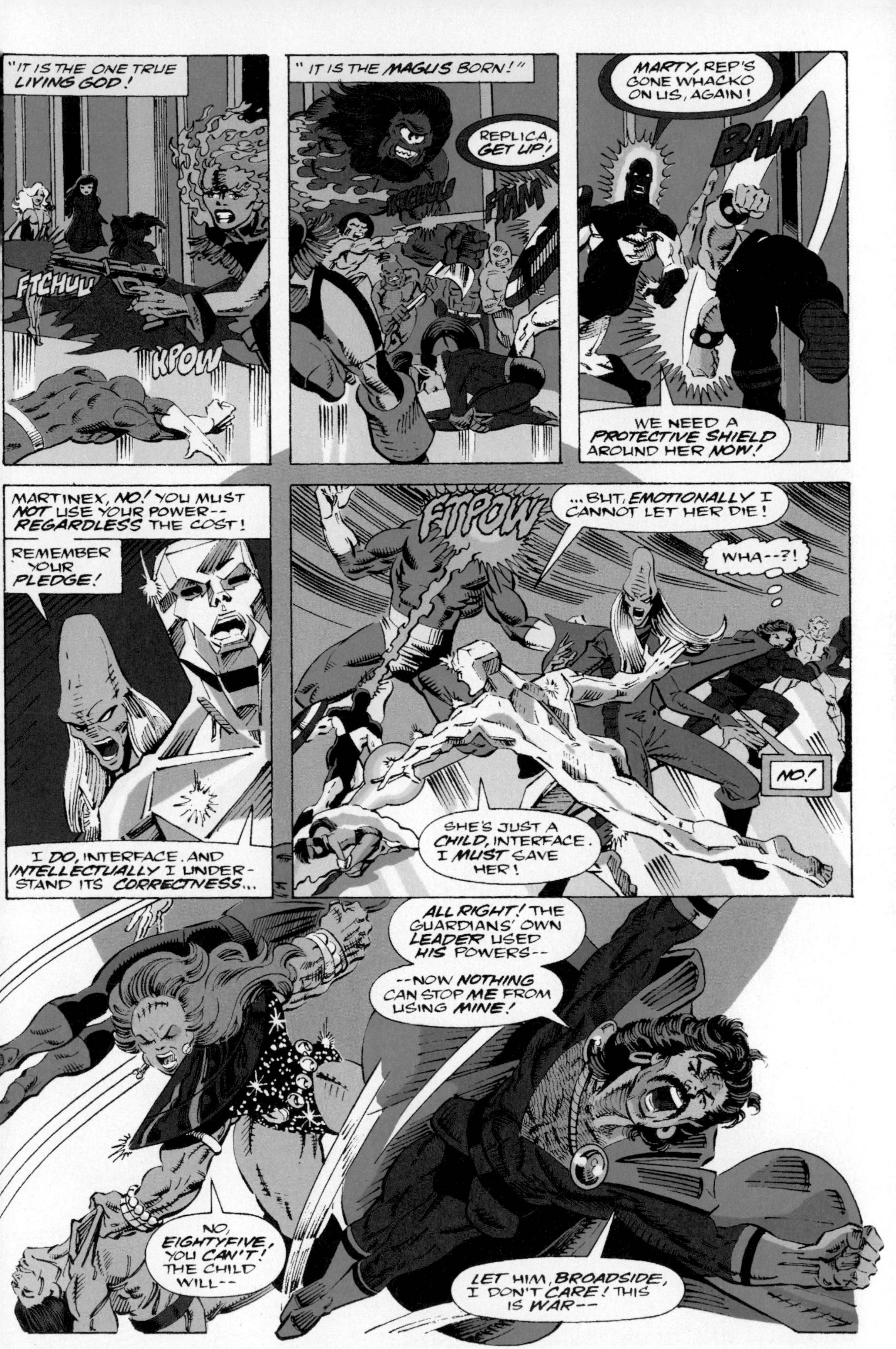
"IT IS THE ONE TRUE LIVING GOD!
FTCHUU
KPOW
"IT IS THE MAGUS BORN!"
REPLICA, GET UP!
FTCHUU
FTAM
MARTY, REP'S GONE WHACKO ON US, AGAIN!
BAM
WE NEED A PROTECTIVE SHIELD AROUND HER NOW!
MARTINEX, NO! YOU MUST NOT USE YOUR POWER-- REGARDLESS THE COST!
REMEMBER YOUR PLEDGE!
I DO, INTERFACE. AND INTELLECTUALLY I UNDER-STAND ITS CORRECTNESS...
FTPOW
...BUT, EMOTIONALLY I CANNOT LET HER DIE!
WHA--?!
NO!
SHE'S JUST A CHILD, INTERFACE. I MUST SAVE HER!
ALL RIGHT! THE GUARDIANS' OWN LEADER USED HIS POWERS--
--NOW NOTHING CAN STOP ME FROM USING MINE!
NO, EIGHTYFIVE, YOU CAN'T! THE CHILD WILL--
LET HIM, BROADSIDE, I DON'T CARE! THIS IS WAR--

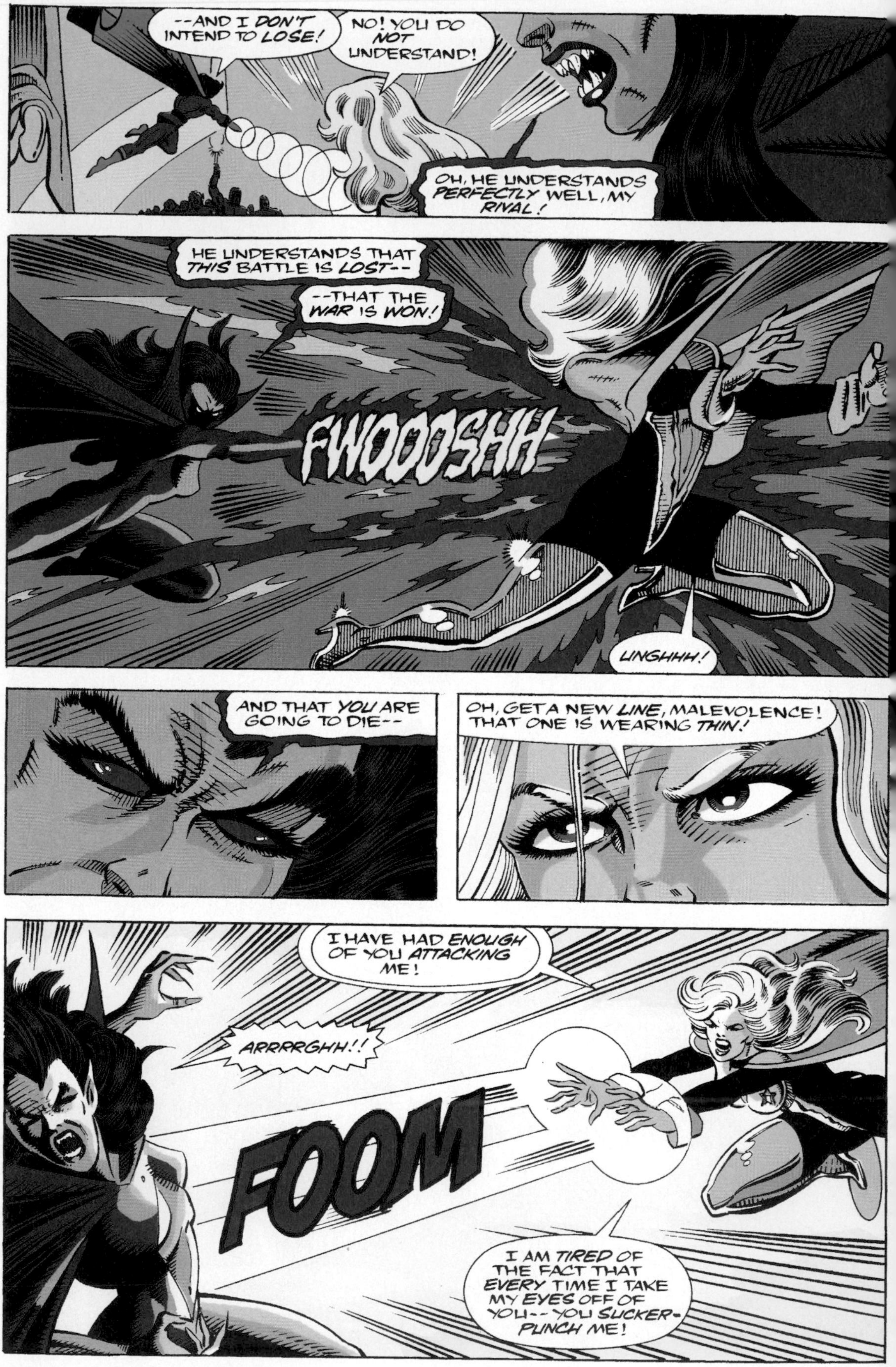
--AND I DON'T INTEND TO LOSE!
NO! YOU DO NOT UNDERSTAND!
OH, HE UNDERSTANDS PERFECTLY WELL, MY RIVAL!
HE UNDERSTANDS THAT THIS BATTLE IS LOST--
--THAT THE WAR IS WON!
FWOOOSHH
UNGHHH!
AND THAT YOU ARE GOING TO DIE--
OH, GET A NEW LINE, MALEVOLENCE! THAT ONE IS WEARING THIN!
I HAVE HAD ENOUGH OF YOU ATTACKING ME!
ARRRRGHH!!
FOOM
I AM TIRED OF THE FACT THAT EVERY TIME I TAKE MY EYES OFF OF YOU--YOU SUCKER-PUNCH ME!

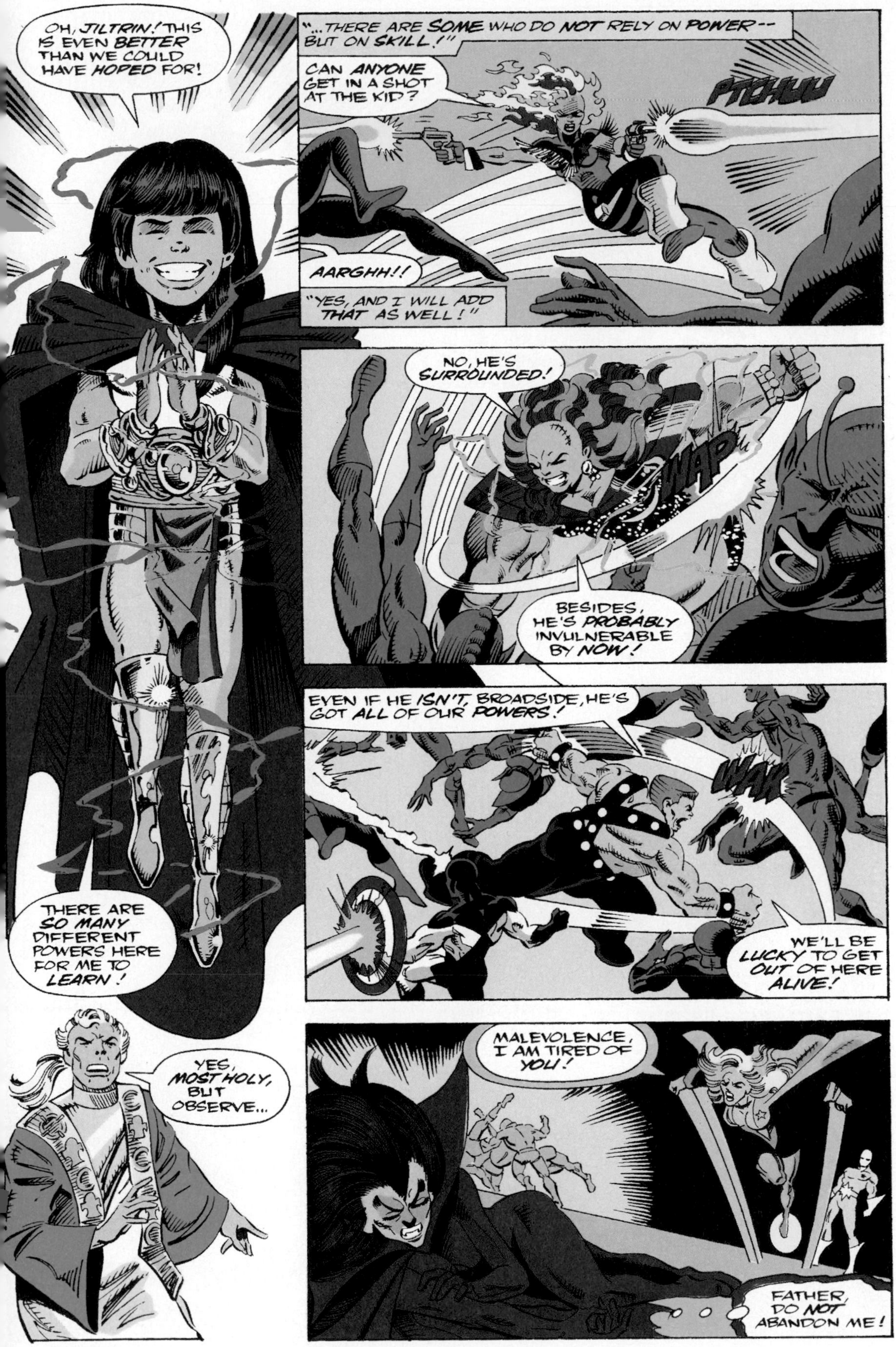
OH, JILTRIN! THIS IS EVEN BETTER THAN WE COULD HAVE HOPED FOR!
"...THERE ARE SOME WHO DO NOT RELY ON POWER-- BUT ON SKILL!"
CAN ANYONE GET IN A SHOT AT THE KID?
PTCHUU
AARGHH!!
"YES, AND I WILL ADD THAT AS WELL!"
NO, HE'S SURROUNDED!
WAP
BESIDES, HE'S PROBABLY INVULNERABLE BY NOW!
EVEN IF HE ISN'T, BROADSIDE, HE'S GOT ALL OF OUR POWERS!
WAK
WE'LL BE LUCKY TO GET OUT OF HERE ALIVE!
THERE ARE SO MANY DIFFERENT POWERS HERE FOR ME TO LEARN!
YES, MOST HOLY, BUT OBSERVE...
MALEVOLENCE, I AM TIRED OF YOU!
FATHER, DO NOT ABANDON ME!

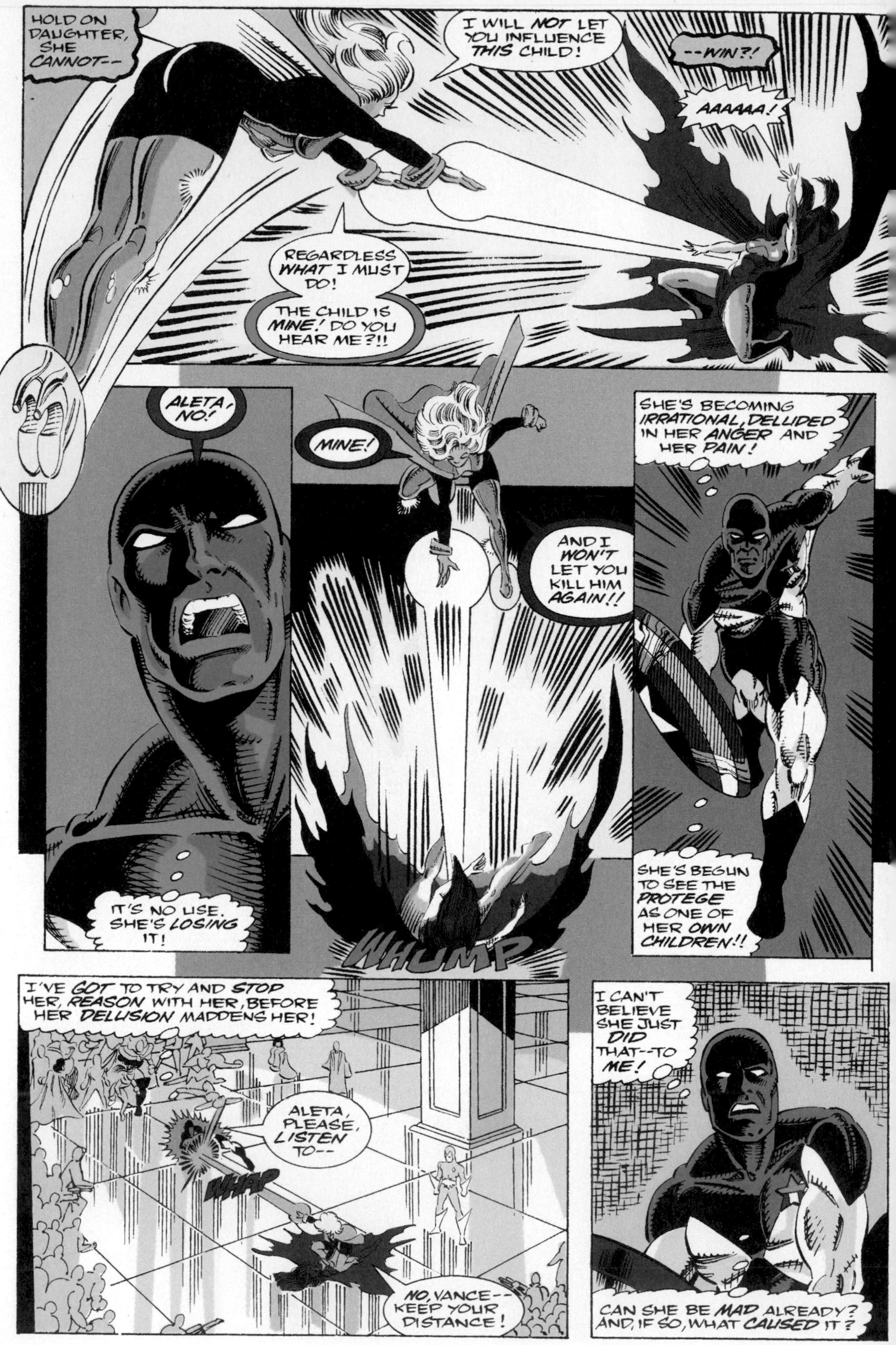
HOLD ON DAUGHTER, SHE CANNOT--
I WILL NOT LET YOU INFLUENCE THIS CHILD!
--WIN?!
AAAAAA!
REGARDLESS WHAT I MUST DO!
THE CHILD IS MINE! DO YOU HEAR ME?!!
ALETA, NO!
IT'S NO USE. SHE'S LOSING IT!
MINE!
AND I WON'T LET YOU KILL HIM AGAIN!!
WHUMP
SHE'S BECOMING IRRATIONAL, DELLUDED IN HER ANGER AND HER PAIN!
SHE'S BEGUN TO SEE THE PROTEGE AS ONE OF HER OWN CHILDREN!!
I'VE GOT TO TRY AND STOP HER, REASON WITH HER, BEFORE HER DELUSION MADDENS HER!
ALETA, PLEASE, LISTEN TO--
WHAP
NO, VANCE--KEEP YOUR DISTANCE!
I CAN'T BELIEVE SHE JUST DID THAT--TO ME!
CAN SHE BE MAD ALREADY? AND, IF SO, WHAT CAUSED IT?

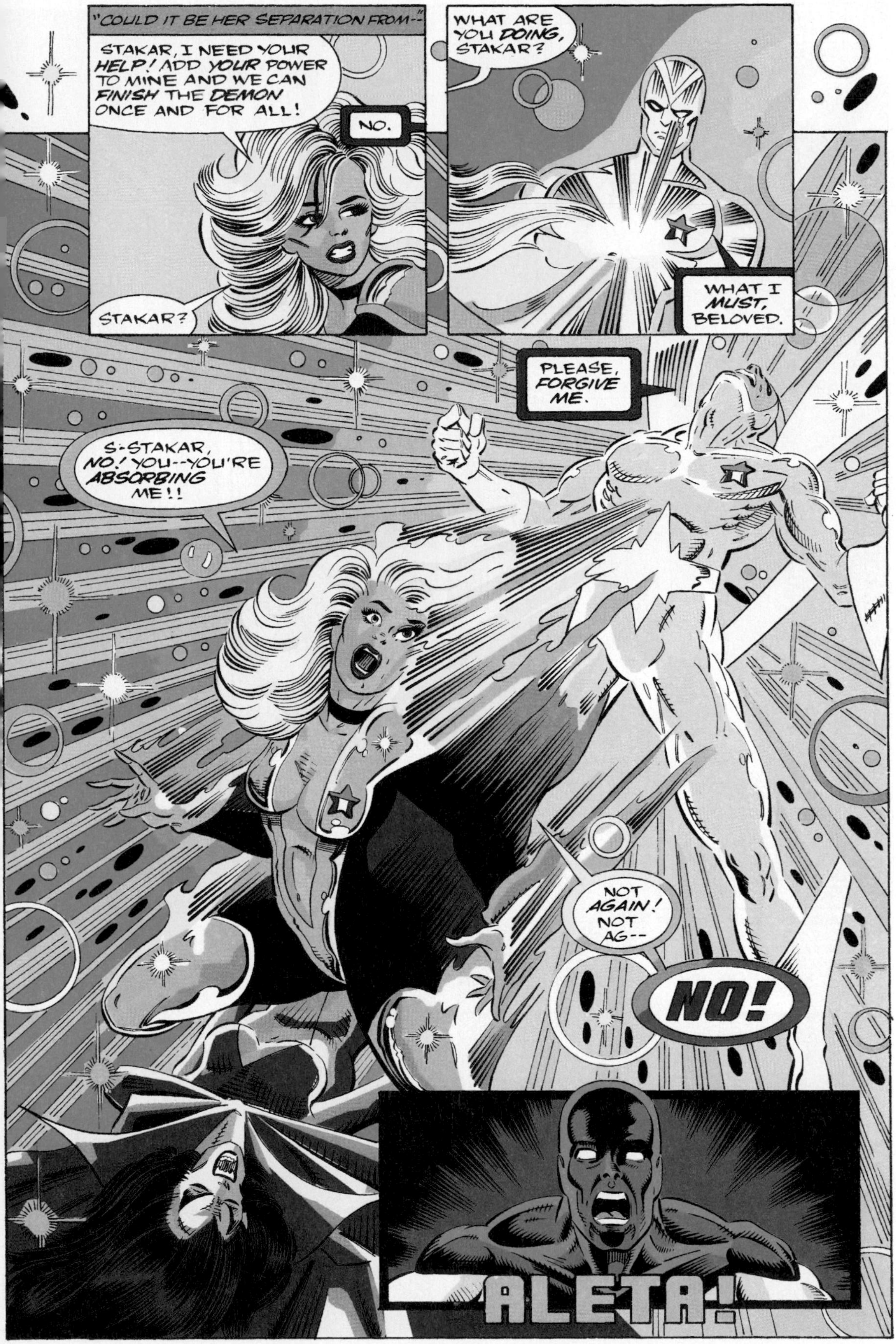
"COULD IT BE HER SEPARATION FROM--"
STAKAR, I NEED YOUR HELP! ADD YOUR POWER TO MINE AND WE CAN FINISH THE DEMON ONCE AND FOR ALL!
NO.
STAKAR?
WHAT ARE YOU DOING, STAKAR?
WHAT I MUST, BELOVED.
PLEASE, FORGIVE ME.
S-STAKAR, NO! YOU--YOU'RE ABSORBING ME!!
NOT AGAIN! NOT AG--
NO!
ALETA!

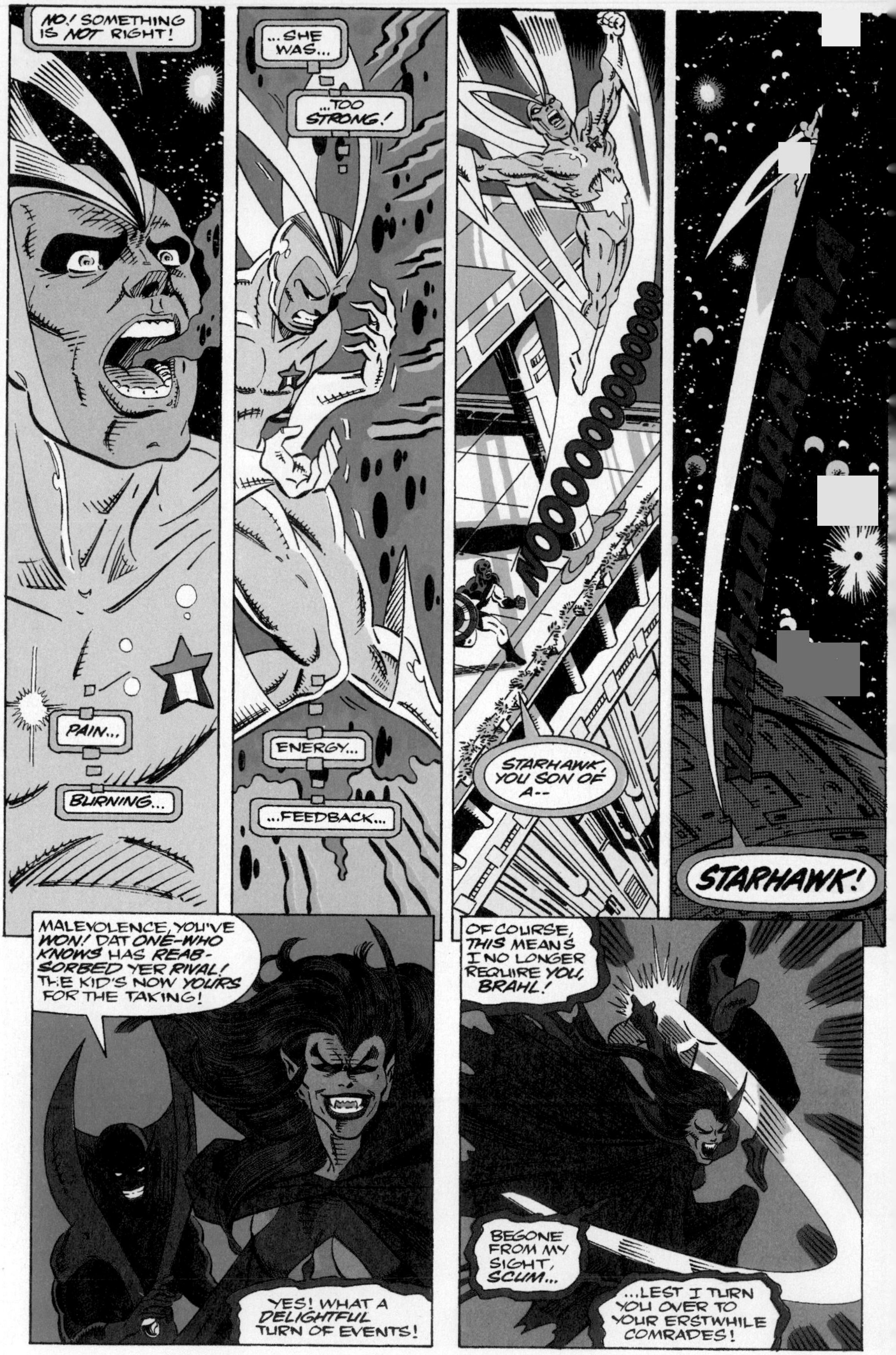
NO! SOMETHING IS NOT RIGHT!
PAIN...
BURNING...
...SHE WAS...
...TOO STRONG!
ENERGY...
...FEEDBACK...
STARHAWK, YOU SON OF A--
STARHAWK!
MALEVOLENCE, YOU'VE WON! DAT ONE-WHO KNOWS HAS REAB-SORBED YER RIVAL! THE KID'S NOW YOURS FOR THE TAKING!
YES! WHAT A DELIGHTFUL TURN OF EVENTS!
OF COURSE, THIS MEANS I NO LONGER REQUIRE YOU, BRAHL!
BEGONE FROM MY SIGHT, SCUM...
...LEST I TURN YOU OVER TO YOUR ERSTWHILE COMRADES!

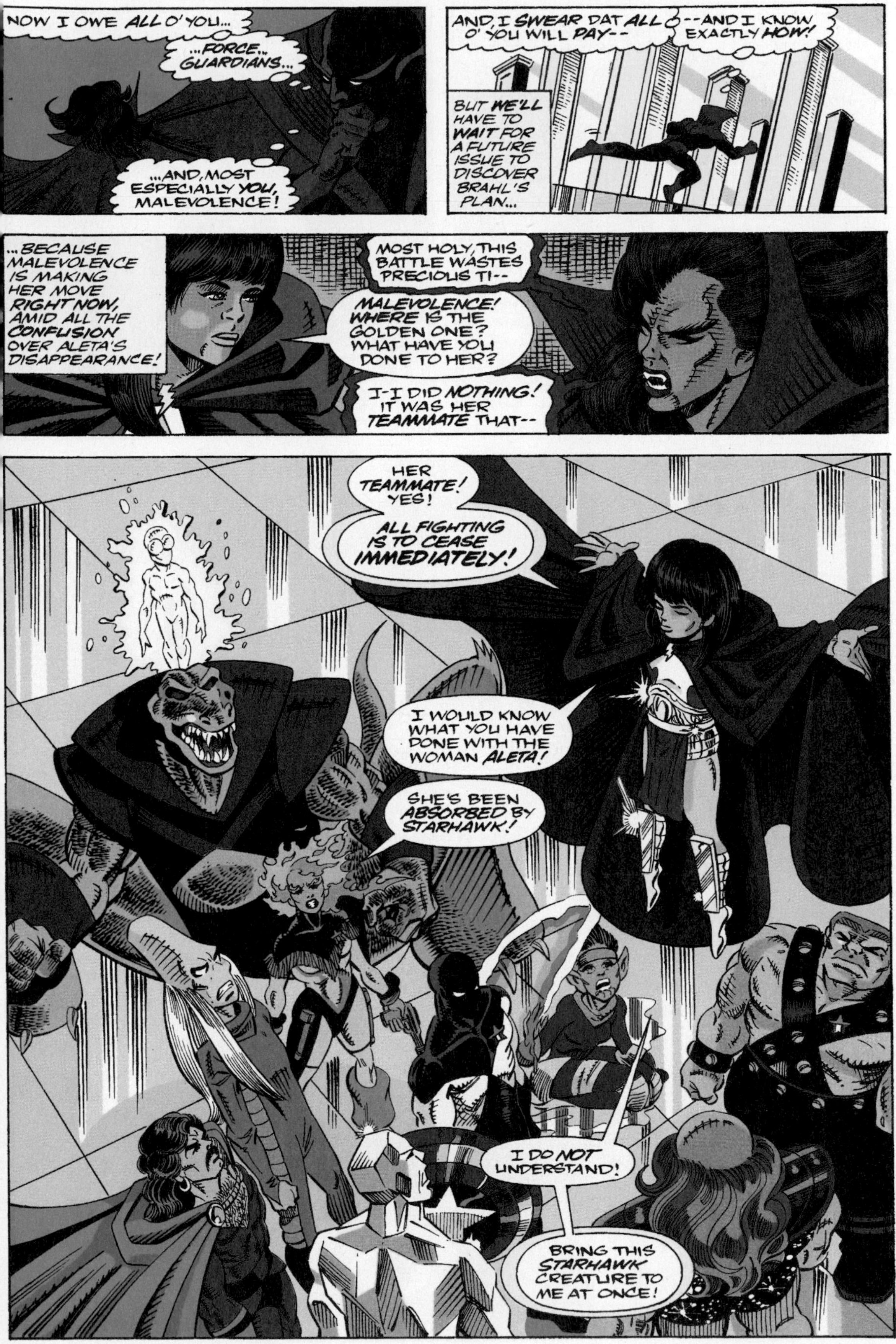

NOW I OWE ALL O' YOU...
...FORCE.. GUARDIANS...
...AND, MOST ESPECIALLY YOU, MALEVOLENCE!
AND, I SWEAR DAT ALL O' YOU WILL PAY--
--AND I KNOW EXACTLY HOW!
BUT WE'LL HAVE TO WAIT FOR A FUTURE ISSUE TO DISCOVER BRAHL'S PLAN...
...BECAUSE MALEVOLENCE IS MAKING HER MOVE RIGHT NOW, AMID ALL THE CONFUSION OVER ALETA'S DISAPPEARANCE!
MOST HOLY, THIS BATTLE WASTES PRECIOUS TI--
MALEVOLENCE! WHERE IS THE GOLDEN ONE? WHAT HAVE YOU DONE TO HER?
I-I DID NOTHING! IT WAS HER TEAMMATE THAT--
HER TEAMMATE! YES!
ALL FIGHTING IS TO CEASE IMMEDIATELY!
I WOULD KNOW WHAT YOU HAVE DONE WITH THE WOMAN ALETA!
SHE'S BEEN ABSORBED BY STARHAWK!
I DO NOT UNDERSTAND!
BRING THIS STARHAWK CREATURE TO ME AT ONCE!

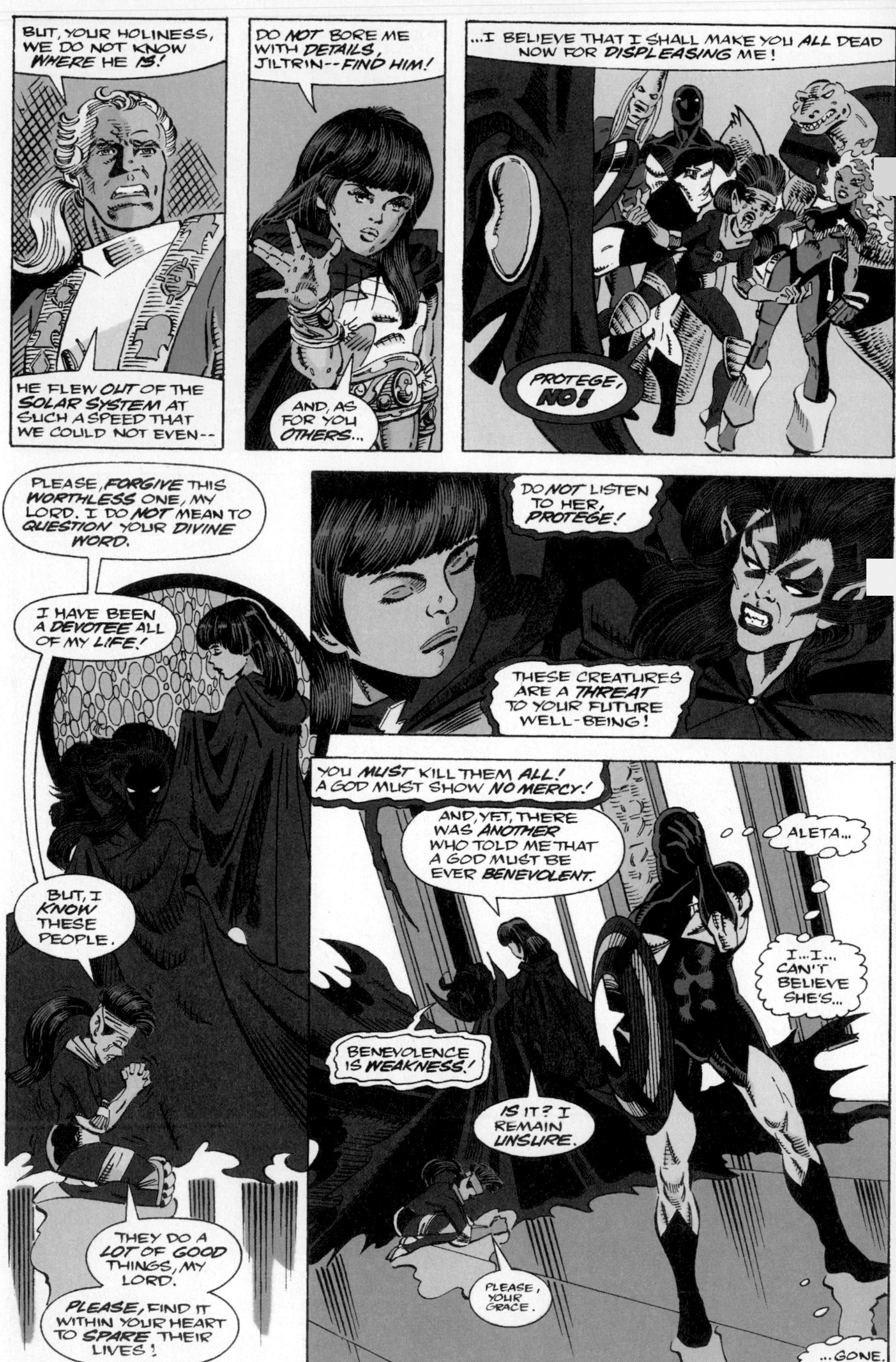
BUT, YOUR HOLINESS, WE DO NOT KNOW WHERE HE IS!
HE FLEW OUT OF THE SOLAR SYSTEM AT SUCH A SPEED THAT WE COULD NOT EVEN--
DO NOT BORE ME WITH DETAILS, JILTRIN--FIND HIM!
AND, AS FOR YOU OTHERS...
...I BELIEVE THAT I SHALL MAKE YOU ALL DEAD NOW FOR DISPLEASING ME!
PROTEGE, NO!
PLEASE, FORGIVE THIS WORTHLESS ONE, MY LORD. I DO NOT MEAN TO QUESTION YOUR DIVINE WORD.
I HAVE BEEN A DEVOTEE ALL OF MY LIFE!
BUT, I KNOW THESE PEOPLE.
THEY DO A LOT OF GOOD THINGS, MY LORD.
PLEASE, FIND IT WITHIN YOUR HEART TO SPARE THEIR LIVES!
DO NOT LISTEN TO HER, PROTEGE!
THESE CREATURES ARE A THREAT TO YOUR FUTURE WELL-BEING!
YOU MUST KILL THEM ALL! A GOD MUST SHOW NO MERCY!
AND, YET, THERE WAS ANOTHER WHO TOLD ME THAT A GOD MUST BE EVER BENEVOLENT.
ALETA...
BENEVOLENCE IS WEAKNESS!
IS IT? I REMAIN UNSURE.
I...I... CAN'T BELIEVE SHE'S...
PLEASE, YOUR GRACE.
...GONE.

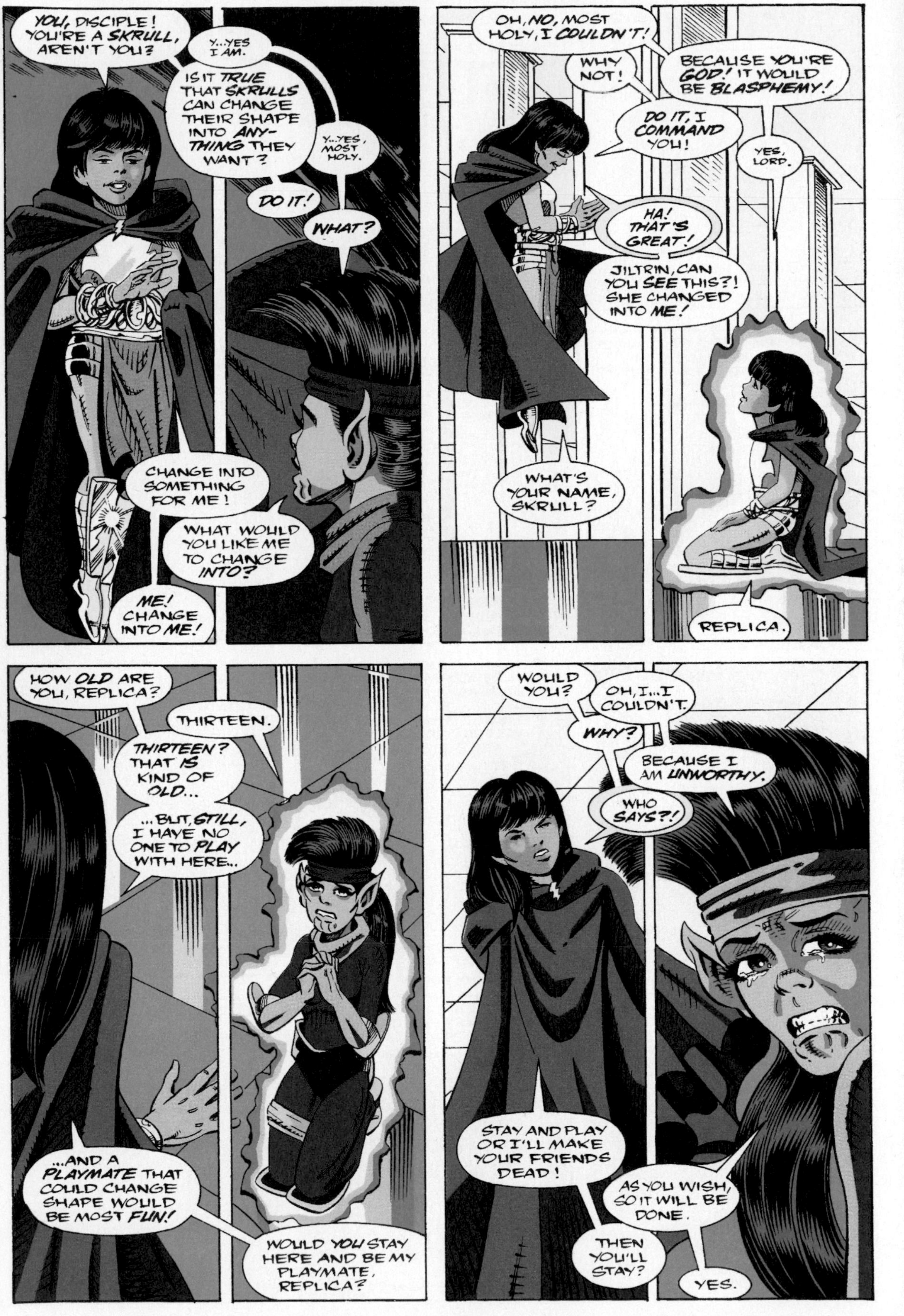
YOU, DISCIPLE! YOU'RE A SKRULL, AREN'T YOU?
Y...YES I AM.
IS IT TRUE THAT SKRULLS CAN CHANGE THEIR SHAPE INTO ANY-THING THEY WANT?
Y...YES, MOST HOLY.
DO IT!
WHAT?
CHANGE INTO SOMETHING FOR ME!
WHAT WOULD YOU LIKE ME TO CHANGE INTO?
ME! CHANGE INTO ME!
OH, NO, MOST HOLY, I COULDN'T!
WHY NOT!
BECAUSE YOU'RE GOD! IT WOULD BE BLASPHEMY!
DO IT, I COMMAND YOU!
YES, LORD.
HA! THAT'S GREAT!
JILTRIN, CAN YOU SEE THIS?! SHE CHANGED INTO ME!
WHAT'S YOUR NAME, SKRULL?
REPLICA.
HOW OLD ARE YOU, REPLICA?
THIRTEEN.
THIRTEEN? THAT IS KIND OF OLD...
...BUT, STILL, I HAVE NO ONE TO PLAY WITH HERE...
...AND A PLAYMATE THAT COULD CHANGE SHAPE WOULD BE MOST FUN!
WOULD YOU STAY HERE AND BE MY PLAYMATE, REPLICA?
WOULD YOU?
OH, I...I COULDN'T.
WHY?
BECAUSE I AM UNWORTHY.
WHO SAYS?!
STAY AND PLAY OR I'LL MAKE YOUR FRIENDS DEAD!
AS YOU WISH, SO IT WILL BE DONE.
THEN YOU'LL STAY?
YES.

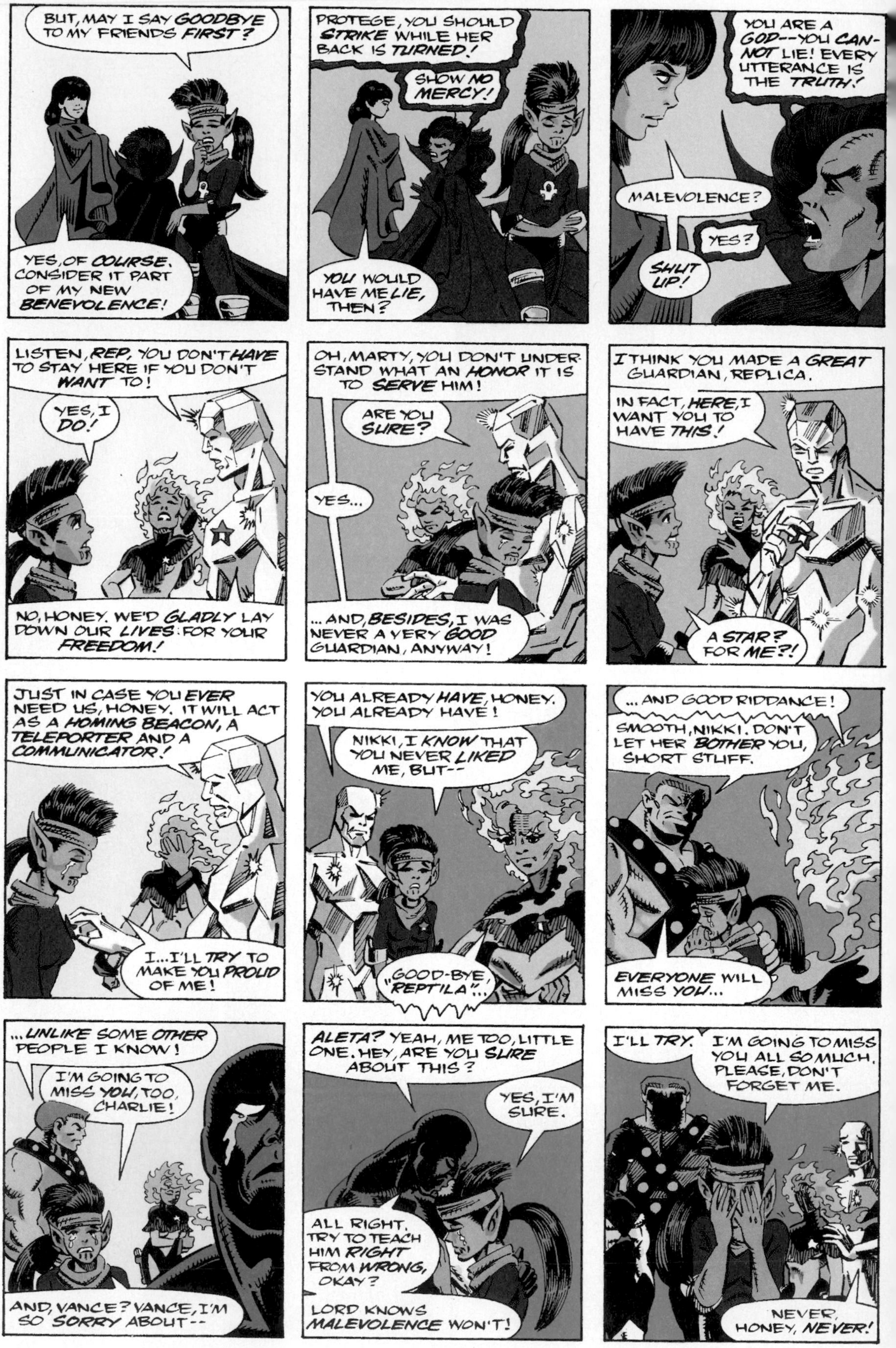
BUT, MAY I SAY GOODBYE TO MY FRIENDS FIRST?
YES, OF COURSE. CONSIDER IT PART OF MY NEW BENEVOLENCE!
PROTEGE, YOU SHOULD STRIKE WHILE HER BACK IS TURNED!
SHOW NO MERCY!
YOU WOULD HAVE ME LIE, THEN?
YOU ARE A GOD--YOU CAN-NOT LIE! EVERY UTTERANCE IS THE TRUTH!
MALEVOLENCE?
YES?
SHUT UP!
LISTEN, REP, YOU DON'T HAVE TO STAY HERE IF YOU DON'T WANT TO!
YES, I DO!
NO, HONEY. WE'D GLADLY LAY DOWN OUR LIVES FOR YOUR FREEDOM!
OH, MARTY, YOU DON'T UNDER-STAND WHAT AN HONOR IT IS TO SERVE HIM!
ARE YOU SURE?
YES...
...AND, BESIDES, I WAS NEVER A VERY GOOD GUARDIAN, ANYWAY!
I THINK YOU MADE A GREAT GUARDIAN, REPLICA.
IN FACT, HERE, I WANT YOU TO HAVE THIS!
A STAR? FOR ME?!
JUST IN CASE YOU EVER NEED US, HONEY. IT WILL ACT AS A HOMING BEACON, A TELEPORTER AND A COMMUNICATOR!
I...I'LL TRY TO MAKE YOU PROUD OF ME!
YOU ALREADY HAVE, HONEY. YOU ALREADY HAVE!
NIKKI, I KNOW THAT YOU NEVER LIKED ME, BUT--
"GOOD-BYE, "REPTILA"...
...AND GOOD RIDDANCE!
SMOOTH, NIKKI. DON'T LET HER BOTHER YOU, SHORT STUFF.
EVERYONE WILL MISS YOU...
...UNLIKE SOME OTHER PEOPLE I KNOW!
I'M GOING TO MISS YOU, TOO, CHARLIE!
AND, VANCE? VANCE, I'M SO SORRY ABOUT--
ALETA? YEAH, ME TOO, LITTLE ONE. HEY, ARE YOU SURE ABOUT THIS?
YES, I'M SURE.
ALL RIGHT. TRY TO TEACH HIM RIGHT FROM WRONG, OKAY?
LORD KNOWS MALEVOLENCE WON'T!
I'LL TRY.
I'M GOING TO MISS YOU ALL SO MUCH. PLEASE, DON'T FORGET ME.
NEVER, HONEY, NEVER!

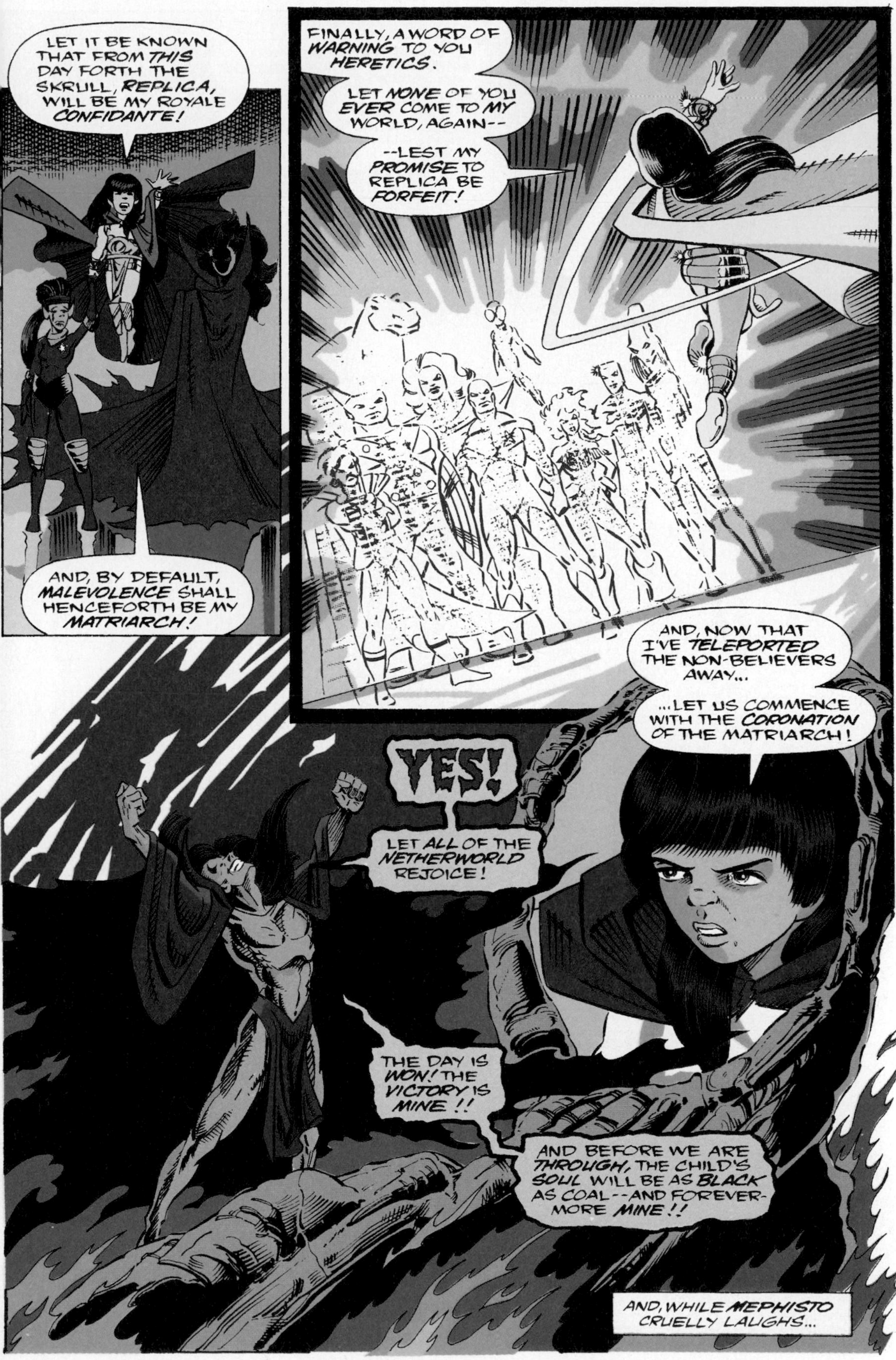
LET IT BE KNOWN THAT FROM THIS DAY FORTH THE SKRULL, REPLICA, WILL BE MY ROYALE CONFIDANTE!
AND, BY DEFAULT, MALEVOLENCE SHALL HENCEFORTH BE MY MATRIARCH!
FINALLY, A WORD OF WARNING TO YOU HERETICS.
LET NONE OF YOU EVER COME TO MY WORLD, AGAIN--
--LEST MY PROMISE TO REPLICA BE FORFEIT!
AND, NOW THAT I'VE TELEPORTED THE NON-BELIEVERS AWAY...
...LET US COMMENCE WITH THE CORONATION OF THE MATRIARCH!
YES!
LET ALL OF THE NETHERWORLD REJOICE!
THE DAY IS WON! THE VICTORY IS MINE!!
AND BEFORE WE ARE THROUGH, THE CHILD'S SOUL WILL BE AS BLACK AS COAL--AND FOREVER-MORE MINE!!
AND, WHILE MEPHISTO CRUELLY LAUGHS...

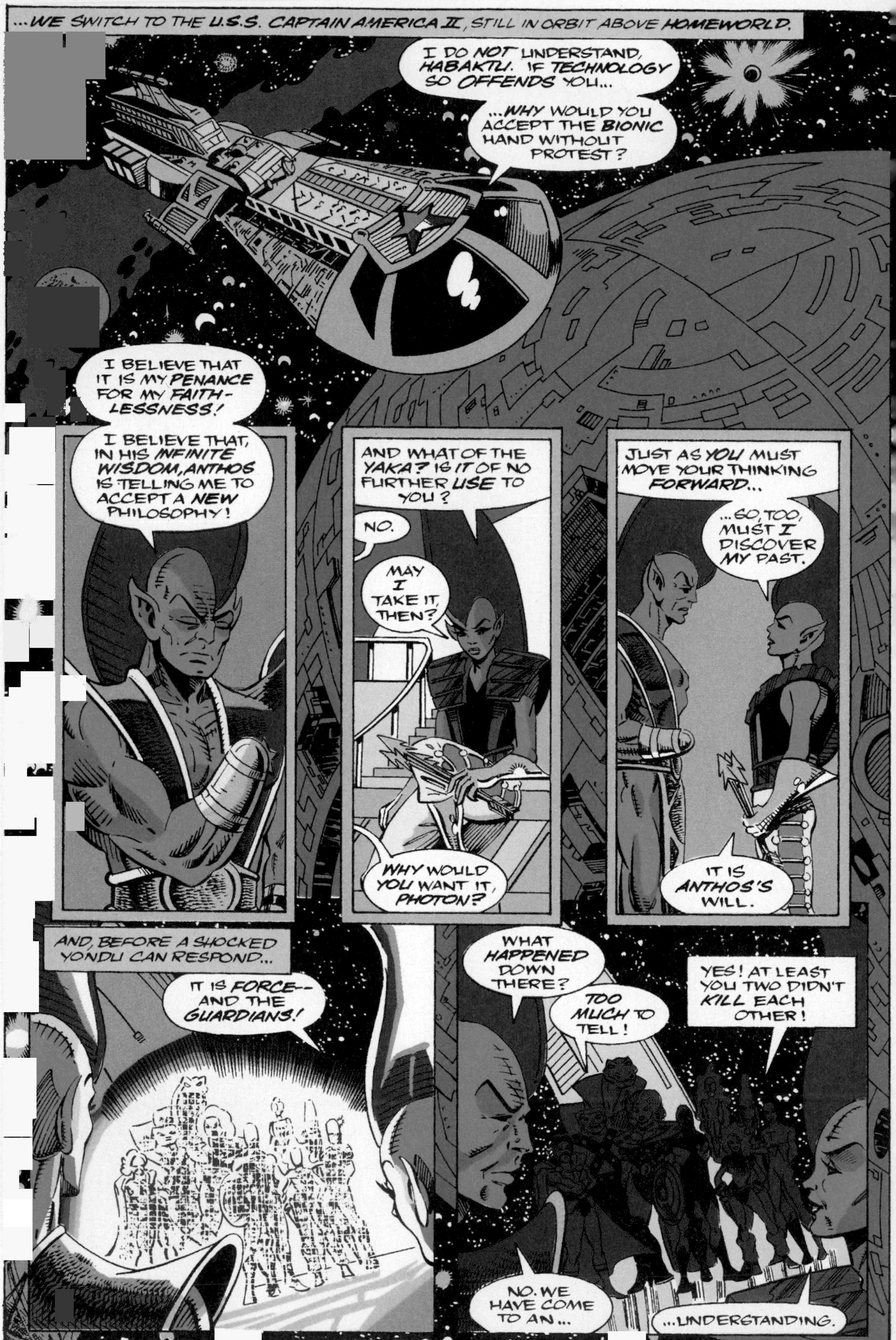
...WE SWITCH TO THE U.S.S. CAPTAIN AMERICA II, STILL IN ORBIT ABOVE HOMEWORLD.
I DO NOT UNDERSTAND, HABAKTU. IF TECHNOLOGY SO OFFENDS YOU...
...WHY WOULD YOU ACCEPT THE BIONIC HAND WITHOUT PROTEST?
I BELIEVE THAT IT IS MY PENANCE FOR MY FAITH-LESSNESS!
I BELIEVE THAT, IN HIS INFINITE WISDOM, ANTHOS IS TELLING ME TO ACCEPT A NEW PHILOSOPHY!
AND WHAT OF THE YAKA? IS IT OF NO FURTHER USE TO YOU?
NO.
MAY I TAKE IT, THEN?
WHY WOULD YOU WANT IT, PHOTON?
JUST AS YOU MUST MOVE YOUR THINKING FORWARD...
...SO, TOO, MUST I DISCOVER MY PAST.
IT IS ANTHOS'S WILL.
AND, BEFORE A SHOCKED YONDU CAN RESPOND...
IT IS FORCE-- AND THE GUARDIANS!
WHAT HAPPENED DOWN THERE?
TOO MUCH TO TELL!
YES! AT LEAST YOU TWO DIDN'T KILL EACH OTHER!
NO. WE HAVE COME TO AN...
...UNDERSTANDING.

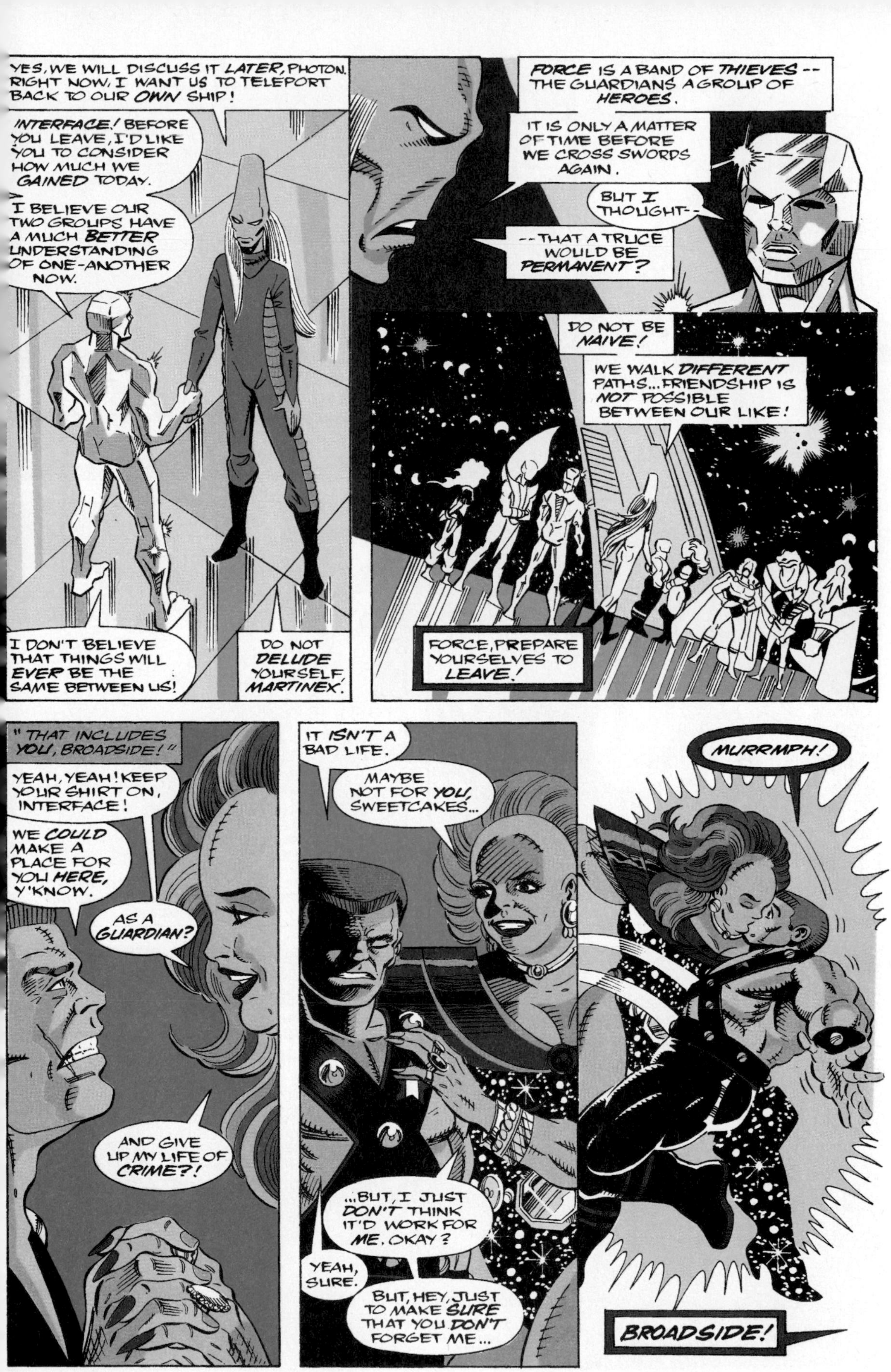

YES, WE WILL DISCUSS IT LATER, PHOTON. RIGHT NOW, I WANT US TO TELEPORT BACK TO OUR OWN SHIP!
INTERFACE! BEFORE YOU LEAVE, I'D LIKE YOU TO CONSIDER HOW MUCH WE GAINED TODAY.
I BELIEVE OUR TWO GROUPS HAVE A MUCH BETTER UNDERSTANDING OF ONE-ANOTHER NOW.
I DON'T BELIEVE THAT THINGS WILL EVER BE THE SAME BETWEEN US!
DO NOT DELUDE YOURSELF, MARTINEX.
FORCE IS A BAND OF THIEVES -- THE GUARDIANS A GROUP OF HEROES.
IT IS ONLY A MATTER OF TIME BEFORE WE CROSS SWORDS AGAIN.
BUT I THOUGHT--
--THAT A TRUCE WOULD BE PERMANENT?
DO NOT BE NAIVE!
WE WALK DIFFERENT PATHS... FRIENDSHIP IS NOT POSSIBLE BETWEEN OUR LIKE!
FORCE, PREPARE YOURSELVES TO LEAVE!
"THAT INCLUDES YOU, BROADSIDE!"
YEAH, YEAH! KEEP YOUR SHIRT ON, INTERFACE!
WE COULD MAKE A PLACE FOR YOU HERE, Y'KNOW.
AS A GUARDIAN?
AND GIVE UP MY LIFE OF CRIME?!
IT ISN'T A BAD LIFE.
MAYBE NOT FOR YOU, SWEETCAKES...
...BUT, I JUST DON'T THINK IT'D WORK FOR ME. OKAY?
YEAH, SURE.
BUT, HEY, JUST TO MAKE SURE THAT YOU DON'T FORGET ME...
MURRMPH!
BROADSIDE!

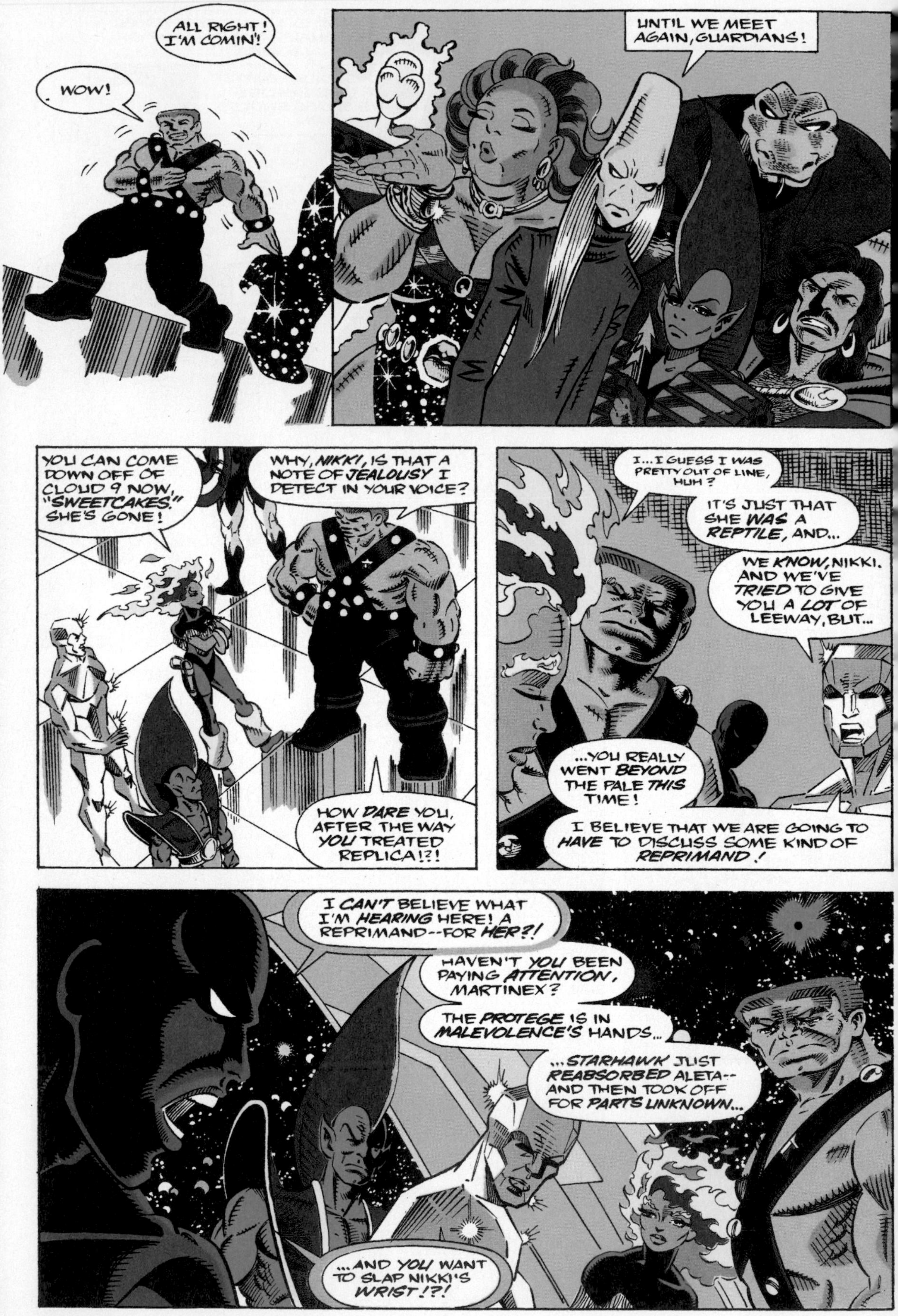
ALL RIGHT! I'M COMIN'!
WOW!
UNTIL WE MEET AGAIN, GUARDIANS!
YOU CAN COME DOWN OFF OF CLOUD 9 NOW, "SWEETCAKES." SHE'S GONE!
WHY, NIKKI, IS THAT A NOTE OF JEALOUSY I DETECT IN YOUR VOICE?
HOW DARE YOU, AFTER THE WAY YOU TREATED REPLICA!?!
I... I GUESS I WAS PRETTY OUT OF LINE, HUH?
IT'S JUST THAT SHE WAS A REPTILE, AND...
WE KNOW, NIKKI. AND WE'VE TRIED TO GIVE YOU A LOT OF LEEWAY, BUT...
...YOU REALLY WENT BEYOND THE PALE THIS TIME!
I BELIEVE THAT WE ARE GOING TO HAVE TO DISCUSS SOME KIND OF REPRIMAND!
I CAN'T BELIEVE WHAT I'M HEARING HERE! A REPRIMAND--FOR HER?!
HAVEN'T YOU BEEN PAYING ATTENTION, MARTINEX?
THE PROTEGE IS IN MALEVOLENCE'S HANDS...
...STARHAWK JUST REABSORBED ALETA-- AND THEN TOOK OFF FOR PARTS UNKNOWN...
...AND YOU WANT TO SLAP NIKKI'S WRIST!?!

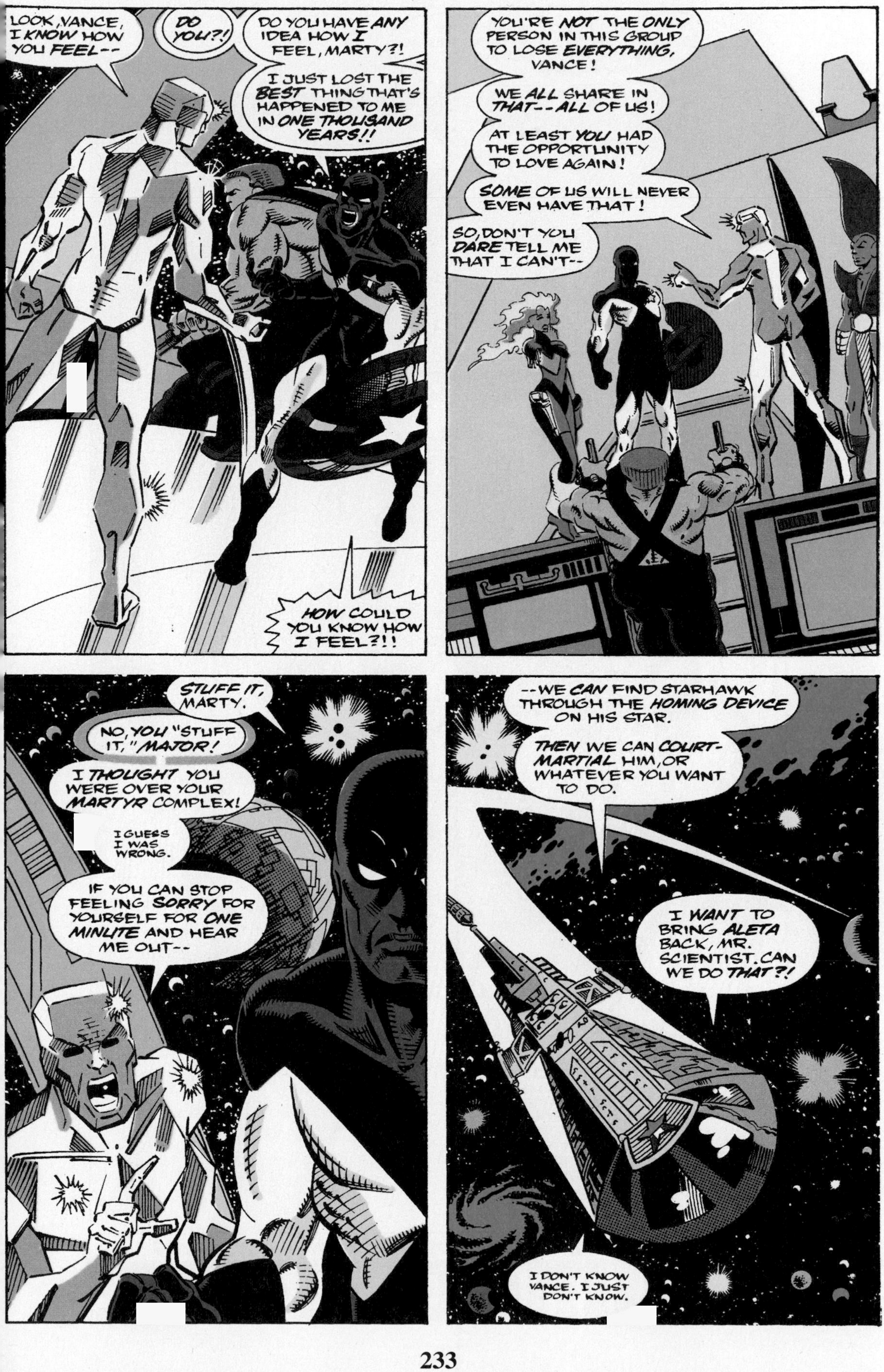

LOOK, VANCE, I KNOW HOW YOU FEEL--
DO YOU?!
DO YOU HAVE ANY IDEA HOW I FEEL, MARTY?!
I JUST LOST THE BEST THING THAT'S HAPPENED TO ME IN ONE THOUSAND YEARS!!
HOW COULD YOU KNOW HOW I FEEL?!!
YOU'RE NOT THE ONLY PERSON IN THIS GROUP TO LOSE EVERYTHING, VANCE!
WE ALL SHARE IN THAT--ALL OF US!
AT LEAST YOU HAD THE OPPORTUNITY TO LOVE AGAIN!
SOME OF US WILL NEVER EVEN HAVE THAT!
SO, DON'T YOU DARE TELL ME THAT I CAN'T--
STUFF IT, MARTY.
NO, YOU "STUFF IT," MAJOR!
I THOUGHT YOU WERE OVER YOUR MARTYR COMPLEX!
I GUESS I WAS WRONG.
IF YOU CAN STOP FEELING SORRY FOR YOURSELF FOR ONE MINUTE AND HEAR ME OUT--
--WE CAN FIND STARHAWK THROUGH THE HOMING DEVICE ON HIS STAR.
THEN WE CAN COURT-MARTIAL HIM, OR WHATEVER YOU WANT TO DO.
I WANT TO BRING ALETA BACK, MR. SCIENTIST. CAN WE DO THAT?!
I DON'T KNOW VANCE. I JUST DON'T KNOW.

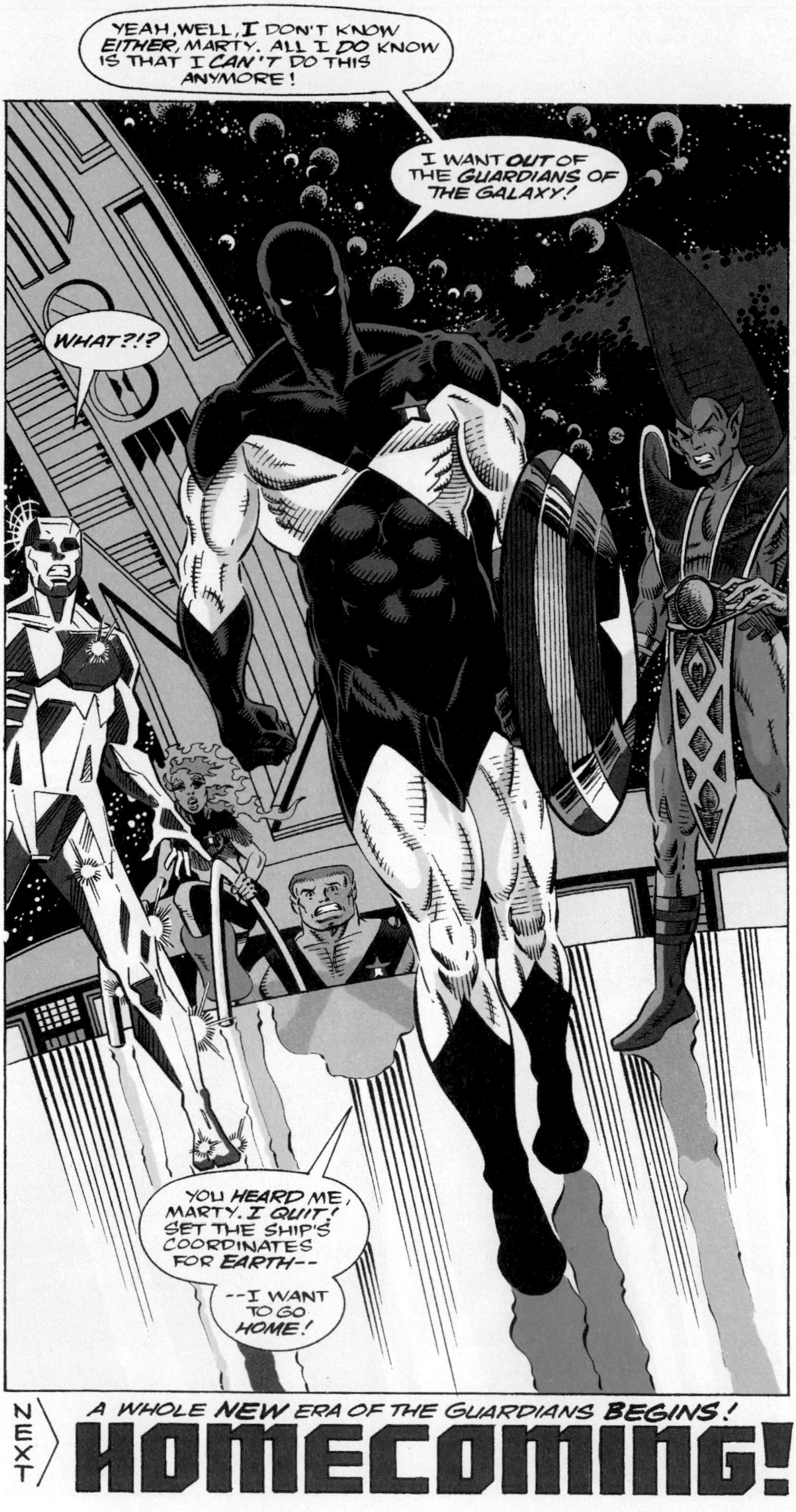
YEAH, WELL, I DON'T KNOW EITHER, MARTY. ALL I DO KNOW IS THAT I CAN'T DO THIS ANYMORE!
I WANT OUT OF THE GUARDIANS OF THE GALAXY!
WHAT?!?
YOU HEARD ME, MARTY. I QUIT! SET THE SHIP'S COORDINATES FOR EARTH--
--I WANT TO GO HOME!
NEXT
A WHOLE NEW ERA OF THE GUARDIANS BEGINS!
HOMECOMING!

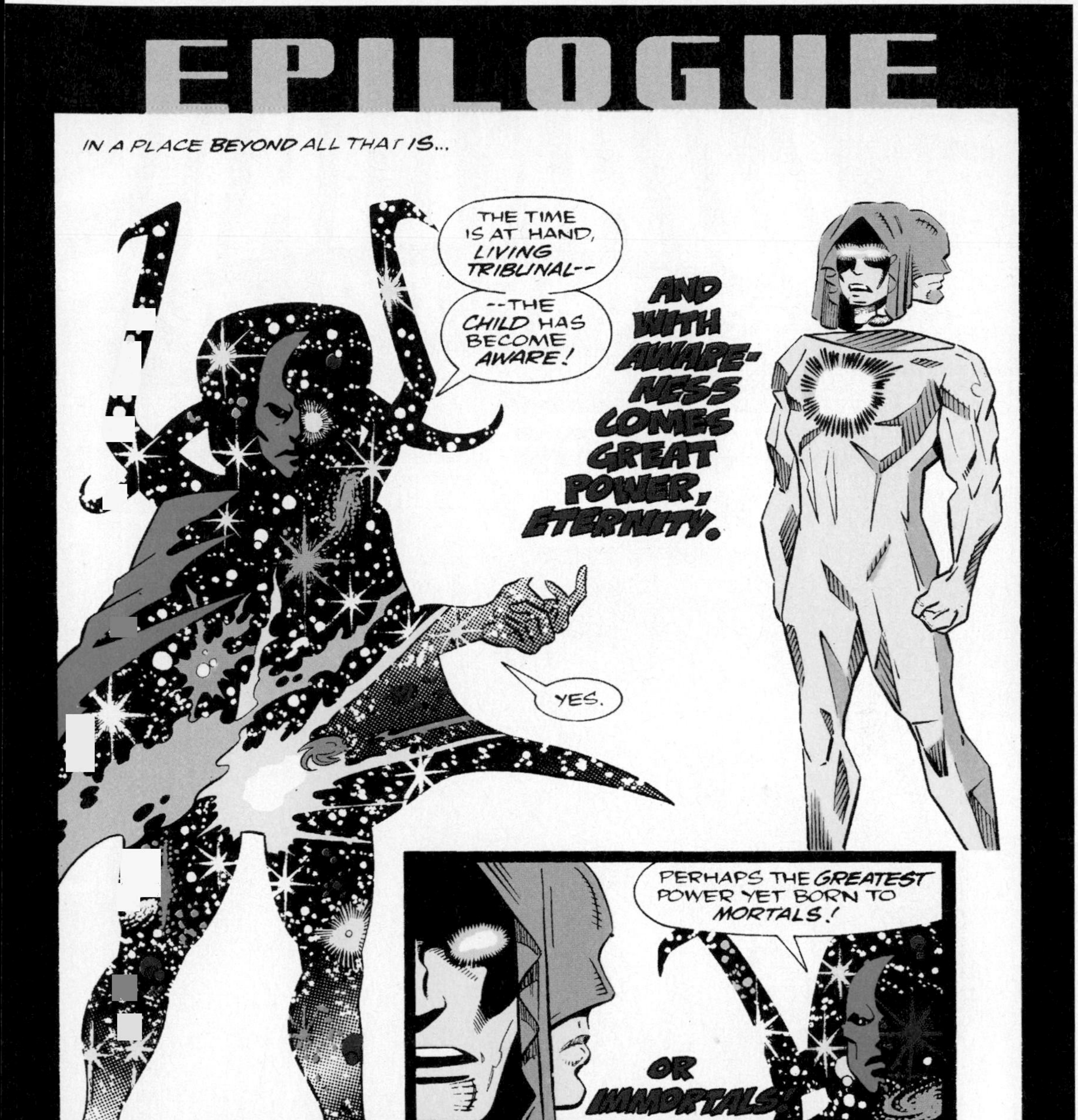
EPILOGUE
IN A PLACE BEYOND ALL THAT IS...
THE TIME IS AT HAND, LIVING TRIBUNAL--
--THE CHILD HAS BECOME AWARE!
AND WITH AWARENESS COMES GREAT POWER, ETERNITY.
YES.
PERHAPS THE GREATEST POWER YET BORN TO MORTALS!
OR IMMORTALS!
IF THERE IS AN IMBALANCE IN THE MULTIVERSE BECAUSE OF THIS CHILD, I WILL INTERVENE, OF COURSE... BUT, IF NOT, THE PROBLEM IS YOURS!
AND, SO, HE-WHO-IS-THE-UNIVERSE PONDERS HIS OPTIONS... PRESUMING, INCORRECTLY, THAT HE HAS AN ETERNITY TO DECIDE THE CHILD'S FATE!
DEFINITELY NOT THE END!

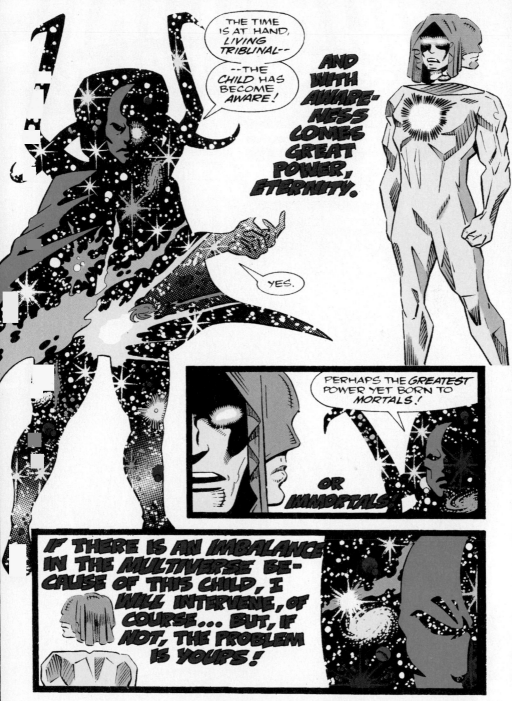

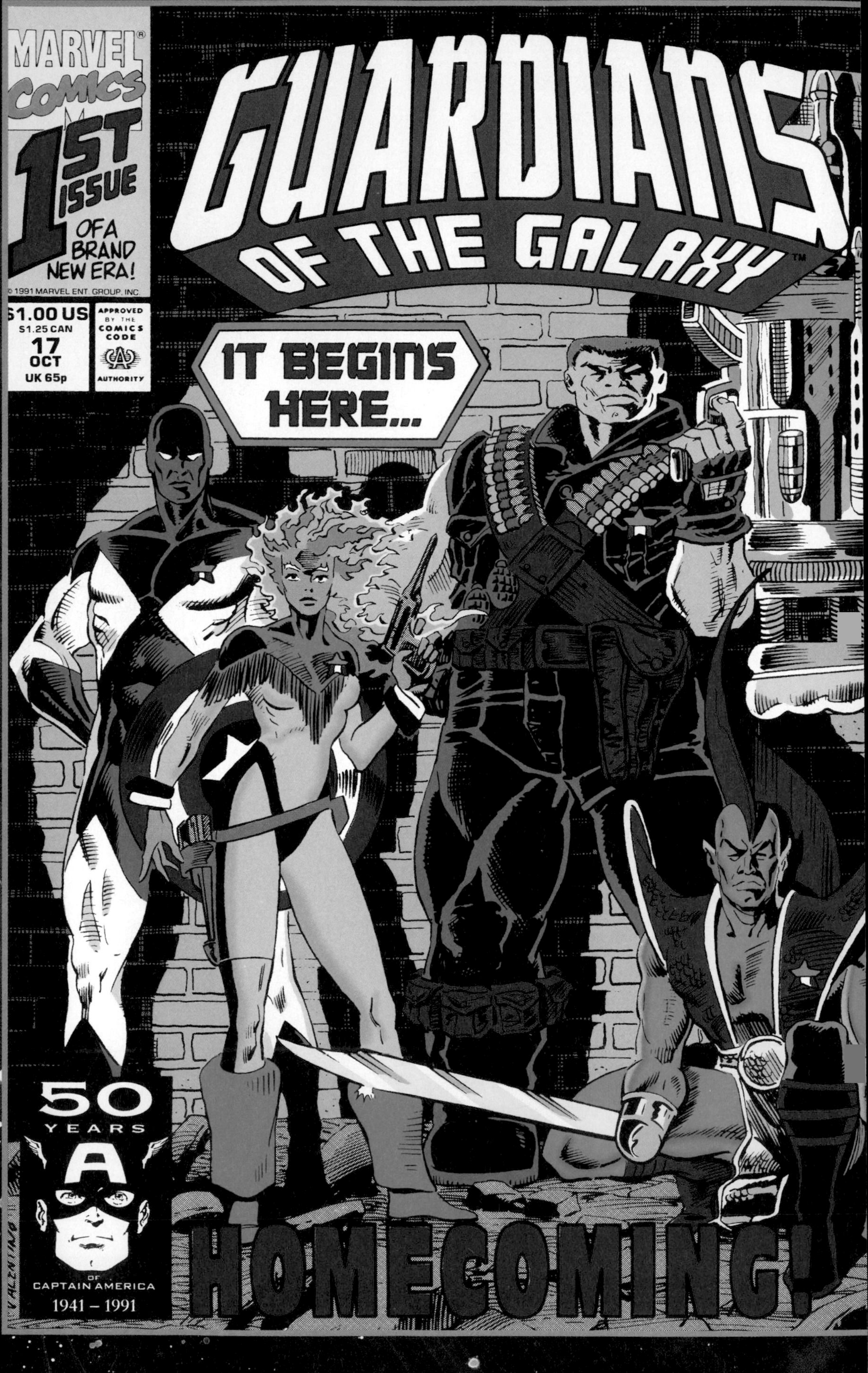

MARVEL COMICS
1ST ISSUE OF A BRAND NEW ERA!
© 1991 MARVEL ENT. GROUP, INC.
$1.00 US
$1.25 CAN
17
OCT
UK 65p
APPROVED BY THE COMICS CODE AUTHORITY
GUARDIANS OF THE GALAXY
IT BEGINS HERE...
50 YEARS
A
OF CAPTAIN AMERICA
1941 – 1991
HOMECOMING!

CHARLIE 27! MARTINEX! NIKKI! VANCE ASTRO! YONDU! ALETA! STARHAWK! SEVEN EXTRAORDINARY SUPER-BEINGS, ALL SURVIVORS OF INTERSTELLAR WAR. NOW THEY ROAM THE COSMOS OF THE 31ST CENTURY ABOARD THE STARSHIP CAPTAIN AMERICA, THEIR MISSION—TO SAFEGUARD THE MILKY WAY! STAN LEE PRESENTS . . . THE GUARDIANS OF THE GALAXY!

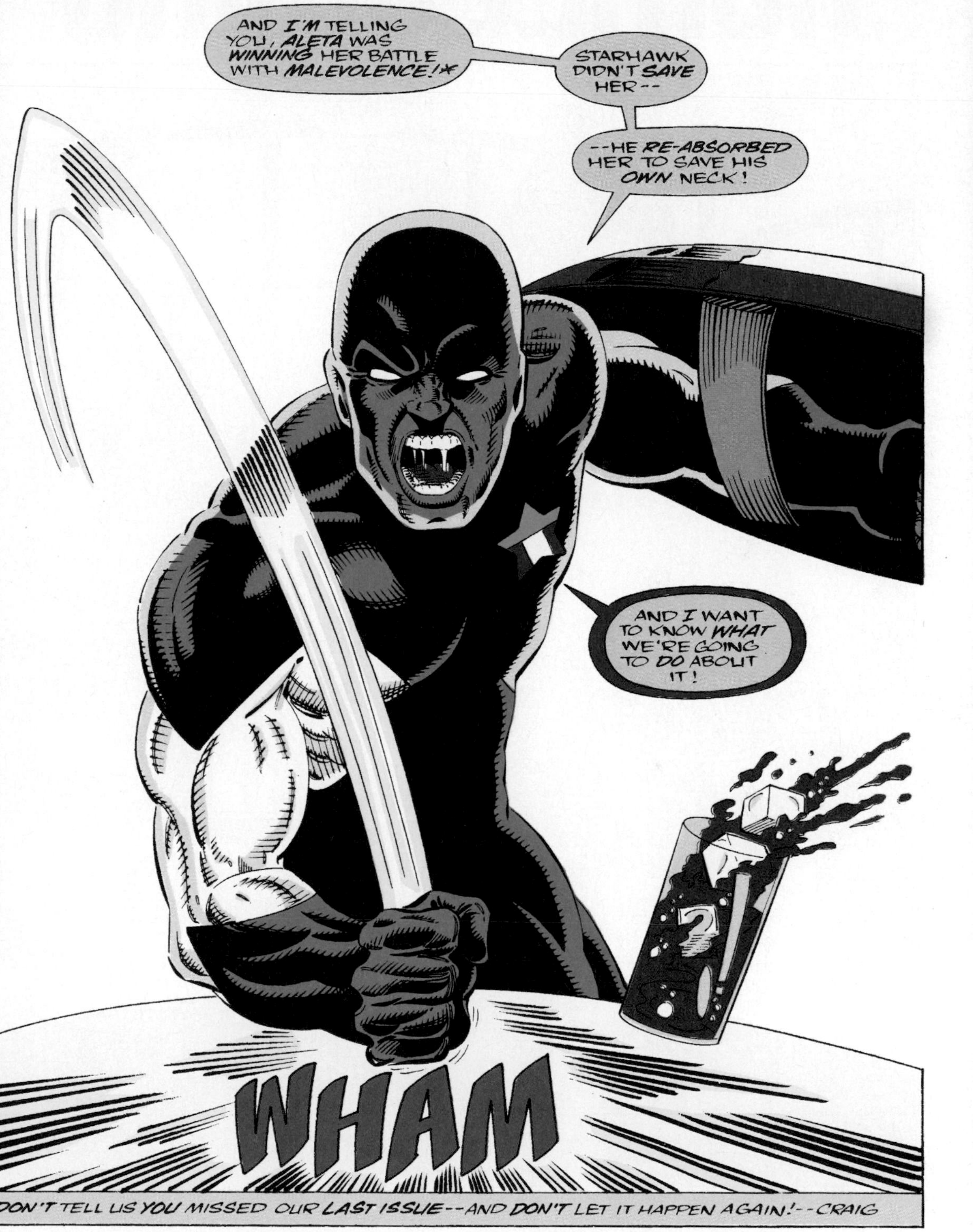
AND I'M TELLING YOU, ALETA WAS WINNING HER BATTLE WITH MALEVOLENCE!*
STARHAWK DIDN'T SAVE HER--
--HE RE-ABSORBED HER TO SAVE HIS OWN NECK!
AND I WANT TO KNOW WHAT WE'RE GOING TO DO ABOUT IT!
WHAM
DON'T TELL US YOU MISSED OUR LAST ISSUE--AND DON'T LET IT HAPPEN AGAIN!--CRAIG

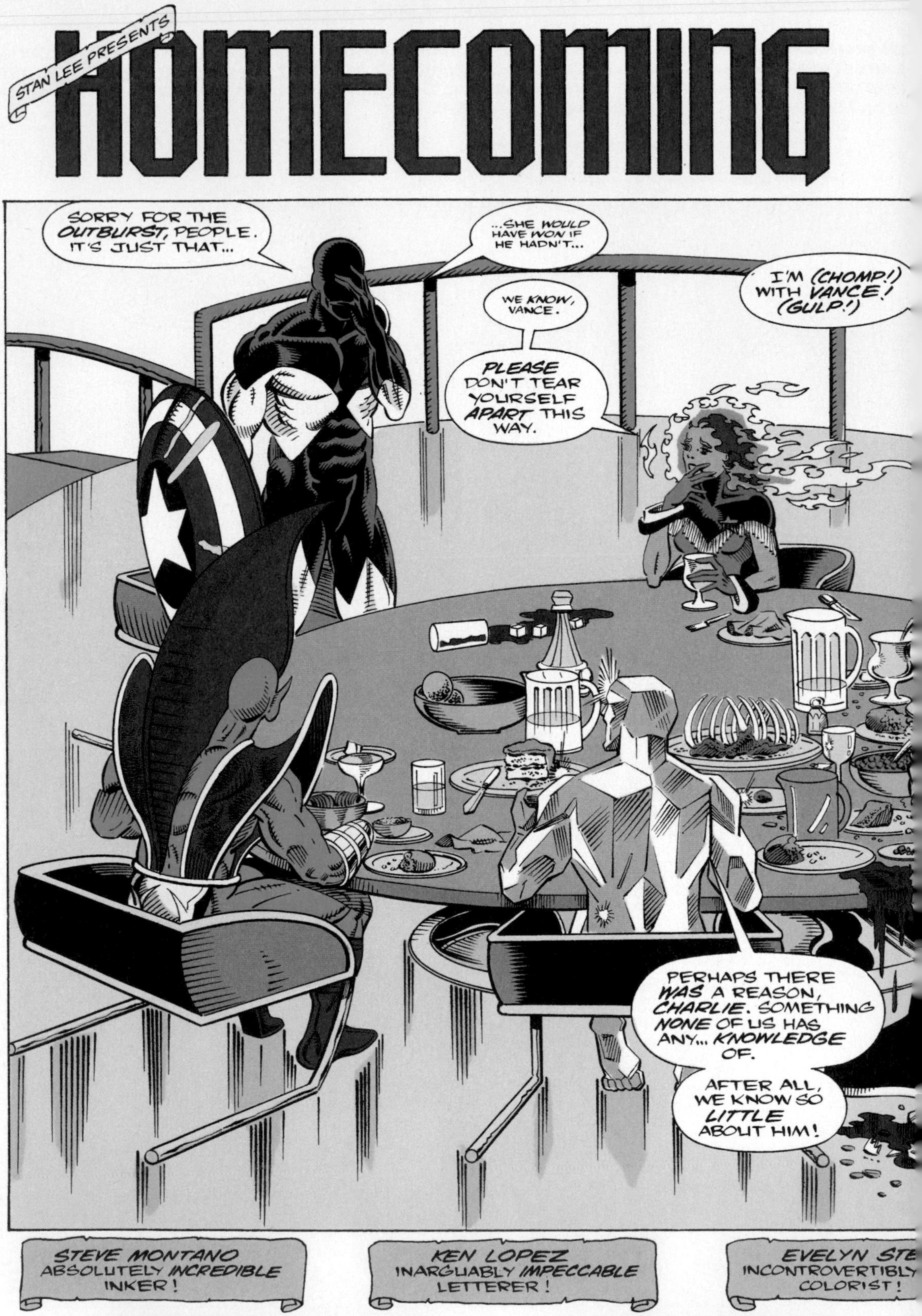
STAN LEE PRESENTS
HOMECOMING
SORRY FOR THE OUTBURST, PEOPLE. IT'S JUST THAT...
...SHE WOULD HAVE WON IF HE HADN'T...
WE KNOW, VANCE.
PLEASE DON'T TEAR YOURSELF APART THIS WAY.
I'M (CHOMP!) WITH VANCE! (GULP!)
PERHAPS THERE WAS A REASON, CHARLIE. SOMETHING NONE OF US HAS ANY... KNOWLEDGE OF.
AFTER ALL, WE KNOW SO LITTLE ABOUT HIM!
STEVE MONTANO ABSOLUTELY INCREDIBLE INKER!
KEN LOPEZ INARGUABLY IMPECCABLE LETTERER!
EVELYN STE INCONTROVERTIBLY COLORIST!
CRAIG ANDERSON INDISPUTABLY INDISPENSABLE EDITOR!
TOM DeFALCO UNBELIEVABLY IMPORTANT EDITOR IN CHIEF!

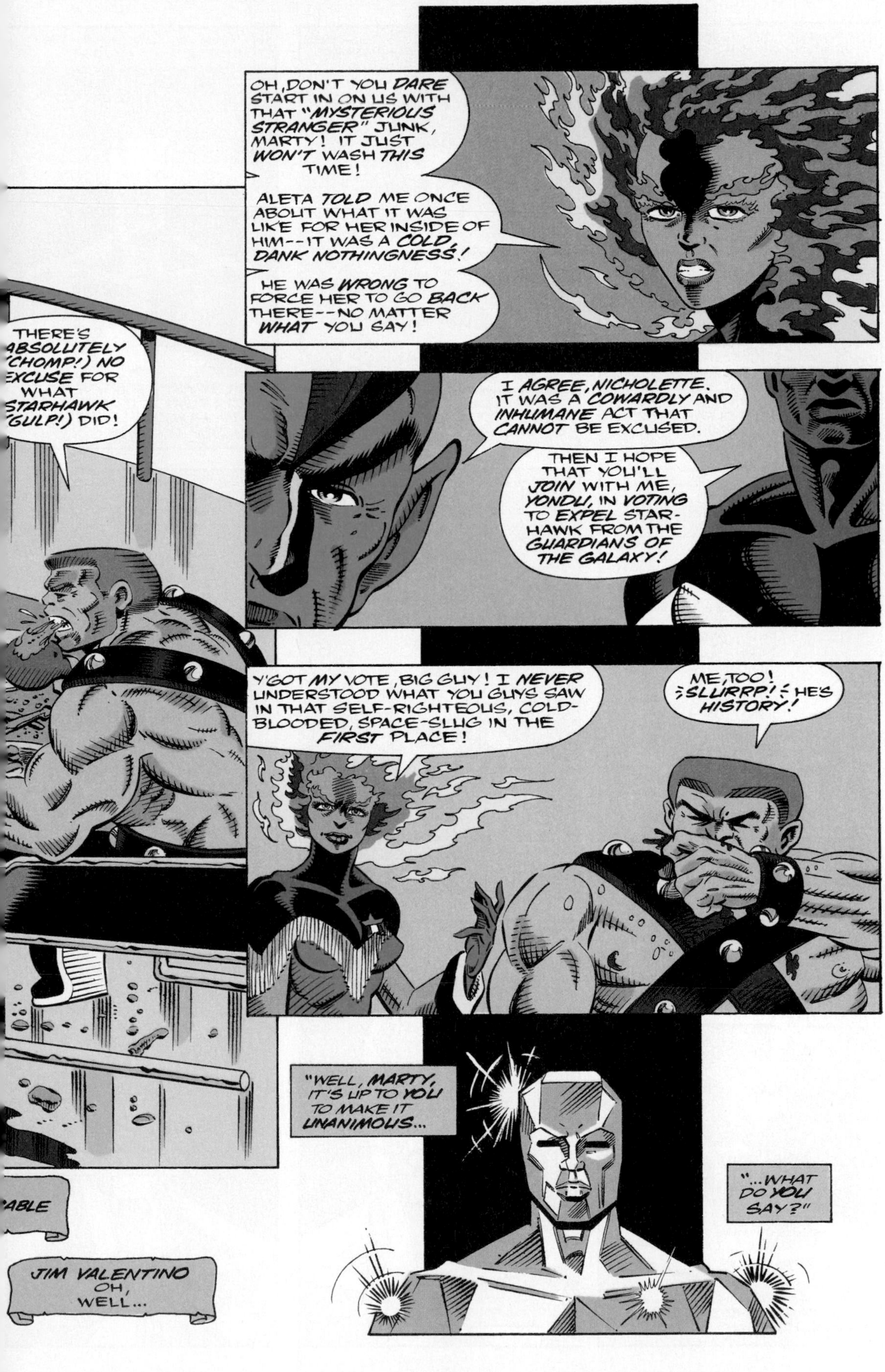
OH, DON'T YOU DARE START IN ON US WITH THAT "MYSTERIOUS STRANGER" JUNK, MARTY! IT JUST WON'T WASH THIS TIME!
ALETA TOLD ME ONCE ABOUT WHAT IT WAS LIKE FOR HER INSIDE OF HIM--IT WAS A COLD, DANK NOTHINGNESS!
HE WAS WRONG TO FORCE HER TO GO BACK THERE--NO MATTER WHAT YOU SAY!
THERE'S ABSOLUTELY (CHOMP!) NO EXCUSE FOR WHAT STARHAWK (GULP!) DID!
I AGREE, NICHOLETTE. IT WAS A COWARDLY AND INHUMANE ACT THAT CANNOT BE EXCUSED.
THEN I HOPE THAT YOU'LL JOIN WITH ME, YONDU, IN VOTING TO EXPEL STAR-HAWK FROM THE GUARDIANS OF THE GALAXY!
Y'GOT MY VOTE, BIG GUY! I NEVER UNDERSTOOD WHAT YOU GUYS SAW IN THAT SELF-RIGHTEOUS, COLD-BLOODED, SPACE-SLUG IN THE FIRST PLACE!
ME, TOO! -SLURRP!- HE'S HISTORY!
"WELL, MARTY, IT'S UP TO YOU TO MAKE IT UNANIMOUS...
"...WHAT DO YOU SAY?"
JIM VALENTINO OH, WELL...

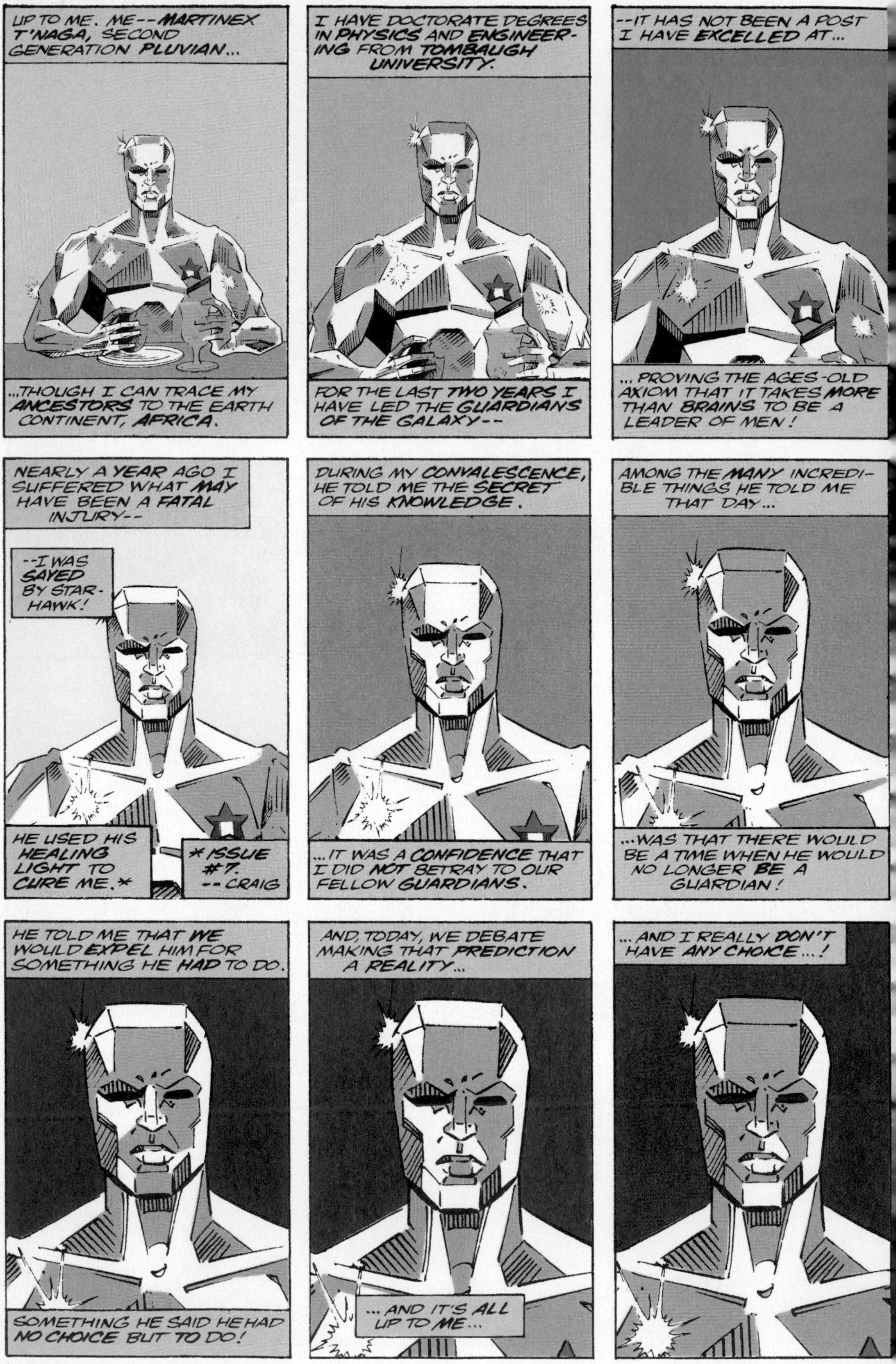
UP TO ME. ME--MARTINEX T'NAGA, SECOND GENERATION PLUVIAN...
...THOUGH I CAN TRACE MY ANCESTORS TO THE EARTH CONTINENT, AFRICA.
I HAVE DOCTORATE DEGREES IN PHYSICS AND ENGINEERING FROM TOMBAUGH UNIVERSITY.
FOR THE LAST TWO YEARS I HAVE LED THE GUARDIANS OF THE GALAXY--
--IT HAS NOT BEEN A POST I HAVE EXCELLED AT...
...PROVING THE AGES-OLD AXIOM THAT IT TAKES MORE THAN BRAINS TO BE A LEADER OF MEN!
NEARLY A YEAR AGO I SUFFERED WHAT MAY HAVE BEEN A FATAL INJURY--
--I WAS SAVED BY STAR-HAWK!
HE USED HIS HEALING LIGHT TO CURE ME.*
*ISSUE #7. --CRAIG
DURING MY CONVALESCENCE, HE TOLD ME THE SECRET OF HIS KNOWLEDGE.
...IT WAS A CONFIDENCE THAT I DID NOT BETRAY TO OUR FELLOW GUARDIANS.
AMONG THE MANY INCREDIBLE THINGS HE TOLD ME THAT DAY...
...WAS THAT THERE WOULD BE A TIME WHEN HE WOULD NO LONGER BE A GUARDIAN!
HE TOLD ME THAT WE WOULD EXPEL HIM FOR SOMETHING HE HAD TO DO.
SOMETHING HE SAID HE HAD NO CHOICE BUT TO DO!
AND, TODAY, WE DEBATE MAKING THAT PREDICTION A REALITY...
...AND IT'S ALL UP TO ME...
...AND I REALLY DON'T HAVE ANY CHOICE...!

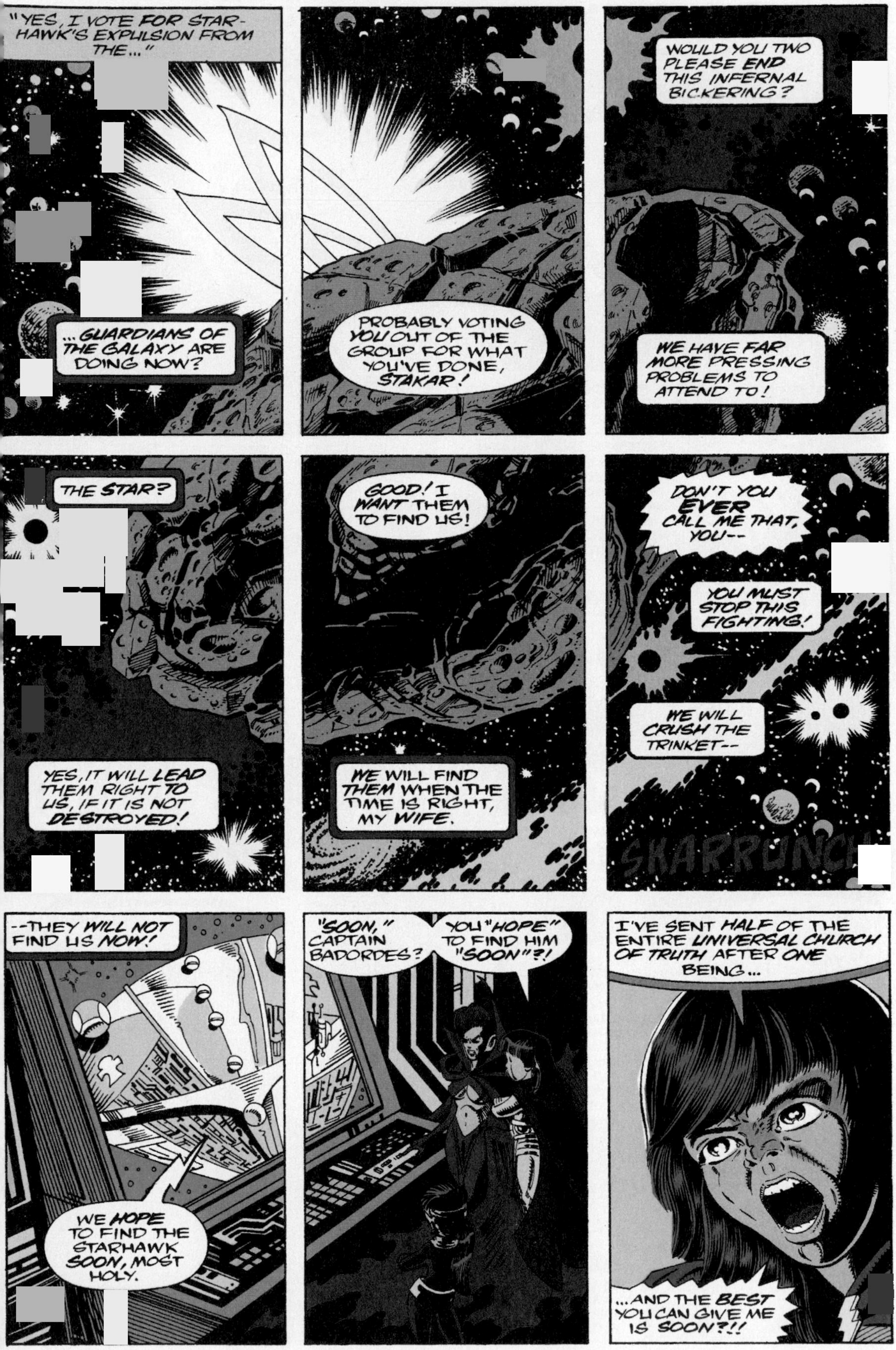
"YES, I VOTE FOR STAR-HAWK'S EXPULSION FROM THE..."
...GUARDIANS OF THE GALAXY ARE DOING NOW?
PROBABLY VOTING YOU OUT OF THE GROUP FOR WHAT YOU'VE DONE, STAKAR!
WOULD YOU TWO PLEASE END THIS INFERNAL BICKERING?
WE HAVE FAR MORE PRESSING PROBLEMS TO ATTEND TO!
THE STAR?
YES, IT WILL LEAD THEM RIGHT TO US, IF IT IS NOT DESTROYED!
GOOD! I WANT THEM TO FIND US!
WE WILL FIND THEM WHEN THE TIME IS RIGHT, MY WIFE.
DON'T YOU EVER CALL ME THAT, YOU--
YOU MUST STOP THIS FIGHTING!
WE WILL CRUSH THE TRINKET--
SKARRUNC
--THEY WILL NOT FIND US NOW!
WE HOPE TO FIND THE STARHAWK SOON, MOST HOLY.
"SOON," CAPTAIN BADORDES?
YOU "HOPE" TO FIND HIM "SOON"?!
I'VE SENT HALF OF THE ENTIRE UNIVERSAL CHURCH OF TRUTH AFTER ONE BEING...
...AND THE BEST YOU CAN GIVE ME IS SOON?!!

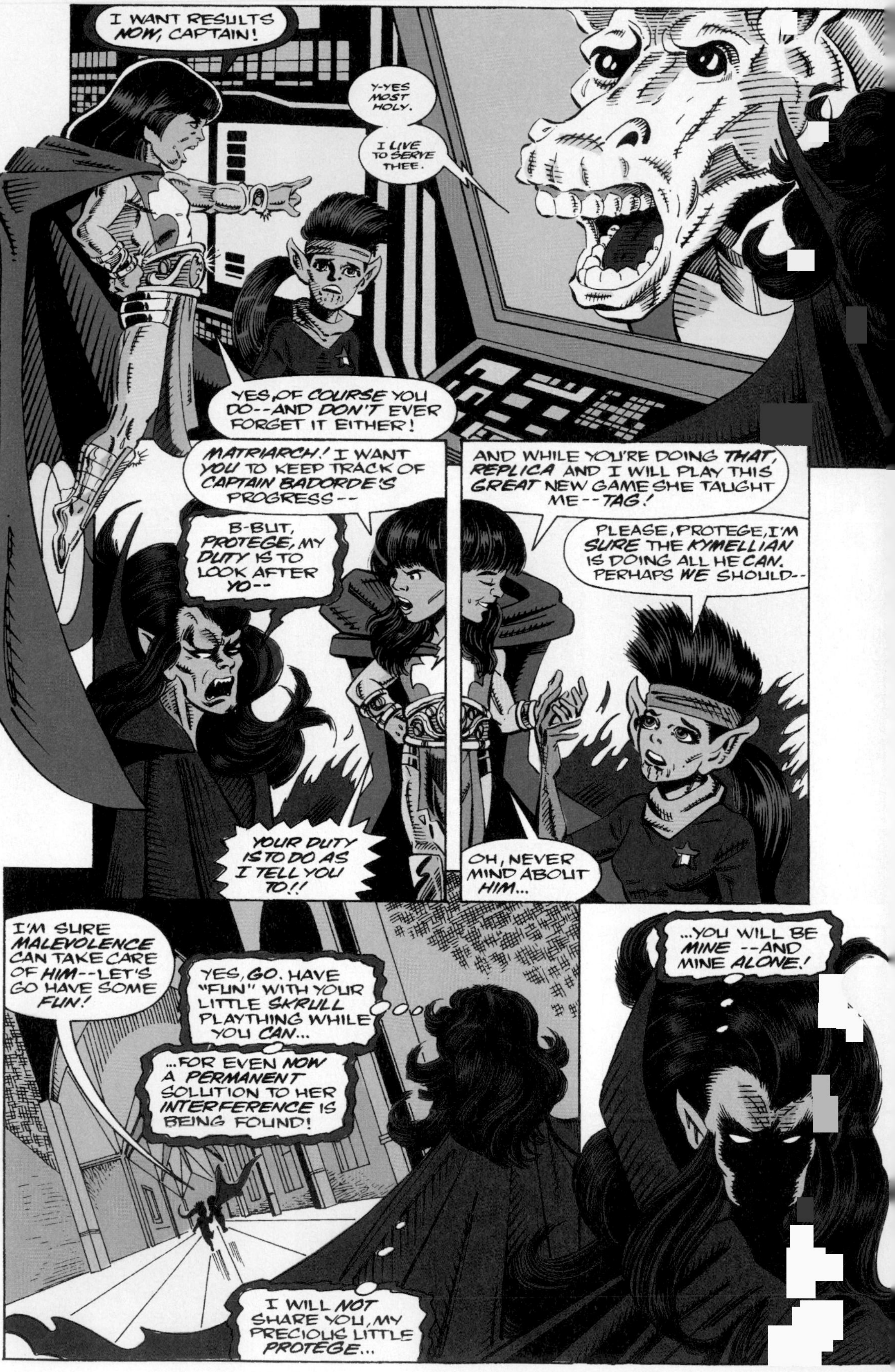
I WANT RESULTS NOW, CAPTAIN!
Y-YES MOST HOLY.
I LIVE TO SERVE THEE.
YES, OF COURSE YOU DO--AND DON'T EVER FORGET IT EITHER!
MATRIARCH! I WANT YOU TO KEEP TRACK OF CAPTAIN BADORDE'S PROGRESS--
B-BUT, PROTEGE, MY DUTY IS TO LOOK AFTER YO--
YOUR DUTY IS TO DO AS I TELL YOU TO!!
AND WHILE YOU'RE DOING THAT, REPLICA AND I WILL PLAY THIS GREAT NEW GAME SHE TAUGHT ME--TAG!
PLEASE, PROTEGE, I'M SURE THE KYMELLIAN IS DOING ALL HE CAN. PERHAPS WE SHOULD--
OH, NEVER MIND ABOUT HIM...
I'M SURE MALEVOLENCE CAN TAKE CARE OF HIM--LET'S GO HAVE SOME FUN!
YES, GO. HAVE "FUN" WITH YOUR LITTLE SKRULL PLAYTHING WHILE YOU CAN...
...FOR EVEN NOW A PERMANENT SOLUTION TO HER INTERFERENCE IS BEING FOUND!
I WILL NOT SHARE YOU, MY PRECIOUS LITTLE PROTEGE...
...YOU WILL BE MINE --AND MINE ALONE!

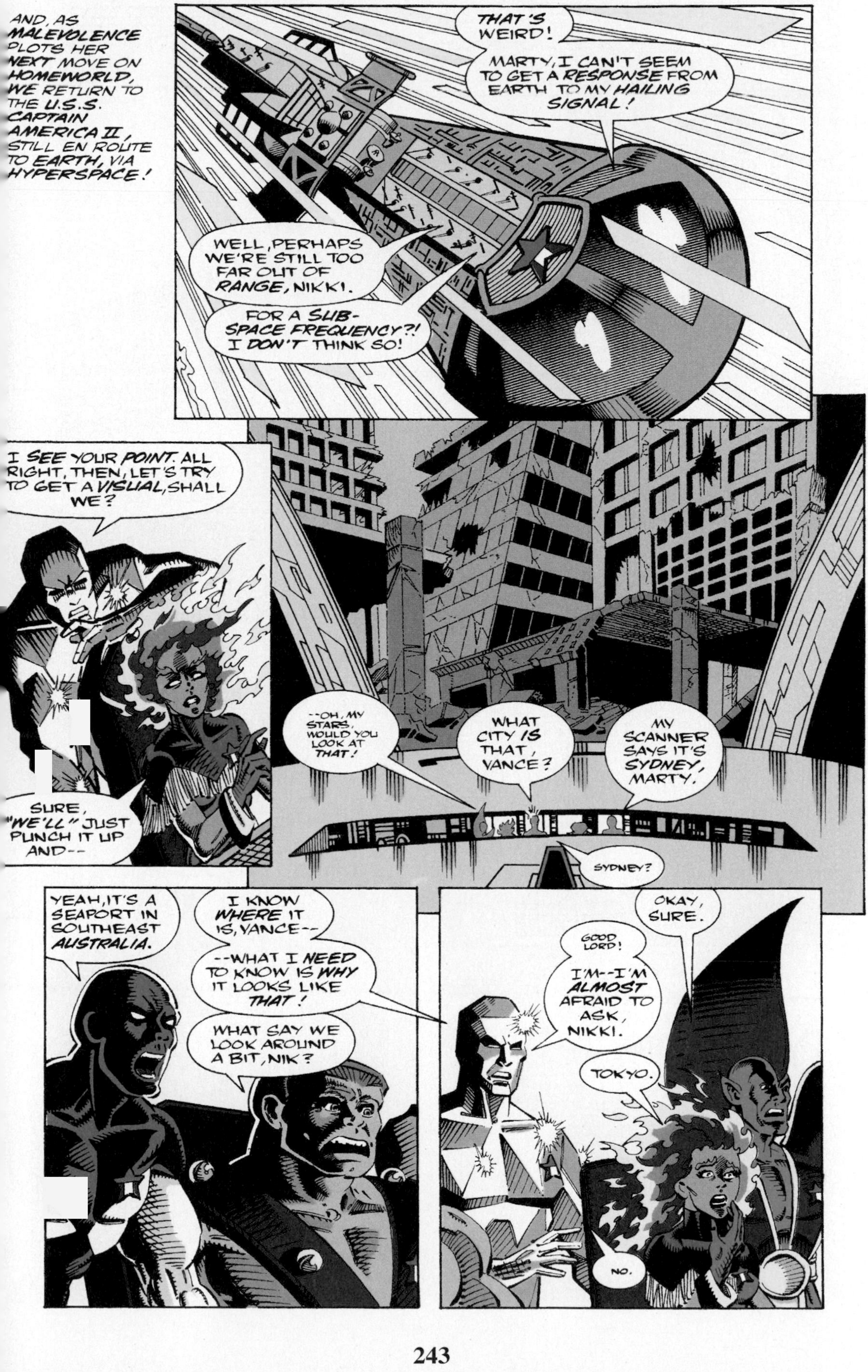
AND, AS MALEVOLENCE PLOTS HER NEXT MOVE ON HOMEWORLD, WE RETURN TO THE U.S.S. CAPTAIN AMERICA II, STILL EN ROUTE TO EARTH, VIA HYPERSPACE!
THAT'S WEIRD!
MARTY, I CAN'T SEEM TO GET A RESPONSE FROM EARTH TO MY HAILING SIGNAL!
WELL, PERHAPS WE'RE STILL TOO FAR OUT OF RANGE, NIKKI.
FOR A SUB-SPACE FREQUENCY?! I DON'T THINK SO!
I SEE YOUR POINT. ALL RIGHT, THEN, LET'S TRY TO GET A VISUAL, SHALL WE?
SURE, "WE'LL" JUST PUNCH IT UP AND--
--OH, MY STARS, WOULD YOU LOOK AT THAT!
WHAT CITY IS THAT, VANCE?
MY SCANNER SAYS IT'S SYDNEY, MARTY.
SYDNEY?
YEAH, IT'S A SEAPORT IN SOUTHEAST AUSTRALIA.
I KNOW WHERE IT IS, VANCE--
--WHAT I NEED TO KNOW IS WHY IT LOOKS LIKE THAT!
WHAT SAY WE LOOK AROUND A BIT, NIK?
OKAY, SURE.
GOOD LORD!
I'M--I'M ALMOST AFRAID TO ASK, NIKKI.
TOKYO.
NO.

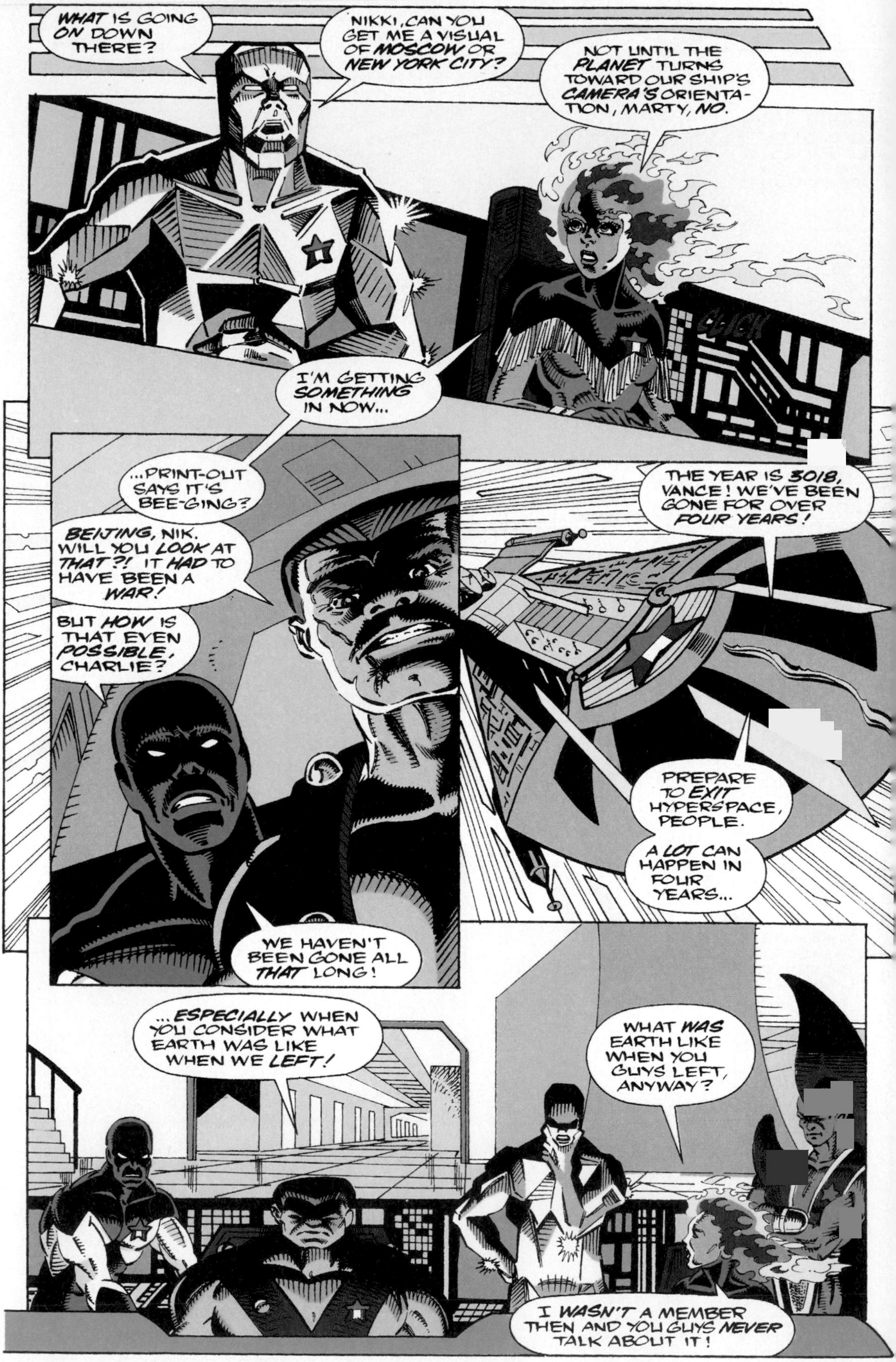
WHAT IS GOING ON DOWN THERE?
NIKKI, CAN YOU GET ME A VISUAL OF MOSCOW OR NEW YORK CITY?
NOT UNTIL THE PLANET TURNS TOWARD OUR SHIP'S CAMERA'S ORIENTATION, MARTY, NO.
I'M GETTING SOMETHING IN NOW...
...PRINT-OUT SAYS IT'S BEE-GING?
BEIJING, NIK. WILL YOU LOOK AT THAT?! IT HAD TO HAVE BEEN A WAR!
BUT HOW IS THAT EVEN POSSIBLE, CHARLIE?
WE HAVEN'T BEEN GONE ALL THAT LONG!
THE YEAR IS 3018, VANCE! WE'VE BEEN GONE FOR OVER FOUR YEARS!
PREPARE TO EXIT HYPERSPACE, PEOPLE.
A LOT CAN HAPPEN IN FOUR YEARS...
...ESPECIALLY WHEN YOU CONSIDER WHAT EARTH WAS LIKE WHEN WE LEFT!
WHAT WAS EARTH LIKE WHEN YOU GUYS LEFT, ANYWAY?
I WASN'T A MEMBER THEN AND YOU GUYS NEVER TALK ABOUT IT!

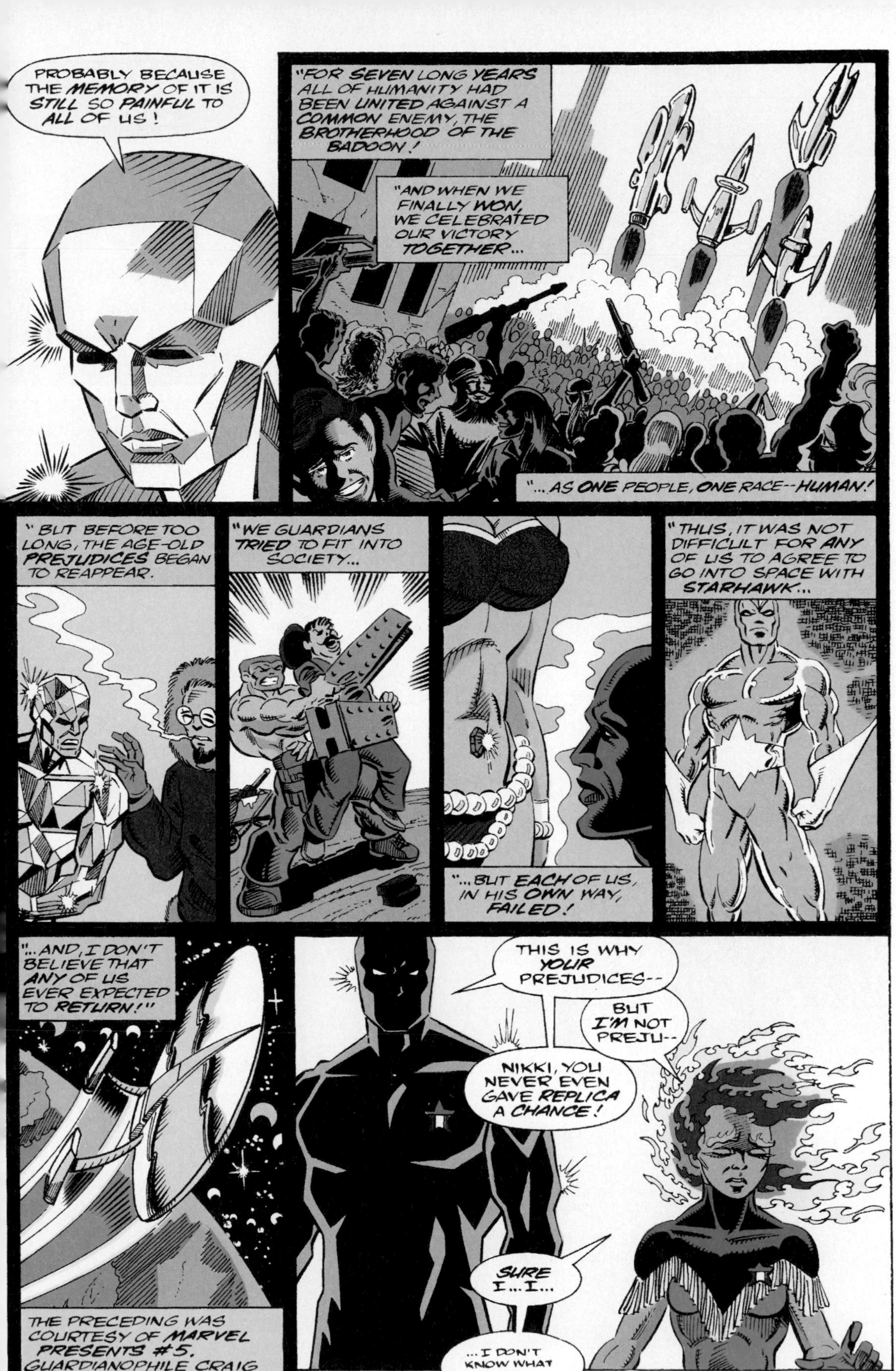
PROBABLY BECAUSE THE MEMORY OF IT IS STILL SO PAINFUL TO ALL OF US!
"FOR SEVEN LONG YEARS ALL OF HUMANITY HAD BEEN UNITED AGAINST A COMMON ENEMY, THE BROTHERHOOD OF THE BADOON!
"AND WHEN WE FINALLY WON, WE CELEBRATED OUR VICTORY TOGETHER...
"...AS ONE PEOPLE, ONE RACE--HUMAN!
"BUT BEFORE TOO LONG, THE AGE-OLD PREJUDICES BEGAN TO REAPPEAR.
"WE GUARDIANS TRIED TO FIT INTO SOCIETY...
"...BUT EACH OF US, IN HIS OWN WAY, FAILED!
"THUS, IT WAS NOT DIFFICULT FOR ANY OF US TO AGREE TO GO INTO SPACE WITH STARHAWK...
"...AND, I DON'T BELIEVE THAT ANY OF US EVER EXPECTED TO RETURN!"
THE PRECEDING WAS COURTESY OF MARVEL PRESENTS #5. GUARDIANOPHILE CRAIG
THIS IS WHY YOUR PREJUDICES--
BUT I'M NOT PREJU--
NIKKI, YOU NEVER EVEN GAVE REPLICA A CHANCE!
SURE I... I...
...I DON'T KNOW WHAT TO SAY...

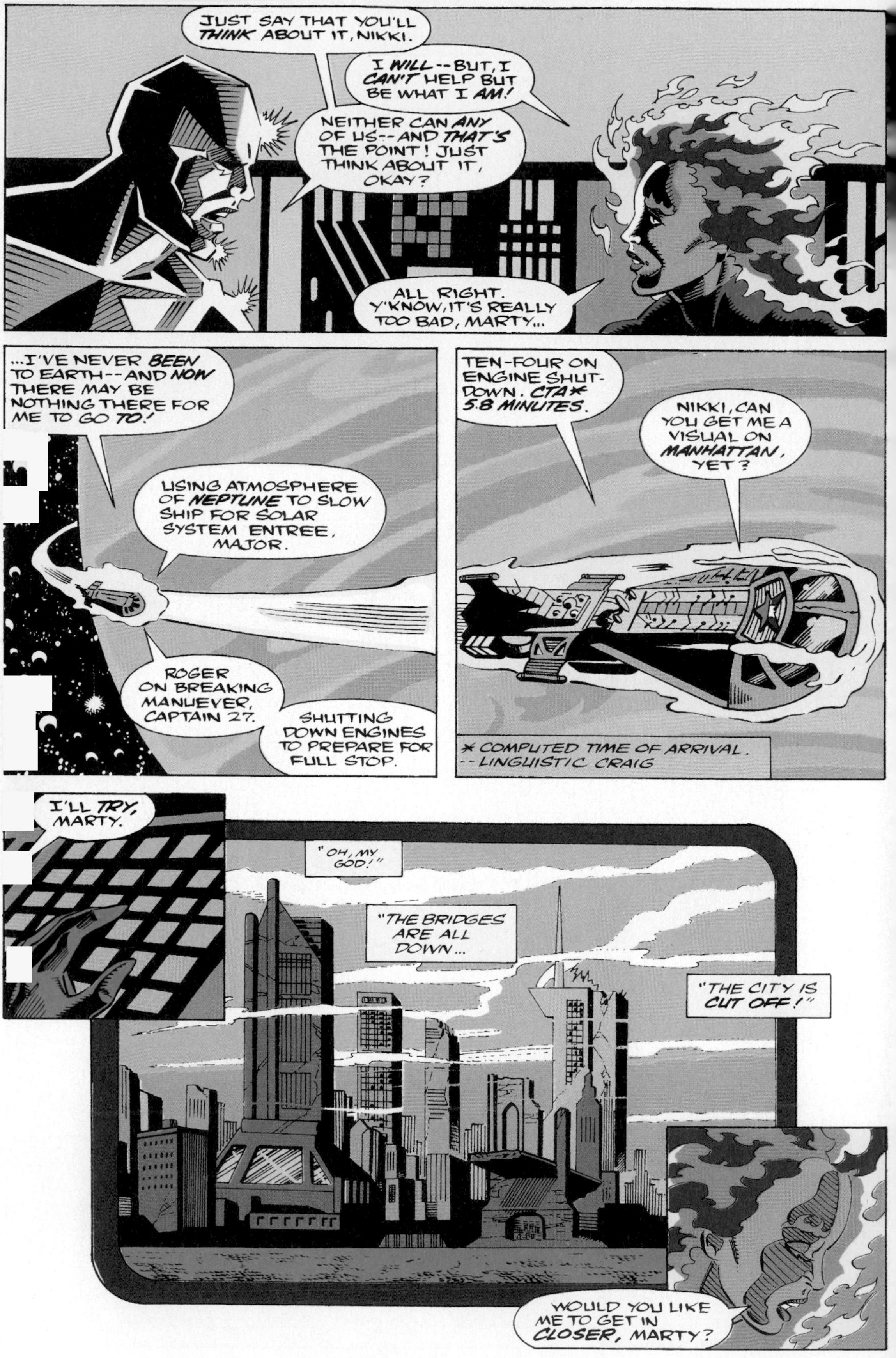
JUST SAY THAT YOU'LL THINK ABOUT IT, NIKKI.
I WILL--BUT, I CAN'T HELP BUT BE WHAT I AM!
NEITHER CAN ANY OF US--AND THAT'S THE POINT! JUST THINK ABOUT IT, OKAY?
ALL RIGHT. Y'KNOW, IT'S REALLY TOO BAD, MARTY...
...I'VE NEVER BEEN TO EARTH--AND NOW THERE MAY BE NOTHING THERE FOR ME TO GO TO!
USING ATMOSPHERE OF NEPTUNE TO SLOW SHIP FOR SOLAR SYSTEM ENTREE, MAJOR.
ROGER ON BREAKING MANUEVER, CAPTAIN 27.
SHUTTING DOWN ENGINES TO PREPARE FOR FULL STOP.
TEN-FOUR ON ENGINE SHUT-DOWN. CTA* 5.8 MINUTES.
NIKKI, CAN YOU GET ME A VISUAL ON MANHATTAN, YET?
* COMPUTED TIME OF ARRIVAL. --LINGUISTIC CRAIG
I'LL TRY, MARTY.
"OH, MY GOD!"
"THE BRIDGES ARE ALL DOWN...
"THE CITY IS CUT OFF!"
WOULD YOU LIKE ME TO GET IN CLOSER, MARTY?

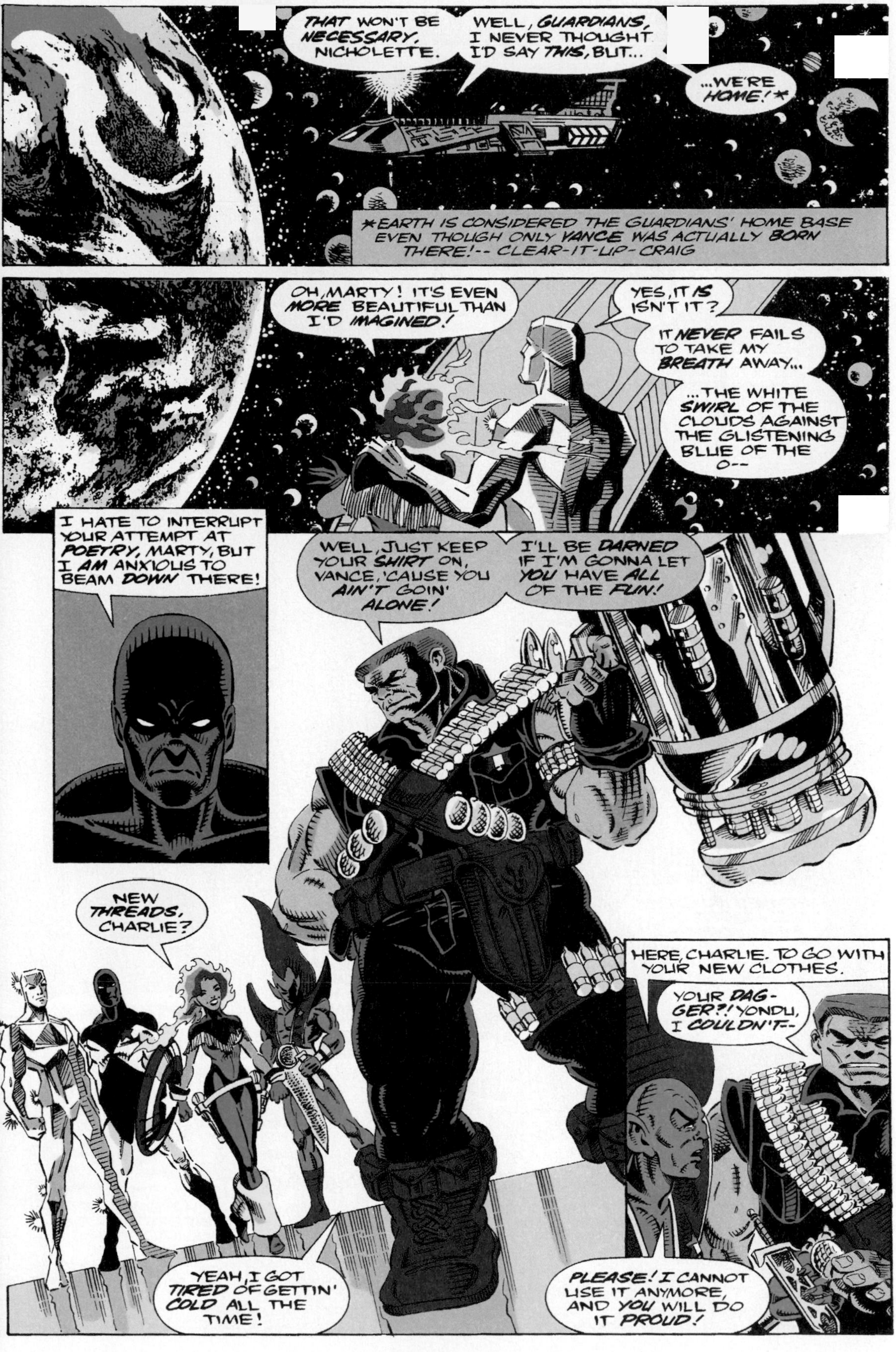
THAT WON'T BE NECESSARY, NICHOLETTE.
WELL, GUARDIANS, I NEVER THOUGHT I'D SAY THIS, BUT...
...WE'RE HOME!*
*EARTH IS CONSIDERED THE GUARDIANS' HOME BASE EVEN THOUGH ONLY VANCE WAS ACTUALLY BORN THERE!-- CLEAR-IT-UP-CRAIG
OH, MARTY! IT'S EVEN MORE BEAUTIFUL THAN I'D IMAGINED!
YES, IT IS ISN'T IT?
IT NEVER FAILS TO TAKE MY BREATH AWAY...
...THE WHITE SWIRL OF THE CLOUDS AGAINST THE GLISTENING BLUE OF THE O--
I HATE TO INTERRUPT YOUR ATTEMPT AT POETRY, MARTY, BUT I AM ANXIOUS TO BEAM DOWN THERE!
WELL, JUST KEEP YOUR SHIRT ON, VANCE, 'CAUSE YOU AIN'T GOIN' ALONE!
I'LL BE DARNED IF I'M GONNA LET YOU HAVE ALL OF THE FUN!
NEW THREADS, CHARLIE?
YEAH, I GOT TIRED OF GETTIN' COLD ALL THE TIME!
HERE, CHARLIE. TO GO WITH YOUR NEW CLOTHES.
YOUR DAGGER?! YONDU, I COULDN'T--
PLEASE! I CANNOT USE IT ANYMORE, AND YOU WILL DO IT PROUD!

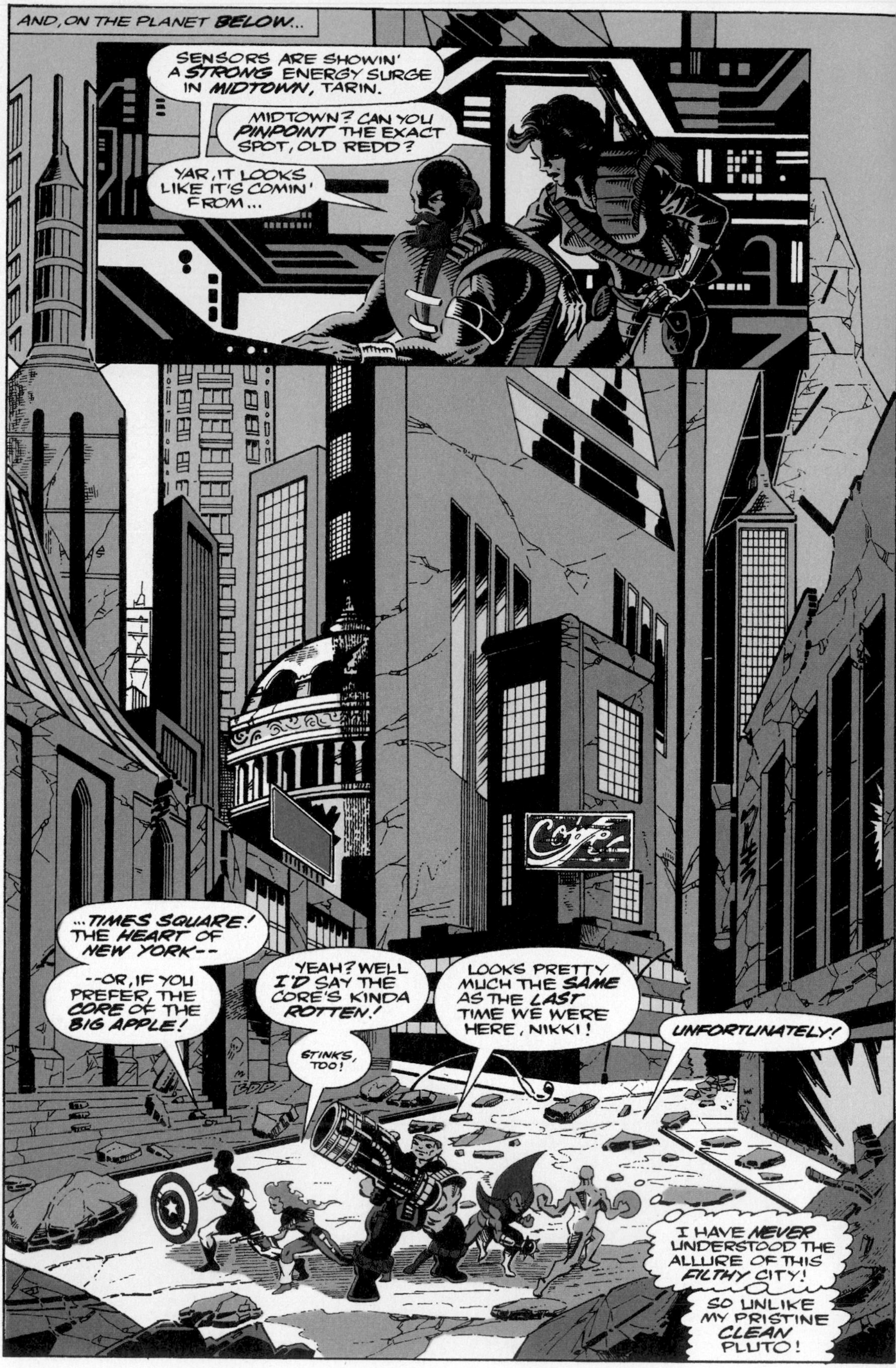
AND, ON THE PLANET BELOW...
SENSORS ARE SHOWIN' A STRONG ENERGY SURGE IN MIDTOWN, TARIN.
MIDTOWN? CAN YOU PINPOINT THE EXACT SPOT, OLD REDD?
YAR, IT LOOKS LIKE IT'S COMIN' FROM...
...TIMES SQUARE! THE HEART OF NEW YORK--
--OR, IF YOU PREFER, THE CORE OF THE BIG APPLE!
YEAH? WELL I'D SAY THE CORE'S KINDA ROTTEN!
STINKS, TOO!
LOOKS PRETTY MUCH THE SAME AS THE LAST TIME WE WERE HERE, NIKKI!
UNFORTUNATELY!
I HAVE NEVER UNDERSTOOD THE ALLURE OF THIS FILTHY CITY!
SO UNLIKE MY PRISTINE CLEAN PLUTO!

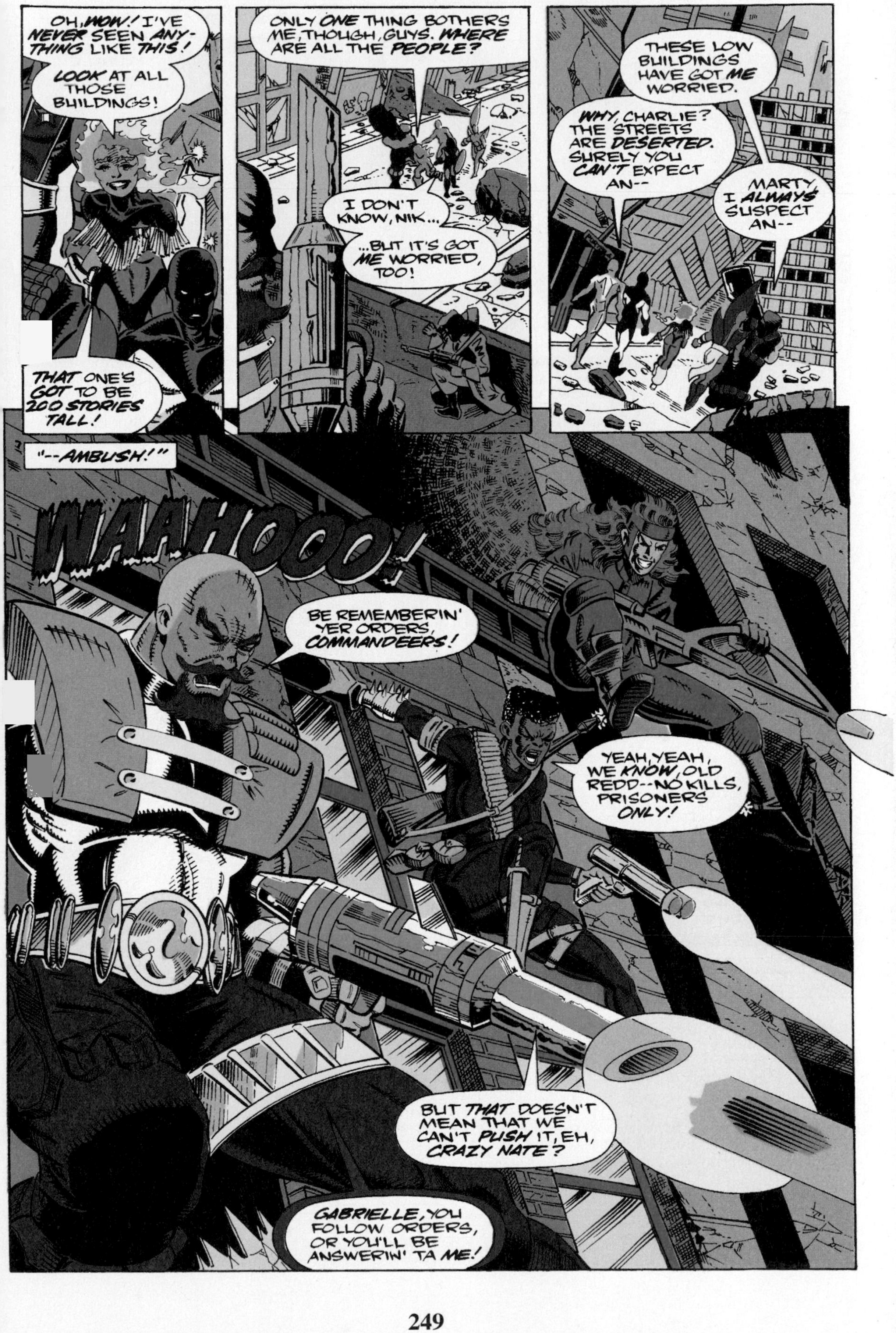

OH, WOW! I'VE NEVER SEEN ANYTHING LIKE THIS!
LOOK AT ALL THOSE BUILDINGS!
THAT ONE'S GOT TO BE 200 STORIES TALL!
ONLY ONE THING BOTHERS ME, THOUGH, GUYS. WHERE ARE ALL THE PEOPLE?
I DON'T KNOW, NIK...
...BUT IT'S GOT ME WORRIED, TOO!
THESE LOW BUILDINGS HAVE GOT ME WORRIED.
WHY, CHARLIE? THE STREETS ARE DESERTED. SURELY YOU CAN'T EXPECT AN--
MARTY, I ALWAYS SUSPECT AN--
"--AMBUSH!"
WAAHOOO!
BE REMEMBERIN' YER ORDERS, COMMANDEERS!
YEAH, YEAH, WE KNOW, OLD REDD--NO KILLS, PRISONERS ONLY!
BUT THAT DOESN'T MEAN THAT WE CAN'T PUSH IT, EH, CRAZY NATE?
GABRIELLE, YOU FOLLOW ORDERS, OR YOU'LL BE ANSWERIN' TA ME!

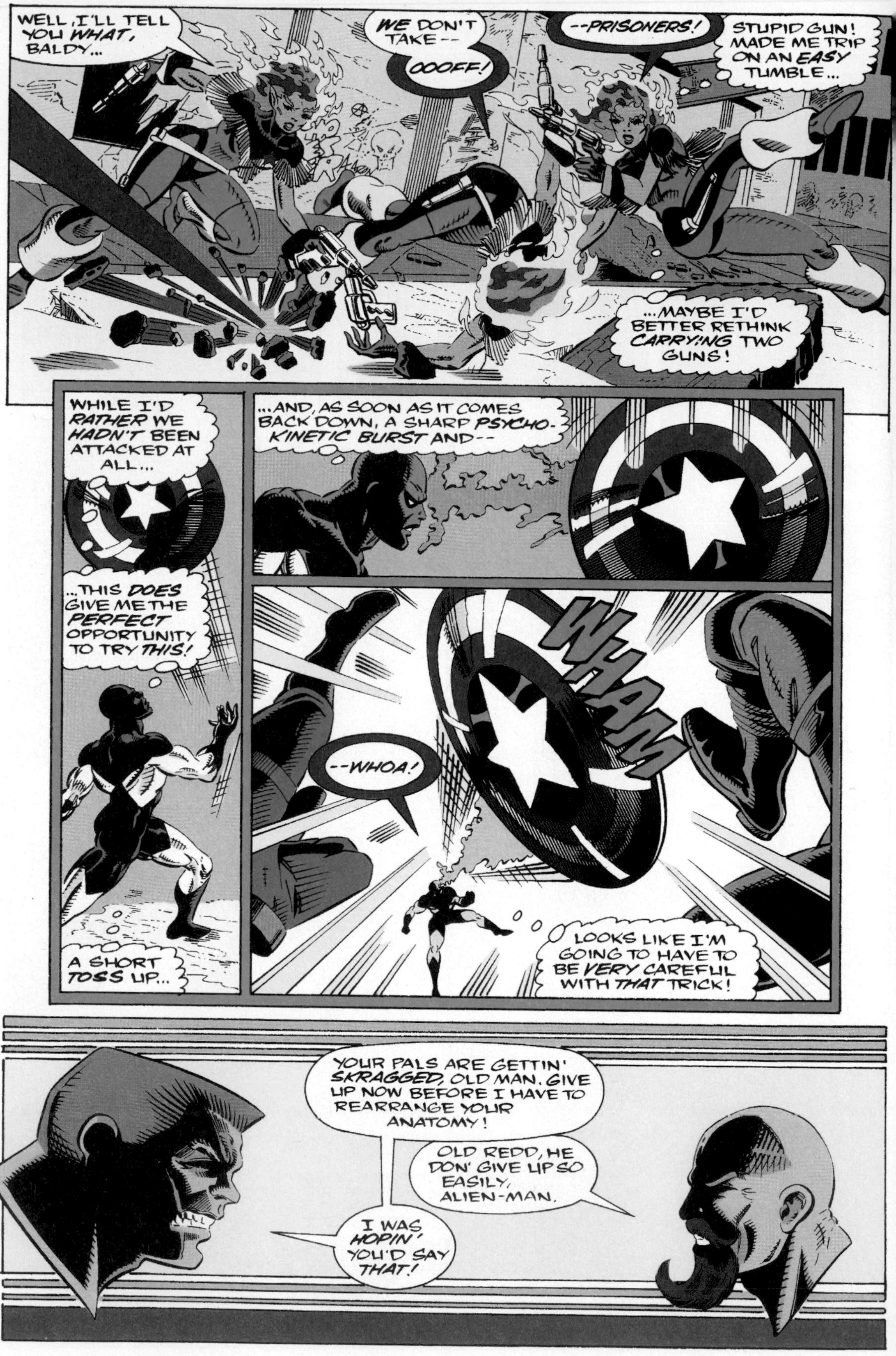
WELL, I'LL TELL YOU WHAT, BALDY...
WE DON'T TAKE--
OOOFF!
--PRISONERS!
STUPID GUN! MADE ME TRIP ON AN EASY TUMBLE...
...MAYBE I'D BETTER RETHINK CARRYING TWO GUNS!
WHILE I'D RATHER WE HADN'T BEEN ATTACKED AT ALL...
...THIS DOES GIVE ME THE PERFECT OPPORTUNITY TO TRY THIS!
A SHORT TOSS UP...
...AND, AS SOON AS IT COMES BACK DOWN, A SHARP PSYCHO-KINETIC BURST AND--
WHAM
--WHOA!
LOOKS LIKE I'M GOING TO HAVE TO BE VERY CAREFUL WITH THAT TRICK!
YOUR PALS ARE GETTIN' SKRAGGED, OLD MAN. GIVE UP NOW BEFORE I HAVE TO REARRANGE YOUR ANATOMY!
OLD REDD, HE DON' GIVE UP SO EASILY, ALIEN-MAN.
I WAS HOPIN' YOU'D SAY THAT!

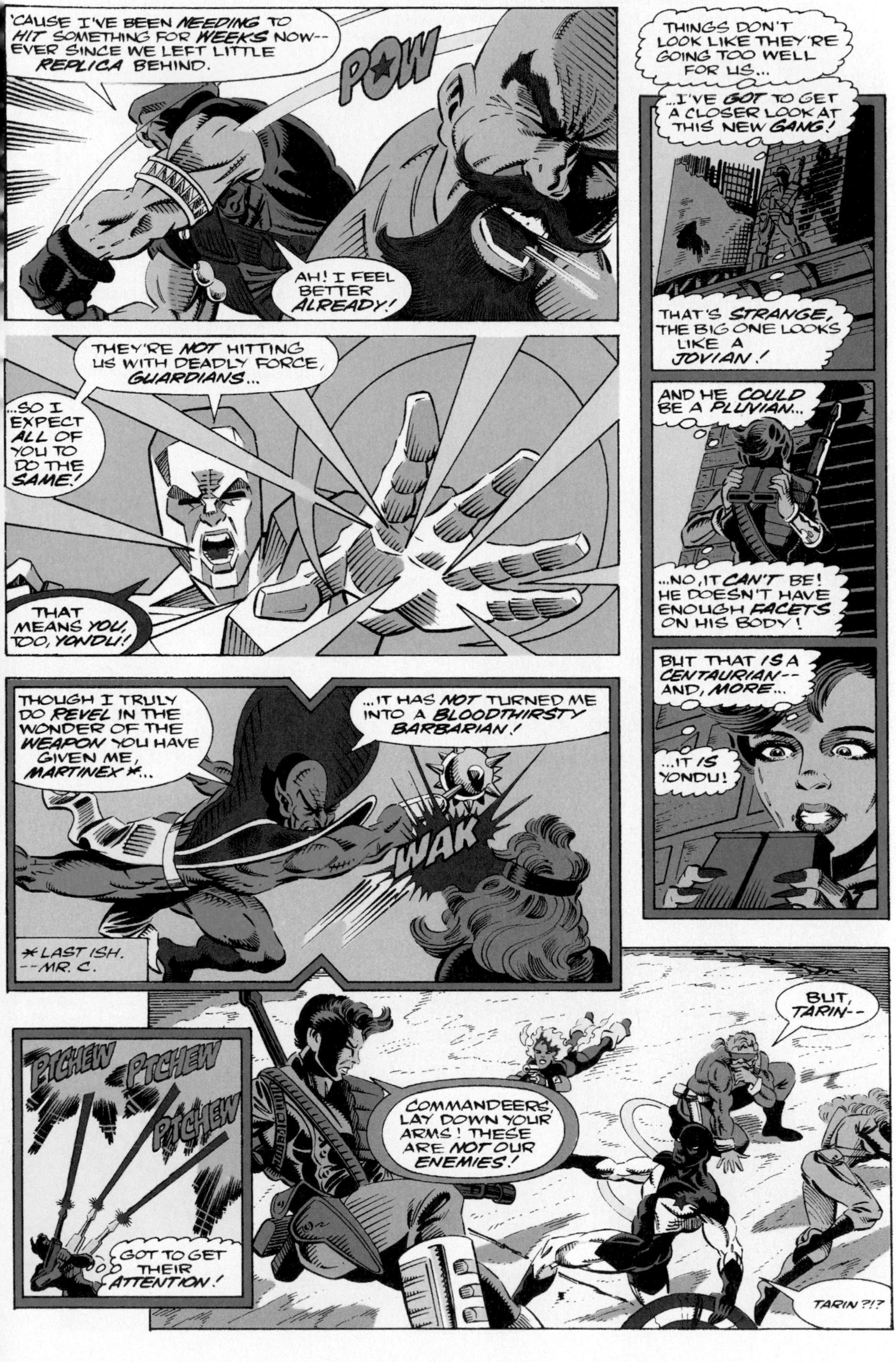
'CAUSE I'VE BEEN NEEDING TO HIT SOMETHING FOR WEEKS NOW-- EVER SINCE WE LEFT LITTLE REPLICA BEHIND.
POW
AH! I FEEL BETTER ALREADY!
THINGS DON'T LOOK LIKE THEY'RE GOING TOO WELL FOR US...
...I'VE GOT TO GET A CLOSER LOOK AT THIS NEW GANG!
THAT'S STRANGE, THE BIG ONE LOOKS LIKE A JOVIAN!
THEY'RE NOT HITTING US WITH DEADLY FORCE, GUARDIANS...
...SO I EXPECT ALL OF YOU TO DO THE SAME!
THAT MEANS YOU, TOO, YONDU!
AND HE COULD BE A PLUVIAN...
...NO, IT CAN'T BE! HE DOESN'T HAVE ENOUGH FACETS ON HIS BODY!
THOUGH I TRULY DO REVEL IN THE WONDER OF THE WEAPON YOU HAVE GIVEN ME, MARTINEX *...
...IT HAS NOT TURNED ME INTO A BLOODTHIRSTY BARBARIAN!
WAK
* LAST ISH. --MR. C.
BUT THAT IS A CENTAURIAN-- AND, MORE...
...IT IS YONDU!
PTCHEW PTCHEW PTCHEW
GOT TO GET THEIR ATTENTION!
COMMANDEERS, LAY DOWN YOUR ARMS! THESE ARE NOT OUR ENEMIES!
BUT, TARIN--
TARIN?!?

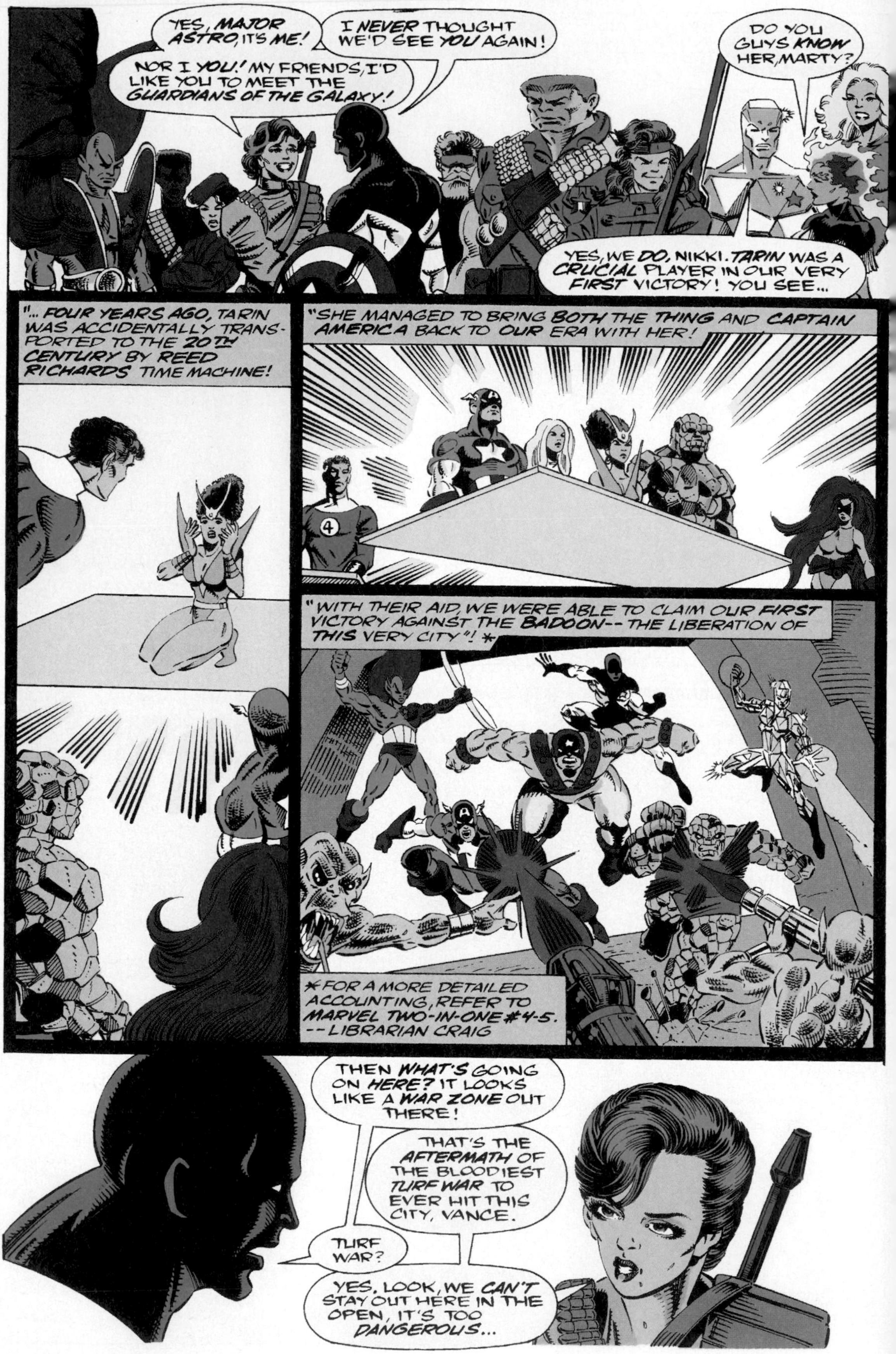
YES, MAJOR ASTRO, IT'S ME!
I NEVER THOUGHT WE'D SEE YOU AGAIN!
NOR I YOU! MY FRIENDS, I'D LIKE YOU TO MEET THE GUARDIANS OF THE GALAXY!
DO YOU GUYS KNOW HER, MARTY?
YES, WE DO, NIKKI. TARIN WAS A CRUCIAL PLAYER IN OUR VERY FIRST VICTORY! YOU SEE...
"...FOUR YEARS AGO, TARIN WAS ACCIDENTALLY TRANSPORTED TO THE 20TH CENTURY BY REED RICHARDS TIME MACHINE!
"SHE MANAGED TO BRING BOTH THE THING AND CAPTAIN AMERICA BACK TO OUR ERA WITH HER!
"WITH THEIR AID, WE WERE ABLE TO CLAIM OUR FIRST VICTORY AGAINST THE BADOON-- THE LIBERATION OF THIS VERY CITY"! *
* FOR A MORE DETAILED ACCOUNTING, REFER TO MARVEL TWO-IN-ONE #4-5. --LIBRARIAN CRAIG
THEN WHAT'S GOING ON HERE? IT LOOKS LIKE A WAR ZONE OUT THERE!
THAT'S THE AFTERMATH OF THE BLOODIEST TURF WAR TO EVER HIT THIS CITY, VANCE.
TURF WAR?
YES. LOOK, WE CAN'T STAY OUT HERE IN THE OPEN, IT'S TOO DANGEROUS...

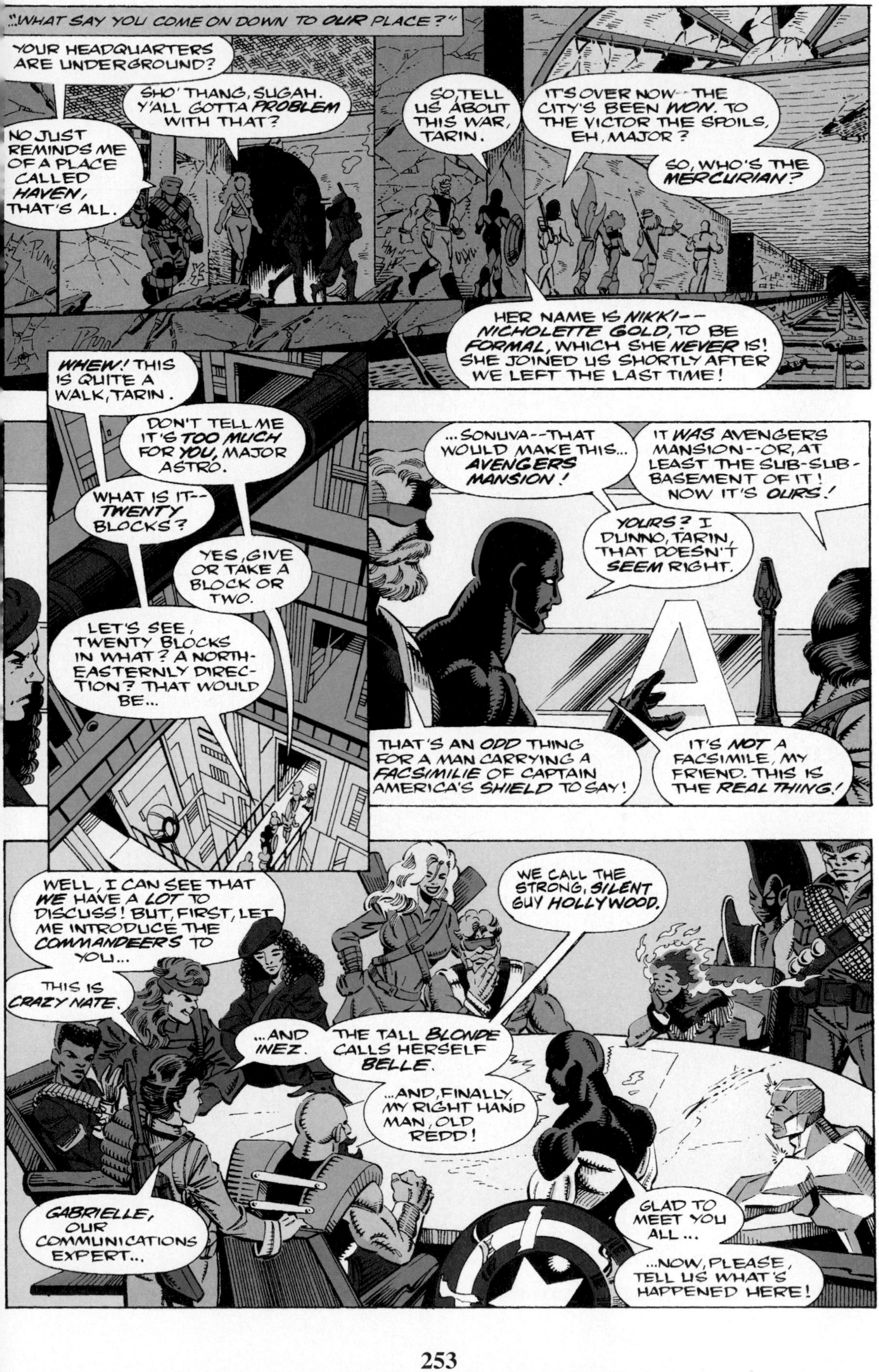
"...WHAT SAY YOU COME ON DOWN TO OUR PLACE?"
YOUR HEADQUARTERS ARE UNDERGROUND?
SHO' THANG, SUGAH. Y'ALL GOTTA PROBLEM WITH THAT?
NO JUST REMINDS ME OF A PLACE CALLED HAVEN, THAT'S ALL.
SO, TELL US ABOUT THIS WAR, TARIN.
IT'S OVER NOW-- THE CITY'S BEEN WON. TO THE VICTOR THE SPOILS, EH, MAJOR?
SO, WHO'S THE MERCURIAN?
HER NAME IS NIKKI-- NICHOLETTE GOLD, TO BE FORMAL, WHICH SHE NEVER IS! SHE JOINED US SHORTLY AFTER WE LEFT THE LAST TIME!
WHEW! THIS IS QUITE A WALK, TARIN.
DON'T TELL ME IT'S TOO MUCH FOR YOU, MAJOR ASTRO.
WHAT IS IT-- TWENTY BLOCKS?
YES, GIVE OR TAKE A BLOCK OR TWO.
LET'S SEE, TWENTY BLOCKS IN WHAT? A NORTH-EASTERNLY DIRECTION? THAT WOULD BE...
...SONUVA--THAT WOULD MAKE THIS... AVENGERS MANSION!
IT WAS AVENGERS MANSION--OR, AT LEAST THE SUB-SUB-BASEMENT OF IT! NOW IT'S OURS!
YOURS? I DUNNO, TARIN, THAT DOESN'T SEEM RIGHT.
THAT'S AN ODD THING FOR A MAN CARRYING A FACSIMILIE OF CAPTAIN AMERICA'S SHIELD TO SAY!
IT'S NOT A FACSIMILE, MY FRIEND. THIS IS THE REAL THING!
WELL, I CAN SEE THAT WE HAVE A LOT TO DISCUSS! BUT, FIRST, LET ME INTRODUCE THE COMMANDEERS TO YOU...
THIS IS CRAZY NATE.
GABRIELLE, OUR COMMUNICATIONS EXPERT...
...AND INEZ.
THE TALL BLONDE CALLS HERSELF BELLE.
WE CALL THE STRONG, SILENT GUY HOLLYWOOD.
...AND, FINALLY MY RIGHT HAND MAN, OLD REDD!
GLAD TO MEET YOU ALL...
...NOW, PLEASE, TELL US WHAT'S HAPPENED HERE!

IT ALL STARTED SHORTLY AFTER YOU *GUARDIANS* LEFT THE EARTH.

A *CONSORTIUM* INTRODUCED A NEW *HOME ENTERTAIN-MENT CENTER* ON THE MARKETPLACE!

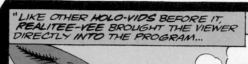

"LIKE OTHER *HOLO-VIDS* BEFORE IT, *REALITEE-VEE* BROUGHT THE VIEWER DIRECTLY *INTO* THE PROGRAM...

"...BUT, *THIS* PRODUCT WAS BASED ON PIRATED *BADOON* TECHNOLOGY...

"...AND WAS *COMPLETELY* INTERACTIVE, AFFECTING *ALL* OF THE VIEWER'S SENSES AT ONCE!

"BUT, MOST INSIDIOUS OF ALL WAS THE FACT THAT THE SET EMITTED A HIGHLY *ADDICTIVE* GAS!

"THE ALIEN NARCOTIC WASN'T DISCOVERED UNTIL IT WAS *TOO LATE!*

"THE DRUG *KEPT* PEOPLE IN *FRONT* OF THEIR SETS. THEY WOULDN'T GET UP TO EAT, SLEEP OR ANYTHING!

"EVENTUALLY, THEY *DIED* IN FRONT OF THEIR SETS!

"AND, WHILE THE *OLDER GENERATION DIED* FOR THEIR ENTERTAINMENT...

"...THE *KIDS* TOOK TO THE STREETS-- AND THE *TURF WAR* BEGAN!

"DURING THE ENSUING *ANARCHY* ON EARTH, THE ENSLAVED COLONY OF *LUNA* ✻ SECEDED FROM THE EARTH-GOV...

"...WITHOUT SHEDDING A DROP OF *BLOOD!*

✻ SEE *GUARDIANS OF THE GALAXY ANNUAL # 1.* CROSS-REFERENCIN'-CRAIG.

"THE SAME COULD *NOT* BE SAID FOR *EARTH!*

"AFTER OVER A *YEAR* OF BLOODY FIGHTING, A *VICTOR* EMERGED...

"...THE MOST *VIOLENT* AND *RUTHLESS STREET ARMY* OF THEM ALL --

PUNISHERS!"

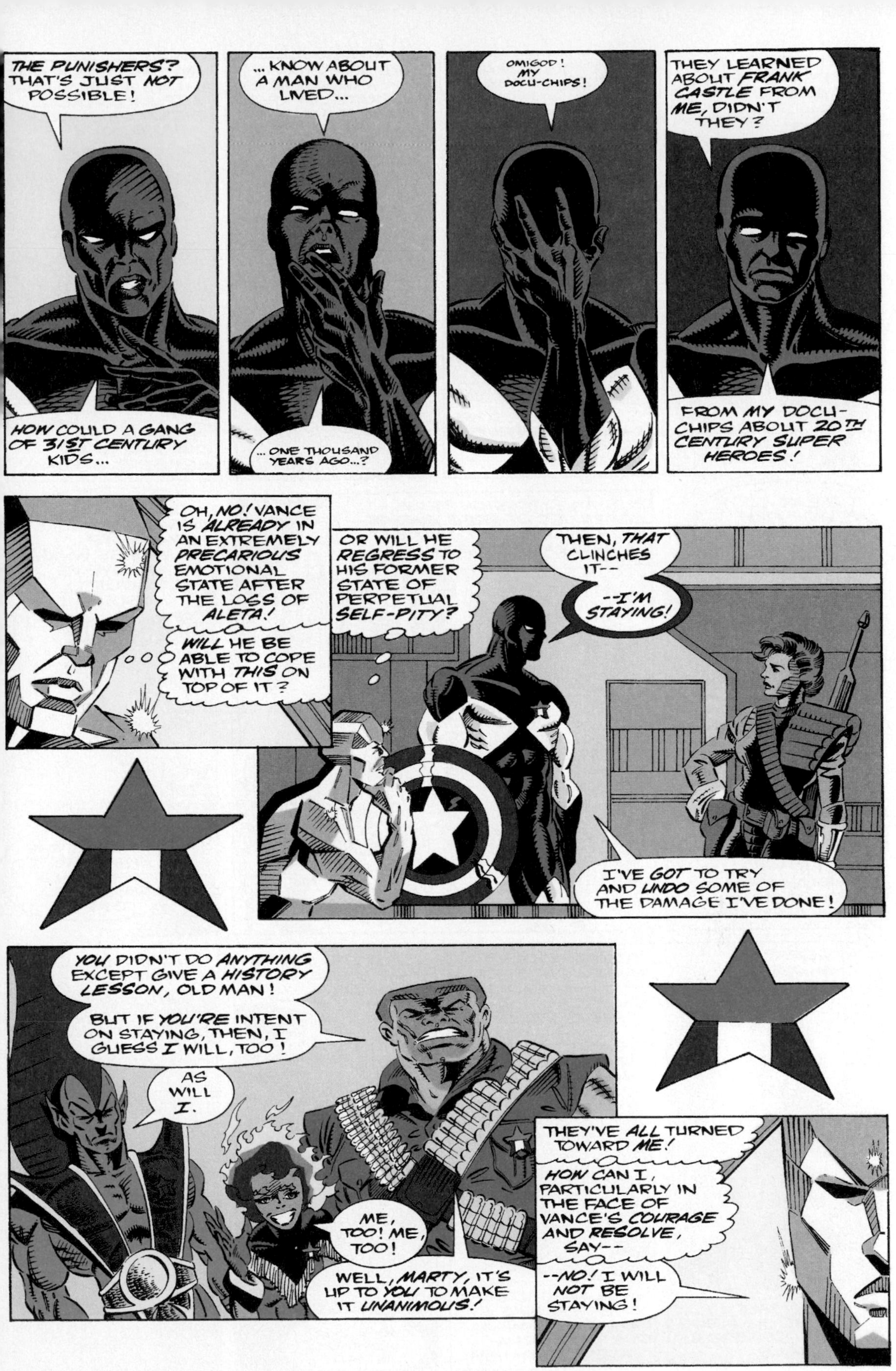
THE PUNISHERS? THAT'S JUST NOT POSSIBLE!
HOW COULD A GANG OF 31ST CENTURY KIDS...
...KNOW ABOUT A MAN WHO LIVED...
...ONE THOUSAND YEARS AGO...?
OMIGOD! MY DOCU-CHIPS!
THEY LEARNED ABOUT FRANK CASTLE FROM ME, DIDN'T THEY?
FROM MY DOCU-CHIPS ABOUT 20TH CENTURY SUPER HEROES!
OH, NO! VANCE IS ALREADY IN AN EXTREMELY PRECARIOUS EMOTIONAL STATE AFTER THE LOSS OF ALETA!
WILL HE BE ABLE TO COPE WITH THIS ON TOP OF IT?
OR WILL HE REGRESS TO HIS FORMER STATE OF PERPETUAL SELF-PITY?
THEN, THAT CLINCHES IT--
--I'M STAYING!
I'VE GOT TO TRY AND UNDO SOME OF THE DAMAGE I'VE DONE!
YOU DIDN'T DO ANYTHING EXCEPT GIVE A HISTORY LESSON, OLD MAN!
BUT IF YOU'RE INTENT ON STAYING, THEN, I GUESS I WILL, TOO!
AS WILL I.
ME, TOO! ME, TOO!
WELL, MARTY, IT'S UP TO YOU TO MAKE IT UNANIMOUS!
THEY'VE ALL TURNED TOWARD ME!
HOW CAN I, PARTICULARLY IN THE FACE OF VANCE'S COURAGE AND RESOLVE, SAY--
--NO! I WILL NOT BE STAYING!

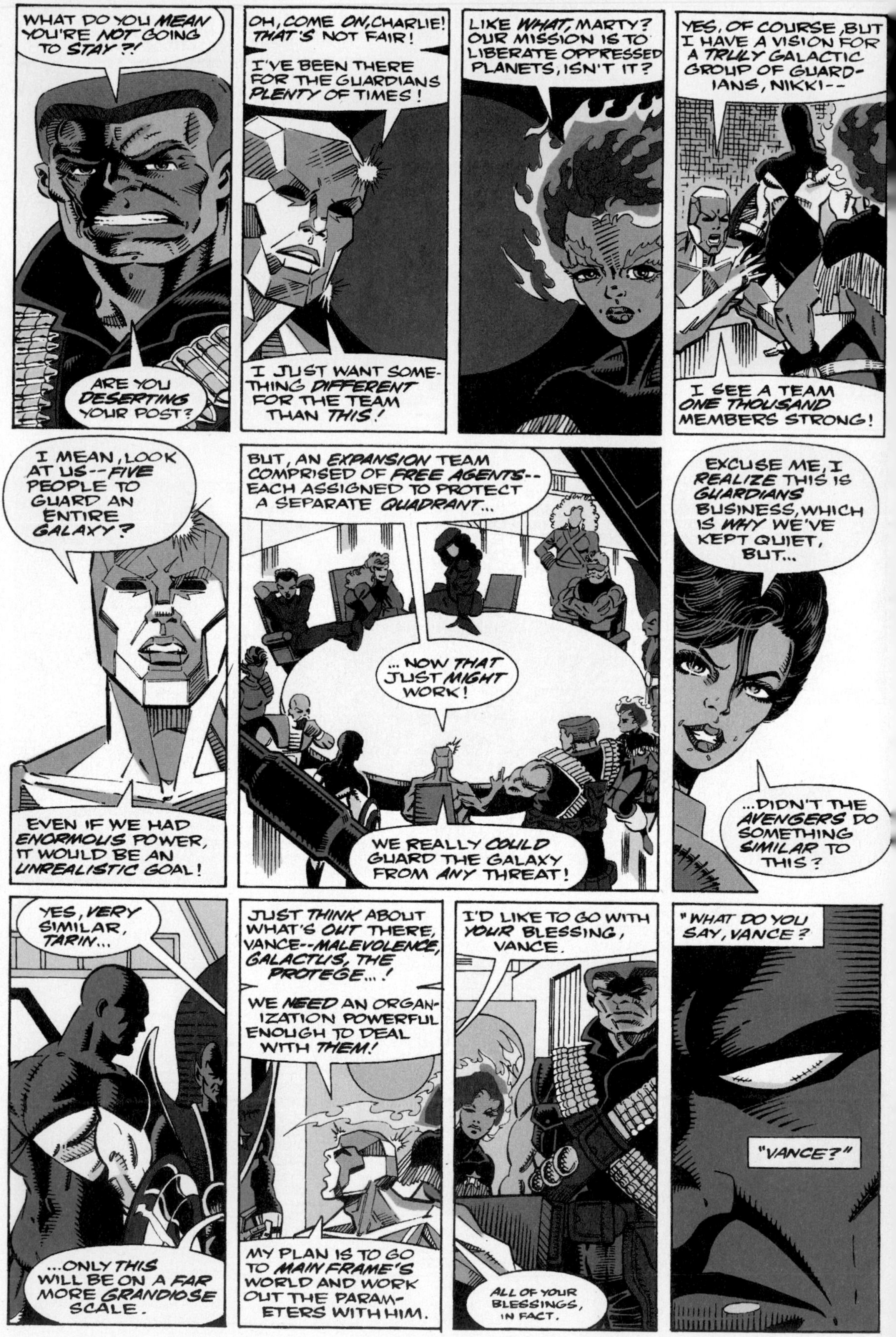
WHAT DO YOU MEAN YOU'RE NOT GOING TO STAY?!
ARE YOU DESERTING YOUR POST?
OH, COME ON, CHARLIE! THAT'S NOT FAIR!
I'VE BEEN THERE FOR THE GUARDIANS PLENTY OF TIMES!
I JUST WANT SOMETHING DIFFERENT FOR THE TEAM THAN THIS!
LIKE WHAT, MARTY? OUR MISSION IS TO LIBERATE OPPRESSED PLANETS, ISN'T IT?
YES, OF COURSE, BUT I HAVE A VISION FOR A TRULY GALACTIC GROUP OF GUARDIANS, NIKKI--
I SEE A TEAM ONE THOUSAND MEMBERS STRONG!
I MEAN, LOOK AT US--FIVE PEOPLE TO GUARD AN ENTIRE GALAXY?
EVEN IF WE HAD ENORMOUS POWER, IT WOULD BE AN UNREALISTIC GOAL!
BUT, AN EXPANSION TEAM COMPRISED OF FREE AGENTS--EACH ASSIGNED TO PROTECT A SEPARATE QUADRANT...
...NOW THAT JUST MIGHT WORK!
WE REALLY COULD GUARD THE GALAXY FROM ANY THREAT!
EXCUSE ME, I REALIZE THIS IS GUARDIANS BUSINESS, WHICH IS WHY WE'VE KEPT QUIET, BUT...
...DIDN'T THE AVENGERS DO SOMETHING SIMILAR TO THIS?
YES, VERY SIMILAR, TARIN...
...ONLY THIS WILL BE ON A FAR MORE GRANDIOSE SCALE.
JUST THINK ABOUT WHAT'S OUT THERE, VANCE--MALEVOLENCE, GALACTUS, THE PROTEGE...!
WE NEED AN ORGANIZATION POWERFUL ENOUGH TO DEAL WITH THEM!
MY PLAN IS TO GO TO MAIN FRAME'S WORLD AND WORK OUT THE PARAMETERS WITH HIM.
I'D LIKE TO GO WITH YOUR BLESSING, VANCE.
ALL OF YOUR BLESSINGS, IN FACT.
"WHAT DO YOU SAY, VANCE?
"VANCE?"

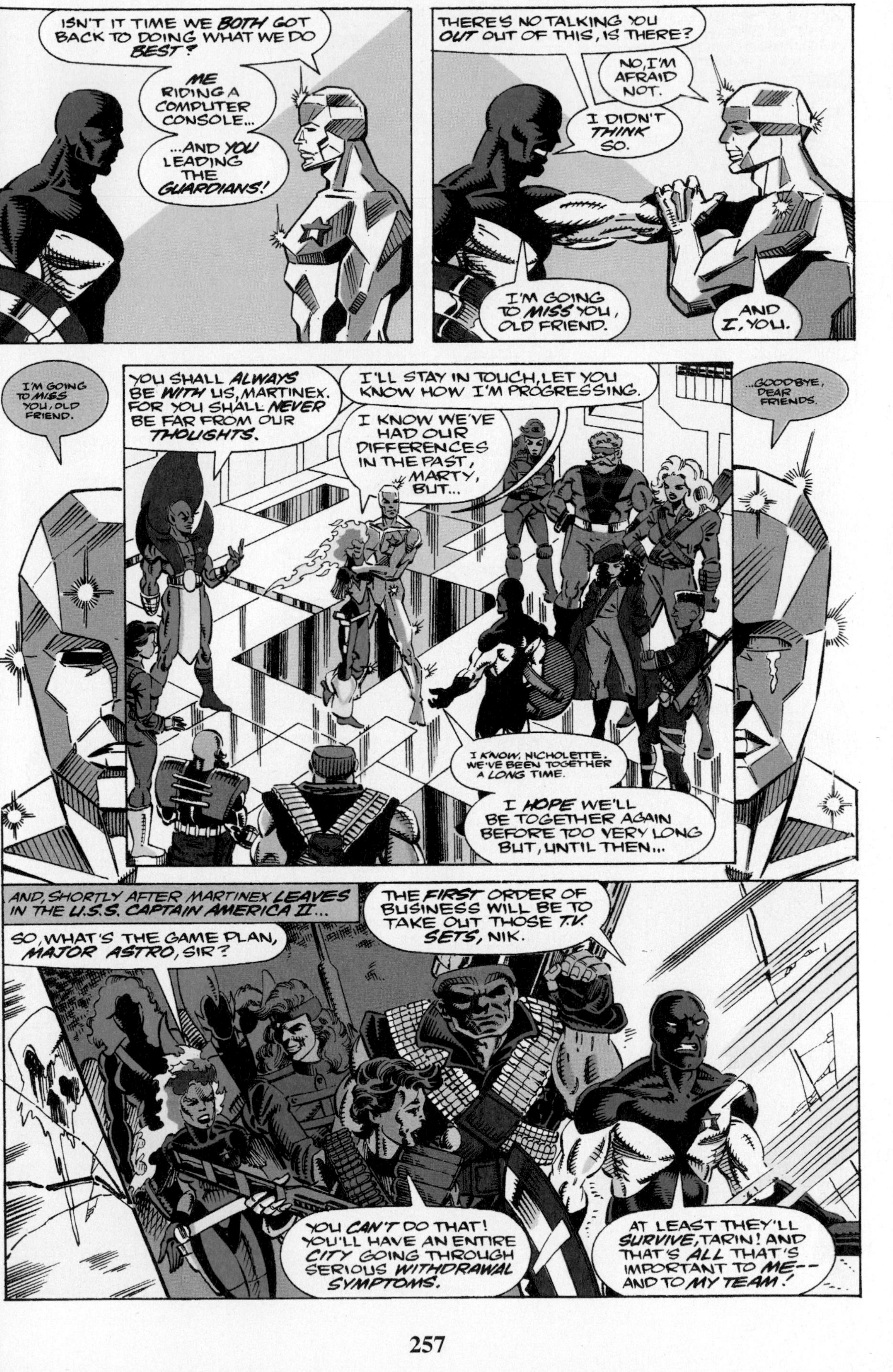
ISN'T IT TIME WE BOTH GOT BACK TO DOING WHAT WE DO BEST?
ME RIDING A COMPUTER CONSOLE...
...AND YOU LEADING THE GUARDIANS!
THERE'S NO TALKING YOU OUT OUT OF THIS, IS THERE?
NO, I'M AFRAID NOT.
I DIDN'T THINK SO.
I'M GOING TO MISS YOU, OLD FRIEND.
AND I, YOU.
I'M GOING TO MISS YOU, OLD FRIEND.
YOU SHALL ALWAYS BE WITH US, MARTINEX. FOR YOU SHALL NEVER BE FAR FROM OUR THOUGHTS.
I'LL STAY IN TOUCH, LET YOU KNOW HOW I'M PROGRESSING.
I KNOW WE'VE HAD OUR DIFFERENCES IN THE PAST, MARTY, BUT...
...GOODBYE, DEAR FRIENDS.
I KNOW, NICHOLETTE. WE'VE BEEN TOGETHER A LONG TIME.
I HOPE WE'LL BE TOGETHER AGAIN BEFORE TOO VERY LONG BUT, UNTIL THEN...
AND, SHORTLY AFTER MARTINEX LEAVES IN THE U.S.S. CAPTAIN AMERICA II...
SO, WHAT'S THE GAME PLAN, MAJOR ASTRO, SIR?
THE FIRST ORDER OF BUSINESS WILL BE TO TAKE OUT THOSE T.V. SETS, NIK.
YOU CAN'T DO THAT! YOU'LL HAVE AN ENTIRE CITY GOING THROUGH SERIOUS WITHDRAWAL SYMPTOMS.
AT LEAST THEY'LL SURVIVE, TARIN! AND THAT'S ALL THAT'S IMPORTANT TO ME-- AND TO MY TEAM!

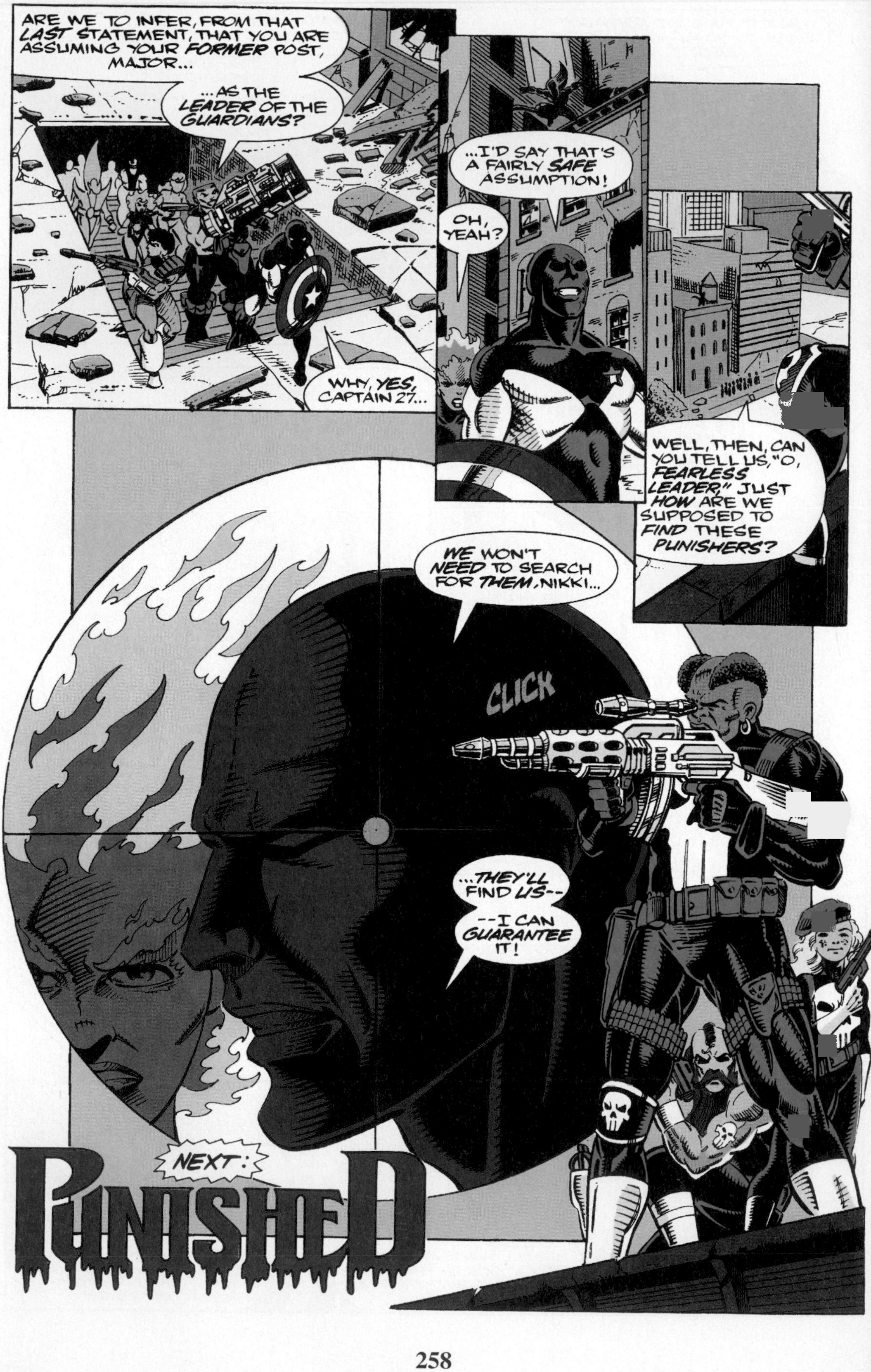
ARE WE TO INFER, FROM THAT LAST STATEMENT, THAT YOU ARE ASSUMING YOUR FORMER POST, MAJOR...
...AS THE LEADER OF THE GUARDIANS?
WHY, YES, CAPTAIN 27...
...I'D SAY THAT'S A FAIRLY SAFE ASSUMPTION!
OH, YEAH?
WELL, THEN, CAN YOU TELL US, "O, FEARLESS LEADER," JUST HOW ARE WE SUPPOSED TO FIND THESE PUNISHERS?
WE WON'T NEED TO SEARCH FOR THEM, NIKKI...
CLICK
...THEY'LL FIND US--
--I CAN GUARANTEE IT!
NEXT:
PUNISHED

GUARDIANS OF THE GALAXY

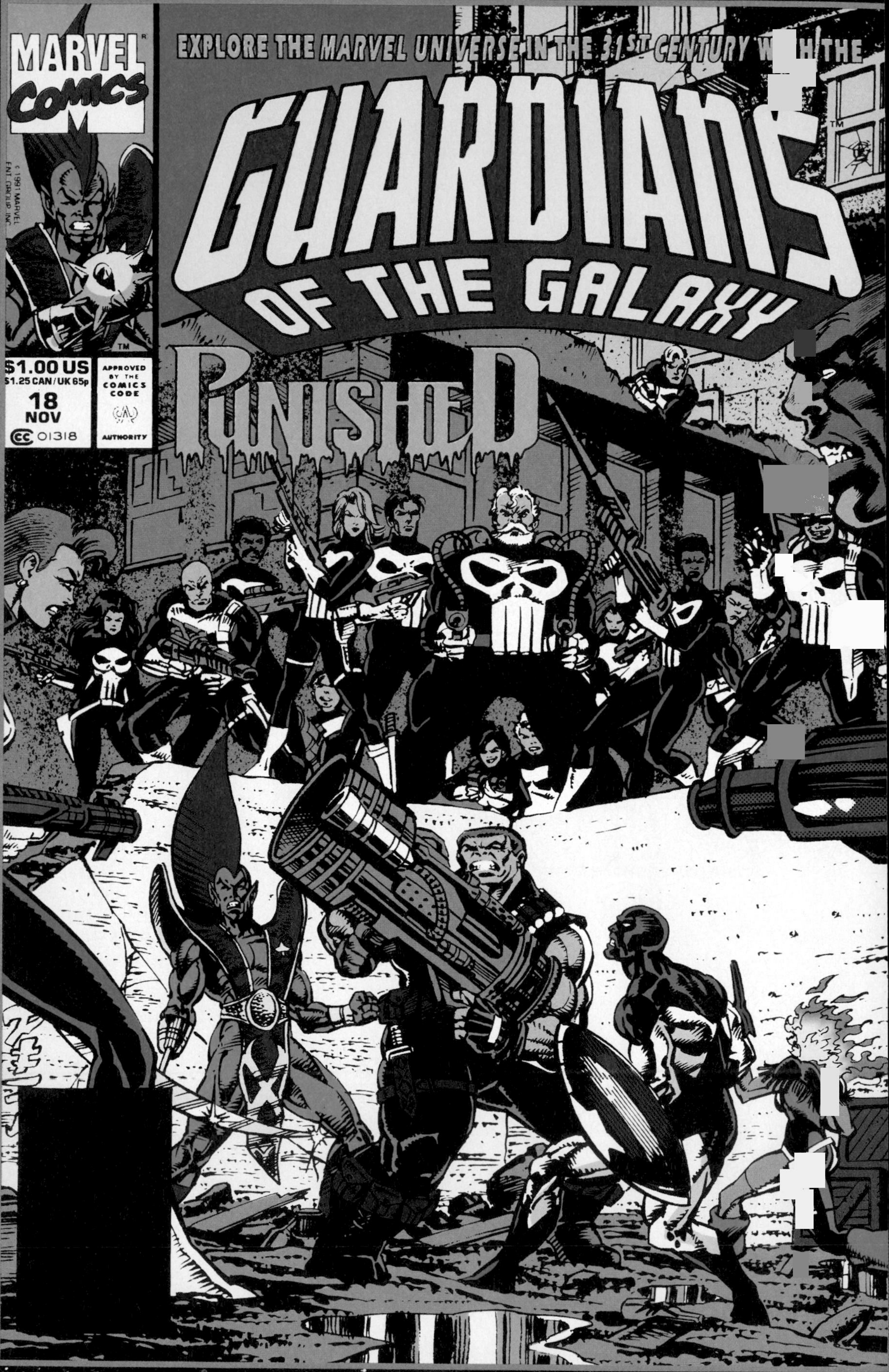
MARVEL COMICS
EXPLORE THE MARVEL UNIVERSE IN THE 31ST CENTURY W H THE
GUARDIANS OF THE GALAXY
© 1991 MARVEL ENT. GROUP, INC.
$1.00 US
$1.25 CAN/UK 65p
18
NOV
01318
APPROVED BY THE COMICS CODE AUTHORITY
PUNISHED

MAJOR VANCE ASTRO! CHARLIE 27! NIKKI! YONDU! FOUR EXTRAORDINARY SUPER-BEINGS, ALL SURVIVORS OF INTERSTELLAR WAR. NOW THEY ROAM THE COSMOS OF THE 31ST CENTURY ABOARD THE STARSHIP CAPTAIN AMERICA, THEIR MISSION—TO SAFEGUARD THE MILKY WAY!
STAN LEE PRESENTS . . . THE GUARDIANS OF THE GALAXY!

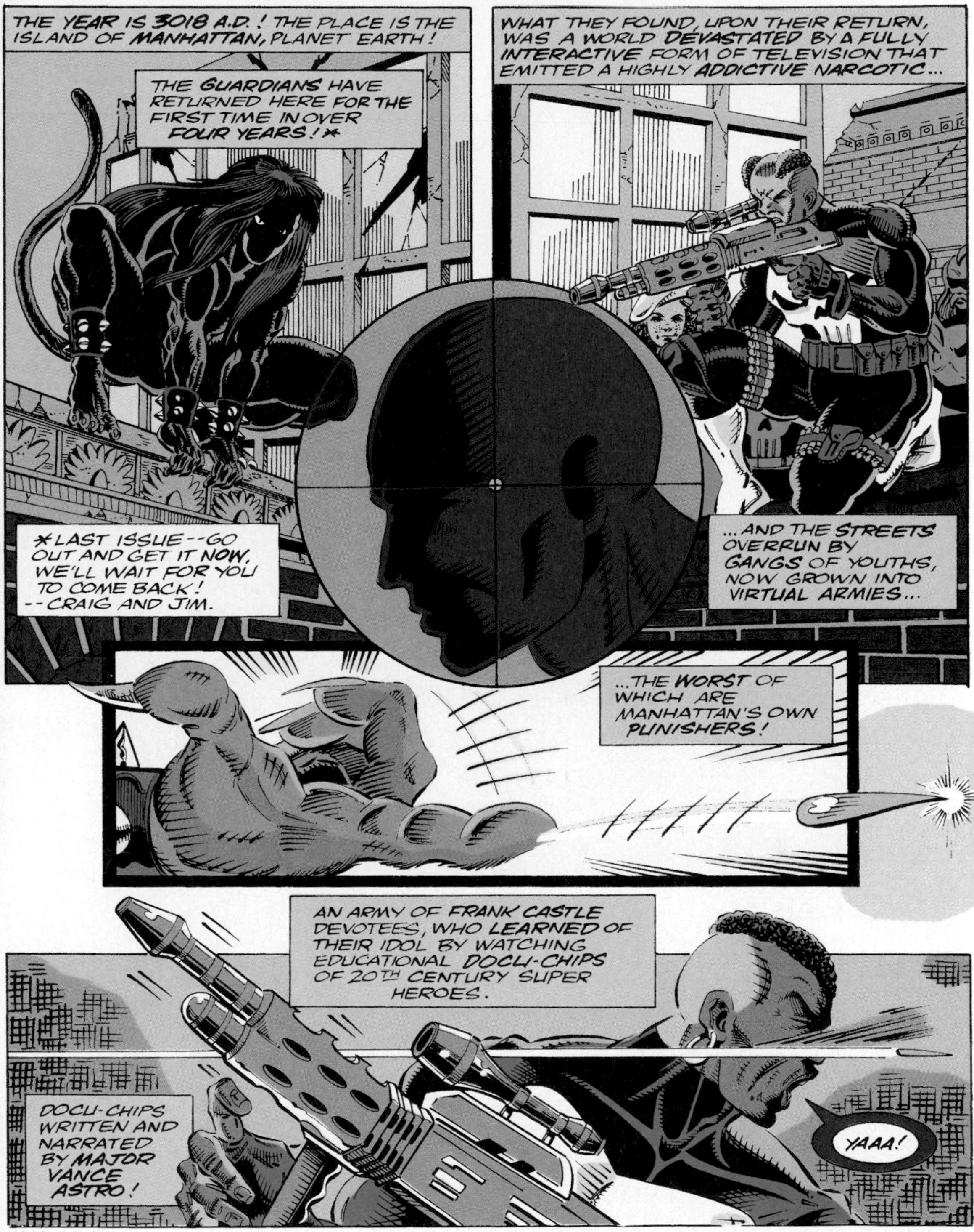
THE YEAR IS 3018 A.D.! THE PLACE IS THE ISLAND OF MANHATTAN, PLANET EARTH!
THE GUARDIANS HAVE RETURNED HERE FOR THE FIRST TIME IN OVER FOUR YEARS!*
*LAST ISSUE--GO OUT AND GET IT NOW. WE'LL WAIT FOR YOU TO COME BACK! --CRAIG AND JIM.
WHAT THEY FOUND, UPON THEIR RETURN, WAS A WORLD DEVASTATED BY A FULLY INTERACTIVE FORM OF TELEVISION THAT EMITTED A HIGHLY ADDICTIVE NARCOTIC...
...AND THE STREETS OVERRUN BY GANGS OF YOUTHS, NOW GROWN INTO VIRTUAL ARMIES...
...THE WORST OF WHICH ARE MANHATTAN'S OWN PUNISHERS!
AN ARMY OF FRANK CASTLE DEVOTEES, WHO LEARNED OF THEIR IDOL BY WATCHING EDUCATIONAL DOCU-CHIPS OF 20TH CENTURY SUPER HEROES.
DOCU-CHIPS WRITTEN AND NARRATED BY MAJOR VANCE ASTRO!
YAAA!

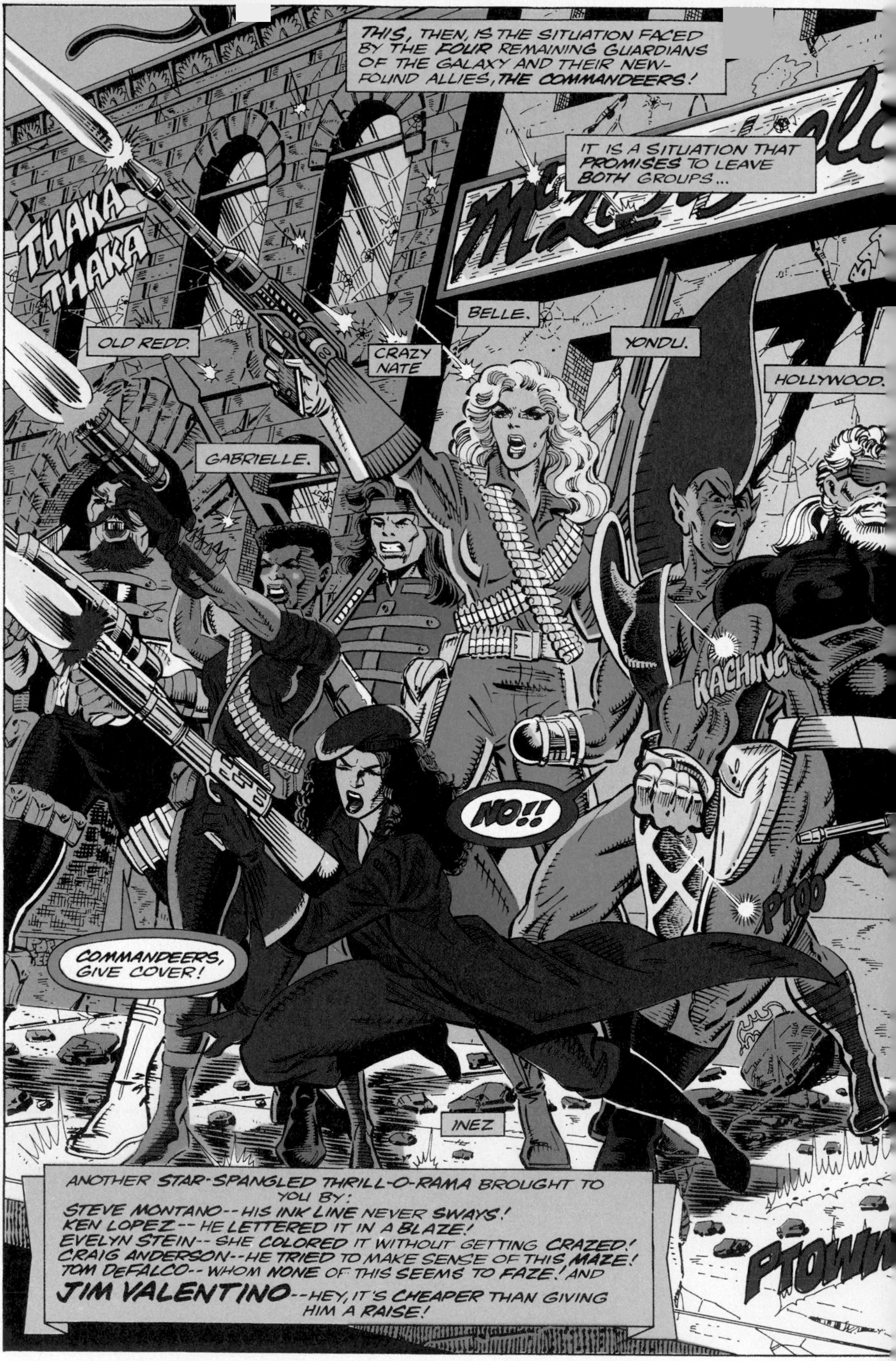
THIS, THEN, IS THE SITUATION FACED BY THE FOUR REMAINING GUARDIANS OF THE GALAXY AND THEIR NEW-FOUND ALLIES, THE COMMANDEERS!
IT IS A SITUATION THAT PROMISES TO LEAVE BOTH GROUPS...
THAKA THAKA
OLD REDD.
CRAZY NATE
BELLE.
YONDU.
HOLLYWOOD.
GABRIELLE.
KACHING
NO!!
PTOO
COMMANDEERS, GIVE COVER!
INEZ
ANOTHER STAR-SPANGLED THRILL-O-RAMA BROUGHT TO YOU BY:
STEVE MONTANO--HIS INK LINE NEVER SWAYS!
KEN LOPEZ--HE LETTERED IT IN A BLAZE!
EVELYN STEIN--SHE COLORED IT WITHOUT GETTING CRAZED!
CRAIG ANDERSON--HE TRIED TO MAKE SENSE OF THIS MAZE!
TOM DeFALCO--WHOM NONE OF THIS SEEMS TO FAZE! AND
JIM VALENTINO--HEY, IT'S CHEAPER THAN GIVING HIM A RAISE!
PTOWW

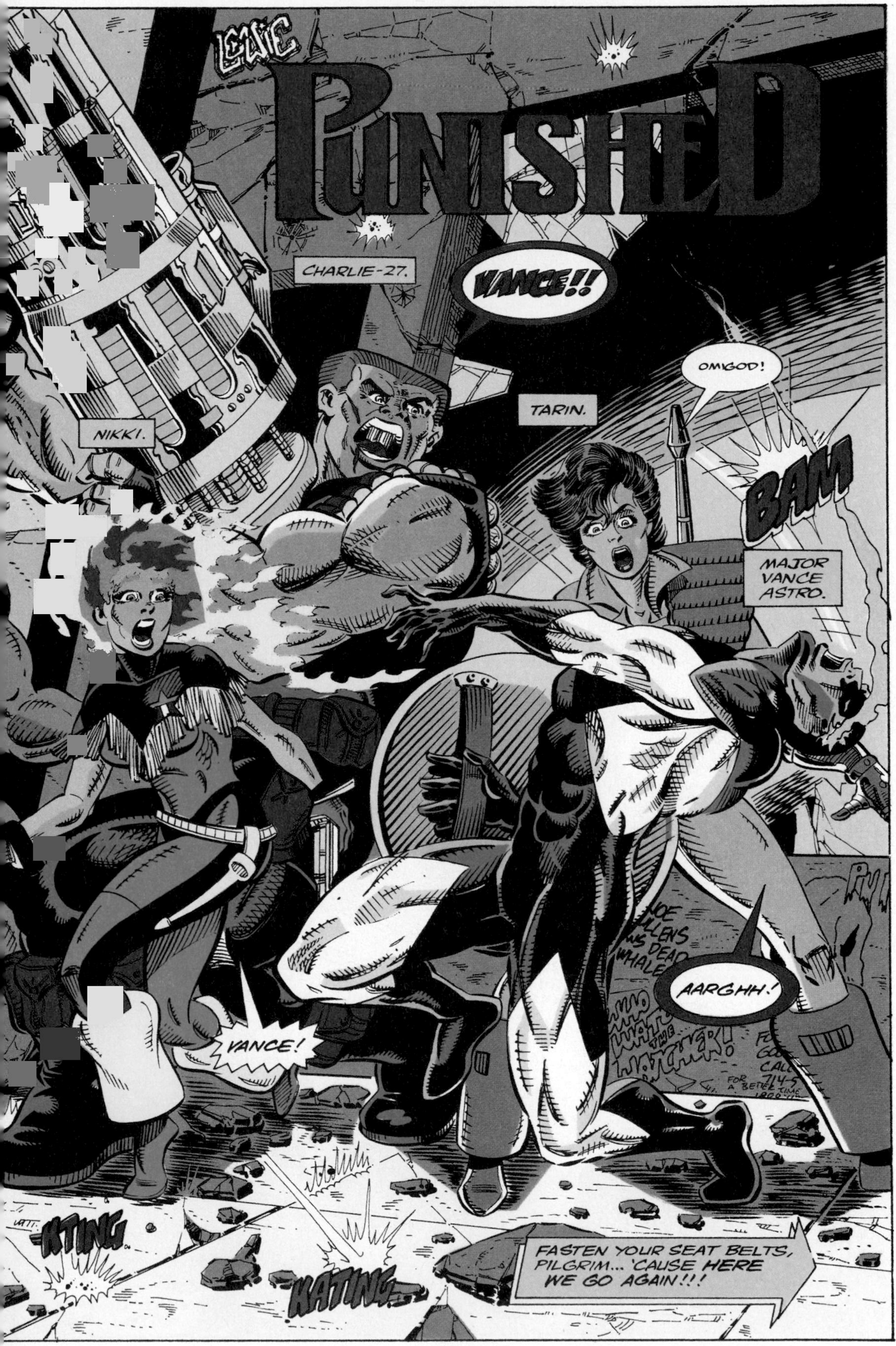

PUNISHED
CHARLIE-27.
VANCE!!
OMIGOD!
TARIN.
NIKKI.
BAM
MAJOR VANCE ASTRO.
AARGHH!
VANCE!
KTING
KATING
FASTEN YOUR SEAT BELTS, PILGRIM... 'CAUSE HERE WE GO AGAIN!!!

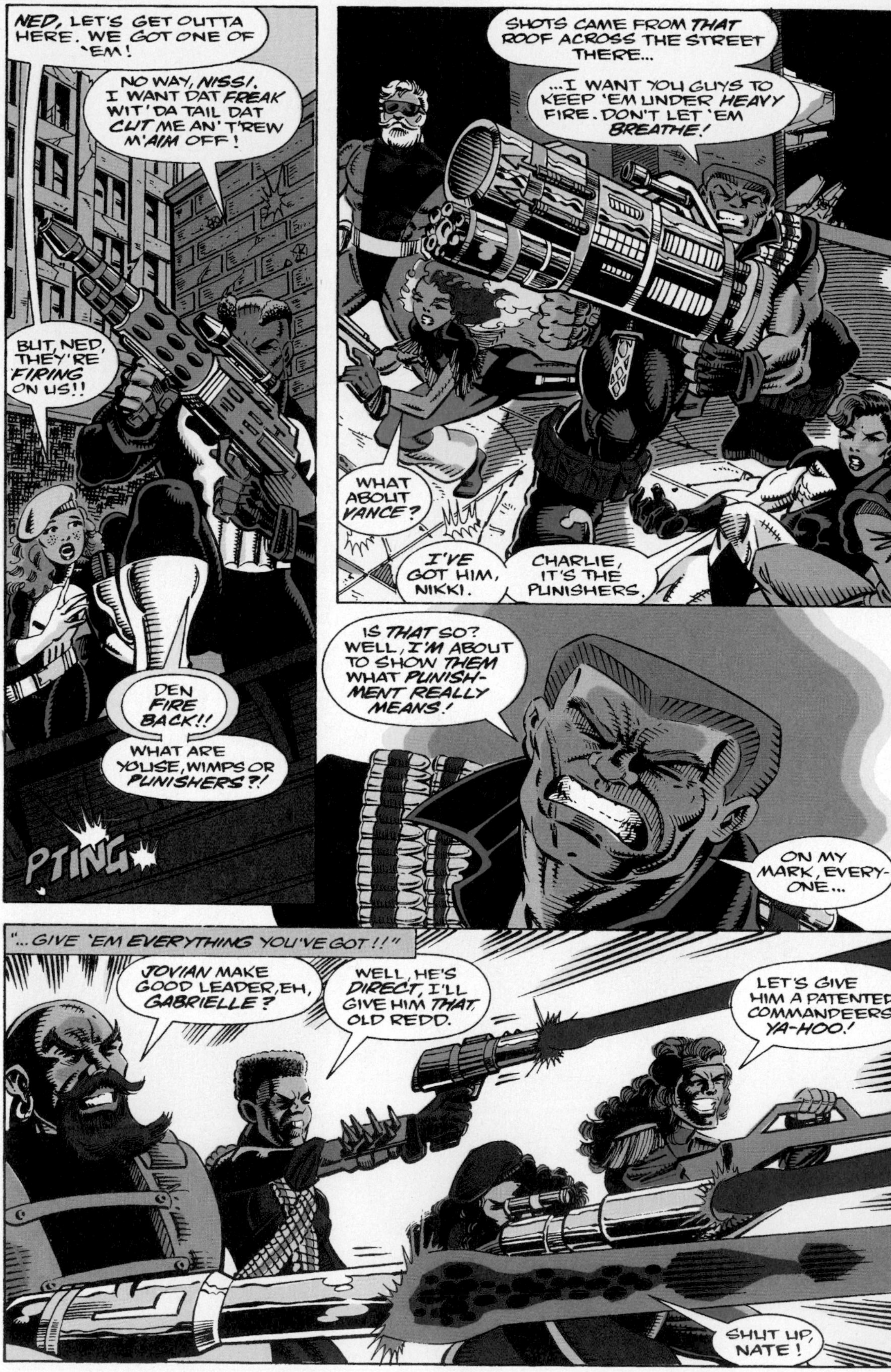
NED, LET'S GET OUTTA HERE. WE GOT ONE OF 'EM!
NO WAY, NISSI. I WANT DAT FREAK WIT' DA TAIL DAT CUT ME AN' T'REW M'AIM OFF!
BUT, NED, THEY'RE FIRING ON US!!
DEN FIRE BACK!!
WHAT ARE YOUSE, WIMPS OR PUNISHERS?!
PTING
SHOTS CAME FROM THAT ROOF ACROSS THE STREET THERE...
...I WANT YOU GUYS TO KEEP 'EM UNDER HEAVY FIRE. DON'T LET 'EM BREATHE!
WHAT ABOUT VANCE?
I'VE GOT HIM, NIKKI.
CHARLIE, IT'S THE PUNISHERS.
IS THAT SO? WELL, I'M ABOUT TO SHOW THEM WHAT PUNISHMENT REALLY MEANS!
ON MY MARK, EVERYONE...
"...GIVE 'EM EVERYTHING YOU'VE GOT!!"
JOVIAN MAKE GOOD LEADER, EH, GABRIELLE?
WELL, HE'S DIRECT, I'LL GIVE HIM THAT, OLD REDD.
LET'S GIVE HIM A PATENTED COMMANDEERS YA-HOO!
SHUT UP, NATE!

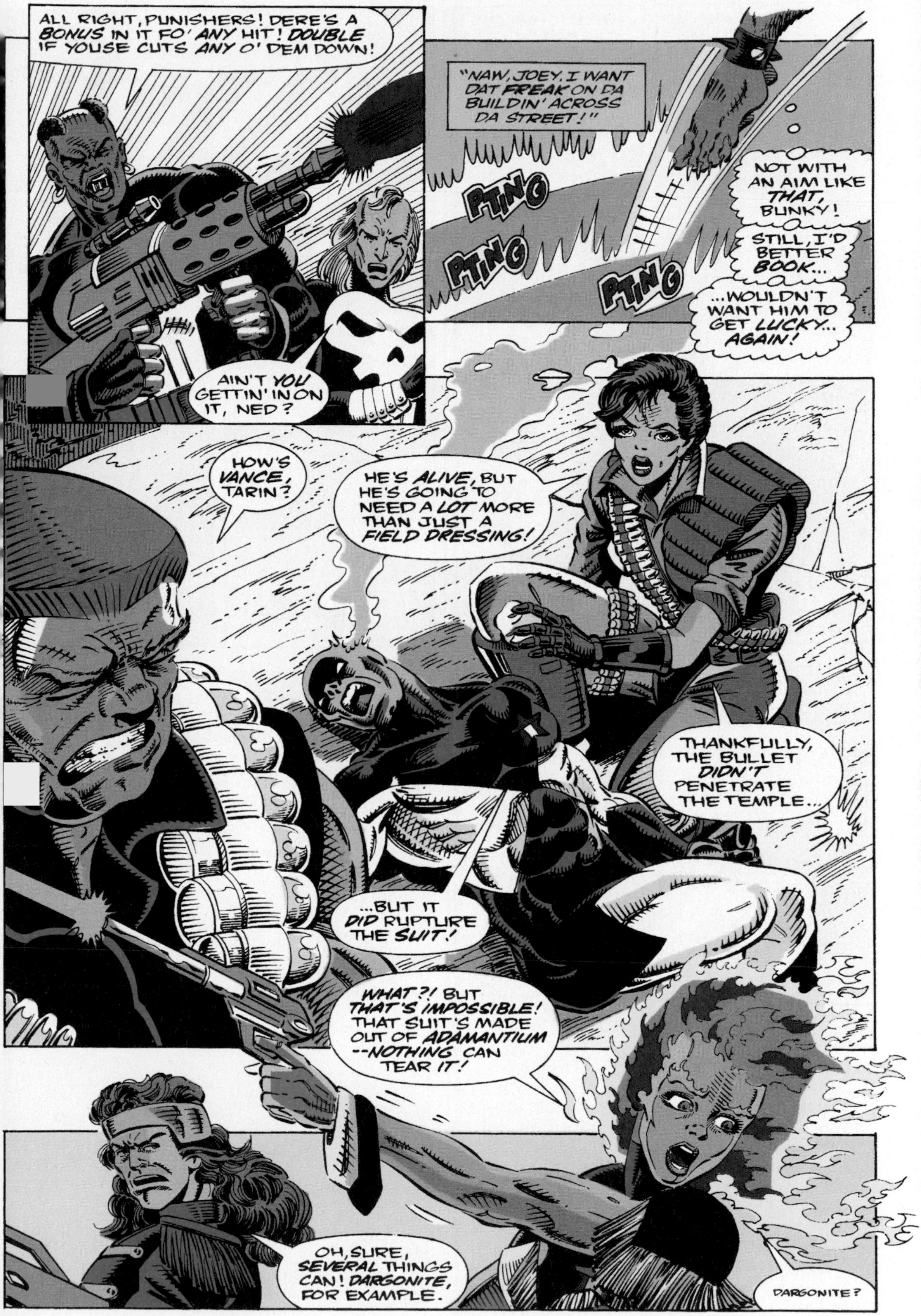
ALL RIGHT, PUNISHERS! DERE'S A BONUS IN IT FO' ANY HIT! DOUBLE IF YOUSE CUTS ANY O' DEM DOWN!
AIN'T YOU GETTIN' IN ON IT, NED?
"NAW, JOEY. I WANT DAT FREAK ON DA BUILDIN' ACROSS DA STREET!"
PTING
PTING
PTING
NOT WITH AN AIM LIKE THAT, BUNKY!
STILL, I'D BETTER BOOK...
...WOULDN'T WANT HIM TO GET LUCKY... AGAIN!
HOW'S VANCE, TARIN?
HE'S ALIVE, BUT HE'S GOING TO NEED A LOT MORE THAN JUST A FIELD DRESSING!
THANKFULLY, THE BULLET DIDN'T PENETRATE THE TEMPLE...
...BUT IT DID RUPTURE THE SUIT!
WHAT?! BUT THAT'S IMPOSSIBLE! THAT SUIT'S MADE OUT OF ADAMANTIUM --NOTHING CAN TEAR IT!
OH, SURE, SEVERAL THINGS CAN! DARGONITE, FOR EXAMPLE.
DARGONITE?

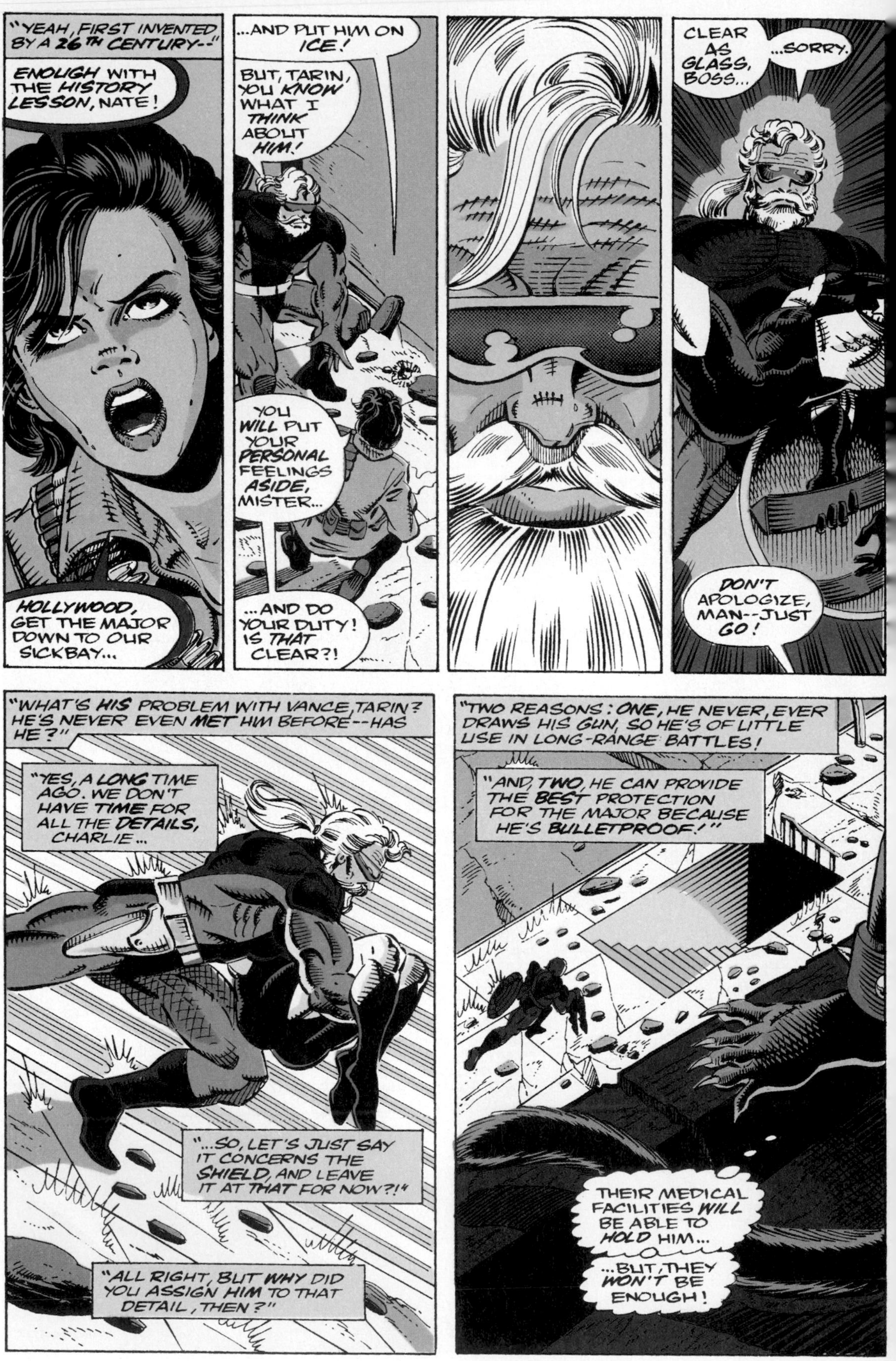
"YEAH, FIRST INVENTED BY A 26TH CENTURY--"
ENOUGH WITH THE HISTORY LESSON, NATE!
HOLLYWOOD, GET THE MAJOR DOWN TO OUR SICKBAY...
...AND PUT HIM ON ICE!
BUT, TARIN, YOU KNOW WHAT I THINK ABOUT HIM!
YOU WILL PUT YOUR PERSONAL FEELINGS ASIDE, MISTER...
...AND DO YOUR DUTY! IS THAT CLEAR?!
CLEAR AS GLASS, BOSS...
...SORRY.
DON'T APOLOGIZE, MAN--JUST GO!
"WHAT'S HIS PROBLEM WITH VANCE, TARIN? HE'S NEVER EVEN MET HIM BEFORE--HAS HE?"
"YES, A LONG TIME AGO. WE DON'T HAVE TIME FOR ALL THE DETAILS, CHARLIE...
"...SO, LET'S JUST SAY IT CONCERNS THE SHIELD, AND LEAVE IT AT THAT FOR NOW?!"
"ALL RIGHT, BUT WHY DID YOU ASSIGN HIM TO THAT DETAIL, THEN?"
"TWO REASONS: ONE, HE NEVER, EVER DRAWS HIS GUN, SO HE'S OF LITTLE USE IN LONG-RANGE BATTLES!
"AND, TWO, HE CAN PROVIDE THE BEST PROTECTION FOR THE MAJOR BECAUSE HE'S BULLETPROOF!"
THEIR MEDICAL FACILITIES WILL BE ABLE TO HOLD HIM...
...BUT, THEY WON'T BE ENOUGH!

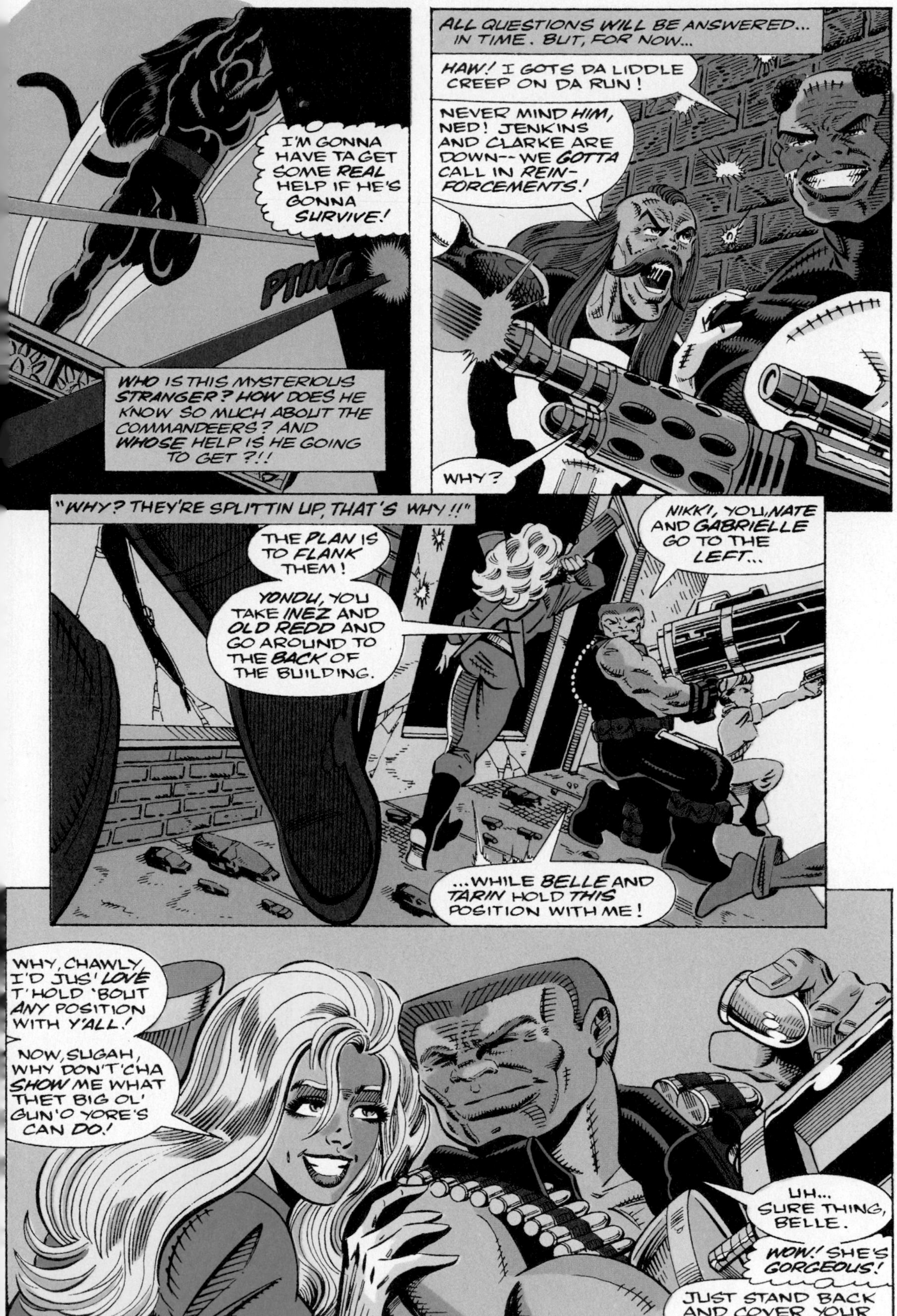
I'M GONNA HAVE TA GET SOME REAL HELP IF HE'S GONNA SURVIVE!
PTING
WHO IS THIS MYSTERIOUS STRANGER? HOW DOES HE KNOW SO MUCH ABOUT THE COMMANDEERS? AND WHOSE HELP IS HE GOING TO GET?!!
ALL QUESTIONS WILL BE ANSWERED... IN TIME. BUT, FOR NOW...
HAW! I GOTS DA LIDDLE CREEP ON DA RUN!
NEVER MIND HIM, NED! JENKINS AND CLARKE ARE DOWN-- WE GOTTA CALL IN REIN-FORCEMENTS!
WHY?
"WHY? THEY'RE SPLITTIN UP, THAT'S WHY!!"
THE PLAN IS TO FLANK THEM!
YONDU, YOU TAKE INEZ AND OLD REDD AND GO AROUND TO THE BACK OF THE BUILDING.
NIKKI, YOU, NATE AND GABRIELLE GO TO THE LEFT...
...WHILE BELLE AND TARIN HOLD THIS POSITION WITH ME!
WHY, CHAWLY, I'D JUS' LOVE T'HOLD 'BOUT ANY POSITION WITH Y'ALL!
NOW, SUGAH, WHY DON'T'CHA SHOW ME WHAT THET BIG OL' GUN'O YORE'S CAN DO!
UH... SURE THING, BELLE.
WOW! SHE'S GORGEOUS!
JUST STAND BACK AND COVER YOUR EARS, LITTLE LADY!

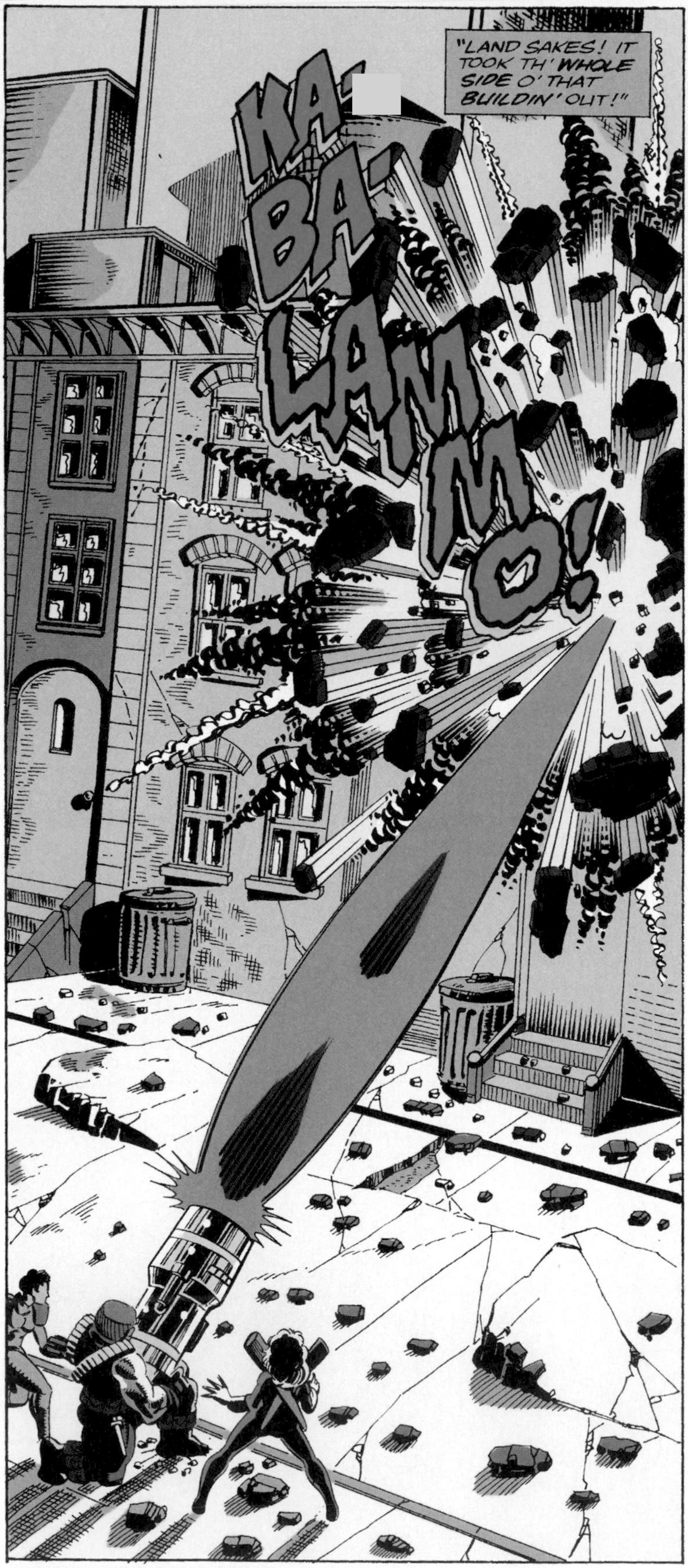
KA-BA-LAM-MO!
"LAND SAKES! IT TOOK TH' WHOLE SIDE O' THAT BUILDIN' OUT!"

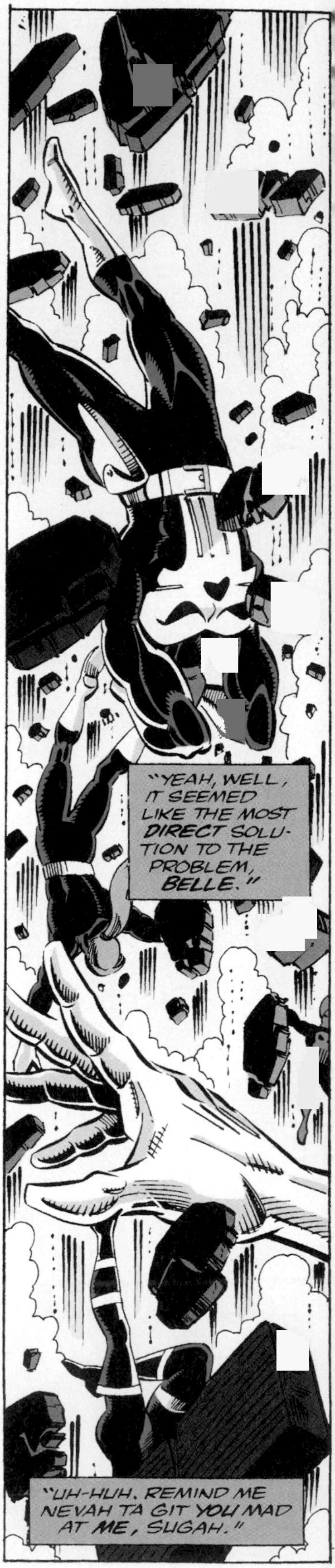
"YEAH, WELL, IT SEEMED LIKE THE MOST DIRECT SOLUTION TO THE PROBLEM, BELLE."
"UH-HUH. REMIND ME NEVAH TA GIT YOU MAD AT ME, SUGAH."

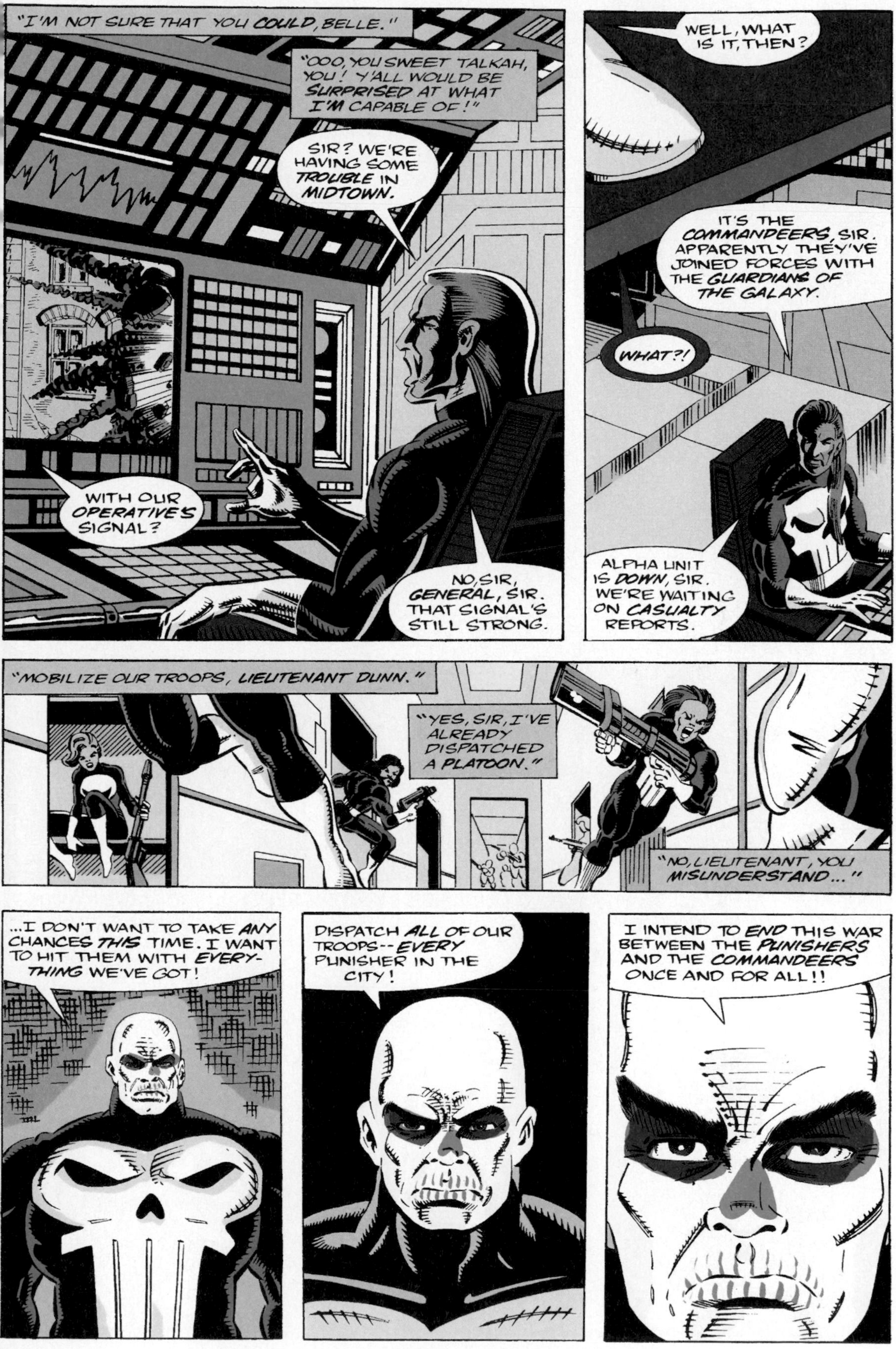
"I'M NOT SURE THAT YOU COULD, BELLE."
"OOO, YOU SWEET TALKAH, YOU! Y'ALL WOULD BE SURPRISED AT WHAT I'M CAPABLE OF!"
SIR? WE'RE HAVING SOME TROUBLE IN MIDTOWN.
WITH OUR OPERATIVE'S SIGNAL?
NO, SIR, GENERAL, SIR. THAT SIGNAL'S STILL STRONG.
WELL, WHAT IS IT, THEN?
IT'S THE COMMANDEERS, SIR. APPARENTLY THEY'VE JOINED FORCES WITH THE GUARDIANS OF THE GALAXY.
WHAT?!
ALPHA UNIT IS DOWN, SIR. WE'RE WAITING ON CASUALTY REPORTS.
"MOBILIZE OUR TROOPS, LIEUTENANT DUNN."
"YES, SIR, I'VE ALREADY DISPATCHED A PLATOON."
"NO, LIEUTENANT, YOU MISUNDERSTAND..."
...I DON'T WANT TO TAKE ANY CHANCES THIS TIME. I WANT TO HIT THEM WITH EVERY-THING WE'VE GOT!
DISPATCH ALL OF OUR TROOPS--EVERY PUNISHER IN THE CITY!
I INTEND TO END THIS WAR BETWEEN THE PUNISHERS AND THE COMMANDEERS ONCE AND FOR ALL!!

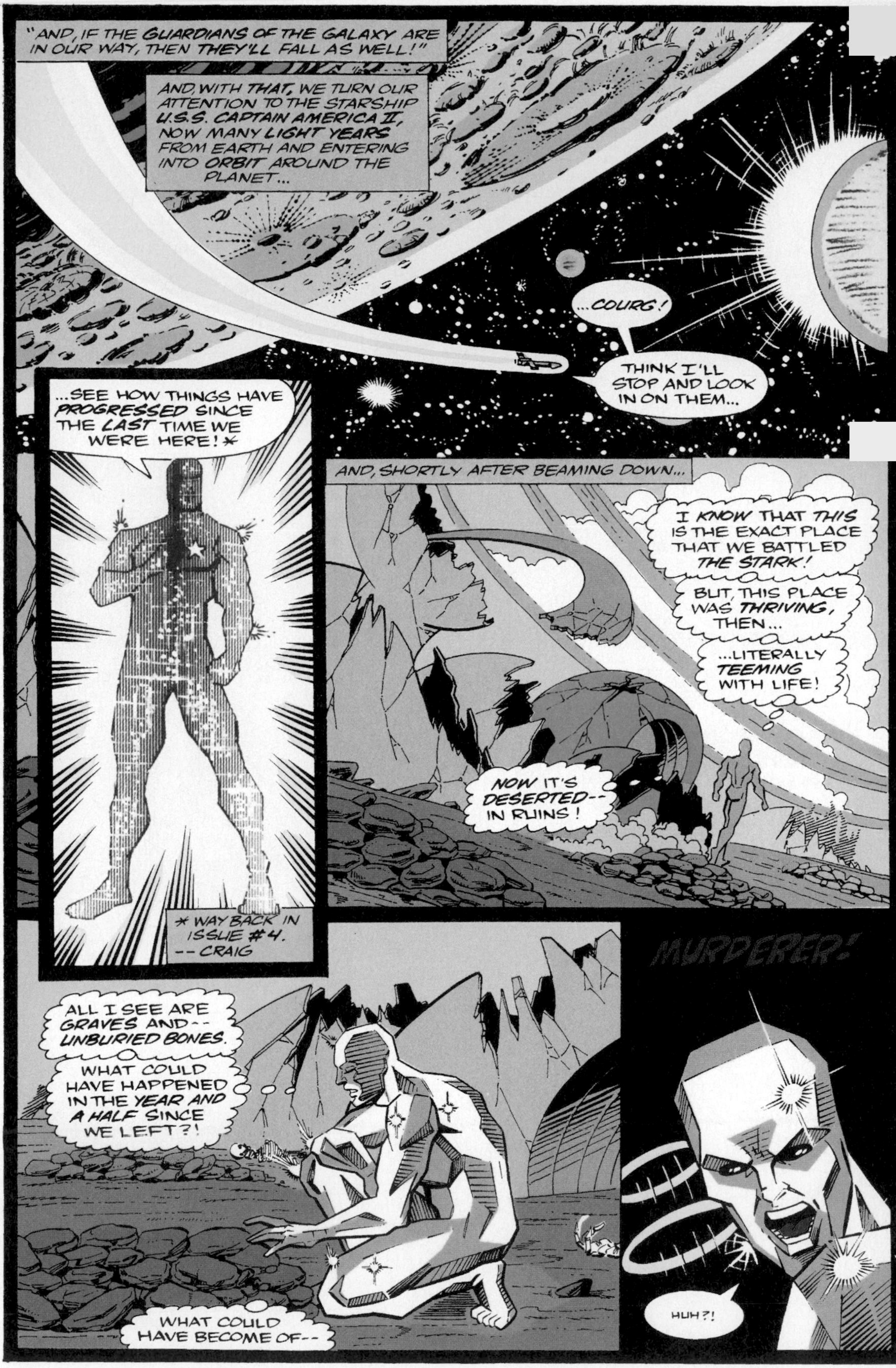
"AND, IF THE GUARDIANS OF THE GALAXY ARE IN OUR WAY, THEN THEY'LL FALL AS WELL!"
AND, WITH THAT, WE TURN OUR ATTENTION TO THE STARSHIP U.S.S. CAPTAIN AMERICA II, NOW MANY LIGHT YEARS FROM EARTH AND ENTERING INTO ORBIT AROUND THE PLANET...
...COURG!
THINK I'LL STOP AND LOOK IN ON THEM...
...SEE HOW THINGS HAVE PROGRESSED SINCE THE LAST TIME WE WERE HERE! *
* WAY BACK IN ISSUE #4. --CRAIG
AND, SHORTLY AFTER BEAMING DOWN...
I KNOW THAT THIS IS THE EXACT PLACE THAT WE BATTLED THE STARK!
BUT, THIS PLACE WAS THRIVING, THEN...
...LITERALLY TEEMING WITH LIFE!
NOW IT'S DESERTED-- IN RUINS!
ALL I SEE ARE GRAVES AND-- UNBURIED BONES.
WHAT COULD HAVE HAPPENED IN THE YEAR AND A HALF SINCE WE LEFT?!
WHAT COULD HAVE BECOME OF--
MURDERER!
HUH?!

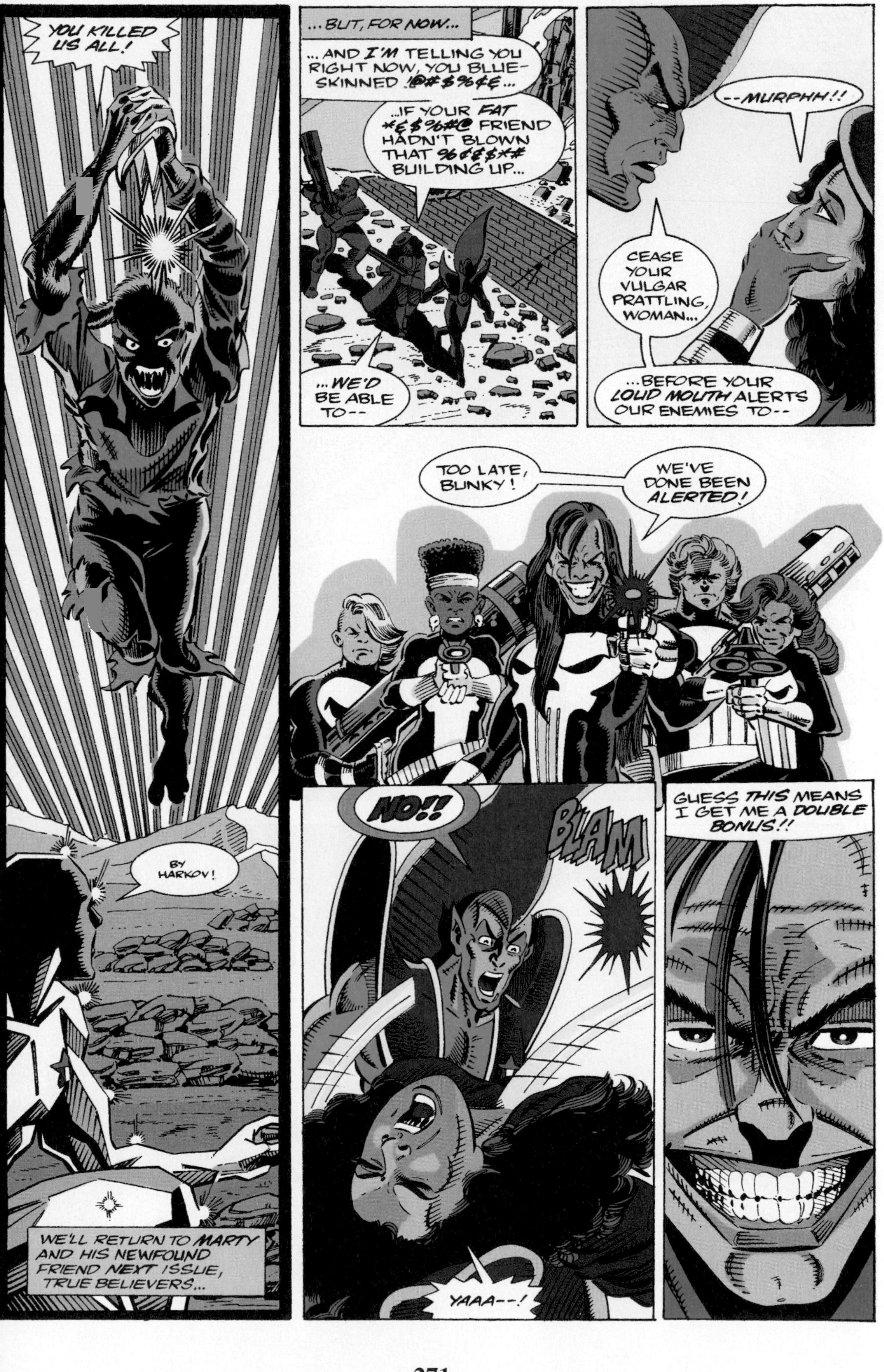
YOU KILLED US ALL!
BY HARKOV!
WE'LL RETURN TO MARTY AND HIS NEWFOUND FRIEND NEXT ISSUE, TRUE BELIEVERS...
...BUT, FOR NOW...
...AND I'M TELLING YOU RIGHT NOW, YOU BLUE-SKINNED !@#$%¢€...
...IF YOUR FAT *€$%#@ FRIEND HADN'T BLOWN THAT %¢€$*# BUILDING UP...
...WE'D BE ABLE TO--
--MURPHH!!
CEASE YOUR VULGAR PRATTLING, WOMAN...
...BEFORE YOUR LOUD MOUTH ALERTS OUR ENEMIES TO--
TOO LATE, BLINKY!
WE'VE DONE BEEN ALERTED!
NO!!
BLAM
YAAA--!
GUESS THIS MEANS I GET ME A DOUBLE BONUS!!

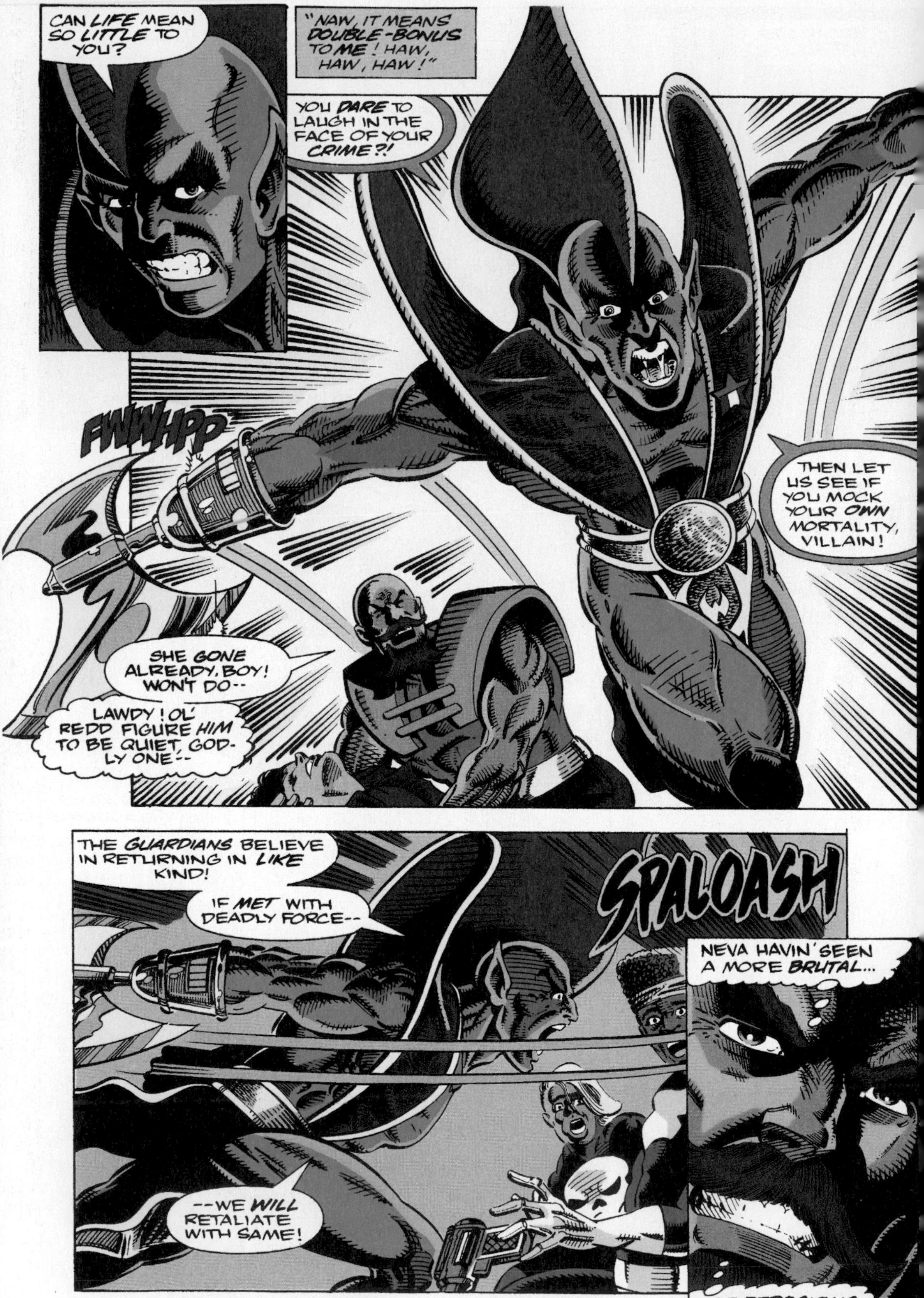
CAN LIFE MEAN SO LITTLE TO YOU?
"NAW, IT MEANS DOUBLE-BONUS TO ME! HAW, HAW, HAW!"
YOU DARE TO LAUGH IN THE FACE OF YOUR CRIME?!
FWWHPP
THEN LET US SEE IF YOU MOCK YOUR OWN MORTALITY, VILLAIN!
SHE GONE ALREADY, BOY! WON'T DO--
LAWDY! OL' REDD FIGURE HIM TO BE QUIET, GODLY ONE--
THE GUARDIANS BELIEVE IN RETURNING IN LIKE KIND!
IF MET WITH DEADLY FORCE--
--WE WILL RETALIATE WITH SAME!
SPALOASH
NEVA HAVIN' SEEN A MORE BRUTAL...
...OR FEROCIOUS ATTACK--

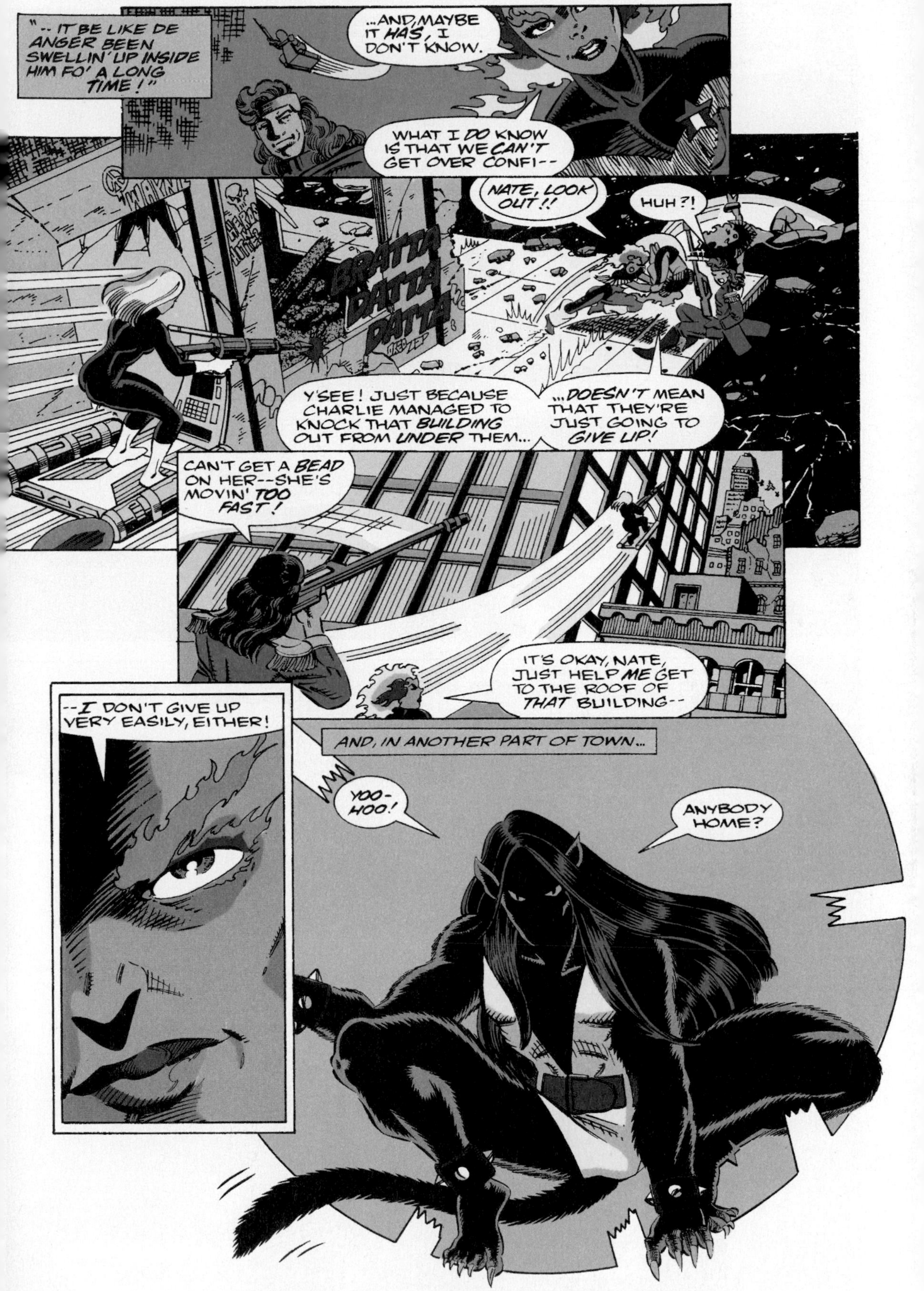
"-- IT BE LIKE DE ANGER BEEN SWELLIN' UP INSIDE HIM FO' A LONG TIME!"
...AND, MAYBE IT HAS, I DON'T KNOW.
WHAT I DO KNOW IS THAT WE CAN'T GET OVER CONFI--
NATE, LOOK OUT!!
HUH?!
BRATTA DATTA DATTA
Y'SEE! JUST BECAUSE CHARLIE MANAGED TO KNOCK THAT BUILDING OUT FROM UNDER THEM...
...DOESN'T MEAN THAT THEY'RE JUST GOING TO GIVE UP!
CAN'T GET A BEAD ON HER--SHE'S MOVIN' TOO FAST!
IT'S OKAY, NATE, JUST HELP ME GET TO THE ROOF OF THAT BUILDING--
--I DON'T GIVE UP VERY EASILY, EITHER!
AND, IN ANOTHER PART OF TOWN...
YOO-HOO!
ANYBODY HOME?

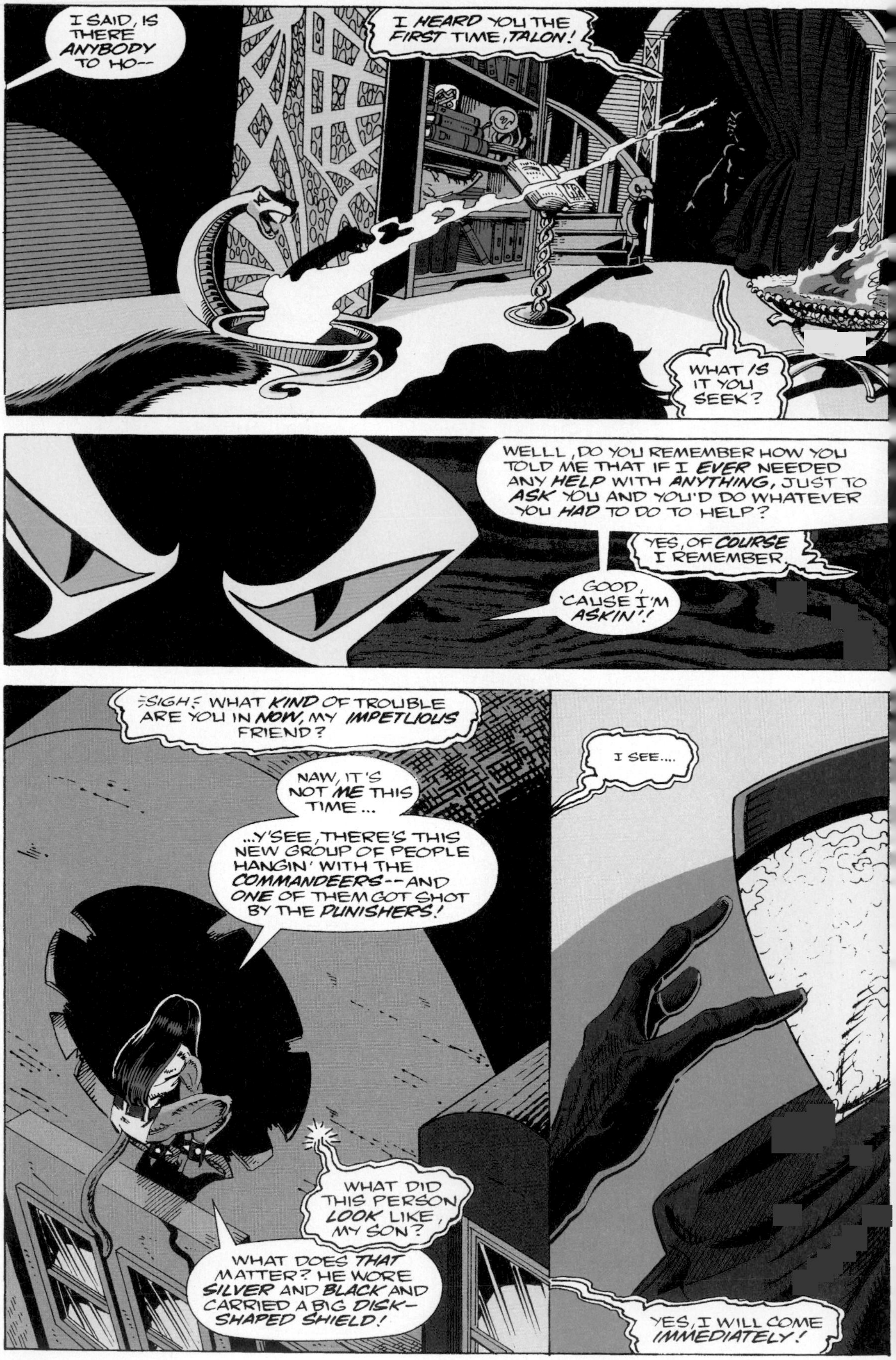

I SAID, IS THERE ANYBODY TO HO--
I HEARD YOU THE FIRST TIME, TALON!
WHAT IS IT YOU SEEK?
WELLL, DO YOU REMEMBER HOW YOU TOLD ME THAT IF I EVER NEEDED ANY HELP WITH ANYTHING, JUST TO ASK YOU AND YOU'D DO WHATEVER YOU HAD TO DO TO HELP?
YES, OF COURSE I REMEMBER.
GOOD, 'CAUSE I'M ASKIN'!
=SIGH= WHAT KIND OF TROUBLE ARE YOU IN NOW, MY IMPETUOUS FRIEND?
NAW, IT'S NOT ME THIS TIME...
...Y'SEE, THERE'S THIS NEW GROUP OF PEOPLE HANGIN' WITH THE COMMANDEERS--AND ONE OF THEM GOT SHOT BY THE PUNISHERS!
WHAT DID THIS PERSON LOOK LIKE, MY SON?
WHAT DOES THAT MATTER? HE WORE SILVER AND BLACK AND CARRIED A BIG DISK-SHAPED SHIELD!
I SEE....
YES, I WILL COME IMMEDIATELY!

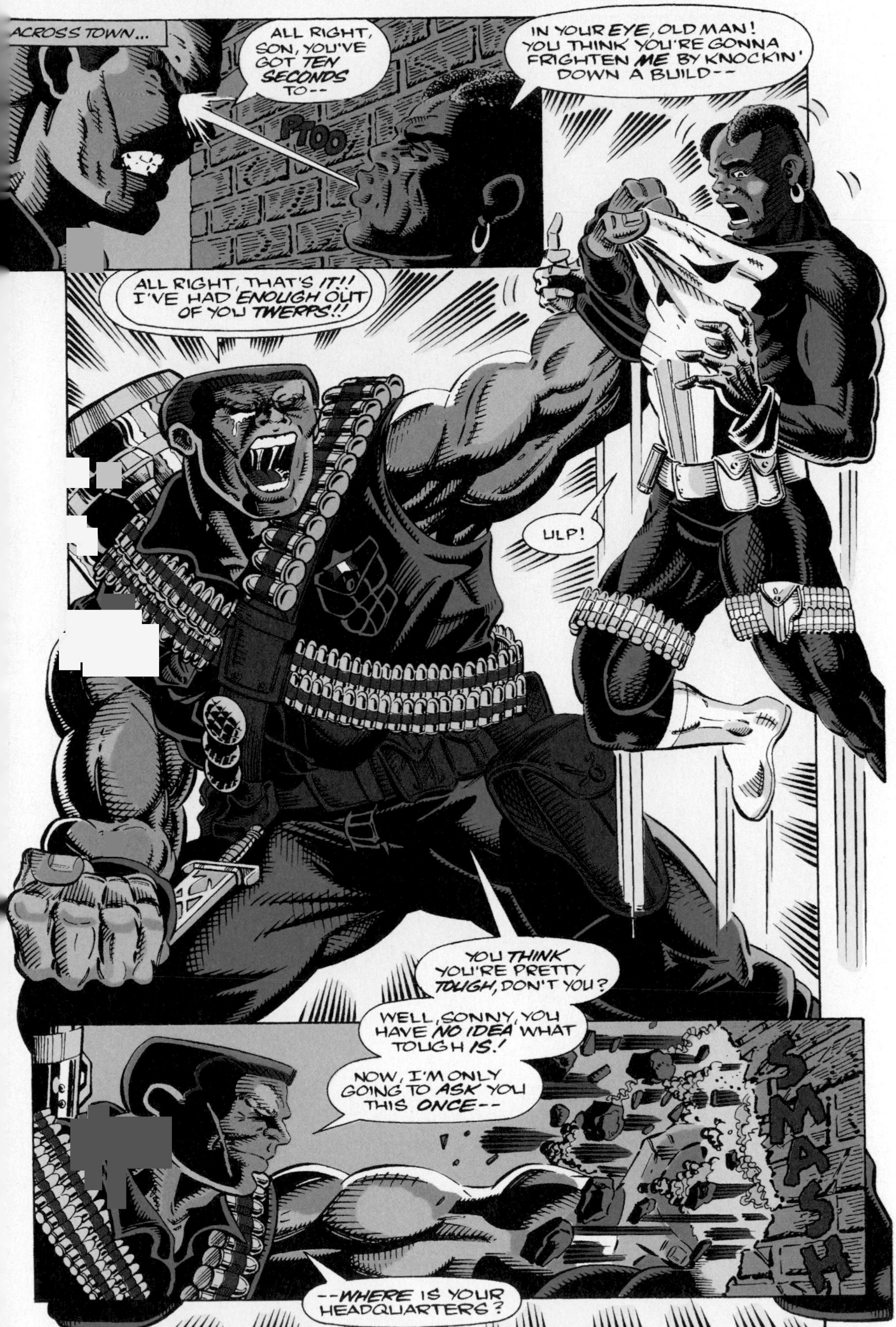

ACROSS TOWN...
ALL RIGHT, SON, YOU'VE GOT TEN SECONDS TO--
PTOO
IN YOUR EYE, OLD MAN! YOU THINK YOU'RE GONNA FRIGHTEN ME BY KNOCKIN' DOWN A BUILD--
ALL RIGHT, THAT'S IT!! I'VE HAD ENOUGH OUT OF YOU TWERPS!!
ULP!
YOU THINK YOU'RE PRETTY TOUGH, DON'T YOU?
WELL, SONNY, YOU HAVE NO IDEA WHAT TOUGH IS!
NOW, I'M ONLY GOING TO ASK YOU THIS ONCE--
SMASH
--WHERE IS YOUR HEADQUARTERS?

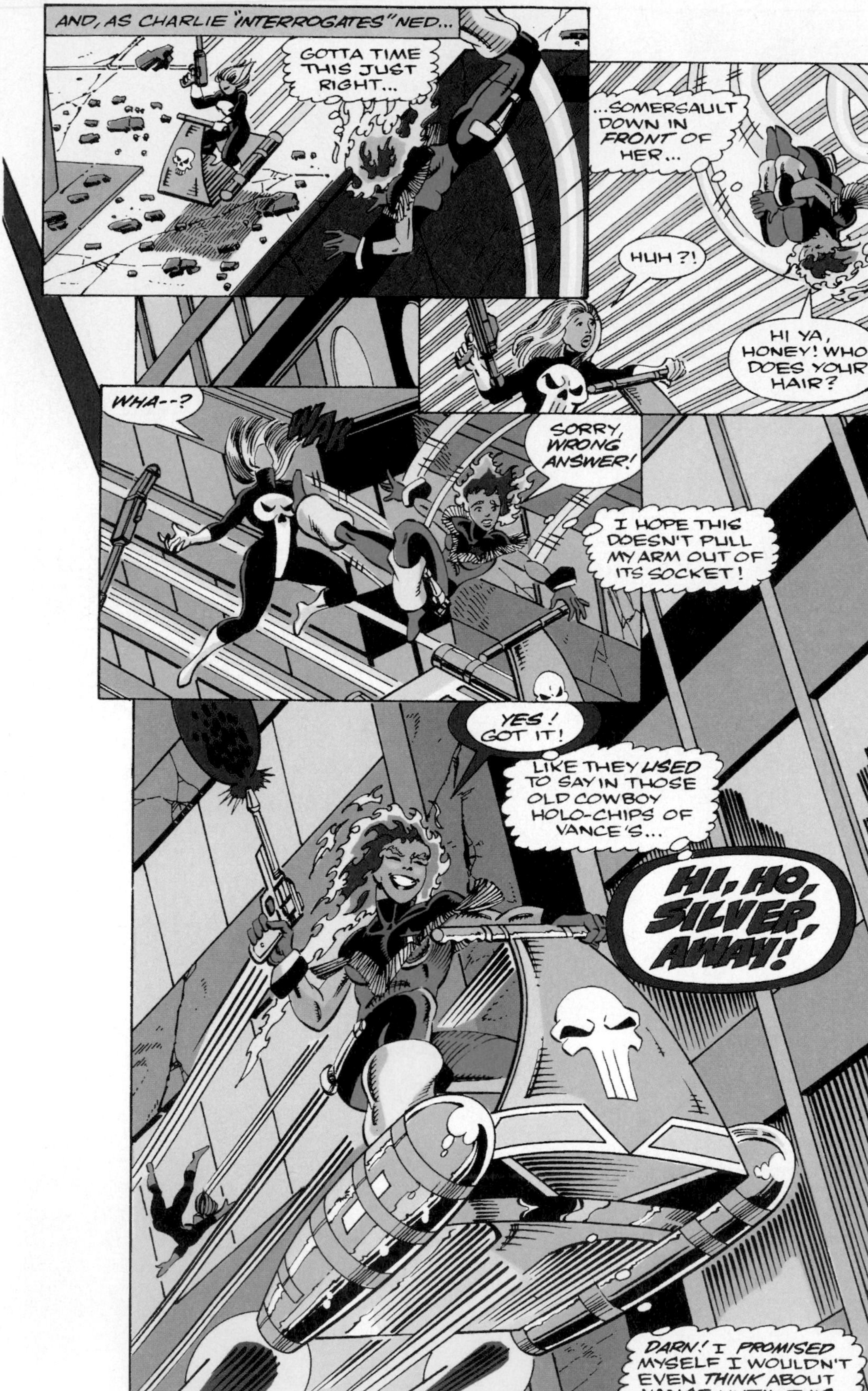
AND, AS CHARLIE "INTERROGATES" NED...
GOTTA TIME THIS JUST RIGHT...
...SOMERSAULT DOWN IN FRONT OF HER...
HUH ?!
HI YA, HONEY! WHO DOES YOUR HAIR?
WHA--?
WAK
SORRY, WRONG ANSWER!
I HOPE THIS DOESN'T PULL MY ARM OUT OF ITS SOCKET!
YES! GOT IT!
LIKE THEY USED TO SAY IN THOSE OLD COWBOY HOLO-CHIPS OF VANCE'S...
HI, HO, SILVER, AWAY!
DARN! I PROMISED MYSELF I WOULDN'T EVEN THINK ABOUT VANCE UNTIL THIS BATTLE WAS OVER!

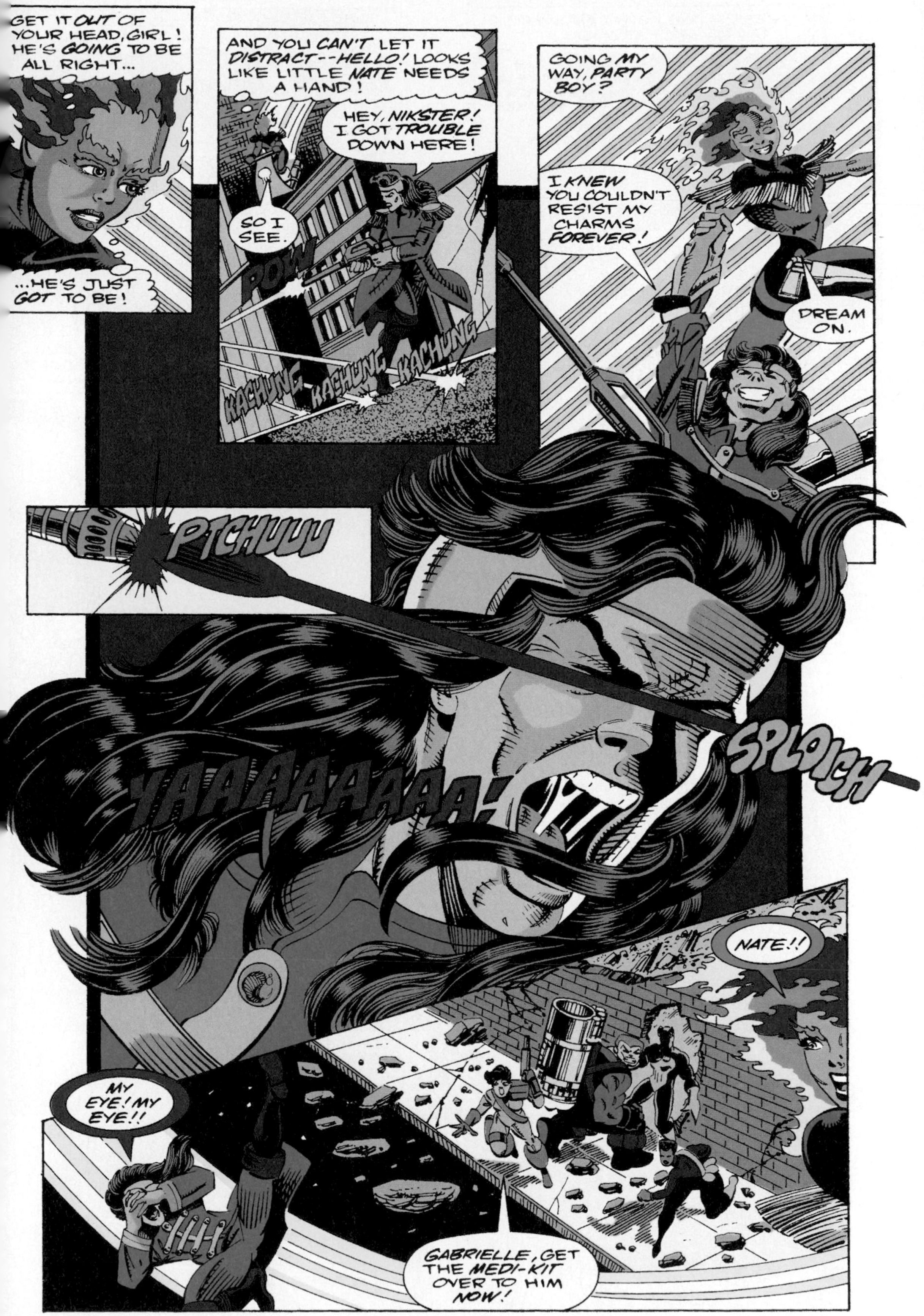
GET IT OUT OF YOUR HEAD, GIRL! HE'S GOING TO BE ALL RIGHT...
...HE'S JUST GOT TO BE!
AND YOU CAN'T LET IT DISTRACT--HELLO! LOOKS LIKE LITTLE NATE NEEDS A HAND!
HEY, NIKSTER! I GOT TROUBLE DOWN HERE!
SO I SEE.
POW
KACHUNG KACHUNG KACHUNG
GOING MY WAY, PARTY BOY?
I KNEW YOU COULDN'T RESIST MY CHARMS FOREVER!
DREAM ON.
PTCHUUU
YAAAAAAAA!
SPLOICH
NATE!!
MY EYE! MY EYE!!
GABRIELLE, GET THE MEDI-KIT OVER TO HIM NOW!

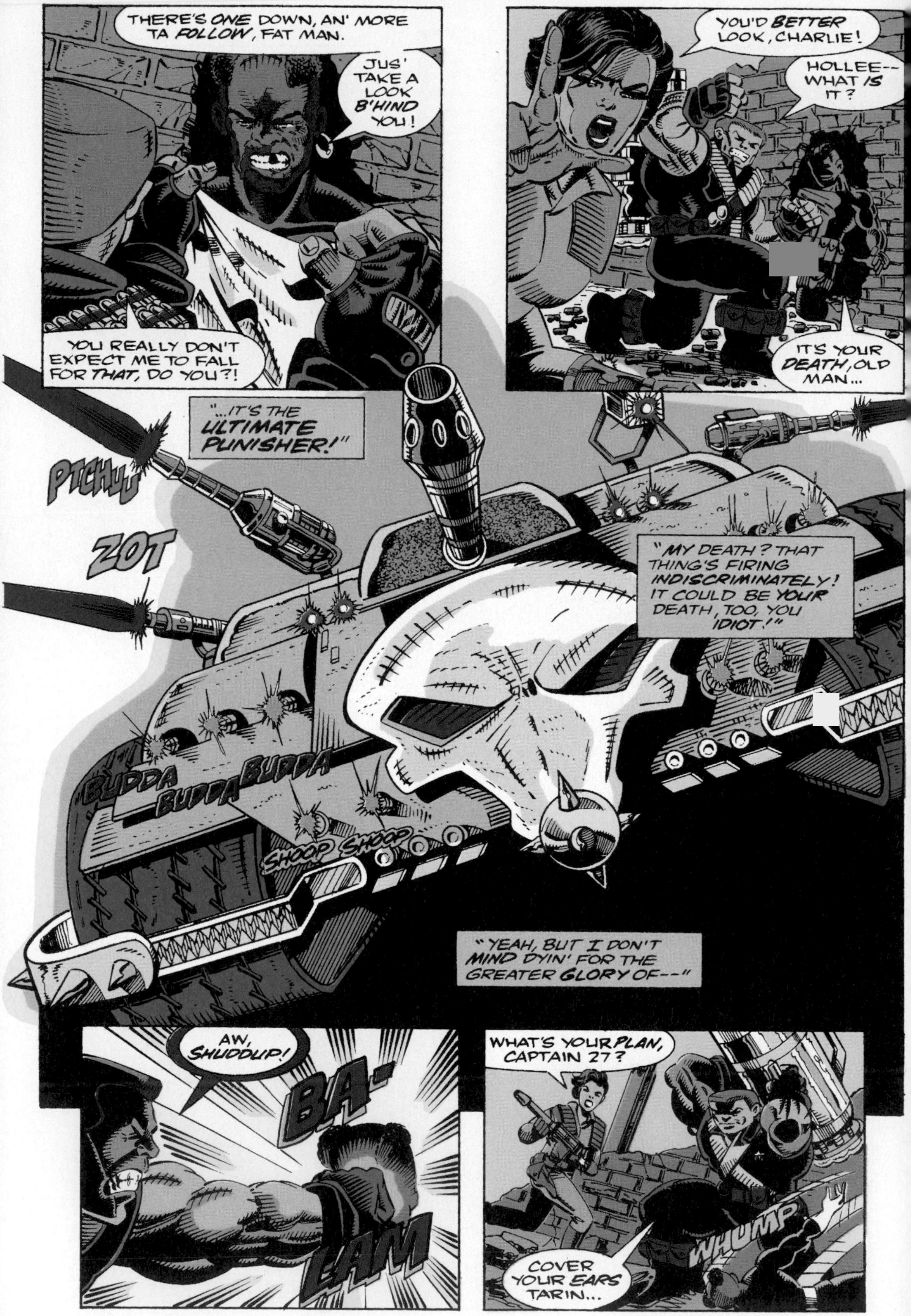

THERE'S ONE DOWN, AN' MORE TA FOLLOW, FAT MAN.
JUS' TAKE A LOOK B'HIND YOU!
YOU REALLY DON'T EXPECT ME TO FALL FOR THAT, DO YOU?!
YOU'D BETTER LOOK, CHARLIE!
HOLLEE-- WHAT IS IT?
IT'S YOUR DEATH, OLD MAN...
"...IT'S THE ULTIMATE PUNISHER!"
PTCHUU
ZOT
"MY DEATH? THAT THING'S FIRING INDISCRIMINATELY! IT COULD BE YOUR DEATH, TOO, YOU IDIOT!"
BUDDA BUDDA BUDDA
SHOOP SHOOP
"YEAH, BUT I DON'T MIND DYIN' FOR THE GREATER GLORY OF--"
AW, SHUDDUP!
BA-LAM
WHAT'S YOUR PLAN, CAPTAIN 27?
COVER YOUR EARS TARIN...
WHUMP

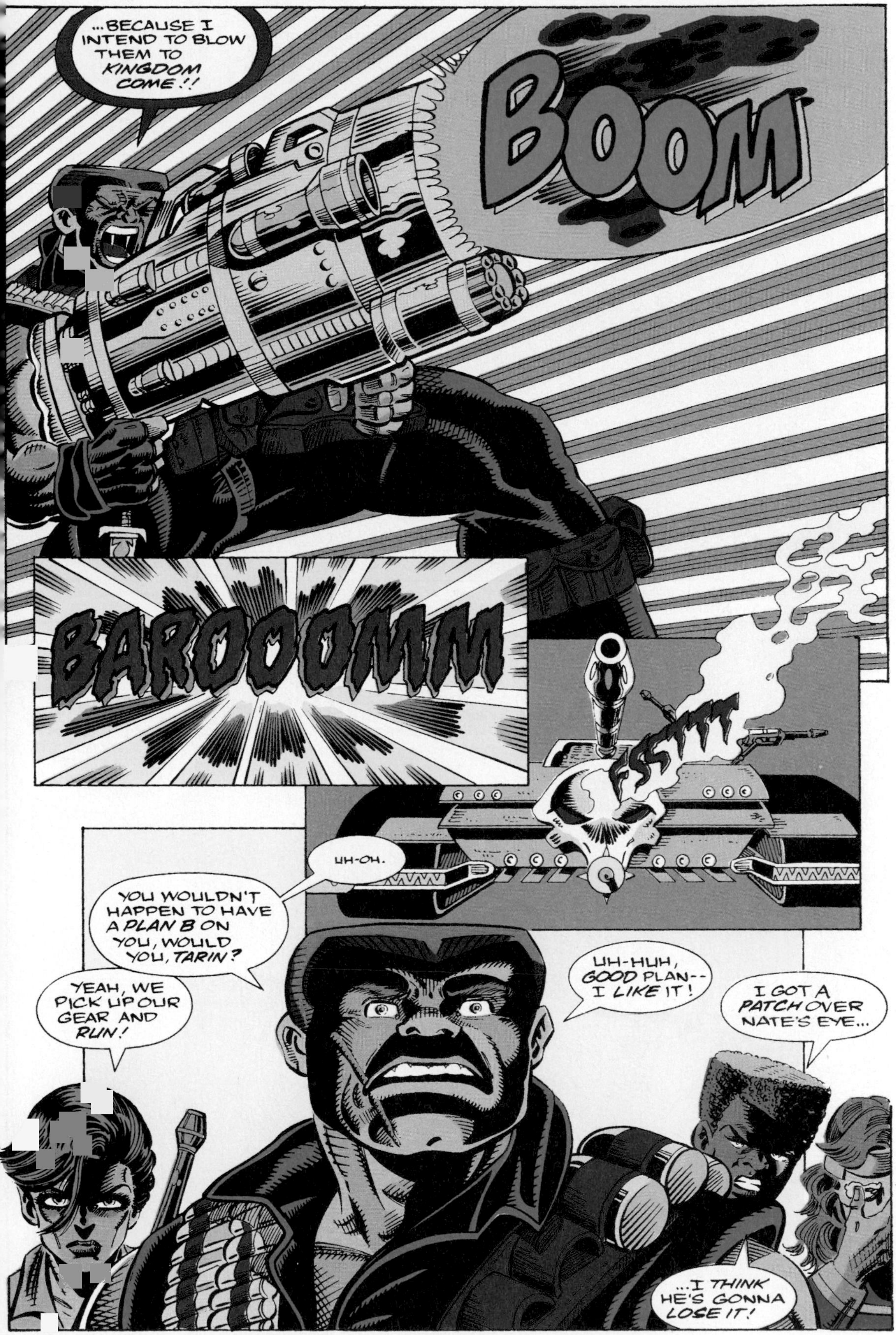
...BECAUSE I INTEND TO BLOW THEM TO KINGDOM COME!!
BOOM
BAROOOMM
FSSTTT
UH-OH.
YOU WOULDN'T HAPPEN TO HAVE A PLAN B ON YOU, WOULD YOU, TARIN?
YEAH, WE PICK UP OUR GEAR AND RUN!
UH-HUH, GOOD PLAN-- I LIKE IT!
I GOT A PATCH OVER NATE'S EYE...
...I THINK HE'S GONNA LOSE IT!

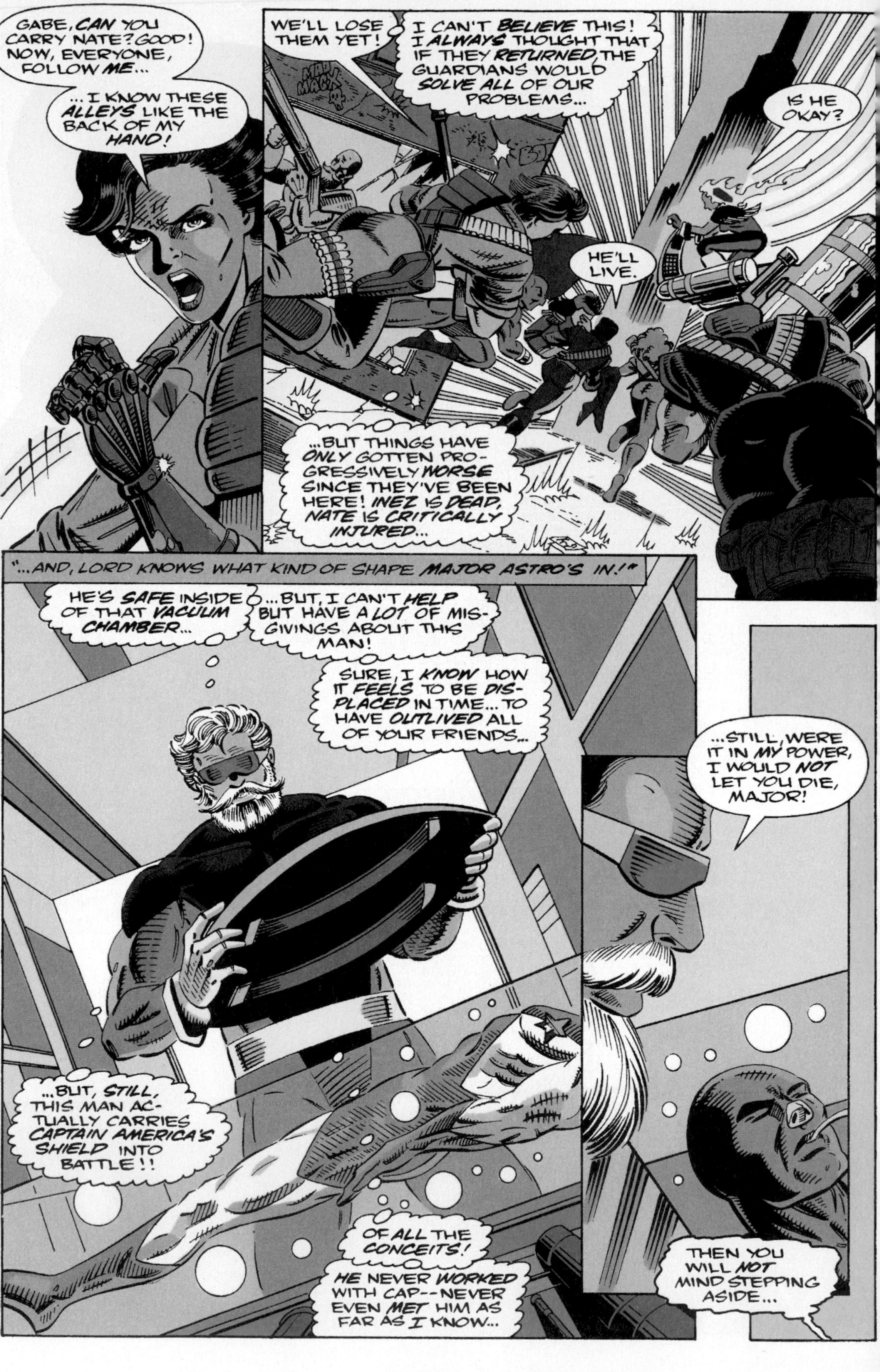
GABE, CAN YOU CARRY NATE? GOOD! NOW, EVERYONE, FOLLOW ME...
...I KNOW THESE ALLEYS LIKE THE BACK OF MY HAND!
WE'LL LOSE THEM YET!
I CAN'T BELIEVE THIS! I ALWAYS THOUGHT THAT IF THEY RETURNED, THE GUARDIANS WOULD SOLVE ALL OF OUR PROBLEMS...
IS HE OKAY?
HE'LL LIVE.
...BUT THINGS HAVE ONLY GOTTEN PROGRESSIVELY WORSE SINCE THEY'VE BEEN HERE! INEZ IS DEAD, NATE IS CRITICALLY INJURED...
"...AND, LORD KNOWS WHAT KIND OF SHAPE MAJOR ASTRO'S IN!"
HE'S SAFE INSIDE OF THAT VACUUM CHAMBER...
...BUT, I CAN'T HELP BUT HAVE A LOT OF MISGIVINGS ABOUT THIS MAN!
SURE, I KNOW HOW IT FEELS TO BE DISPLACED IN TIME... TO HAVE OUTLIVED ALL OF YOUR FRIENDS...
...BUT, STILL, THIS MAN ACTUALLY CARRIES CAPTAIN AMERICA'S SHIELD INTO BATTLE!!
OF ALL THE CONCEITS!
HE NEVER WORKED WITH CAP--NEVER EVEN MET HIM AS FAR AS I KNOW...
...STILL, WERE IT IN MY POWER, I WOULD NOT LET YOU DIE, MAJOR!
THEN YOU WILL NOT MIND STEPPING ASIDE...

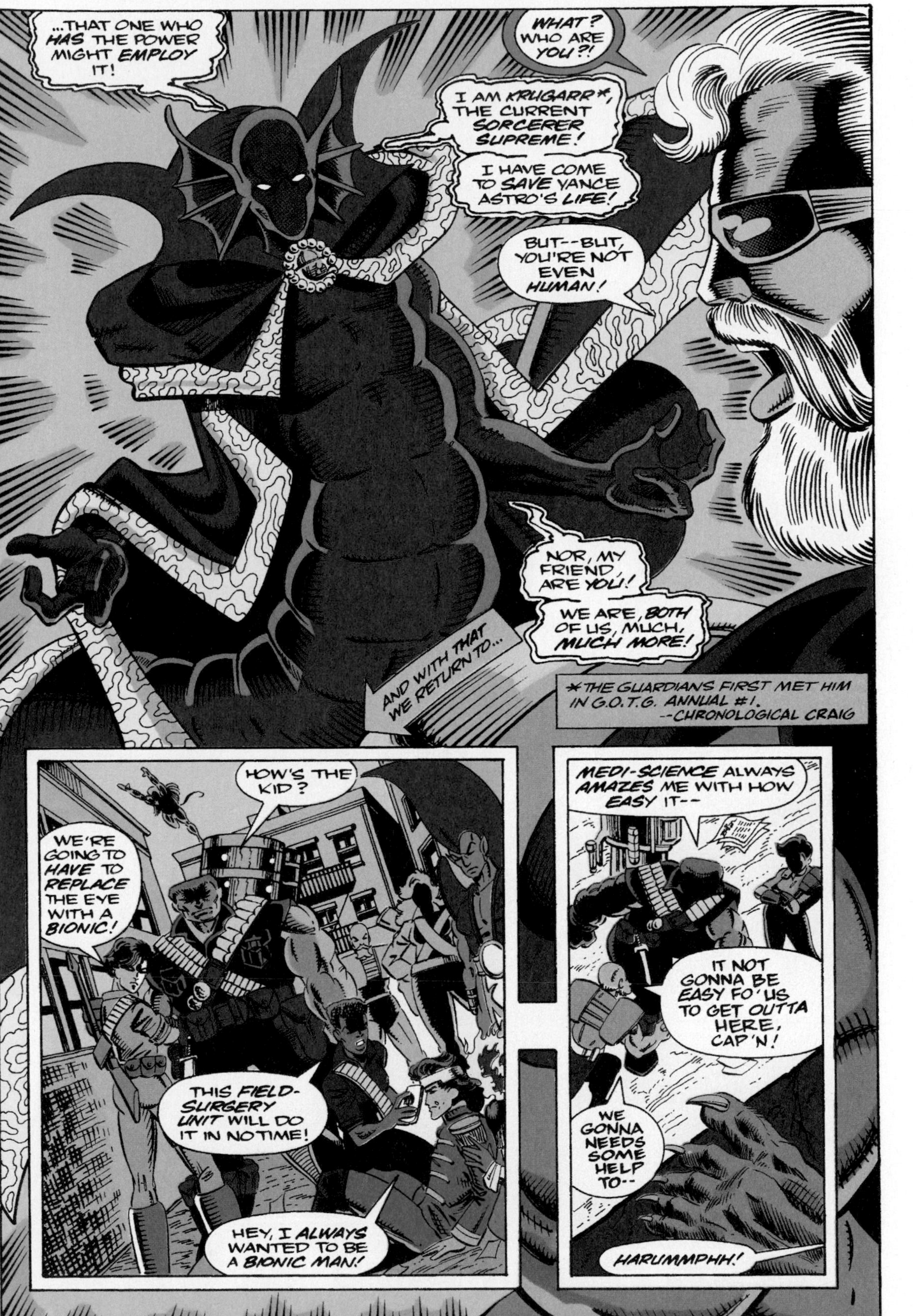

...THAT ONE WHO HAS THE POWER MIGHT EMPLOY IT!
WHAT? WHO ARE YOU?!
I AM KRUGARR*, THE CURRENT SORCERER SUPREME!
I HAVE COME TO SAVE YANCE ASTRO'S LIFE!
BUT--BUT, YOU'RE NOT EVEN HUMAN!
NOR, MY FRIEND, ARE YOU!
WE ARE, BOTH OF US, MUCH, MUCH MORE!
AND WITH THAT WE RETURN TO...
*THE GUARDIANS FIRST MET HIM IN G.O.T.G. ANNUAL #1. --CHRONOLOGICAL CRAIG
HOW'S THE KID?
WE'RE GOING TO HAVE TO REPLACE THE EYE WITH A BIONIC!
THIS FIELD-SURGERY UNIT WILL DO IT IN NO TIME!
HEY, I ALWAYS WANTED TO BE A BIONIC MAN!
MEDI-SCIENCE ALWAYS AMAZES ME WITH HOW EASY IT--
IT NOT GONNA BE EASY FO' US TO GET OUTTA HERE, CAP'N!
WE GONNA NEEDS SOME HELP TO--
HARUMMPHH!

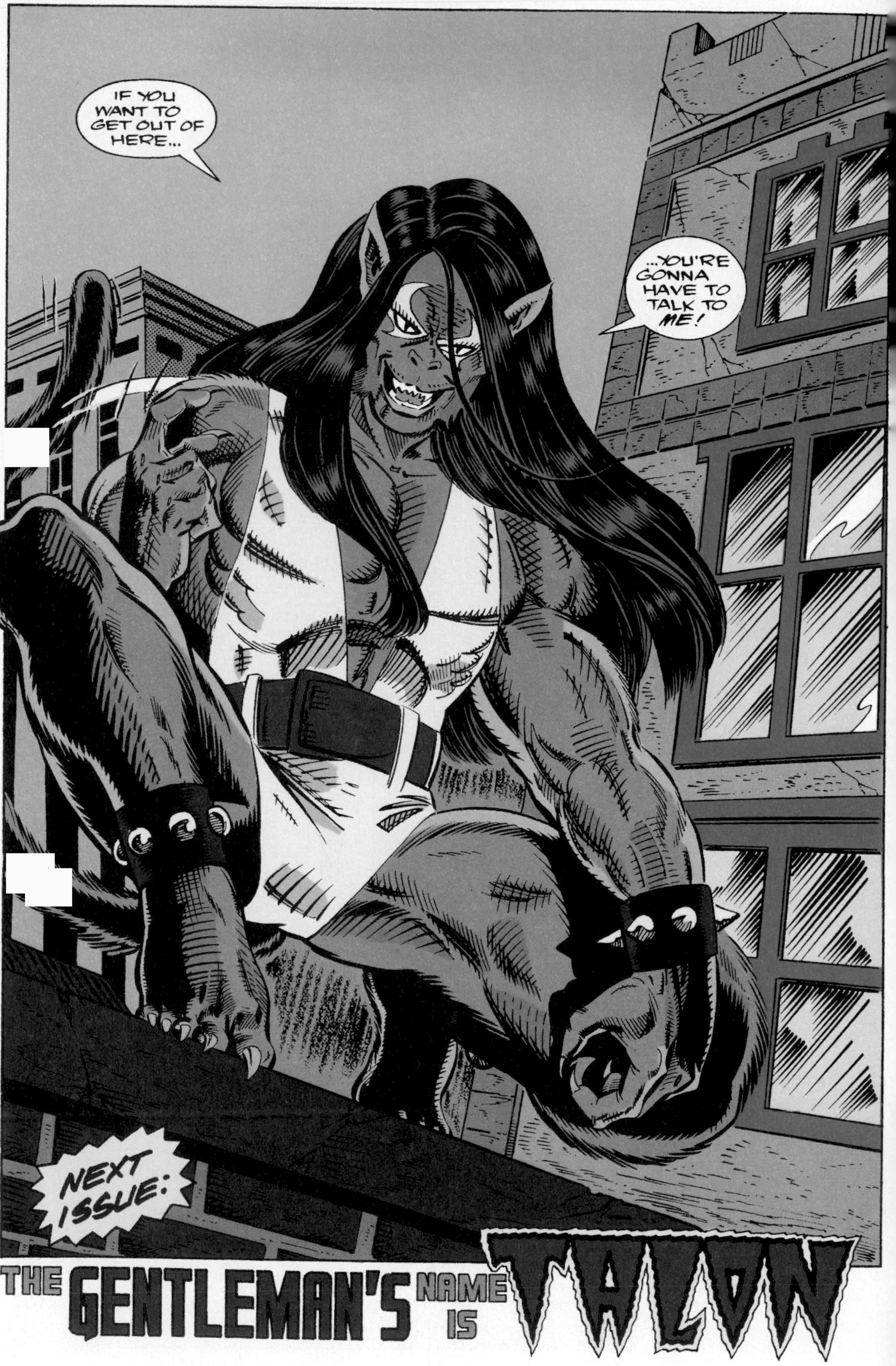
IF YOU WANT TO GET OUT OF HERE...
...YOU'RE GONNA HAVE TO TALK TO ME!
NEXT ISSUE:
THE GENTLEMAN'S NAME IS TALON

GUARDIANS
OF THE GALAXY

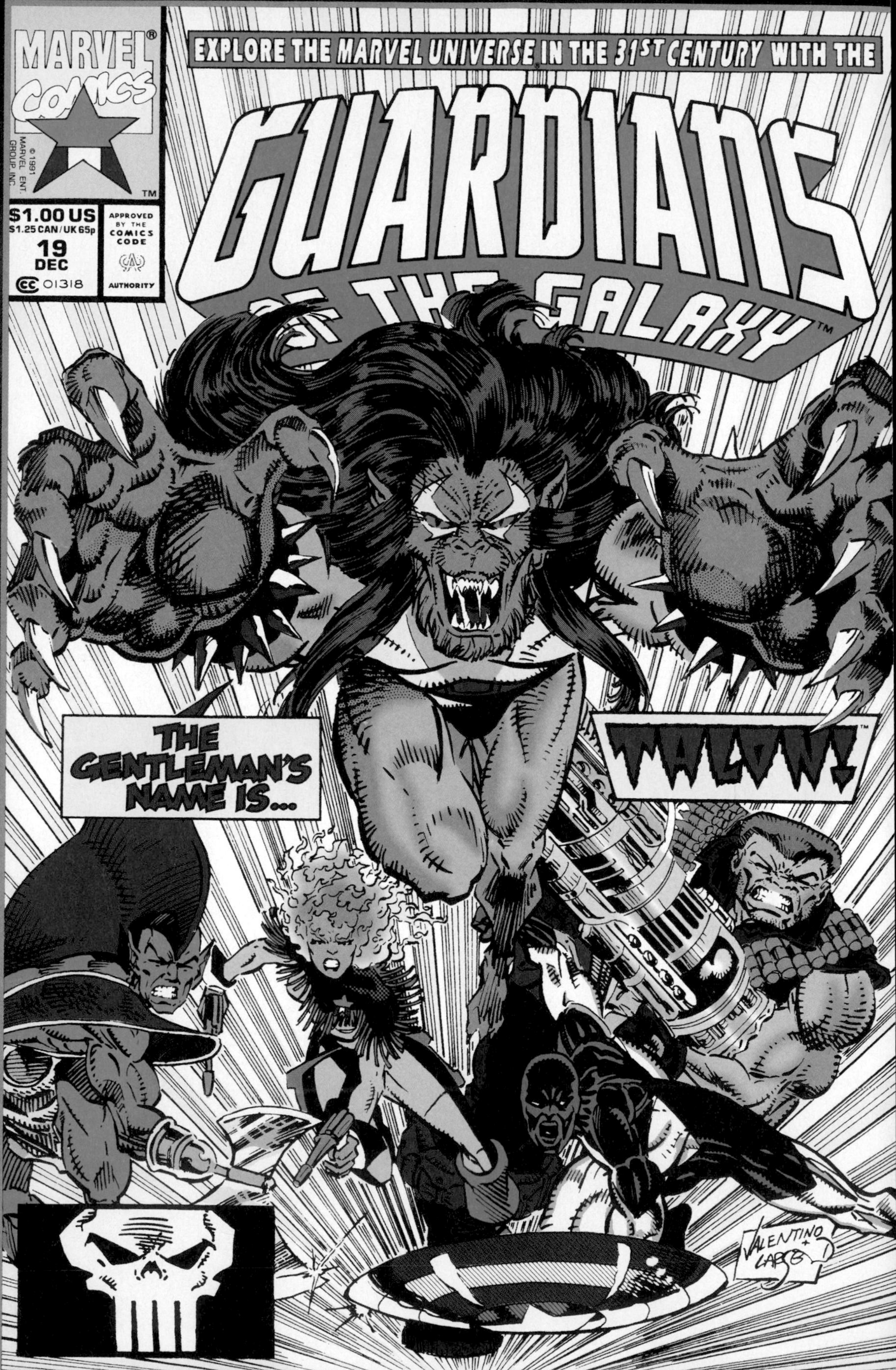
MARVEL COMICS
© 1991 MARVEL ENT. GROUP INC.
$1.00 US
$1.25 CAN/UK 65p
19
DEC
CC 01318
APPROVED BY THE COMICS CODE AUTHORITY
EXPLORE THE MARVEL UNIVERSE IN THE 31ST CENTURY WITH THE
GUARDIANS OF THE GALAXY
THE GENTLEMAN'S NAME IS...
TALON!
VALENTINO + GARCIA

MAJOR VANCE ASTRO! CHARLIE 27! NIKKI! YONDU! FOUR EXTRAORDINARY SUPER-BEINGS, ALL SURVIVORS OF INTERSTELLAR WAR. NOW THEY ROAM THE COSMOS OF THE 31ST CENTURY ABOARD THE STARSHIP CAPTAIN AMERICA, THEIR MISSION—TO SAFEGUARD THE MILKY WAY!
STAN LEE PRESENTS . . . THE GUARDIANS OF THE GALAXY!

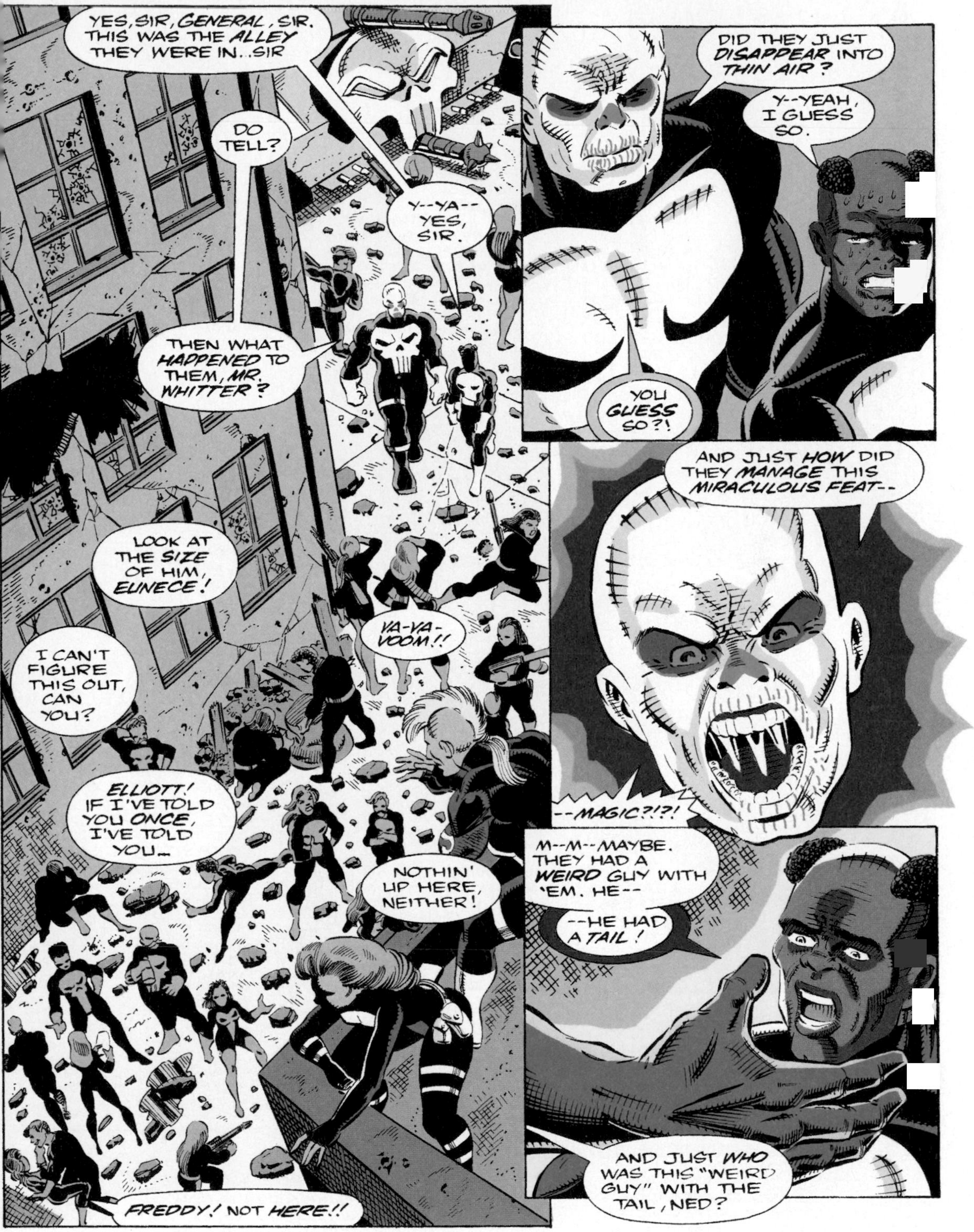

YES, SIR, GENERAL, SIR. THIS WAS THE ALLEY THEY WERE IN...SIR
DO TELL?
Y--YA--YES, SIR.
THEN WHAT HAPPENED TO THEM, MR. WHITTER?
LOOK AT THE SIZE OF HIM, EUNECE!
VA-VA-VOOM!!
I CAN'T FIGURE THIS OUT, CAN YOU?
ELLIOTT! IF I'VE TOLD YOU ONCE, I'VE TOLD YOU...
NOTHIN' UP HERE, NEITHER!
FREDDY! NOT HERE!!
DID THEY JUST DISAPPEAR INTO THIN AIR?
Y--YEAH, I GUESS SO.
YOU GUESS SO?!
AND JUST HOW DID THEY MANAGE THIS MIRACULOUS FEAT--
--MAGIC?!?!
M--M--MAYBE. THEY HAD A WEIRD GUY WITH 'EM. HE--
--HE HAD A TAIL!
AND JUST WHO WAS THIS "WEIRD GUY" WITH THE TAIL, NED?

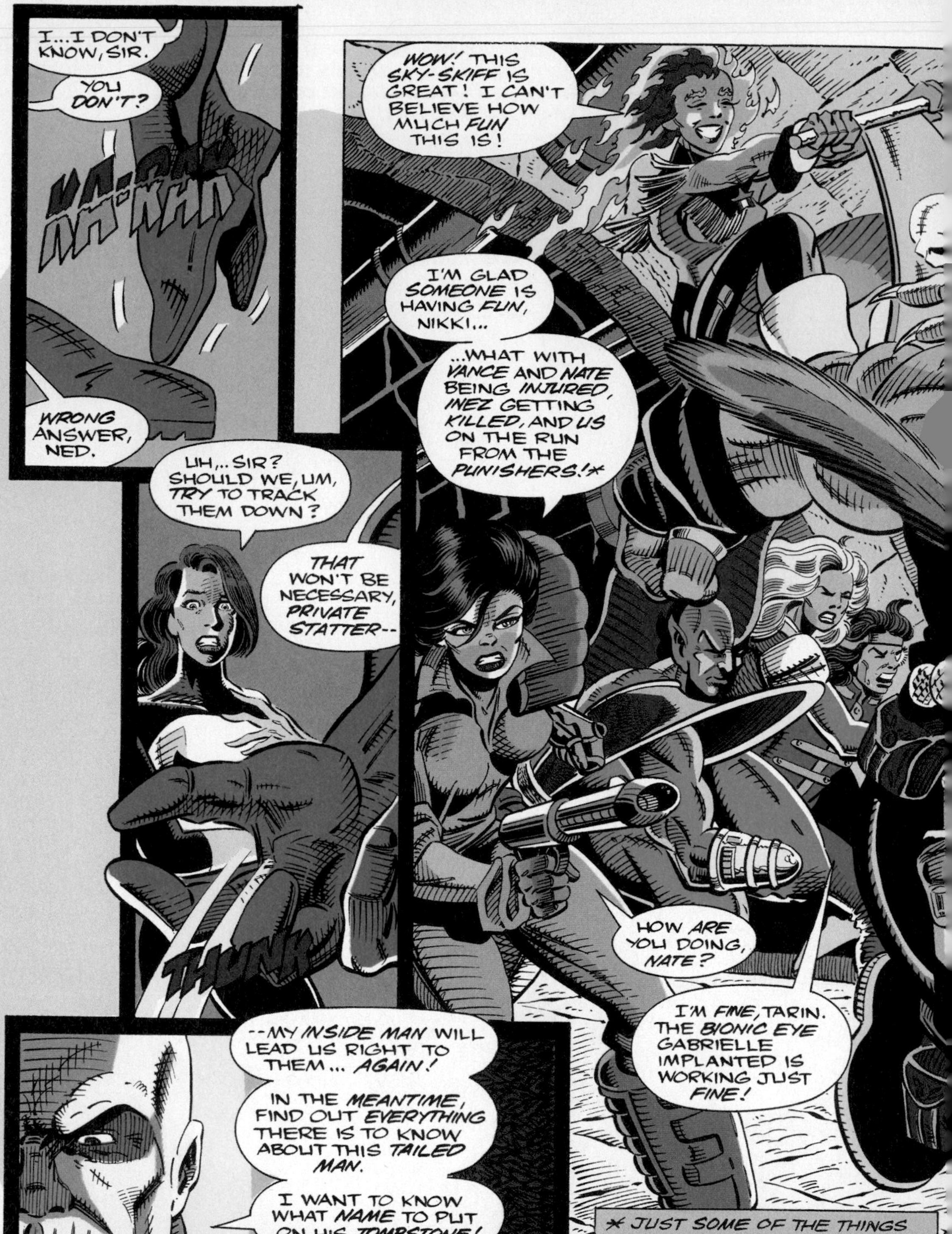
I...I DON'T KNOW, SIR.
YOU DON'T?
WRONG ANSWER, NED.
WOW! THIS SKY-SKIFF IS GREAT! I CAN'T BELIEVE HOW MUCH FUN THIS IS!
I'M GLAD SOMEONE IS HAVING FUN, NIKKI...
...WHAT WITH VANCE AND NATE BEING INJURED, INEZ GETTING KILLED, AND US ON THE RUN FROM THE PUNISHERS!*
UH,.. SIR? SHOULD WE, UM, TRY TO TRACK THEM DOWN?
THAT WON'T BE NECESSARY, PRIVATE STATTER--
THUNK
HOW ARE YOU DOING, NATE?
I'M FINE, TARIN. THE BIONIC EYE GABRIELLE IMPLANTED IS WORKING JUST FINE!
--MY INSIDE MAN WILL LEAD US RIGHT TO THEM... AGAIN!
IN THE MEANTIME, FIND OUT EVERYTHING THERE IS TO KNOW ABOUT THIS TAILED MAN.
I WANT TO KNOW WHAT NAME TO PUT ON HIS TOMBSTONE!
* JUST SOME OF THE THINGS THAT HAPPENED LAST ISH-- NOW, AREN'T YOU SORRY YOU MISSED IT?-- CRAIG

INCREDIBLE INKING BY **STEVE MONTANO**
IMPECCABLE LETTERING BY **KEN LOPEZ**
INCOMPARABLE COLORING BY **EVELYN STEIN**

INDISPENSABLE EDITING BY **CRAIG ANDERSON**
INCALCULABLE CHIEFING BY **TOM DeFALCO**
INEVITABLE PROCRASTINATION BY **JIM VALENTINO**

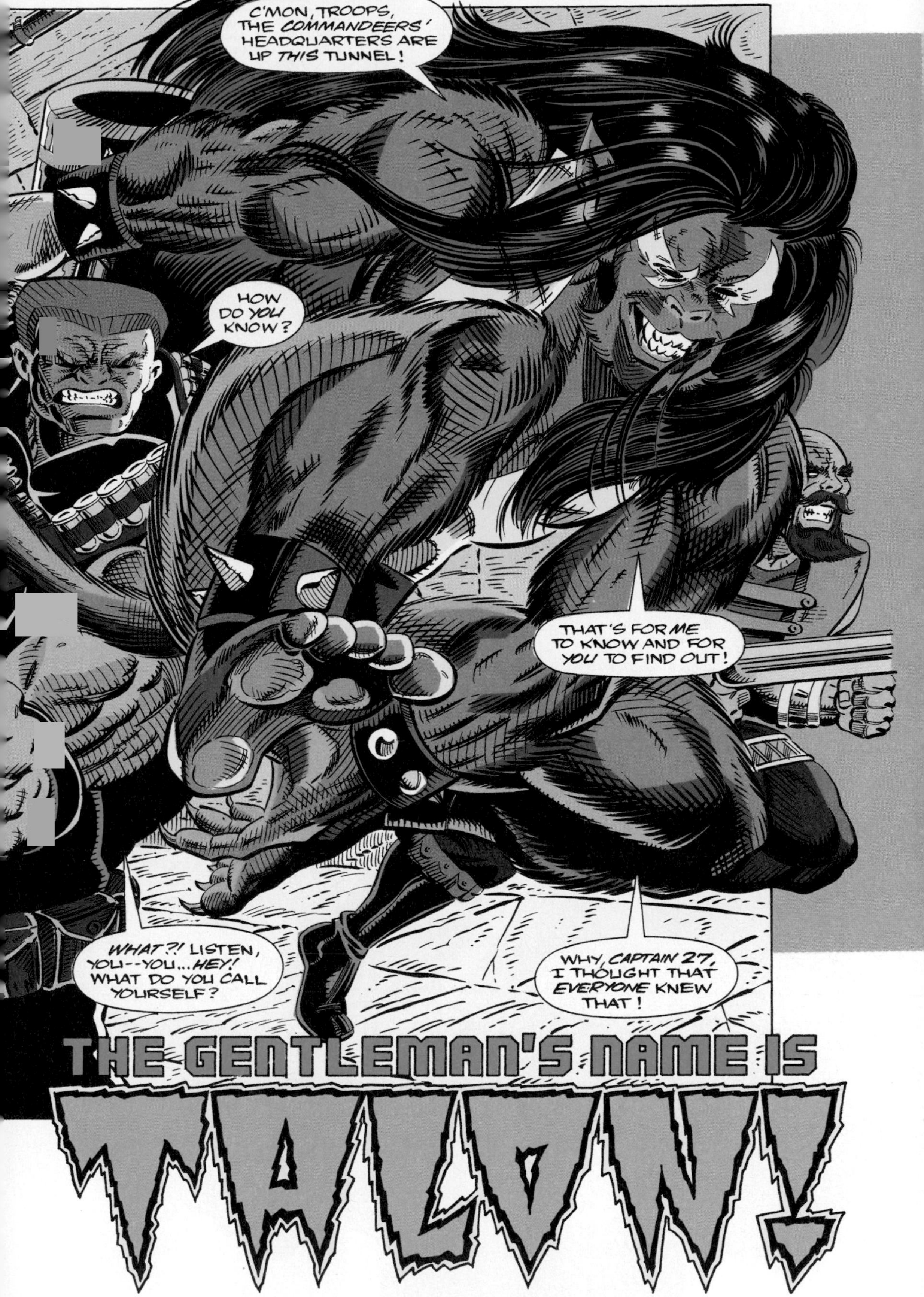
C'MON, TROOPS, THE COMMANDEERS' HEADQUARTERS ARE UP THIS TUNNEL!
HOW DO YOU KNOW?
THAT'S FOR ME TO KNOW AND FOR YOU TO FIND OUT!
WHAT?! LISTEN, YOU--YOU...HEY! WHAT DO YOU CALL YOURSELF?
WHY, CAPTAIN 27, I THOUGHT THAT EVERYONE KNEW THAT!
THE GENTLEMAN'S NAME IS
TALON!

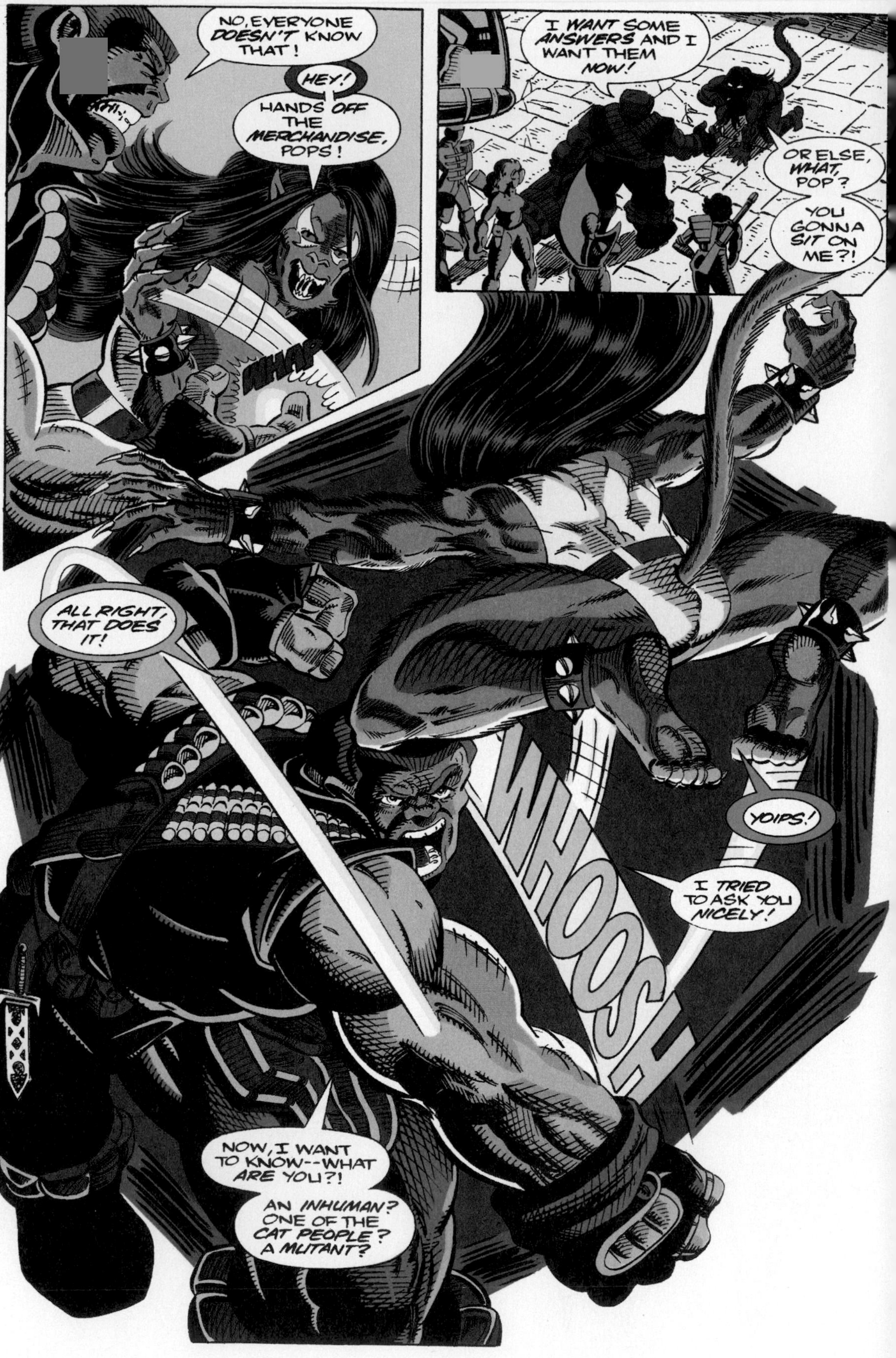
NO, EVERYONE DOESN'T KNOW THAT!
HEY!
HANDS OFF THE MERCHANDISE, POPS!
WHAP
I WANT SOME ANSWERS AND I WANT THEM NOW!
OR ELSE, WHAT, POP?
YOU GONNA SIT ON ME?!
ALL RIGHT, THAT DOES IT!
WHOOSH
YOIPS!
I TRIED TO ASK YOU NICELY!
NOW, I WANT TO KNOW--WHAT ARE YOU?!
AN INHUMAN? ONE OF THE CAT PEOPLE? A MUTANT?

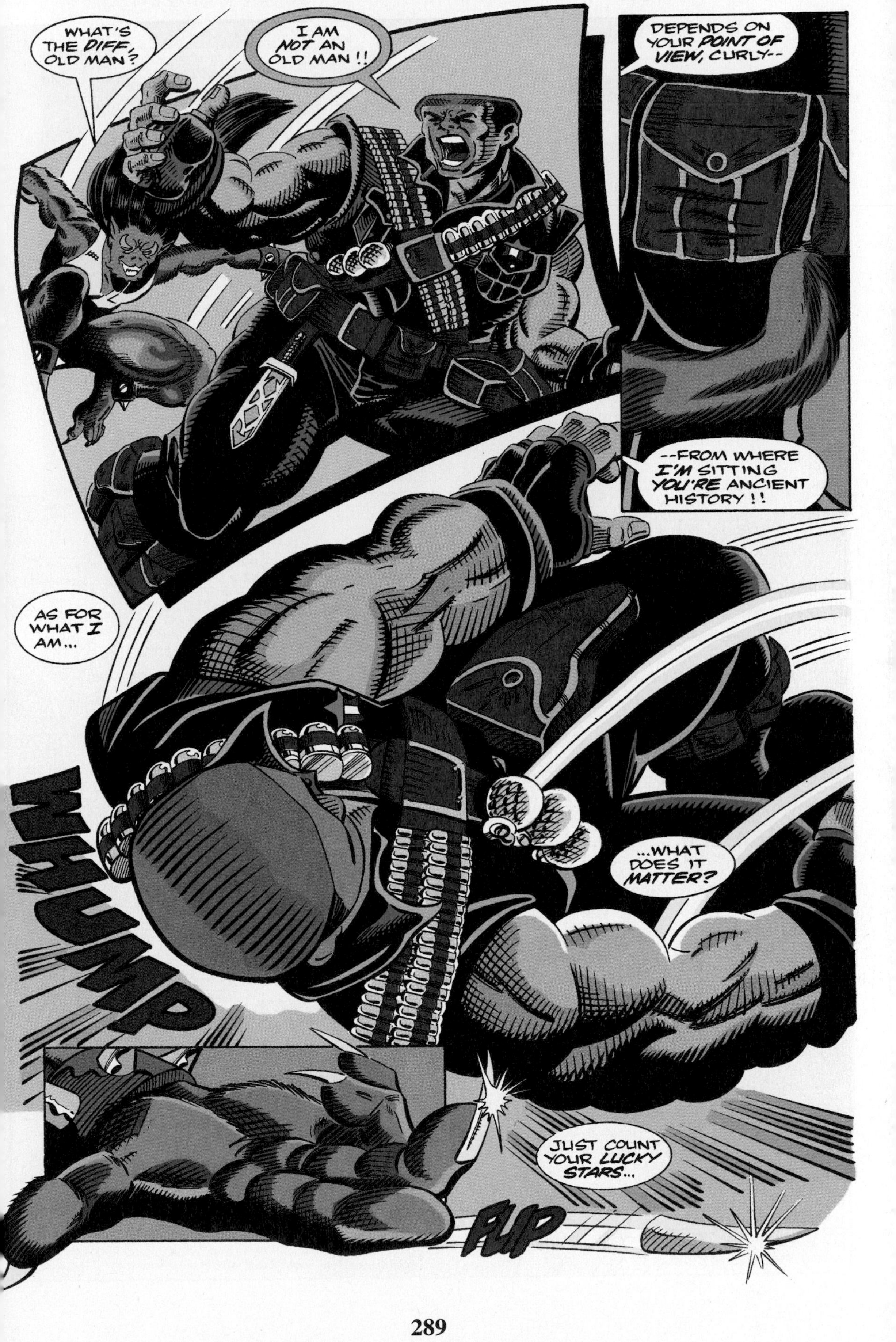
WHAT'S THE DIFF, OLD MAN?
I AM NOT AN OLD MAN!!
DEPENDS ON YOUR POINT OF VIEW, CURLY--
--FROM WHERE I'M SITTING YOU'RE ANCIENT HISTORY!!
AS FOR WHAT I AM...
WHUMP
...WHAT DOES IT MATTER?
JUST COUNT YOUR LUCKY STARS...
FLIP

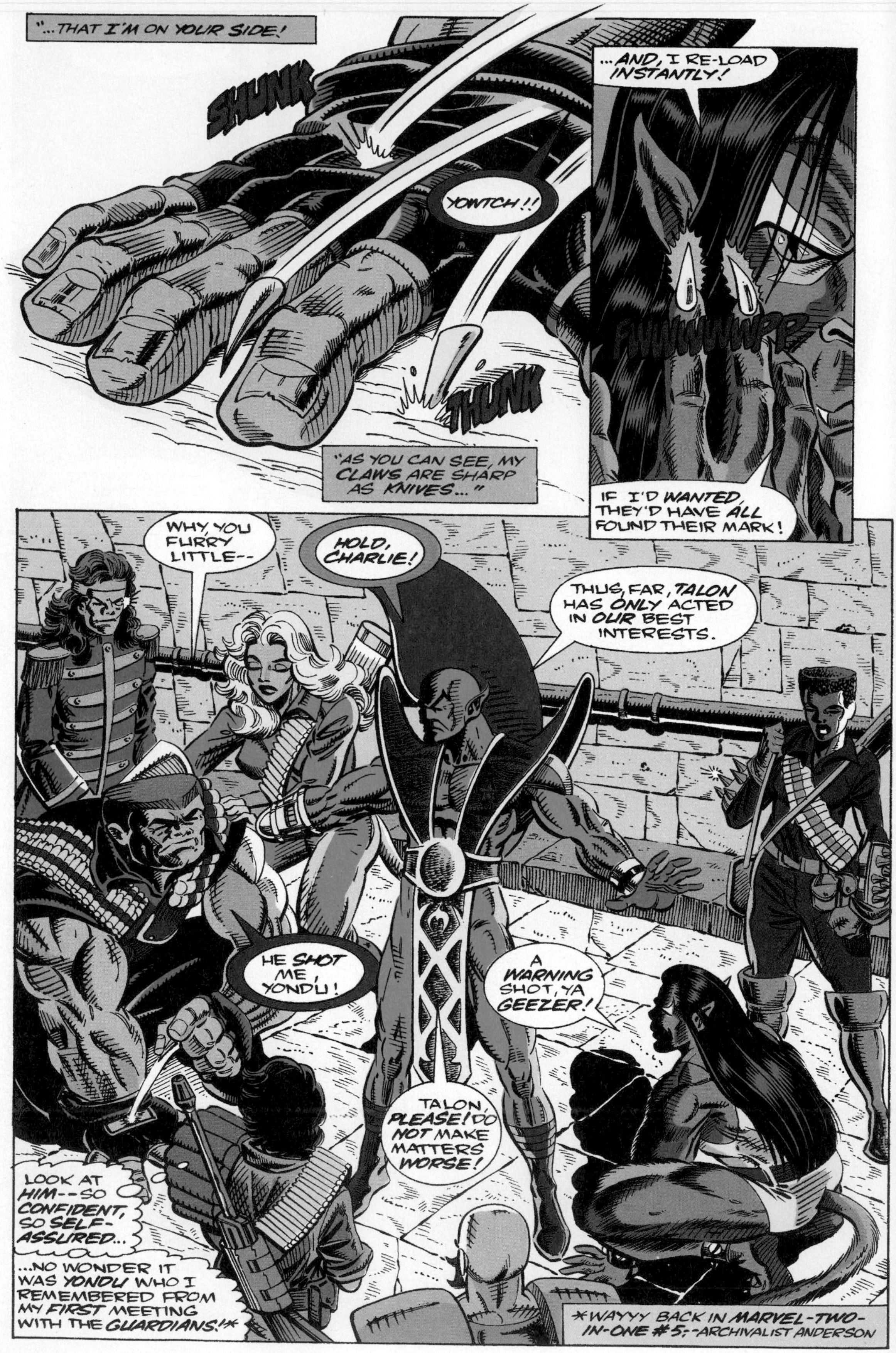
"...THAT I'M ON YOUR SIDE!
SHUNK
YOWTCH!!
THUNK
"AS YOU CAN SEE, MY CLAWS ARE SHARP AS KNIVES..."
...AND, I RE-LOAD INSTANTLY!
FWWWWWPP
IF I'D WANTED, THEY'D HAVE ALL FOUND THEIR MARK!
WHY, YOU FURRY LITTLE--
HOLD, CHARLIE!
THUS, FAR, TALON HAS ONLY ACTED IN OUR BEST INTERESTS.
HE SHOT ME, YONDU!
A WARNING SHOT, YA GEEZER!
TALON, PLEASE! DO NOT MAKE MATTERS WORSE!
LOOK AT HIM--SO CONFIDENT, SO SELF-ASSURED...
...NO WONDER IT WAS YONDU WHO I REMEMBERED FROM MY FIRST MEETING WITH THE GUARDIANS!*
*WAYYY BACK IN MARVEL-TWO-IN-ONE #5.-ARCHIVALIST ANDERSON

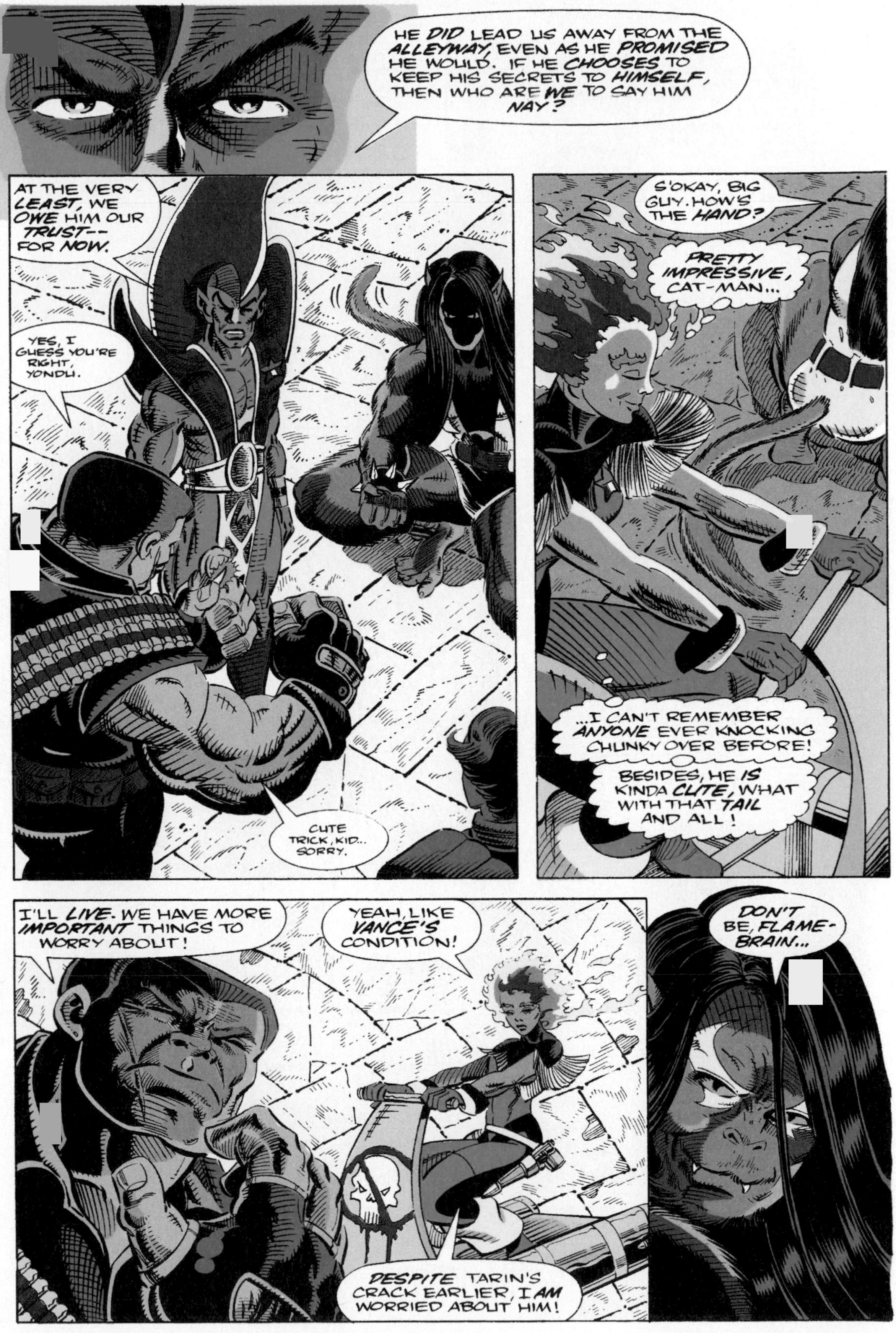
HE DID LEAD US AWAY FROM THE ALLEYWAY, EVEN AS HE PROMISED HE WOULD. IF HE CHOOSES TO KEEP HIS SECRETS TO HIMSELF, THEN WHO ARE WE TO SAY HIM NAY?
AT THE VERY LEAST, WE OWE HIM OUR TRUST-- FOR NOW.
YES, I GUESS YOU'RE RIGHT, YONDU.
CUTE TRICK, KID.. SORRY.
S'OKAY, BIG GUY. HOW'S THE HAND?
PRETTY IMPRESSIVE, CAT-MAN...
...I CAN'T REMEMBER ANYONE EVER KNOCKING CHUNKY OVER BEFORE!
BESIDES, HE IS KINDA CUTE, WHAT WITH THAT TAIL AND ALL!
I'LL LIVE. WE HAVE MORE IMPORTANT THINGS TO WORRY ABOUT!
YEAH, LIKE VANCE'S CONDITION!
DON'T BE, FLAME-BRAIN...
DESPITE TARIN'S CRACK EARLIER, I AM WORRIED ABOUT HIM!

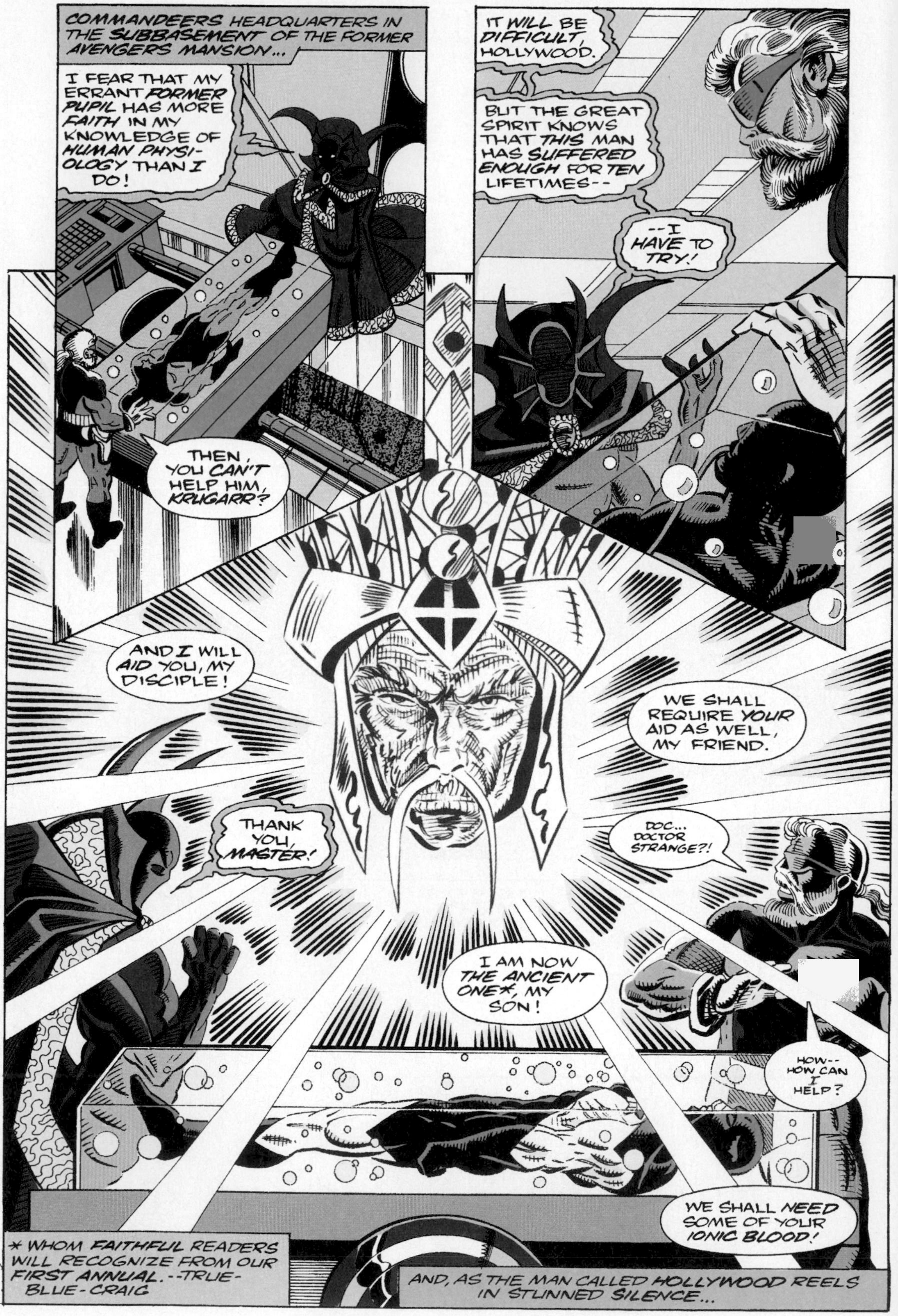
COMMANDEERS HEADQUARTERS IN THE SUBBASEMENT OF THE FORMER AVENGERS MANSION...
I FEAR THAT MY ERRANT FORMER PUPIL HAS MORE FAITH IN MY KNOWLEDGE OF HUMAN PHYSI-OLOGY THAN I DO!
IT WILL BE DIFFICULT, HOLLYWOOD.
BUT THE GREAT SPIRIT KNOWS THAT THIS MAN HAS SUFFERED ENOUGH FOR TEN LIFETIMES--
--I HAVE TO TRY!
THEN, YOU CAN'T HELP HIM, KRUGARR?
AND I WILL AID YOU, MY DISCIPLE!
WE SHALL REQUIRE YOUR AID AS WELL, MY FRIEND.
THANK YOU, MASTER!
DOC... DOCTOR STRANGE?!
I AM NOW THE ANCIENT ONE*, MY SON!
HOW-- HOW CAN I HELP?
WE SHALL NEED SOME OF YOUR IONIC BLOOD!
* WHOM FAITHFUL READERS WILL RECOGNIZE FROM OUR FIRST ANNUAL. --TRUE-BLUE-CRAIG
AND, AS THE MAN CALLED HOLLYWOOD REELS IN STUNNED SILENCE...

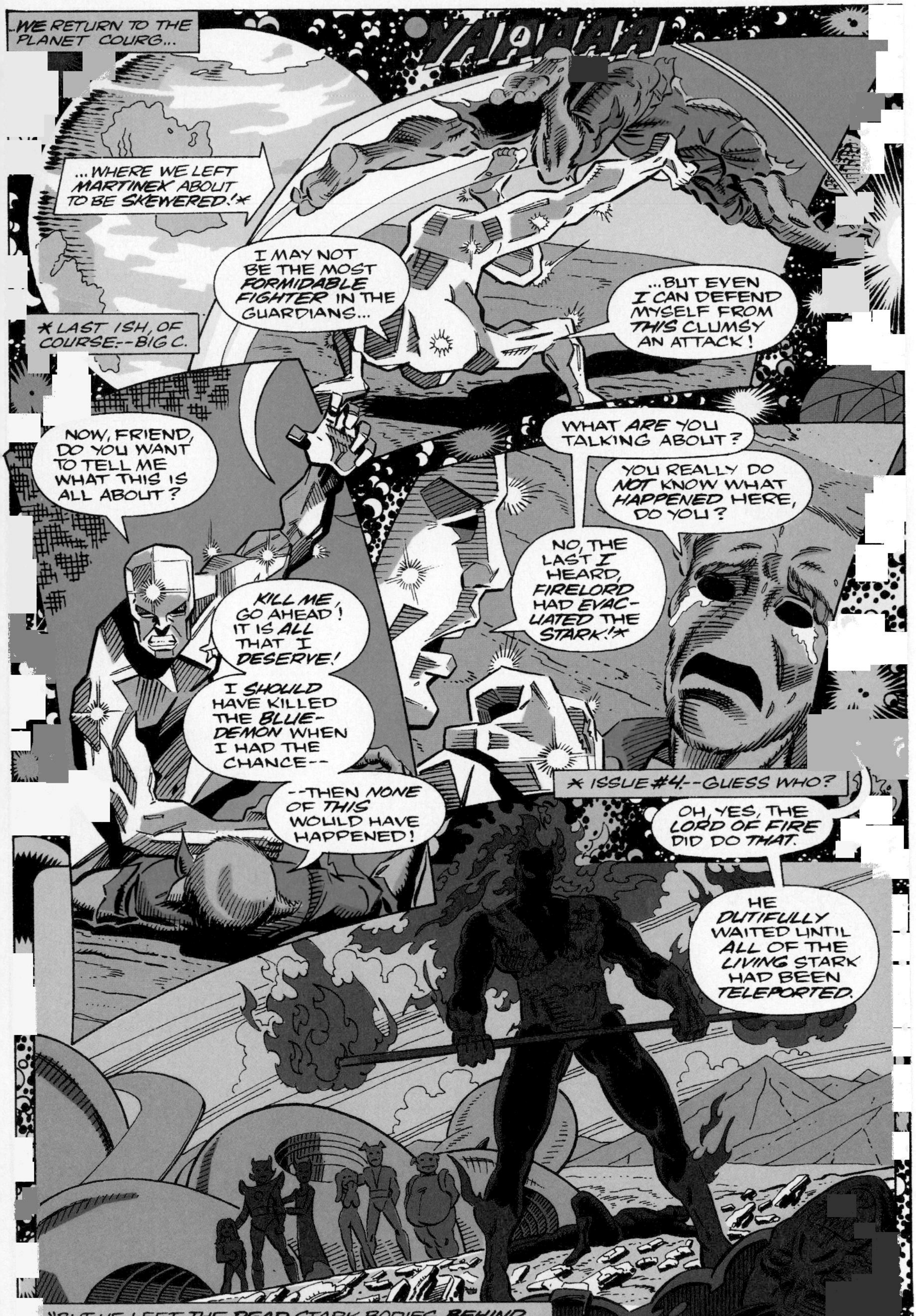
...WE RETURN TO THE PLANET COURG...
YAAAAA
...WHERE WE LEFT MARTINEX ABOUT TO BE SKEWERED!*
I MAY NOT BE THE MOST FORMIDABLE FIGHTER IN THE GUARDIANS...
...BUT EVEN I CAN DEFEND MYSELF FROM THIS CLUMSY AN ATTACK!
*LAST ISH, OF COURSE:--BIG C.
NOW, FRIEND, DO YOU WANT TO TELL ME WHAT THIS IS ALL ABOUT?
KILL ME, GO AHEAD! IT IS ALL THAT I DESERVE!
I SHOULD HAVE KILLED THE BLUE-DEMON WHEN I HAD THE CHANCE--
--THEN NONE OF THIS WOULD HAVE HAPPENED!
WHAT ARE YOU TALKING ABOUT?
YOU REALLY DO NOT KNOW WHAT HAPPENED HERE, DO YOU?
NO, THE LAST I HEARD, FIRELORD HAD EVACUATED THE STARK!*
* ISSUE #4.--GUESS WHO?
OH, YES, THE LORD OF FIRE DID DO THAT.
HE DUTIFULLY WAITED UNTIL ALL OF THE LIVING STARK HAD BEEN TELEPORTED.
"BUT HE LEFT THE DEAD STARK BODIES BEHIND...

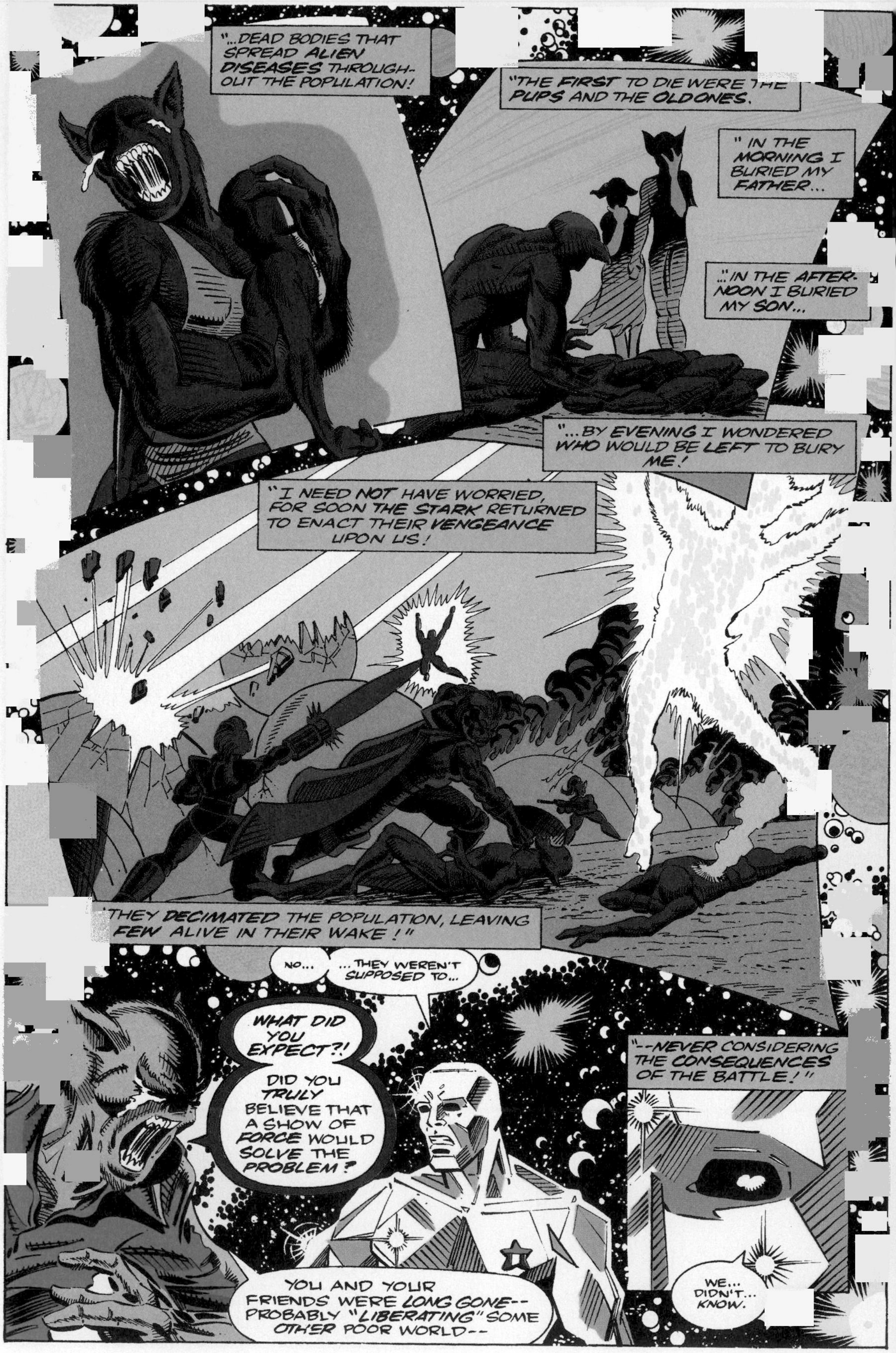
"...DEAD BODIES THAT SPREAD ALIEN DISEASES THROUGH-OUT THE POPULATION!
"THE FIRST TO DIE WERE THE PUPS AND THE OLD ONES.
" IN THE MORNING I BURIED MY FATHER...
"...IN THE AFTER-NOON I BURIED MY SON...
"...BY EVENING I WONDERED WHO WOULD BE LEFT TO BURY ME!
"I NEED NOT HAVE WORRIED, FOR SOON THE STARK RETURNED TO ENACT THEIR VENGEANCE UPON US!
"THEY DECIMATED THE POPULATION, LEAVING FEW ALIVE IN THEIR WAKE!"
NO...
...THEY WEREN'T SUPPOSED TO...
WHAT DID YOU EXPECT?!
DID YOU TRULY BELIEVE THAT A SHOW OF FORCE WOULD SOLVE THE PROBLEM?
YOU AND YOUR FRIENDS WERE LONG GONE-- PROBABLY "LIBERATING" SOME OTHER POOR WORLD--
"--NEVER CONSIDERING THE CONSEQUENCES OF THE BATTLE!"
WE... DIDN'T... KNOW.

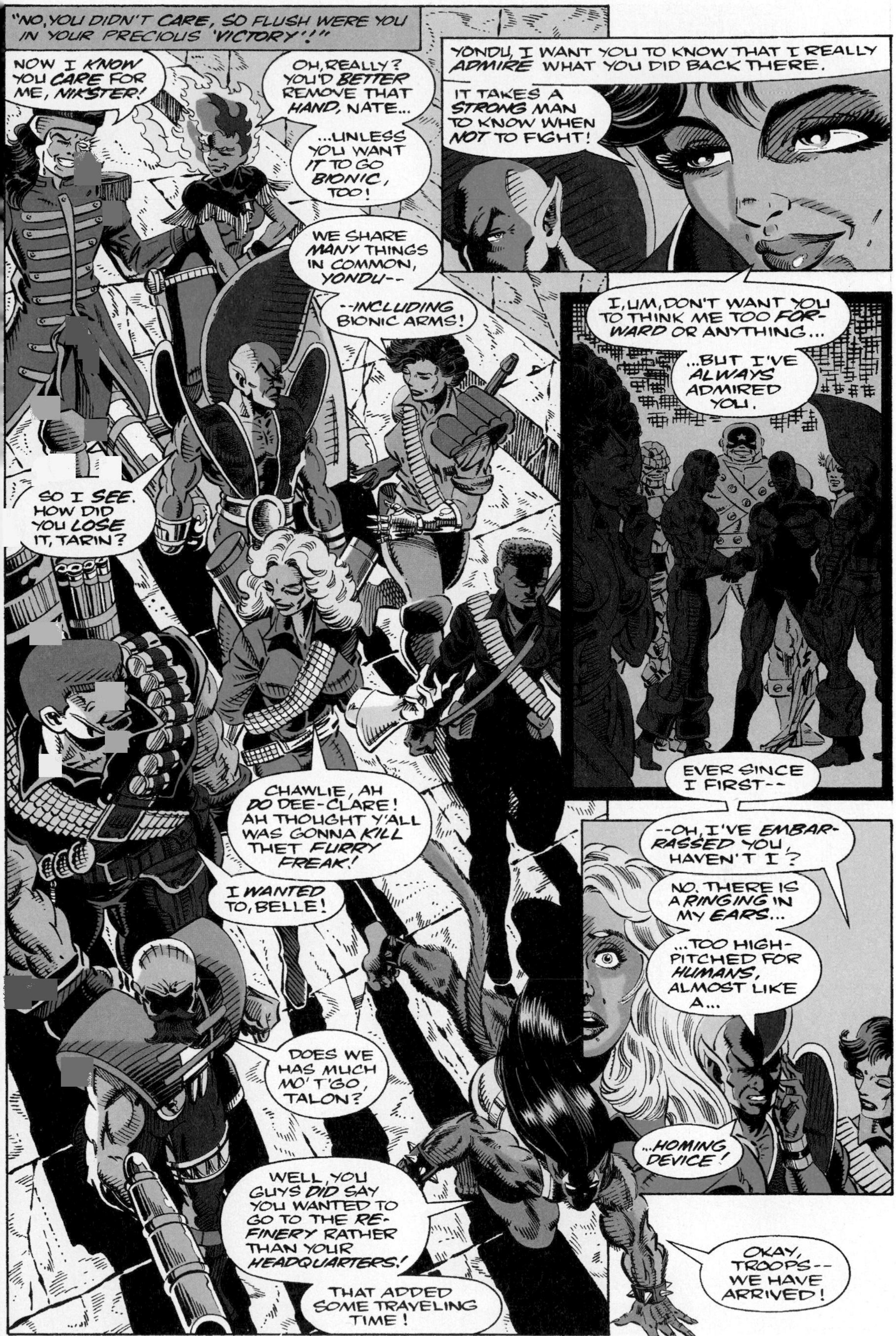
"NO, YOU DIDN'T CARE, SO FLUSH WERE YOU IN YOUR PRECIOUS 'VICTORY'!"
NOW I KNOW YOU CARE FOR ME, NIKSTER!
OH, REALLY? YOU'D BETTER REMOVE THAT HAND, NATE...
...UNLESS YOU WANT IT TO GO BIONIC, TOO!
YONDU, I WANT YOU TO KNOW THAT I REALLY ADMIRE WHAT YOU DID BACK THERE.
IT TAKES A STRONG MAN TO KNOW WHEN NOT TO FIGHT!
WE SHARE MANY THINGS IN COMMON, YONDU--
--INCLUDING BIONIC ARMS!
I, UM, DON'T WANT YOU TO THINK ME TOO FOR-WARD OR ANYTHING...
...BUT I'VE ALWAYS ADMIRED YOU.
SO I SEE. HOW DID YOU LOSE IT, TARIN?
EVER SINCE I FIRST--
--OH, I'VE EMBAR-RASSED YOU, HAVEN'T I?
NO. THERE IS A RINGING IN MY EARS...
...TOO HIGH-PITCHED FOR HUMANS, ALMOST LIKE A...
...HOMING DEVICE!
CHAWLIE, AH DO DEE-CLARE! AH THOUGHT Y'ALL WAS GONNA KILL THET FURRY FREAK!
I WANTED TO, BELLE!
DOES WE HAS MUCH MO' T'GO, TALON?
WELL, YOU GUYS DID SAY YOU WANTED TO GO TO THE RE-FINERY RATHER THAN YOUR HEADQUARTERS!
THAT ADDED SOME TRAVELING TIME!
OKAY, TROOPS-- WE HAVE ARRIVED!

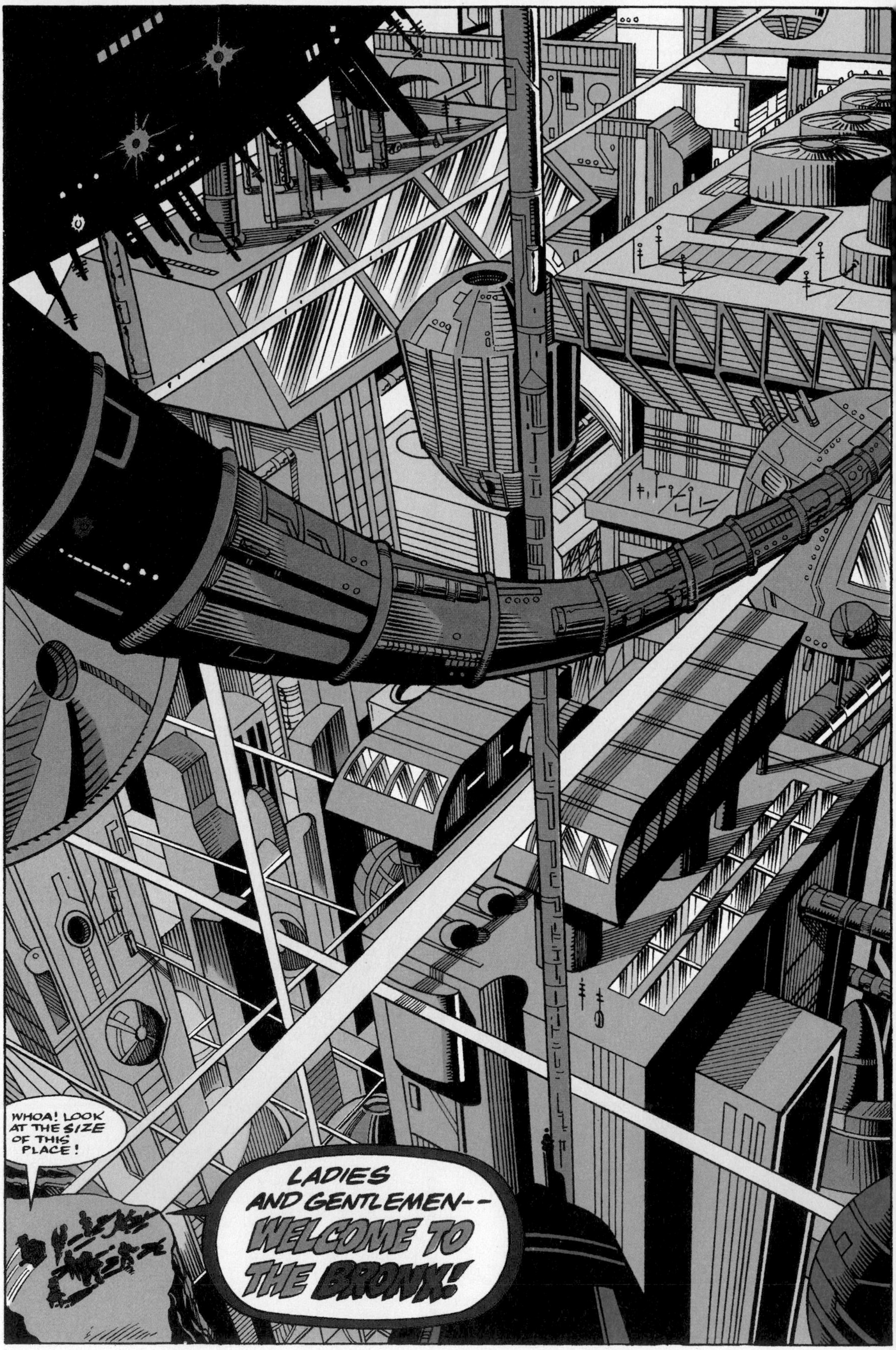
WHOA! LOOK AT THE SIZE OF THIS PLACE!
LADIES AND GENTLEMEN-- WELCOME TO THE BRONX!

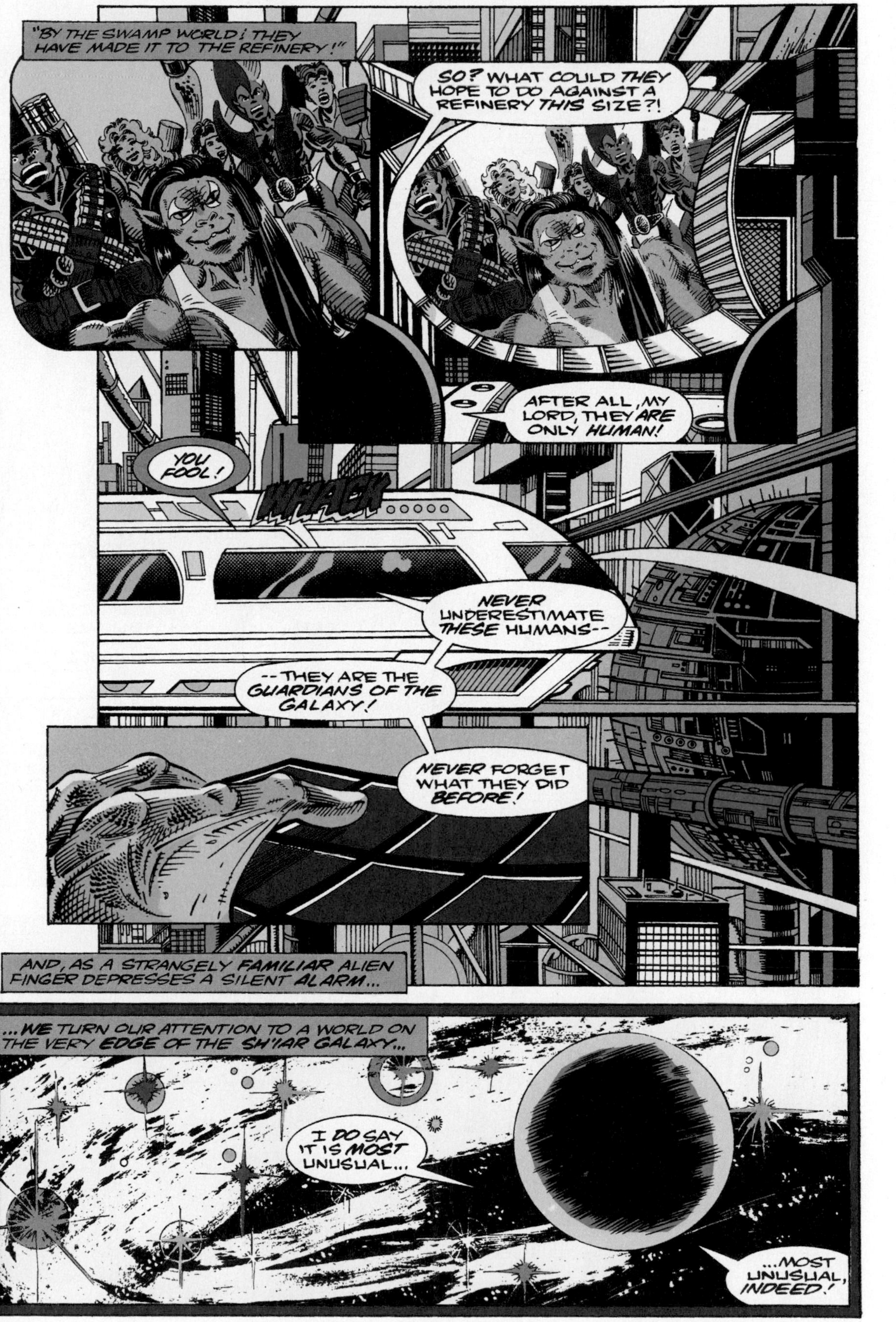

"BY THE SWAMP WORLD! THEY HAVE MADE IT TO THE REFINERY!"
SO? WHAT COULD THEY HOPE TO DO AGAINST A REFINERY THIS SIZE?!
AFTER ALL, MY LORD, THEY ARE ONLY HUMAN!
YOU FOOL!
WHACK
NEVER UNDERESTIMATE THESE HUMANS--
--THEY ARE THE GUARDIANS OF THE GALAXY!
NEVER FORGET WHAT THEY DID BEFORE!
AND, AS A STRANGELY FAMILIAR ALIEN FINGER DEPRESSES A SILENT ALARM...
...WE TURN OUR ATTENTION TO A WORLD ON THE VERY EDGE OF THE SH'IAR GALAXY...
I DO SAY IT IS MOST UNUSUAL...
...MOST UNUSUAL, INDEED!

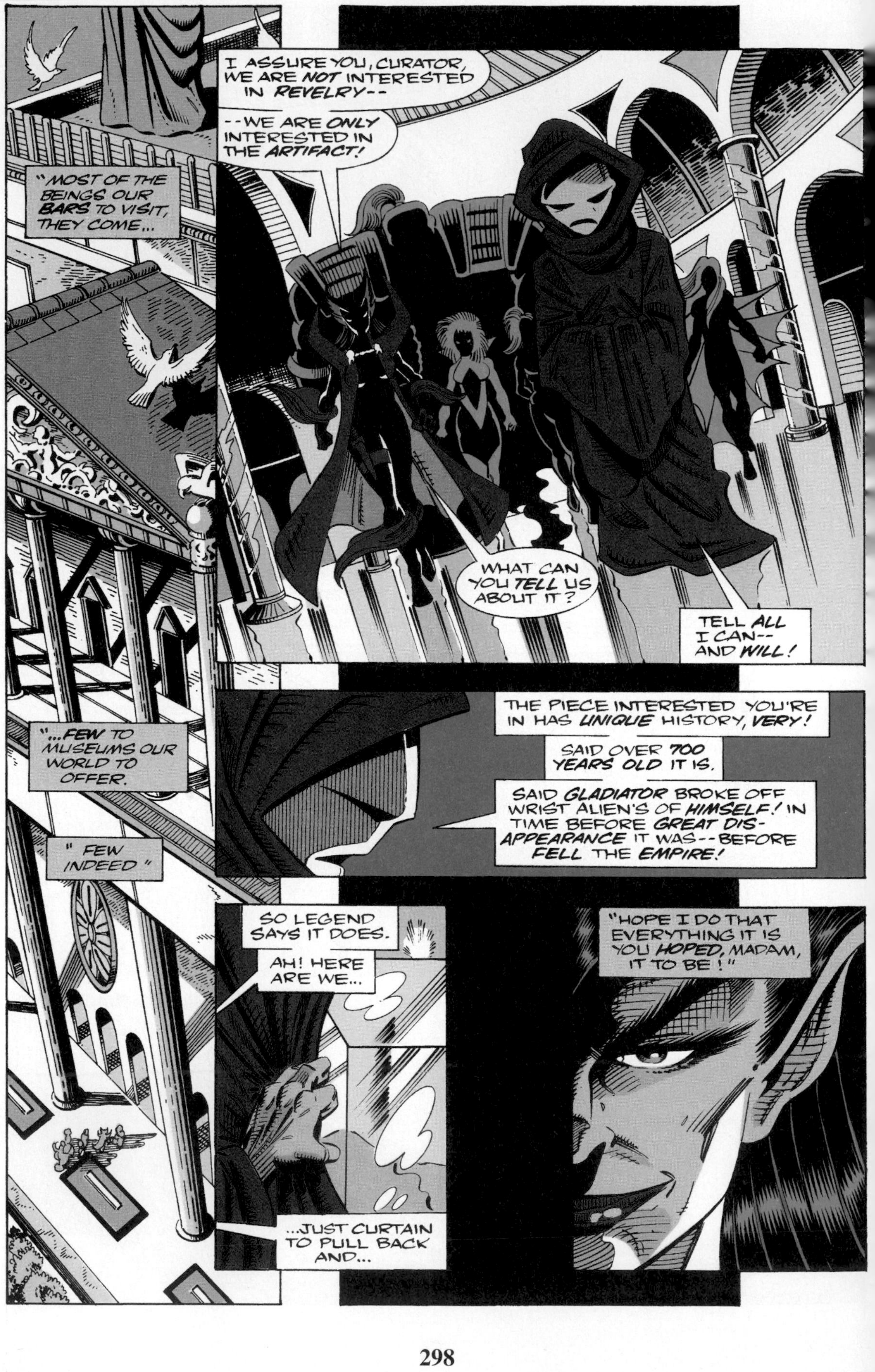
"MOST OF THE BEINGS OUR BARS TO VISIT, THEY COME...
"...FEW TO MUSEUMS OUR WORLD TO OFFER.
" FEW INDEED "
I ASSURE YOU, CURATOR, WE ARE NOT INTERESTED IN REVELRY--
--WE ARE ONLY INTERESTED IN THE ARTIFACT!
WHAT CAN YOU TELL US ABOUT IT?
TELL ALL I CAN-- AND WILL!
THE PIECE INTERESTED YOU'RE IN HAS UNIQUE HISTORY, VERY!
SAID OVER 700 YEARS OLD IT IS.
SAID GLADIATOR BROKE OFF WRIST ALIEN'S OF HIMSELF! IN TIME BEFORE GREAT DIS-APPEARANCE IT WAS--BEFORE FELL THE EMPIRE!
SO LEGEND SAYS IT DOES.
AH! HERE ARE WE...
...JUST CURTAIN TO PULL BACK AND...
"HOPE I DO THAT EVERYTHING IT IS YOU HOPED, MADAM, IT TO BE!"

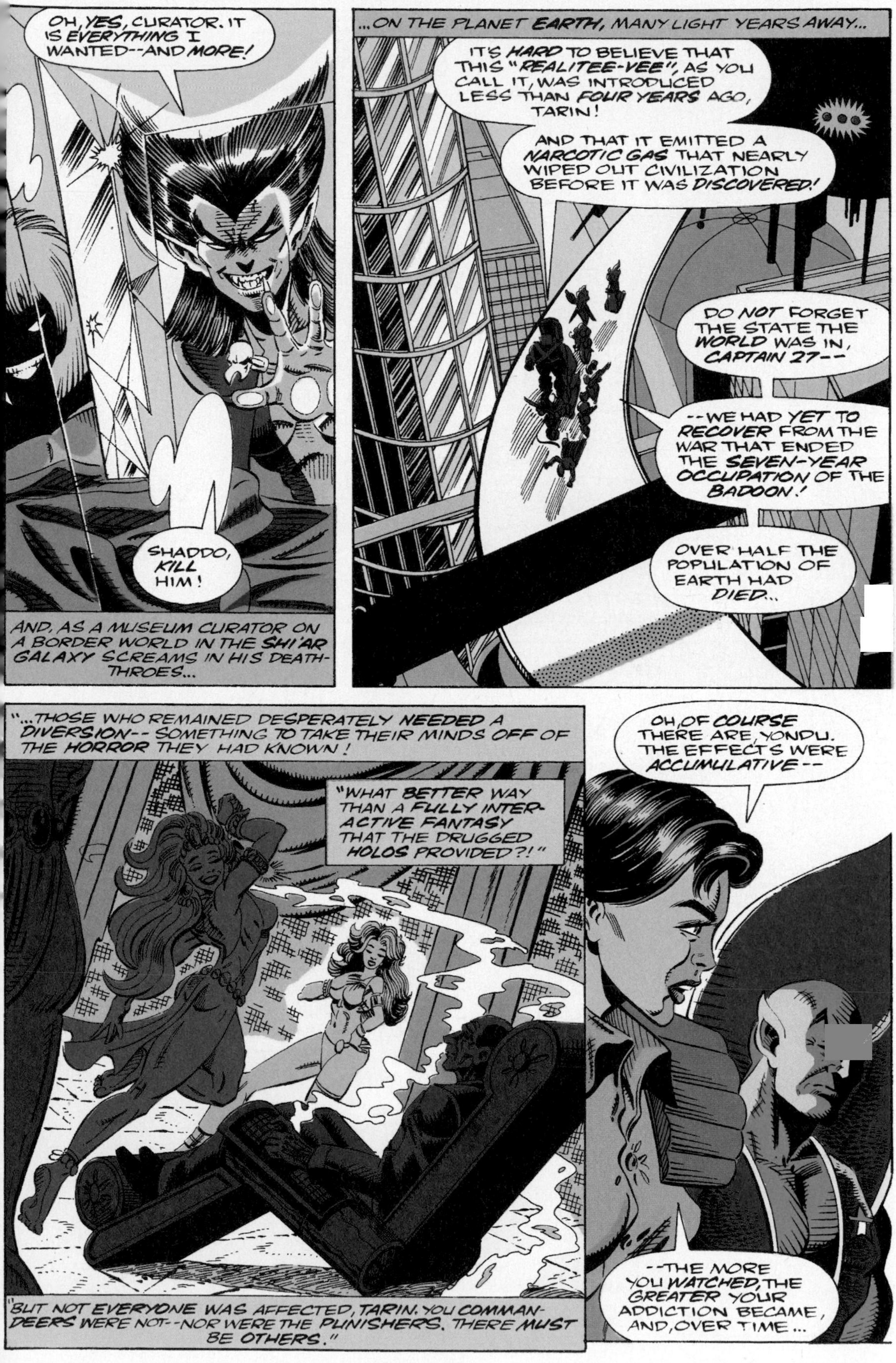
OH, YES, CURATOR. IT IS EVERYTHING I WANTED--AND MORE!
SHADDO, KILL HIM!
AND, AS A MUSEUM CURATOR ON A BORDER WORLD IN THE SHI'AR GALAXY SCREAMS IN HIS DEATH-THROES...
...ON THE PLANET EARTH, MANY LIGHT YEARS AWAY...
IT'S HARD TO BELIEVE THAT THIS "REALITEE-VEE", AS YOU CALL IT, WAS INTRODUCED LESS THAN FOUR YEARS AGO, TARIN!
AND THAT IT EMITTED A NARCOTIC GAS THAT NEARLY WIPED OUT CIVILIZATION BEFORE IT WAS DISCOVERED!
DO NOT FORGET THE STATE THE WORLD WAS IN, CAPTAIN 27--
--WE HAD YET TO RECOVER FROM THE WAR THAT ENDED THE SEVEN-YEAR OCCUPATION OF THE BADOON!
OVER HALF THE POPULATION OF EARTH HAD DIED...
"...THOSE WHO REMAINED DESPERATELY NEEDED A DIVERSION-- SOMETHING TO TAKE THEIR MINDS OFF OF THE HORROR THEY HAD KNOWN!
"WHAT BETTER WAY THAN A FULLY INTER-ACTIVE FANTASY THAT THE DRUGGED HOLOS PROVIDED?!"
"BUT NOT EVERYONE WAS AFFECTED, TARIN. YOU COMMAN-DEERS WERE NOT--NOR WERE THE PUNISHERS. THERE MUST BE OTHERS."
OH, OF COURSE THERE ARE, YONDU. THE EFFECTS WERE ACCUMULATIVE--
--THE MORE YOU WATCHED, THE GREATER YOUR ADDICTION BECAME, AND, OVER TIME...

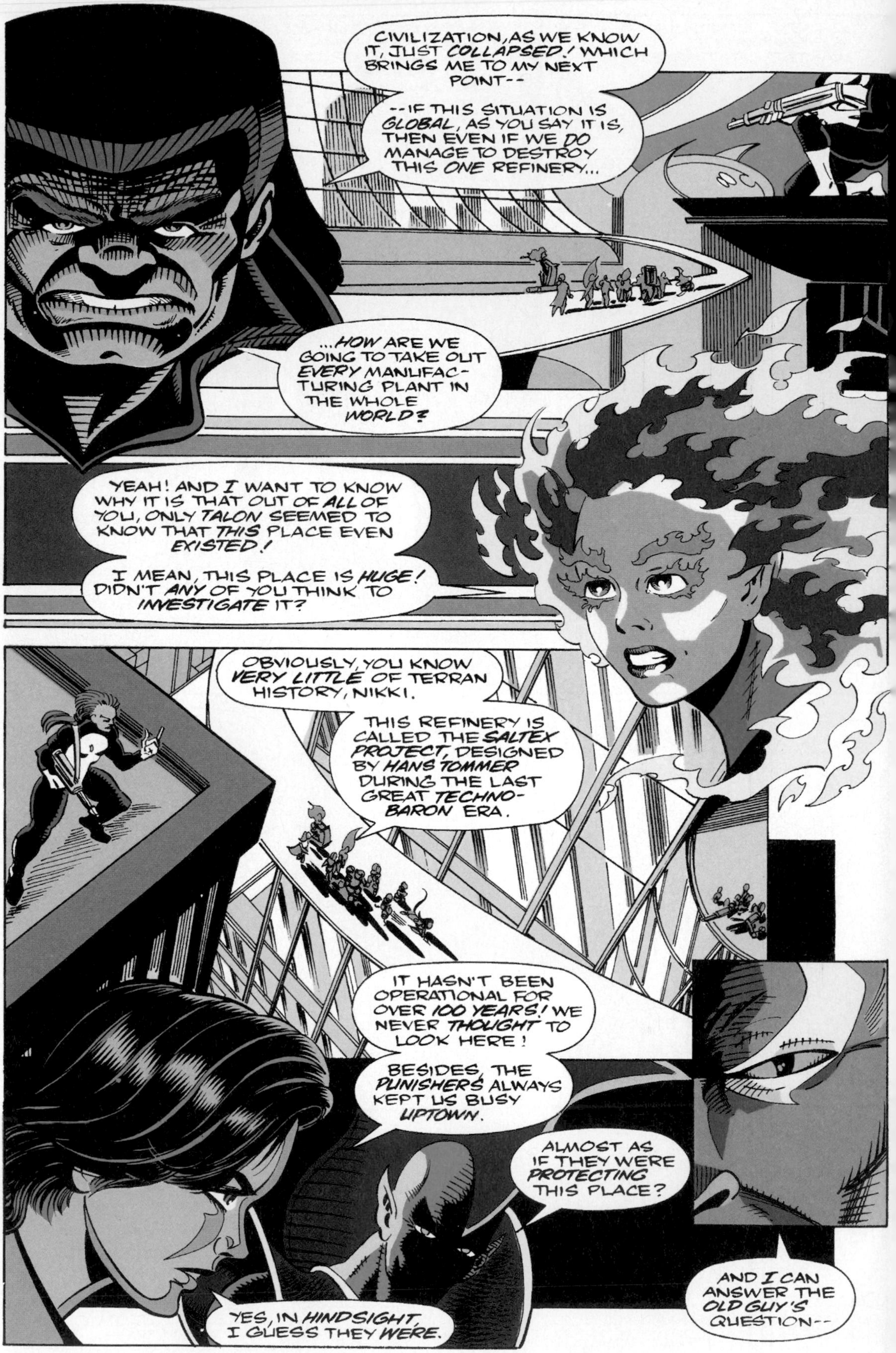
CIVILIZATION, AS WE KNOW IT, JUST COLLAPSED! WHICH BRINGS ME TO MY NEXT POINT--
--IF THIS SITUATION IS GLOBAL, AS YOU SAY IT IS, THEN EVEN IF WE DO MANAGE TO DESTROY THIS ONE REFINERY...
...HOW ARE WE GOING TO TAKE OUT EVERY MANUFACTURING PLANT IN THE WHOLE WORLD?
YEAH! AND I WANT TO KNOW WHY IT IS THAT OUT OF ALL OF YOU, ONLY TALON SEEMED TO KNOW THAT THIS PLACE EVEN EXISTED!
I MEAN, THIS PLACE IS HUGE! DIDN'T ANY OF YOU THINK TO INVESTIGATE IT?
OBVIOUSLY, YOU KNOW VERY LITTLE OF TERRAN HISTORY, NIKKI.
THIS REFINERY IS CALLED THE SALTEX PROJECT, DESIGNED BY HANS TOMMER DURING THE LAST GREAT TECHNO-BARON ERA.
IT HASN'T BEEN OPERATIONAL FOR OVER 100 YEARS! WE NEVER THOUGHT TO LOOK HERE!
BESIDES, THE PUNISHERS ALWAYS KEPT US BUSY UPTOWN.
ALMOST AS IF THEY WERE PROTECTING THIS PLACE?
YES, IN HINDSIGHT, I GUESS THEY WERE.
AND I CAN ANSWER THE OLD GUY'S QUESTION--

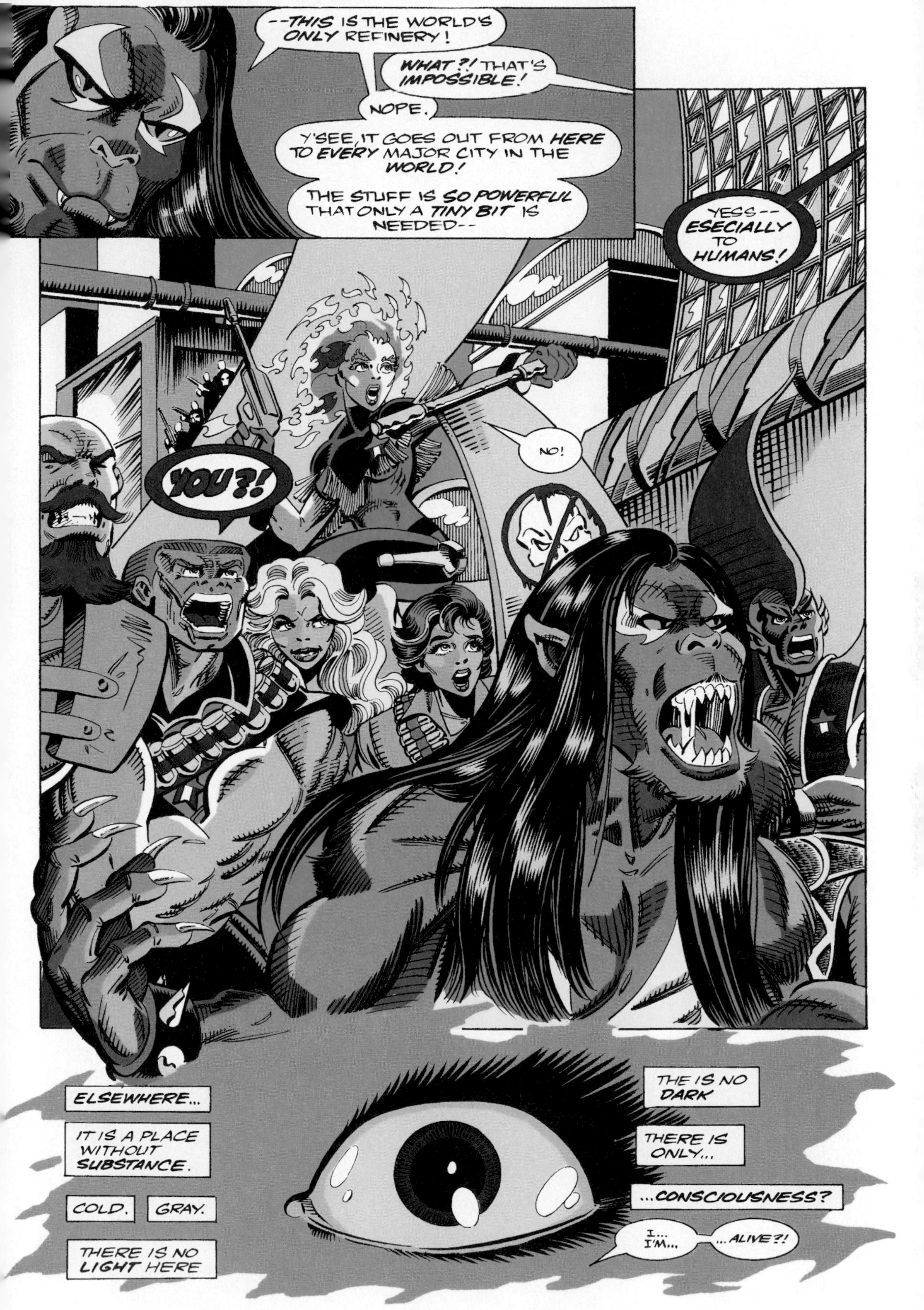
--THIS IS THE WORLD'S ONLY REFINERY!
WHAT?! THAT'S IMPOSSIBLE!
NOPE.
Y'SEE, IT GOES OUT FROM HERE TO EVERY MAJOR CITY IN THE WORLD!
THE STUFF IS SO POWERFUL THAT ONLY A TINY BIT IS NEEDED--
YESS-- ESECIALLY TO HUMANS!
NO!
YOU?!
ELSEWHERE...
IT IS A PLACE WITHOUT SUBSTANCE.
COLD.
GRAY.
THERE IS NO LIGHT HERE
THE IS NO DARK
THERE IS ONLY...
...CONSCIOUSNESS?
I... I'M...
...ALIVE?!

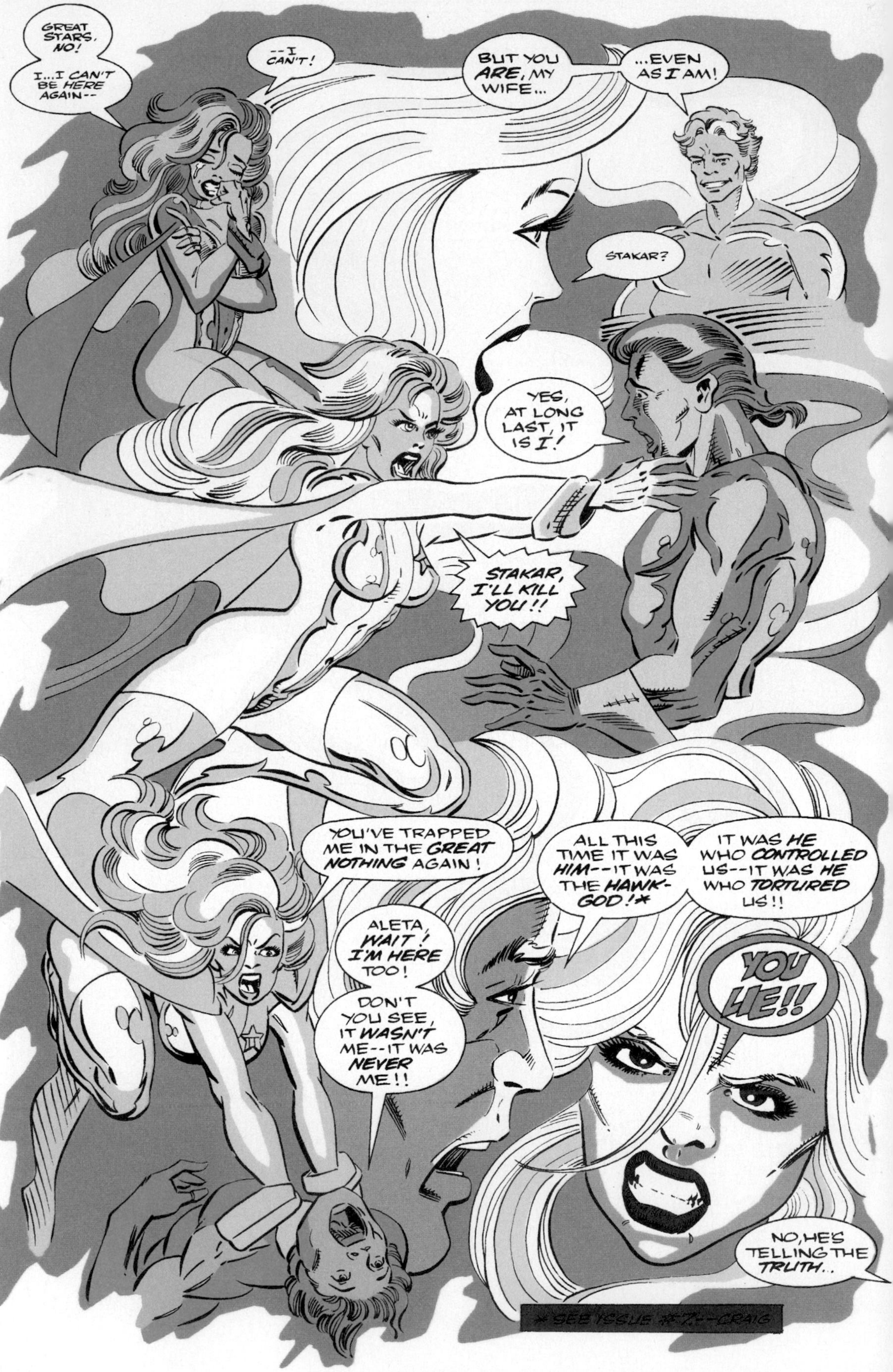
GREAT STARS, NO!
I...I CAN'T BE HERE AGAIN--
--I CAN'T!
BUT YOU ARE, MY WIFE...
...EVEN AS I AM!
STAKAR?
YES, AT LONG LAST, IT IS I!
STAKAR, I'LL KILL YOU!!
YOU'VE TRAPPED ME IN THE GREAT NOTHING AGAIN!
ALL THIS TIME IT WAS HIM--IT WAS THE HAWK-GOD!*
IT WAS HE WHO CONTROLLED US--IT WAS HE WHO TORTURED US!!
ALETA, WAIT! I'M HERE TOO!
DON'T YOU SEE, IT WASN'T ME--IT WAS NEVER ME!!
YOU LIE!!
NO, HE'S TELLING THE TRUTH...
* SEE ISSUE #7.--CRAIG

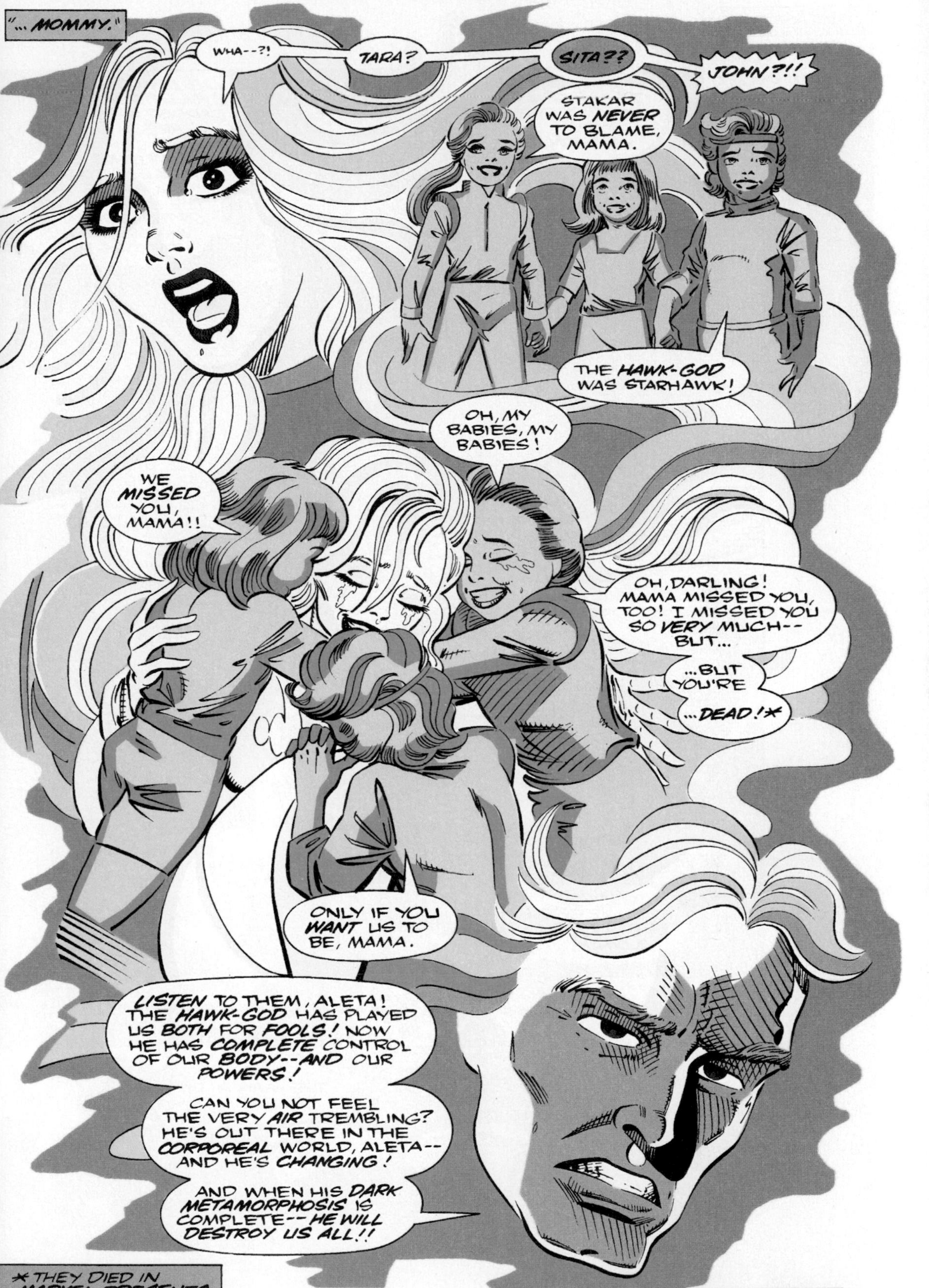
"... MOMMY."
WHA--?!
TARA?
SITA??
JOHN?!!
STAKAR WAS NEVER TO BLAME, MAMA.
THE HAWK-GOD WAS STARHAWK!
OH, MY BABIES, MY BABIES!
WE MISSED YOU, MAMA!!
OH, DARLING! MAMA MISSED YOU, TOO! I MISSED YOU SO VERY MUCH-- BUT...
...BUT YOU'RE
...DEAD!*
ONLY IF YOU WANT US TO BE, MAMA.
LISTEN TO THEM, ALETA! THE HAWK-GOD HAS PLAYED US BOTH FOR FOOLS! NOW HE HAS COMPLETE CONTROL OF OUR BODY--AND OUR POWERS!
CAN YOU NOT FEEL THE VERY AIR TREMBLING? HE'S OUT THERE IN THE CORPOREAL WORLD, ALETA-- AND HE'S CHANGING!
AND WHEN HIS DARK METAMORPHOSIS IS COMPLETE-- HE WILL DESTROY US ALL!!
*THEY DIED IN MARVEL PRESENTS #11.-- CRAIG
WE'LL RETURN HERE NEXT ISSUE...

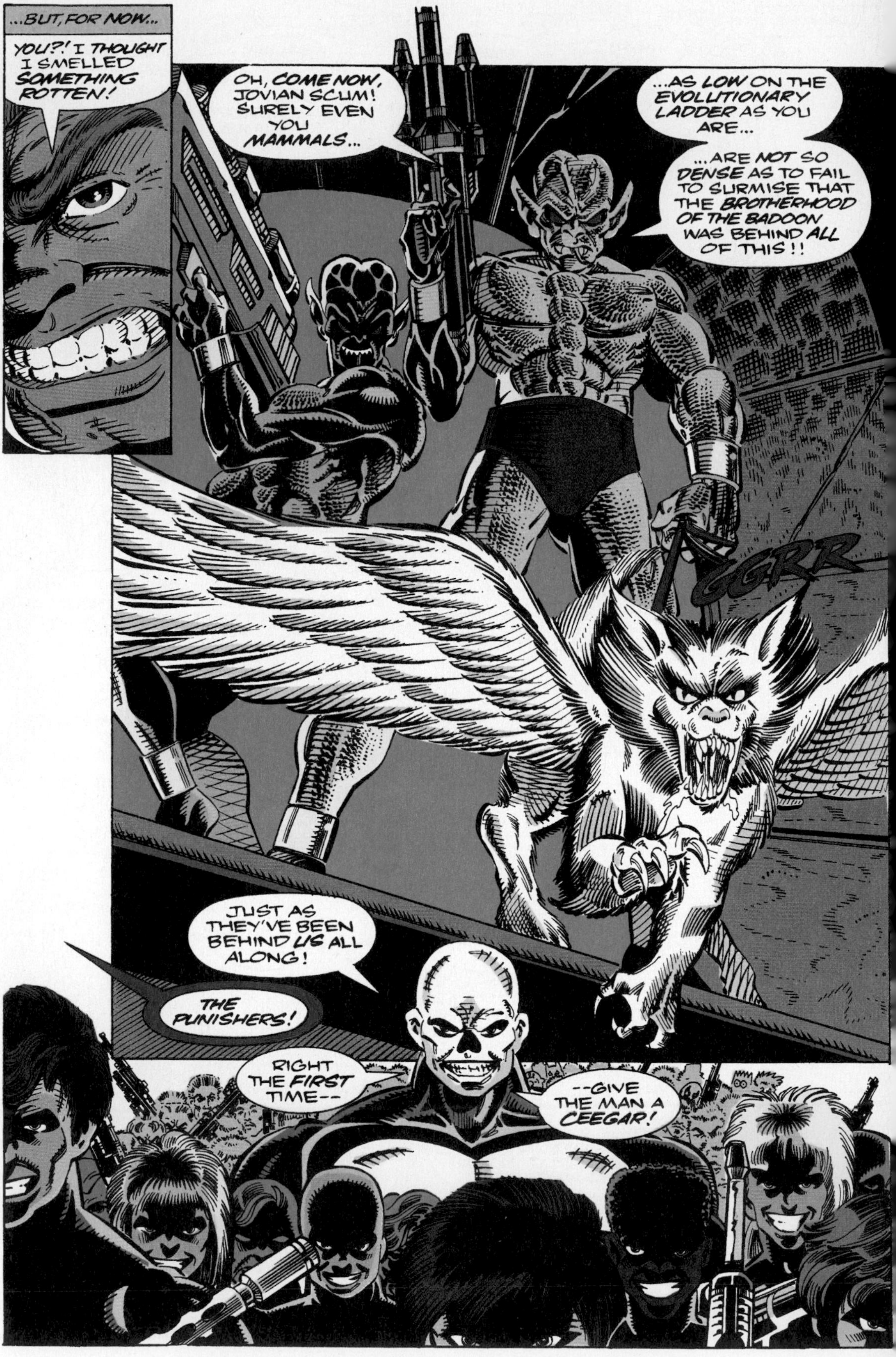
...BUT, FOR NOW...
YOU?! I THOUGHT I SMELLED SOMETHING ROTTEN!
OH, COME NOW, JOVIAN SCUM! SURELY EVEN YOU MAMMALS...
...AS LOW ON THE EVOLUTIONARY LADDER AS YOU ARE...
...ARE NOT SO DENSE AS TO FAIL TO SURMISE THAT THE BROTHERHOOD OF THE BADOON WAS BEHIND ALL OF THIS!!
GGRR
JUST AS THEY'VE BEEN BEHIND US ALL ALONG!
THE PUNISHERS!
RIGHT THE FIRST TIME--
--GIVE THE MAN A CEEGAR!

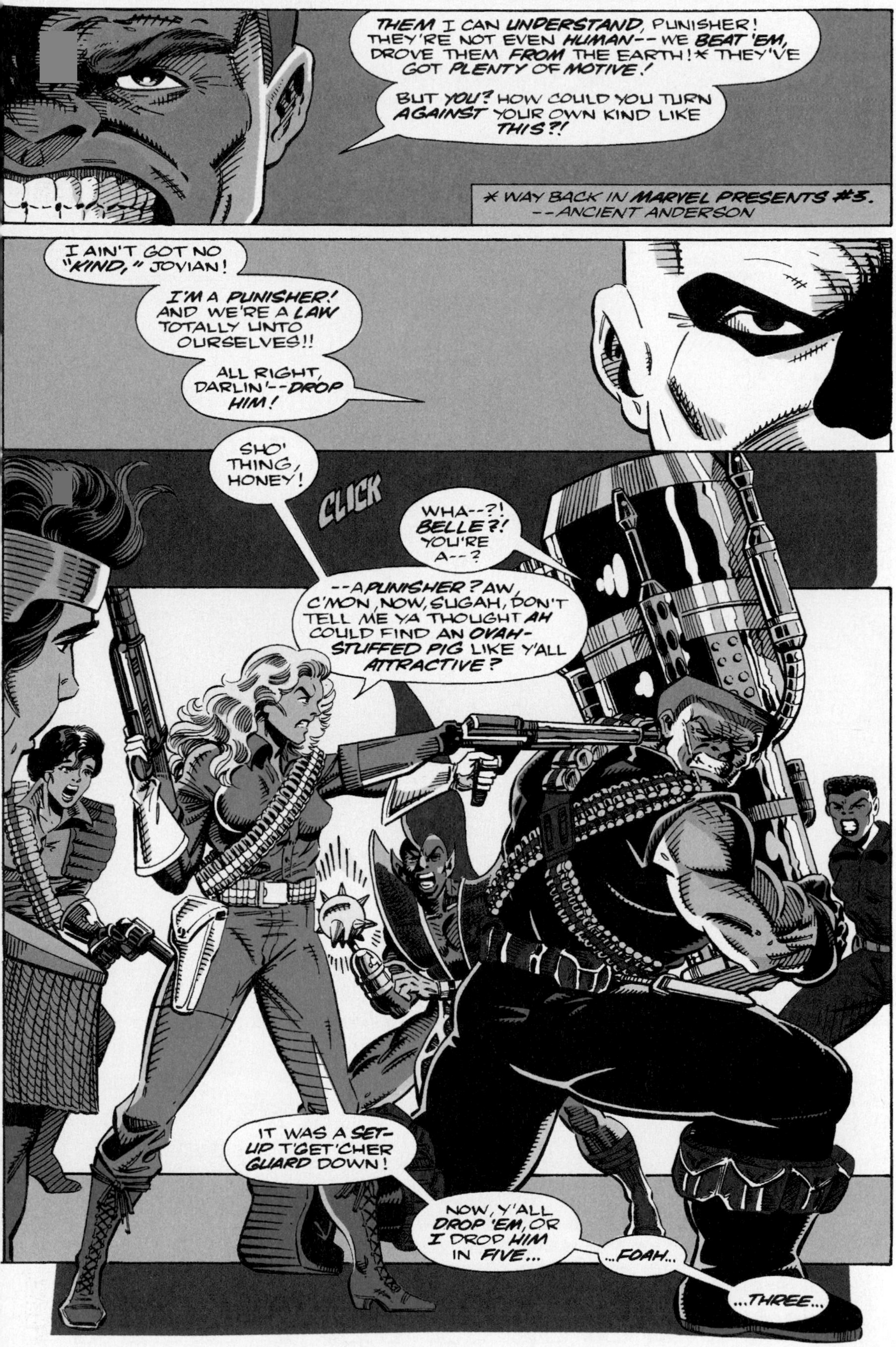
THEM I CAN UNDERSTAND, PUNISHER! THEY'RE NOT EVEN HUMAN-- WE BEAT 'EM, DROVE THEM FROM THE EARTH!* THEY'VE GOT PLENTY OF MOTIVE!
BUT YOU? HOW COULD YOU TURN AGAINST YOUR OWN KIND LIKE THIS?!
* WAY BACK IN MARVEL PRESENTS #3. --ANCIENT ANDERSON
I AIN'T GOT NO "KIND," JOVIAN!
I'M A PUNISHER! AND WE'RE A LAW TOTALLY UNTO OURSELVES!!
ALL RIGHT, DARLIN'--DROP HIM!
SHO' THING, HONEY!
CLICK
WHA--?! BELLE?! YOU'RE A--?
--A PUNISHER? AW, C'MON, NOW, SUGAH, DON'T TELL ME YA THOUGHT AH COULD FIND AN OVAH-STUFFED PIG LIKE Y'ALL ATTRACTIVE?
IT WAS A SET-UP T'GET'CHER GUARD DOWN!
NOW, Y'ALL DROP 'EM, OR I DROP HIM IN FIVE...
...FOAH...
...THREE...

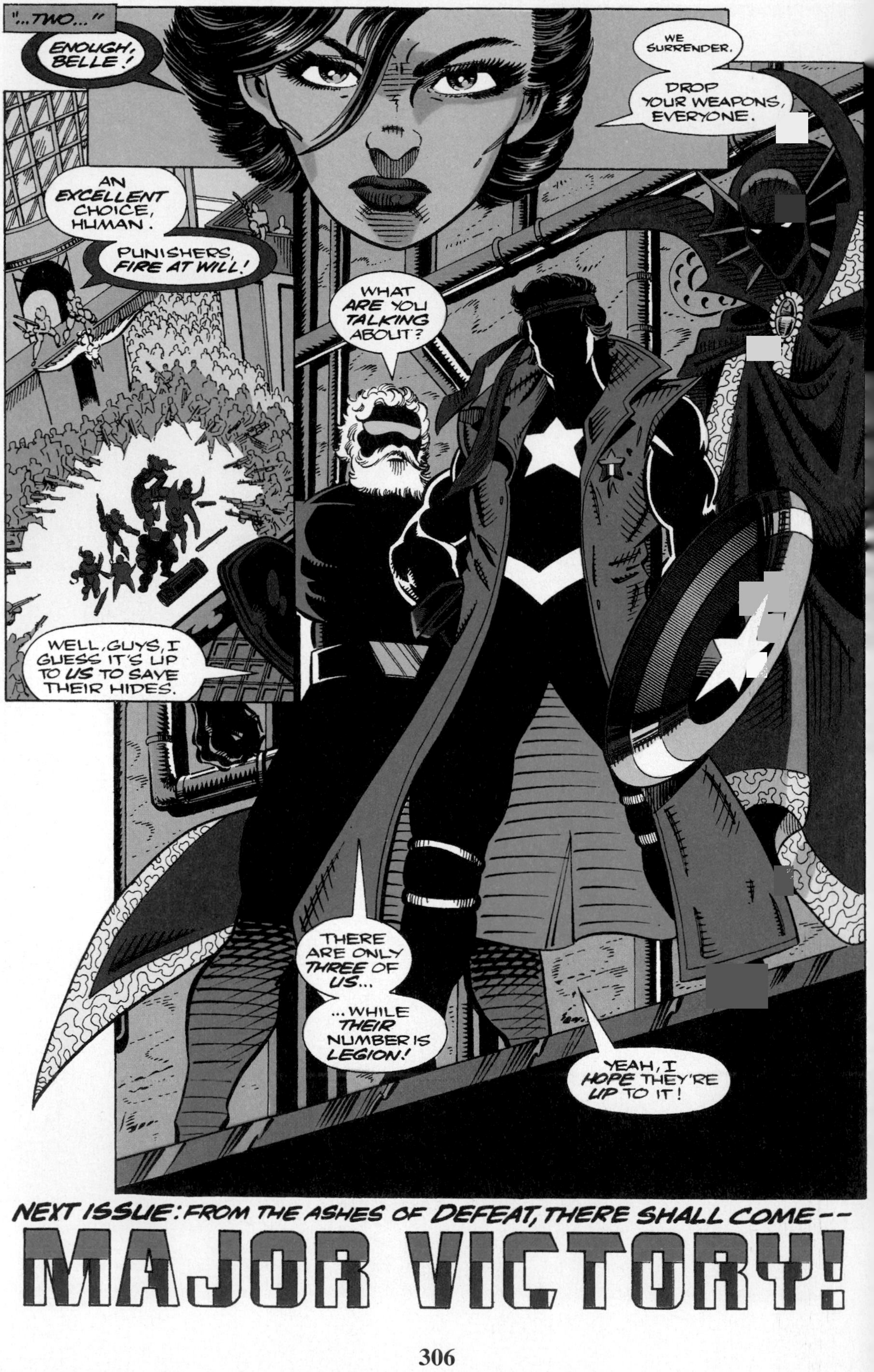
"...TWO..."
ENOUGH, BELLE!
WE SURRENDER.
DROP YOUR WEAPONS, EVERYONE.
AN EXCELLENT CHOICE, HUMAN.
PUNISHERS, FIRE AT WILL!
WHAT ARE YOU TALKING ABOUT?
WELL, GUYS, I GUESS IT'S UP TO US TO SAVE THEIR HIDES.
THERE ARE ONLY THREE OF US...
...WHILE THEIR NUMBER IS LEGION!
YEAH, I HOPE THEY'RE UP TO IT!

NEXT ISSUE: FROM THE ASHES OF DEFEAT, THERE SHALL COME--

MAJOR VICTORY!

GUARDIANS
OF THE GALAXY

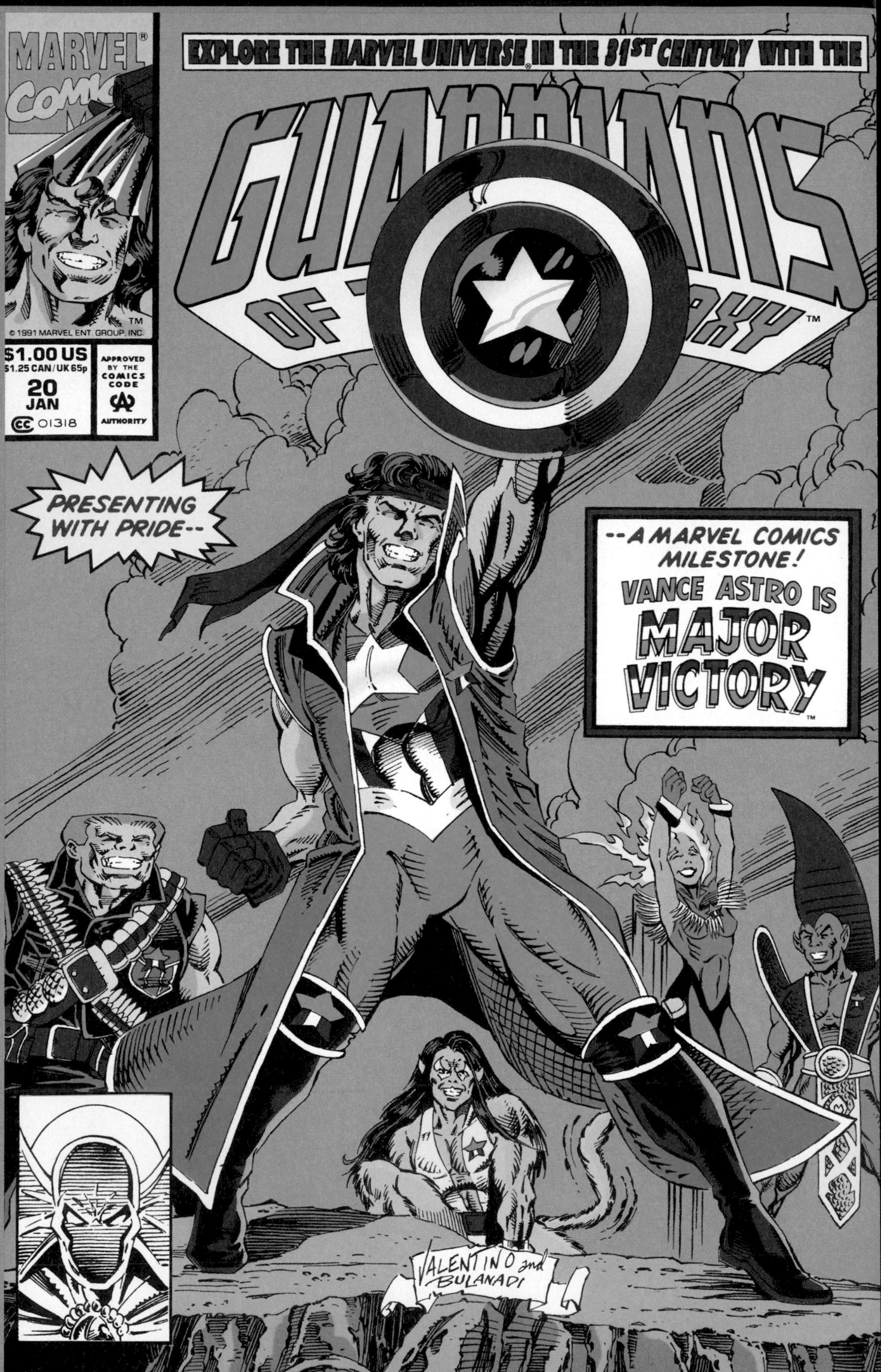

MARVEL®
EXPLORE THE MARVEL UNIVERSE® IN THE 31ST CENTURY WITH THE
TM
© 1991 MARVEL ENT. GROUP, INC.
$1.00 US
$1.25 CAN/UK 65p
20
JAN
01318
APPROVED BY THE COMICS CODE AUTHORITY
PRESENTING WITH PRIDE--
--A MARVEL COMICS MILESTONE!
VANCE ASTRO IS
MAJOR VICTORY™
VALENTINO and BULANADI

MAJOR VANCE ASTRO! CHARLIE 27! NIKKI! YONDU! FOUR EXTRAORDINARY SUPER-BEINGS, ALL SURVIVORS OF INTERSTELLAR WAR. NOW THEY ROAM THE COSMOS OF THE 31ST CENTURY ABOARD THE STARSHIP CAPTAIN AMERICA, THEIR MISSION—TO SAFEGUARD THE MILKY WAY! STAN LEE PRESENTS . . . THE GUARDIANS OF THE GALAXY!

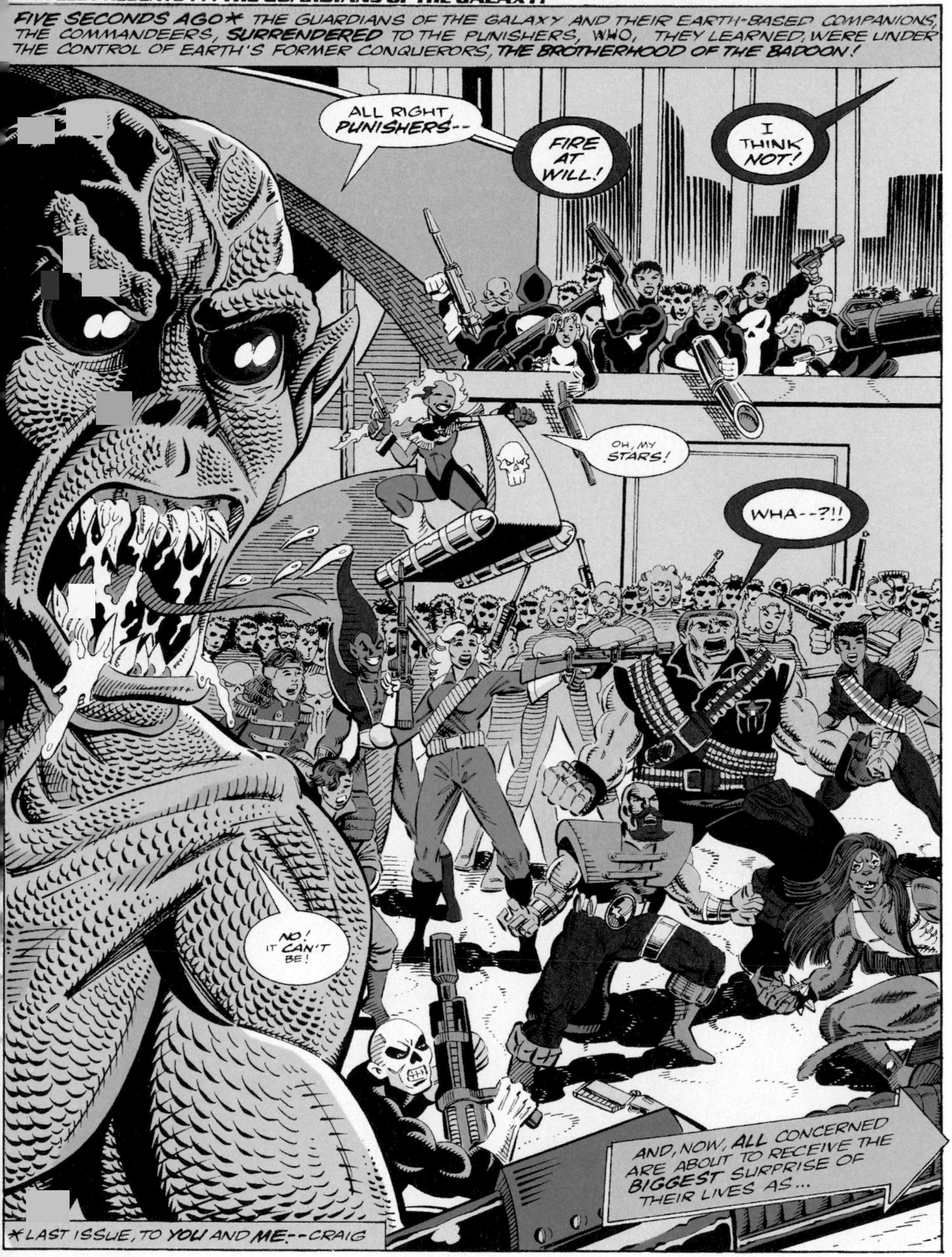
FIVE SECONDS AGO* THE GUARDIANS OF THE GALAXY AND THEIR EARTH-BASED COMPANIONS, THE COMMANDEERS, SURRENDERED TO THE PUNISHERS, WHO, THEY LEARNED, WERE UNDER THE CONTROL OF EARTH'S FORMER CONQUERORS, THE BROTHERHOOD OF THE BADOON!
ALL RIGHT, PUNISHERS--
FIRE AT WILL!
I THINK NOT!
OH, MY STARS!
WHA--?!!
NO! IT CAN'T BE!
AND, NOW, ALL CONCERNED ARE ABOUT TO RECEIVE THE BIGGEST SURPRISE OF THEIR LIVES AS...
*LAST ISSUE, TO YOU AND ME.--CRAIG

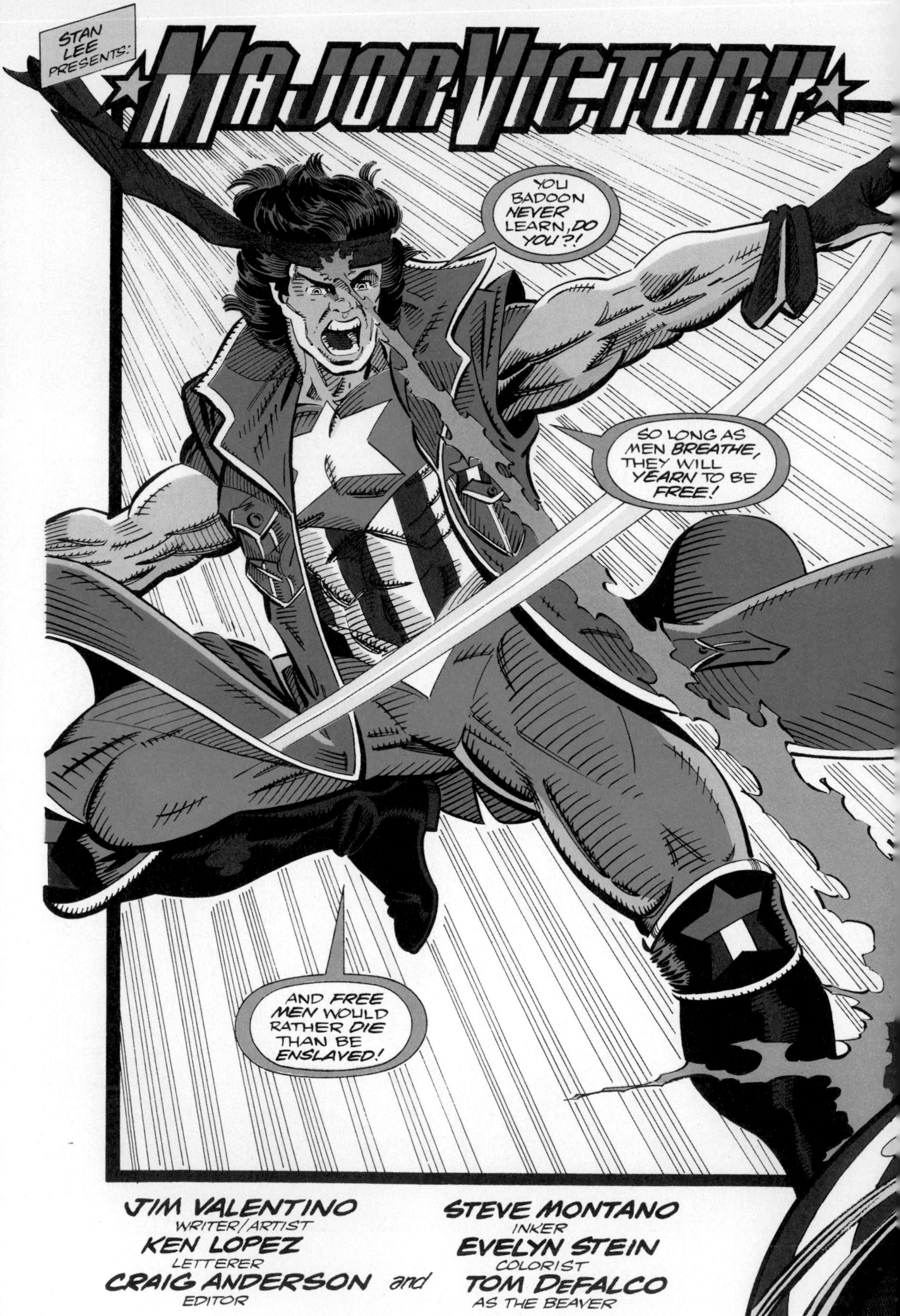
STAN LEE PRESENTS:
MAJOR VICTORY
YOU BADOON NEVER LEARN, DO YOU?!
SO LONG AS MEN BREATHE, THEY WILL YEARN TO BE FREE!
AND FREE MEN WOULD RATHER DIE THAN BE ENSLAVED!
JIM VALENTINO WRITER/ARTIST
KEN LOPEZ LETTERER
CRAIG ANDERSON EDITOR
and
STEVE MONTANO INKER
EVELYN STEIN COLORIST
TOM DeFALCO AS THE BEAVER

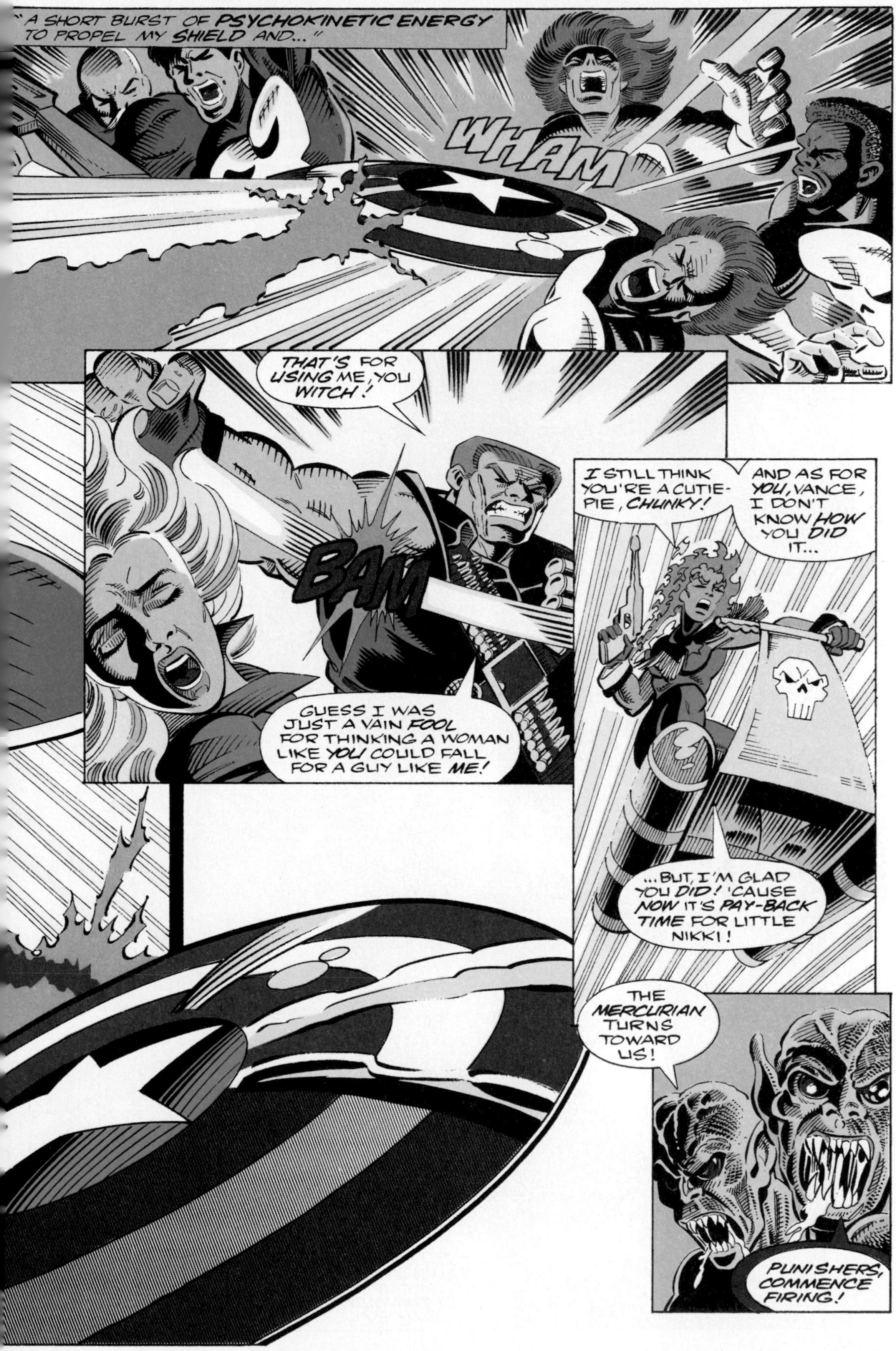
"A SHORT BURST OF PSYCHOKINETIC ENERGY TO PROPEL MY SHIELD AND..."
WHAM
THAT'S FOR USING ME, YOU WITCH!
BAM
GUESS I WAS JUST A VAIN FOOL FOR THINKING A WOMAN LIKE YOU COULD FALL FOR A GUY LIKE ME!
I STILL THINK YOU'RE A CUTIE-PIE, CHUNKY!
AND AS FOR YOU, VANCE, I DON'T KNOW HOW YOU DID IT...
...BUT, I'M GLAD YOU DID! 'CAUSE NOW IT'S PAY-BACK TIME FOR LITTLE NIKKI!
THE MERCURIAN TURNS TOWARD US!
PUNISHERS, COMMENCE FIRING!

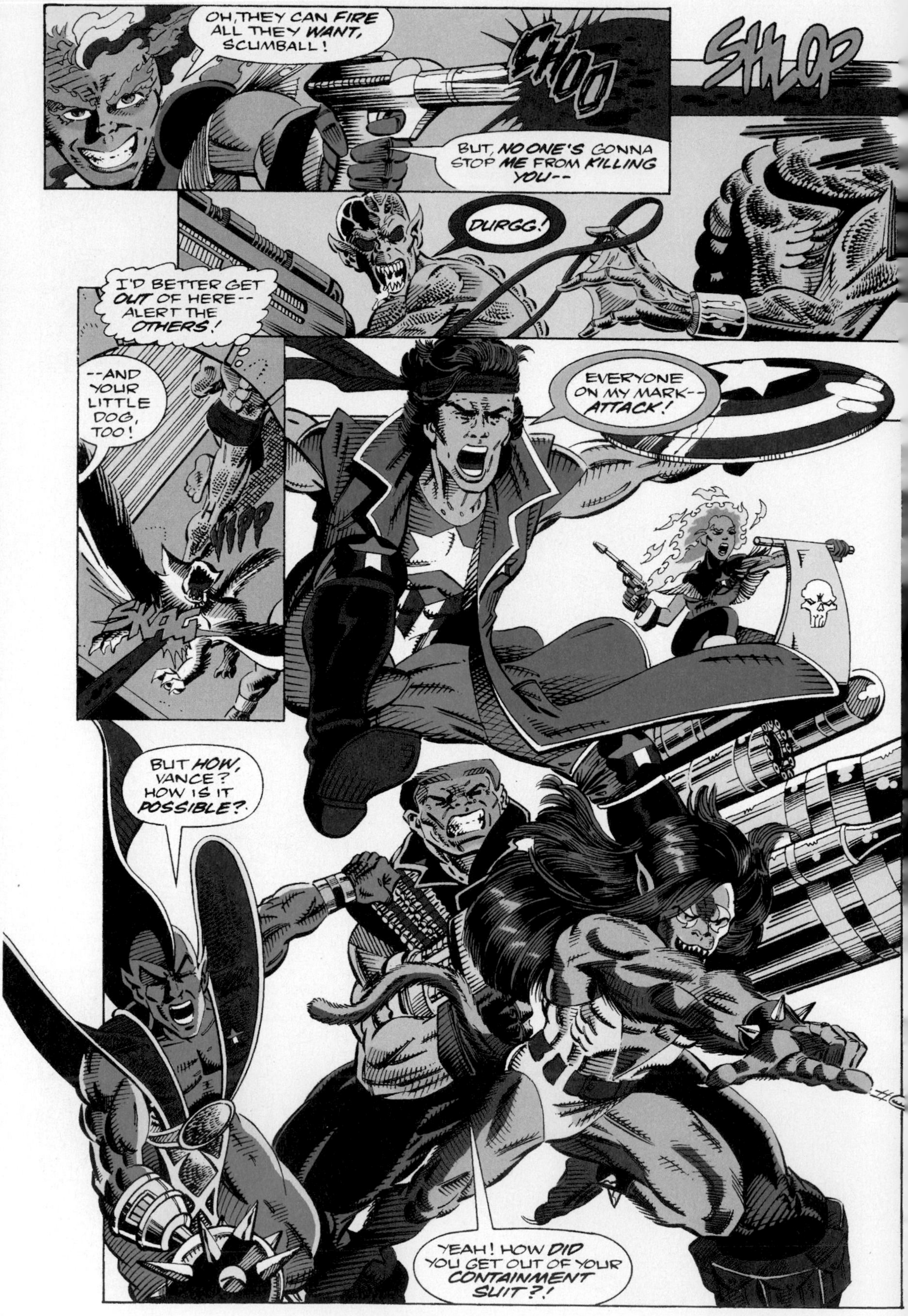
OH, THEY CAN FIRE ALL THEY WANT, SCUMBALL!
CHOO
SHLOP
BUT, NO ONE'S GONNA STOP ME FROM KILLING YOU--
DURGG!
I'D BETTER GET OUT OF HERE-- ALERT THE OTHERS!
--AND YOUR LITTLE DOG, TOO!
YIPP
SKAG
EVERYONE ON MY MARK-- ATTACK!
BUT HOW, VANCE? HOW IS IT POSSIBLE?
YEAH! HOW DID YOU GET OUT OF YOUR CONTAINMENT SUIT?!

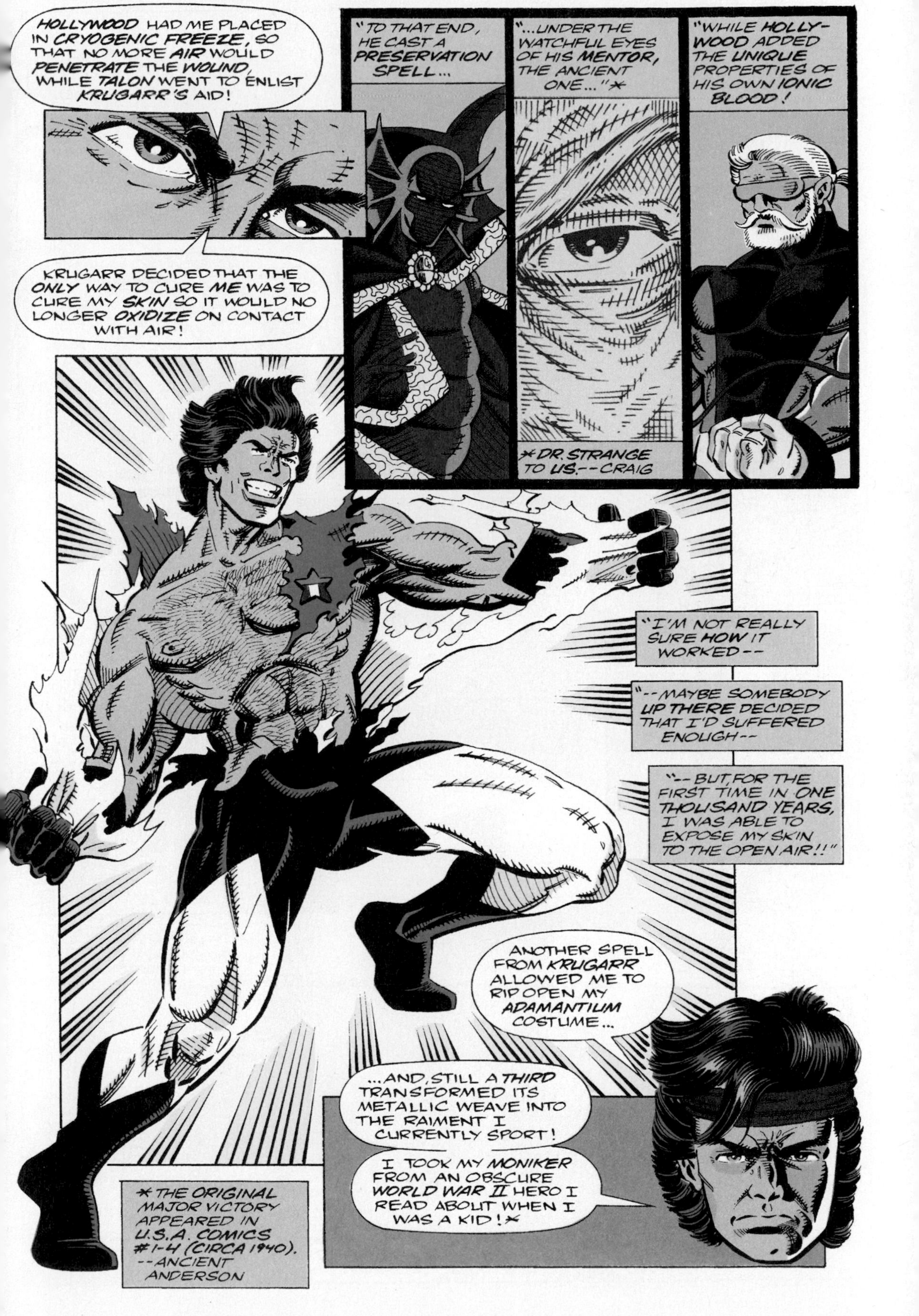
HOLLYWOOD HAD ME PLACED IN CRYOGENIC FREEZE, SO THAT NO MORE AIR WOULD PENETRATE THE WOUND, WHILE TALON WENT TO ENLIST KRUGARR'S AID!
KRUGARR DECIDED THAT THE ONLY WAY TO CURE ME WAS TO CURE MY SKIN SO IT WOULD NO LONGER OXIDIZE ON CONTACT WITH AIR!
"TO THAT END, HE CAST A PRESERVATION SPELL...
"...UNDER THE WATCHFUL EYES OF HIS MENTOR, THE ANCIENT ONE..."*
*DR. STRANGE TO US.--CRAIG
"WHILE HOLLYWOOD ADDED THE UNIQUE PROPERTIES OF HIS OWN IONIC BLOOD!
"I'M NOT REALLY SURE HOW IT WORKED--
"--MAYBE SOMEBODY UP THERE DECIDED THAT I'D SUFFERED ENOUGH--
"--BUT, FOR THE FIRST TIME IN ONE THOUSAND YEARS, I WAS ABLE TO EXPOSE MY SKIN TO THE OPEN AIR!!"
ANOTHER SPELL FROM KRUGARR ALLOWED ME TO RIP OPEN MY ADAMANTIUM COSTUME...
...AND, STILL A THIRD TRANSFORMED ITS METALLIC WEAVE INTO THE RAIMENT I CURRENTLY SPORT!
I TOOK MY MONIKER FROM AN OBSCURE WORLD WAR II HERO I READ ABOUT WHEN I WAS A KID!*
*THE ORIGINAL MAJOR VICTORY APPEARED IN U.S.A. COMICS #1-4 (CIRCA 1940). --ANCIENT ANDERSON

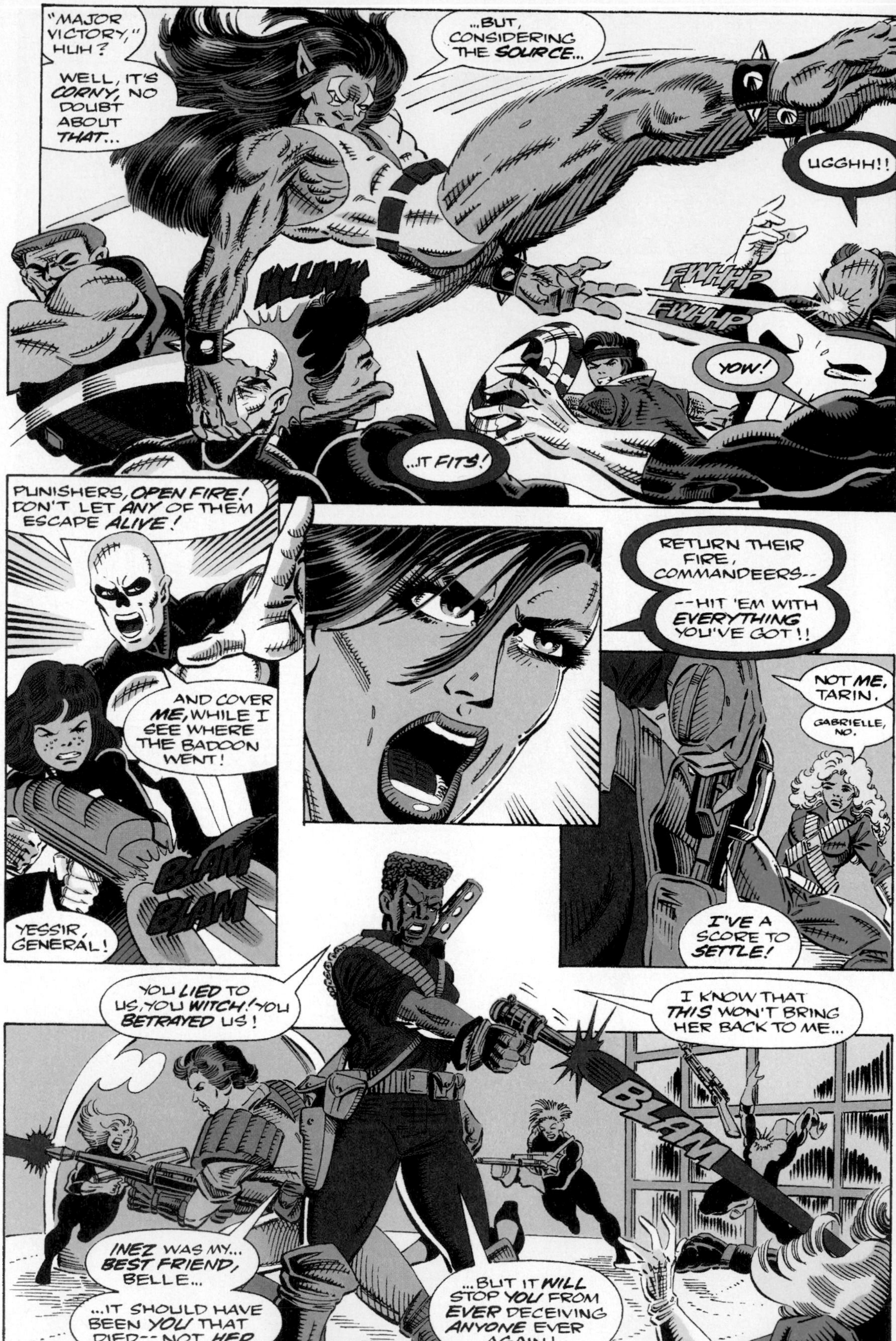
"MAJOR VICTORY," HUH?
WELL, IT'S CORNY, NO DOUBT ABOUT THAT...
...BUT, CONSIDERING THE SOURCE...
UGGHH!!
HUNK
FWHP
FWHP
YOW!
...IT FITS!
PUNISHERS, OPEN FIRE! DON'T LET ANY OF THEM ESCAPE ALIVE!
AND COVER ME, WHILE I SEE WHERE THE BADOON WENT!
BLAM
BLAM
YESSIR, GENERAL!
RETURN THEIR FIRE, COMMANDEERS--
--HIT 'EM WITH EVERYTHING YOU'VE GOT!!
NOT ME, TARIN.
GABRIELLE, NO.
I'VE A SCORE TO SETTLE!
YOU LIED TO US, YOU WITCH! YOU BETRAYED US!
I KNOW THAT THIS WON'T BRING HER BACK TO ME...
BLAM
INEZ WAS MY... BEST FRIEND, BELLE...
...IT SHOULD HAVE BEEN YOU THAT DIED-- NOT HER.
...BUT IT WILL STOP YOU FROM EVER DECEIVING ANYONE EVER AGAIN!

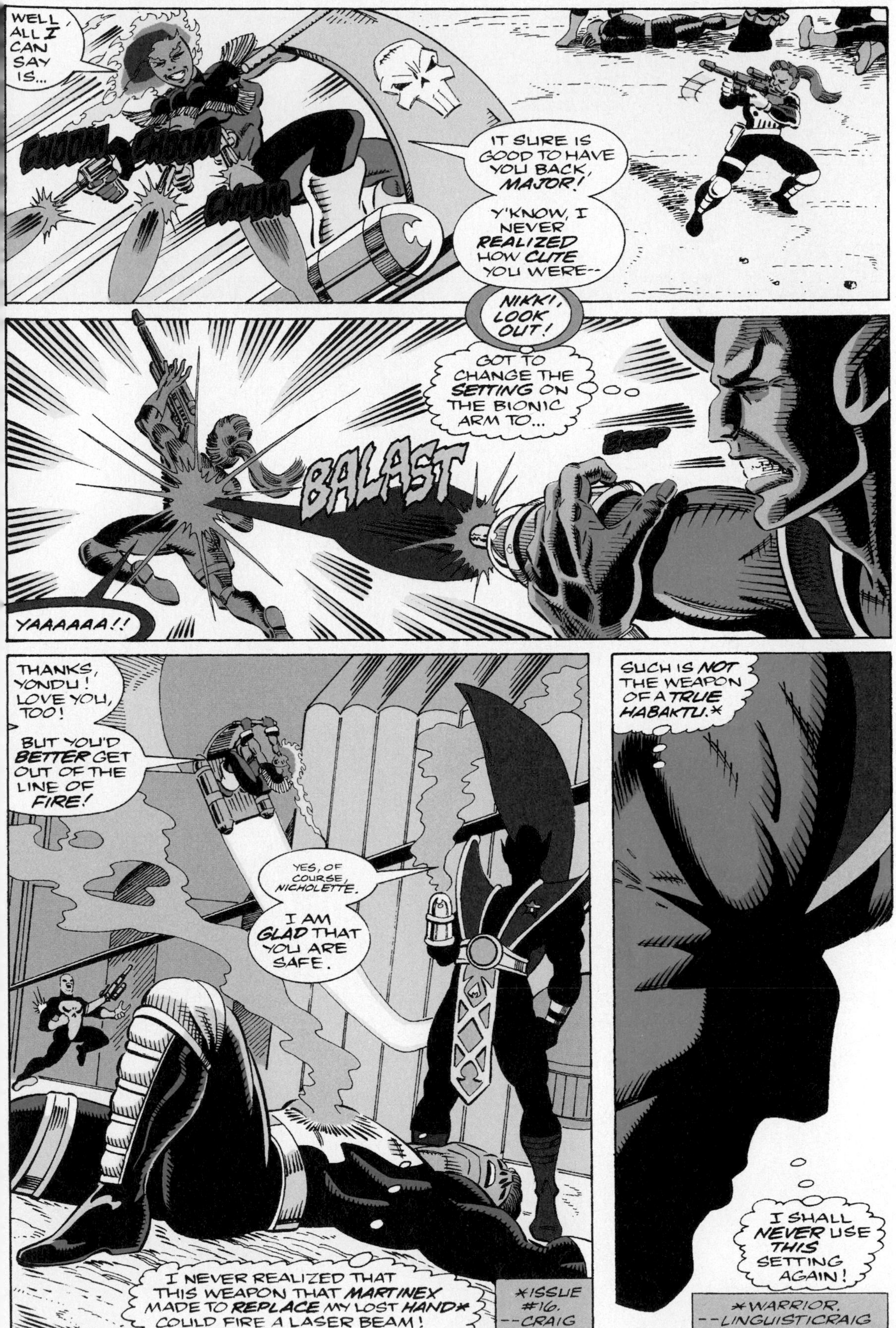
WELL ALL I CAN SAY IS...
CHOOM CHOOM CHOOM
IT SURE IS GOOD TO HAVE YOU BACK, MAJOR!
Y'KNOW, I NEVER REALIZED HOW CUTE YOU WERE--
NIKKI, LOOK OUT!
GOT TO CHANGE THE SETTING ON THE BIONIC ARM TO...
BALAST
YAAAAAA!!
THANKS, YONDU! LOVE YOU, TOO!
BUT YOU'D BETTER GET OUT OF THE LINE OF FIRE!
YES, OF COURSE, NICHOLETTE.
I AM GLAD THAT YOU ARE SAFE.
I NEVER REALIZED THAT THIS WEAPON THAT MARTINEX MADE TO REPLACE MY LOST HAND* COULD FIRE A LASER BEAM!
*ISSUE #16. --CRAIG
SUCH IS NOT THE WEAPON OF A TRUE HABAKTU.*
I SHALL NEVER USE THIS SETTING AGAIN!
*WARRIOR. --LINGUISTICRAIG

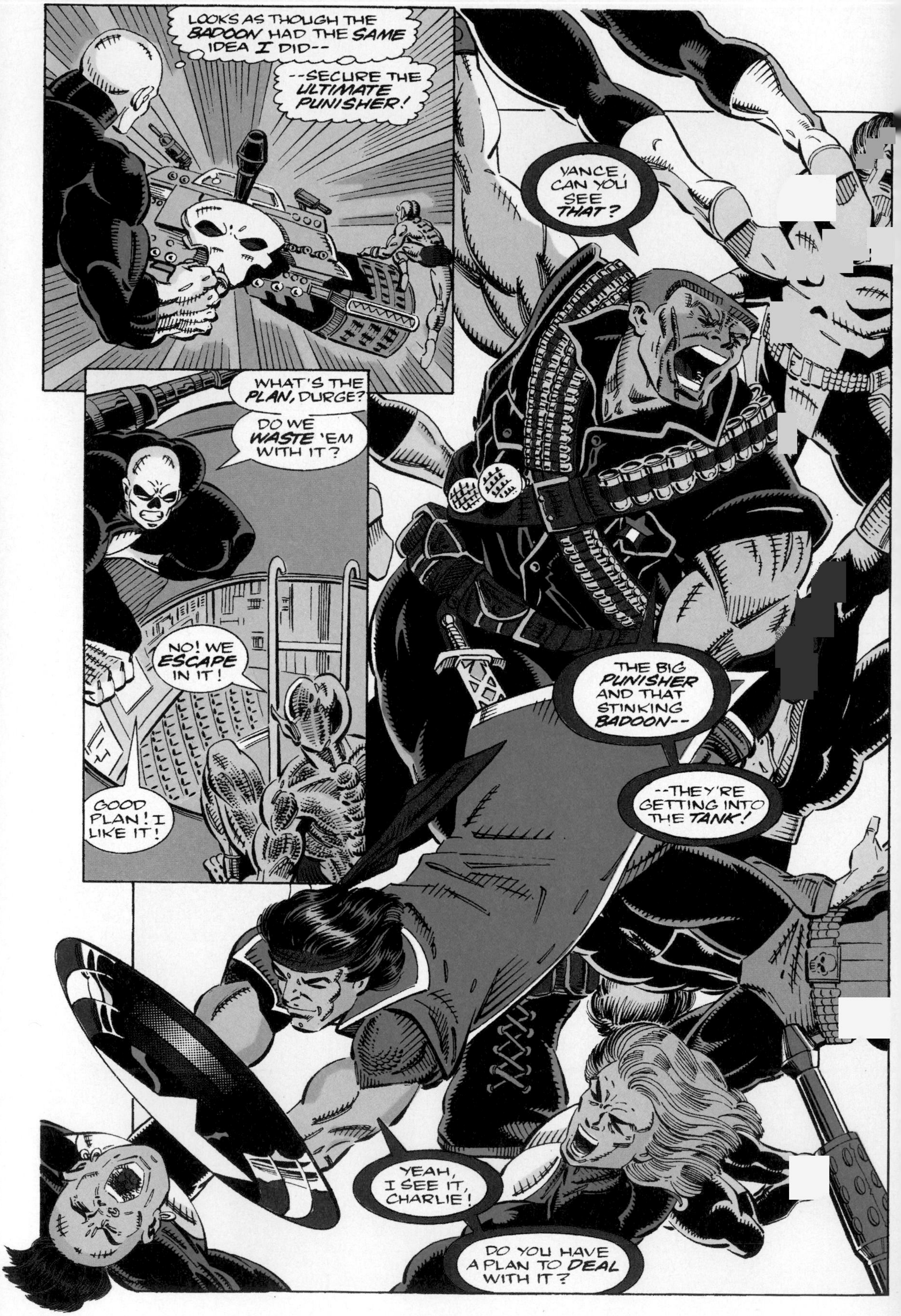
LOOKS AS THOUGH THE BADOON HAD THE SAME IDEA I DID--
--SECURE THE ULTIMATE PUNISHER!
YANCE, CAN YOU SEE THAT?
WHAT'S THE PLAN, DURGE?
DO WE WASTE 'EM WITH IT?
NO! WE ESCAPE IN IT!
GOOD PLAN! I LIKE IT!
THE BIG PUNISHER AND THAT STINKING BADOON--
--THEY'RE GETTING INTO THE TANK!
YEAH, I SEE IT, CHARLIE!
DO YOU HAVE A PLAN TO DEAL WITH IT?

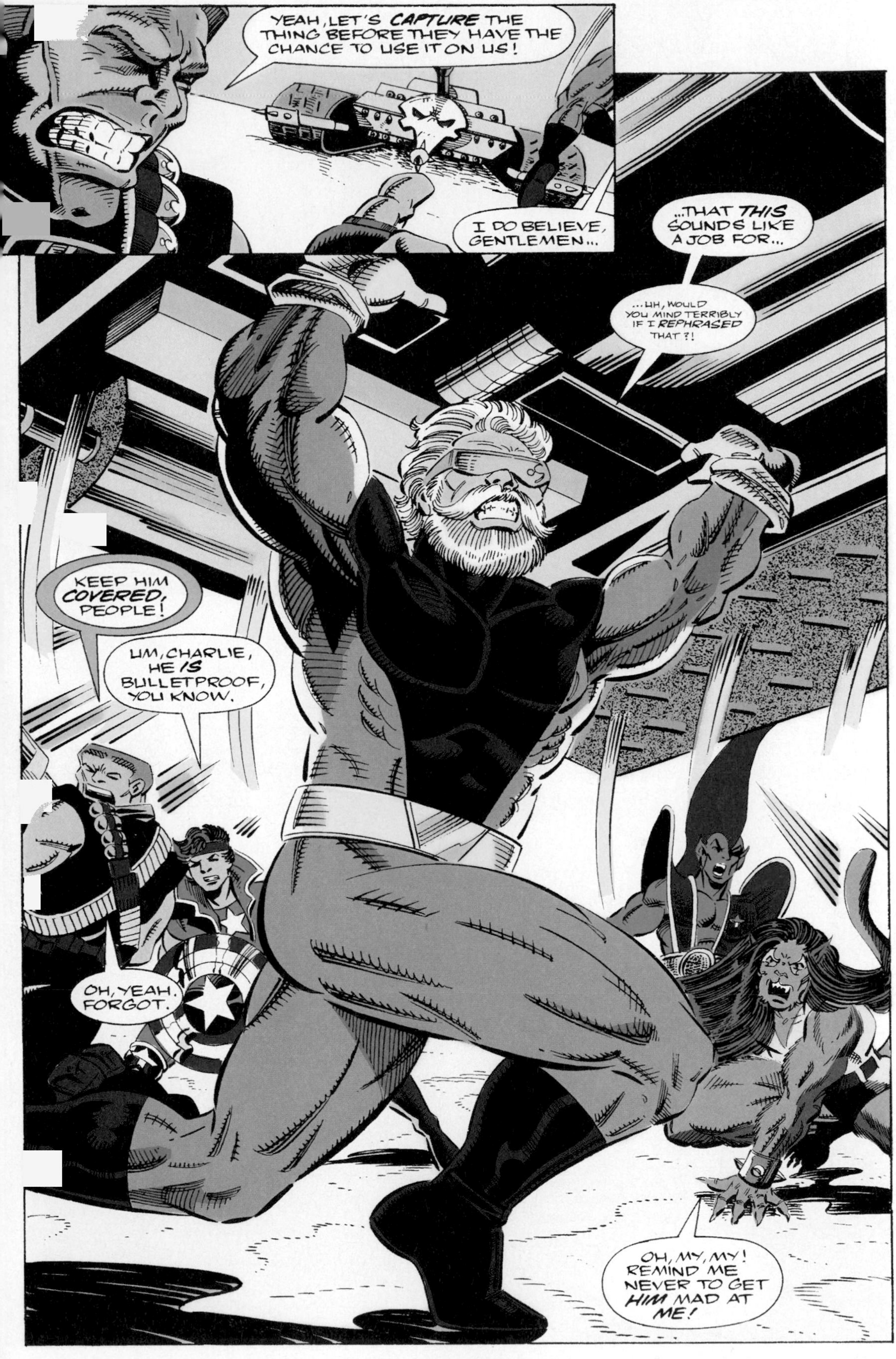
YEAH, LET'S CAPTURE THE THING BEFORE THEY HAVE THE CHANCE TO USE IT ON US!
I DO BELIEVE, GENTLEMEN...
...THAT THIS SOUNDS LIKE A JOB FOR...
...UH, WOULD YOU MIND TERRIBLY IF I REPHRASED THAT?!
KEEP HIM COVERED, PEOPLE!
UM, CHARLIE, HE IS BULLETPROOF, YOU KNOW.
OH, YEAH. FORGOT.
OH, MY, MY! REMIND ME NEVER TO GET HIM MAD AT ME!

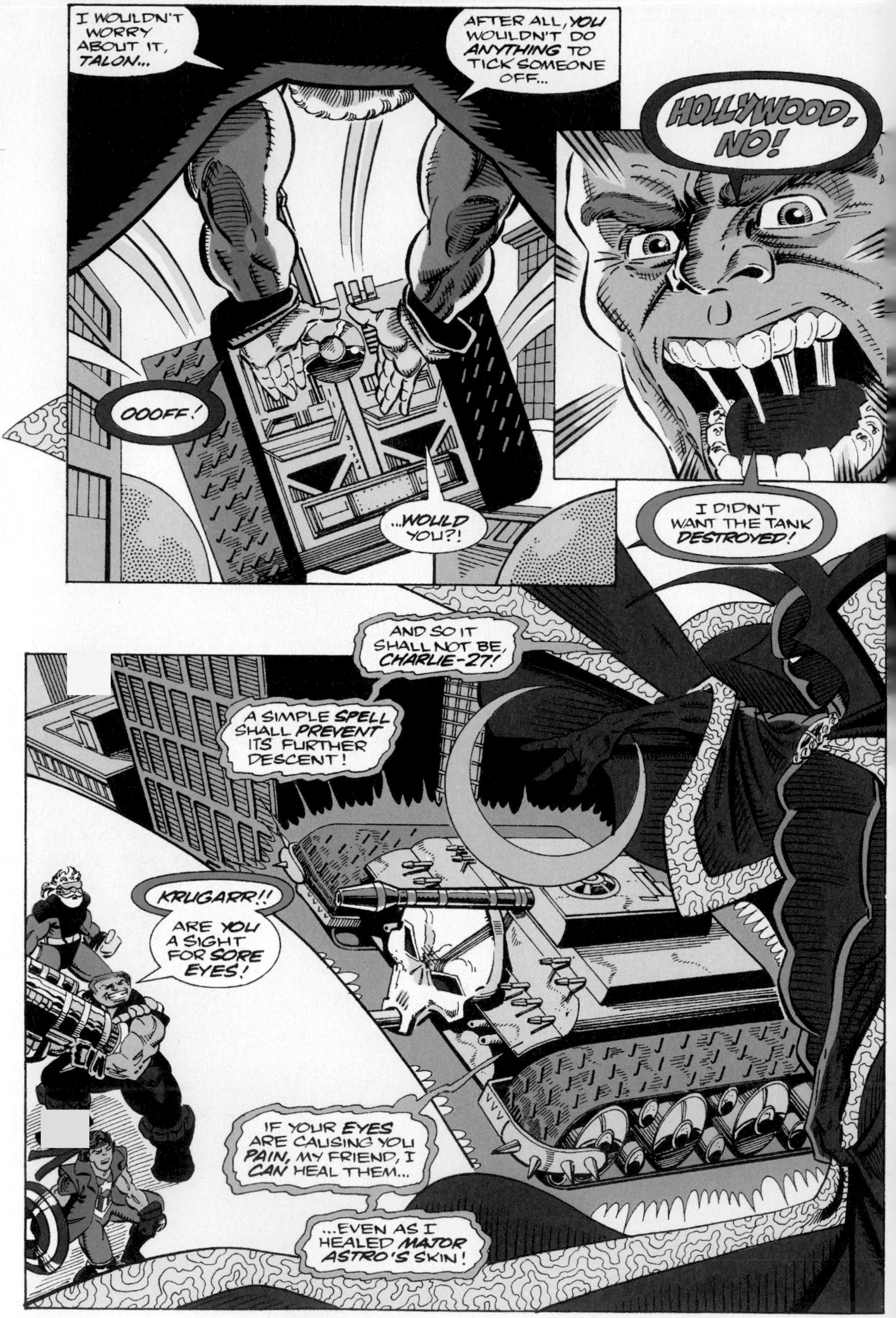
I WOULDN'T WORRY ABOUT IT, TALON...
AFTER ALL, YOU WOULDN'T DO ANYTHING TO TICK SOMEONE OFF...
HOLLYWOOD, NO!
OOOFF!
...WOULD YOU?!
I DIDN'T WANT THE TANK DESTROYED!
AND SO IT SHALL NOT BE, CHARLIE-27!
A SIMPLE SPELL SHALL PREVENT ITS FURTHER DESCENT!
KRUGARR!! ARE YOU A SIGHT FOR SORE EYES!
IF YOUR EYES ARE CAUSING YOU PAIN, MY FRIEND, I CAN HEAL THEM...
...EVEN AS I HEALED MAJOR ASTRO'S SKIN!

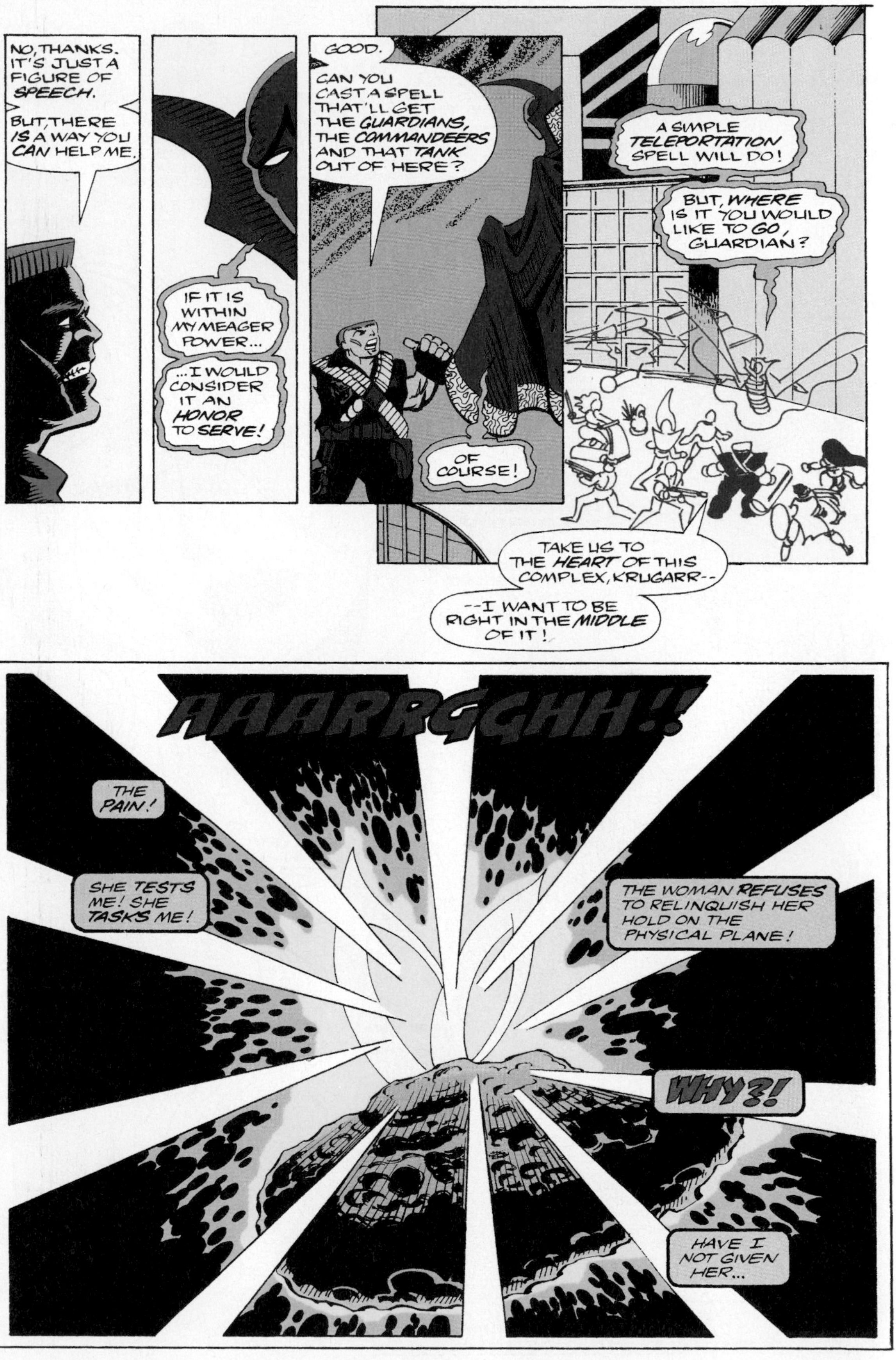
NO, THANKS. IT'S JUST A FIGURE OF SPEECH.
BUT, THERE IS A WAY YOU CAN HELP ME.
IF IT IS WITHIN MY MEAGER POWER...
...I WOULD CONSIDER IT AN HONOR TO SERVE!
GOOD.
CAN YOU CAST A SPELL THAT'LL GET THE GUARDIANS, THE COMMANDEERS AND THAT TANK OUT OF HERE?
OF COURSE!
A SIMPLE TELEPORTATION SPELL WILL DO!
BUT, WHERE IS IT YOU WOULD LIKE TO GO, GUARDIAN?
TAKE US TO THE HEART OF THIS COMPLEX, KRUGARR--
--I WANT TO BE RIGHT IN THE MIDDLE OF IT!
AAARRGGHH!!
THE PAIN!
SHE TESTS ME! SHE TASKS ME!
THE WOMAN REFUSES TO RELINQUISH HER HOLD ON THE PHYSICAL PLANE!
WHY?!
HAVE I NOT GIVEN HER...

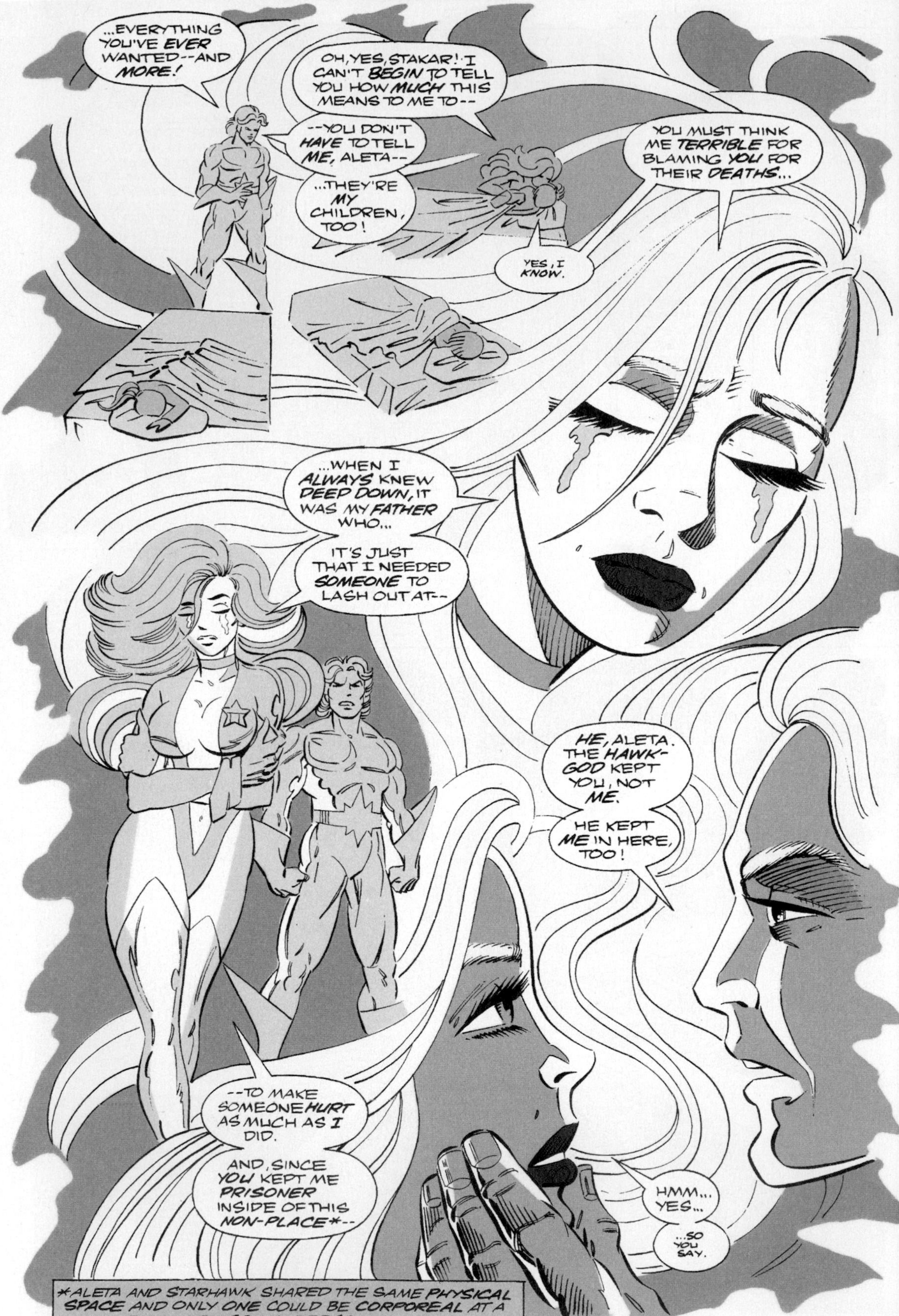
...EVERYTHING YOU'VE EVER WANTED--AND MORE!
OH, YES, STAKAR! I CAN'T BEGIN TO TELL YOU HOW MUCH THIS MEANS TO ME TO--
--YOU DON'T HAVE TO TELL ME, ALETA--
...THEY'RE MY CHILDREN, TOO!
YOU MUST THINK ME TERRIBLE FOR BLAMING YOU FOR THEIR DEATHS...
YES, I KNOW.
...WHEN I ALWAYS KNEW DEEP DOWN, IT WAS MY FATHER WHO...
IT'S JUST THAT I NEEDED SOMEONE TO LASH OUT AT--
HE, ALETA. THE HAWK-GOD KEPT YOU, NOT ME.
HE KEPT ME IN HERE, TOO!
--TO MAKE SOMEONE HURT AS MUCH AS I DID.
AND, SINCE YOU KEPT ME PRISONER INSIDE OF THIS NON-PLACE*--
HMM... YES...
...SO YOU SAY.
*ALETA AND STARHAWK SHARED THE SAME PHYSICAL SPACE AND ONLY ONE COULD BE CORPOREAL AT A TIME. --EDISON ANDERSON

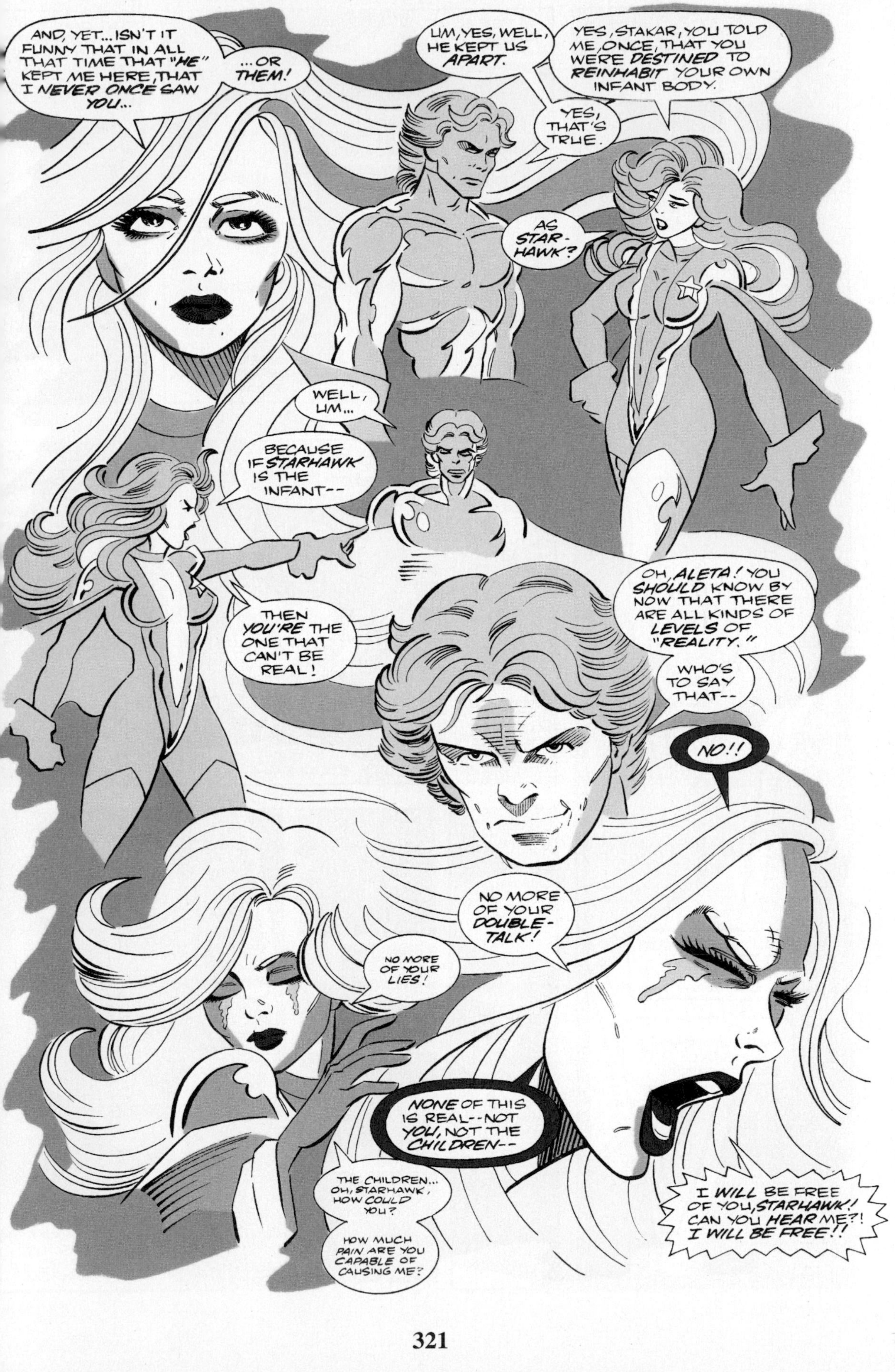
AND, YET... ISN'T IT FUNNY THAT IN ALL THAT TIME THAT "HE" KEPT ME HERE, THAT I NEVER ONCE SAW YOU...
...OR THEM!
UM, YES, WELL, HE KEPT US APART.
YES, STAKAR, YOU TOLD ME, ONCE, THAT YOU WERE DESTINED TO REINHABIT YOUR OWN INFANT BODY.
YES, THAT'S TRUE.
AS STAR-HAWK?
WELL, UM...
BECAUSE IF STARHAWK IS THE INFANT--
THEN YOU'RE THE ONE THAT CAN'T BE REAL!
OH, ALETA! YOU SHOULD KNOW BY NOW THAT THERE ARE ALL KINDS OF LEVELS OF "REALITY."
WHO'S TO SAY THAT--
NO!!
NO MORE OF YOUR DOUBLE-TALK!
NO MORE OF YOUR LIES!
NONE OF THIS IS REAL--NOT YOU, NOT THE CHILDREN--
THE CHILDREN... OH, STARHAWK, HOW COULD YOU?
HOW MUCH PAIN ARE YOU CAPABLE OF CAUSING ME?
I WILL BE FREE OF YOU, STARHAWK! CAN YOU HEAR ME?! I WILL BE FREE!!

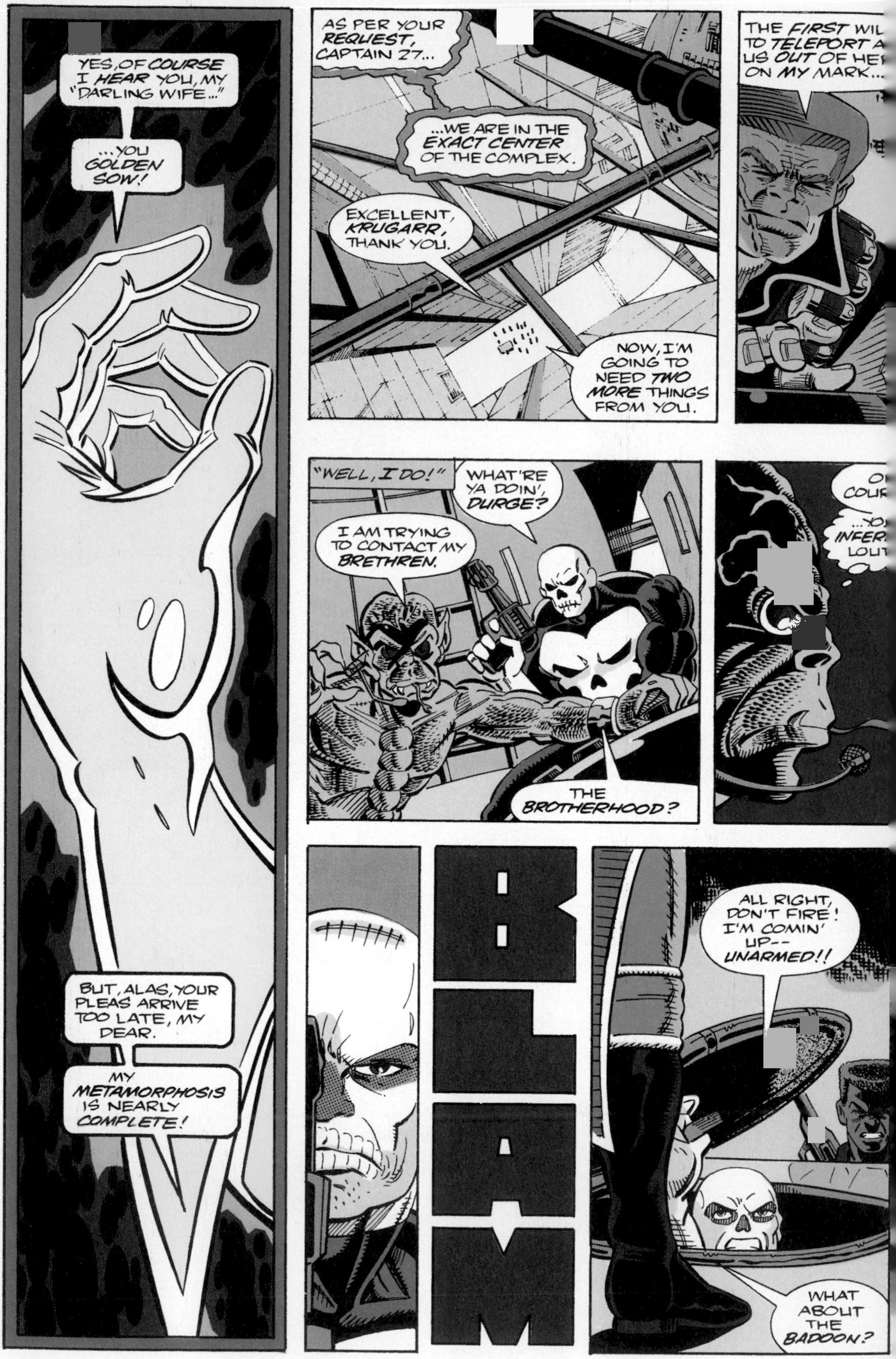

YES, OF COURSE I HEAR YOU, MY "DARLING WIFE..."
...YOU GOLDEN SOW!
BUT, ALAS, YOUR PLEAS ARRIVE TOO LATE, MY DEAR.
MY METAMORPHOSIS IS NEARLY COMPLETE!
AS PER YOUR REQUEST, CAPTAIN 27...
...WE ARE IN THE EXACT CENTER OF THE COMPLEX.
EXCELLENT, KRUGARR, THANK YOU.
NOW, I'M GOING TO NEED TWO MORE THINGS FROM YOU.
THE FIRST WIL
TO TELEPORT A
US OUT OF HE
ON MY MARK...
"WELL, I DO!"
WHAT'RE YA DOIN', DURGE?
I AM TRYING TO CONTACT MY BRETHREN.
THE BROTHERHOOD?
BLAM
ALL RIGHT, DON'T FIRE! I'M COMIN' UP-- UNARMED!!
WHAT ABOUT THE BADOON?

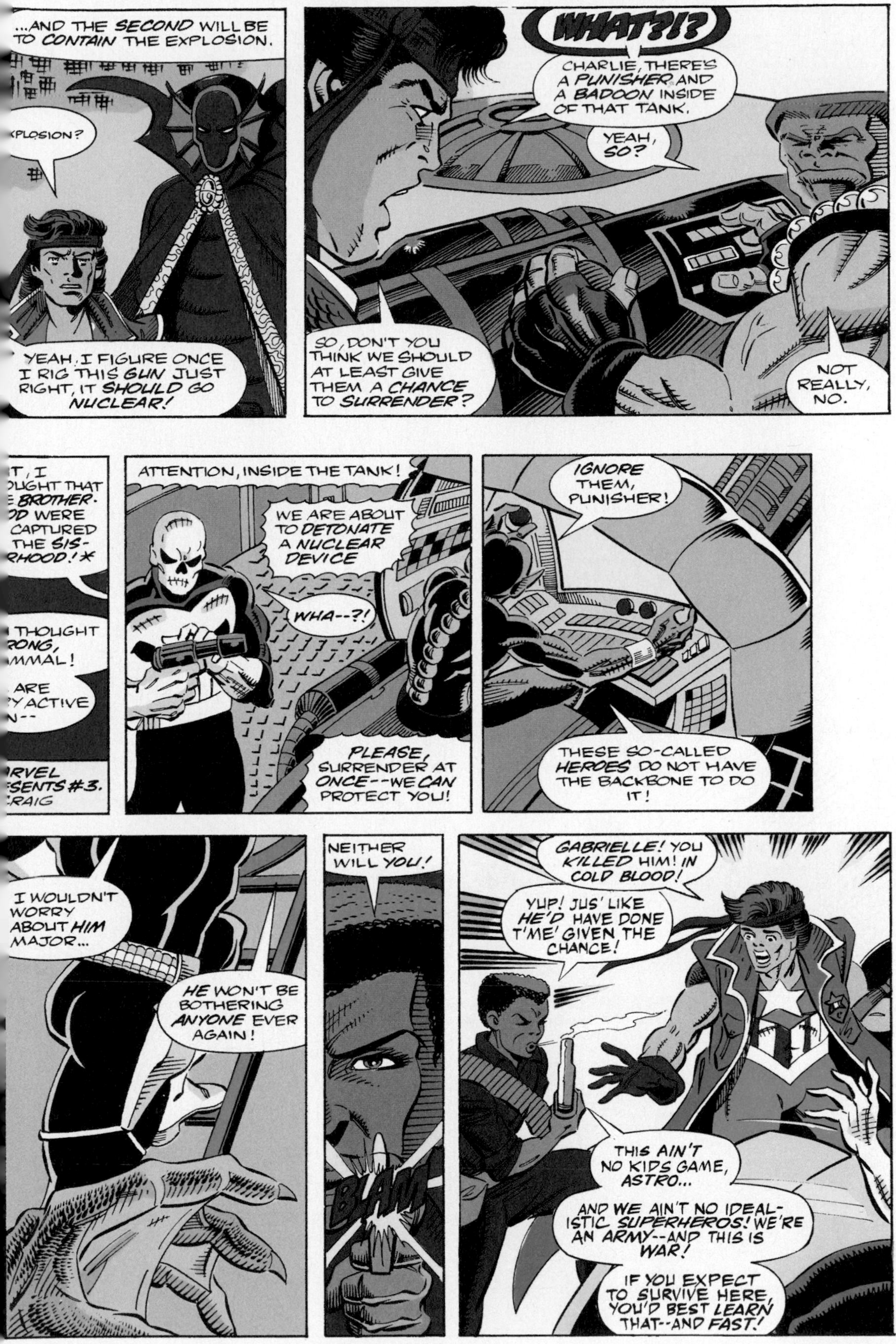
...AND THE SECOND WILL BE TO CONTAIN THE EXPLOSION.
XPLOSION?
YEAH. I FIGURE ONCE I RIG THIS GUN JUST RIGHT, IT SHOULD GO NUCLEAR!
WHAT?!?
CHARLIE, THERE'S A PUNISHER AND A BADOON INSIDE OF THAT TANK.
YEAH, SO?
SO, DON'T YOU THINK WE SHOULD AT LEAST GIVE THEM A CHANCE TO SURRENDER?
NOT REALLY, NO.
T, I OUGHT THAT BROTHER- OD WERE CAPTURED THE SIS- RHOOD! *
THOUGHT RONG, MMAL!
ARE Y ACTIVE N--
RVEL SENTS #3. CRAIG
ATTENTION, INSIDE THE TANK!
WE ARE ABOUT TO DETONATE A NUCLEAR DEVICE
WHA--?!
PLEASE, SURRENDER AT ONCE--WE CAN PROTECT YOU!
IGNORE THEM, PUNISHER!
THESE SO-CALLED HEROES DO NOT HAVE THE BACKBONE TO DO IT!
I WOULDN'T WORRY ABOUT HIM MAJOR...
HE WON'T BE BOTHERING ANYONE EVER AGAIN!
NEITHER WILL YOU!
BLAM
GABRIELLE! YOU KILLED HIM! IN COLD BLOOD!
YUP! JUS' LIKE HE'D HAVE DONE T'ME' GIVEN THE CHANCE!
THIS AIN'T NO KIDS GAME, ASTRO...
AND WE AIN'T NO IDEAL- ISTIC SUPERHEROS! WE'RE AN ARMY--AND THIS IS WAR!
IF YOU EXPECT TO SURVIVE HERE, YOU'D BEST LEARN THAT--AND FAST!

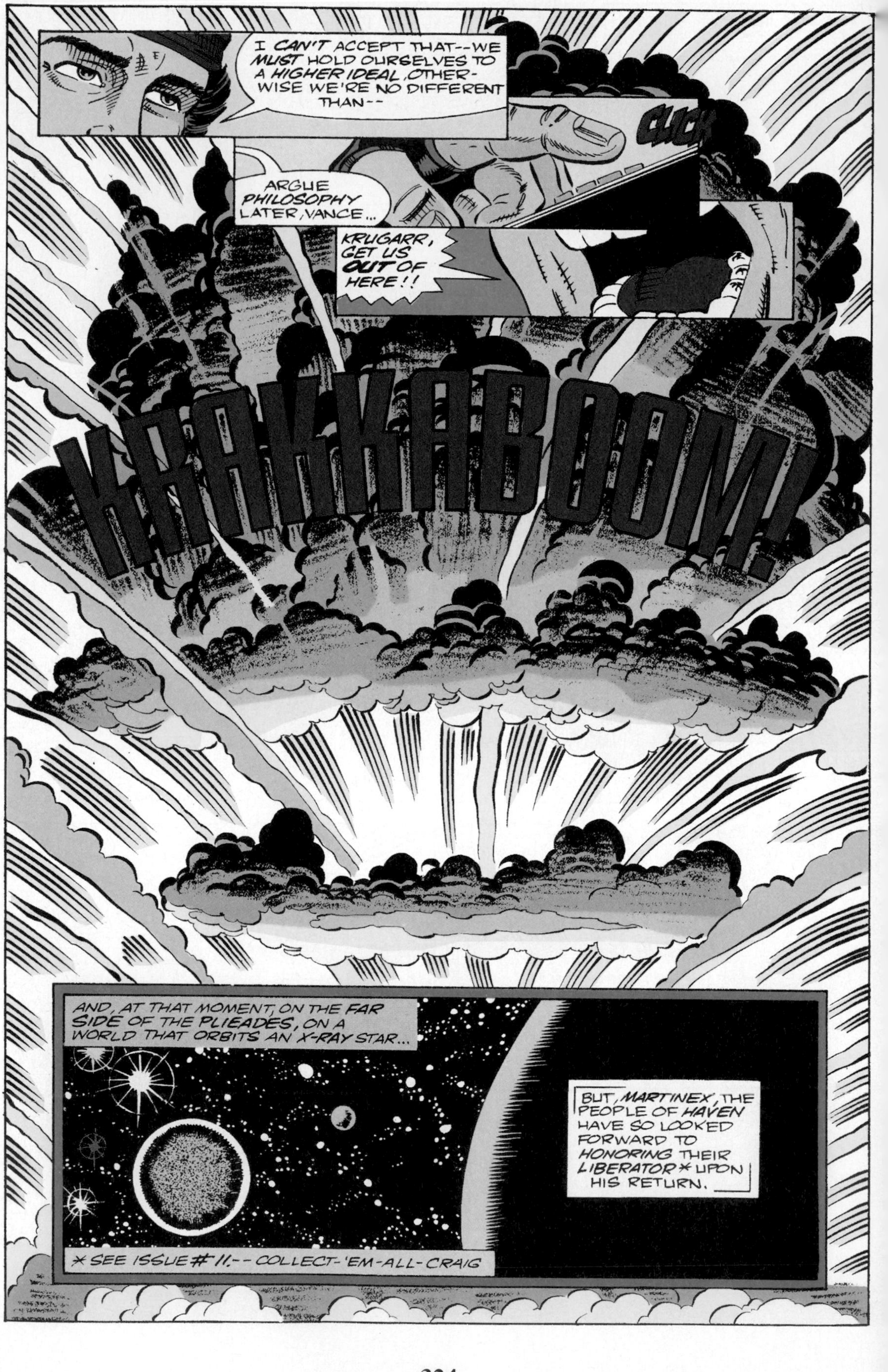
I CAN'T ACCEPT THAT--WE MUST HOLD OURSELVES TO A HIGHER IDEAL, OTHERWISE WE'RE NO DIFFERENT THAN--
CLICK
ARGUE PHILOSOPHY LATER, VANCE...
KRUGARR, GET US OUT OF HERE!!
KRAKKABOOM!
AND, AT THAT MOMENT, ON THE FAR SIDE OF THE PLIEADES, ON A WORLD THAT ORBITS AN X-RAY STAR...
BUT, MARTINEX, THE PEOPLE OF HAVEN HAVE SO LOOKED FORWARD TO HONORING THEIR LIBERATOR* UPON HIS RETURN.
* SEE ISSUE #11.-- COLLECT-'EM-ALL-CRAIG

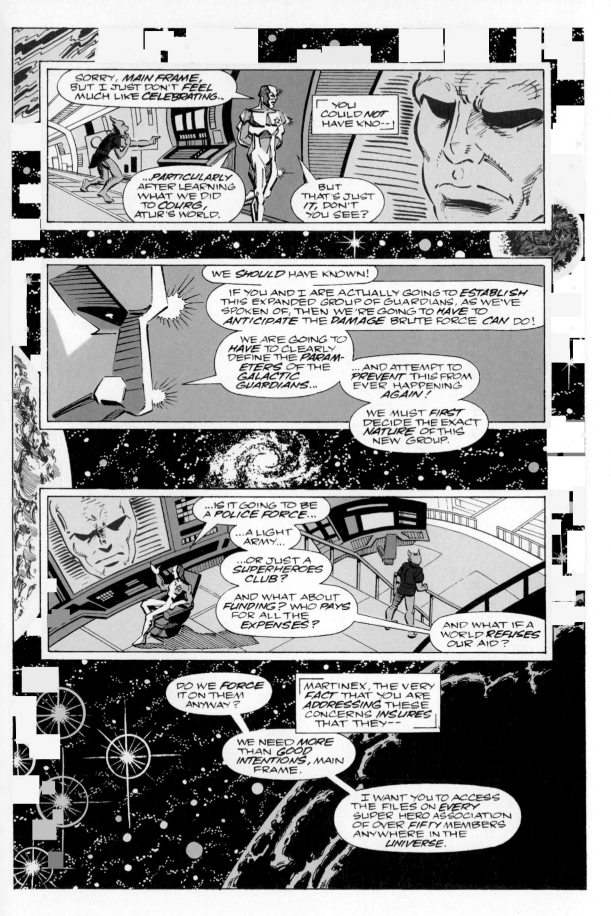

SORRY, *MAIN FRAME,* BUT I JUST DON'T *FEEL* MUCH LIKE *CELEBRATING...*

...*PARTICULARLY* AFTER LEARNING WHAT WE DID TO *COURG,* ATUR'S WORLD.

YOU COULD *NOT* HAVE KNO---

BUT THAT'S JUST *IT,* DON'T YOU SEE?

WE *SHOULD* HAVE KNOWN! IF YOU AND I ARE ACTUALLY GOING TO *ESTABLISH* THIS EXPANDED GROUP OF GUARDIANS, AS WE'VE SPOKEN OF, THEN WE'RE GOING TO *HAVE* TO *ANTICIPATE* THE *DAMAGE* BRUTE FORCE *CAN* DO!

WE ARE GOING TO *HAVE* TO CLEARLY DEFINE THE *PARAMETERS* OF THE *GALACTIC GUARDIANS...*

...AND ATTEMPT TO *PREVENT* THIS FROM EVER HAPPENING *AGAIN!*

WE MUST *FIRST* DECIDE THE EXACT *NATURE* OF THIS NEW GROUP.

...IS IT GOING TO BE A *POLICE FORCE...*

...A *LIGHT* ARMY...

...OR JUST A *SUPERHEROES* CLUB?

AND WHAT ABOUT *FUNDING?* WHO *PAYS* FOR ALL THE *EXPENSES?*

AND WHAT IF A WORLD *REFUSES* OUR AID?

DO WE *FORCE* IT ON THEM ANYWAY?

MARTINEX, THE VERY *FACT* THAT YOU ARE *ADDRESSING* THESE CONCERNS *INSURES* THAT THEY---

WE NEED *MORE* THAN *GOOD* INTENTIONS, MAIN FRAME.

I WANT YOU TO ACCESS THE FILES ON *EVERY* SUPER HERO ASSOCIATION OF OVER *FIFTY* MEMBERS ANYWHERE IN THE *UNIVERSE.*

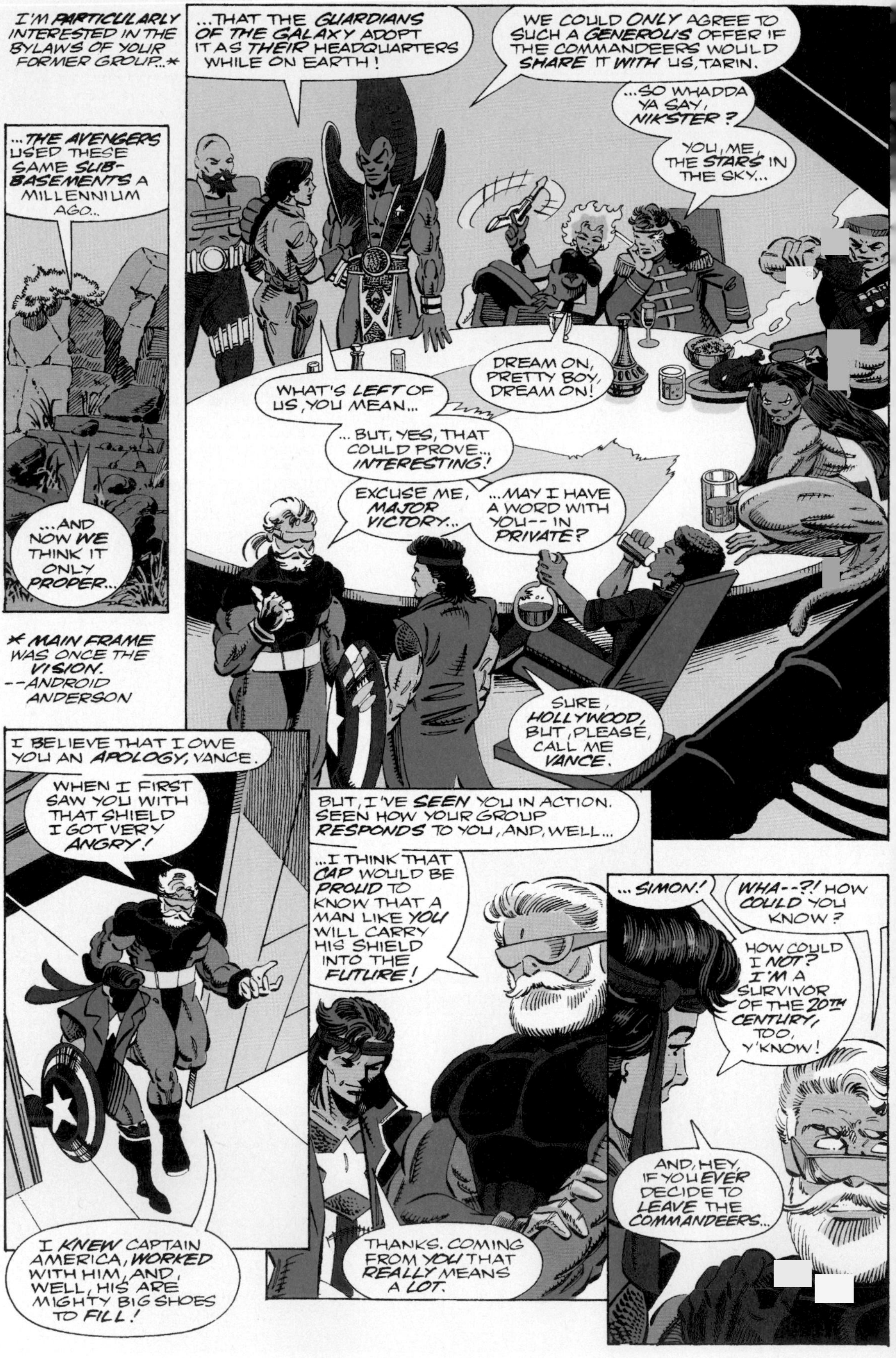
I'M PARTICULARLY INTERESTED IN THE BYLAWS OF YOUR FORMER GROUP...*
...THAT THE GUARDIANS OF THE GALAXY ADOPT IT AS THEIR HEADQUARTERS WHILE ON EARTH!
WE COULD ONLY AGREE TO SUCH A GENEROUS OFFER IF THE COMMANDEERS WOULD SHARE IT WITH US, TARIN.
...SO WHADDA YA SAY, NIKSTER?
YOU, ME, THE STARS IN THE SKY...
...THE AVENGERS USED THESE SAME SUB-BASEMENTS A MILLENNIUM AGO...
...AND NOW WE THINK IT ONLY PROPER...
DREAM ON, PRETTY BOY, DREAM ON!
WHAT'S LEFT OF US, YOU MEAN...
...BUT, YES, THAT COULD PROVE... INTERESTING!
EXCUSE ME, MAJOR VICTORY...
...MAY I HAVE A WORD WITH YOU-- IN PRIVATE?
* MAIN FRAME WAS ONCE THE VISION. --ANDROID ANDERSON
SURE, HOLLYWOOD, BUT, PLEASE, CALL ME VANCE.
I BELIEVE THAT I OWE YOU AN APOLOGY, VANCE.
WHEN I FIRST SAW YOU WITH THAT SHIELD I GOT VERY ANGRY!
I KNEW CAPTAIN AMERICA, WORKED WITH HIM, AND, WELL, HIS ARE MIGHTY BIG SHOES TO FILL!
BUT, I'VE SEEN YOU IN ACTION. SEEN HOW YOUR GROUP RESPONDS TO YOU, AND, WELL...
...I THINK THAT CAP WOULD BE PROUD TO KNOW THAT A MAN LIKE YOU WILL CARRY HIS SHIELD INTO THE FUTURE!
THANKS. COMING FROM YOU THAT REALLY MEANS A LOT.
... SIMON!
WHA--?! HOW COULD YOU KNOW?
HOW COULD I NOT? I'M A SURVIVOR OF THE 20TH CENTURY, TOO, Y'KNOW!
AND, HEY, IF YOU EVER DECIDE TO LEAVE THE COMMANDEERS...

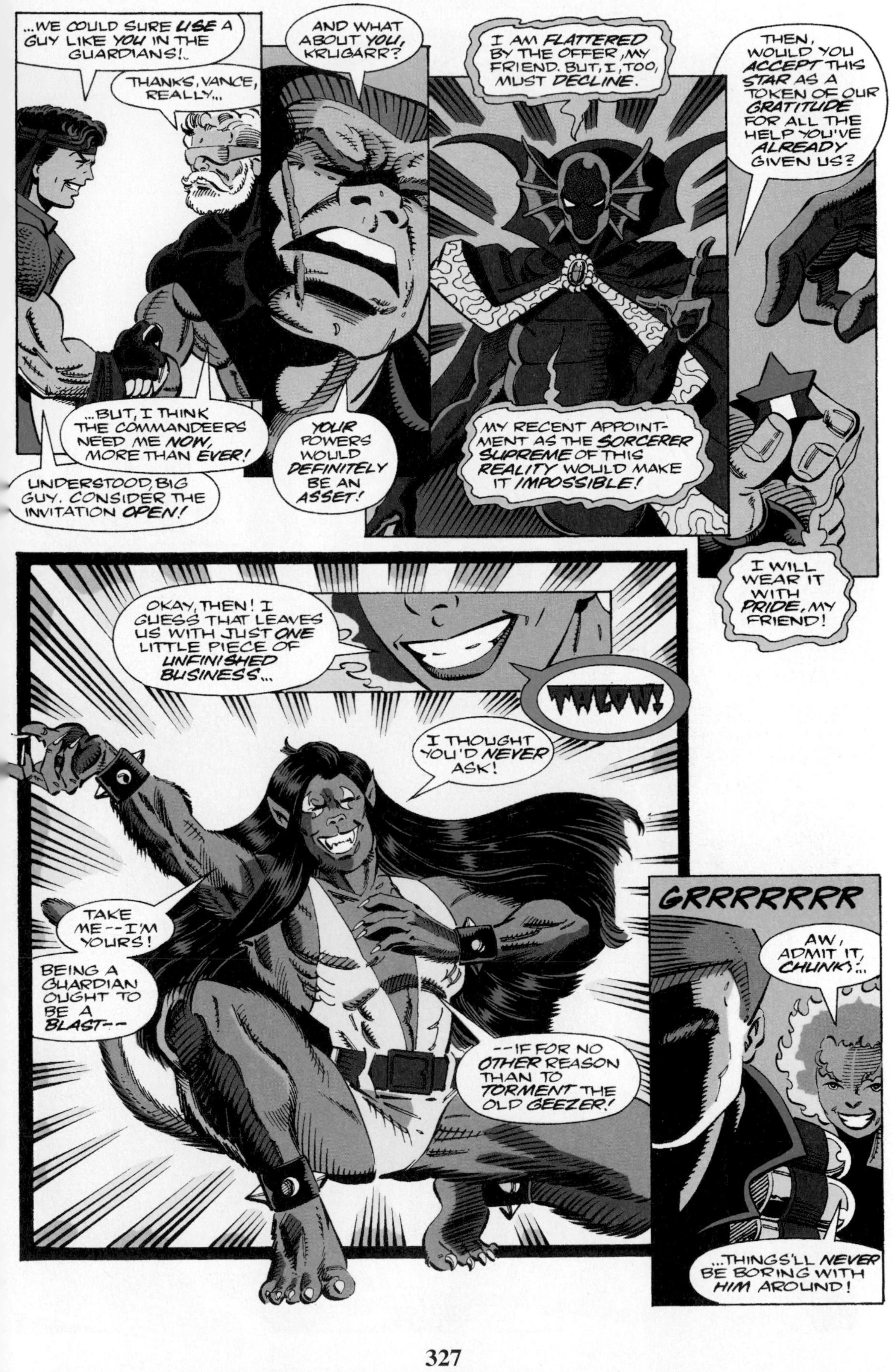
...WE COULD SURE USE A GUY LIKE YOU IN THE GUARDIANS!..
THANKS, VANCE, REALLY...
...BUT, I THINK THE COMMANDEERS NEED ME NOW, MORE THAN EVER!
UNDERSTOOD, BIG GUY. CONSIDER THE INVITATION OPEN!
AND WHAT ABOUT YOU, KRUGARR?
YOUR POWERS WOULD DEFINITELY BE AN ASSET!
I AM FLATTERED BY THE OFFER, MY FRIEND. BUT, I, TOO, MUST DECLINE.
MY RECENT APPOINTMENT AS THE SORCERER SUPREME OF THIS REALITY WOULD MAKE IT IMPOSSIBLE!
THEN, WOULD YOU ACCEPT THIS STAR AS A TOKEN OF OUR GRATITUDE FOR ALL THE HELP YOU'VE ALREADY GIVEN US?
I WILL WEAR IT WITH PRIDE, MY FRIEND!
OKAY, THEN! I GUESS THAT LEAVES US WITH JUST ONE LITTLE PIECE OF UNFINISHED BUSINESS...
TALON!
I THOUGHT YOU'D NEVER ASK!
TAKE ME--I'M YOURS!
BEING A GUARDIAN OUGHT TO BE A BLAST--
--IF FOR NO OTHER REASON THAN TO TORMENT THE OLD GEEZER!
GRRRRRRR
AW, ADMIT IT, CHUNKY...
...THINGS'LL NEVER BE BORING WITH HIM AROUND!

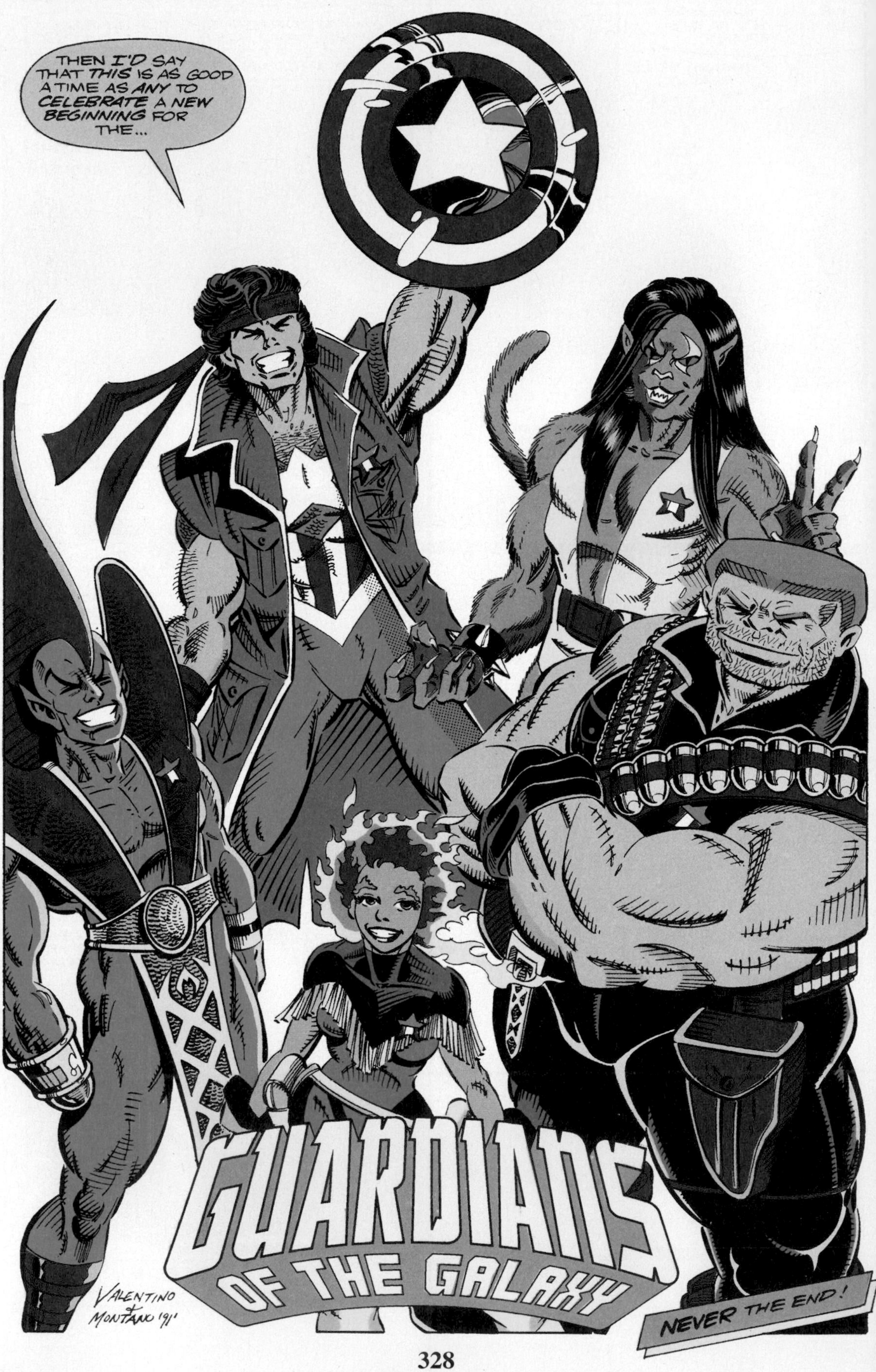
THEN I'D SAY THAT THIS IS AS GOOD A TIME AS ANY TO CELEBRATE A NEW BEGINNING FOR THE...
GUARDIANS OF THE GALAXY
NEVER THE END!
VALENTINO & MONTANO '91'

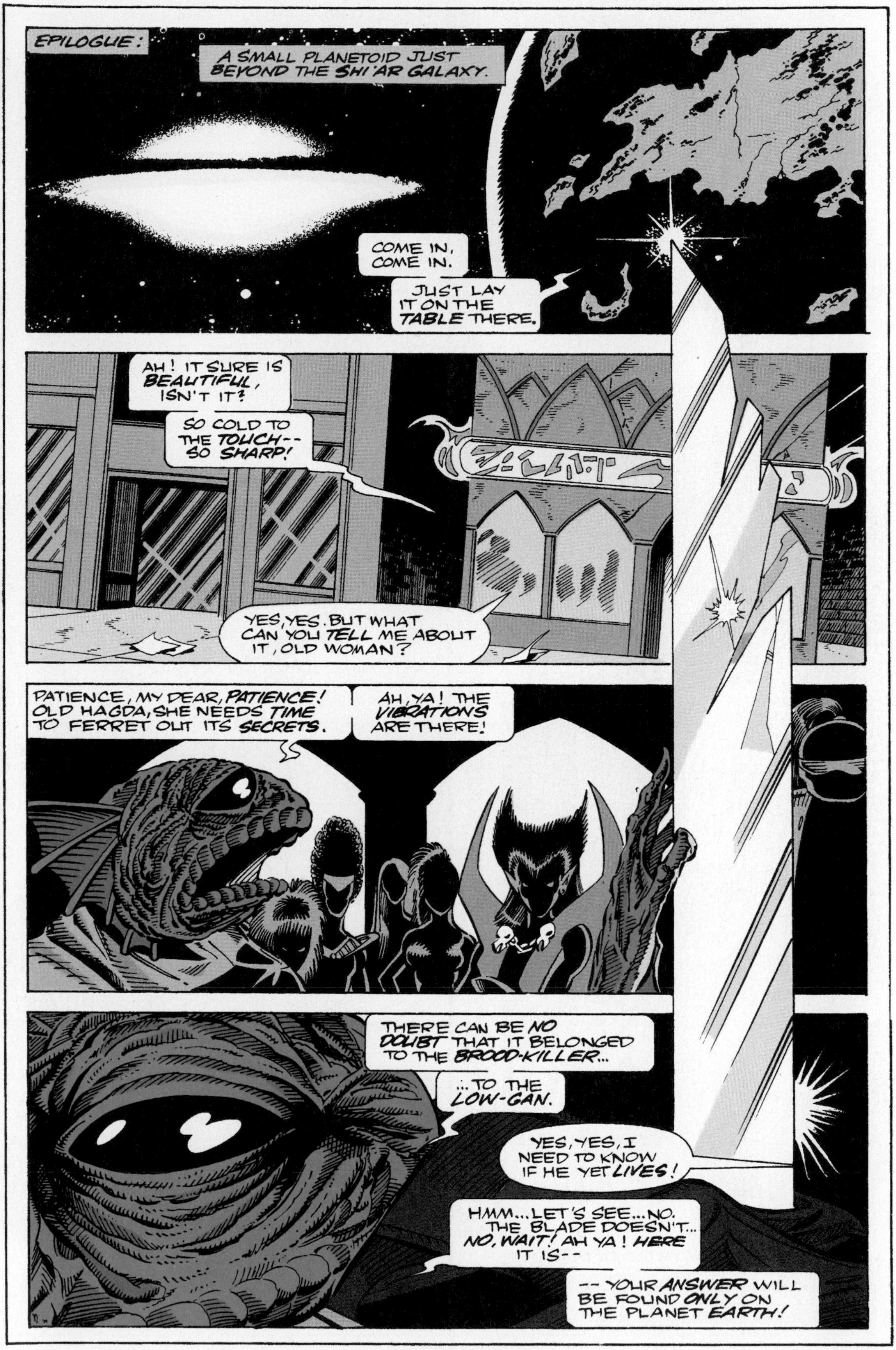
EPILOGUE:
A SMALL PLANETOID JUST BEYOND THE SHI'AR GALAXY.
COME IN. COME IN.
JUST LAY IT ON THE TABLE THERE.
AH! IT SURE IS BEAUTIFUL, ISN'T IT?
SO COLD TO THE TOUCH-- SO SHARP!
YES, YES. BUT WHAT CAN YOU TELL ME ABOUT IT, OLD WOMAN?
PATIENCE, MY DEAR, PATIENCE! OLD HAGDA, SHE NEEDS TIME TO FERRET OUT ITS SECRETS.
AH, YA! THE VIBRATIONS ARE THERE!
THERE CAN BE NO DOUBT THAT IT BELONGED TO THE BROOD-KILLER...
...TO THE LOW-GAN.
YES, YES, I NEED TO KNOW IF HE YET LIVES!
HMM... LET'S SEE... NO. THE BLADE DOESN'T... NO, WAIT! AH YA! HERE IT IS--
-- YOUR ANSWER WILL BE FOUND ONLY ON THE PLANET EARTH!

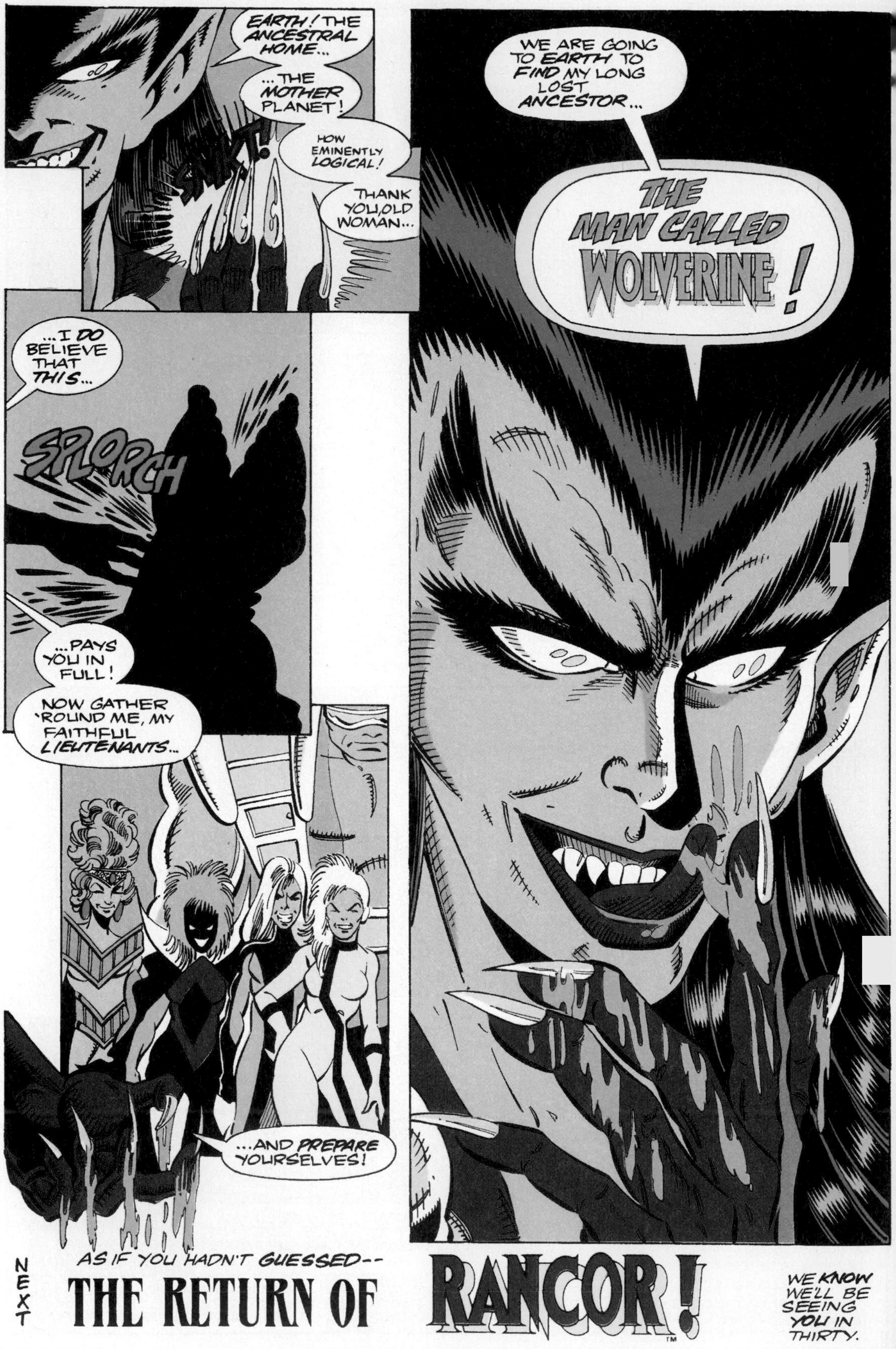
EARTH! THE ANCESTRAL HOME...
...THE MOTHER PLANET!
SNIKT!
HOW EMINENTLY LOGICAL!
THANK YOU, OLD WOMAN...
...I DO BELIEVE THAT THIS...
SPLORCH
...PAYS YOU IN FULL!
NOW GATHER 'ROUND ME, MY FAITHFUL LIEUTENANTS...
...AND PREPARE YOURSELVES!
WE ARE GOING TO EARTH TO FIND MY LONG LOST ANCESTOR...
THE MAN CALLED WOLVERINE!
NEXT
AS IF YOU HADN'T GUESSED--
THE RETURN OF RANCOR!™
WE KNOW WE'LL BE SEEING YOU IN THIRTY.

X-TRA   THE *MUTANT* REPORT   X-TRA

VOLUME 5   "THE ??? STEP IN NEWS EVOLUTION"   **NUMBER 9**

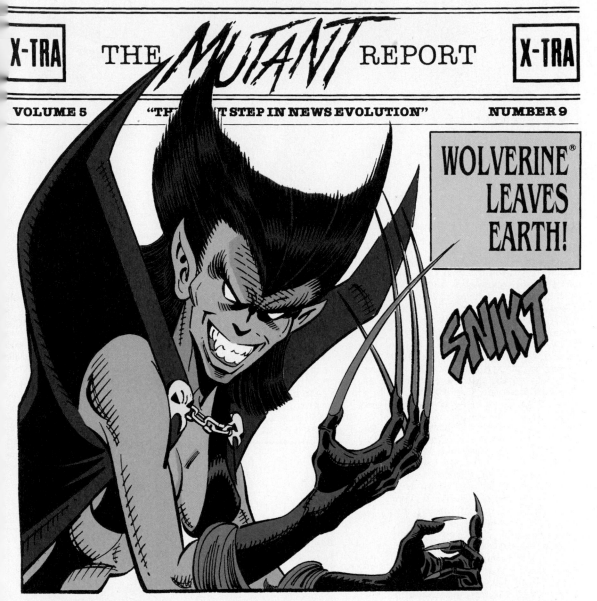

WOLVERINE® LEAVES EARTH!

SNIKT

Magneto Masterminds Mutant Exodus!
RE: Guardians Of The Galaxy #9-11 since their first appearance in MARVEL SUPER HEROES, Vol. 1, Number 18 (Jan. 1969), The Guardians of the Galaxy have been the foundation of the future in the Marvel Universe. The group, a collection of aliens and earth's descendants, drawn from colonies on different planets, were brought together for a specific purpose — to find The Lost Colony of Free Earthmen.

Over the years, their mission has taken a back seat to more pressing adventures. Twice, they have journeyed back into our time-line and saved the galaxy; once, teaming-up with the now defunct Defenders to battle the Badoon, and another time teaming with the Avengers to defeat the all powerful Korvac. Now, having successfully battled The Stark, a race developed from the genius of industrialist Tony Stark,

and having found the legendary shield of Captain America, the Guardians journey with renewed hope to seek out the Lost Colony of Free Earthmen.

"But," I can hear you screaming, "what does this have to do with Mutants?!" Patience, Marvelites. The powers that be at ole MARVEL AGE MAGAZINE have not confused their articles. Relax while I disclose the mutant angle to this masterful Guardians storyline. Are you seated? The Lost Colony of Earth Freemen are discovered to be the descendants of Earth's twentieth century mutants! In order to avoid the political genocide that resulted from the 'Days of Future Past' storyline, most of Earth's mutants, led by Magneto (No, you're not hearing things, I did say Magneto), fled Earth to find another planet suitable for colonization amongst the stars.

Their first stop was the ice covered

Europa, one of Jupiter's moons. Under the ice, the mutants begin to construct three ships to further their trek. Unfortunately, with only two ships completed, Apocalypse attacks the complex. As the mutants flee, Magneto valiantly battles Apocalypse, providing valuable time for the mutants to make their escape. And what of Magneto and that third ship? While the latter question was answered in the Guardians' original series (the third ship became their very own Captain America I), the former, concerning the Mutant Master of Magnetism, is never revealed.

Several generations later, the mutants would arrive upon a planet called Haven. Haven is a planet tearing itself apart due to intense geo-thermic activity. Not one's first choice for a new home, but unfortunately the only planet the mutants found inhabitable when their ships finally could go no

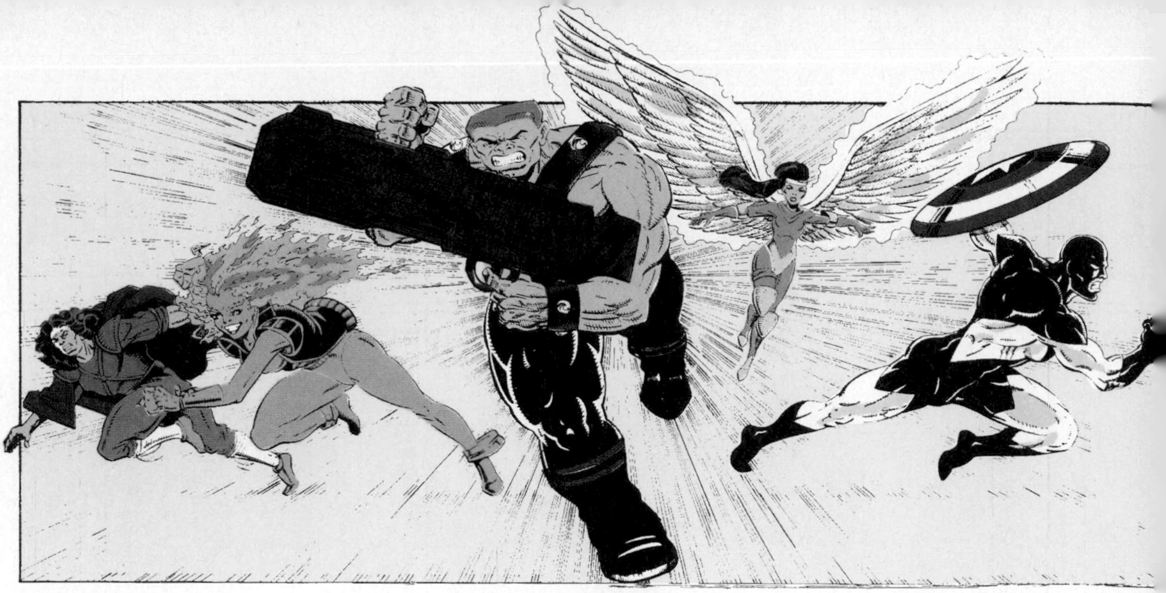

further.

Leading up the charge from Europa, and the only twentieth century survivor of this ardous journey is none other than Wolverine himself (Wolverine originally followed Magneto from Earth as a means to keep an eye on the former leader of the Brotherhood of Evil Mutants). Any true maven of Merry Marvel Mutantdom can tell you that Wolverine, though one of the wisest and most feared fighters in the world, has always deigned to let others lead. Well, A Wolverine can't change its claws. Thus, as soon as he led the descendants of his teammates and enemies to a peaceful valley on Haven where they would build their own city, Wolverine fled to the wilds. This was not before he had the chance to have a few offspring of his own. Unlike their dad, the children of Wolverine had no such inhibitions about leading the mutants and did so with an iron fist (or claw, as it were).

While generation after generation passed, the mutant causing X-Factor gene was slowly bred out of the population. Fewer and fewer mutants were born with each succeeding generation and those mutants who were born lorded over their non-mutant brethren, in a perverted realization of Magneto's long held dream!

This is the world that The Guardians of the Galaxy discover; a world now terrorized by its absolute monarch, the fifth generation descendant of Wolverine: Rancor! Rancor makes her great great granddaddy seem like Willie Lumpkin. I mean, this young woman ripped her father's heart from his chest and took over his throne as a present to herself on her sixteenth birthday! Rancor, who has all of the animal instincts and intensity of Wolverine, but not his hard won honor or conscience, was born with organic fingernails that she can lengthen into razor sharp talons at will. She leads a small band of bloodthirsty mutants she calls her "Lieutenants." They are: Shaddo, whose 'living cape' wraps itself around its intended victims and slithers down their throat to asphyxiate them; Blockade, whose body can expand in height and width until he becomes a moveable living wall; Side-Step, who can teleport by walking diagonally; Mindscan, a telepath; Blaster, who flies and emits deadly bursts of ionic energy from his hands; and the two junior members: Bat-Wing, who flies and emits deadly bio-blasts, and Rhodney, a super strong-man.

The Guardians find allies in the poorly organized, greatly over-powered resistance movement in the persons of: Replica, a young girl able to alter her shape into any form she desires; ar Giraud, a third generation resistanc fighter who will become the new Pheoni:

A plethora of future mutants, one whom will become the newest memb of The Guardians of the Galaxy, a pear in this storyline which begins issue number nine. Special gue cover inkers for this series-with -a-series are mutant artist Rob Liefe (#9), Jim Lee (#10), and Bob Wiace (#11). THE GUARDIANS OF TH GALAXY is written and penciled by Ji Valentino and inked by Steve Montano.

Steve Vrattc

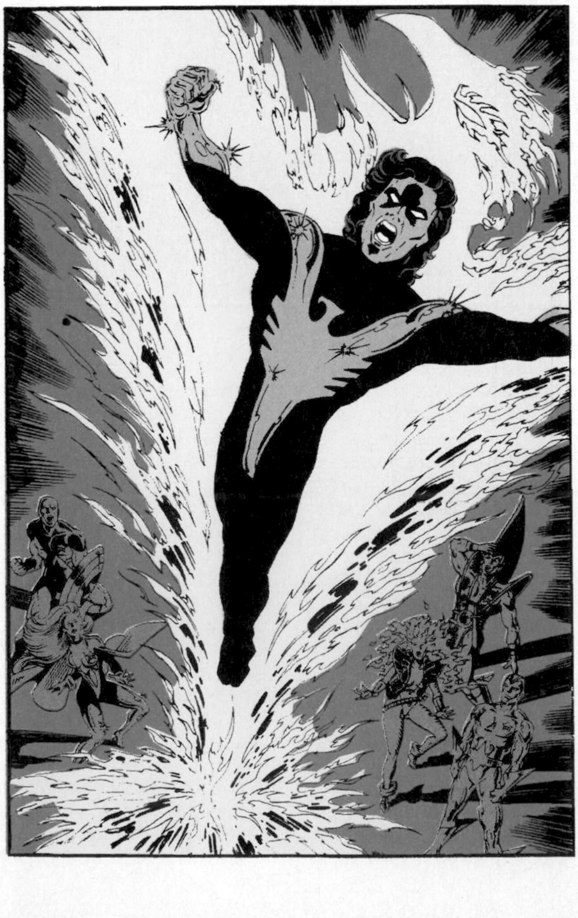

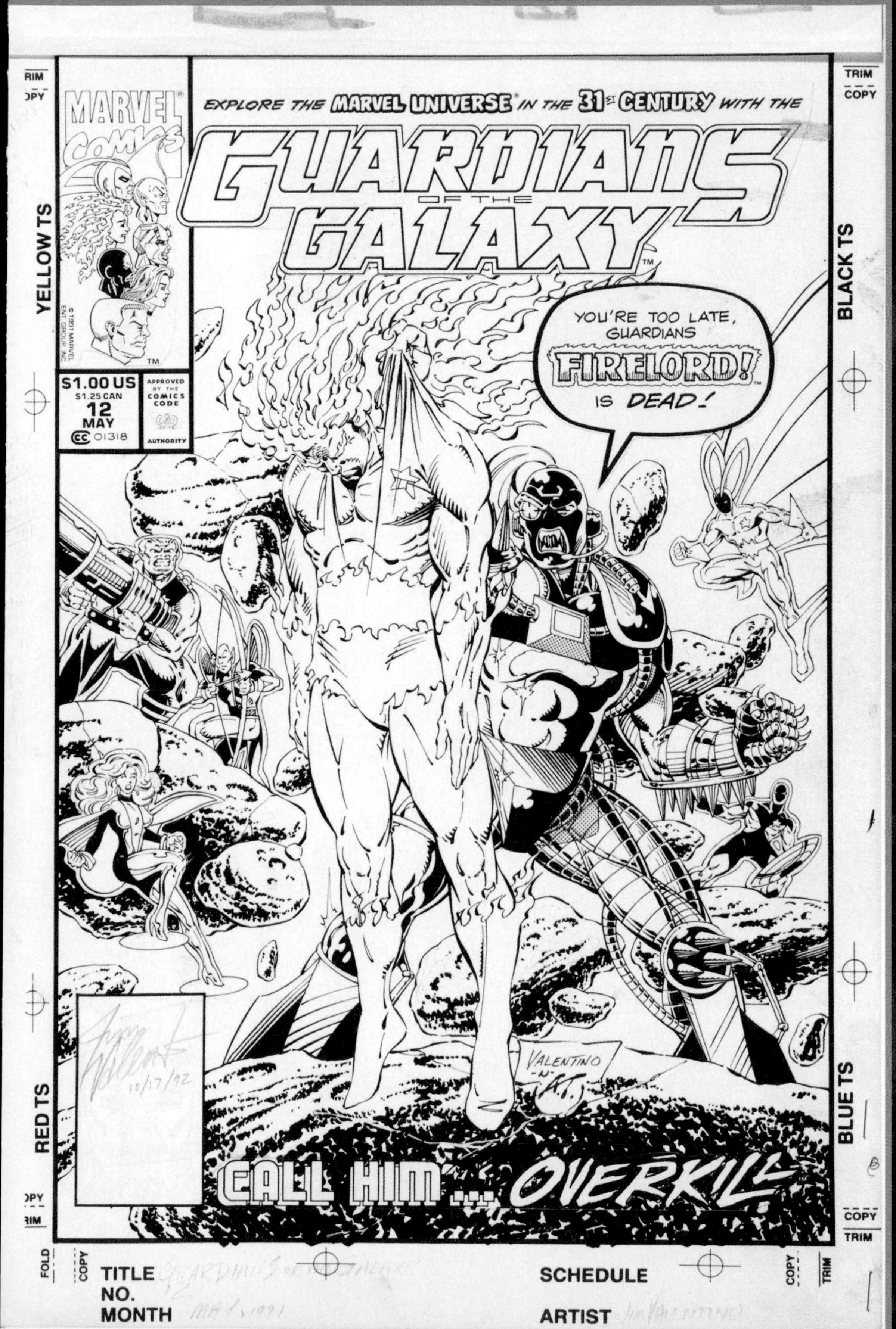
MARVEL COMICS
EXPLORE THE MARVEL UNIVERSE IN THE 31ST CENTURY WITH THE
GUARDIANS OF THE GALAXY
$1.00 US
$1.25 CAN
12
MAY
APPROVED BY THE COMICS CODE AUTHORITY
YOU'RE TOO LATE, GUARDIANS
FIRELORD!
IS DEAD!
VALENTINO -N- A.T.
CALL HIM... OVERKILL
TITLE
NO.
MONTH
SCHEDULE
ARTIST

GUARDIANS OF THE GALAXY #12 COVER ART BY JIM VALENTINO & ART THIBERT
IMAGE COURTESY OF HERITAGEAUCTIONS.COM

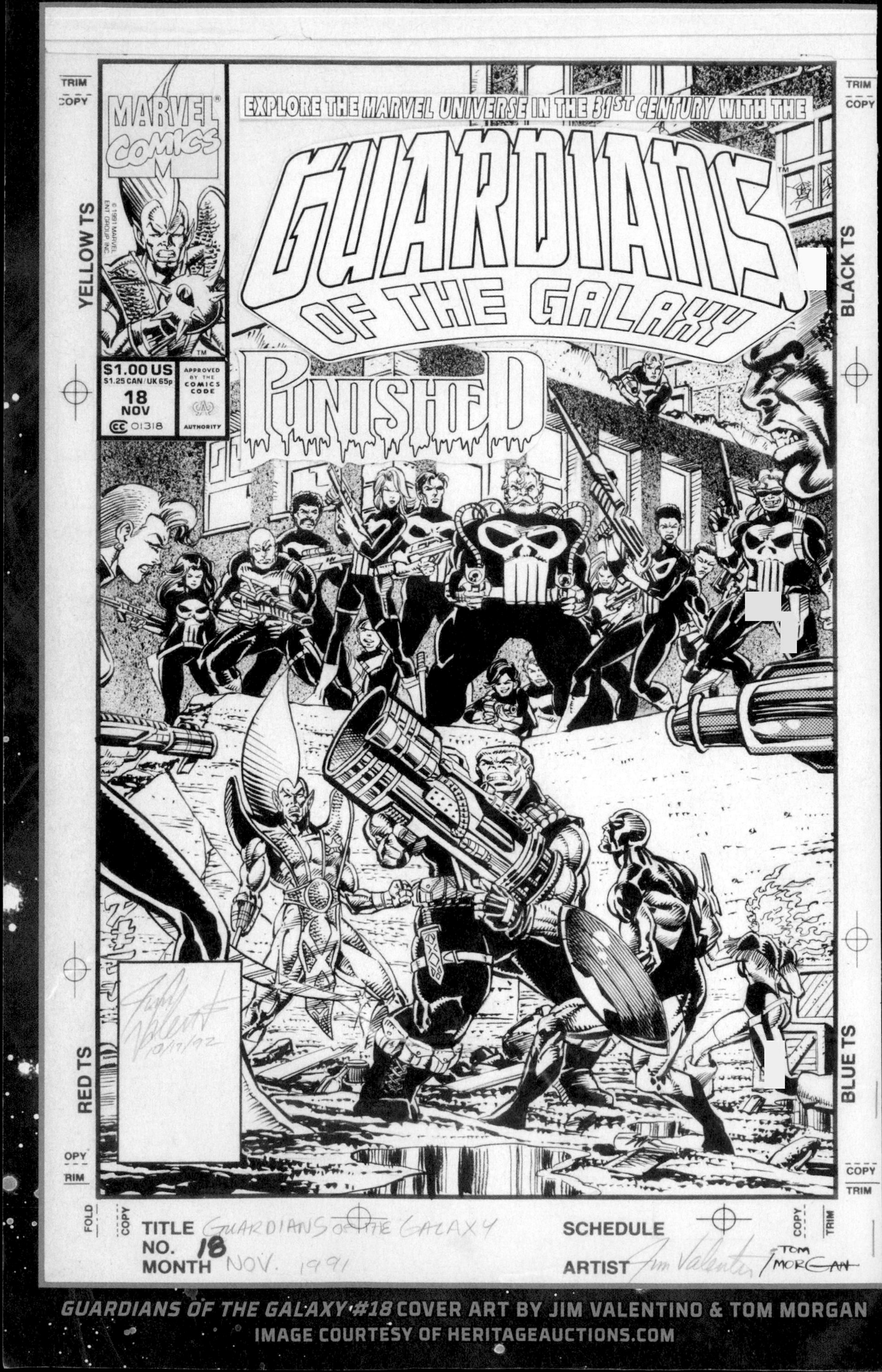

MARVEL COMICS
EXPLORE THE MARVEL UNIVERSE IN THE 31ST CENTURY WITH THE
GUARDIANS OF THE GALAXY
PUNISHED
$1.00 US
$1.25 CAN / UK 65p
18
NOV
01318
APPROVED BY THE COMICS CODE AUTHORITY
TRIM
COPY
YELLOW TS
BLACK TS
RED TS
BLUE TS
FOLD
TITLE GUARDIANS OF THE GALAXY
NO. 18
MONTH NOV. 1991
SCHEDULE
ARTIST Jim Valentino / TOM MORGAN

GUARDIANS OF THE GALAXY #18 COVER ART BY JIM VALENTINO & TOM MORGAN
IMAGE COURTESY OF HERITAGEAUCTIONS.COM

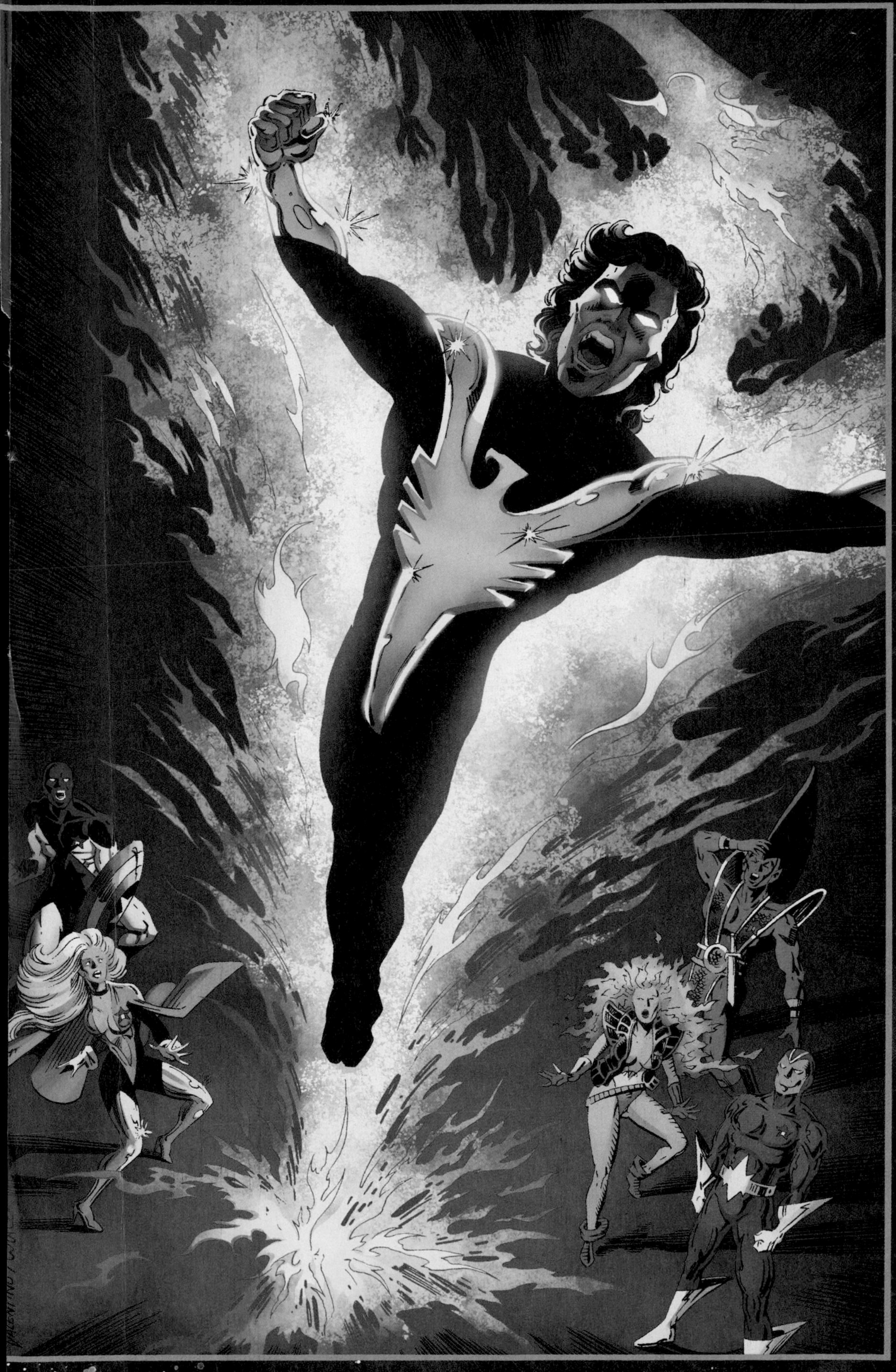

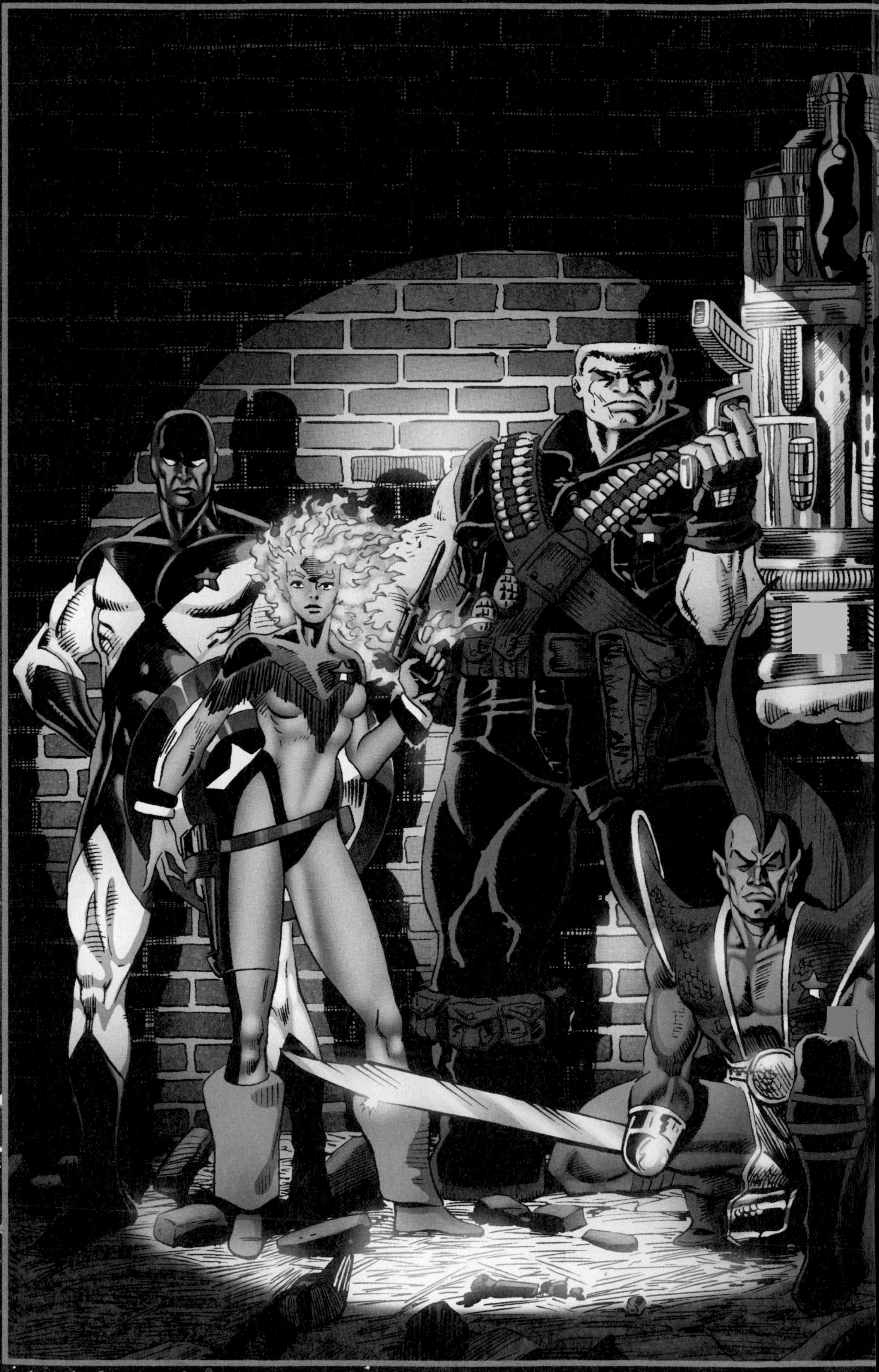